The CMA Companion

The CMA Companion

A Guide to the Cleveland Museum of Art

The Cleveland Museum of Art

in association with

Scala Arts Publishers

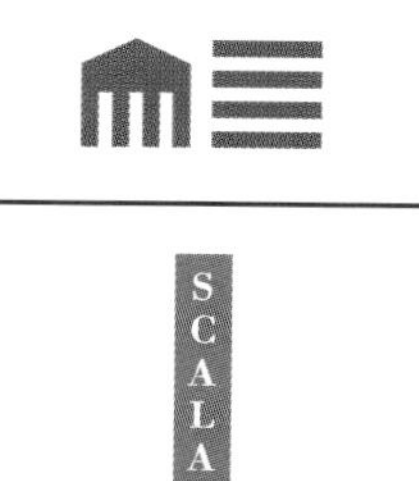

This publication is made possible in part by the Andrew W. Mellon Foundation.

The Cleveland Museum of Art is generously funded by Cuyahoga County residents through Cuyahoga Arts and Culture. The Ohio Arts Council helps fund the museum with state dollars to encourage economic growth, educational excellence, and cultural enrichment for all Ohioans.

Library of Congress Control Number: 2013950681
ISBN (softcover): 978-1-85759-891-9

First published in 2014 by
Scala Arts Publishers, Inc.
141 Wooster Street, Suite 4D
New York, NY 10012
www.scalapublishers.com

Distributed in the book trade by
Antique Collectors' Club Limited
6 West 18th Street, 4th Floor
New York, NY 10011
United States of America

All measurements are in centimeters followed by inches; height precedes width precedes depth, unless noted otherwise.

Edited by Barbara J. Bradley and Kathleen Mills
Designed by Laurence Channing
Produced by Scala Arts Publishers
Printed and bound in China

Contents

Director's Foreword 7
A Brief History of the Museum 9

African Art 27
American Art 43
Ancient Art 65
Chinese Art 91
Contemporary Art 113
Decorative Art and Design 129
Drawings 153
European Painting and Sculpture 171
Indian and Southeast Asian Art 199
Islamic Art 223
Japanese Art 233
Korean Art 247
Medieval Art 257
Modern European Art 285
Photography 303
Pre-Columbian and
Native North American Art 321
Prints 345
Textiles 361

Gallery Maps 376
Index 378
Contributors 383
Board of Trustees 384

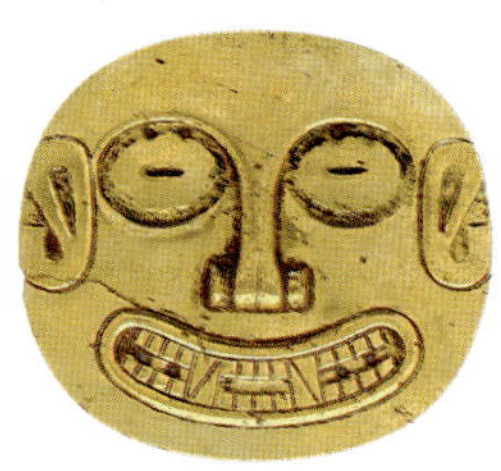

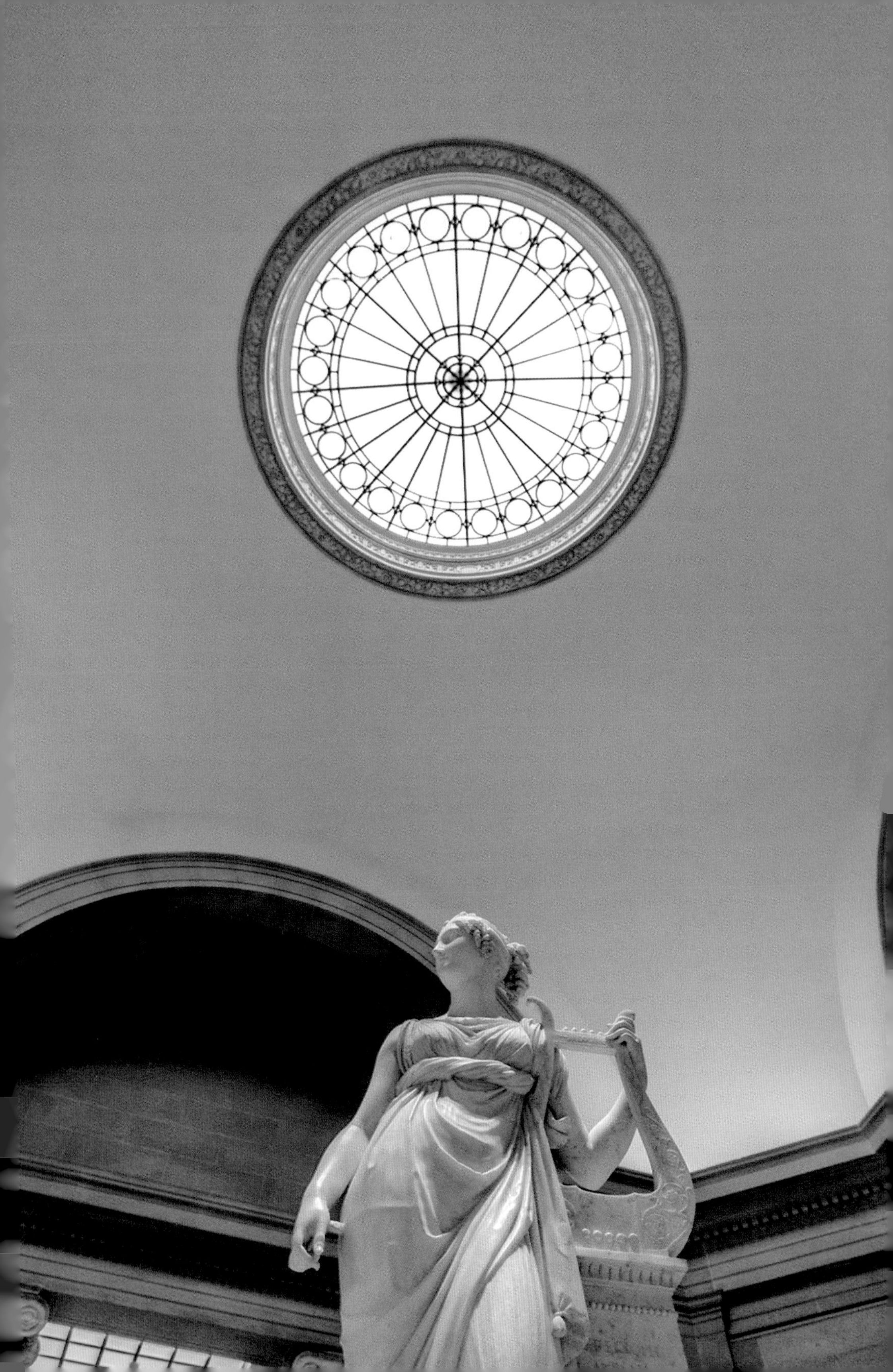

Welcome to the Cleveland Museum of Art

This new guide to the collection of the Cleveland Museum of Art is published at a turning point in the history of the institution. The year 2014 marks the end of an extensive renovation and expansion project and the beginning of centennial celebrations commemorating the opening of the museum in 1916. The entire collection is now sensitively displayed in a building that matches the quality of the art it houses.

Of the museum's more than 45 thousand works of art only a selection is on view. Your favorite painting or sculpture may not be on display since the galleries change continuously, with new objects entering the collection and others going out for exhibition at other museums. Further, objects such as works on paper and textiles are fragile and can only be shown for short periods of time to protect them from damage due to light.

Throughout this guide, the museum's distinctive personality emerges. Clusters of works from a particular culture or historical epoch reveal unexpected strengths, especially for a museum that does not specialize in any one area. Each in its own way, singular objects illuminate the standards associated with the term "Cleveland quality."

This guide is arranged alphabetically by curatorial area; objects within each area are presented by culture and/or chronologically. We hope the brief descriptions will introduce you to unfamiliar cultures and works of art, provide a reference for objects you know and love, and encourage you to return again and again.

■ Frederick E. Bidwell, Interim Director

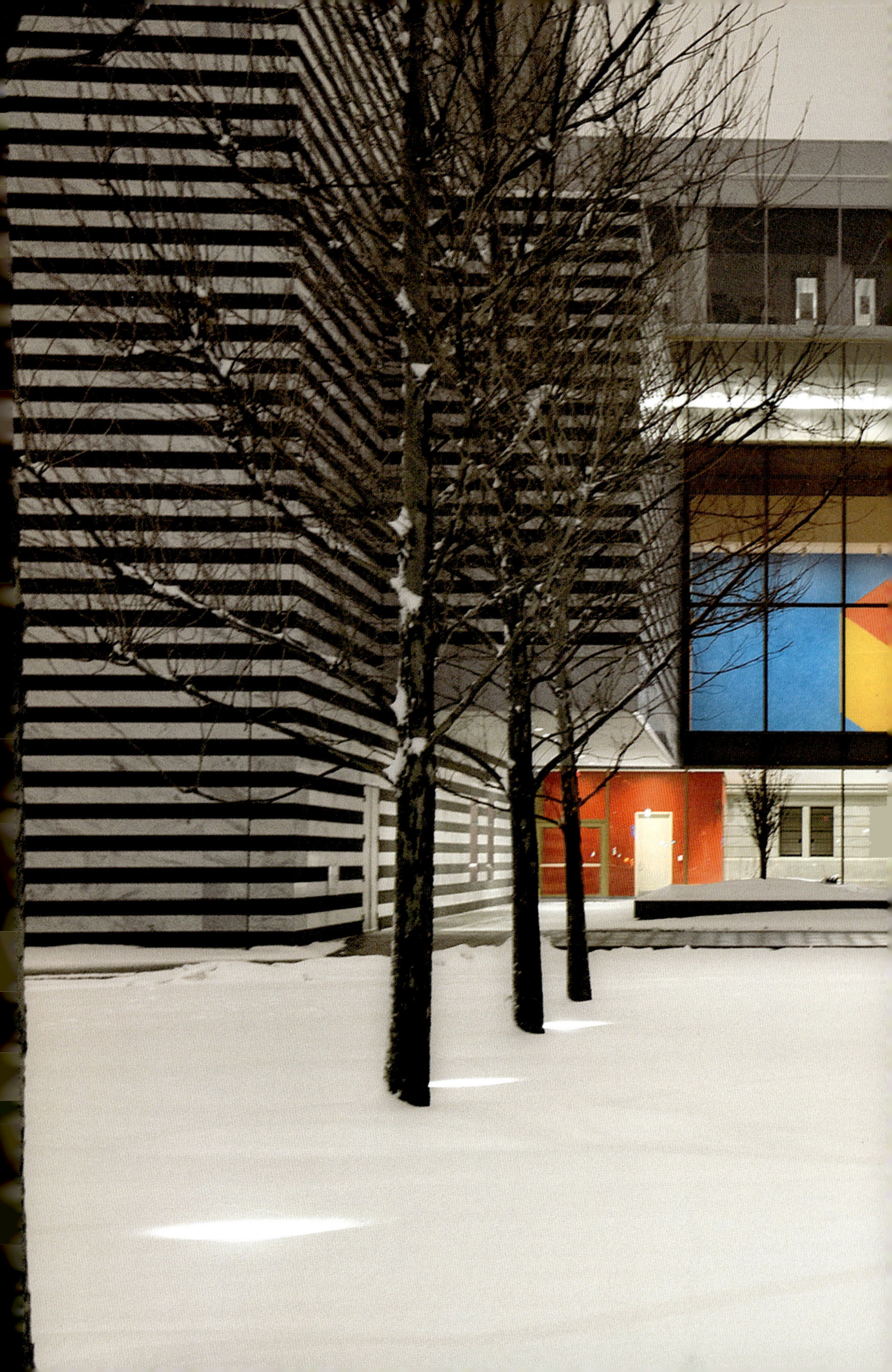

A Brief History of the Museum

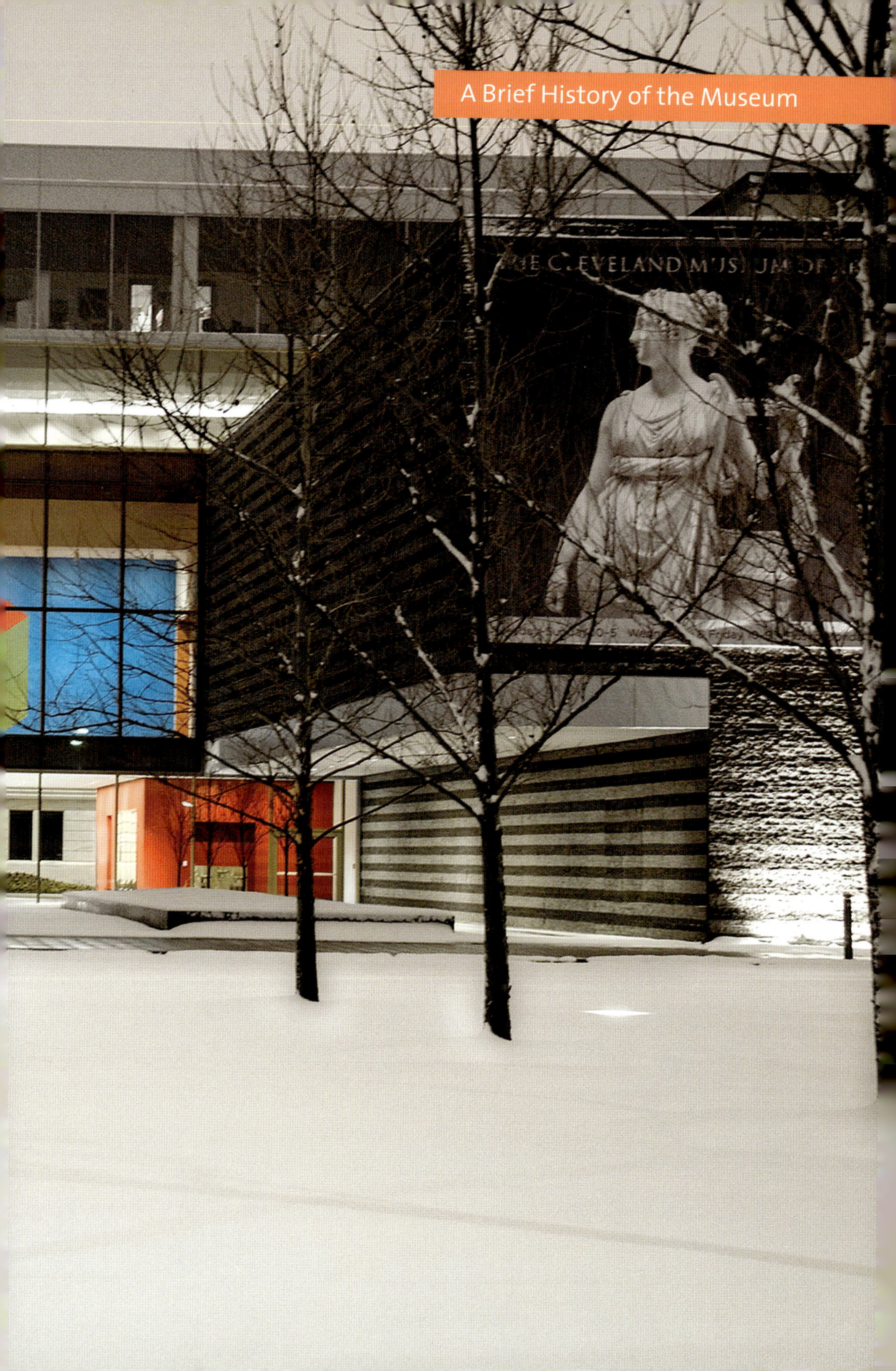

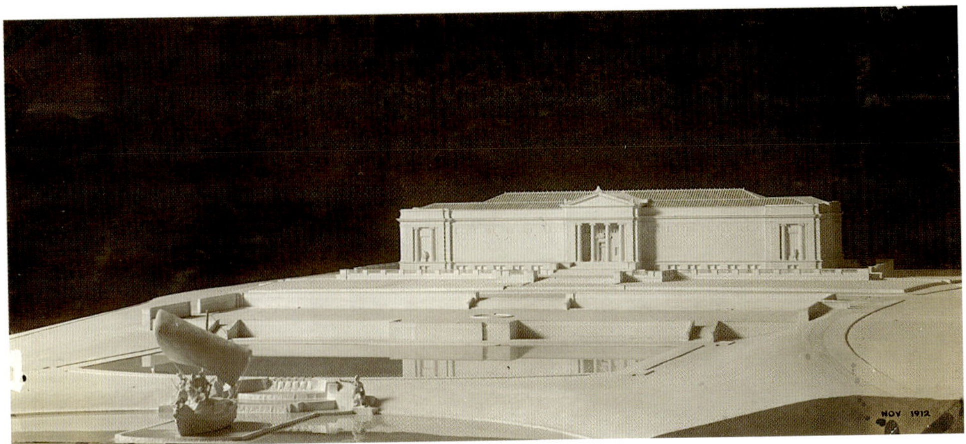

As with many museums established at the time, museum architects Benjamin S. Hubbell and W. Dominick Benes designed the Cleveland Museum of Art in the monumental classical style.

The Cleveland Museum of Art came into being at the dawn of the 20th century. The founders had a simple plan: build a beautiful building, fill it with great art, and open the doors to everyone free of charge. Over the years, generous and loyal benefactors have continued in their footsteps, endowing the museum with both singular works of art and the funds to keep admission to the museum free to all in perpetuity.

Three of the four founders whose names are memorialized in the museum rotunda never saw plans for or stepped inside the Cleveland Museum of Art. Their visions for an art gallery weren't realized until many years after their deaths. Horace A. Kelley, John Huntington, and Hinman B. Hurlbut, men of wealth and taste in the 19th century, each unbeknown to the others, bequeathed funds to erect an art museum to house their personal collections as well as other objects that would be purchased with funds endowed for the purpose. It took 25 years for the trustees of these estates to reconcile them into one magnificent museum.

The man who most significantly set the tone for the new museum, however, was Jeptha Homer Wade II, the grandson of Jepha Homer Wade, one of the founders of Western Union Telegraph and an artist in his own right. The junior Wade gave the land upon which the museum sits, located in his grandfather's 1882 gift of Wade Park to the city of Cleveland. He also encouraged the appointment of local architects Hubbell and Benes, whose landmark buildings include the West Side Market and Wade Memorial Chapel in Lake View Cemetery. They were assisted by Henry W. Kent of the Metropolitan Museum of Art in New York in

Overleaf: Sol LeWitt's Wall Drawing 590A, *first drawn in 1989 and created again in 2013 for the grand opening of the renovated and expanded Cleveland Museum of Art*

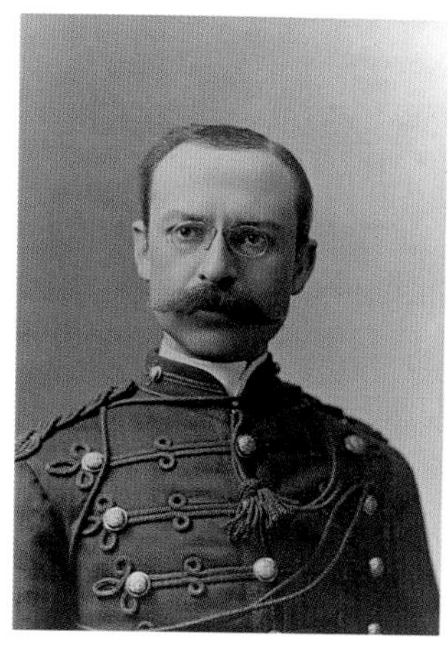

Founder Jeptha Wade's interest in art and gemstones began when he was only 13 during a family tour of Europe where he became acquainted with and thoroughly disliked old master paintings, which he described in his journal as "old, faded, dull, gross, and nude." He much preferred "something new and natural . . . scenery from the present age, bright, cheerful, natural, and elegant." Wade and his family traveled the world collecting many works that made their way into the museum's collection.

designing the building. The floor plan occupied only two stories in order to provide as much natural light as possible in the galleries. The symmetrical arrangement included a central rotunda flanked by two main galleries intended to exhibit classical and medieval casts of famous European artworks. This plan was very deliberately thwarted by the museum's first director, Frederic Allen Whiting, who was determined that the new museum exhibit only the finest examples of the art of all ages and places.

Wade also had the most significant influence on collecting of any early benefactor. Although he confessed to no particular knowledge of art history, he amassed significant collections of decorative art, paintings, Far Eastern art, and gemstones. Wade's love of textiles influenced the museum's commitment to lace, embroideries, woven and printed fabrics, tapestries, and rugs over the costumes found in most American museums at the time. His first gift to the museum in 1914 was a group of 532 type pieces of lace. By his death in 1926, Wade had donated 2,855 works of art. In order to ensure the continued development of the collection he established the J. H. Wade Purchase Fund in 1920, the museum's first endowment.

The new museum's board of trustees (primarily trustees from the Huntington and Kelley trusts) and advisory council consisted of important Cleveland collectors, including Dr. Dudley Peter Allen, Samuel Mather, Ralph King, Worcester R. Warner, and John L. Severance, whose tastes influenced early acquisitions and gifts. It

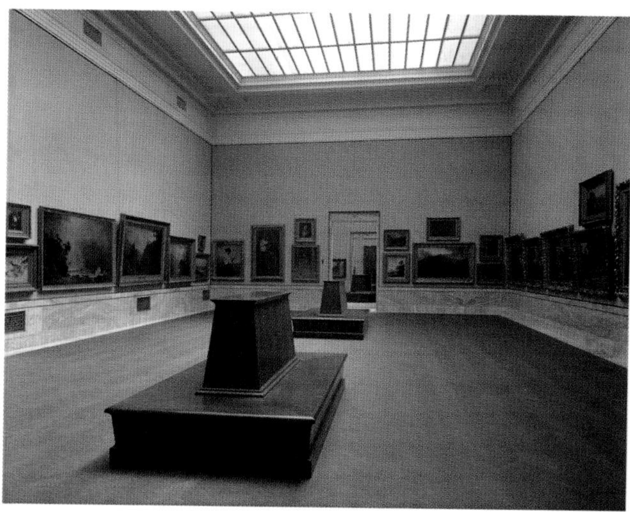

The inaugural exhibition in 1916 featured numerous objects loaned by dealers in the hopes that wealthy Clevelanders would be inspired to purchase them for the collection.

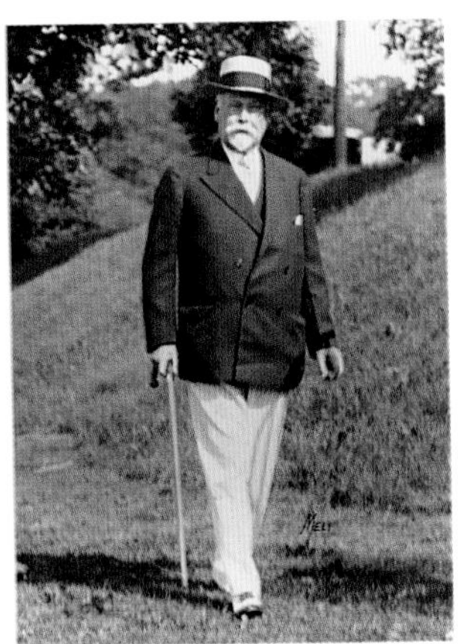

John L. Severance served on the museum advisory council and board of trustees for many years. His generous donations included the original armor collection. He built his private art collection with the expectation that the works would pass to the museum after his death.

was Whiting, though, who gave voice to the museum's collecting goals. From the outset his aspiration was for an encyclopedic collection, ambitious, but common for nascent museums of the time. Over time three goals have remained constant: achieving and maintaining a balance among parts of the collections, the quality of individual works, and a conservative sensibility. To achieve a degree of specialization and set the museum apart, he also advocated the acquisition of Indian art, an aspiration not fulfilled until after World War II.

The importance of acquiring only the best examples of artworks was expressed in the founders' wills and made museum policy from the outset, but works of art were not sought after only for their own sake. Whiting's interest in art was educational. He was influenced by his early social work in the textile mills of Lowell, Massachusetts. The museum's early Asian and primitive art collections were acquired primarily for historical interest and education value. From the beginning the museum has maintained two collections: the primary art collection and the education art collection, which originally had its own "museum" in the education wing.

Whiting also believed that "the modern museum should bind itself in the most intimate way to the life and industry of the community. . . . The CMA desires to build up, with the cooperation of the manufacturers of Cleveland, a number of important collections for the special benefit of local industries" (*Bulletin of the Cleveland Museum of Art* 5, no. 10 [1918]). Achieving these goals was a daunting task given the size of the museum organization. The staff included only one curator and one field worker who was responsible for managing agents hired to select and purchase works of art using funds from the founders' trusts.

Despite the museum's small size, the sheer number of artworks entering the collection was significantly higher in its infancy than in later years from the generosity of early benefactors and their tendency to donate many works of a particular type, such as the Wade laces. In paintings, the museum focused on American, both colonial and contemporary, to complement the collection amassed by founder Hinman Hurlbut and to support American artists. Portraits by Charles Wilson Peale and John Singleton Copley were early acquisitions. The museum was enticed into purchasing George Bellows's *Stag at Sharkey's*, 1909 (p. 54) by the artist's dealer, Mrs. Albert Sterner, when she loaned it to the *Second Annual Exhibition of Contemporary American Painting* in 1922 and declared

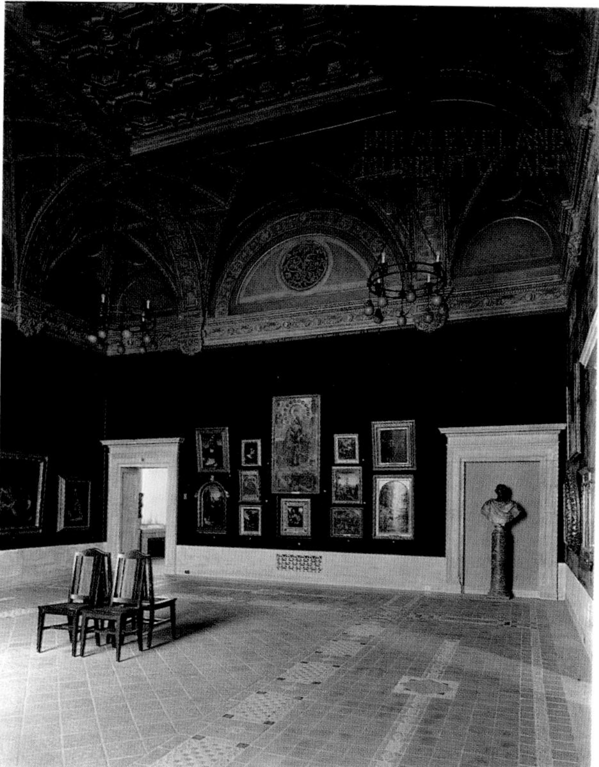

Mrs. Liberty Holden's Italian pre-Raphaelite paintings became the foundation of the museum's European paintings collection.

that it had been turned down by the Metropolitan as being too brutal. The accessions committee jumped at the chance to prove Clevelanders were not so squeamish.

At the time the museum was founded the prevailing wisdom held that old master paintings were firmly ensconced in European museums and private collections, well beyond the reach of American museums. Cleveland was fortunate that a collection of Italian pre-Raphaelite paintings, part of the 19th-century collection of James Jackson Jarvis, was owned by Delia Holden, whose husband, Liberty, had been chairman of the museum's building committee until his death in 1913. The CMA successfully courted Mrs. Holden for the collection with an entire gallery designed just for those works of art. This was a coup for the museum as Mrs. Holden had a personal relationship with Henry Kent, who flattered her unashamedly in his own attempt to lure the collection to New York. The strategy, recommended by Mrs. Holden's daughter, Roberta Bole, was to construct the gallery without her knowledge—a real gamble as the cost exceeded $15,000, a staggering amount at the time.

By 1920, mostly through the efforts of benefactor and board member Ralph King, the museum owned 555 prints and 21 drawings. King was not only a voracious collector of graphic arts but served voluntarily as curator of prints for two years following

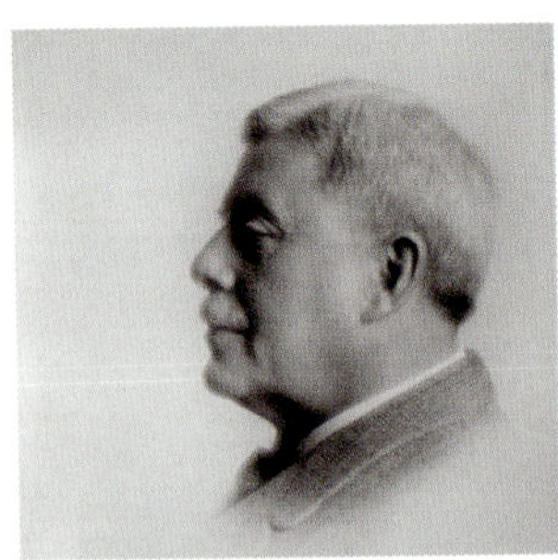

Benefactor Ralph King was a founder and board member of the Print Club of Cleveland, the oldest museum affiliate club in the nation.

the establishment of the department in 1919. When the museum purchased the first work by Henri de Toulouse-Lautrec to enter an American museum (*Monsieur Boileau at the Café,* 1893), King became intrigued by the artist and decided to augment the one Toulouse-Lautrec lithograph in his personal collection. He traveled to New York and, starting at Knoedler's, purchased every Toulouse-Lautrec they had. According to an unpublished manuscript on museum collections by William Milliken, the museum's second director, word quickly spread up Fifth Avenue to "get out your Toulouse-Lautrecs. Ralph King is coming!" By the end of his visit he had bought every work by Toulouse-Lautrec in New York City. A short time later his interest in Odilon Redon lithographs sparked the same type of buying spree. Although best known for his interest in prints, King was an avid collector of every artistic genre and he donated enthusiastically to build up museum collections. His largesse included paintings, decorative art, Asian art, and Auguste Rodin's *The Thinker,* 1880–81, which has graced the south terrace since 1917. At the time of his death in 1926 King had personally donated more than 850 items.

In keeping with his desire to bind the museum to the life of the community, Whiting was particularly anxious to acquire armor for the collection with the expectation that it would

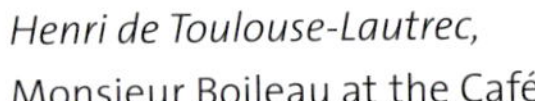

Henri de Toulouse-Lautrec, Monsieur Boileau at the Café

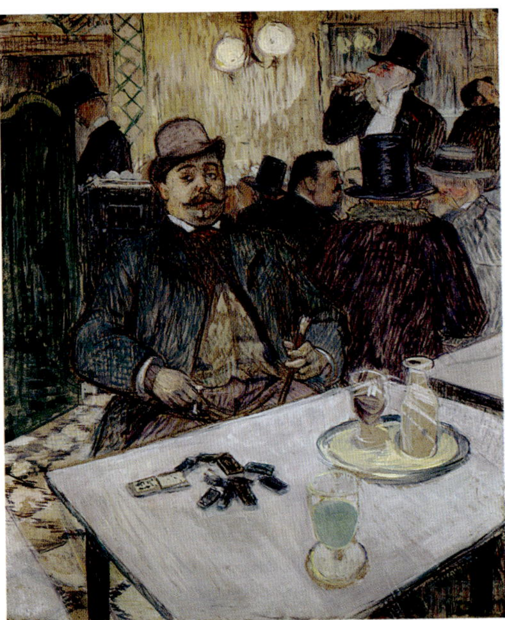

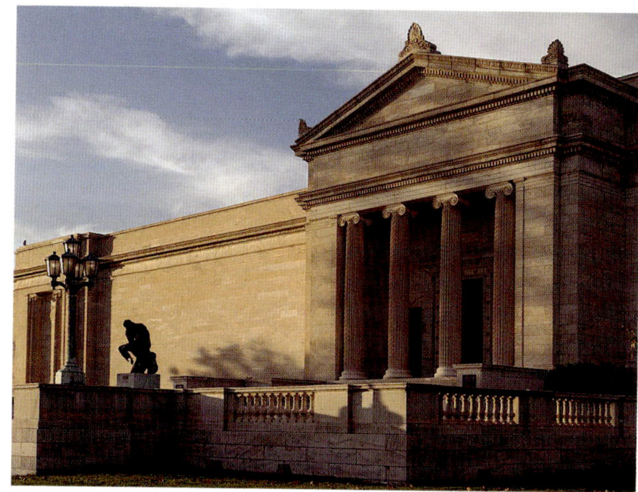

The bottom of Auguste Rodin's The Thinker *was destroyed by a bomb in 1970. Sherman E. Lee, director at the time, decided to leave the sculpture in its damaged state and keep it on the south terrace, where it has been a sentinel since 1917: "If we did repair it, what we would have in effect would be a new cast. We would rather have the original cast. Despite its damage, we feel it is still a significant and moving work of art."*

inspire local steelworkers by restoring an artisan's sense of pride in workmanship. He was supported by trustee Dudley Allen, who advocated the acquisition of collections of particular interest and usefulness to the city's industrial workers. His untimely death in January 1915 inspired a gift by his widow, Elisabeth Severance Allen, of eight 17th-century tapestries depicting the story of Dido and Aeneas. Whiting quickly saw that the tapestries fit the gallery of medieval casts almost as if made for the space. He used the tapestries in his campaign with the board of trustees for an armor court, eventually bringing them around to his point of view. An intact collection owned by Frank Gair Macomber of Boston became the nucleus of the armor collection.

The Jack, Joseph, and Morton Mandel Armor Court has thrilled museum visitors since 1916.

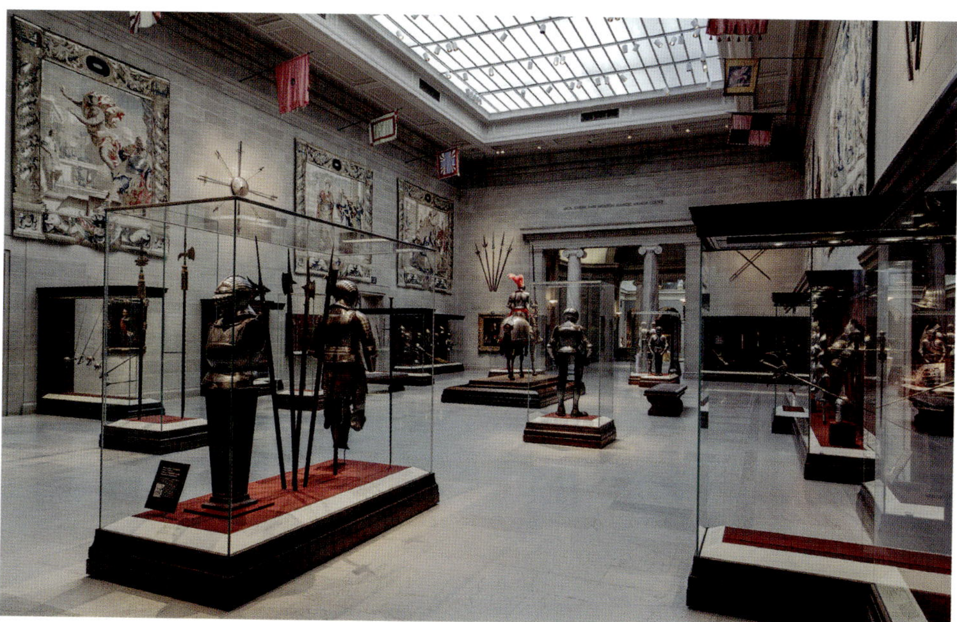

Frederic Whiting to Howard Carter, 12 January 1923

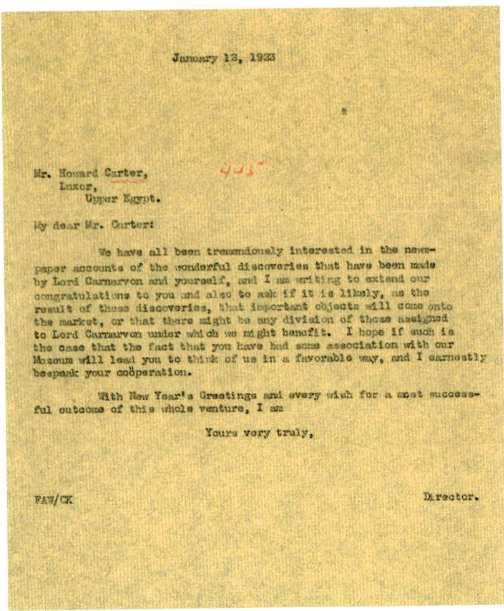

January 12, 1923

Mr. Howard Carter,
Luxor,
Upper Egypt.

My dear Mr. Carter:

We have all been tremendously interested in the newspaper accounts of the wonderful discoveries that have been made by Lord Carnarvon and yourself, and I am writing to extend our congratulations to you and also to ask if it is likely, as the result of these discoveries, that important objects will come onto the market, or that there might be any division of those assigned to Lord Carnarvon under which we might benefit. I hope if such is the case that the fact that you have had some association with our Museum will lead you to think of us in a favorable way, and I earnestly bespeak your coöperation.

With New Year's Greetings and every wish for a most successful outcome of this whole venture, I am

Yours very truly,

FAW/CK

Director.

The museum's interest in antiquities was stimulated by a purchase by the Huntington trust in 1913 of a collection that had been intended for J. P. Morgan, who had died in Rome unexpectedly. To round out that collection, the museum hired Howard Carter in 1918 to act on its behalf in Egypt. Regrettably he was not working for the CMA when he discovered the tomb of King Tutankamen, although the museum sent very polite letters trying to benefit from the find.

In 1919 Whiting established three curatorial departments—oriental art, decorative art, and colonial arts, followed in 1920 by the print department. He left the curators to develop collections in their areas without his interference. Significantly, the curator of decorative arts was Milliken. He and Wade visited New York and European dealers together and set the tone for museum collecting for years. Both men emphasized the importance of emotional responses to works of art and evaluated potential acquisitions by relying on their initial gut reactions. They also tended to purchase clusters of related objects. Milliken favored medieval art. He had less regard for paintings (even though he was curator of paintings for a number of years), and none for early American decorative art.

Milliken became director in 1930, at the height of the Great Depression. Ironically, he made the most important acquisition in the museum's history at this time. Because of the world calamities of war and depression, the German owners of 82 sacred relics from

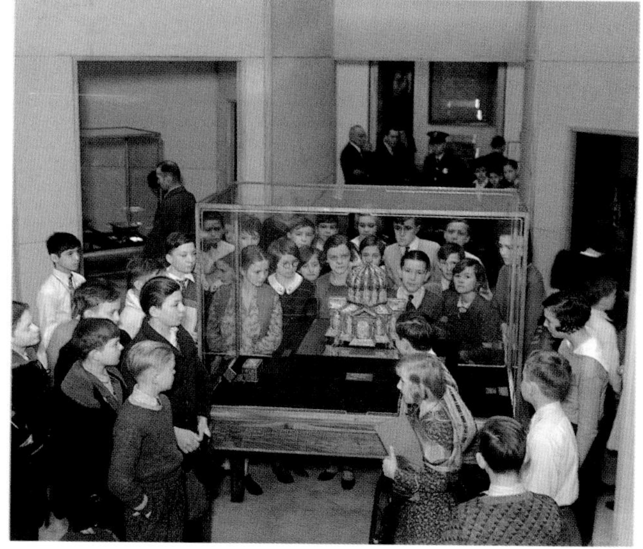

One of the most significant occasions in museum history was the Guelph Treasure exhibition featuring the entire collection of a medieval cathedral treasury.

the Cathedral of Saint Blaise in Brunswick—the finest medieval works of art in the world—were forced to sell. The family turned the objects, called the Guelph Treasure, over to a consortium of dealers, and Milliken campaigned with museum trustees for the considerable amount of money needed to purchase from the collection. His relationship with the dealers netted him first pick, and he was astounded that no other buyers were clamoring at the door (see pp. 264–65).

In Milliken's words, "Here was the opportunity to make the Cleveland Museum a world museum. With unique and famous objects such as these, Cleveland could take rank with the greatest museums." He wanted to purchase the entire collection but was limited by funds to six objects, a book reliquary, an arm reliquary, the Paten of St. Bernwald, a portable altar, a medallion of Christ, and the ivory horn of St. Blasius, which Milliken offered to blow on the saint's day to cure Clevelanders of sinusitis. The entire collection was brought to Cleveland by the dealers brokering the sale. Thousands of visitors lined up on opening day. Enthusiasm was so great that museum trustees contributed additional funds to purchase the two crosses of Countess Gertrude and the greatest work in the collection, the portable altar, the only gold portable altar in existence. While over the years the CMA had strived to collect the best examples of the arts of all ages, this purchase elevated its prestige in the museum world.

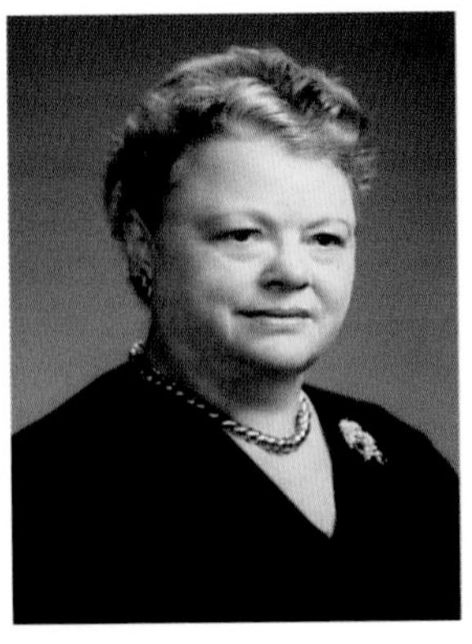

Emery May Norweb was not only an important museum benefactor but the first woman president of the board of trustees. In 1969 she and Sherman Lee selected Marcel Breuer to design a work of architectural art to accommodate the expanding needs of the museum.

During a visit to Cleveland in 1939, art dealer John Wise stopped by, unexpectedly, to see Milliken, and the collection of Pre-Columbian art got a tremendous boost by "chance and good fortune." Wise had brought with him in his pocket a small gold piece that Milliken immediately coveted. At that very moment museum trustee Emery May [Mrs. R. Henry] Norweb, granddaughter of Liberty and Delia Holden, arrived at the museum and upon seeing the piece purchased it for the museum.

Milliken did not then know that Mrs. Norweb had a substantial personal collection of Pre-Columbian art that she had amassed during her husband's diplomatic career as an American ambassador. She invited Milliken to inspect a trunk of items from Mexico, Peru, and Portugal that she had been "carrying all over the face of the earth for about five years." As Milliken recounted later, "A most remarkable treasure emerged from it. . . . I was breathless . . . finally, as at the end of a display of fireworks, the final burst overwhelmed me. . . . I was transfixed, beside myself with excitement." His reaction amused Mrs. Norweb, who became fond of telling the story of how she had cast a spell on him. The collection became the cornerstone of the museum's Pre-Columbian collection.

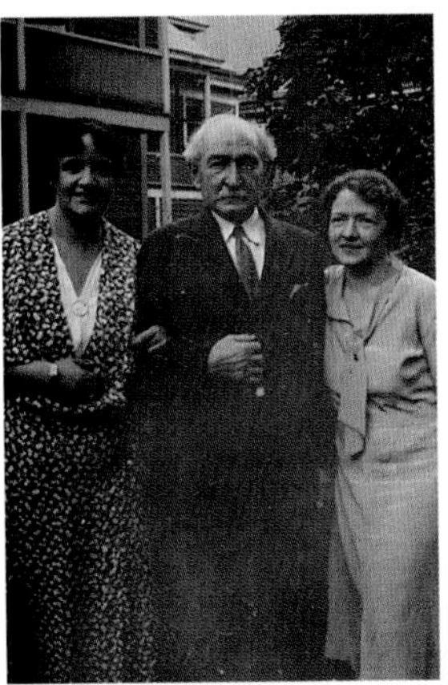

Cleveland public school teacher Helen Humphreys (left) with her father and a friend, n.d.

Another major benefactor of Pre-Columbian art was Helen Humphreys, a Spanish teacher with the Cleveland public schools who was interested in establishing a memorial to her parents with works that would inspire children's imaginations. For more than 20 years Humphreys saved what she could from her schoolteacher's salary and acquired one piece after another as the funds accumulated. The memorial consists of 49 works.

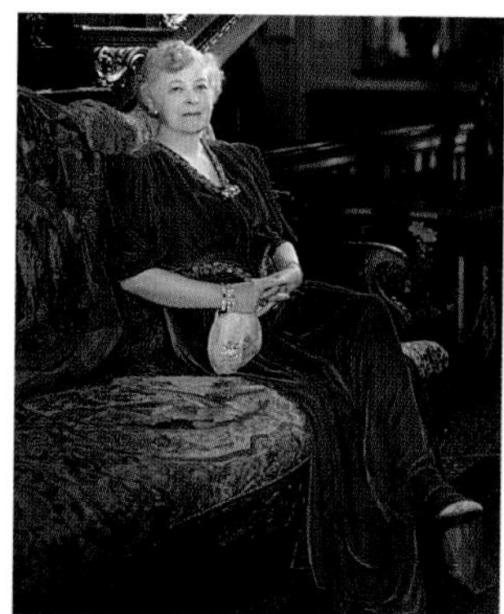

Elisabeth Severance Allen Prentiss and her brother, John L. Severance, had a friendly rivalry that ultimately benefited the museum. When one bought a great piece of art the other inevitably countered with what he or she felt was a better work.

The year 1939 marked a turning point for the museum. Over the next 10 years the deaths of early benefactors resulted in significant bequests of personal art collections, ensuring the museum's future. Industrialist Leonard C. Hanna Jr. established the Coralie Walker Hanna Memorial Collection of Italian Renaissance furniture in memory of his mother. He also established the Hanna Fund, which made possible the acquisition of many great works, culminating in his final bequest of more than $30 million in 1957. Shortly thereafter, the death of Julia Morgan Marlatt brought an unexpected windfall to the museum with her bequest of nearly $2 million. Although Mr. and Mrs. Marlatt had been frequent museum visitors, Director Milliken's only memory of them was as interested patrons of the arts. The bequests of John Severance and his sister, Elisabeth Severance Allen Prentiss, were received in the 1940s. Their friendly competition to outdo each other in collecting important works of art was well known in the community. The great art from these and other personal collections came to the museum not unexpectedly. Both Milliken and subsequent director Sherman E. Lee served as consultants to private collectors. Museum acquisition policy was shaped, in part, with the knowledge of benefactions to be made.

With much more money now available, the museum's focus shifted from American painting and medieval decorative art to the art of the ancient Americas, Islamic art, and Western art of the Renaissance. Most important was growth in European paintings thanks to the Marlatt and Hanna funds, which were specified for this purpose. The Hanna Fund is the largest bequest to have come to the museum. For the first time, and well into the future, the museum could compete for artwork on equal terms with larger and older museums. The museum's board president, Harold T. Clark, wisely convinced Hanna to specify half the bequest for acquisitions and half for operations in order to properly support the works of art. The Hanna Fund also provided most of the funding for a much-needed addition to the building. Designed by the Cleveland firm Hayes and Ruth,

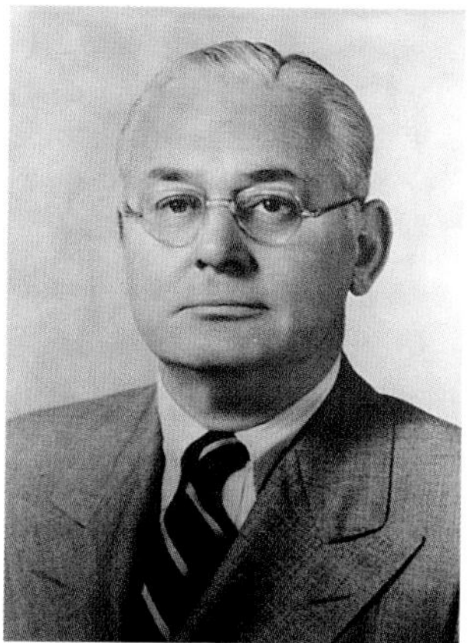

Leonard C. Hanna Jr.

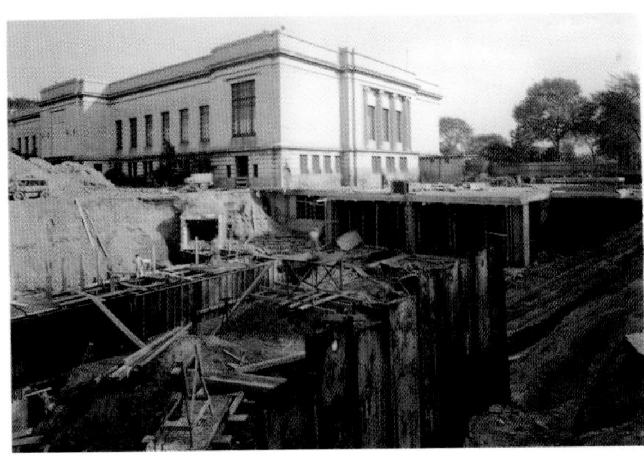

The first expansion and renovation project, funded primarily by Leonard Hanna, opened in 1958 and featured an outdoor sculpture court and the museum's first conservation laboratories.

the expansion doubled the size of the museum and included space for the newly established conservation department. Unfortunately, Hanna did not live to see the opening of this building in 1958.

In 1958, Sherman Lee, curator of oriental art, became the museum's third director. Unlike previous directors, Lee had formal art historical training and a PhD from Western Reserve University. Although his dissertation was on American watercolors, his primary interest was in Asian art. His knowledge of Japanese art had greatly advanced just after World War II when he served as a civilian adviser on collections in the Department of Arts and Monuments of the Supreme Allied Command in Tokyo.

Lee's assessment of the collection at the time of his appointment as director was that the museum had superb holdings in medieval art, European decorative art, Pre-Columbian art, textiles, and prints and drawings. He felt the small ancient and Asian collections were excellent but lacked in depth and breadth. Most significant, post-Renaissance art was unevenly represented in both quality and quantity with a significant absence of 20th-century art, especially abstract art. His master plan for acquisition funds called for at least 50 percent to be spent on Western paintings with other collecting areas sharing the remainder. With the Hanna bequest as a foundation, the museum continued to build collections of the highest quality with less reliance on individual benefactors.

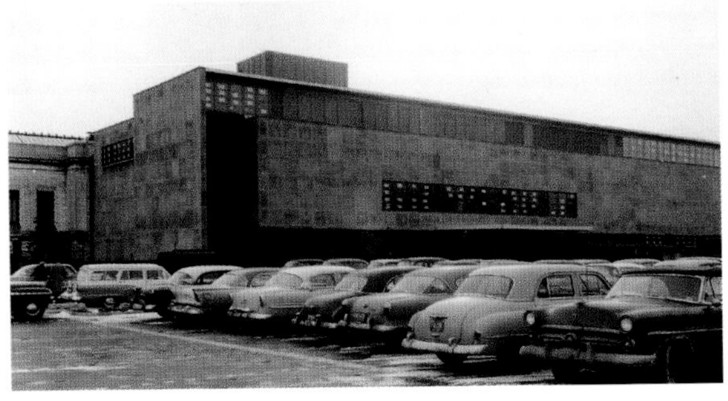

Among the most significant of the four thousand objects added to the collection during Lee's tenure are: Nicolas Poussin's *Holy Family on the Steps*, 1648 (p. 187), which, although purchased and exported legally so irked the French government that an international warrant was issued for Lee's arrest; Caravaggio's *The Crucifixion of Saint Andrew*, 1606–7 (p. 181), which had been lost for three hundred years and then rejected as a fake by several museums when it resurfaced; the

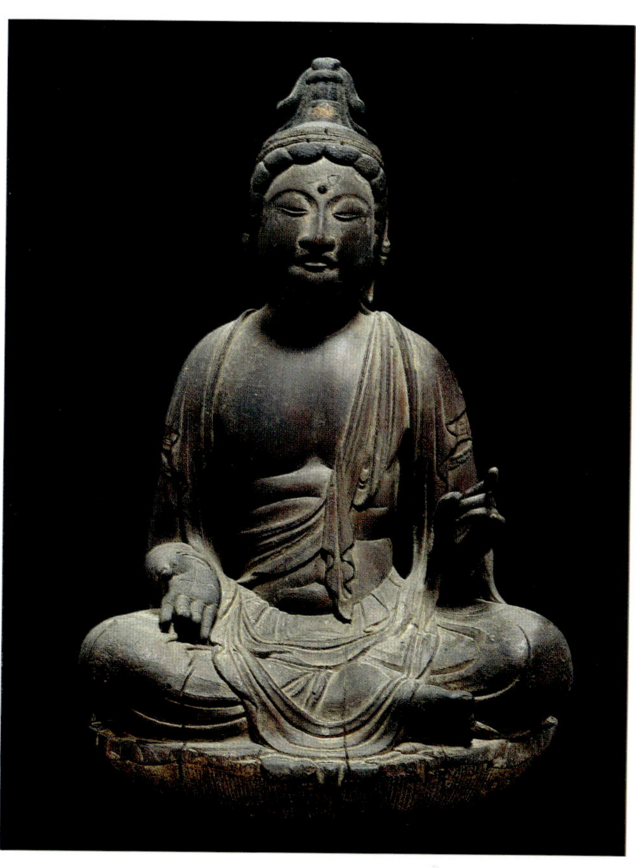

Japan, Heian period, Nikko, the Sun Bodhisattva

Meissonnier *Tureen,* 1735–38 (p. 135); and Antonio Pollaiuolo's *Battle of the Nudes,* 1470s–80s (p. 347), which had been on the museum's wish list for many years.

Of his Asian acquisitions Lee's favorite was *Nikko, the Sun Bodhisattva,* c. 800, which he summarized as "compassion and mercy tenderly expressed in precious wood" (*Bulletin of the Cleveland Museum of Art* 48, no. 10 [1961]) and identified as the piece he would rescue first in an emergency. Lee acquired the head and torso of the *Krishna Govardhana,* 500s–600s (p. 214), only after long negotiations with the owner's heirs. They suggested that missing parts of the sculpture also survived; after much research and negotiation the pieces were indeed found and excavated from the garden of the owner's next-door neighbors. The acquisition of significant works of Indian art was finally realized through the efforts of benefactor and board member George P. Bickford,

Marcel Breuer's concrete canopy has marked the main entrance to the museum since 1971.

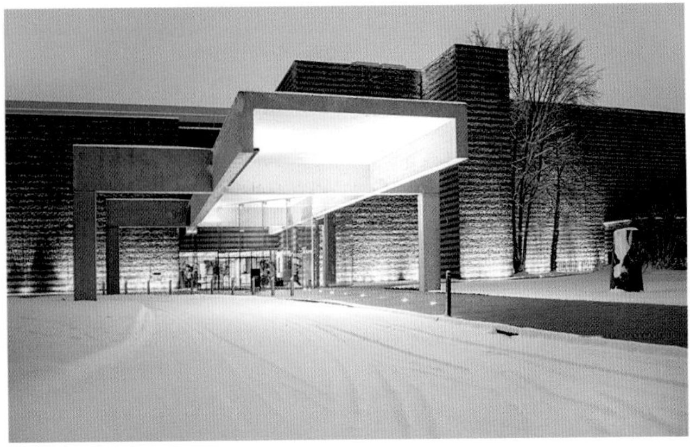

Henri Matisse, Two Women

whose interest and expertise in all areas of Indian art resulted in many donations and culminated in his endowing the museum's first curatorial chair, the George P. Bickford Chair of Indian and Southeast Asian Art, in 1990.

During Lee's directorship the trustees were unenthusiastic about purchasing modern art, believing it had not stood the test of time. In fact, the Matisse bronze *Two Women,* c. 1908, owned by board president Harold Clark, was being used as a doorstop when Lee offered to take it off his hands. In an oral history conducted by UCLA, Lee described himself as a "red hot radical" in the board's eyes but he nonetheless persuaded them to establish a director's discretionary fund for modern art. From 1961 to 1971 nearly 30 works were purchased using this fund, among them pieces by Jean Arp, Anthony Caro, Joseph Cornell, Stuart Davis, Willem de Kooning, Arshile Gorky, Paul Klee, Joan Miró, Piet Mondrian, Robert Motherwell, Isamu Noguchi, and Mark Rothko.

Lee believed that the museum's responsibility was to the object and to an individual's private response to that object. He objected to what were becoming known as blockbuster exhibitions as mere show business rather than the scholarly pursuit of artistic excellence. This continued pursuit of excellence through collecting and educational programming necessitated the construction of two additional wings to the building before he retired in 1983. Marcel Breuer was the only architect invited to submit a design for the 1971 education wing. His artistic aesthetic and understanding of museum needs as expressed in the Whitney Museum of American Art in New York made him the only logical candidate for Cleveland. The public relations

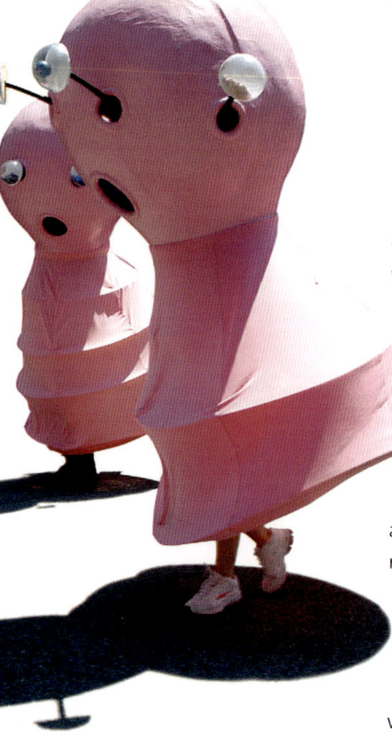

The masks, costumes, and giant puppets created for Parade the Circle get more numerous and more inventive every year. The parade has set off on the first Saturday in June for more than 20 years.

department later described the Breuer wing as the most expensive work of art ever acquired. Further expansion was necessary near the end of Lee's tenure and another addition housing nine galleries and the Ingalls Library was constructed.

Evan Turner's tenure as director (1983–93) was marked by soaring art prices and increased competition in the art market not only among museums but among private collectors as well. He remained committed to established collecting goals and focused on expanding the classical and Asian collections. By this time the one area in which the museum lacked a comprehensive collection was photography. While the CMA had acquired its first photographs, by Alfred Stieglitz, following its first exhibition of photography in 1934, photographs were collected only sporadically for the next several decades. Between 1973 and 1983 a few noteworthy prints were acquired but without a specific plan. Beginning in 1983 the museum began collecting photography with purpose, focusing on works made before World War II with the goal of documenting the aesthetic and technical milestones of the genre and supplying the necessary references for understanding this art form.

Turner's ten years as director was a period of escalating operating costs and cuts in federal and state arts funding. It was also the time of blockbuster exhibitions and the museum's 75th anniversary, which saw the founding of events such as Parade the Circle designed to bring the museum out from behind its hallowed walls and into the community. This visitor-centered orientation

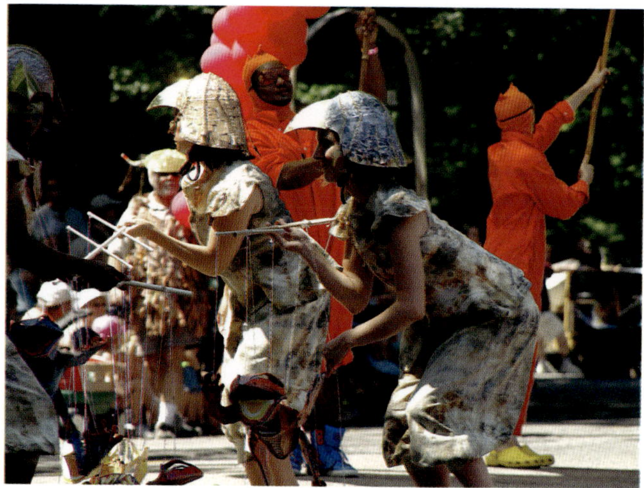

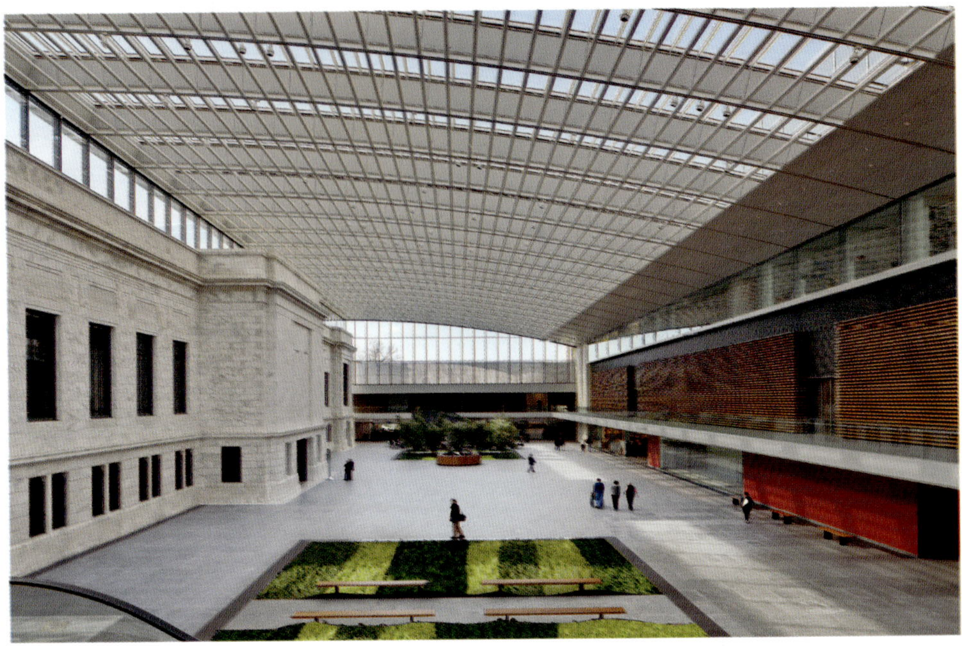

Rafael Viñoly's soaring atrium, named the Ames Family Atrium in 2013, unites the museum's four wings and allows visitors to choose a chronological path through the galleries or go directly to a favorite work of art.

continued under the leadership of Bob Bergman, who served as director from 1993 to 1999. The museum began a significant gallery renovation project at that time, culminating in the reinstallation of the armor court in 1998.

But the mosaic of buildings that the museum had become was a challenge both to staff trying to manage a great collection and to visitors trying to find their way. A vision of a more engaging and multifaceted museum for the 21st century was needed. A strategic planning process begun in 1995 was articulated in a 1999 facilities master plan. The initial step in enacting this plan, taken by the board of trustees on Katharine Lee Reid's first day as museum director in 2000, was the approval for the restoration of the original 1916 neoclassical building and fine arts garden. The project took three years to complete.

The second step followed quickly in 2001 with the selection of renowned architect Rafael Viñoly, whose visionary design to marry the 1916 building and the modernist Breuer wing came to fruition before the community's eyes at a public forum in 2002 where he voiced his perceptive understanding that "the collection is really what needs to be heard . . . it doesn't really quite need a building that assumes that it's going to be, by itself, a source of attraction. We're here to support something that already exists." With the

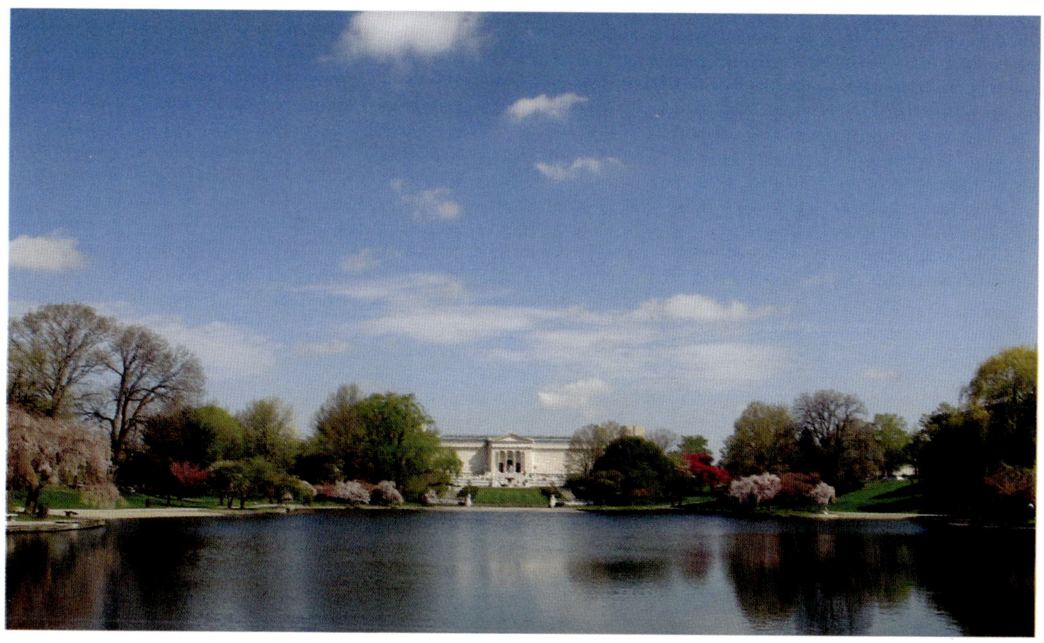

The museum is located in a park-like setting, with the original 1916 entrance overlooking a lagoon circled by cherry trees.

collection as his guide and the 1916 building as the anchor, Viñoly designed symmetrical wings on either side connecting all to the Breuer building with a soaring glass-enclosed atrium. This design achieved the museum's goal of weaving the experience of art into the fabric of the community through an inviting light-filled civic space from which visitors can engage with the collection through galleries, exhibitions, and programs.

The museum's ninth director, David Franklin, an internationally known scholar in Italian Renaissance and Baroque art, guided the completion of the construction project. Interim Director Fred Bidwell, a business leader with deep roots in the arts, continues to lead the transformation that will distinguish the museum as it enters its second century. Today the extraordinary works of art beloved by the local community and revered throughout the museum world beckon visitors into sumptuous galleries. This handbook is an introduction to these works, many lovingly collected by benefactors and generously given to the people of Cleveland and the world. On the eve of its centennial, the museum has rededicated itself to the community by honoring the aspirations of the founders and benefactors who endowed this museum as a living legacy for the benefit of all the people forever.

■ Leslie Cade, Archivist

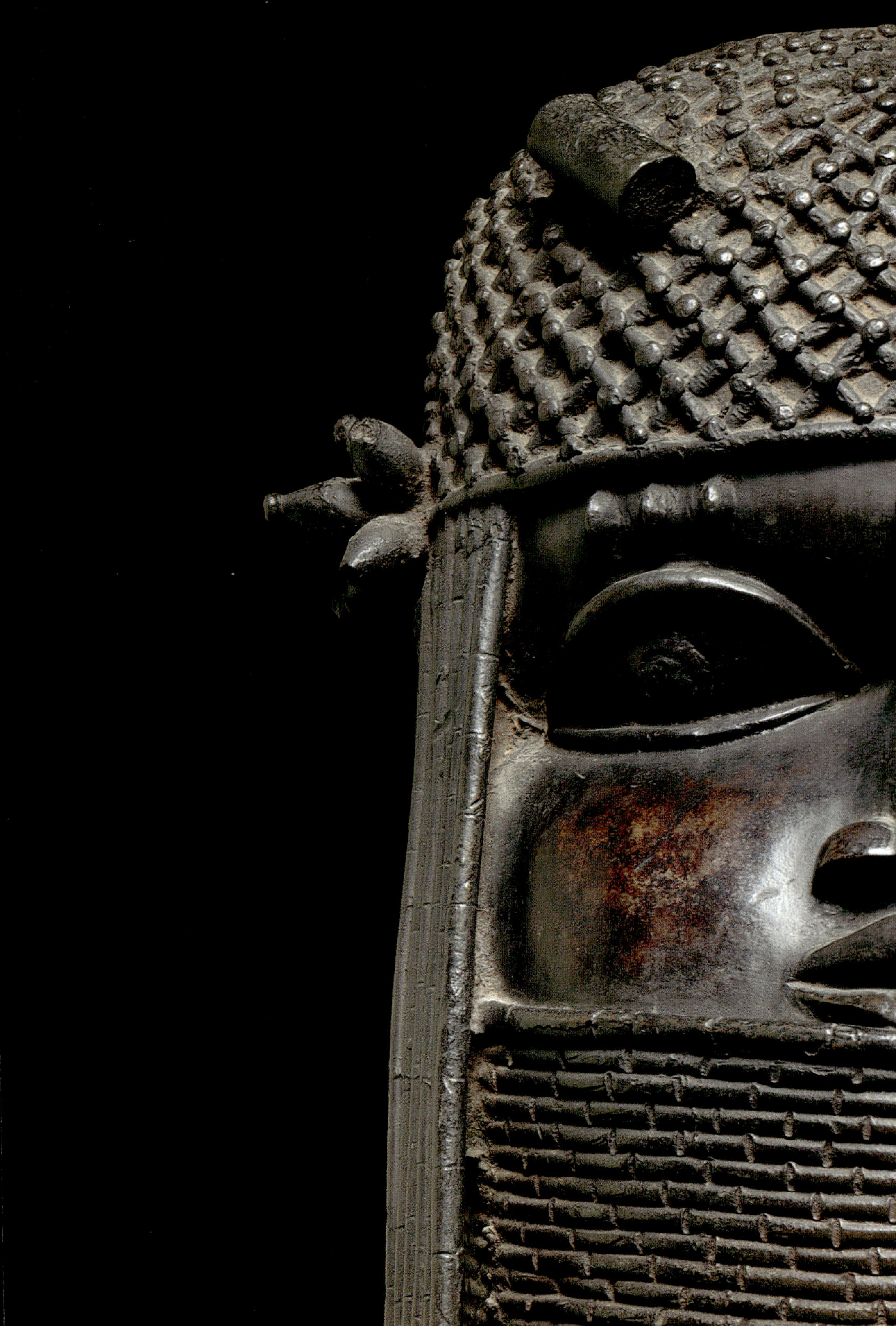

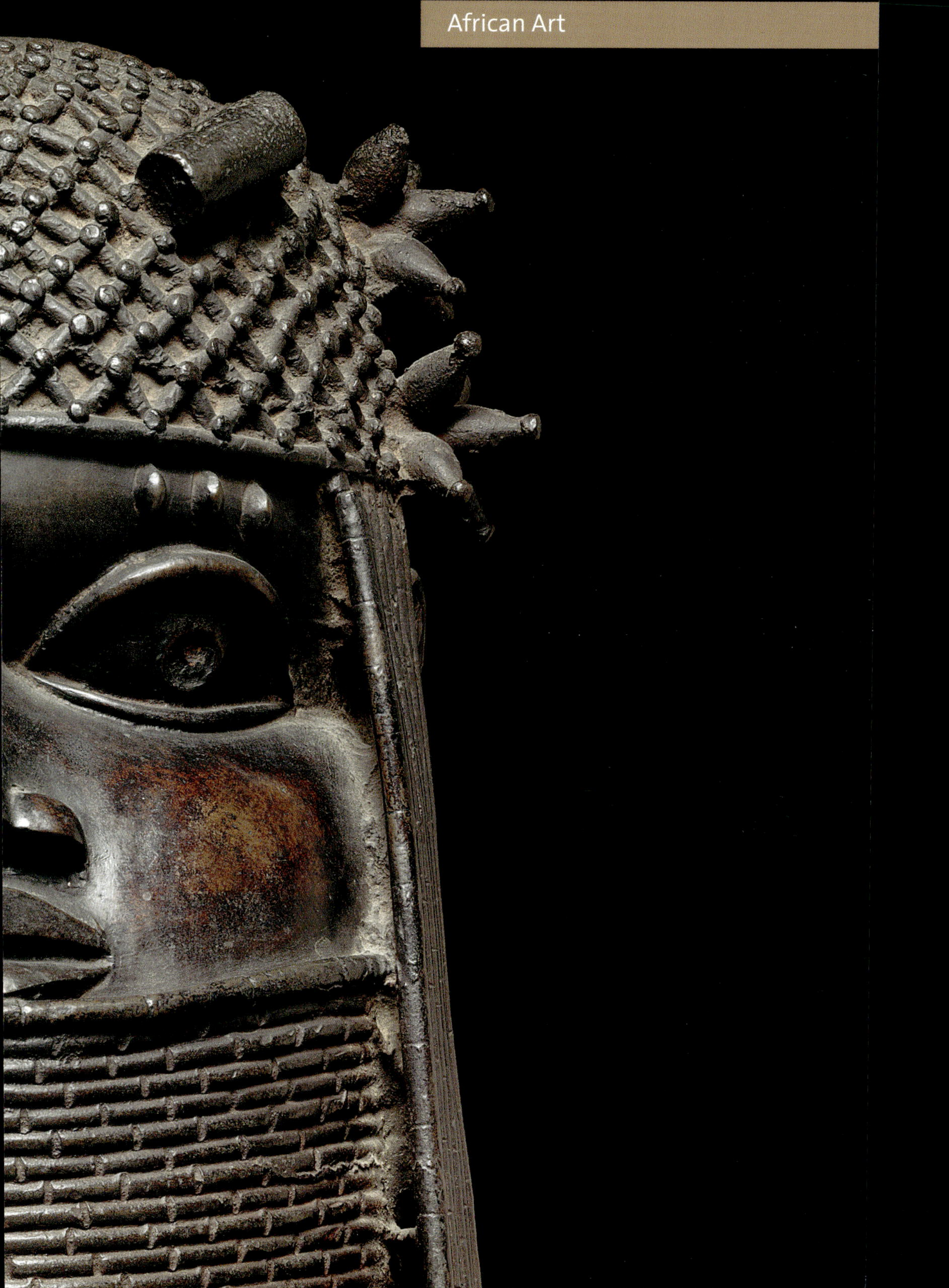

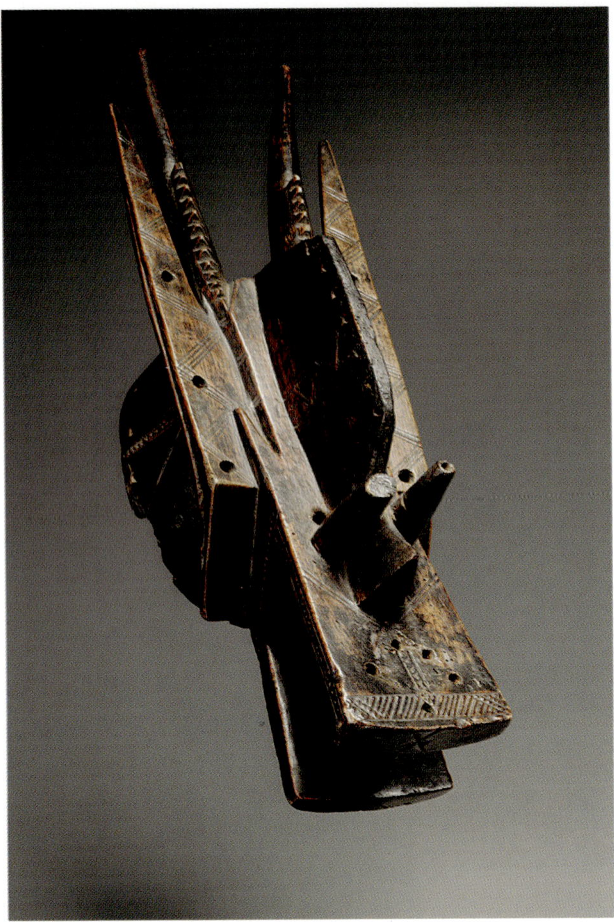

Helmet Mask mid to late 1800s

MALI, PROBABLY MALINKE PEOPLE

Combining animal and human features with abstract elements, this mask in a style characterized by angular volumes and planes is part of a small corpus tentatively attributed to the little-known Malinke people of Mali. Also called Mandinka or Maninka, their name designates speakers of the Manding language who are descendants of the Mali Empire, the powerful Muslim state in northwestern Africa that flourished from the 13th to the 15th century. Instead, many Malinke, like their closely related Bamana neighbors, adhere to the religion of their ancestors and belong to non-Islamic associations generically called *jow* (sing. *jo*). This mask most probably belonged to one of these jow, an interethnic initiation society known as Kore and shared between the Bamana and Malinke. One of six so-called power associations, Kore used to be responsible for organizing the transition rites that ensured the transformation of young boys into responsible adults. Secluded in a secret space in the bush, a group of teenagers was subjected to physical hardships and psychological challenges while being instructed in a variety of subjects that included herbal medicine, sexuality, the cycle of life, and correct behavior toward elders and ancestors. Kore initiates were divided into three distinct classes with their own symbols and masks. This helmet mask is believed to represent one of those classes, the hyena, even though it combines different animal traits.

WOOD; 17.5 X 14.8 X 47 CM (6-7/8 X 5-7/8 X 18-1/2 IN.)

ANDREW R. AND MARTHA HOLDEN JENNINGS FUND

2004.84

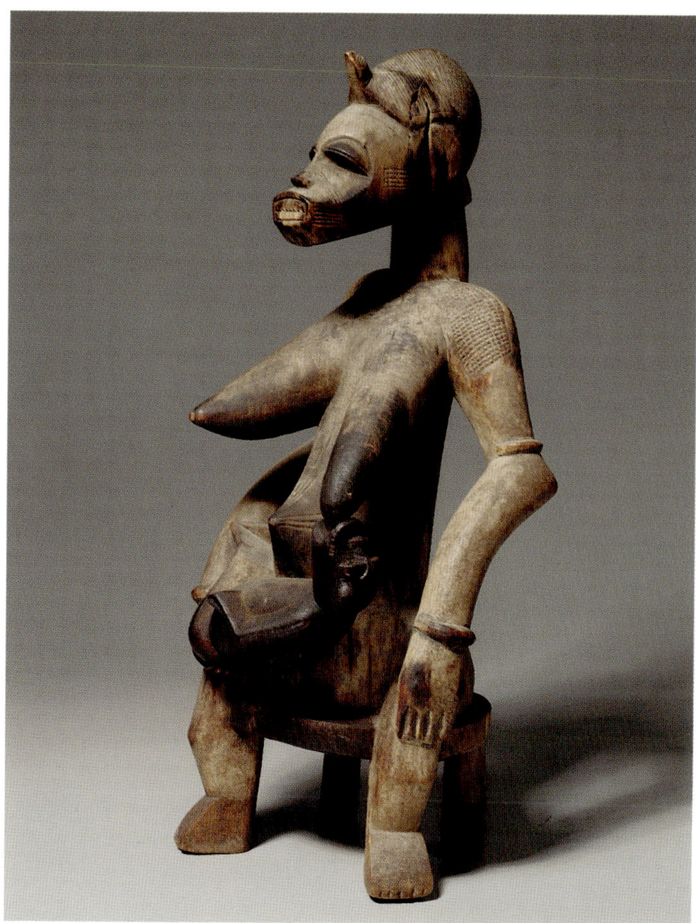

Mother-and-Child Figure late 1800s–mid 1900s

IVORY COAST, SENUFO PEOPLE

Among the Fodonon, a southern Senufo subgroup, large-scale seated mother-and-child figures are related to the female initiation association called Tyekpa and play a role in funerary ceremonies, where they are carried on the participating women's heads. The four-legged stool on which this mother-and-child figure is seated may help balance it on a dancer's head. Among the central Senufo, however, similar female figures were used as stationary display sculpture for Poro, the men's initiation society. Although economy of detail and stylization sometimes indicate a specific function, in practice it is impossible to determine the use of a particular figure based only on its style and degree of elaboration. Both types of figurative carvings belong to a broad category of sculptures designated with the class name *pombibele* (children of Poro). In the context of Poro and Tyekpa, mother-and-child figures probably refer to Ancient Mother (or Woman), the central deity of the Poro initiation cycle who is responsible for the protection and instruction of the initiates, her "children"; she nurses them with the milk of knowledge and thus transforms them into perfect human beings. The dominant context in which the figures appear, either in a static way displayed in an architectural setting, or in a dynamic way in dances and processions, is the commemorative funeral.

WOOD; H. 63.6 CM (25 IN.)

JAMES ALBERT AND MARY GARDINER FORD MEMORIAL FUND 1961.198

Helmet early to mid 1900s

IVORY COAST, SENUFO PEOPLE

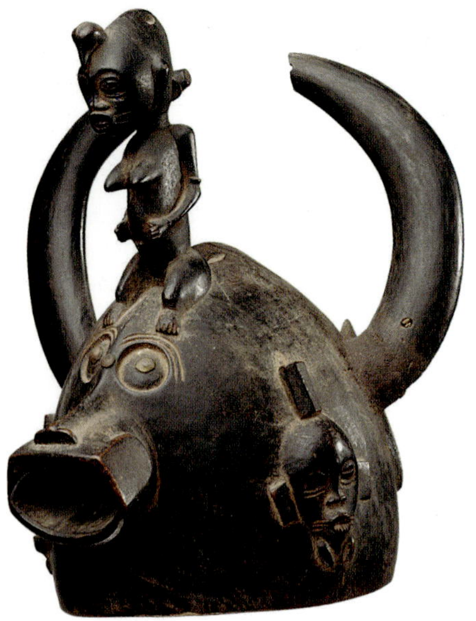

This helmet, decorated with horns and a female figure carved from the same piece of wood, is a rare example of a wooden headdress type from the Boundiali region. Called *daagu,* helmets like this one seem to have been worn in rituals that emphasize the transition from one age group to the next, before their initiation into Poro. Having passed a physical ordeal, young men are permitted to sing songs that criticize the old men of the community and the rituals of the Poro society. When they perform with their age group, each of two men chosen as lead singers wears a daagu headdress festooned with cowrie shells, strips of fabrics, long white feathers, and other accessories. A long train attached to the bottom rim on the back of the helmet is decorated with cowries and fringe with little brass bells. Accompanied by drums and wind instruments, the singing, dances, and sketches start in the early evening and often last until the following morning. The old men of the village are the subject of parody, ridicule, and even insult, with the weaknesses of a particular individual often a target. Though some elders are offended by the criticism and leave the village square in anger, others are honored by the special attention they receive as a result of their many years of service to the Poro society and the community at large.

WOOD; H. 34.9 CM (13-3/4 IN.)

GIFT OF KATHERINE C. WHITE 1975.152

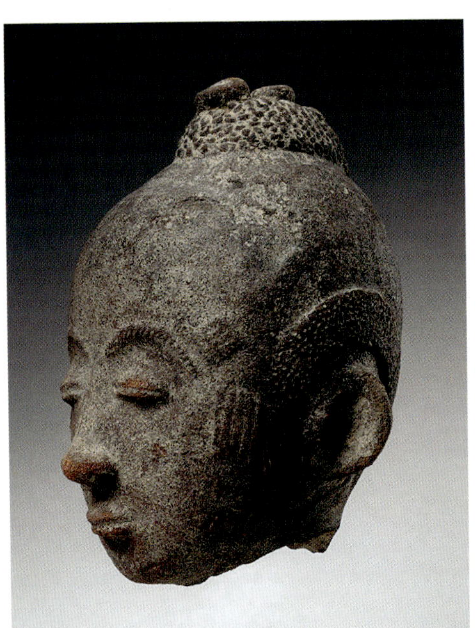

Head late 1600s–early 1700s

GHANA, AKAN PEOPLE

Both Akan divinities and distinguished mortals were once memorialized through terracotta effigies. Akan elites commissioned terracotta portraits from female artists to be used after they died. These terracotta substitutes were placed in sacred groves outside the village days, or even months, after the burial of an individual. Periodically, rituals comprising libations, offerings, and prayers were performed at these groves in honor of the ancestors, expressing the belief in a continuum between life and death. Terracotta busts, standing and seated figures, and figuratively decorated vessels populated such groves along with freestanding heads like this example with its striking serene, introspective expression. Generally called *mma,* meaning "infants," these terracotta memorials were viewed as idealized portraits of the deceased, with the ancestor's identity suggested by the representation of cosmetic adornments, including scarification patterns and symbols of rank and prestige. The curly knobs here imitate a male Akan hairstyle consisting of a shaved and tufted pattern that has been out of fashion since the beginning of the 20th century. Stylistically, it is related to pieces that were accidentally discovered in an archaeological site in the vicinity of the town of Heman in southern Ghana and dated from 1690 to about 1730. The head's refined facial features are typical of a regional style called Twifo, referring to an Akan state positioned along the trade route between the Asante and the Fante.

TERRACOTTA; 19.1 X 13.6 X 15.5 CM (7-1/2 X 5-3/8 X 6-1/8 IN.)

EDWIN R. AND HARRIET PELTON PERKINS MEMORIAL FUND 1990.22

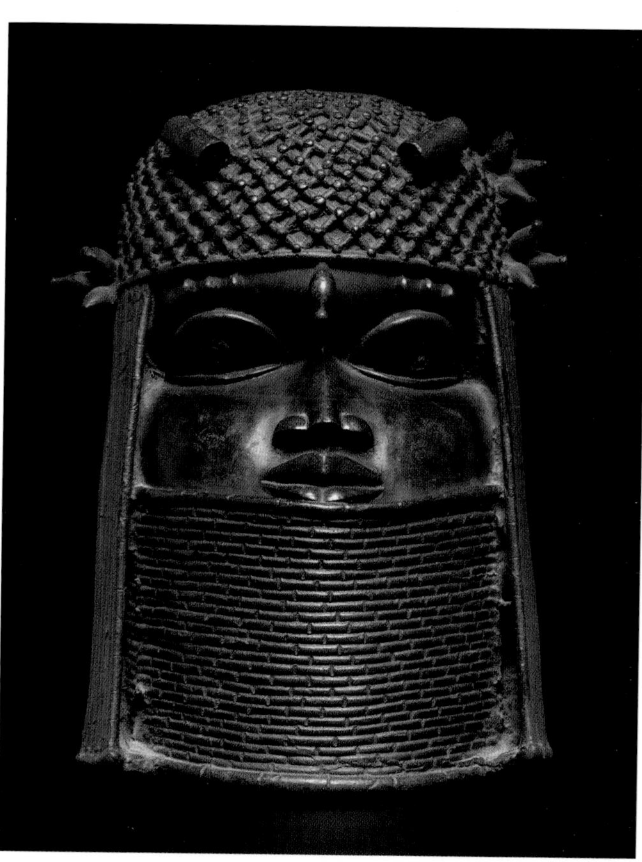

Head possibly mid 1500s or early 1600s

NIGERIA, BENIN KINGDOM, EDO PEOPLE

Metal arts flourished in the Benin kingdom from the 15th century until 1897, when the British sacked the royal palace and exiled the reigning *oba* (king) in retribution for the killing of British officials. The majority of the so-called Benin bronzes are in fact brasses, made of an alloy of copper and zinc. This cast-metal head, made by a highly skilled artist using the lost-wax method, depicts the divine oba cloaked in a ritual headdress and collar of red coral beads. The beads, imported from the Mediterranean and thus testifying to early contacts between the Benin kingdom and Europe, were reserved for the oba and indicated his wealth and status.

Heads were ordered by every new oba as centerpieces for the ancestral altar in honor of his deceased predecessor. The altar commemorating the king's ancestors and glorifying the power of the kingdom was a raised earthen platform on which were displayed a wide variety of objects, such as carved ivory tusks and metal swords and bells. These memorial heads are not real portraits, but standardized representations meant to celebrate royal insignia. This head has been tentatively dated to the mid 16th or early 17th century on stylistic grounds and related to an intermediate or "classical" period. From that time on, altar heads were conceived to support carved ivory tusks.

BRASS; 29.9 X 21.6 X 20.4 CM (11-3/4 X 8-1/2 X 8 IN.)

DUDLEY P. ALLEN FUND 1938.6

Head 600 BC–AD 250

NIGERIA, NOK REGION

Nok is the name of a town on the Jos Plateau in central Nigeria where fragments of terracotta sculptures were found in 1928. Many more fragments and intact figures, both animal and human, as well as heads have come to light in subsequent years. While sharing the same style, called Nok after the site where the discovery was made, the findings show a striking variety. The culture from which these terracotta works come once occupied a vast territory along both sides of the Benue River, an area today inhabited by various ethnic groups. Most of the terracottas were found in open tin mines, but some were discovered in riverbeds or under the roots of trees. Radiocarbon and thermoluminescence dating methods have revealed that the sculptures were made between 600 BC and AD 250. Probably a fragment of an almost life-size male seated figure, this example is remarkably well preserved, its glossy surface largely intact. It was shaped by hand from coarse-grained clay, covered with slip, and then burnished. The production of terracottas of this size was a challenging enterprise, requiring sophisticated technical skill. The identities of the portrayed figures remain unknown, but the adornments and elaborate hairstyles and headdresses of many of the larger figures seem to indicate that they represent notables or even leaders. Some scholars have suggested they served ritual purposes and may have been part of a shrine or temple, or even placed on a tomb.

TERRACOTTA; 38.2 X 20 CM (15-1/2 X 7-7/8 IN.)

ANDREW R. AND MARTHA HOLDEN JENNINGS FUND

1995.21

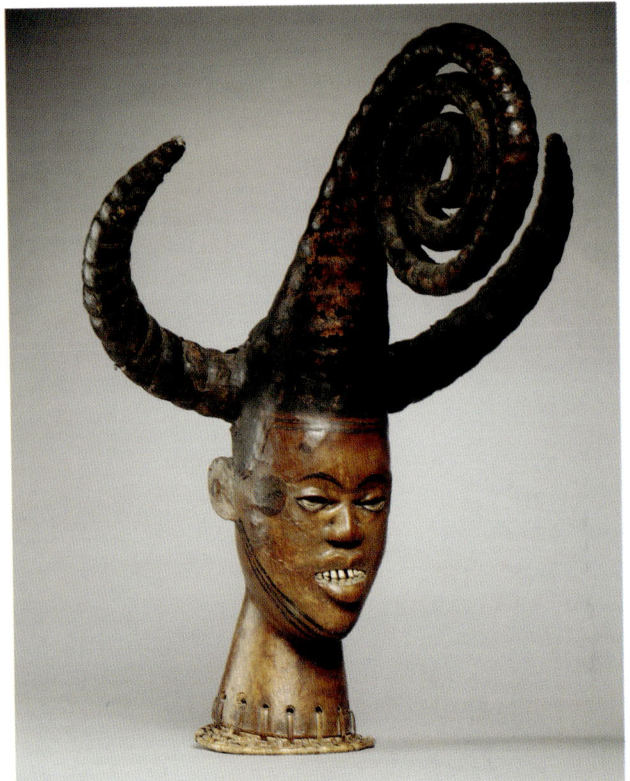

Headdress early 1900s

NIGERIA, EJAGHAM PEOPLE

Skin-covered headdresses or crest masks made of fresh, uncured antelope skin stretched over a carved head are a distinctive naturalistic art form of the Cross River area in the southeastern part of Nigeria and western Cameroon. This crest mask depicts a woman's head with a long neck, rounded facial features, realistically rendered teeth of strips of cane, and a faithful imitation of a horned coiffure. The wickerwork skullcap at the base of the neck would have been secured on the wearer's head by a string under his chin. That such headdresses were originally covered with human skin is not impossible given that they are said to represent heads of enemies killed during wars, and thus attest to their owners' exceptional powers. Such headdresses were used in different secret societies of the region among various peoples. The style of this headdress is characteristic of the lower Cross River area, in or around the town of Calabar in Nigeria. The elaborate hairstyle with down-curving "horns" and the head's facial features indicate that this headdress was most probably used in the context of the Ekpa, a society of Ejagham women responsible for the education of girls in preparation for marriage. The headdress could represent a girl who embodies ideal female beauty and is ready for marriage. The hairstyle depicted was actually worn during the coming-out ceremony following the girls' seclusion in the "fattening-house."

WOOD, ANTELOPE SKIN, BASKETRY, CANE, METAL; 67.3 X 43.2 X 43.2 CM (26-1/2 X 17 X 17 IN.)

ANDREW R. AND MARTHA HOLDEN JENNINGS FUND 1990.23

Male Figure mid 1800s–early 1900s

CAMEROON, BANGWA PEOPLE, PROBABLY CARVED BY ATEU ATSA (ACTIVE 1840–1910) OR HIS WORKSHOP

This figure, adorned with royal attire of cap, beaded necklace, folded loincloth, and drinking horn, belongs to a group of about 25 stylistically related works that have been tentatively attributed to a sculptor named Ateu Atsa and his workshop. While the accuracy of his name has been recently questioned, Ateu Atsa worked for chief Assunganyi of Fontem, one of nine Bangwa chiefdoms. His work is distinguished from that of his colleagues by its sense of realism and the attention devoted to the facial expression.

The Bangwa are especially well known for their royal figure sculptures, such as the example shown here, which represent kings, queens, princesses, and certain high dignitaries. Commemorative works, they are kept by members of a secret association called Lefem, which gathers weekly in a sacred bush to discuss matters related to the survival of the kingdom and to perform sacred music in honor of the royal ancestors. The figures are kept in shrines, where they are silent witnesses to the sacrifices made to the skulls of the chief's ancestors. Exhibited on the occasion of funerals or royal cults, these figures are believed to safeguard the kingdom and protect the fecundity of the people, the animal world, and the soil. As ancestral receptacles, the sculptures evoke the memory of previous chiefs while serving as a vehicle for communication with them.

WOOD; 92.1 X 23.3 X 21 CM (36-1/4 X 9 X 8-1/4 IN.)

PURCHASE FROM THE J. H. WADE FUND 1987.62

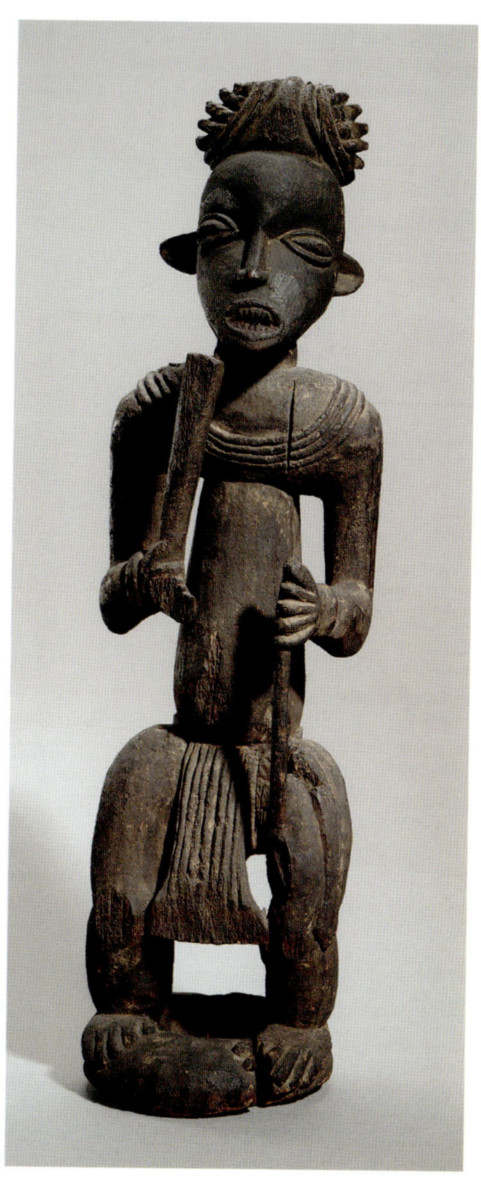

Mother-and-Child Figure mid to late 1800s

DEMOCRATIC REPUBLIC OF THE CONGO, YOMBE PEOPLE

The Yombe are one of the many Kikongo-speaking peoples that at one point in their history were part of, or strongly influenced by, the former kingdom of Kongo, which flourished from at least 1400 through the late 1600s. After the introduction of Christianity and the baptism of King Nzinga a Nkuwa on 3 May 1491, Kongo artists were influenced by the iconography of the new faith. The mother-and-child theme and the naturalism in Yombe art may also reflect the influence of European models and tastes. This mother-and-child figure was probably used in a women's cult concerned with the enhancement of fertility and the treatment of infertility. The cross-legged seated pose atop a square base and the various body adornments, including the miter-shaped cap, filed teeth, firm breasts, and raised scarification marks, convey ideals of beauty and high status; they may also reveal that the woman incarnates the founding ancestor of a kinship group. The double bracelets around her upper arms imitate protective charms made of plaited or braided raffia fibers worn by religious experts and by ill people as a cure. During ritual use, the surfaces of such figures were rubbed with a reddish mixture of oil and camwood powder, both a cosmetic and a sign of mediation; in Yombe thought red indicates transitional conditions such as death and birth.

WOOD; H. 26 CM (10-1/4 IN.)

ANDREW R. AND MARTHA HOLDEN JENNINGS FUND 2003.35

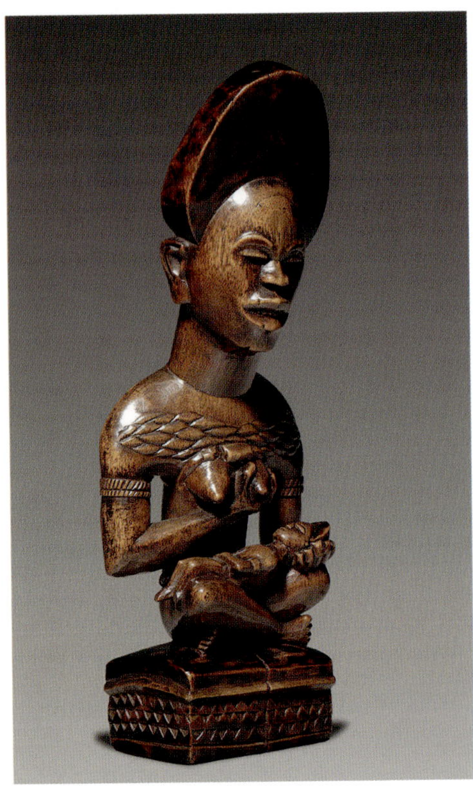

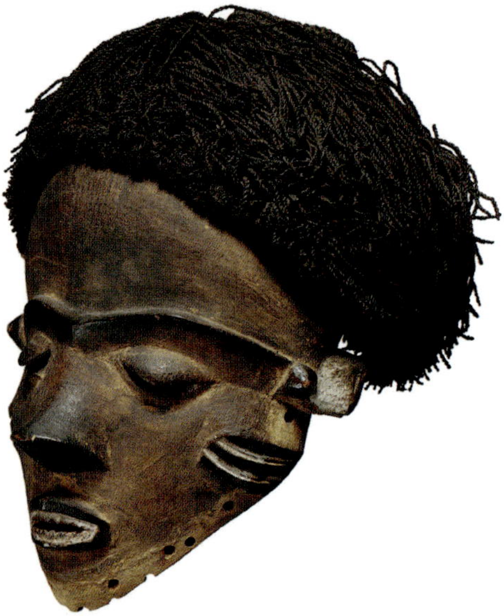

Face Mask early 1900s

DEMOCRATIC REPUBLIC OF THE CONGO, PENDE PEOPLE

This face mask in Central Pende style is an exquisite example of a mask identified as *gambanda,* the wife of the chief or, more generally, the contemporary fashionable woman. Its smooth forehead, softly modeled cheekbones, and oval silhouette are hallmarks of beauty. A wig of hundreds of small braids that imitates a once-fashionable hairdo is another much admired feature. The artist has been especially successful in capturing the seductive gaze present in the greatest renderings of feminine physiognomy. For the Pende, physiognomy and gender are related and gender reflects inner character. Accordingly, women are seen as gentle, self-controlled, and socially responsible, and their masks are characterized by soft modulations and modest features. Before masquerades became largely secular events meant to entertain and amuse the community, they constituted a place of communion between the living and the dead. The masks commemorated deceased family members who were said to return to the village to dance among their living descendants. Originally organized after the ritual renewal of the village to thank the ancestors for past assistance and to request their continued benevolence, masquerades would occur when the millet was sowed or harvested, when the chief fell ill, or when an epidemic threatened the well-being of the community.

WOOD, FIBER; 27 X 22 X 28.5 CM
(10-7/8 X 8-5/8 X 11-1/4 IN.)
LEONARD C. HANNA JR. FUND 2008.150

Male Figure possibly early 1900s
DEMOCRATIC REPUBLIC OF THE CONGO, SONGYE PEOPLE

Songye magical figures, *mankishi* (sing. *nkishi*), characterized by their bold aesthetic expression, are used as devices for protection, healing, or therapy. Their value resides in supernatural ingredients of animal, vegetal, and mineral origin, most commonly concealed in the abdominal cavity or in a horn set into the skull. Meant to solicit the powers of the spirit world, these ingredients are selected and assembled according to prescribed formulas by a practitioner whose personal reputation will greatly determine the figure's success. The visual impact and workmanship of this figure and its intermediate size—between smaller, personal objects and larger, community objects—suggest it was used by an extended family rather than an individual. Though its skeletal facial forms attest to influence of the Tempa subgroup in western Songyeland, it was most probably made among the Central Songye. Its external attachments are meant to augment its visual impact. The raffia skirt around the waist and the blue and white beads are indicators of leadership. The metal appliqué covering the face and the metal blades edging the headgear specifically refer to the blacksmith, a culture hero celebrated in a Songye myth of state formation. The metal strips on the face are said to relate to lightning, signaling the figure's role as a powerful anti-sorcerer, able to counteract and redirect aggressive action against the evildoer. Yet, the contrast between white iron and red copper symbolically alludes to ambivalent powers.

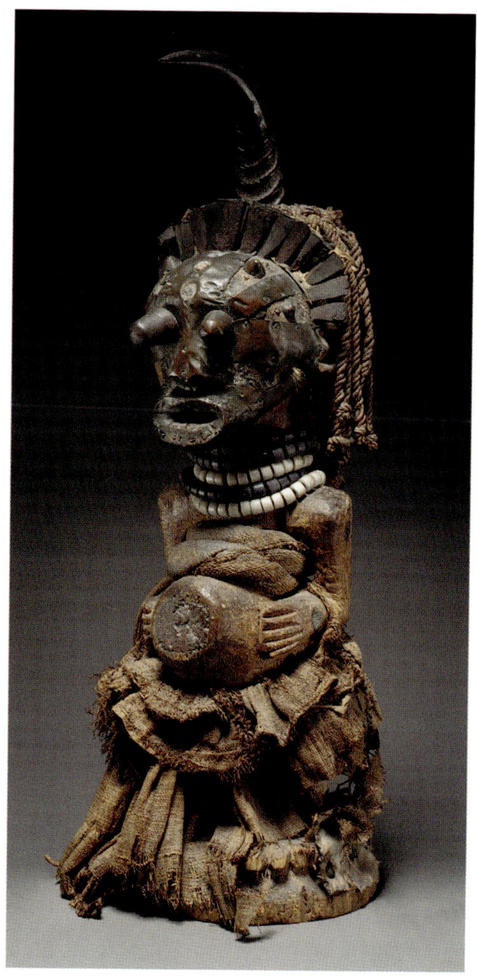

WOOD, GLASS BEADS, COPPER ALLOY, IRON ALLOY, HUMAN TEETH, ANTELOPE HORN, HIDE, ANIMAL HAIR, MINERALS, WOVEN PLANT FIBERS; 64 X 24.5 X 24 CM
(25-1/4 X 9-5/8 X 9-1/2 IN.)
RENÉ AND ODETTE DELENNE COLLECTION, LEONARD C. HANNA JR. FUND 2010.451

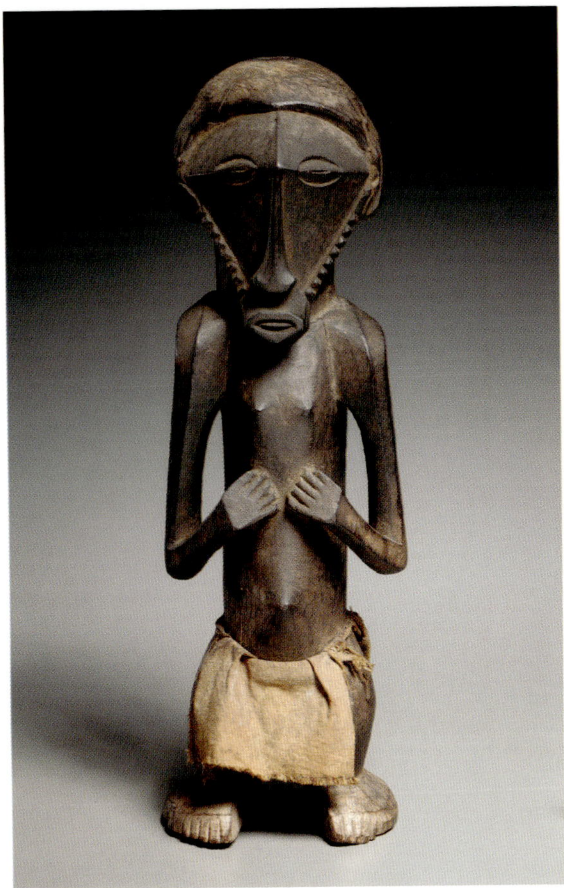

Male Figure late 1800s–early 1900s

DEMOCRATIC REPUBLIC OF THE CONGO, SO-CALLED PRE-BEMBE PEOPLE

This male figure is the work of a sculptor of one of the so-called Pre-Bembe hunters. The Pre-Bembe people include different groups, such as the Basikasingo, Bahutshwe, and Babwari, and live dispersed among the Bembe, Boyo, and other peoples near Lake Tanganyika. Figures such as this example have often been misattributed to the Bembe proper. While the Pre-Bembe have been strongly influenced by the Bembe, the hunter groups have preserved their cultural autonomy. Standing Pre-Bembe figures, male or female, are used within the framework of an ancestor cult and are dedicated to the founders of small political groupings. They are usually kept in a shrine with a number of stylistically related figures that represent named and genealogically related ancestors. Such ensembles serve as intermediaries between the ancestors and their living descendants. At times of crisis, the custodian of the shrine, who is often the village headman, spends the night very near the images and invokes and brings offerings to the ancestors in exchange for their support. Among the neighboring and closely related Boyo, a figure's size indicates chronological sequence, with the largest figures in an ensemble being the oldest and depicting founding ancestors. These central figures serve as models or prototypes for the smaller figures that represent successive generations of chiefs.

WOOD, CLOTH; 48.6 X 15.6 X 17.2 CM (19-1/4 X 6-1/4 X 6-3/4 IN.)

GIFT OF KATHERINE C. WHITE 1969.10

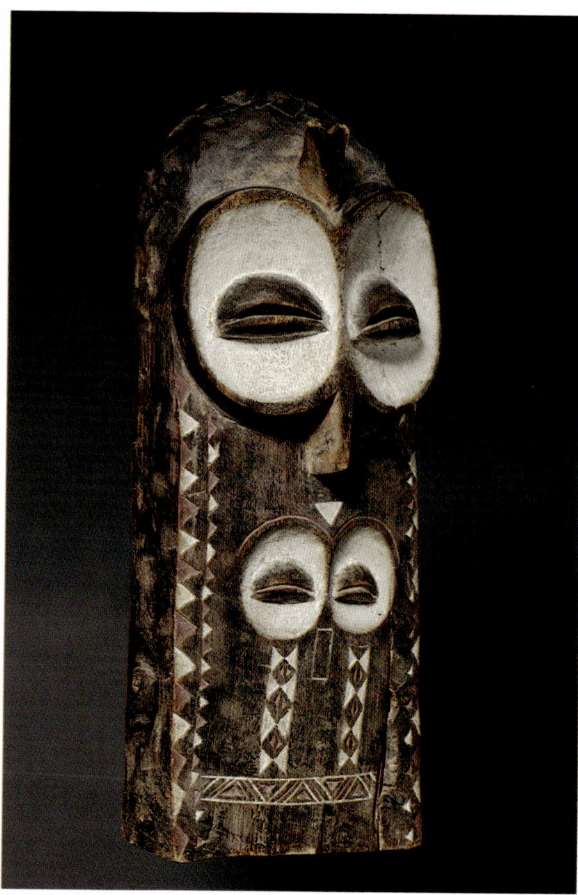

Plank Mask possibly early 1900s

DEMOCRATIC REPUBLIC OF THE CONGO, BEMBE PEOPLE

Though the Bembe are culturally and historically related to the neighboring Lega people, sharing the Bwami association as one of their premier art patrons, they incorporated and assimilated many other influences. Polychrome and nearly rectangular plank masks, used in one of two types of men's puberty rites among southwestern Bembe groups, are rare. Attached to a large banana-leaf and barkstrip costume hiding the wearer's identity, or sometimes affixed to a cone-shaped bark hat, the mask would be donned by a recently circumcised youth during his seclusion, when disguised (and thus incognito) he would leave the bush where he temporarily resided and venture out in nearby villages to beg for food.

Combining human and animal traits in a highly stylized shape, this mask has two pairs of coffee-bean–shaped eyes in white oval planes, its face bordered with a frieze of white and red triangles. Elusive and tentative, some interpretations have suggested the two pairs of eyes refer to the dichotomy between male and female or to opposing forces in nature, while others have drawn a connection with the practice of divination and the idea of enhanced perception in both the past and the future. The two excrescences above the forehead have been identified as representing the tufts of an owl, possibly in reference to the forest as a source of mystic power. In some parts of Bembeland, however, similar masks were attached to offering tables on which libations were made to deceased relatives.

WOOD; 46.5 X 19 X 10 CM (18-1/4 X 7-1/2 X 4 IN.)

LEONARD C. HANNA JR. FUND 2006.116

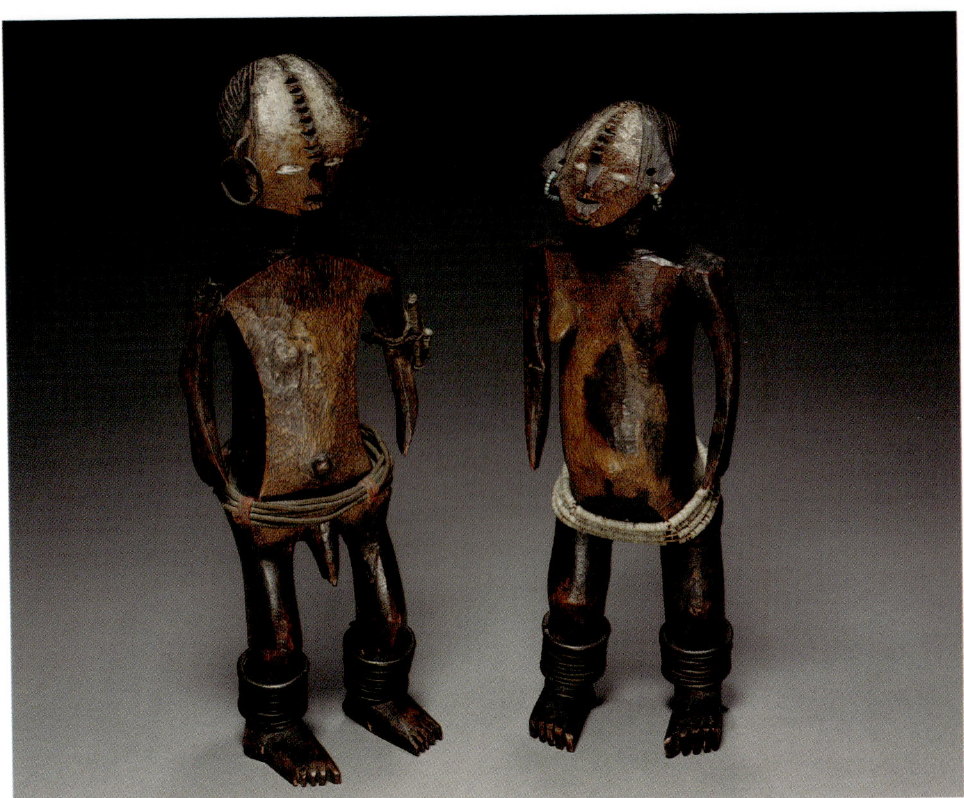

Male and Female Figure Pair possibly early 1900s
DEMOCRATIC REPUBLIC OF THE CONGO, PROBABLY NGBANDI PEOPLE

On the basis of stylistic features, the origin of this pair can be situated in the Ubangi River region, a little-researched area in the heart of Africa. Because of the limited field investigations, many questions remain regarding the provenance, usage, meaning, and function of the region's art. A cultural crucible, it was shaped by numerous exchanges in religious and ritual matters resulting from a long history of migrations and assimilations. The sculpture of the Ubangi region—masks, musical instruments, figures—displays several interrelated styles. Though this couple has been attributed to the Ngbandi, many of the characteristics identified as typical of the Ngbandi are in fact shared by their neighbors. While carving paired figures is well documented for the Ngbaka-Minagende, where such sculptures are said to represent the mythical ancestor Seto and his sister-wife, Nabo, no field-based research to date has been able to confirm the existence of figurative couples among the Ngbandi. The literature does mention clay or wooden figures placed near the shrine of an ancestor as well as wooden sculptures employed by magic practitioners and trance diviners. However, some of the earliest figures in Ngbandi style to enter European collections were opposite-sex pairs like this example. Were all such Ngbandi-style couples perhaps created by Ngbandi artists for a neighboring Ngbaka-Minagende community (or another Ubangi group where the use of such sculptures was common practice), or do they instead refer to a more localized tradition that was never documented by foreign observers?

WOOD, COPPER ALLOY, IRON ALLOY, SHELL AND GLASS BEADS, FABRIC, PLANT FIBER, PIGMENT; 45 X 15.5 X 9.2 CM (17-3/4 X 6-1/2 X 3-5/8 IN.) AND 41 X 13 X 11.5 CM (16-1/4 X 5-1/8 X 4-1/2 IN.)

RENÉ AND ODETTE DELENNE COLLECTION, LEONARD C. HANNA JR. FUND 2010.459.1–2

Fertility Figure late 1800s or early 1900s

LESOTHO, SOUTHERN SOTHO PEOPLE

This stylized representation of a human body can be identified as stemming from the Southern Sotho on the basis of the abstract geometric patterns of its beaded designs, as well as the typical, often bold, color sequences. It is constructed around a wooden core carved by a man; a woman was responsible for the wrapping of the core in cloth and the intricate beading. While beads were greatly valued as adornment throughout southern Africa, they were originally bartered and acquired from foreign explorers, traders, and missionaries. Fertility figures like this example were used during the initiation ceremonies of pubescent girls. Integrating talismanic materials in their fabrication, they were meant to guarantee fertility and to prevent or cure barrenness. Expressing the desire to bear children, the figures are sometimes also called child figures—rather than dolls—because young brides would care for them as they would for their children, carrying them on their backs and sleeping with them until their first child was born, who is named after the doll. After they had served their purpose these dolls were either destroyed or left at sacred sites as offerings to the spirits. Despite being called child figures, such images never represent children but instead take the form of adult women capable of procreation. Their female gender can usually be determined on the basis of their beaded dress or ornaments.

WOOD, GLASS BEADS, FIBER; H. 26 CM (10-1/4 IN.), DIAM. 8.2 CM (3-1/4 IN.)

LEONARD C. HANNA JR. FUND 2010.208

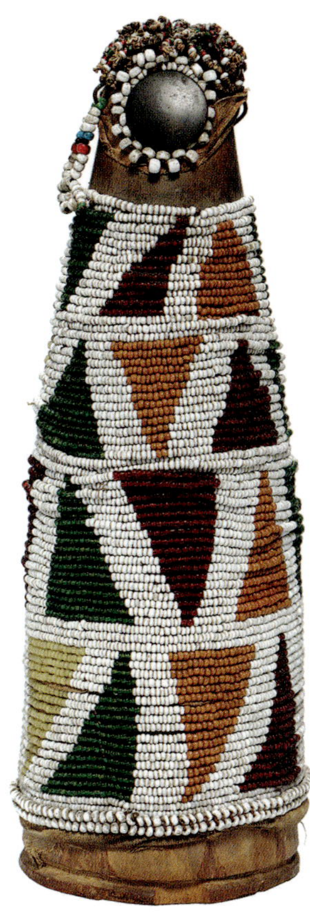

African Art: More Than Figures and Masks

The exhibition *African Textiles and Decorative Arts,* hosted by the Cleveland Museum of Art in 1973, was a landmark in the field of African art. It was curated by Indiana University professor Roy Sieber—one of the founding fathers of African art studies in this country—for the Museum of Modern Art in New York, but Cleveland collector Katherine "Kat" White played a discreet yet important behind-the-scenes role in the exhibition's conception and organization. One of this country's most important postwar private collectors of African art, Kat White donated more than 100 works to our museum. She also lent some textiles and decorative arts to the 1973 exhibition. Despite the transformative impact of the show on the appreciation of nonsculptural and nonfigurative forms of African art as worthy of both collectors' and scholars' attention, it took two more decades before Cleveland pursued the more systematic acquisition of textiles and decorative arts for its African collection. However, not coincidentally, some of the museum's earliest African acquisitions, dating to 1915, consisted of a group of Kuba textiles and Chokwe decorative works of art, such as a comb or hair ornament topped

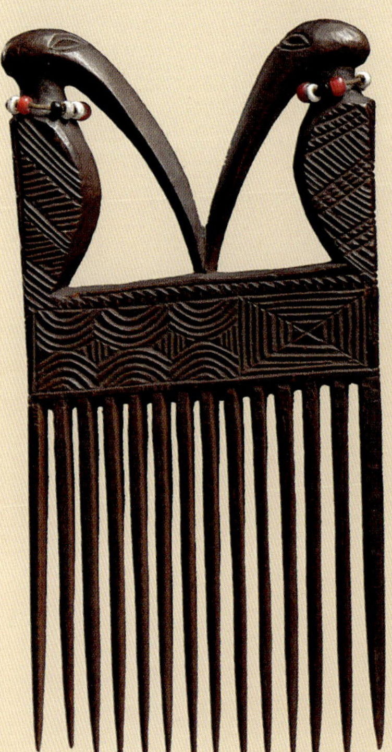

Comb or Hair Ornament, mid to late 1800s. Angola or Democratic Republic of the Congo, Chokwe people. Wood; 13.3 x 8 x 1.4 cm (5-1/4 x 3-1/8 x 1/2 in.). The Harold R. Clark Educational Extension Fund 1915.453

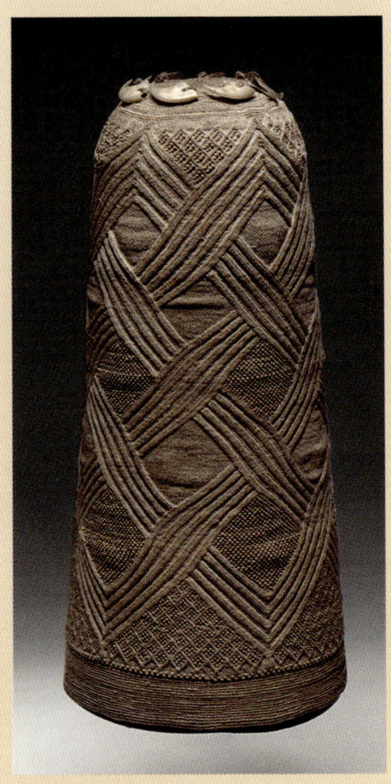

Hat, late 1800s–early 1900s. Democratic Republic of the Congo, possibly Yombe people. Raffia palm fiber, leopard claws; 42 x 19.3 x 19 cm (16-1/2 x 7-5/8 x 7-1/2 in.). John L. Severance Fund 1997.180

with two birds. In those early days such object types were not fully considered art but were instead added to the museum's education collection. Some of the most recent acquisitions in the areas of textiles and decorative arts—all originating from today's Democratic Republic of the Congo—are a finely woven chief's hat of the Yombe people decorated with a rim of leopard claws, a strikingly unusual hand-shaped pipe of possible Luntu origin, and a woman's skirt of the Mbuun people, one of a handful of such textiles to be preserved outside of Europe. The expanded recognition of what constitutes African art beyond the familiar genres of wooden masks and figure sculptures has also led to an interest in new geographic areas with different forms of visual art. Illustrative of southern Africa's rich artistic legacy are a newly acquired Southern Nguni apron made of leather and glass beads, and a Southern Sotho snuff container carved from cattle horn.

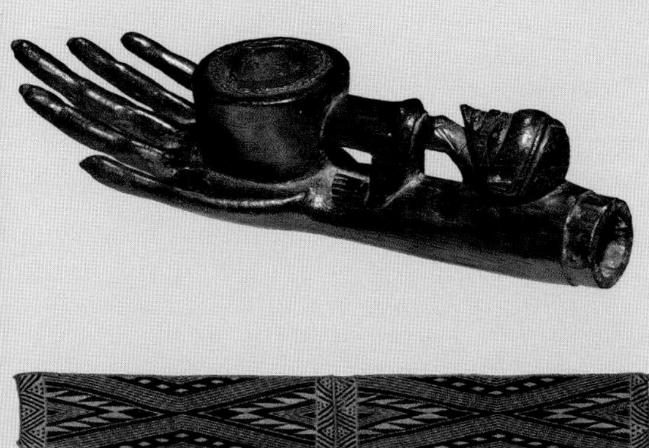

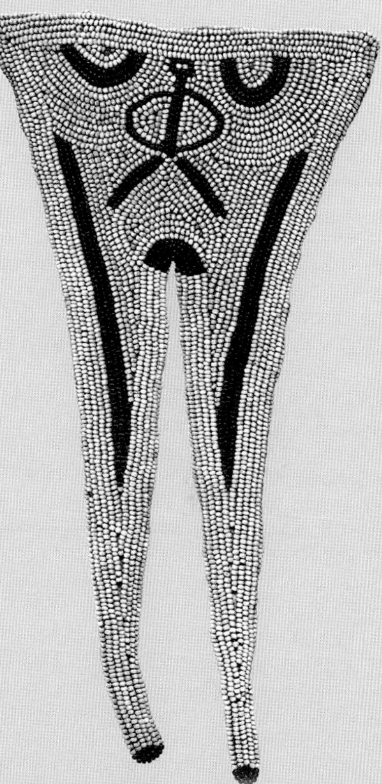

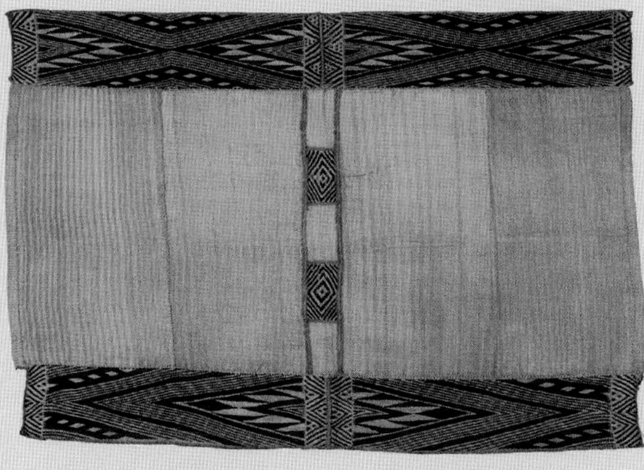

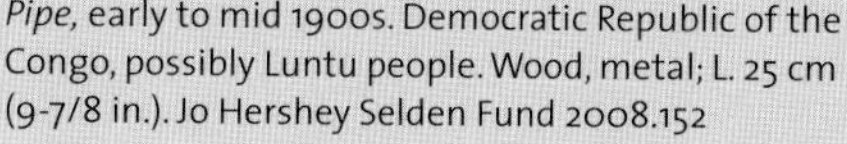

Pipe, early to mid 1900s. Democratic Republic of the Congo, possibly Luntu people. Wood, metal; L. 25 cm (9-7/8 in.). Jo Hershey Selden Fund 2008.152

Woman's Skirt, late 1800s–early 1900s. Democratic Republic of the Congo, Mbuun people. Raffia palm fiber; 73.7 x 102.9 cm (29 x 40-1/2 in.). Alma Kroeger Fund 2013.5

Snuff Container, 1800s–1900s. Lesotho, Southern Sotho people. Cattle horn; H. 10.8 cm (4-1/4 in.). Leonard C. Hanna Jr. Fund 2010.202

Apron, 1800s–1900s. South Africa, Southern Nguni people. Leather, glass, beads; H. 35.6 cm (14 in.). Leonard C. Hanna Jr. Fund 2010.206

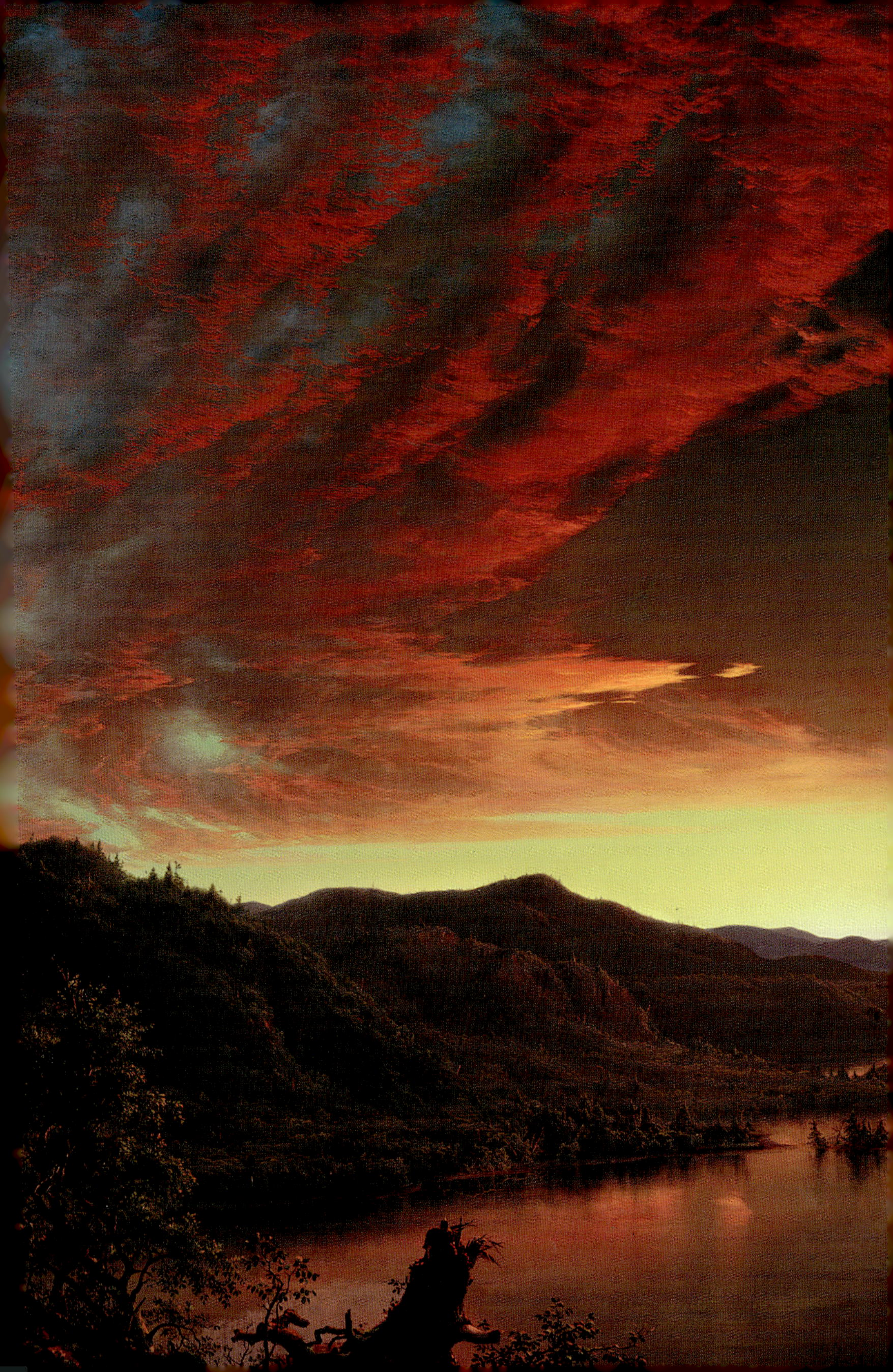

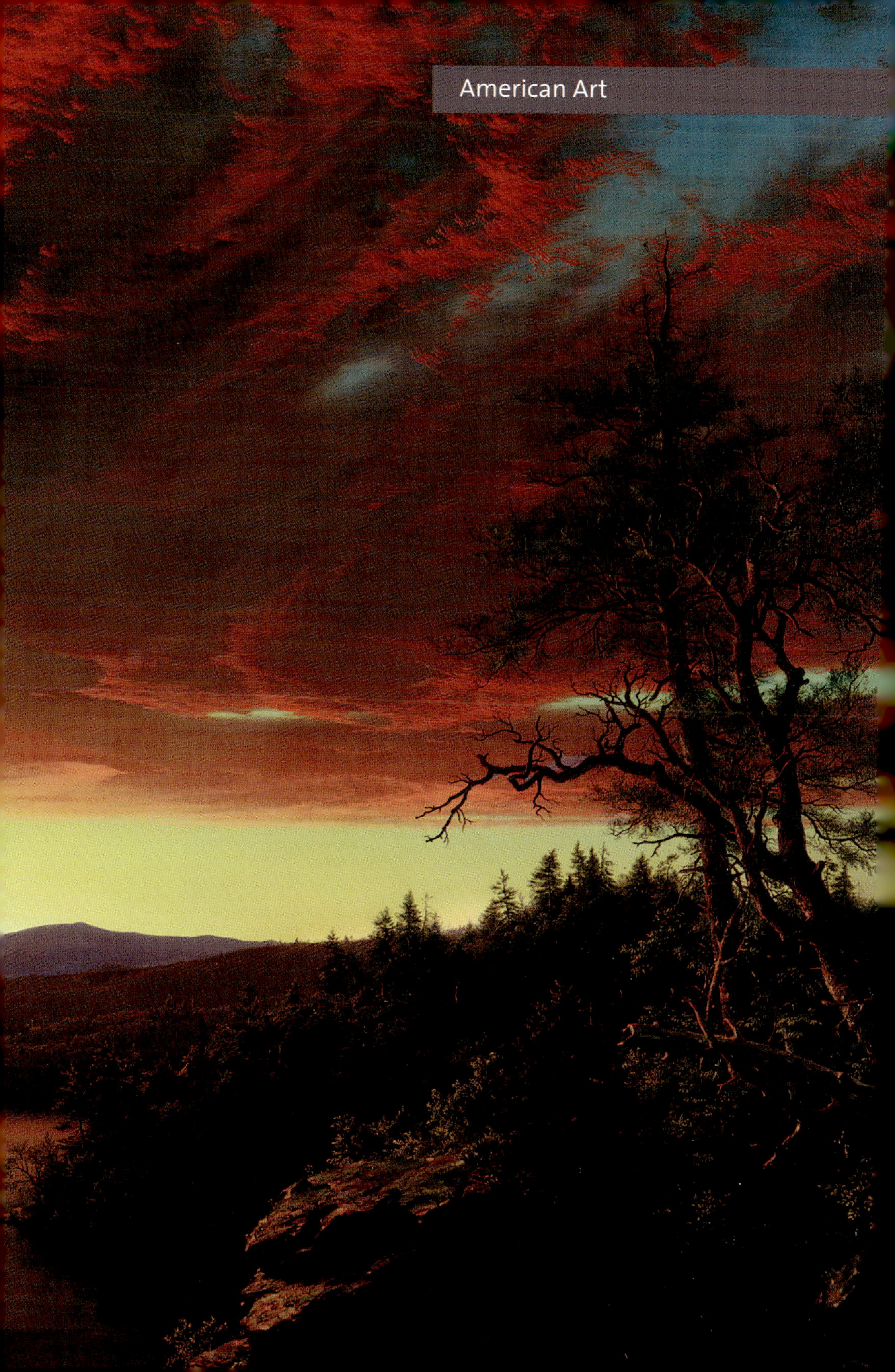

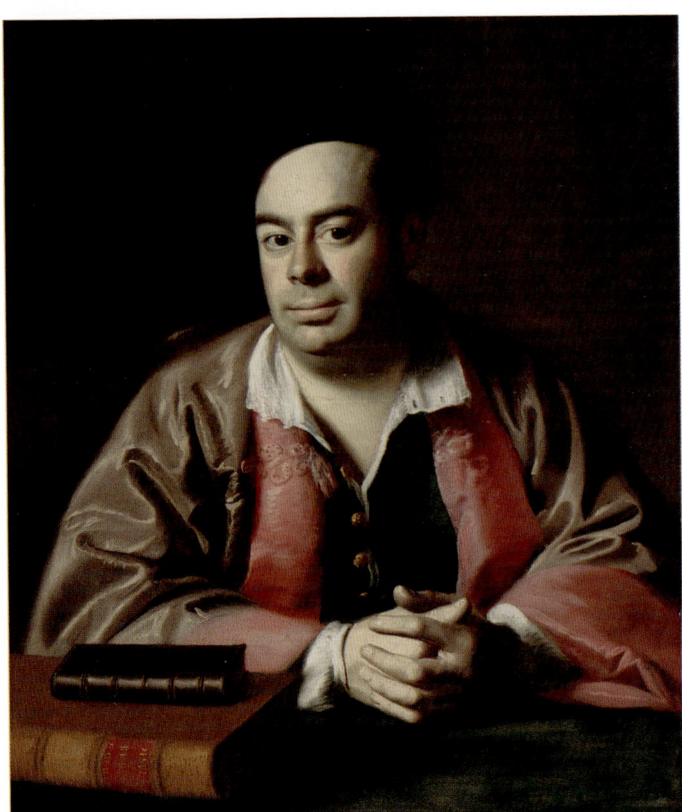

Portrait of Nathaniel Hurd about 1765
JOHN SINGLETON COPLEY (AMERICAN, 1738–1815)
Hurd was a prominent silversmith and engraver in Boston, and the warm gaze and unforced smile in his portrait by Copley suggest the friendship between the two artists. Hurd's open-collared shirt and the rakishly tilted turban that covers his shaved head in place of a ceremonial powdered wig create an air of informality that is unusual for a portrait of this time.
OIL ON CANVAS; 76.2 X 64.8 CM (30 X 25-1/2 IN.)
GIFT OF THE JOHN HUNTINGTON ART AND POLYTECHNIC TRUST 1915.534

Portrait of Elizabeth Shewell West and Her Son, Raphael about 1770
BENJAMIN WEST (AMERICAN, 1738–1820)
West was the first American artist to study in Italy, where he spent three years before permanently settling in London. He so admired the artistic ideals of the Italian Renaissance master Raphael that he named his eldest son after him, and he imitated Raphael's celebrated *Madonna of the Chair* when composing this tender double portrait of his wife and child.
OIL ON CANVAS; 66.5 X 66.3 CM (26-1/8 X 26-1/8 IN.)
THE CHARLES W. HARKNESS GIFT 1927.393

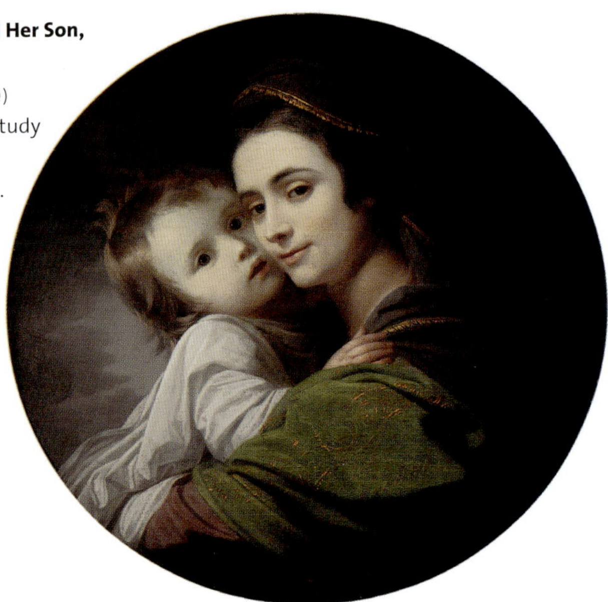

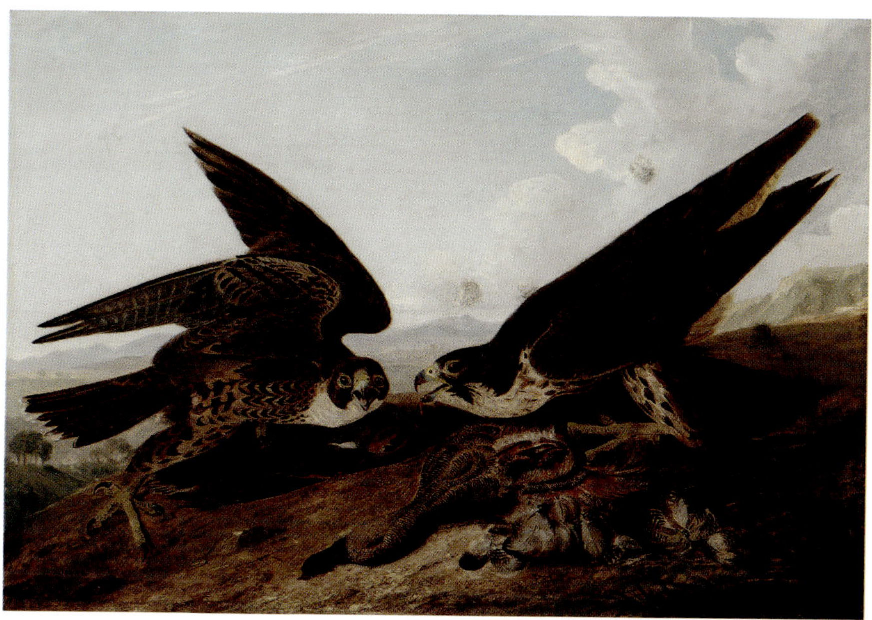

Peregrine Falcons (Duck Hawks) about 1827
JOHN JAMES AUDUBON (AMERICAN, B. HAITI, 1785–1851)

Combining his interests in nature and art, Audubon sought to depict every species of native North American birds posed in action with elements of their habitats. His efforts resulted in the four-volume publication *The Birds of America,* which contains more than 435 hand-colored engravings after his watercolor renderings. Occasionally the artist, sometimes with the help of assistants, made oil versions of his watercolors, of which this image of two falcons feasting on fresh duck carcasses is an early and especially lively example.

OIL ON CANVAS; 64.5 X 91.5 CM (25-3/8 X 36 IN.)
GIFT OF THE AMERICAN FOUNDATION FOR THE MAUD E. AND WARREN H. CORNING BOTANICAL COLLECTION
1964.351

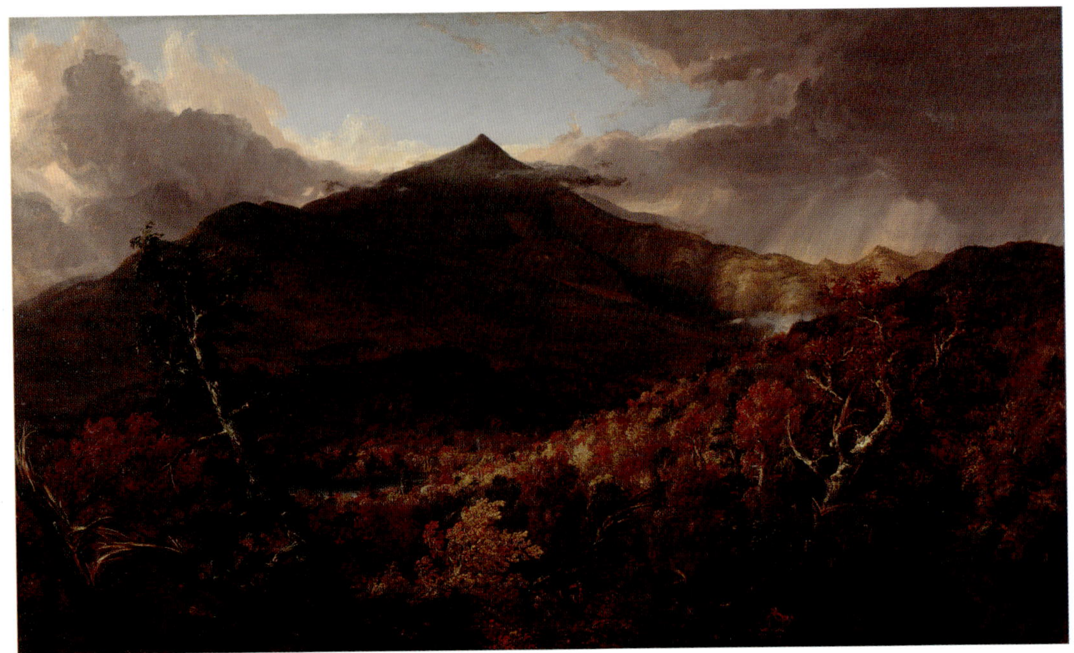

View of Schroon Mountain, Essex County, New York, After a Storm 1838

THOMAS COLE (AMERICAN, B. ENGLAND, 1801–1848)

Championing the unspoiled American wilderness, Cole declared, "We are still in Eden," in his "Essay on American Scenery," published two years before he painted this view of the Adirondacks. The artist sketched the scene in early summer, but when he created the painting in his Catskill studio, he rendered it in a dramatic blaze of fall colors. Such a choice likely had nationalistic overtones, for Cole once proclaimed that autumn was "one season where the American forest surpasses all the world in gorgeousness." The artist further underscored the New World character of his scene by depicting Native Americans in the right foreground foliage. At this time, the presence of Native Americans in the Adirondacks—as in most areas east of the Mississippi River—was rapidly diminishing due to forced resettlement and repression.

OIL ON CANVAS; 99.8 X 160.6 CM (39-1/4 X 63-1/4 IN.)

HINMAN B. HURLBUT COLLECTION 1335.1917

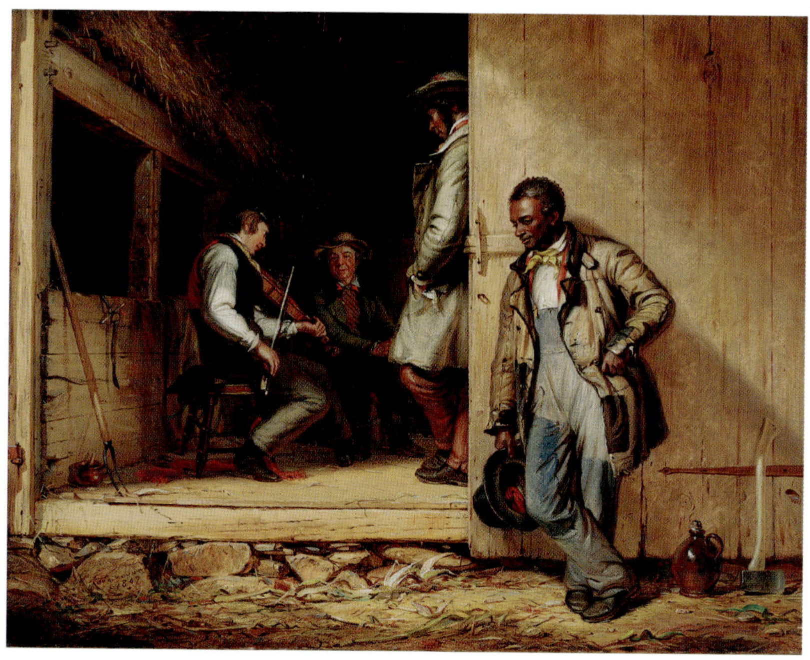

The Power of Music 1847

WILLIAM SIDNEY MOUNT (AMERICAN, 1807–1868)

Set in rural Long Island before the Civil War, this scene of an African American laborer eavesdropping on a fiddle tune suggests the divisive race relations in America at the time. While a love of music connects the men and acknowledges their common humanity, they nevertheless occupy different spaces. The barn door that separates the laborer likely serves as a symbolic reminder that he lacked the political rights and social privileges of the group of white men inside.

OIL ON CANVAS; 43.4 X 53.5 CM (17-1/8 X 21-1/8 IN.)

LEONARD C. HANNA JR. FUND 1991.110

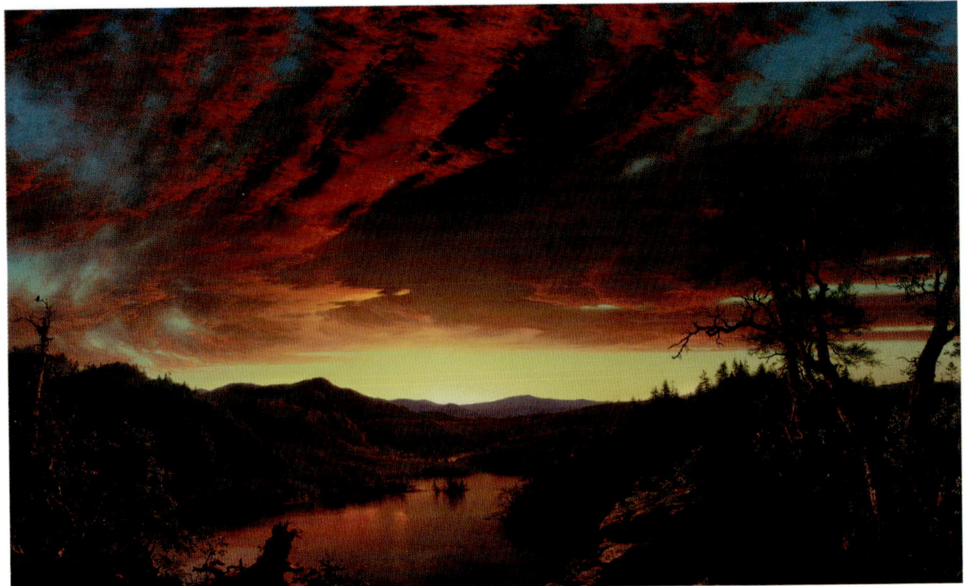

Twilight in the Wilderness 1860

FREDERIC EDWIN CHURCH (AMERICAN, 1826–1900)

In his New York studio, Church painted this spectacular view of a blazing sunset over wilderness near Mount Katahdin in Maine, which he had sketched during a visit nearly two years earlier. Although Church often extolled the grandeur of pristine American landscape in his work, this painting appears to have additional overtones. Created on the eve of the Civil War, the painting's subject can be interpreted as symbolically evoking the coming conflagration. Church's considerable technical skills and clever showmanship contributed to his fame as the premier artist of his generation. Rather than debut this painting in an annual exhibition with works by other artists as was the custom, Church instead exhibited it by itself at a prestigious art gallery. Coaxed by advance publicity and highly favorable press reviews, several hundred spectators flocked to admire it during its seven-week run.

OIL ON CANVAS; 101.6 X 162.6 CM (40 X 64 IN.)

MR. AND MRS. WILLIAM H. MARLATT FUND 1965.233

Indian Combat 1868

EDMONIA LEWIS (AMERICAN, ABOUT 1844–1907)

Lewis studied at Oberlin College and apprenticed with a sculptor in Boston before relocating to Rome in 1866. Of Native American (Ojibwe) and African American ancestry, she became the first nonwhite American sculptor to achieve international renown. Her most popular works

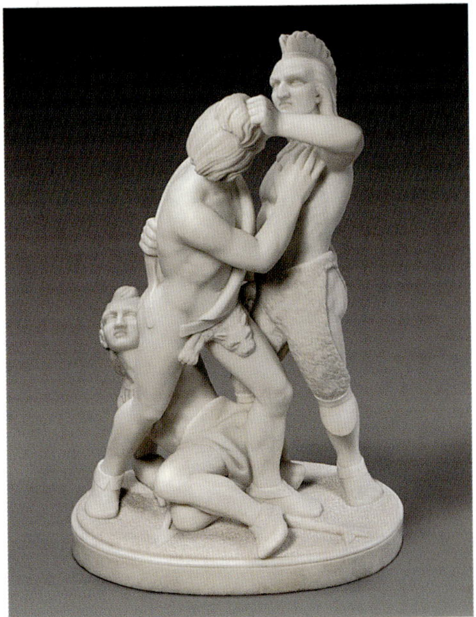

were Native American subjects, readily purchased by patrons on both sides of the Atlantic. *Indian Combat,* a spiraling composition with three intertwined figures, ranks as her most dynamic and complex creation. Although Lewis's sculptures of Native Americans typically exist in multiple versions, this example appears to be unique.

MARBLE; 76.2 X 48.3 X 36.5 CM (30 X 19 X 14-3/8 IN.)
AMERICAN PAINTING AND SCULPTURE SUNDRY PURCHASE FUND AND PURCHASE FROM THE J. H. WADE FUND 2011.110

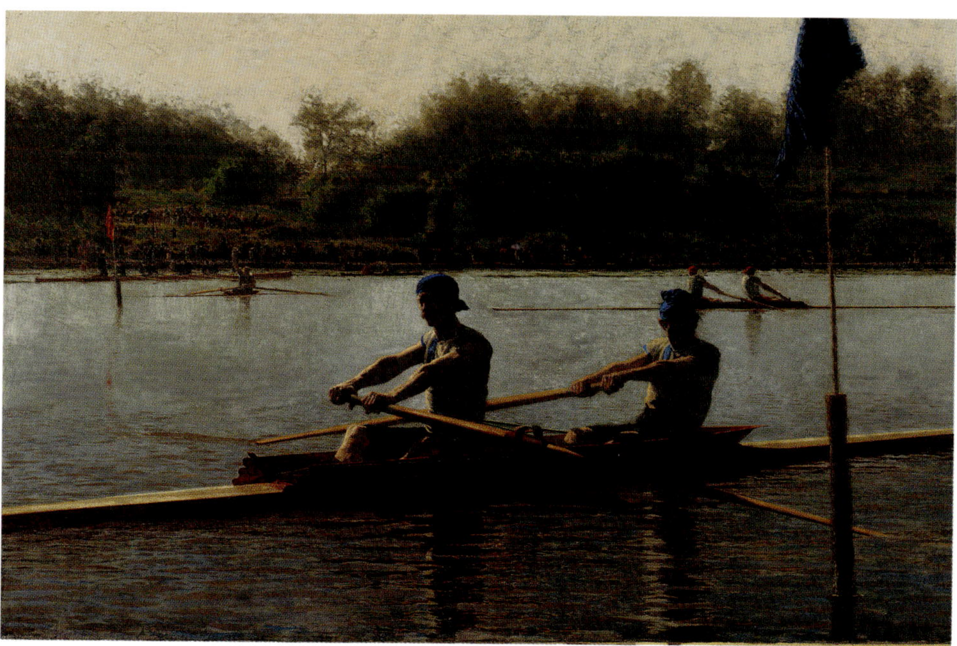

The Biglin Brothers Turning the Stake 1873
THOMAS EAKINS (AMERICAN, 1844–1916)
Eakins's painting celebrates athletic teamwork while commemorating a famous rowing race that took place on the Schuylkill River in Philadelphia during May 1872. Throngs of spectators line the riverbank and watch as Barney and John Biglin negotiate the tricky turn around a stake marking the halfway point in the contest. Their competitors, seen in the middle distance at the right, lag behind. The Biglin brothers won the race, cementing their status as the most celebrated oarsmen of the era. Trained in the United States and France, Eakins spent almost his entire artistic career in his hometown of Philadelphia. He is renowned for the unsentimental realism in his paintings, whose compositions he developed through painstakingly prepared figure and perspective drawings.

OIL ON CANVAS; 101.3 X 151.4 CM (39-7/8 X 59-5/8 IN.)
HINMAN B. HURLBUT COLLECTION 1984.1927

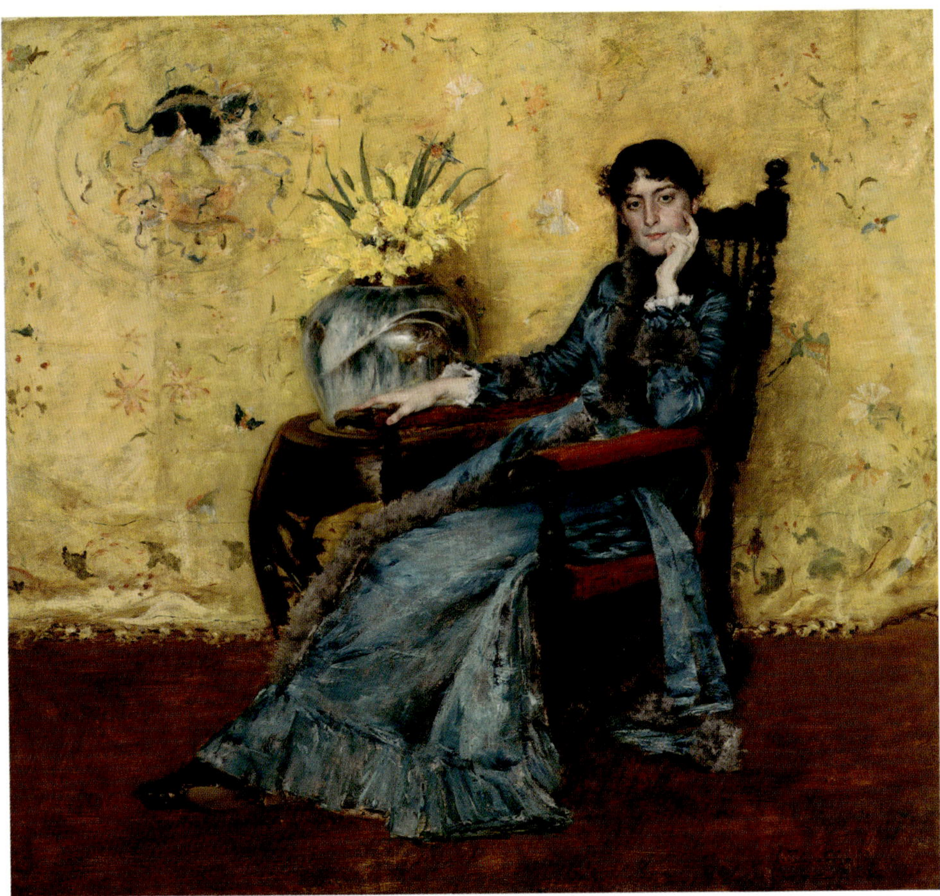

Portrait of Dora Wheeler 1882–83

WILLIAM MERRITT CHASE (AMERICAN, 1849–1916)

Dora Wheeler became Chase's first student when he returned from overseas study in Munich and set up a teaching studio in New York. At the time, few American artists accepted women as private pupils. After her course of study, Wheeler joined her mother in launching a successful decorating firm, one of the first businesses in the country to be operated entirely by women. For the firm, she designed luxurious textiles, and the embroidered silk tapestry that fills the background in her portrait references her occupational interest. Chase's portrait was awarded a gold medal at an international survey of contemporary art in Munich in 1883, and later that year was also shown in Paris. At some later point, the painting was acquired by the sitter, who subsequently donated it to the museum.

OIL ON CANVAS; 159 X 165.5 CM (62-5/8 X 65-1/8 IN.)
GIFT OF MRS. BOUDINOT KEITH IN MEMORY OF MR. AND MRS. J. H. WADE 1921.1239

Portrait of Lisa Colt Curtis 1898

JOHN SINGER SARGENT (AMERICAN, B. ITALY, 1856–1925)

One of the most sought-after painters of his era, Sargent achieved considerable critical and financial success portraying cosmopolitan members of high society on both sides of the Atlantic. Here, the artist depicts an acquaintance—an heir to the Colt firearms fortune—who had recently married his distant cousin Ralph. In her portrait, Curtis wears an elegant satin dress and poses as if she were welcoming guests into her palatial Venetian home. The painting apparently was a wedding gift to the couple by the artist; its inscription at the top right reads, "To Ralph and Mrs. Ralph, John S. Sargent 1898."

OIL ON CANVAS; 219.3 X 104.8 CM (86-3/8 X 41-1/4 IN.)
LEONARD C. HANNA JR. FUND 1998.168

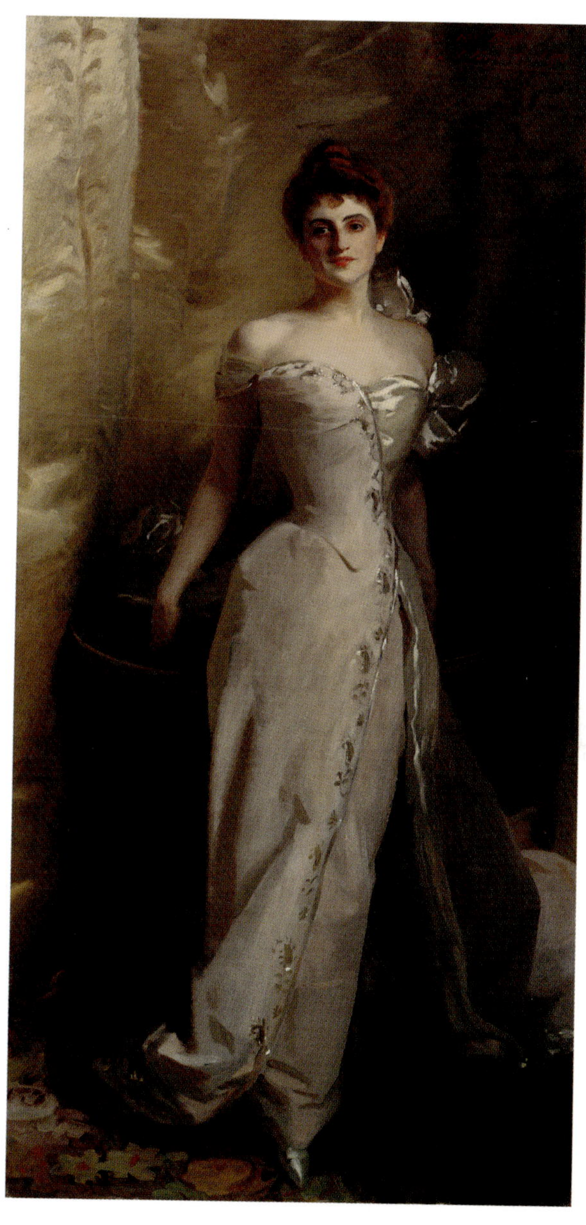

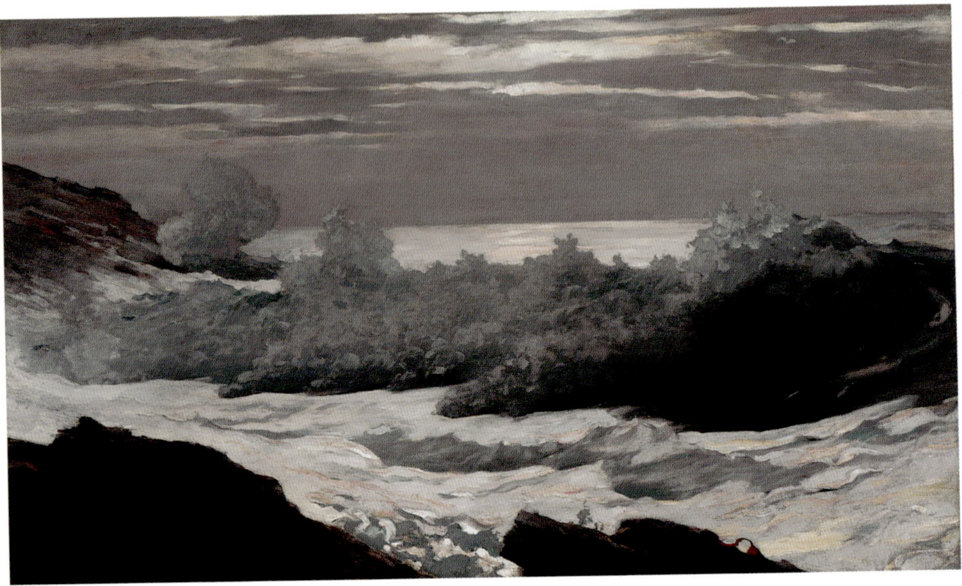

Early Morning after a Storm at Sea 1900–1903

WINSLOW HOMER (AMERICAN, 1836–1910)

The powerful Atlantic surf pounding against the desolate coast of Prouts Neck, Maine, provided primary subject matter for the dramatic paintings that Homer created during his final decades. This example, which the artist proclaimed as "the best picture of the sea that I have painted," was initially conceived as a watercolor. Undertaking the composition in oil after a lapse of nearly two decades, Homer patiently waited for the appropriate atmospheric conditions, executing the work in six different sessions spread over three years.

OIL ON CANVAS; 76.8 X 127 CM (30-1/4 X 50 IN.)

GIFT OF J. H. WADE 1924.195

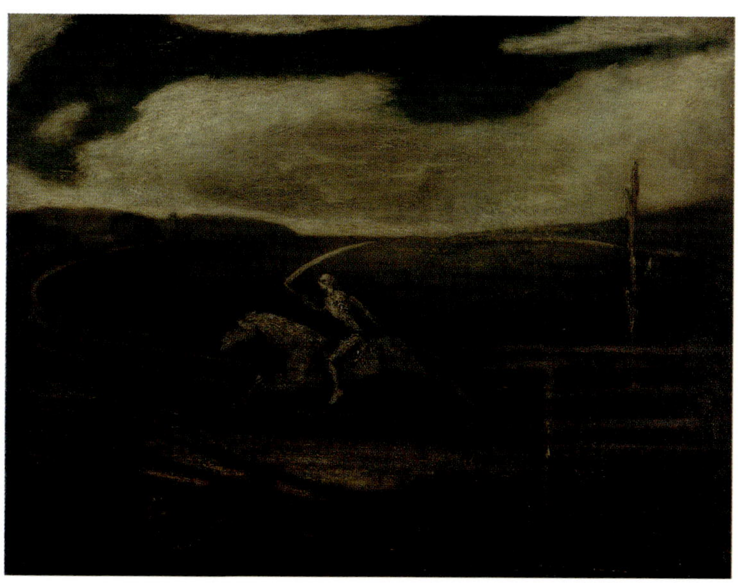

The Race Track (Death on a Pale Horse) about 1896–1908

ALBERT PINKHAM RYDER (AMERICAN, 1847–1917)

Ryder's subject was inspired by a horse race that took place in New York during 1888. One of the artist's friends wagered $500 on the race and then committed suicide after the horse lost. Medieval symbolism infuses the composition: Death appears as a skeleton on horseback holding a scythe with which he cuts down the living, while a snake—a sign of temptation and evil—slithers in the foreground. An intense man, Ryder worked on the painting for several years and was deeply reluctant to part with it.

OIL ON CANVAS; 70.5 X 90 CM (27-3/4 X 35-3/8 IN.)

PURCHASE FROM THE J. H. WADE FUND 1928.8

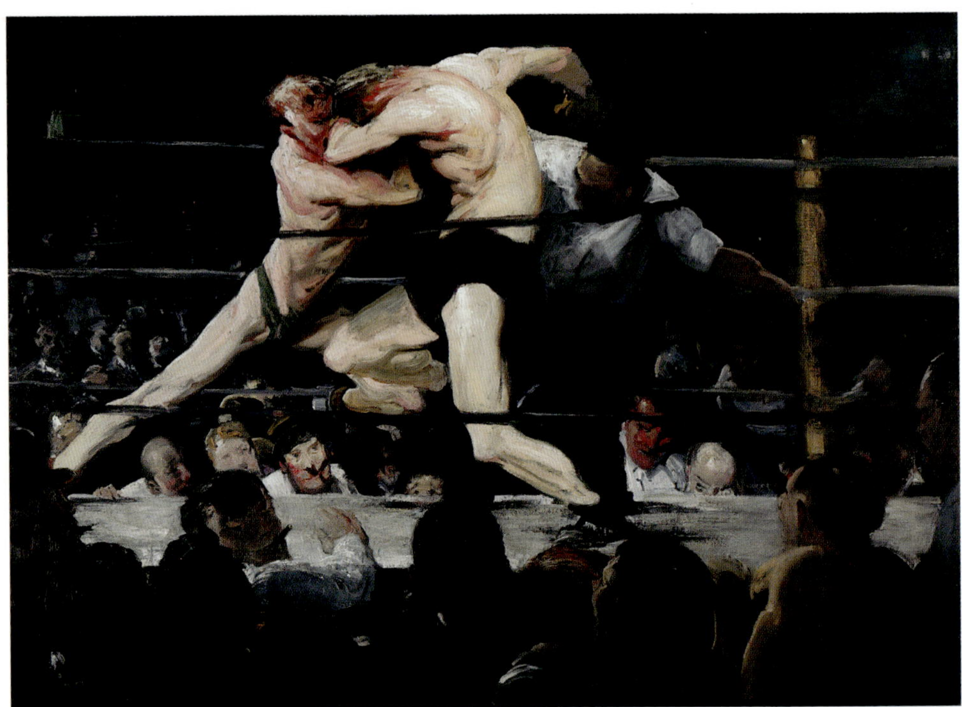

Stag at Sharkey's 1909

GEORGE BELLOWS (AMERICAN, 1882–1925)

An avid fan of boxing, Bellows recorded several images of the sport throughout his career, and *Stag at Sharkey's* is his most famous. Sharkey's Athletic Club, located across the street from the artist's Manhattan studio, was actually a tavern with a back room that accommodated a boxing ring. Because public prizefighting was illegal in New York at the time, private events had to be arranged in order for a match to take place. Participation in the ring was limited to members of the club, a loosely organized group of local semiprofessionals. Whenever an outsider competed at the club, he was given temporary membership and known as a "stag."

OIL ON CANVAS; 92 X 122.6 CM (36-1/4 X 48-1/4 IN.)

HINMAN B. HURLBUT COLLECTION 1133.1922

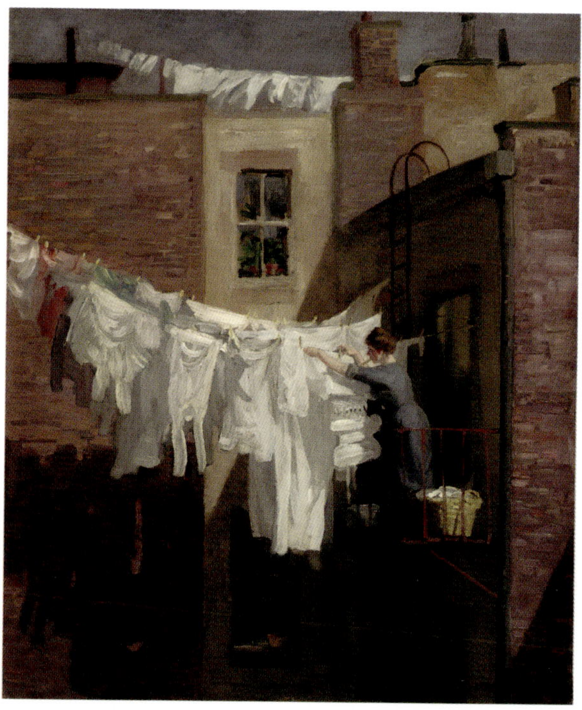

A Woman's Work 1912

JOHN SLOAN (AMERICAN, 1871–1951)

Trained as a journalist, the young Sloan explored social issues more vigorously than most of the painters of his time, portraying working-class urbanites engaged in ordinary activities. He observed this particular scene through a rear window of his Greenwich Village apartment. Perched on a narrow fire escape, a woman hangs fresh laundry on clotheslines strung between tenements. As evidenced by the painting, the labors of American women at the turn of the 1900s were most often confined to the domestic realm.

OIL ON CANVAS; 80.3 X 65.4 CM (31-5/8 X 25-3/4 IN.)

GIFT OF AMELIA ELIZABETH WHITE 1964.160

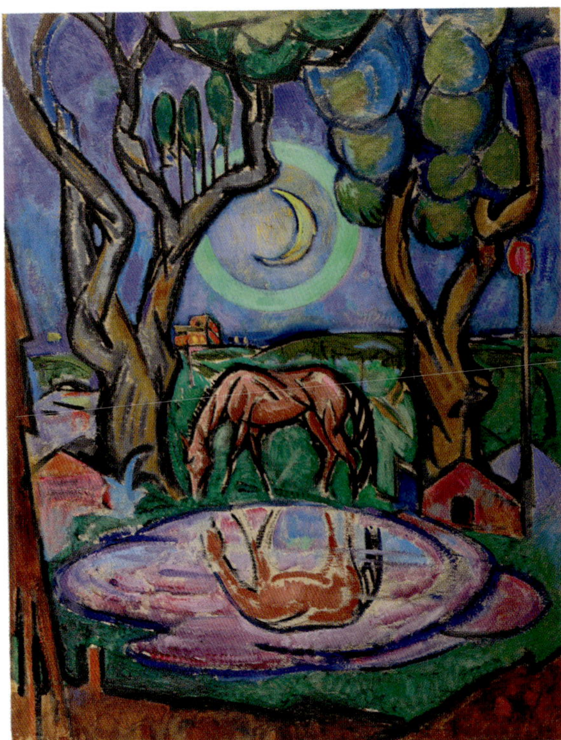

The Pool about 1916–19

WILLIAM SOMMER (AMERICAN, 1867–1949)

In 1914, Cleveland-based Sommer moved to Brandywine, Ohio, where he converted an abandoned schoolhouse into a studio that became an important meeting place for modern artists, poets, and musicians. This rural community provided inspirational subject matter for much of his subsequent work, including *The Pool,* which also reveals his stylistic debt to French avant-garde art. Seeking freedom from convention by immersing himself in nature, Sommer explained, "I believe art should be as spontaneous as the song of a bird."

OIL ON PANEL; 80.7 X 60 CM (31-3/4 X 23-5/8 IN.)

SILVER JUBILEE TREASURE FUND 1945.46.A

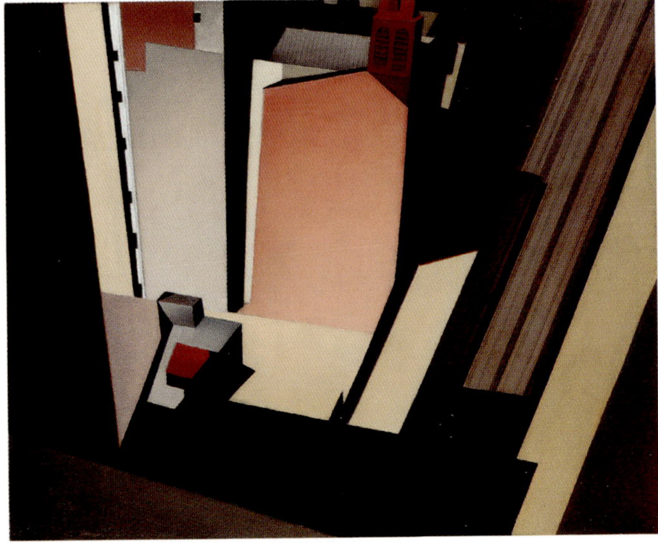

Church Street El 1920

CHARLES SHEELER (AMERICAN, 1883–1965)

Capturing the soaring heights of New York City, this painting is a dramatic bird's-eye view of Broadway at Wall Street, showing a conglomeration of buildings at left and center, and the Church Street elevated train at right. Sheeler based his composition on an image from the short movie *Manhatta* (1920), which he made with the photographer Paul Strand. One of the first avant-garde American films, *Manhatta* celebrates the dynamic metropolis through a series of carefully composed shots of Lower Manhattan. As typical with Sheeler's work, the artist simplified forms and eliminated textures in *Church Street El* to concentrate on rhythmic interplays of shapes and color, as well as patterns of light and shadow.

OIL ON CANVAS; 41 X 48.5 CM (16-1/8 X 19-1/8 IN.)

MR. AND MRS. WILLIAM H. MARLATT FUND 1977.43

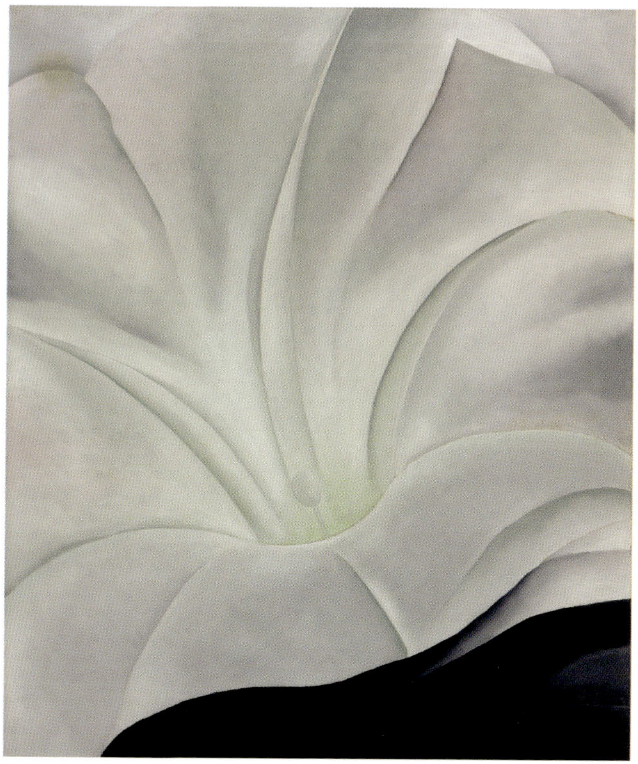

Morning Glory with Black 1926

GEORGIA O'KEEFFE (AMERICAN, 1887–1986)

O'Keeffe is best known for close-up flower subjects whose magnified forms fill the entire space of each canvas. Likely inspired by similar compositions in modern photography, these images are not only celebrations of natural forms, but also striking essays in abstract design. Although many critics interpreted O'Keeffe's flower paintings as reflections of femininity in general and female sexuality in particular, the artist strongly opposed such readings. Throughout most of her career, she frequently attempted to persuade others to discuss her work without referring to her gender, writing on one occasion, "I have always been very annoyed at being referred to as a 'woman artist' rather than an 'artist.'"

OIL ON CANVAS; 91 X 75.5 CM (35-7/8 X 29-3/4 IN.)

BEQUEST OF LEONARD C. HANNA JR. 1958.42

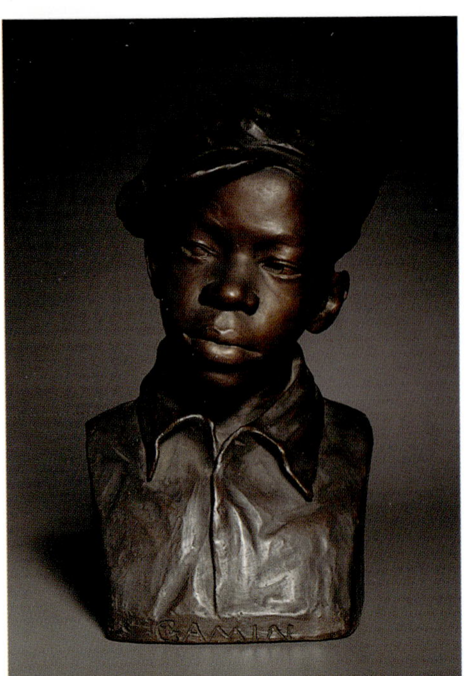

Gamin about 1929

AUGUSTA SAVAGE (AMERICAN, 1892–1962)

Savage was the most acclaimed sculptor working during the Harlem Renaissance of the 1920s and 1930s, and *Gamin* is her most famous work. It was long thought that the image was a generic figure; however, recent research reveals that it depicts her nephew. The warm characterization likely arises from the close bond shared between artist and model. Although several small versions of the sculpture were produced, this life-size, hand-painted plaster is unique and likely the oldest surviving example of the subject.

HAND-PAINTED PLASTER; 44.5 X 24.2 X 20.4 CM (17-1/2 X 9-1/2 X 8 IN.)

PURCHASE FROM THE J. H. WADE FUND 2003.40

A Paramount Picture 1934

REGINALD MARSH (AMERICAN, B. FRANCE, 1898–1954)

Contrasting the real lives of everyday people with the reel lives of movie stars, this painting portrays a working-class woman standing by a Times Square theater in front of a large poster advertising Cecil B. DeMille's blockbuster movie *Cleopatra,* starring Claudette Colbert in the title role. Enormously popular, such film spectacles offered escapist glamour, romance, and power amid the challenges of the Great Depression. Yet, despite the distraction of the city and its entertainments, the woman appears weary and is essentially alone in the crowd.

TEMPERA ON MASONITE; 90.8 X 70.5 CM (35-3/4 X 27-3/4 IN.)

LEONARD C. HANNA JR. FUND 2006.137

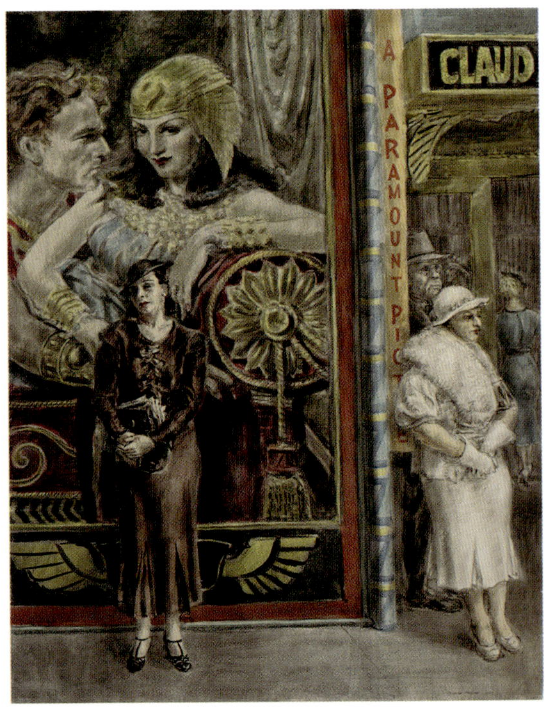

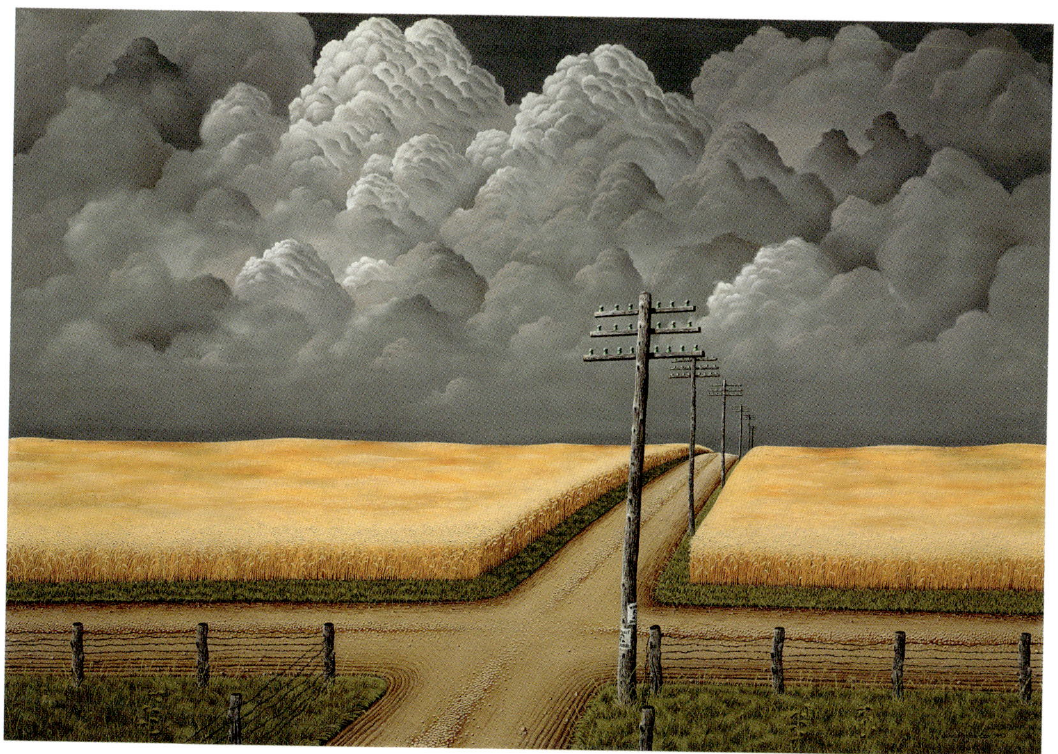

Gray and Gold 1942

JOHN ROGERS COX (AMERICAN, 1915–1990)

Cox painted *Gray and Gold* shortly after the United States joined the Second World War, and its image of amber waves of grain threatened by ominous storm clouds likely has symbolic overtones. The painting's foreground features an intersection of two dirt lanes, as well as a telephone pole emblazoned with political campaign posters. The artist seems to imply that American democracy is at a crossroads during this time of combat against the spread of fascism in Europe and Asia. Interestingly, the work was inspired by the landscape around Cox's hometown of Terre Haute, Indiana, a location nicknamed "The Crossroads of America" because the junction of major north-south and east-west national highways was within its city limits. The museum purchased this painting out of a traveling exhibition entitled *Artists for Victory*, which consisted of works by artists who wanted to assist in the war effort. The exhibition opened at the Metropolitan Museum of Art in New York on the first anniversary of the bombing at Pearl Harbor.

OIL ON CANVAS; 91.5 X 151.8 CM (36 X 59-3/4 IN.)

MR. AND MRS. WILLIAM H. MARLATT FUND 1943.60

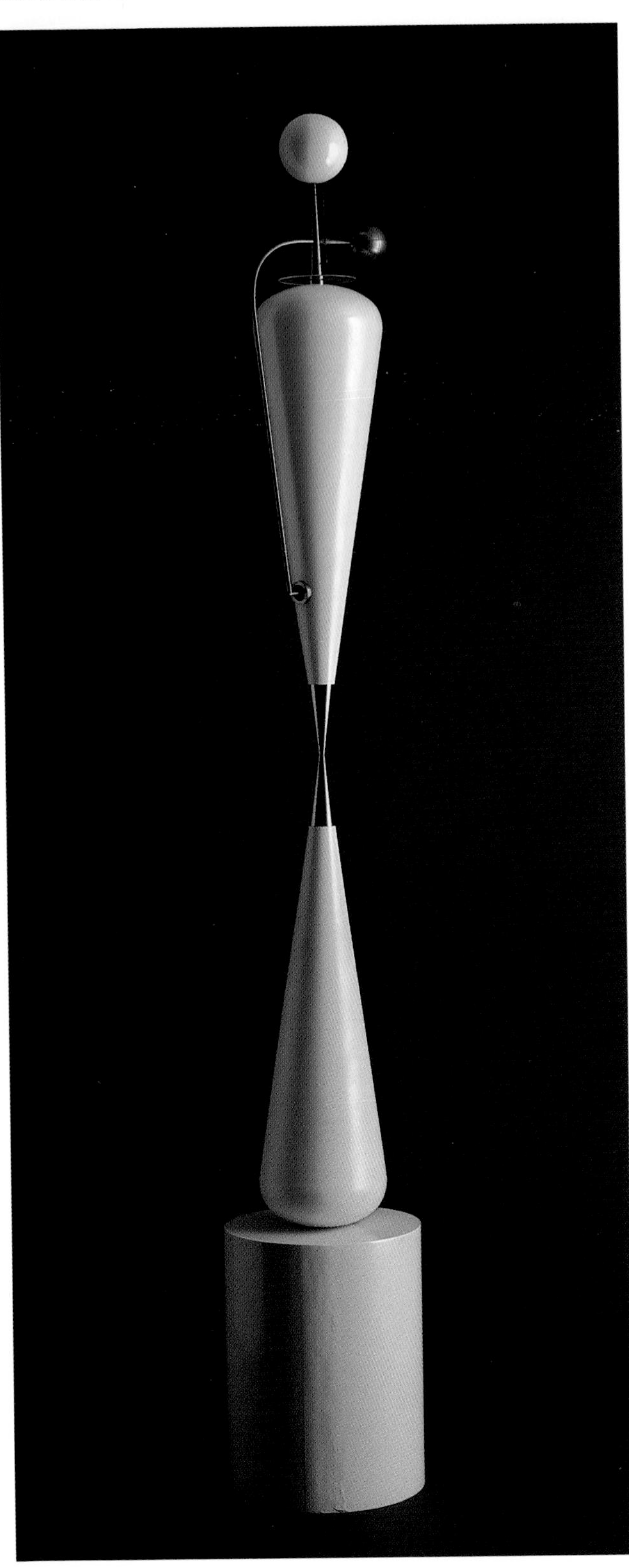

White and Steel Polars 1945

THEODORE ROSZAK (AMERICAN, B. POLAND, 1907–1981)

An artist who once worked in the aeronautics industry, Roszak emerged during the 1930s as one of America's premier modernist sculptors. In an era when most sculpture was made by traditional methods such as carving or casting, he instead employed industrial techniques to create his inventive works. His studio was more akin to a machine shop, complete with drill presses, lathes, and dies. *White and Steel Polars* illustrates the goal of integrating art and technology that several artists began to share between World Wars I and II. By virtue of its industrial materials and techniques, streamlined design, and impressive scale, the sculpture stands as an exuberant monument to America's machine age.

PAINTED WOOD, STEEL, IRON, AND PLEXIGLASS; 271.8 X 40.6 X 40.6 CM (107 X 15 X 15 IN.)

LEONARD C. HANNA JR. FUND 2005.144

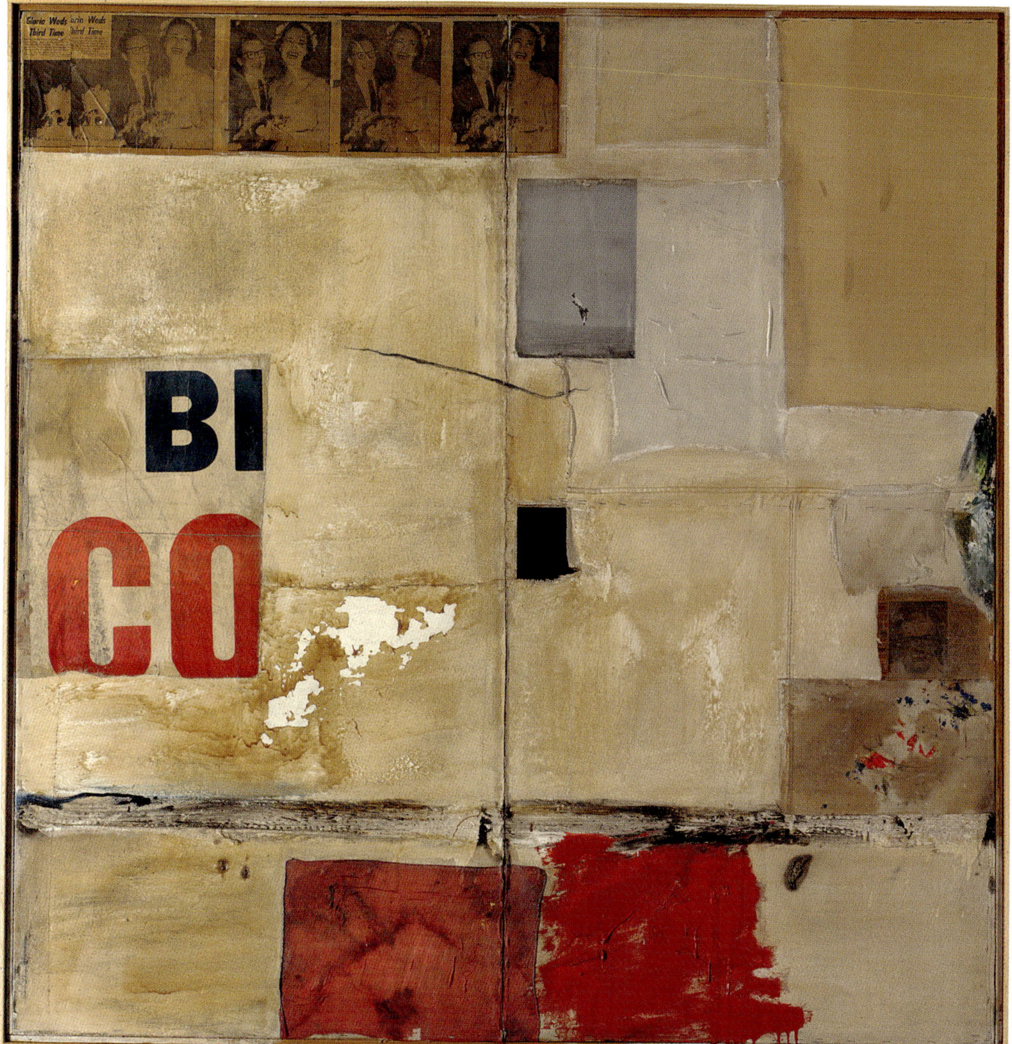

Gloria 1956

ROBERT RAUSCHENBERG (AMERICAN, 1925–2008)

Gloria exemplifies Rauschenberg's compositions of the mid 1950s that combine ephemera and abstract painting. By juxtaposing a photograph, a fragment of printed cardboard, newspaper clippings of New York socialite Gloria Vanderbilt, and passages of thickly applied, dripping paint, Rauschenberg dismissed traditional hierarchies of artistic materials and blurred boundaries between everyday life and art. As he famously said, "A pair of socks is no less suitable to make a painting with than wood, nails, turpentine, oil, and fabric."

OIL AND PAPER COLLAGE ON CANVAS; 168.2 X 160.6 CM (66-1/4 X 63-1/4 IN.)

GIFT OF THE CLEVELAND SOCIETY FOR CONTEMPORARY ART 1966.333

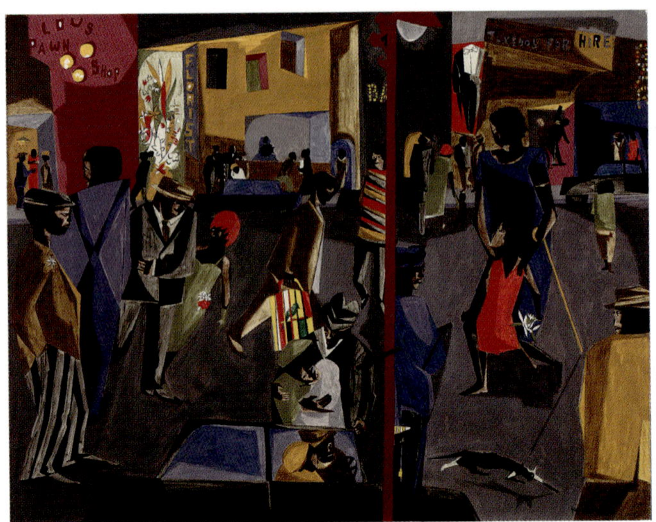

Fulton and Nostrand 1958

JACOB LAWRENCE (AMERICAN, 1917–2000)

Having moved to Harlem as a teenager, Lawrence would become the first major artist trained entirely within the neighborhood's African American community. Throughout his long career he believed art should be a quest for both self and social identity, a notion reflected in this work, one of his liveliest and largest paintings. Teeming with more than 40 figures, it depicts the vibrant streetscape at the intersection of Fulton Street (now Harriet Tubman Avenue) and Nostrand Avenue in Brooklyn, near where the artist lived at the time.

TEMPERA ON MASONITE; 60.9 X 76.2 CM (23 X 30 IN.)

MR. AND MRS. WILLIAM H. MARLATT FUND 2007.158

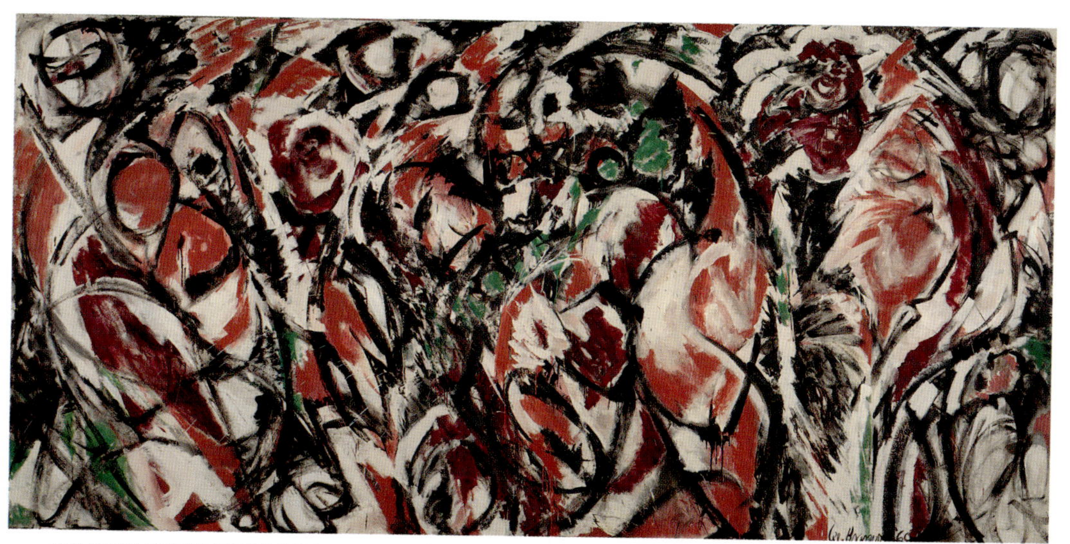

Celebration 1960

LEE KRASNER (AMERICAN, 1908–1984)

Krasner once proclaimed, "I swing from the lyric to the dramatic," and her mature style consists of highly gestural brushwork that can be alternately blissful and ferocious within the same composition. *Celebration* embodies this approach particularly well, combining gentler organic shapes with frenzied thrusts, whiplashes, and spatters of paint. Its expansive scale fills the visual field of observers who stand a customary distance from it, providing an uncanny experience of envelopment.

OIL ON CANVAS; 234.3 X 468.6 CM (92-1/4 X 184-1/2 IN.)

PURCHASE FROM THE J. H. WADE FUND 2003.227

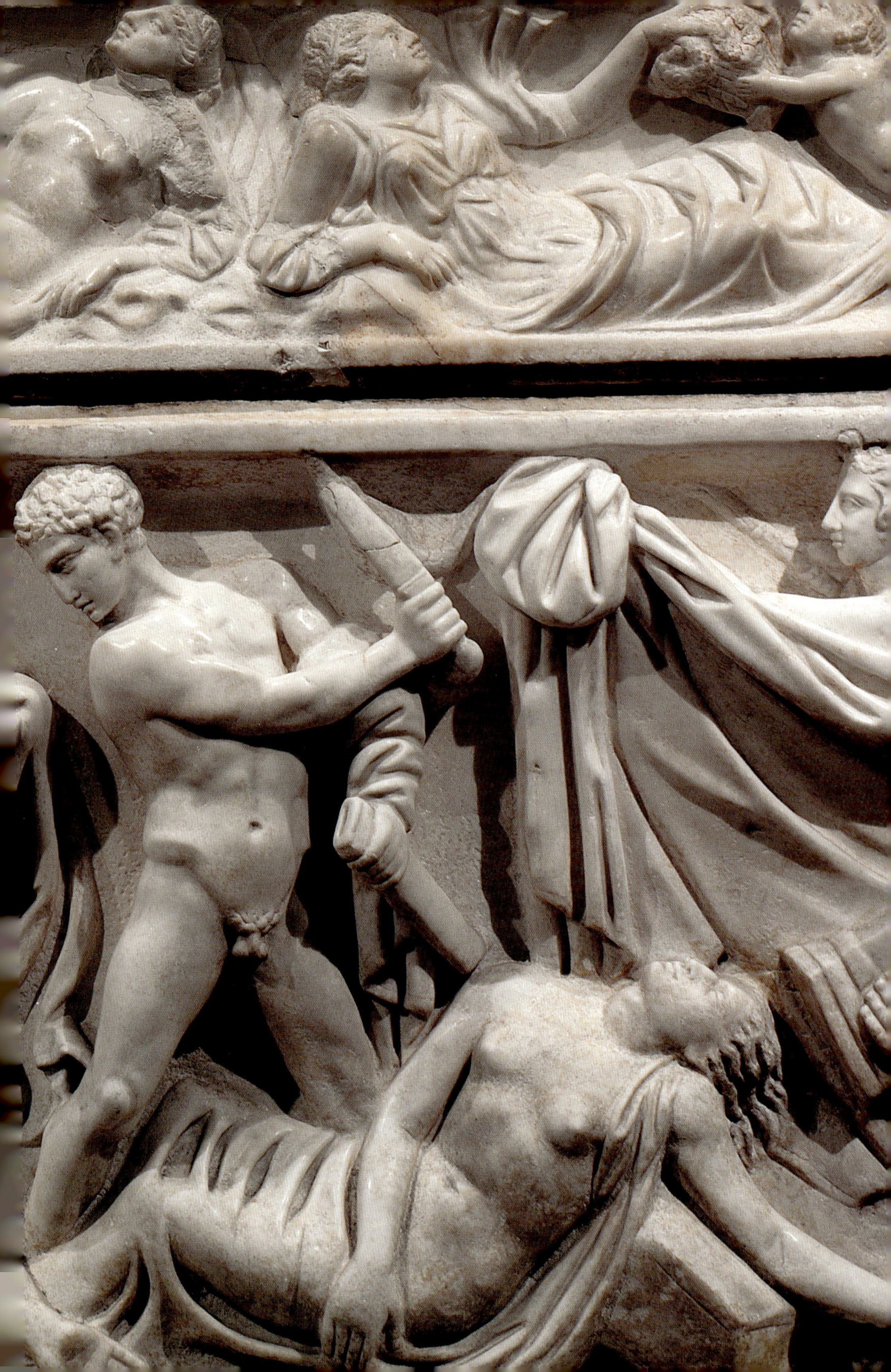

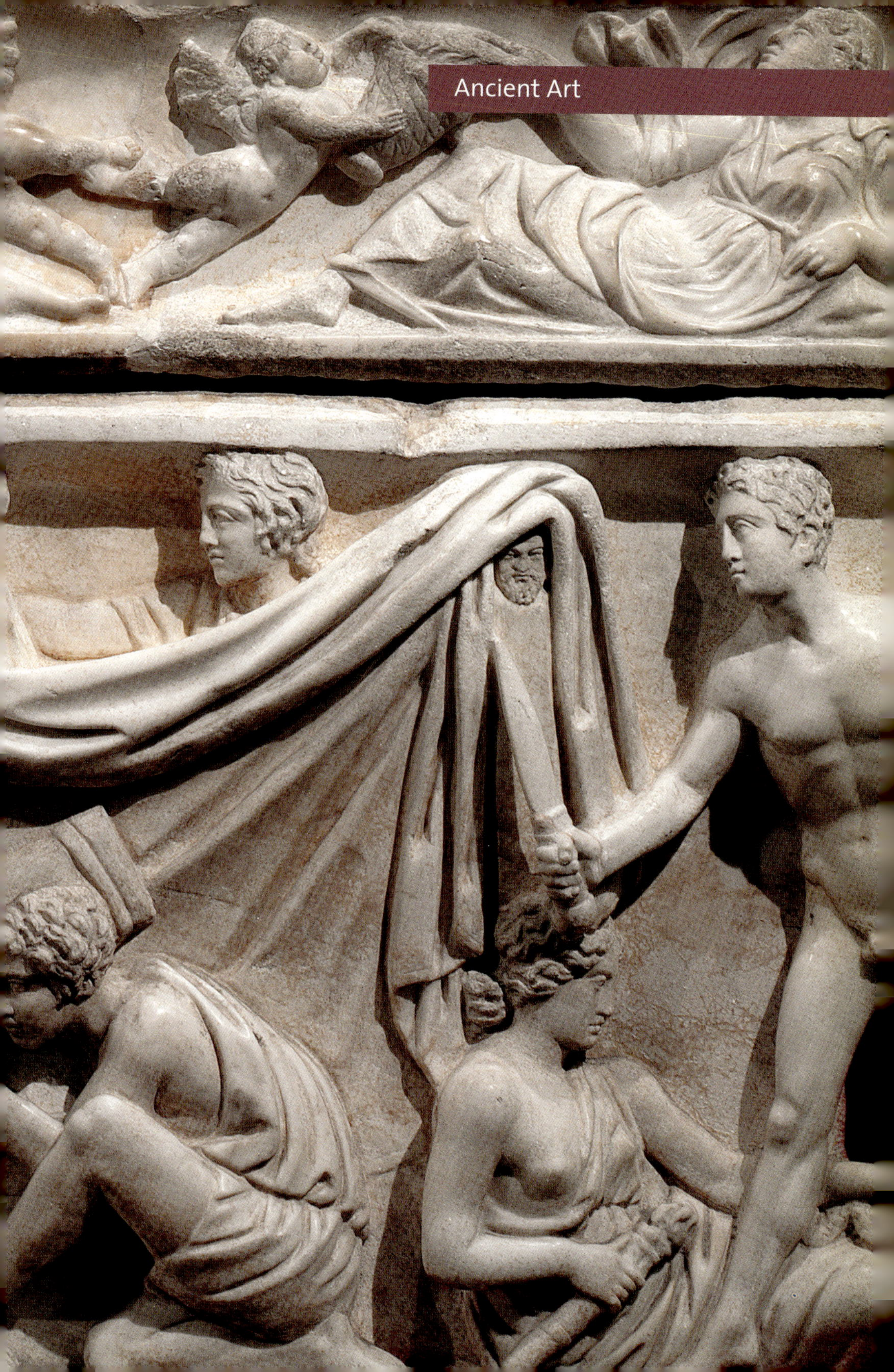

Statuette of a Woman: "The Stargazer" about 3000 BC
WESTERN ANATOLIA(?)

One of only about 15 complete or nearly complete such figures known, this marble statuette is also one of the museum's oldest representations of the human figure. Statuettes of this type have been discovered in western Anatolia in the areas around Troy, and in Thrace and elsewhere.

Brilliantly stylized, the figure is composed of just a few abstracted forms within elegantly resolved contours. Head tilted dramatically back, this stargazer appears to gaze heavenward. Rounded at the bottom and pointed at the back, the head is out of all proportion to the body. The tiny eyes are in relief, the nose is a long ridge, and the mouth is missing. A tall cylindrical neck supports the oversized head on a petite body. Frontally conceived, the body contrasts with the more three-dimensional head. Rounded shoulders arc down, ending in oblique cuts separating the forearms, rendered as raised diagonals, from the torso. The torso is widest at the angled width of the hips, from where the figure's contours narrow to the feet, held close together. Incision separates the legs and defines the pelvic area.

The Stargazer appeals to modern viewers because of its strong design qualities and evocative pose. This graceful figure's remote antiquity and upturned head encourage meditation on the mystery of humankind's place and role in a larger cosmos.

MARBLE; 17.2 X 6.5 X 6.3 CM (6-3/4 X 2-5/8 X 2-1/2 IN.)
LEONARD C. HANNA JR. FUND AND JOHN L. SEVERANCE FUND 1993.165

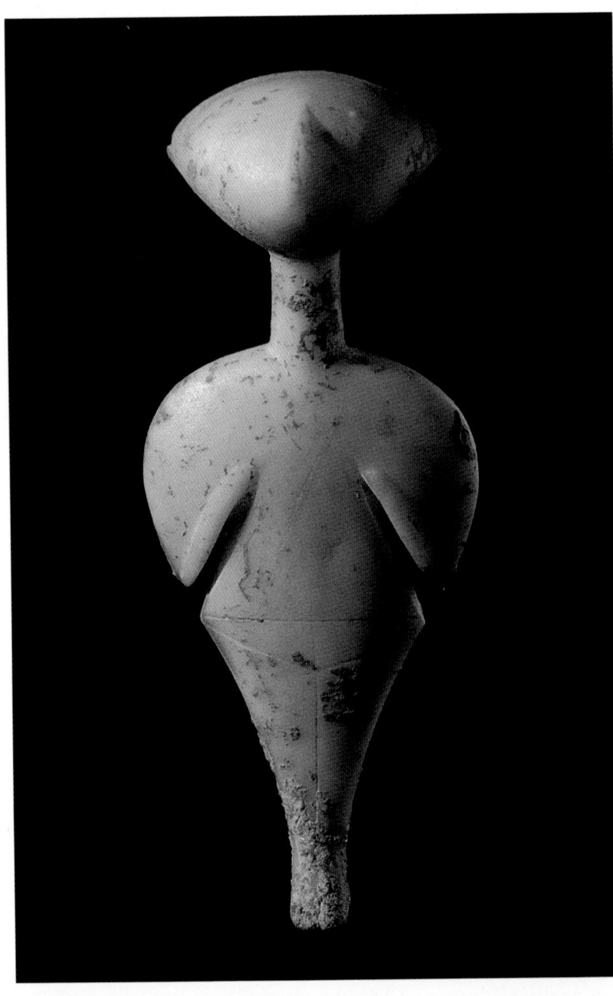

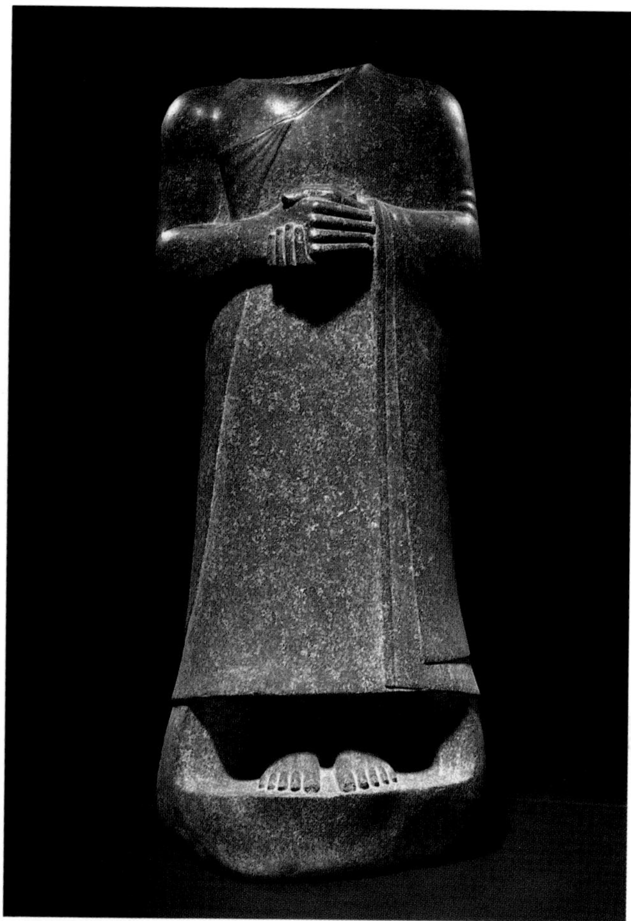

Statue of Gudea 2143–2124 BC

IRAQ, GIRSU, NEO-SUMERIAN, REIGN OF GUDEA

Gudea was an important contributor to the so-called Neo-Sumerian Renaissance, a period of high artistic and literary achievement. One of the most enlightened rulers of the ancient Near East, he was the religious and political governor of Lagash, among the oldest Sumerian cities. More than 2,400 inscriptions mention him by name and recount his 20-year building campaign of public works and city improvements. His long reign continuously enhanced the city's physical and cultural infrastructure, leaving a distinguished legacy.

Of the more than 30 statues of Gudea that have survived, this figure is one of the most outstanding in its refined craftsmanship and artistry. While it has no identifying inscription, 12 other statues of nearly identical pose, execution, and material on display at the Louvre and elsewhere provide ample evidence for a secure identification. Like many Gudea statues, this one's head was broken off in an attempt to cancel its ritual power. The figure is barefoot and stands within a bow-shaped plinth with rounded corners. He wears a finely woven, close-fitting linen cloak. A subtly carved garment drapes over his shoulders. His hands are clasped in front in an unnatural gesture that surely had a specific meaning as it often appears in Gudea statues, both seated and standing. It has been variously interpreted as a gesture of humility, devotion, piety, and an attitude of passive attendance.

DOLORITE; 126 X 55 X 36 CM (49-5/8 X 21-5/8 X 14-1/8 IN.)

PURCHASE FROM THE J. H. WADE FUND 1963.154

Priest-King or Deity about 1600 BC

NORTH SYRIA, HITTITE

The Hittites migrated into Anatolia in the third millennium BC. Technologically advanced, they were the first ancient people to use iron for weapons. From 1600 to 1200 BC their empire was at its apogee, encompassing central Anatolia and extending to Syria and south along the eastern Mediterranean. This vast territory and their commercial interests permitted the Hittites to extend Mesopotamian cultural ideas throughout the ancient Mediterranean world.

Hittite sculpture in the round is extremely rare. Surface marks on this carved basalt statue indicate millennia of burial in damp conditions. The figure holds a small bowl in his right hand, and the pose of his left fist, drilled through, suggests that he originally held a long instrument such as a flail, wand, scepter, or sword. He wears a horned conical crown and a long robe trimmed with what appears to be fur, leaving his shoulders bare. His feet are also bare and he wears a false beard. The head was violently removed from the body but fortunately survived and was reattached. The figure's wedge-shaped feet are set into a block base, whose back is attached to the lower legs. It is unclear whether this is a cult figure of a god or a worshiper. While a royal personage cannot be eliminated as a possibility, the horned crown, fringed cloak, and bowl are appropriate for a religious figure, perhaps a god or priest.

BASALT WITH BONE EYES; H. 87.6 CM (34-1/2 IN.)

LEONARD C. HANNA FUND 1971.45

Saluting Protective Spirit 883–859 BC

IRAQ, NIMRUD, NEO-ASSYRIAN, NORTHWEST PALACE, REIGN OF ASHURNASIRPAL II

The Assyrian Empire was the largest before the rise of Persia in the sixth century BC. It embraced lands extending from Iran to Egypt. During the last three centuries of Assyrian rule—known as the Neo-Assyrian Empire—more than a dozen lavish royal palaces were constructed, richly decorated with ivory inlays, exotic woods, precious stones, gilding, and numerous brightly painted carved reliefs and sculptures in the round. This large relief is one of a substantial number that have been preserved in museum collections.

This towering stone slab depicting a saluting, protective spirit was part of an extensive series of reliefs that embellished the interior of the royal palace complex constructed by Ashurnasirpal II at Calah (modern Nimrud). It decorated the wall of a chamber near the king's throne room. Carved in low relief, it depicts a supernatural spirit with double wings raising a right hand, held open to the viewer. His facial features closely resemble those of the king, as does the coiffed hair and beard arranged in rows of curls. Fine incision renders details worked into the woven fabric of his garments: palmettes, rosettes, pomegranates, cedar trees, geometric lozenges, and kneeling bulls. He wears sandals with wedge-shaped heels, a headband, a dangling earring, bracelets with rosette insets, and armbands with calf-head finials. The exaggerated musculature adds to the impression of otherworldly ferocity. The entire surface was brightly painted. The lines of cuneiform script proclaim the king's unrivaled authority.

GYPSUM; 229.9 X 137 CM (90-1/2 X 53-7/8 IN.)

PURCHASE FROM THE J. H. WADE FUND 1943.246

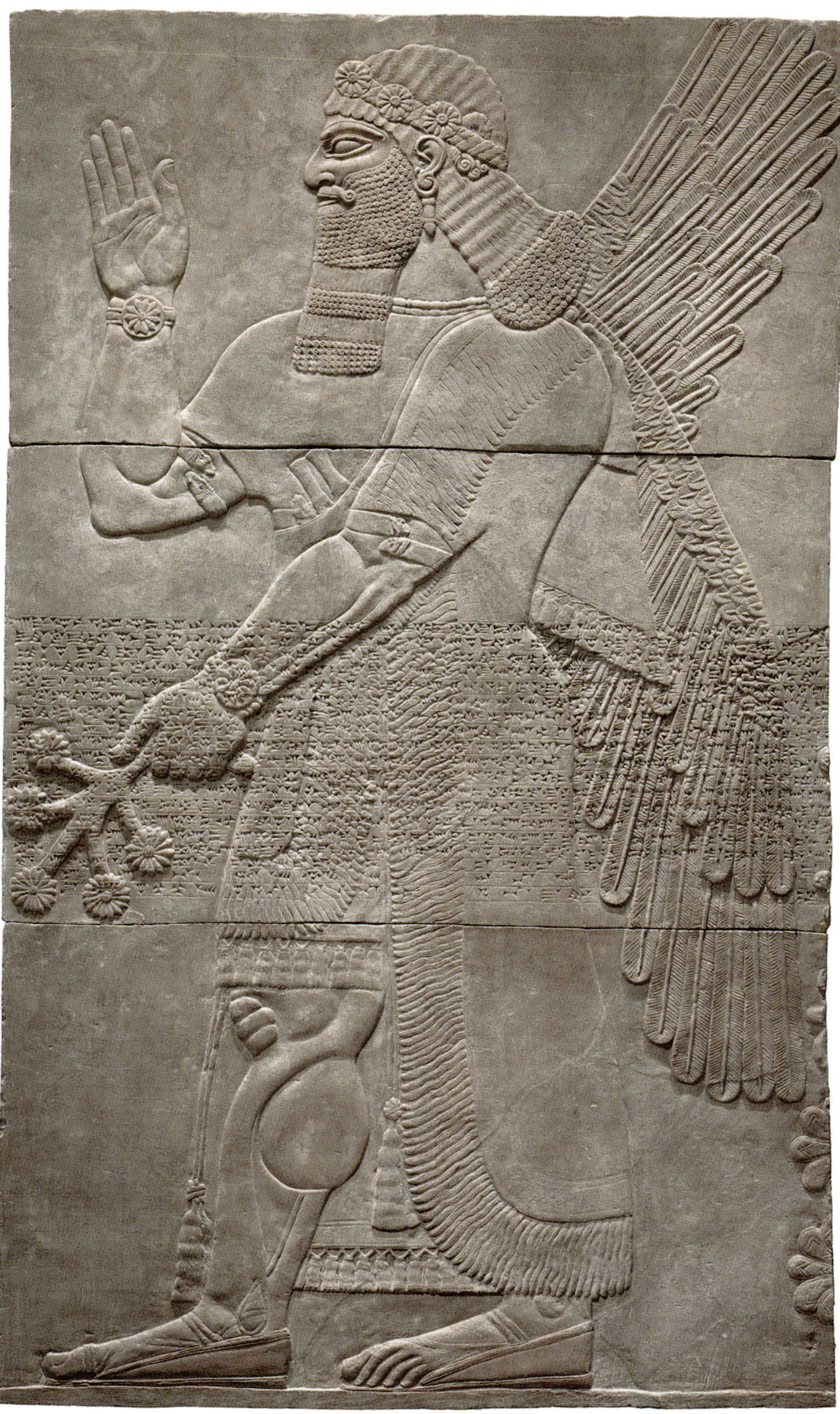

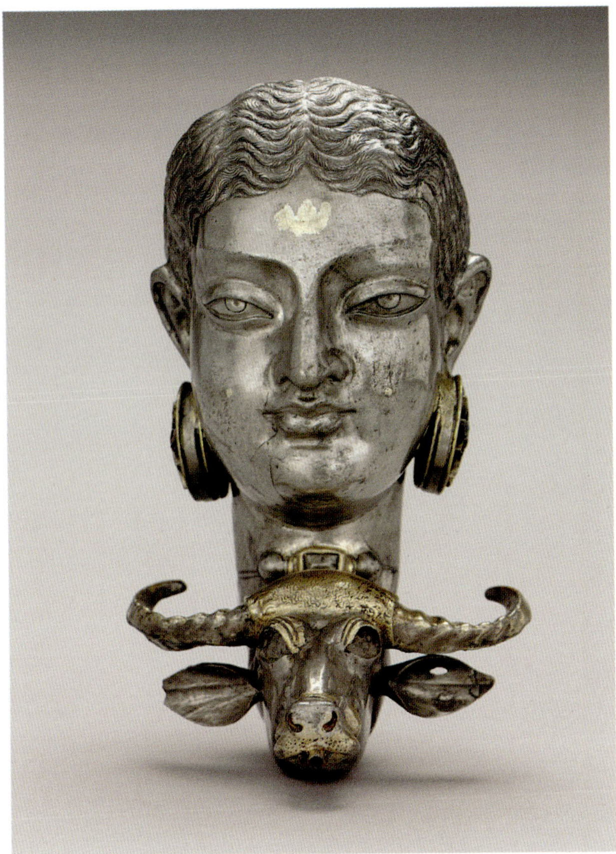

Woman and Water Buffalo Rhyton about AD 600–700

POSSIBLY EASTERN IRAN, SASANIAN

Crafted of silver repoussé, this luxurious rhyton, or drinking vessel, displays a mixture of cultural influences current in the last decades of the Sasanian Empire, the last Persian empire before the Muslim conquest in the seventh century AD. The techniques and materials point to Sasanian workshop traditions, but the style and formal elements combine Greco-Roman and Gupta Indian influences.

Rhyta were popular drinking vessels in the ancient Near East; this elaborate example joins a woman's head with that of a horned water buffalo. The woman's facial features compare with Gupta Indian sculptural prototypes, while the animal is rendered in a style influenced by Greco-Roman sculpture. The elegant lady wears large earrings with lotus flowers inlaid with green glass paste. The crescent-shaped mark on her forehead, areas on her cheeks, her earrings, and the bezel of the central jewel of her necklace all show mercury gilding. The buffalo horns, textured pate, eyelids, and muzzle also retain signs of gilding. The upper and lower parts of the rhyton are soldered together. Wine poured into the woman's head flowed out of the spout at the buffalo's mouth.

The rhyton may have been used in religious rituals associated with the cult of the Hindu god Shiva and the goddess Durga, known as Nana in Iran. According to a fifth-century AD Sanskrit text, Durga drank a cup of divine wine and thereafter beheaded a fearsome buffalo demon. She was afterward known as the Buffalo Demon Slayer.

SILVER WITH MERCURY GILDING AND GLASS INLAYS; 19.1 X 20 X 12.5 CM (7-1/2 X 7-7/8 X 5 IN.)

LEONARD C. HANNA JR. FUND 1964.96

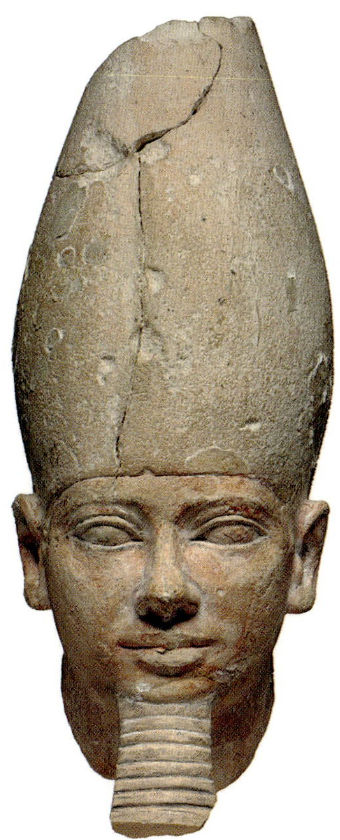

Head of King Userkaf 2454–2447 BC

EGYPT, DYNASTY 5, REIGN OF USERKAF

This masterfully carved limestone head is of Userkaf, the first king of Dynasty 5. He wears the White Crown, the topknot of which has been broken off. His false beard is striped by a series of raised horizontal registers and connected to the neck by a thin webbing of stone. The false beard was likely attached by painted chin straps. The lower tabs of the crown, shown reaching around the earlobes, were perhaps painted on as well. The stone webbing that once secured the statue to its back slab has largely broken off. The facial features closely compare with other portraits of Userkaf, such as the colossal red granite head of the king from his pyramid temple at Saqqara, the life-size graywacke head from his sun temple at Abusir, and a fragmentary life-size head of travertine from the same temple.

Unfinished chisel marks on the back of the king's crown at the proper right side is evidence that another figure was once seated on that side. If so, that figure must have been a god or goddess because only an image of a deity could appear at the dominant, right side of the king. Comparisons with other sculptural groups raise the possibility that this head of Userkaf might well have been part of a larger figural group.

PAINTED LIMESTONE; 17.2 X 6.5 X 7.2 CM (6-3/4 X 2-5/8 X 2-7/8 IN.)

LEONARD C. HANNA JR. FUND 1979.2

Statue of Minemheb 1391–1353 BC

EGYPT, DYNASTY 18, REIGN OF AMENHOTEP III

Minemheb, a scribe working for Amenhotep III, oversaw the construction of buildings connected with the king's jubilee, or sed-festival, including a palace and great festival hall among other royal structures. Here Minemheb is shown kneeling, back held upright. Between his knees is an altar on which the god Thoth, represented as a hamadryas baboon, squats. Inscribed hieroglyphs on the back pillar identify the scribe by name and rank. This is the only known sculptural image of Minemheb.

The statuette is nearly completely preserved, and the carving is of the very highest quality. Unlike other sculpted images of private individuals, which closely resemble royal portraits, Minemheb's features are individualized. He wears a two-part wig and a short-sleeved long tunic. His expression and pose mirror those of the baboon, giving the impression that the two are somehow intimates. The inscription on

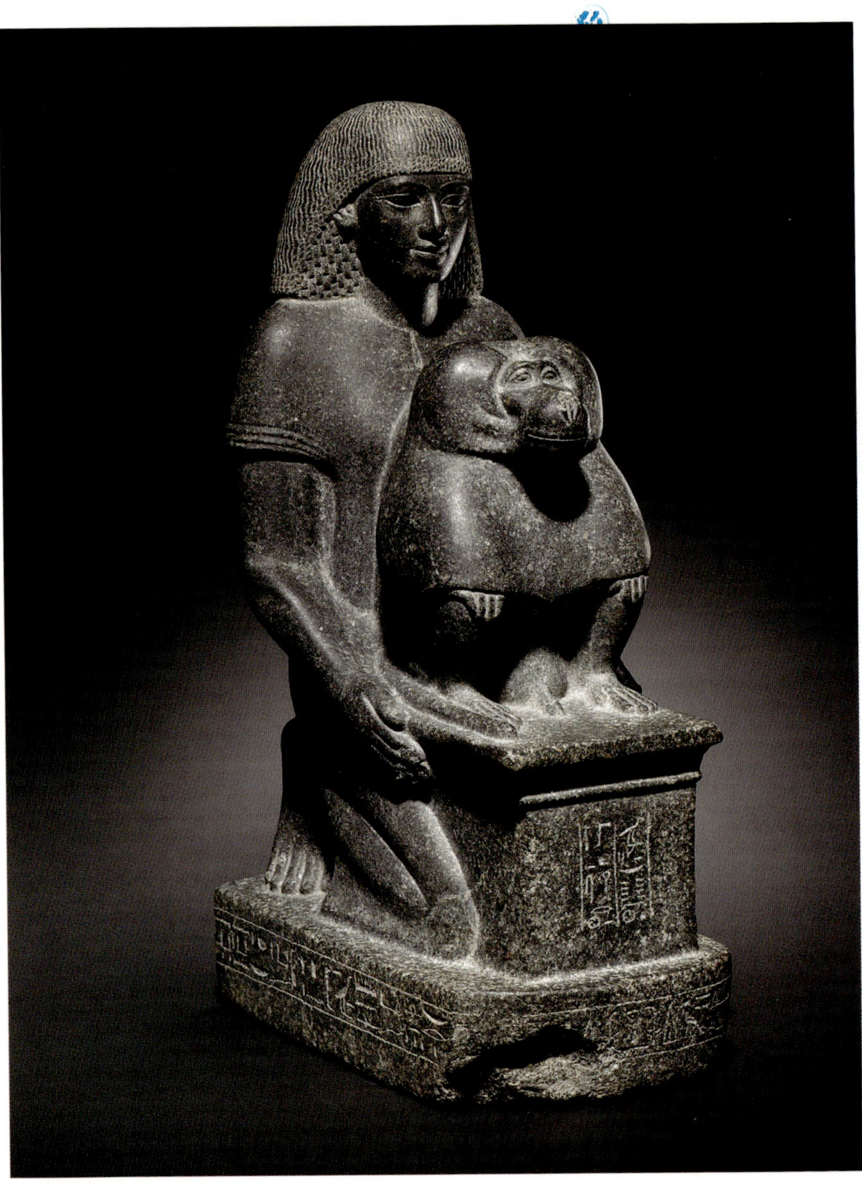

the front of the altar reveals the baboon's true identity and hints at Minemheb's home: "Thoth, lord of Hermopolis, the great god, foremost of Hesret." Thoth was the god of wisdom and knowledge and, most appropriately for a statuette of Minemheb, the patron god of scribes. Minemheb possibly once lived near Hermopolis in Middle Egypt and dedicated this statuette to Thoth at his temple at Hesret, a cemetery there.

The inscription on the left side of the base makes clear the statuette's function: "An offering that the king gives Ra-Horakhty, that he may cause the remembrance of me to be beautiful and enduring forever and that I may see his beauty daily, for the ka of the chief of works in the mansion of the sed-festival, Minemheb."

GRANODIORITE; 45 X 16.6 X 28.3 CM (17-3/4 X 6-1/2 X 11-1/8 IN.)

LEONARD C. HANNA JR. FUND 1996.28

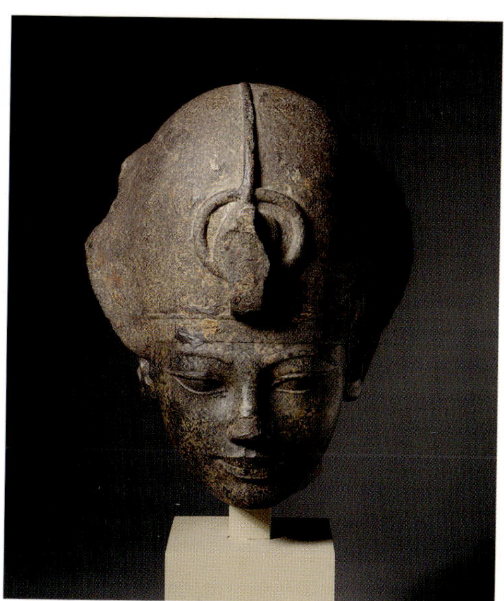

Head of Amenhotep III Wearing the Blue Crown

1391–1353 BC

EGYPT, DYNASTY 18, REIGN OF AMENHOTEP III

Details indicate the extremely high standard of workmanship of this monumental portrait head: the precisely carved line defining the full lips of the mouth (the upper thicker than the lower), the gently raised ridge of the arched eyebrows, tapering gradually to a subtly raised point, and the long, slanted almond-shaped eyes. Amenhotep III appears very youthful. His face is flawlessly smooth, with hardly a trace of the underlying bone structure. He wears the Blue Crown embellished with the uraeus (sacred serpent). At the back of the crown and nape of the neck are the broken traces of the back pillar that supported the statue. The crown was originally painted blue and the brow band yellow. It is impossible to know whether the figure was originally seated or standing.

This portrait is one of three that show Amenhotep III wearing this headdress. Of the other two, the one at the Louvre is also granodiorite and the one at the Metropolitan Museum of Art is brown quartzite. The Louvre portrait is closest stylistically to the Cleveland head. Both are finished similarly, with the flesh areas given a smooth polished surface, while the eyeballs and crown are left somewhat roughened. For the crown, this distressed treatment was clearly done intentionally as a preparation for the application of paint.

GRANODIORITE; 39.1 X 30.3 X 27.7 CM (15-3/8 X 11-7/8 X 10-7/8 IN.). GIFT OF THE HANNA FUND 1952.51

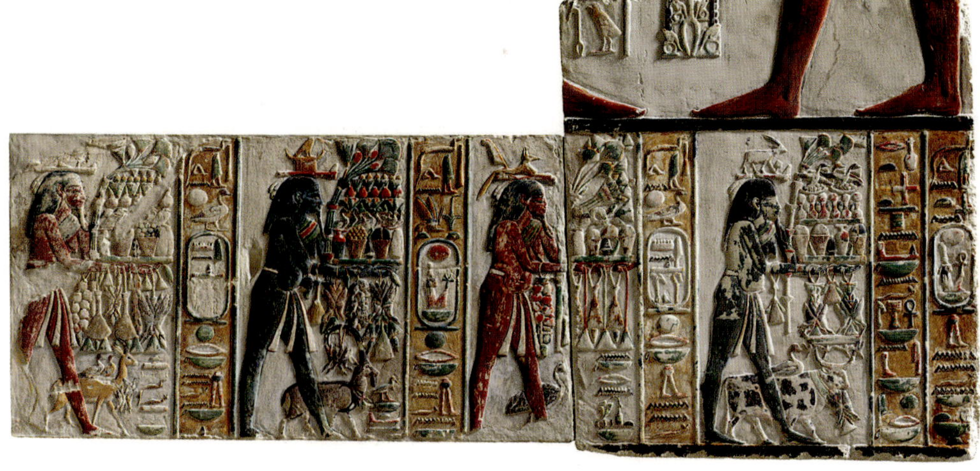

Nome Gods Bearing Offerings 1391–1353 BC

EGYPT, DYNASTY 18, REIGN OF AMENHOTEP III

The high quality of the carving, clever inventiveness of the figural imagery, and excellent state of preservation distinguish these wall reliefs as the finest dating from the reign of Amenhotep III outside of Egypt. Painted and carved in exacting low relief, these two fragmentary adjoining blocks represent four Egyptian nome gods proceeding to the right and addressing a god, probably Horus. Provincial districts within pharaoh's kingdom were known as nomes, and each had its eponymous deity. The reliefs once graced the wall of a royal temple. They might have come from a temple dedicated to the god Horus in Middle Egypt, at Hebenu.

Two scenes are preserved. The lower register represents the four nome gods carrying offerings of food piled atop offering mats while leading sacrificial animals. Together with their abundant offerings and sacrificial animals, these gods represent the vast wealth of the kingdom as reckoned by its abundant agricultural produce and varieties of wildlife. Nowhere else are nome gods depicted with such lively detail.

Each nome god has the pharaoh Amenhotep III's facial features and wears the royal beard. All likely address the god Horus, whose shins and feet are preserved in the top register at the right. The single foot in front probably belongs to the king.

PAINTED LIMESTONE; H. 66 CM (26 IN.), L. 133 CM (52-3/8 IN.) OVERALL. JOHN L. SEVERANCE FUND 1961.205, 1976.51

Coffin of Bakenmut 976–889 BC

EGYPT, LATE DYNASTY 21 TO EARLY DYNASTY 22

This elaborate, densely decorated painted coffin is one of the finest made for priests of Amen and their families at Thebes during Dynasty 21 and early Dynasty 22. Anthropoid in shape, it depicts the deceased in the form of a mummy. A complete set of coffins would have included an outer coffin, inner coffin, and mummy board. The generous proportions suggest an outer coffin. Every available surface is adorned with religious scenes, depictions of funerary gods and goddesses, magical and religious symbols, and intricate protective spells. The lid shows Bakenmut wearing a striped divine wig and false beard attached with chin straps. Over his crossed arms covering his chest and upper abdomen is a massive floral collar, leaving visible only his separately attached hands (now missing). Crossing the collar are depictions of red "mummy braces" that would have been secured around the neck of the mummy. At the intersection is a winged sun disk with uraei (sacred serpents). The bottom of the lid is crowded with tiny figures applied in gesso against a gold background. The effect is similar to gold inlaid with semiprecious stones or glass.

The painted interior features two deified kings of Dynasty 18. The main upper scene depicts Tuthmosis III, a pharaoh who lived 500 years before Bakenmut, holding the crook and flail and wearing a brightly colored feathered garment enveloping him in falcon's wings. In the scene below, demarcated by a winged sun disk and pendant uraei, are two back-to-back images of the deified Amenhotep I, who was considered a patron of the Theban cemetery and worshiped locally as a god.

GESSOED AND PAINTED SYCAMORE; L. 208 CM (81-7/8 IN.), W. 68 CM (26-3/4 IN)

GIFT OF THE JOHN HUNTINGTON ART AND POLYTECHNIC TRUST 1914.561.A–B

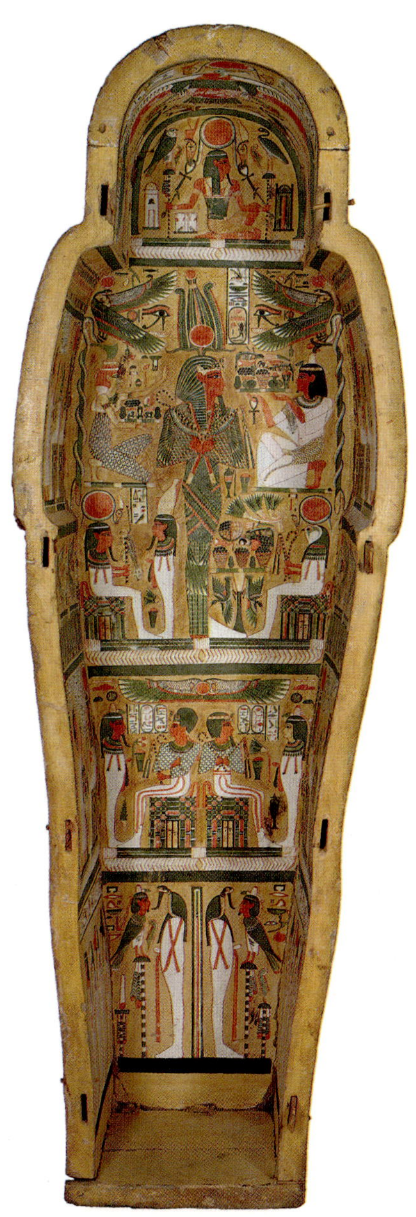

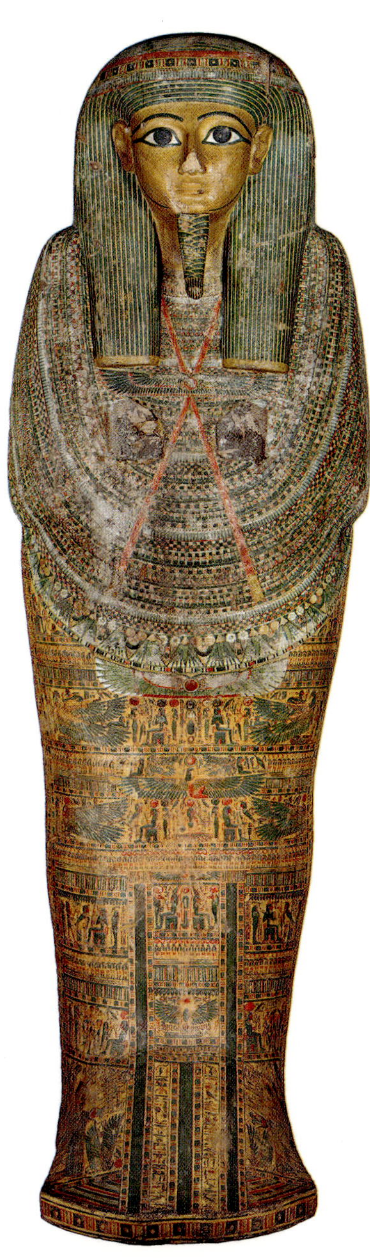

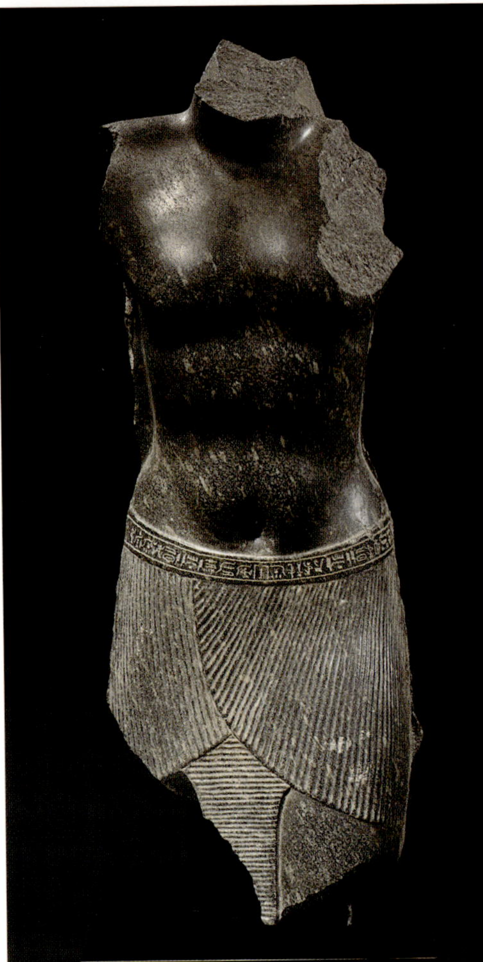

Torso of Amenpayom probably 200–100 BC

EGYPT, PTOLEMAIC DYNASTY

From the inscription on his belt, which gives his titles and filiation, this superb life-size torso is identified as Amenpayom, the great army general of the district of Mendes in the Nile Delta. The belt secures a neatly pleated kilt, a mainstay of pharaonic dress used in this late period for images of private persons for their tomb statues. Despite its fragmentary state, the figure was certainly represented in the traditional Egyptian striding pose with arms pressed to the sides and left foot forward.

The hard stone is carved and finished with extraordinary sensitivity. The anatomical structure of the torso—pectorals, rib cage, and abdominal muscles—are sculpted so that transitions merge into one another seamlessly, creating an undulating surface pulsing with life. This impression is enhanced by the highly polished surface on the flesh areas. While the question of Greek influence in the carving is difficult to assess, clearly it is a product of the Hellenistic age and could have been made in no other period.

On the back at the top is a scene with four figures. At the right, Amenpayom, shown with head shaved and wearing a kilt, worships the triad of Mendes: Harpocrates, Banebdjedet (the ram-headed figure), and his consort Hatmehit, wearing the nome emblem of Mendes on her head (a fish on a standard). Below is an inscription: "The priest, overseer of troops, king's brother Amenpayom, son of Paimyroihu and the lady of the house Nebettekhet." Amenpayom is known from one other statue found at Tanis.

GRANODIORITE; 96.4 X 32.3 X 28.6 CM (38 X 12-3/4 X 11-1/4 IN.)

GIFT OF HANNA FUND 1948.141

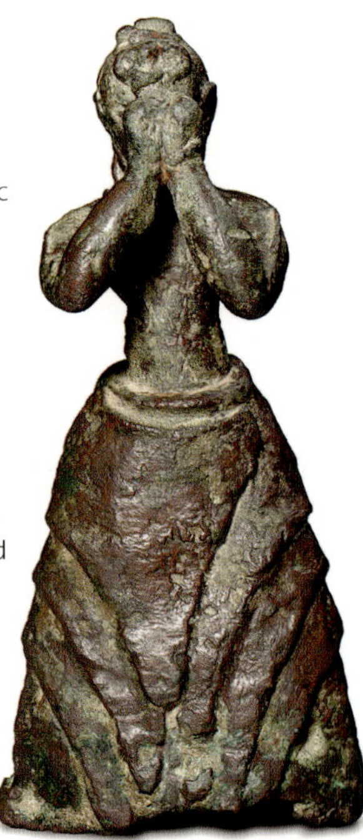

Girl about 1600–1500 BC

CRETE, MINOAN

This Minoan bronze statuette is unique in its depiction of a preadolescent girl worshiping a deity. It dates to the Neo-Palatial period, when a sophisticated urbanized civilization flourished on the island of Crete. During this time of high cultural achievement, refined works of art in a number of media were produced: wall paintings and sculpture as well as functional objects of great charm and beauty. Urban life centered on grand sprawling palaces, and a precocious pictographic script, known as "Linear A," was used by palace scribes.

While the statuette was made by a Minoan artist, the subject finds its closest parallel on the island of Thera (Santorini), some 60 miles north of Crete. Contemporary fresco paintings discovered there in a building constructed of carefully cut stone masonry depict girls from preadolescence past the age of puberty engaged in ritual activities, including presenting crocus flowers to a seated divine female figure. One of these girls—shrouded in a bejeweled, transparent veil—matches this bronze exactly.

The statuette and fresco painting are the only representations of such a distinctively dressed and adorned young girl. Most unusual is her jewelry: large hoop earrings, segmented necklace, and heavy bracelets. Equally rare is her hairstyle: shaved in certain places and in other areas allowed to grow into long tresses. Given the correspondence between the fresco and the statuette it is likely that its maker, who was from Crete, was familiar with rituals popular on Thera. Perhaps he visited there before the eruption of the Thera volcano in the second half of the 16th century BC.

BRONZE; H. 14 CM (5-1/2 IN.)

PURCHASE FROM THE J. H. WADE FUND 2002.89

Horse 750–700 BC

CORINTH, GREEK, GEOMETRIC STYLE

During the Geometric period, regional workshops produced numerous cast-bronze horse statuettes that are freestanding (with or without bases), mounted on openwork spheres, or attached to the ring handles of tripod cauldrons. They were among the most popular dedications at Greek sanctuaries, such as the pan-Hellenic sanctuaries at Olympia and Delphi, as well as other temple precincts throughout the Greek world. Clearly, the bronze horse statuette was something of an icon of the period, a pervasive symbol of status and power.

This bronze horse is one of the most outstanding produced in a Corinthian workshop, owing to its finely balanced proportions, large size, and excellent state of preservation. It is also one of the largest and is completely intact. In its reduction and stylization of the form to its essence, it appears strikingly modern. Conceived in profile, the formal elements of the body are abstracted and balanced in a remarkable proportional harmony. The wide thin neck and swelling foreparts form a unit connected to the voluminous hindquarters by the radically constricted cylindrical central section of the body. The tail is continuous with the body and drops in a graceful curve to the openwork base. Muzzle and ears are of a piece, terminating the forward arc of the neck. Stamps of concentric circles with internal dots are visible on both sides of the neck, in addition to other surface incision and embellishment.

Horses were also carved on articles of personal adornment, painted on vases, and sculpted in terracotta in the Geometric period.

BRONZE; 11.5 X 10 X 2.6 CM (4-1/2 X 3-7/8 X 1 IN.)

JOHN L. SEVERANCE FUND 1998.173

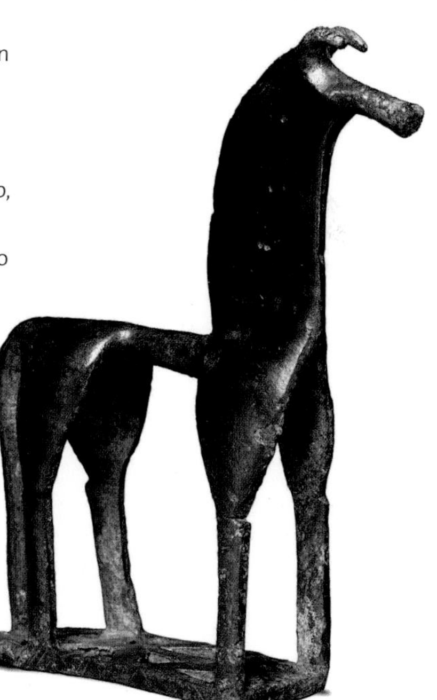

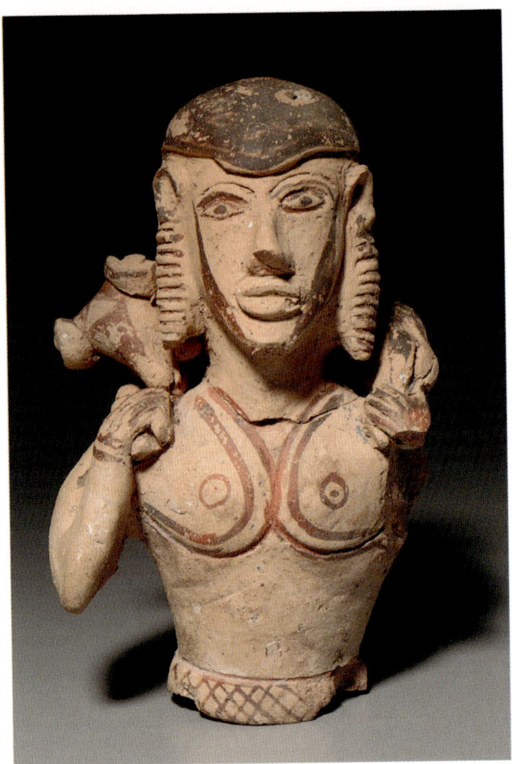

Kriophoros Statuette (Ram-Bearer) about 650–600 BC

CRETE, GREEK

The only known representation of a warrior-hero presenting a ram for sacrifice to a god, this terracotta statuette was intentionally made as a half-figure, perhaps part of a sculptural group. The animal draped across his shoulders classifies the figure as a *kriophoros* (ram-bearer). The statuette stands at the beginning of a sculptural tradition, including the depiction of the god Hermes as ram-bearer, that continued into the sixth and fifth centuries BC.

The protective panoply identifies him as a Homeric hero. He wears a cap-like helmet with a painted chin strap. Instead of a bronze corslet, he wears curious breastplates that leave his midriff bare. His waistbelt (zoster) is modeled in relief and decorated with painted cross-hatchings. The zoster is the most characteristic attribute of the Homeric hero, both in epic poetry and in Greek art of the eighth and seventh centuries BC. In the epic poems the fundamental aspects of the heroic, kingly persona—warrior, charioteer, and athlete—are distinguished by the wearing of waistbelts.

The ram was a popular sacrificial animal. It also had heroic associations. In book 3 of the *Iliad,* King Priam compares Odysseus to a "deep fleeced" ram when he and Helen look down on the Achaean warriors from the walls of Troy. In book 9 of the *Odyssey,* Odysseus clings to the belly of a ram, "far the finest of the flock," in order to escape from the one-eyed giant Polyphemos. Odysseus later sacrifices this ram to Zeus. In Greek art of the fifth and fourth centuries BC, warriors are depicted killing rams in a *sphagion,* a ritual sacrifice conducted just before battle.

TERRACOTTA; 17.5 X 9.6 X 8 CM (6-7/8 X 3-3/4 X 3-1/8 IN.)

JOHN L. SEVERANCE FUND 1998.172

Kouros 575–550 BC

GREEK

In the sixth century BC, Greek sculptors created images of young men in marble. These figures (sing. *kouros*; pl. *kouroi*) were depicted nude and without attributes. Scholars have therefore felt free to speculate about whom they were meant to represent and on their function. Sometimes they have been called "Apollo" when a connection can be made to his cult. Other times they are thought to be funerary memorials to young men, perhaps fallen in battle. All kouroi are presented in the bloom of their manly beauty and doubtless were admired for aesthetic qualities that in Greek culture were conflated with other virtues. For the ancient Greeks, beauty implied goodness.

The extremely high quality of this kouros is manifest in its meticulously carved and finished surface. For Greek kouroi of the Archaic period, much of the sculptor's attention was concentrated on the surface. When compared with surviving contemporary kouroi, the precise, stylized articulation of the male anatomy distinguishes this kouros, especially evident in the way the pectorals are defined, the raised arched ridge defining the thorax, the iliac bulges, and also the sensitively rendered musculature of the back and buttocks. The fastidious stylization is reminiscent of a bronze corslet, an article of protective armor worn by Greek warriors over the torso. In this resemblance there may be an allusion to heroism and prowess in war. A preoccupation with surface pattern is also seen in the treatment of the long hair, arranged down the back into neat horizontal bands.

MARBLE; H. 62.5 CM (24-5/8 IN.), W. 33.6 CM (13-1/4 IN.)
LEONARD C. HANNA JR. FUND 1953.125

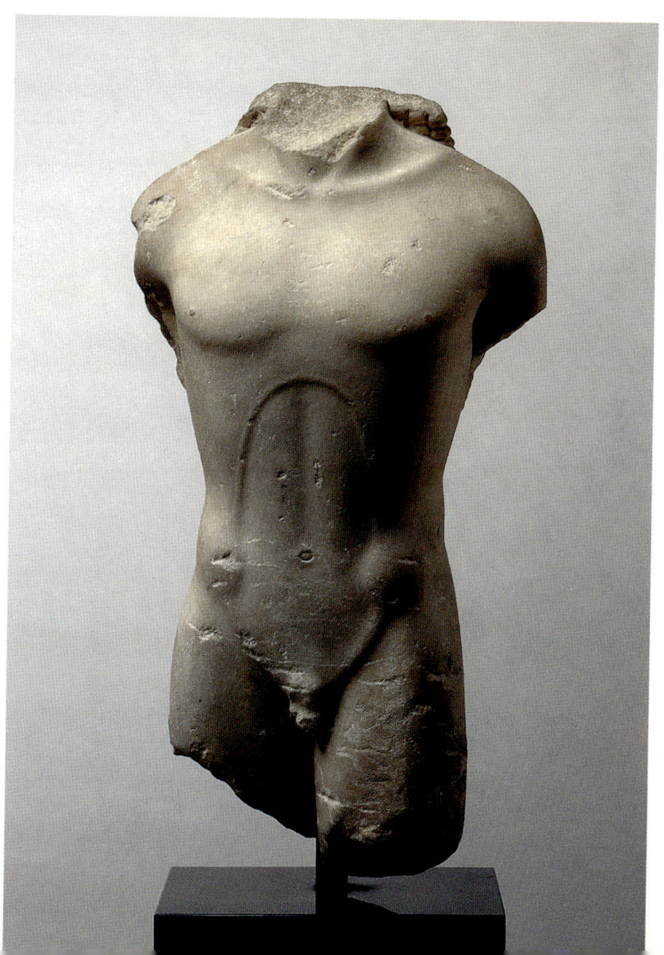

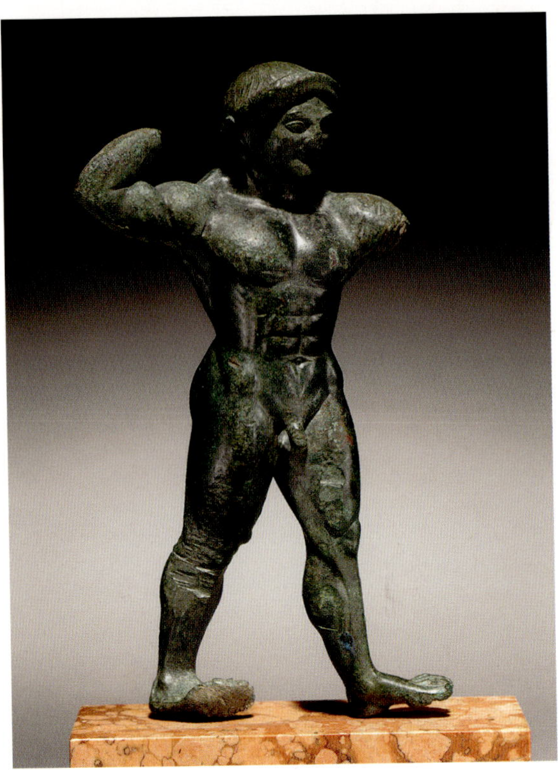

Statuette of an Athlete about 510–500 BC

PELOPONNESE, GREEK

In the late sixth century BC, Greek sculptors were finding new ways to represent the human body in motion. By the beginning of the fifth century BC, a conceptual breakthrough led to an unprecedented naturalism and a fundamentally new style. This rare solid-cast bronze figure captures the transition between a dominant interest in surface and pattern toward an innovative understanding of the human figure animated and enlivened from within. In retrospect, it is possible to detect in this figure the precise transitional moment when the key features of the classical style are first recognizable. With its weight shifted to the right leg, the figure strides forward with right arm raised. From the front, the schematic modeling still harkens back to older conventions, but from the back it is evident that its maker was among a small number of pioneering Greek artists experimenting with novel ways to depict the effects of motion on the human body. The statuette is one of a very few sculptures that clearly illuminate the origins of Greek classicism, a style that would have a deep and lasting legacy in the art of the Western world.

The figure's nudity, muscular physique, and hairstyle identify him as an athlete. He once held a javelin or a discus, and therefore represents a victorious pentathlete. The Pentathelon was an event at the Olympic Games combining the javelin-throw, long jump, discus, foot race, and wrestling. Thus in all likelihood the statuette depicts an Olympic champion. Nothing in Greek life was more celebrated or glorious than being an Olympic victor. Such an achievement was immortalized in verse and song and could be rewarded with large sums of money, a pension, a home, a lifetime supply of olive oil, and meals at public expense.

BRONZE; H. 21.5 CM (8-1/2 IN.), W. 10.5 CM (4-1/8 IN.)

JOHN L. SEVERANCE FUND 2000.6

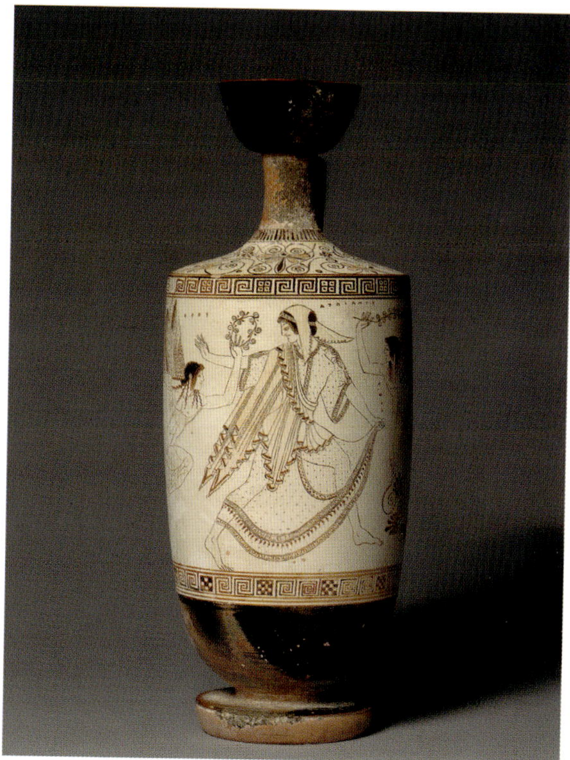

Atalanta Lekythos about 500–490 BC
ATTRIBUTED TO DOURIS (GREEK, ACTIVE 500–460 BC)

The bold composition, confident draftsmanship, and excellent state of preservation rate this Greek vase among the best executed in the white-ground technique to have survived. The white color is a clay slip on which the figures were painted with black glaze, also a clay solution. The black glaze was further diluted with water for the brownish painted lines describing fine details of musculature and dress. The vessel is a *lekythos* (oil flask). Conventionally, *lekythoi* (pl.) have figural decoration on one side only, but the figures on this unusual lekythos wrap around the vase entirely. They are identified by inscriptions. Three winged personifications of love (erotes) pursue the running figure of Atalanta. Eros was the son of Aphrodite, goddess of love, and Ares, god of warfare. Atalanta, accomplished in such masculine pursuits as wrestling, archery, and running, preferred to spend her time in the wild countryside. She would marry only the suitor who could beat her in a footrace. Aphrodite gave a challenger three golden apples that he dropped during his race, distracting Atalanta long enough to win.

Whether the scene should be read as a continuous narrative or as a series of individual vignettes is not clear. Atalanta wears a diaphanous chiton that she holds at its bottom edge while running to the right. She looks back toward the figure of Eros behind her, who holds up a garland in his left hand. In his right hand he once held a whip, now repainted as a tendril. Two other erotes appear in positions and poses less obviously associated with Atalanta and the footrace. Perhaps all three erotes are one and the same, rendered as in a timed sequence.

CERAMIC, WHITE-GROUND; H. 32.5 CM (12-1/2 IN.), DIAM. 8.8 CM (3-1/2 IN.) FOOT
LEONARD C. HANNA JR. FUND 1966.114

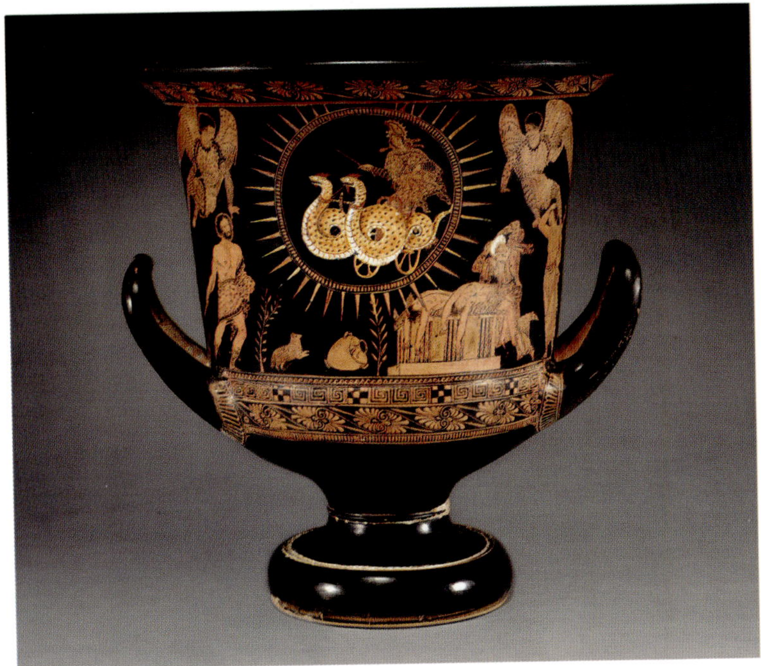

Calyx-Krater about 400 BC

SOUTH ITALY, LUCANIAN, ATTRIBUTED TO NEAR THE POLICORO PAINTER

This elaborately decorated calyx-krater is a vessel designed for mixing wine with water, a typical practice for the Greeks. It was made in Lucania in South Italy and features two scenes taken from plays of Euripides, an Athenian playwright popular with the Greek colonists of South Italy and Sicily.

On the front is the final scene from *Medea.* She flies across the sky in a chariot driven by two coiled snakes, surrounded by a radiate nimbus, perhaps an attribute of her grandfather, the sun god Helios. She wears a Phrygian helmet, cloak, tunic, and sleeved undergarment. Above to the left and right are winged Erinyes, grotesque hags with hooked noses, there to avenge Medea's unspeakable crime: the bloody bodies of her two murdered sons are draped over an altar in the lower right corner. At the lower left her husband, Jason, looks up at her helplessly as his dog leaps up in front of him. Euripides' *Medea* was first staged in Athens in 431 BC.

The back features a scene from the legend of Telephus and Orestes, the subject of a lost Euripidean tragedy of 438 BC. Telephus, shown nude and bearded, holds the infant Orestes in his left hand and grasps an upright sword in his right; his bent left leg rests on a blood-stained altar. The infant extends his arms toward his parents at the right. His father, Agamemnon, threatens Telephus with sword drawn; Agamemnon's wife, Clytemnestra, gestures in alarm. Wounded by Achilles, Telephus took Orestes hostage in order to force Agamemnon to heal the injury.

CERAMIC, RED-FIGURE, WITH ADDED RED, WHITE, AND YELLOW; H. 50.5 CM (19-7/8 IN.), DIAM. 49.9 CM (19-5/8 IN.) MOUTH
LEONARD C. HANNA JR. FUND 1991.1

Apollo the Python-Slayer (formerly **Apollo Sauroktonos**) about 350 BC

ATTRIBUTED TO PRAXITELES (GREEK, ABOUT 400–330 BC)

The technical features, condition, and sensitive modeling of this life-size bronze sculpture are consistent with a mid fourth-century BC date. The sculptural type has been attributed to the famous Athenian sculptor Praxiteles since the first century AD, when the Roman author Pliny the Elder described what is thought to have been the original (*Natural History* 34.70) as a "sauroktonos" (lizard-slayer). He wrote that the sculpture depicted an adolescent Apollo waiting to stab a reptile with an arrow. Roman marble copies show a youthful Apollo leaning on a heavy tree trunk to which a large lizard clings. Until the appearance of this version, there was no reason to question the accuracy of Pliny's epithet. Yet this bronze Apollo is compelling evidence that Pliny did not examine the original closely or perhaps was repeating a popular nickname or misnomer for the sculptural type. The reptilian creature here cannot be called a lizard. In fact, its fantastical composite anatomy is deliberately unnatural. The body is a coiled snake, to which limbs of different sizes are attached asymmetrically. The feet are strangely flattened and oddly formed.

It is in fact the Python that Apollo had to kill before becoming the presiding deity at the Delphi sanctuary. Praxiteles created the bronze original, likely this very statue, in commemoration of the sanctuary's foundation myth. At Delphi, both the Septerion and Pythian festivals celebrated Apollo's triumph over the Python, son of Mother Earth. At Delphi, Apollo the Python-Slayer stood as a monument to the victory of order (Apollo signifying *kosmos*) over disorder (the Python denoting *chaos*) at the center (navel) of the world.

BRONZE, COPPER, AND STONE INLAY; FIGURE, H. 150 CM (59 IN.); LEFT HAND AND FOREARM, L. 25.9 CM (10-1/4 IN.); PYTHON, L. 14.8 CM (5-7/8 IN.)

SEVERANCE AND GRETA MILLIKIN PURCHASE FUND 2004.30. A–C

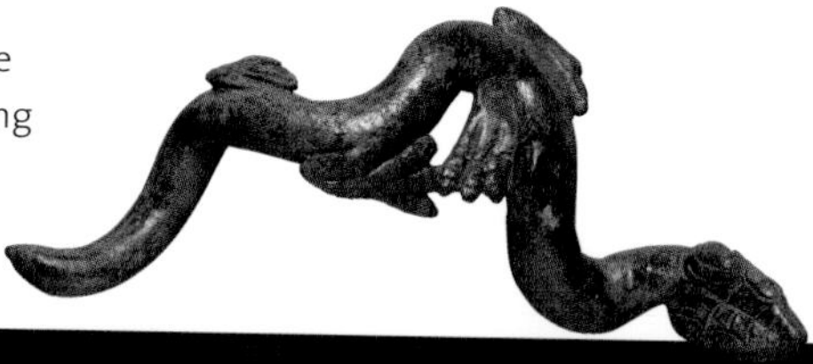

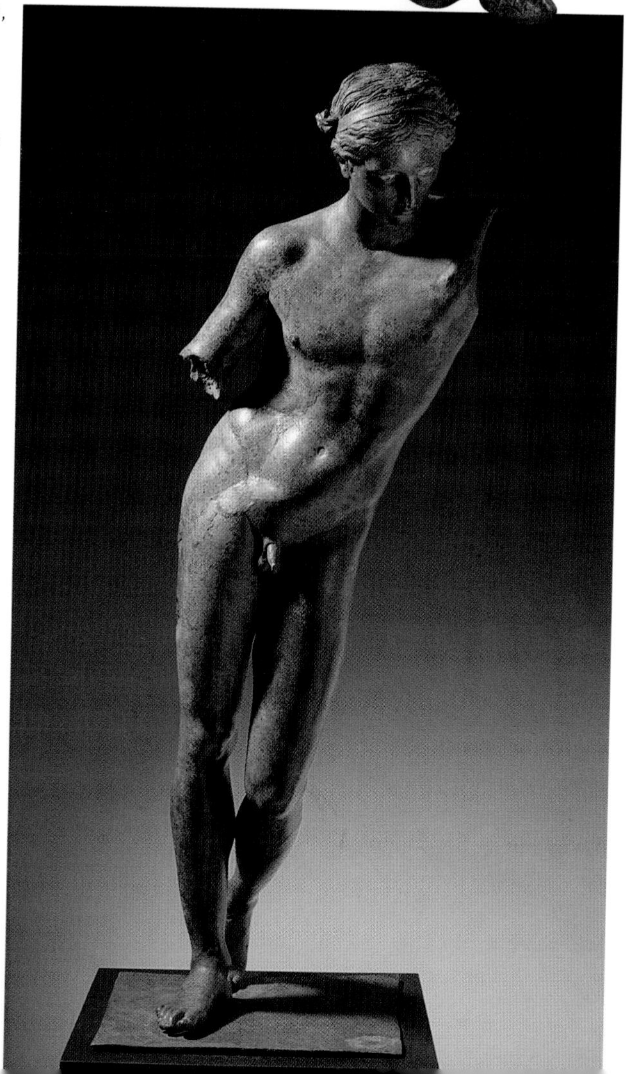

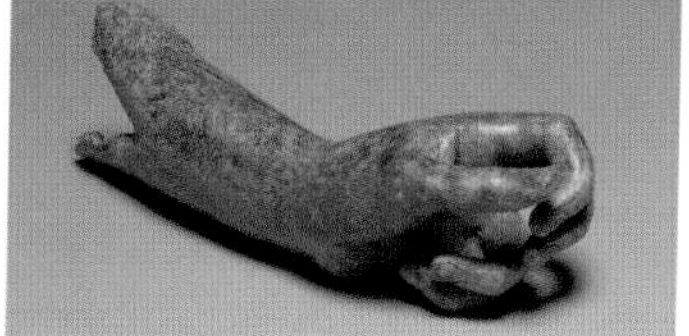

Statuette of a Nanny Goat about 120–100 BC

GREEK

Domesticated early, goats were commonly featured in Greek art and myth. This large hollow-cast statuette, with its curly beard and backswept horns, is not a ram but a pregnant doe, as indicated by her swollen flanks and pendulous teats. The work of a master bronze sculptor, it was probably worshiped as a cult image, made to either stand alone or be part of a larger sculptural group. The greatest Greek sculptors created sculptures of animals. Ancient authors mention several lost masterworks such as Myron's cow (mid 5th century BC), Skopas's goat (late 4th century BC), and Boethus's goose (4th–3rd century BC), all considered among these masters' greatest works.

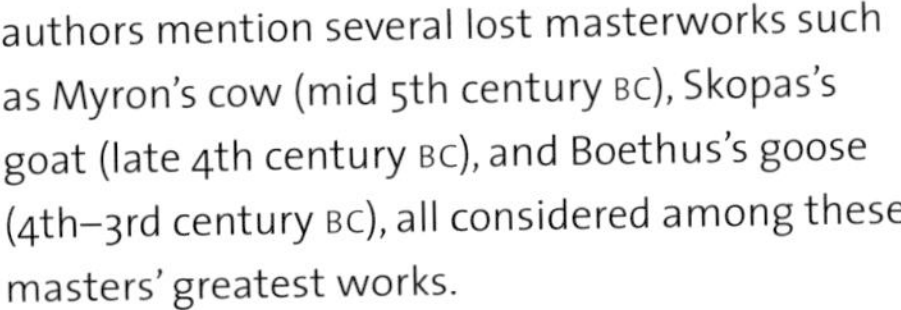

The statuette's large size, dynamic modeling, and realistic appearance make it one of the most important representations of an animal to have survived from classical antiquity in any medium. The rounded pupils are deeply recessed under carefully rendered lids and brows, giving the goat a lively expression as it turns its head subtly to the right. The modeling is more complex and varied on the right side of the body, indicating that the statuette was designed to be seen primarily from that side. Overall the modeling is meticulously executed and convincingly describes the bone structure and masses of muscle under the skin covered in thick, beautifully textured fleece. The concave areas at the tail and hips and the parted mouth are signs that birth is imminent. All these sculptural qualities point to a date in the second century BC.

BRONZE; H. 30.5 (12 IN.), L. 31.1 CM (12-1/4 IN.)

LEONARD C. HANNA JR. FUND 1990.32

Cista Handle: Sleep and Death Carrying Off the Slain Sarpedon 400–380 BC

ITALY, ETRUSCAN

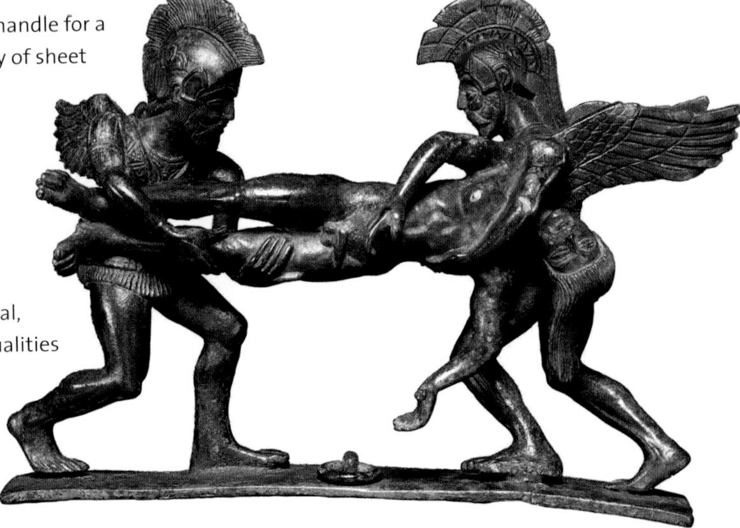

This sculptural group was a handle for a cista, a container with a body of sheet bronze and cast feet used to store precious personal belongings. It was made in the workshop of a skilled Etruscan artist, influenced by Greek artistic models inspired by epic poetry. Although perfectly functional, its outstanding aesthetic qualities distinguish it among small classical bronzes.

Concentrated in northern and central Italy, the Etruscans were passionate admirers of Greek art and culture. This expressive small bronze sculpture eloquently demonstrates how a confluence of cultural traditions can mingle to produce a transcendent work of art. The figures illustrate a passage from Homer's *Iliad:* the brothers Hypnos (Sleep) and Thanatos (Death) gently raising the body of Sarpedon, the son of Zeus who has been killed by the Greek warrior Patroclus. Alarmed that his son's corpse would soon attract dogs and birds, Zeus instructed Apollo to take the body away, wash it in a river, anoint it, dress it in clean clothes, and then hand it over to the brothers who were to convey it to Lycia for a proper burial.

Departing somewhat from the Homeric account, the artist omitted the role of Apollo and, instead of showing Sarpedon's body clothed, represents it nude. This vulnerable nudity, together with the sensitive depiction of the winged brothers, adds a plaintive note of tragic heroism to the scene. Sarpedon's flaccid body provokes sadness and compassion in the viewer. The sentiment is expressed by the Greek word *pathos,* a weighty sorrow provoking deep sympathy. The Greek hero must face death, giving the bloody reality of death in battle a gloss of noble dignity.

BRONZE; H. 14 (5-1/2 IN), L. 17.4 CM (6-7/8 IN.)

PURCHASE FROM THE J. H. WADE FUND 1945.13

Portrait Head of Drusus Minor probably after AD 23

NORTH AFRICA, ROMAN

This imposing marble portrait of Drusus Minor (Nero Claudius Drusus, 13 BC–AD 23) is the most outstanding of the approximately 30 large-scale portraits of the son of the emperor Tiberius known to have survived. The masterful carving, superb state of preservation, and monumental scale set it apart. It is one of the finest Julio-Claudian portraits in America. The Julio-Claudian dynasty (about 27 BC–AD 68) began the Roman Imperial period with the rule of Augustus, who was followed by Tiberius, Caligula, Claudius, and Nero. The portrait was carved during a consequential period in world history, roughly contemporary with the ministry of Jesus Christ.

The impression of great power held in reserve, amplified by massive size, gives the portrait its brooding presence. It combines the cool idealization of Greek classical prototypes with the emotionality of Hellenistic sculptural styles, judiciously employed to describe the subject's features—broad, undulating forehead, pronounced brow, large hooked nose, thin lips, small round chin, and muscular neck—known from other portraits and coins. Augustus had made the distinctive hairstyle popular.

The portrait's noble presence belies Drusus Minor's sordid nature. He had a violent temper, often drank to excess, and enjoyed gladiatorial blood sport to a degree that dismayed his father. Still, he was an able military commander and delivered a funeral oration for Augustus from the rostra in the Roman forum at age 28. In line to become emperor, he was reportedly poisoned by his wife, Livilla, who was having an affair with the general Sejanus.

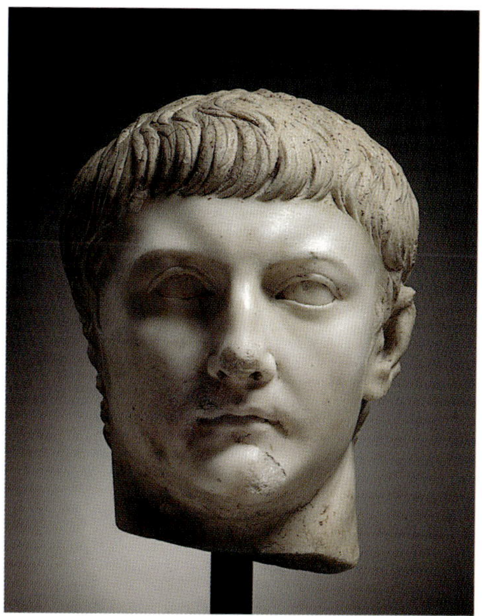

MARBLE; H. 35 CM (13-3/4 IN.), DIAM. 29 CM (11-1/2 IN.)

LEONARD C. HANNA JR. FUND 2012.29

Orestes Sarcophagus AD 100–200

ITALY, ROMAN

The scenes carved in high relief on the front of this sarcophagus—a handsome example of the enduring popularity and influence of Greek myth and literature well into the Roman Imperial period—illustrate a story from Greek epic poetry.

Roman burial practices changed in the early second century AD, when inhumation became more popular than cremation. This richly carved sarcophagus would have been placed in an underground burial chamber outside the city, most likely Rome. Because it was protected from vandalism and the elements in such an environment, it is in excellent condition. It is decorated on only three sides because one side would have been against a wall. On the front are scenes from the myth of Orestes, first told in the *Odyssey* of Homer. Orestes killed his mother, Clytemnestra, because she conspired to murder his father, Agamemnon, king of Mycenae, while carrying on an affair with his cousin Aegisthus.

The narrative unfolds from the left. Three furies, who avenge crimes of murder between relatives, sleep in a rocky landscape. In the next scene, Orestes kills Aegisthus. Then Orestes stands above Clytemnestra, whom he has just killed. And finally, at the right, Orestes appears at the Delphi sanctuary to seek atonement for his crimes. He rests his left hand on the Delphic tripod while stepping over an apparently pacified fury sitting on the ground. On the front surface of the lid are personifications of the four seasons, running chronologically from right to left: Winter, Spring, Summer, and Autumn. Winged putti present each with offerings. At the left and right corners are large heads, perhaps sirens.

MARBLE; 80 X 210 X 55.5 CM (31-1/2 X 82-7/8 X 21-7/8 IN.) GIFT OF THE JOHN HUNTINGTON ART AND POLYTECHNIC TRUSTS 1928.856

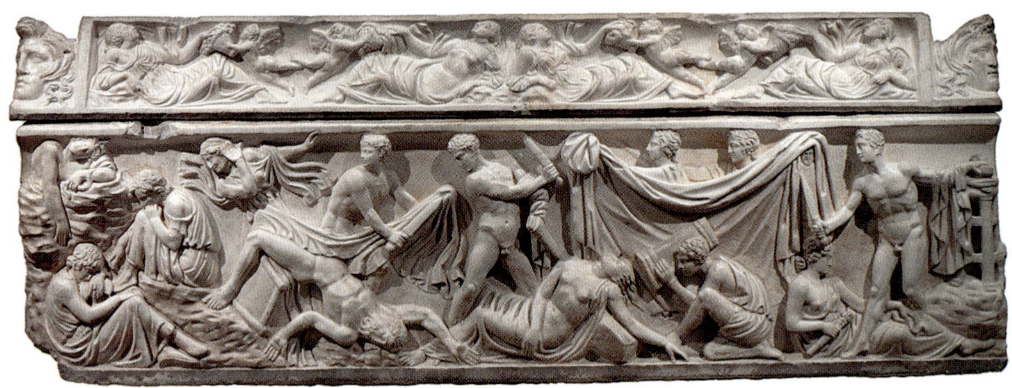

The Emperor as Philosopher, Probably Marcus Aurelius about AD 180–200

ITALY, ROMAN

Scholars are virtually certain that this over-life-size draped bronze figure is a portrait of the Antonine emperor Marcus Aurelius (r. AD 161–80) dressed as a Greek philosopher. The massive, headless figure rests comfortably on the right leg while the left steps forward. He wears a chiton under a himation, and his feet are shod in traveler's sandals. The himation is cleverly modeled to show creases in the fabric, perhaps the result of the laundered fabric being pressed and stored prior to use. The right arm is wrapped in a swath of the himation draping from the right shoulder, revealing the exquisitely modeled right hand. The left hand, hidden under the heavy drapery, appears to be held in a fist and propped against the left hip. The assured contrapposto pose lends the figure an air of authority and confidence.

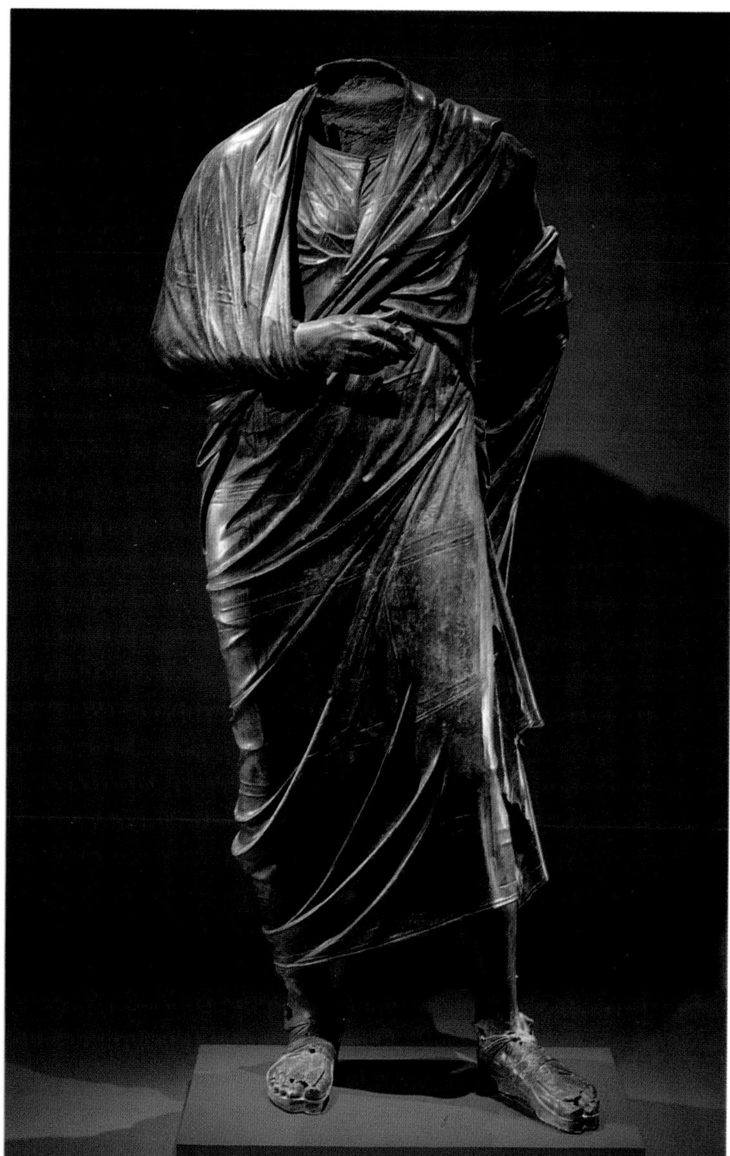

Marcus Aurelius was a devoted student of Stoicism, a dominant set of philosophical beliefs first developed in the Hellenistic period but lasting into the early Roman Empire. He wrote a philosophical work now known as *Meditations*, a kind of self-help guide to living ethically in an often unethical world. He was said to have been influenced by the Greek philosopher Plato, who believed that for harmonious governance philosophers should become rulers. Although the ruler of antiquity's greatest empire, Marcus Aurelius preferred to be portrayed as a humble philosopher and seeker of truth. This remarkable achievement of bronze casting technique is also an iconic image of the Greco-Roman nature of Roman culture among its ruling class at this time.

BRONZE; H. 193 CM (76 IN.)

LEONARD C. HANNA FUND 1986.5

Personal Ornaments from Ancient Greece

Prized emblems of status, cleverly designed and decorated, these four bronze personal ornaments tell us much about early Greek beliefs and customs. The *Zone (Woman's Belt Hanger)* was probably deposited in the grave of its owner. It is one of the largest known and is completely intact. It was worn either suspended from or otherwise attached to a belt as its central ornament. The incised and punched front surface features a central radiate circle flanked by symmetrical groups of smaller circles. Both the form and decoration suggest that it symbolized a woman's reproductive anatomy. The *Fibula with Solar Design* was used to fasten clothing and it, too, is decorated with incision and punch marks. On its crescent "bow" section is a schematic diagram of the route of Helios (the sun), from dawn in

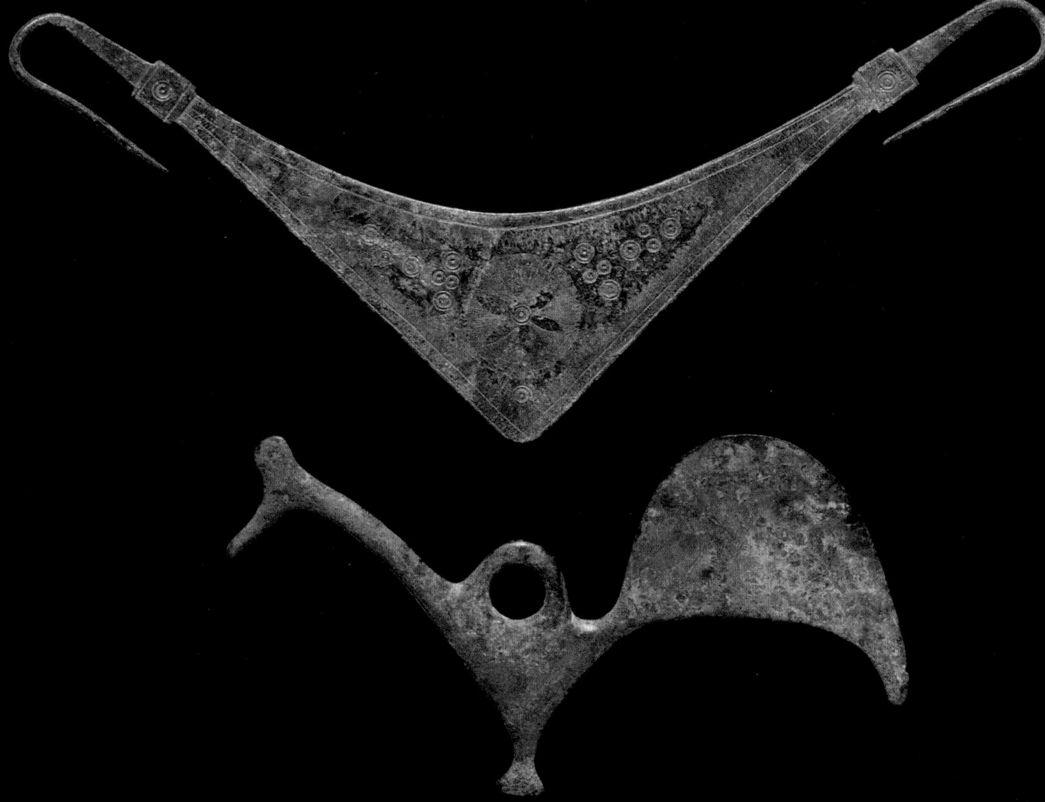

Zone (Woman's Belt Hanger), about 725–675 BC. Northern Greece, Geometric style. Bronze; W. 32.5 cm (12-3/4 in.). The Jane B. Tripp Charitable Lead Annuity Trust 2006.5

Bird Pendant, 800–700 BC. Northern Greece, Geometric style. Bronze; H. 5 cm (2 in.), W. 9 cm (3-1/2 in.). John L. Severance Fund 1999.249

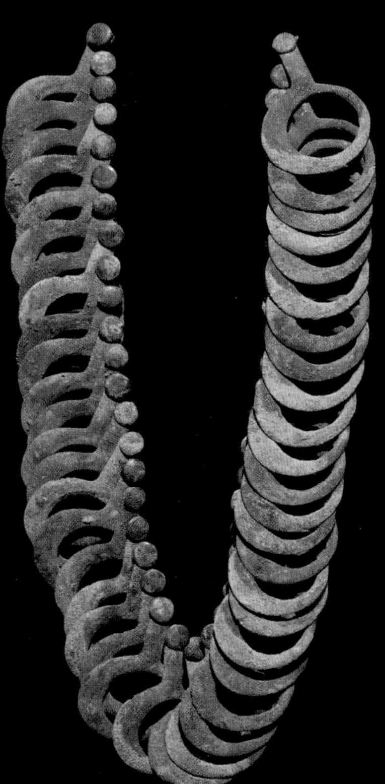

the east to dusk in the west. Arrows indicate the direction of the sun's course to mid heaven; the direction is then reversed until sunset, resulting in a "linear ring." The fibula's decoration relates to the *Homeric Hymn to Helios* and to Homeric descriptions of battles calibrated to the sun's course, with noon marking the moment when Zeus weighs the fates of heroes on the battlefield. A brilliant demonstration of design serving function, the rare *Necklace with Hanging Pendants* combines 45 separately cast pendants that overlap one another, creating a pleasing pattern that reverses itself at the bottom of the necklace. The subject of the *Bird Pendant* is likely a rooster. It is the largest and best preserved of its type known. The rooster's flattened body is radically abstracted into three component parts: the long neck, head, beak, and comb at the top of the head; the small triangular body incorporating a suspension hole; finally, the expansive contours of the arched tail feathers.

Ornament with Hanging Pendants, about 725 BC. Northern Greece, Geometric style. Bronze; L. 40.6 cm (16 in.) overall; H. 5.9 cm (2-3/8 in.), W. 4.3 cm (1-1/8 in.) each pendant. Gift of Bruce Ferrini in honor of Trustee Emeritus Dr. Norman Zaworski on the occasion of his 80th birthday 2000.105

Fibula with Solar Design, 700–675 BC. Greece, Boeotia; Geometric style. Bronze; H. 15.4 cm (6-1/8 in.), W. 11.2 cm (4-3/8 in.). The John L. Severance Fund 1999.9

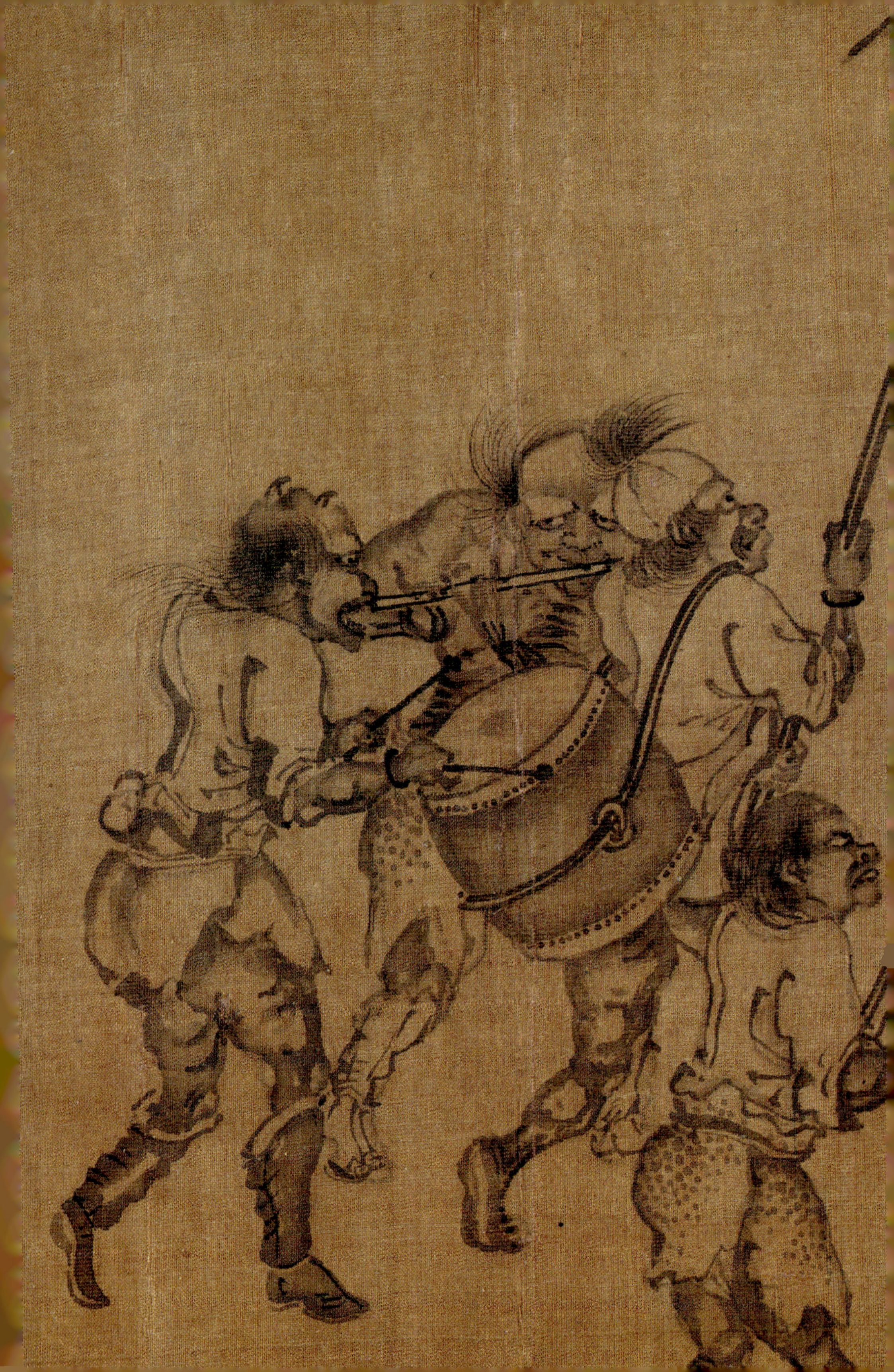

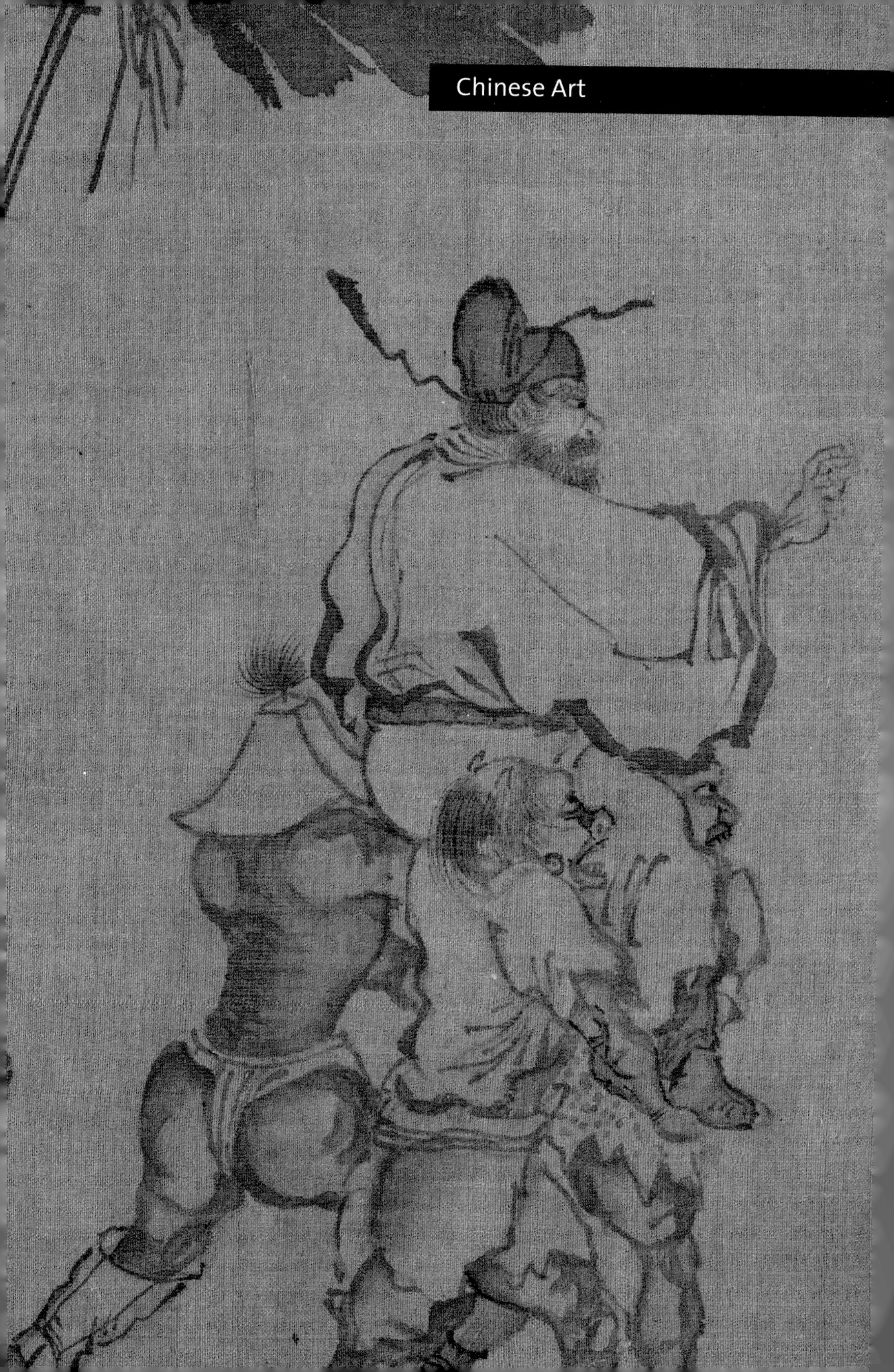

Chinese Art

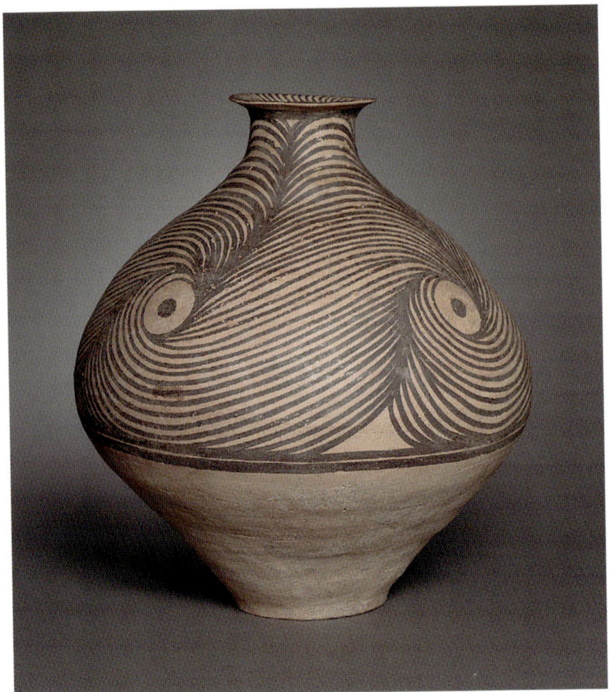

Jar with Spiral Designs about 3300–2650 BC

NORTHWEST CHINA, NEOLITHIC PERIOD, MAJIAYAO CULTURE, MAJIAYAO PHASE

Made of fine clay, this jar is painted with spiral patterns on its smooth burnished surfaces. It is a spectacular example of painted pottery from the Majiayao culture that existed in the northwestern region of China, one of the regional cultures representing the late stage of China's prehistory. The bold, curvilinear decoration and straw-colored body are characteristic of Majiayao pottery. Concentric markings indicate the use of a wheel while the spiral circles and linear patterns suggest a primitive type of brush. In its original context Neolithic painted pottery was functional; now it is esteemed on aesthetic grounds.

The archaeological evidence for pottery making was associated with the appearance of sedentary villages and an agricultural lifestyle. One of the significant contributions of archaeology to the knowledge of prehistoric China is to reveal the confluence of cultures in various regions, challenging the long-held assumption that Chinese civilization originated solely along the Yellow River. Archaeological discoveries show that societies developed along the Yangzi River, in northeastern China, and also in other regions. The artifacts of these various regional cultures manifest distinctive characteristics; each culture played a role in the formation of the Chinese civilization.

EARTHENWARE PAINTED IN DARK BROWN SLIP; H. 45.2 CM (17-3/4 IN.), DIAM. 39.1 CM (15-3/8 IN.)

GIFT OF DONNA S. AND JAMES S. REID JR. IN HONOR OF DR. JU-HSI CHOU 2004.64

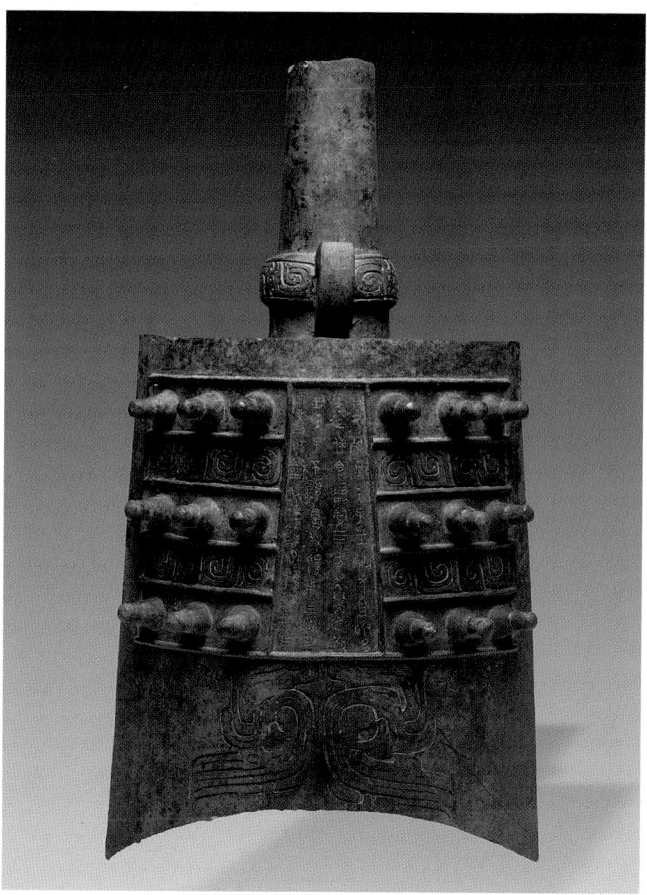

Bell (Lai Zhong) 8th century BC

CHINA, SHAANXI PROVINCE, MEIXIAN, WESTERN ZHOU DYNASTY (ABOUT 1046–771 BC)

This ancient bronze bell, an instrument of Chinese ritual music, was part of a graduated set of eight bells arranged according to size and pitch. When played by a court musician in a ritual ceremony, the bell was suspended diagonally on a frame from the loop at its top and was sounded by striking the exterior of the bottom rims with a mallet.

A commemorative inscription of 129 characters appears on this bell telling of its owner, Lai, and why it was cast. According to the inscription, Lai's ancestors dutifully served the Zhou royal court and he was granted a hereditary position by the Son of Heaven (King Xuanwang, r. 827–782 BC) to manage fisheries and forests. To express filial piety, Lai commissioned a set of harmonized bells as offerings to his father, Gongshu, in the hope that the bronzes would be forever treasured by future generations. Not only is this inscription a significant historical document, offering insights into the ancient Chinese ideas about the Son of Heaven, ancestral sacrifices, and ritual duties, it also provides an example of ancient Chinese calligraphy for our appreciation of the purely abstract lines and the construction of characters.

BRONZE; 70.3 X 37 X 26.6 CM (27-3/4 X 14-5/8 X 10-1/2 IN.)

LEONARD C. HANNA JR. FUND 1989.3

Mat Weight in the Form of a Bear 1st century AD

CHINA, WESTERN HAN DYNASTY (206 BC–AD 9)

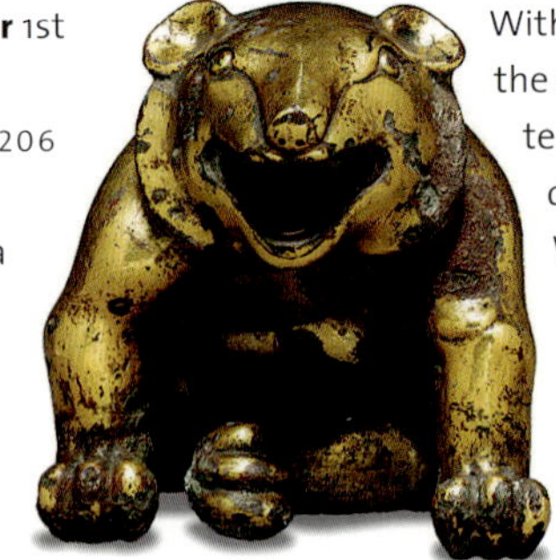

Squatting on its haunches with a back leg bent and head thrust forward, this solid gilt-bronze bear marks a stylistic departure from the previous solemnity of animal-shaped bronze vessels to animal sculpture in the round. Its naturalism and light humor reflect the new worldly tastes of the time. The modeling is simple but vivid, and gilding has replaced the earlier intricate patterns for surface decoration.

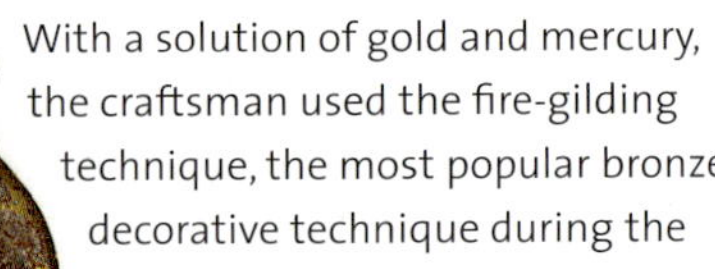

With a solution of gold and mercury, the craftsman used the fire-gilding technique, the most popular bronze decorative technique during the Western Han dynasty.

In its original context this small sculpture was probably used as a mat weight or a supporting element. Bear imagery was particularly popular during the Han and was likely a metaphor for heroic power. The Chinese word for "bear" is pronounced the same as the word "hero." This rebus thus conveyed meaning.

GILT BRONZE; 15.7 X 14.6 X 17.3 CM (6-1/8 X 5-3/4 X 6-7/8 IN.) JOHN L. SEVERANCE FUND 1994.203

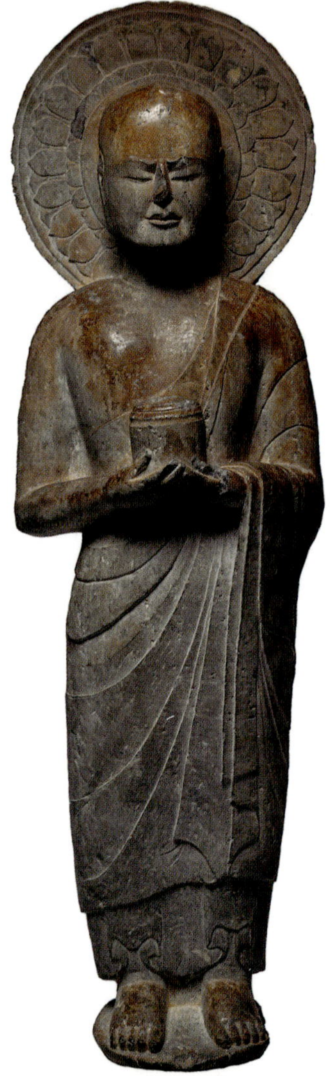

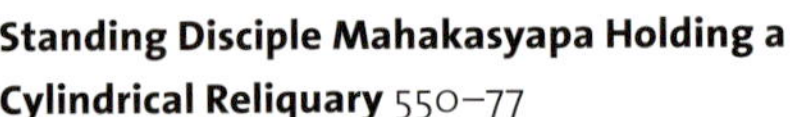

Standing Disciple Mahakasyapa Holding a Cylindrical Reliquary 550–77

CHINA, HEBEI PROVINCE, SOUTHERN XIANGTANGSHAN CAVES, NORTHERN QI DYNASTY (550–577)

Mahakasyapa, a disciple of the Buddha Shakyamuni, stands on a base, eyes closed in an expression of meditative concentration and holding a reliquary for the Buddha's ashes. A halo is attached to the back of his head and shoulders. The entire sculpture is carved from a single block of stone, obviously the work of a master. The artistic simplicity, serene and absorbed expression, and dignified pose accentuate the figure's spiritual content.

This image appears to be a pair with a freestanding sculpture of another disciple, Ananda, currently at the Villa I Tatti, Harvard University Center for Italian Renaissance Studies, in Florence, Italy. Apparently from the southern Xiangtangshan caves, the two were commissioned and donated by the nobility of the Northern Qi dynasty. At Buddhist sites in Xiangtangshan, the ruling class supported temple construction and image making in caves, suggesting that the Buddhist faith had been embraced as the ideal for governance. For individual donors, patronage of Buddhist art was believed to promote benefits for self, family, and state.

LIMESTONE WITH TRACES OF PIGMENT; 116 X 33 X 25 CM (45-3/4 X 13 X 9-7/8 IN.)

LEONARD C. HANNA JR. FUND 1972.166

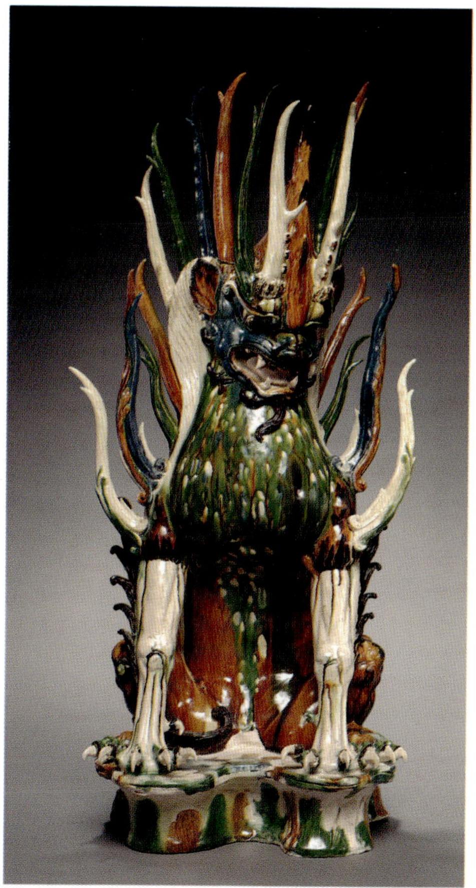

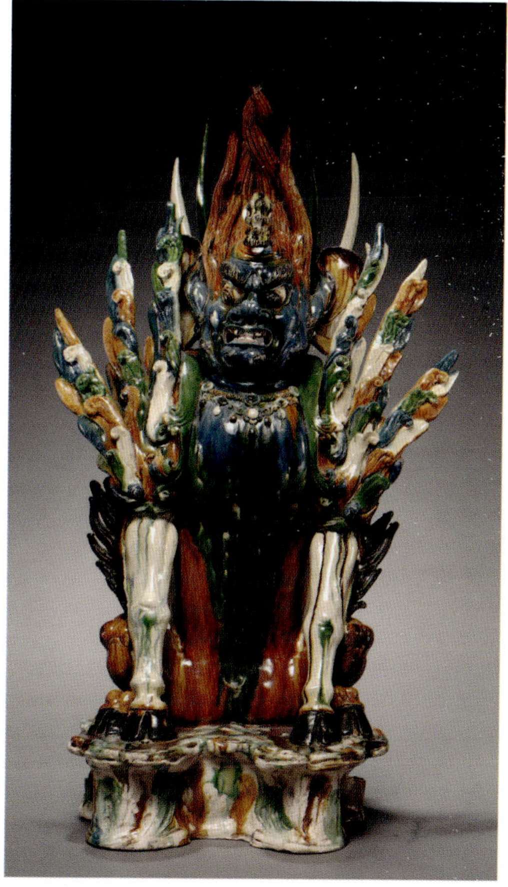

Tomb Guardians early 8th century

CHINA, SHAANXI PROVINCE, XI'AN, TANG DYNASTY (618–907)

Depicted with astonishing power and imagination, these two tomb figurines are magnificent examples of Tang-dynasty glazed ceramic sculptures that accompany the deceased in the afterlife. Known as *qitou* (earth spirits), these two fantastic guardian creatures have different characteristics: one has an animal face and a pair of antlers growing above its eyebrows; the other sports a human face with huge protruding ears and a short horn surrounded by fiery, twisting hair. The numerous elongated spikes on both heighten their fearful intensity.

With their fierce expressions and exaggerated physical features, these statues were intended to guard the entrance to a tomb, warding off evil as well as keeping the soul of the deceased from wandering. Completely covered with the *sancai* (three-color) glaze, they display incomparable vigor and energy. Here, the sancai palette includes not only amber, green, and cream but also a more precious color, blue. The lavish use of the valuable cobalt blue imported from Persia, coupled with the superb workmanship, suggest that the sculptures were reserved for use by the imperial family or high officials.

GLAZED EARTHENWARE, *SANCAI* (THREE-COLOR) WARE; 92.3 X 43.8 X 41.9 CM (36-3/8 X 17-1/4 X 16-1/2 IN.) LEFT, 88.9 X 41 X 50.8 CM (35 X 16-1/8 X 20 IN.) RIGHT

GIFT OF VARIOUS DONORS TO THE DEPARTMENT OF ASIAN ART (BY EXCHANGE) 2000.118.1–2

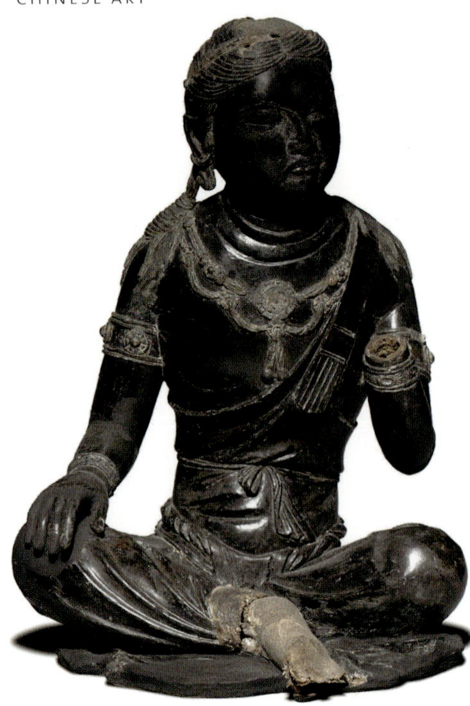

Bodhisattva 8th century

CHINA, TANG DYNASTY (618–907)

A bodhisattva is an enlightened being dedicated to the spiritual awakening of all beings. This example sits in a relaxed pose, head tilted to one side, eyes half-closed and cast down in an expression of profound thought. The graceful posture gives a sense of calm and stately dignity, heightening the transcendental beauty of a sacred image.

Modeled in a sensuous manner, this figure was made using the dry lacquer technique in which a clay core is overlaid with strips of cloth that have been saturated with lacquer. Once the additional lacquer layers are applied and set, the core is removed. Hollow dry-lacquer Buddhist statues like this one are light and easy to carry. The technique is highly suitable for portable statues and was widely adopted in Tang China and spread during the eighth century to Nara, Japan.

When this statue became part of the collection, its original beauty had been distorted by severe retouching. Conservation work removed coats of overpainting and excessive restoration, revealing the true appearance of its highly plastic form, the finishing details, as well as the glossy black lacquer surface with traces of cut-gold decoration and pigments.

DRY LACQUER; 44 X 37 CM (17-3/8 X 14-5/8 IN.)

GIVEN IN MEMORY OF HOWARD PARMELEE EELLS JR. BY HIS WIFE, ADELE CHISHOLM EELLS 1983.86

Bodhisattva 8th century

CHINA, HEBEI PROVINCE, TANG DYNASTY (618–907)

This exquisite and sensuous white marble torso exemplifies the quest for refinement and plasticity of form in eighth-century Chinese Buddhist sculpture. Both the posture and garment are typical of the freestanding bodhisattva statues that mark the golden era of Tang Buddhist sculpture. The figure has an elongated body, broad shoulders, and a narrow waist. The torso leans forward, and the slight sway of the hip on one side and upraised shoulder on the other result in an elegant S-curve in the profile. The body is draped with a chest cloth and a skirt rolled at the waist. The fluid, linear folds of the skirt together with the pearl chains and looping stoles create rhythmic patterns over the body.

The statue was conceived with great power and grandeur. The heavy, emphatic lines cut into the stone reveal the sculptor's skill and sureness of execution. Stylistically, this sculpture is related to the other extant works from Baoding and Dingzhou in Hebei province.

MARBLE; 177.8 X 64 X 58.5 CM (70 X 25-1/4 X 23 IN.)

PURCHASE FROM THE J. H. WADE FUND 1929.981

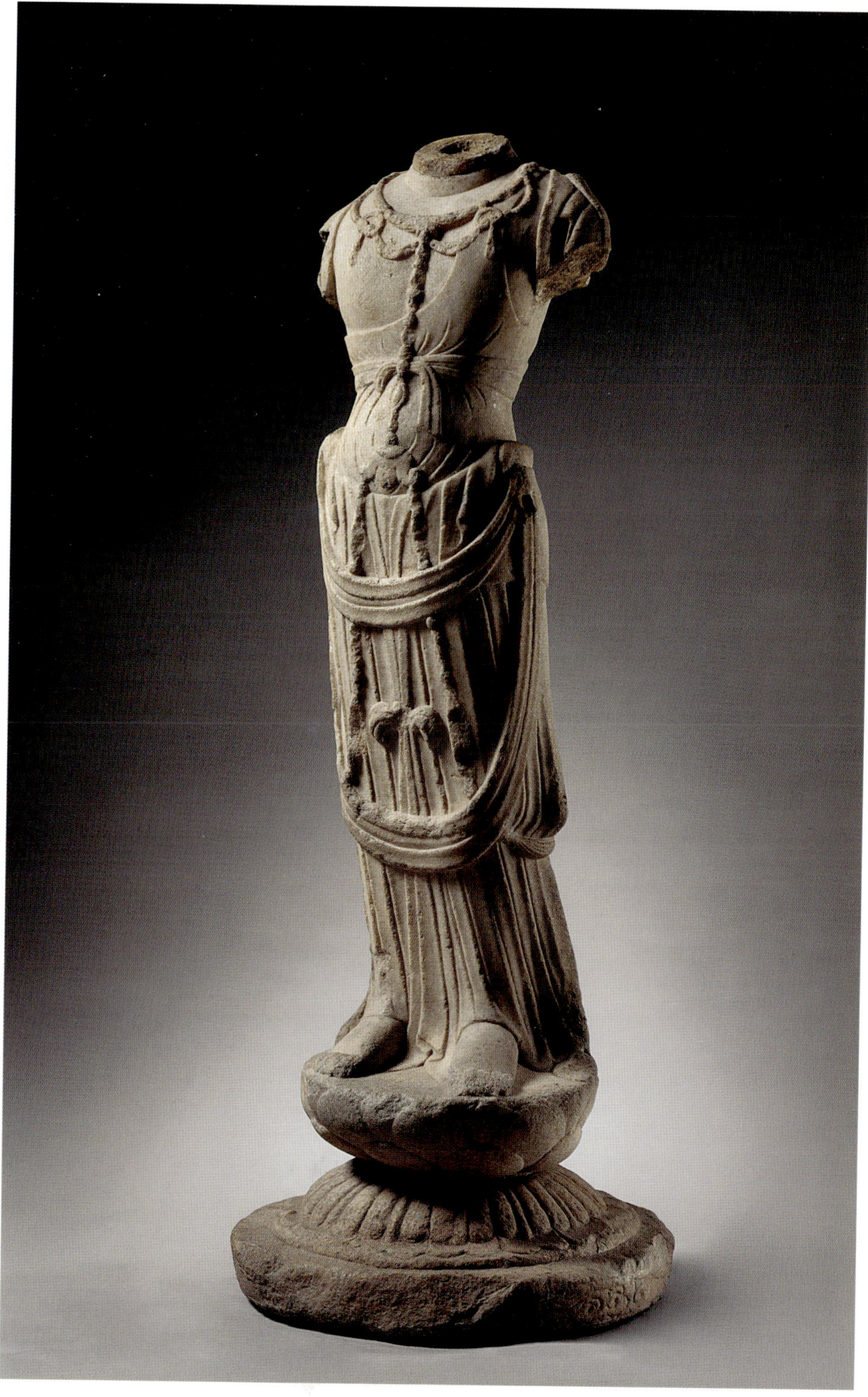

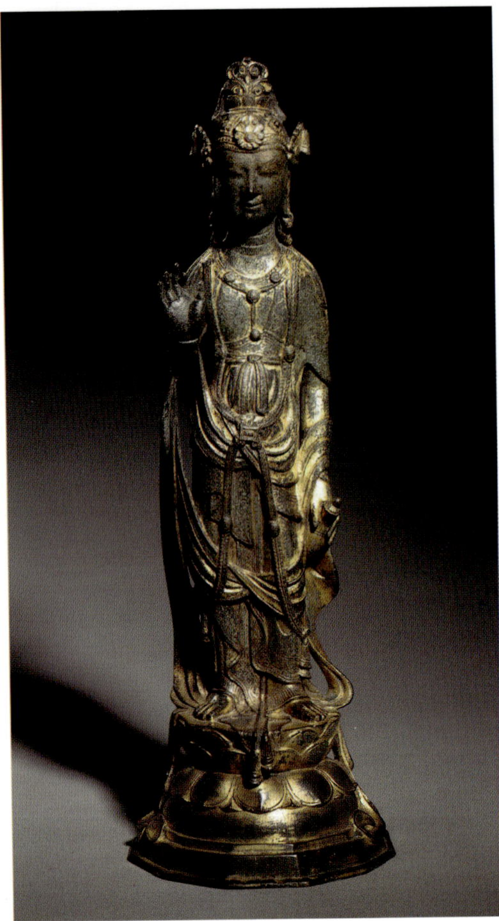

Guanyin 10th century
CHINA, LIAO DYNASTY (916–1125)
This delicately crafted but now corroded gilt-bronze statue of Guanyin (Bodhisattva Avalokiteshvara) bears testimony to the florescence of Buddhist art under the Liao Empire established by the nomadic Khitans (Chinese: Qidan) after the Tang persecution of Buddhism in 845. The Liao rulers were devout Buddhists who commissioned substantial religious projects within the territory. An expanded Liao Empire, including an area of northern China, provided the political background for cultural borrowing from the Chinese. Liao artifacts reflecting close ties to the Tang artistic traditions were most likely executed by displaced or enslaved artisans as a result of mass deportation of populations following the Khitan conquest of northern China.

This gilt-bronze statue is based on the classic Tang style, yet it demonstrates the conception of a different kind of art. Unlike the forcefully modeled Tang gilt-bronze bodhisattvas, which often have a full, round form with a pronounced sway of the body and fluttering scarves, this Liao statue is marked with restrained sensuality. The figure has an oval face and sloping shoulders. The subtle sway and the flow of the scarves close to the body result in a contained, columnar form. Particularly noticeable is its high, ornate diadem bearing a lotus throne and a cloud-like design, a bejeweled medallion in the center, and leaf-shaped embellishments with tassels on both sides, which is a Liao innovative design.

GILT BRONZE; H. 43.8 CM (17-1/4 IN.)
THE SEVERANCE AND GRETA MILLIKIN PURCHASE FUND
1976.14

Brush Washer late 11th century–1127
CHINA, HENAN PROVINCE, BAOFENG COUNTY, NORTHERN SONG DYNASTY (960–1127)
Simplicity and refined elegance are the hallmarks of Ru ware. Other characteristics include an ash-gray body, soft blue-gray glaze with a fine crackle, and small sesame-seed spur marks on the base. The graceful shape, soft luster, and subtle color variation of the glaze interact in perfect unity.

The rarest and most celebrated of all Chinese imperial wares, Ru ware was made for the late Northern Song court for a very short time. The kiln site was located at Qingliangsi, Baofeng county, in Henan province. As recorded in a 12th-century Chinese source, Ru ware ranked at the top, above all other green-glazed ceramic wares produced in the north. It was therefore chosen as an imperial ware to replace white-glazed Ding ware, as the unglazed mouth rim of Ding ware was considered unsuitable for imperial use.

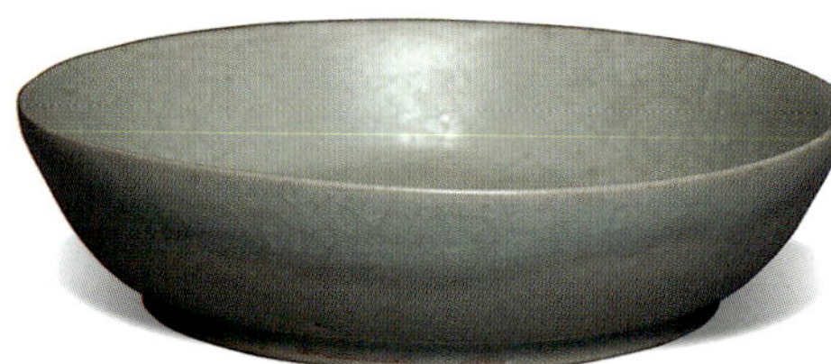

A Southern Song period (1127–1279) writer recorded that this precious ceramic ware, with a glaze containing agate, had been forbidden outside the palace. Only those pieces rejected by the court were circulated, making the ware particularly difficult to obtain. Another literary source mentions the tribute of Ru pieces from a Southern Song official to Emperor Gaozong (r. 1127–62). Such records denote how precious Ru ware was during the Southern Song, especially since it represented the epitome of Northern Song imperial art patronage that was brought to an end with the Jurchen invasion of northern China, when the Song court was forced to flee to the south. Because it was also used for diplomatic gifts, Ru ware inspired celadon production in Goryeo period (918–1392) Korea.

PORCELANEOUS STONEWARE, RU WARE; DIAM. 12.8 CM (5 IN.), H. 3.8 CM (1-1/2 IN.)

JOHN L. SEVERANCE FUND 1957.40

Vase with Floral Scrolls 10th–11th century

CHINA, HENAN PROVINCE, NORTHERN SONG DYNASTY (960–1127)

The rich decoration and robust character of popular Cizhou wares contrast markedly with the understated monochrome wares selected for imperial use. Cizhou wares show the use of slip coating, bold designs, and contrasting color to achieve stunning visual effects. Technically, their decoration is the most varied of any ceramic type produced in China.

This splendid example of Cizhou ware is particularly distinguished by the remarkable rhythmic control of the floral decoration and the combined use of slip coating and inlaid decoration. Slip is an aqueous solution of very finely prepared clay that is often used to coat the ceramic body in order to conceal an undesirable color or coarseness in the clay. Here, the potter first incised the floral-scroll designs before applying a thick white slip. The slip was allowed to dry and the layer over the incised decoration was then removed, revealing the white inlays set against the gray stoneware body. The vase was then covered with a clear glaze. After firing, the slip and the inlaid decoration assumed a soft ivory color while the exposed clay body became a warm cinnamon brown. This vase's long neck and dished mouth echo Tang and Liao ceramics in the shapes of metalwork—traditions that long existed in north China.

As a ceramic type, Cizhou ware takes its name from a ceramic-producing district in Hebei province, but the name has been used more broadly for similar types produced at various kiln sites in Hebei, Henan, and Shanxi provinces.

GLAZED STONEWARE WITH INCISED AND SLIP-INLAID DECORATION, CIZHOU WARE; H. 41.3 CM (16-1/4 IN.), DIAM. 12.7 CM (5 IN.) AT MOUTH

PURCHASE FROM J. H. WADE FUND 1948.226

Jar with Lion-Head Handles 14th century

CHINA, JIANGXI PROVINCE, JINGDEZHEN KILNS, YUAN DYNASTY (1271–1368)

This handsome jar is a classic example of Yuan dynasty blue-and-white porcelain and is particularly appreciated for its strong profile, brilliant blue color, and firm delineation of the decorative motifs. Its striking shape was built up from various thrown parts carefully joined together one on top of another; two lion-head handles are attached. The decorative motifs are rich and diverse: key-fret border, wave patterns, floral scrolls, phoenixes amid flowers within cloud-collar patterns, classic scrolls, and a band of lotus-petal panels filled with symbolic Buddhist emblems.

The introduction of cobalt blue for underglaze painted decoration of the already admired white porcelain of Jingdezhen created a new direction in Chinese ceramic manufacture. Blue-and-white ware was produced no later than the 1330s. The kilns have been found at various sites of Jingdezhen, including Hutian, Luomaqiao, and Zhushan.

Blue-and-white porcelain was made not only for domestic use (for the court and commoners alike) but also for overseas trade, which was much encouraged by the Yuan government as a major source of revenue. The export of Yuan blue-and-white porcelain was supported by archaeological finds along the Mongol trade routes, including the land routes in the north as well as the sea routes in the south. Significantly, Yuan blue-and-white porcelain testified to the transmission of artistic ideas and techniques between China and the rest of the great Mongol Empire. For example, the cobalt that was used as a blue colorant for underglaze painting was imported, likely from mines near Kashan in Iran. The band of cloud-collar motifs with phoenixes set against floral grounds, as illustrated in this jar, is an artistic vocabulary also found in the arts of Ilkhanid period (1256–1353) Iran.

PORCELAIN WITH UNDERGLAZE PAINTED DECORATION, BLUE-AND-WHITE WARE; H. 39.4 CM (15-1/2 IN.), DIAM. 37.5 CM (14-3/4 IN.)

JOHN L. SEVERANCE FUND 1962.154

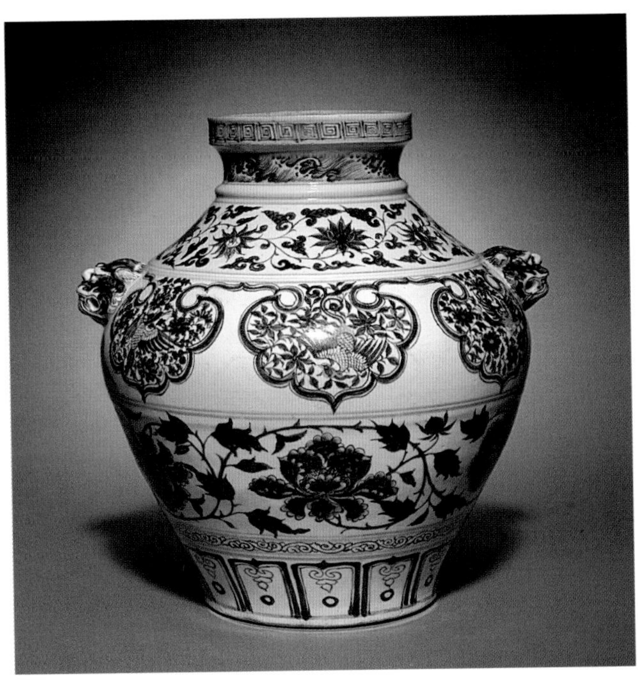

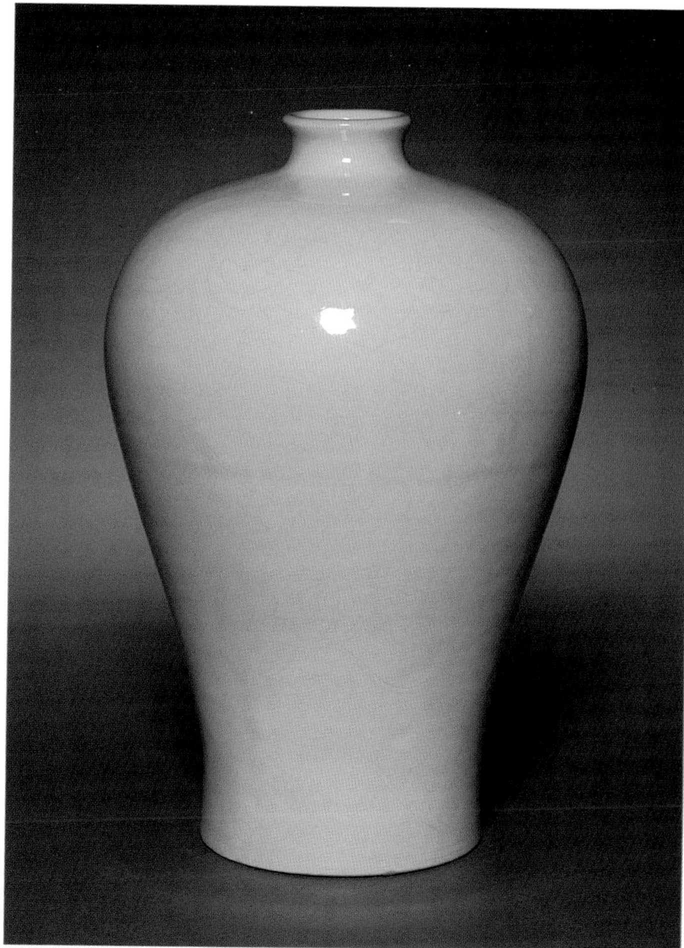

Meiping Vase with Cloud Collars and Peony Sprays 1403–24

CHINA, JIANGXI PROVINCE, JINGDEZHEN KILNS, MING DYNASTY, YONGLE PERIOD (1403–24)

The extremely high standards demanded for imperial white porcelain made during the Yongle period are obvious in this beautiful vase. Exquisitely potted, it is subtly ornamented with "hidden decoration" (*anhua*) finely incised into the body. The high rounded shoulder is incised with the cloud-collar motifs and balanced at the base by the stylized floral scrolls. Between these decorative bands are sprays of peonies, much more freely drawn and realistically represented. The clear glaze over the white body has a luster and purity unequaled in any other period; the white color radiates with a soft glow like melting snow, described by the Chinese connoisseurs as *tianbai*, or "sweet-white." The tianbai ware was a triumph of technology and sensitivity of design. It was produced for use in imperial sacrifices and has always been considered a great achievement of the Yongle period.

The white porcelain of the Ming and the subsequent Qing dynasties represented the ongoing quest for technical perfection in monochrome wares, so that the body became increasingly white and refined, and the glaze more translucent and colorless.

PORCELAIN WITH INCISED DECORATION AND WHITE GLAZE; H. 32.1 CM (12-5/8 IN.), DIAM. 20.3 CM (8 IN.)
SEVERANCE AND GRETA MILLIKIN COLLECTION 1964.167

Collecting Chinese Ceramics

Throughout history, China has impressed the rest of the world with the technical and artistic excellence of its ceramic production. Long a specialized craft and industry, pottery making requires extensive knowledge of the physical and chemical properties of materials that affect quality and appearance. A pot is appreciated for its shape, glaze, decoration, and their interaction to achieve unity. Chinese connoisseurs tend to come up with poetic metaphors for specific glaze effects that conjure nature and appreciation of its aesthetic qualities.

Since the early years of collecting Chinese art at the museum, a great number of ceramics have come as gifts and through bequests of trustees and prominent Cleveland collectors, including Worcester R. Warner, J. H. Wade, John L. Severance, Ralph King, and Elisabeth S. Prentiss, to name just a few. Significant purchases have also been made, with curators widening the scope beyond the later decorative porcelains that

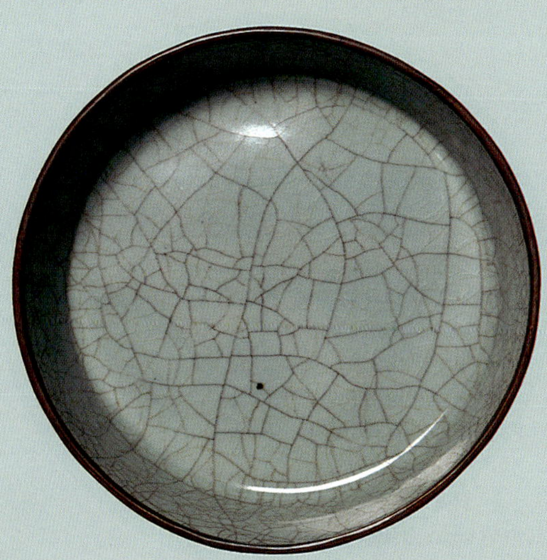

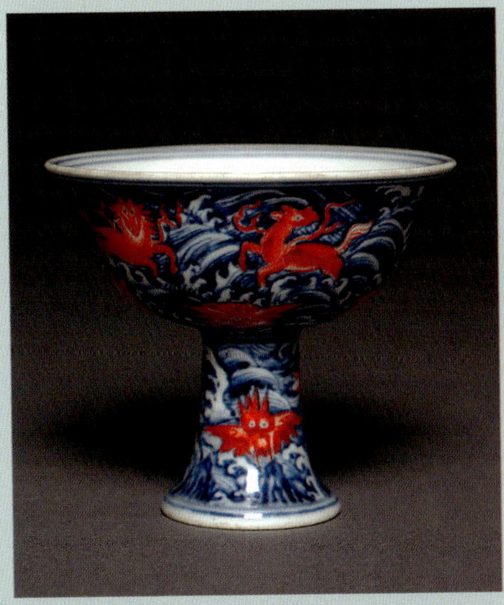

Candlestand, 7th century. China, Sui dynasty (581–618) or early Tang dynasty (618–906). Glazed stoneware with applied and carved decoration, H. 29.8 cm (11-3/4 in.). Charles W. Harkness Endowment Fund 1930.322

Basin, 1127–1279. China, Zhejiang province, Hangzhou, Southern Song dynasty (1127–1279). Porcelaneous stoneware, Guan ware, Diam. 24.2 cm (9-1/2 in.). John L. Severance Fund 1957.48

Stem-Cup with Sea Monsters, 1426–35. China, Jiangxi province, Jingdezhen kilns, Ming dynasty, Xuande mark and period (1426–35). Porcelain decorated in underglaze blue and overglaze red enamel, Diam. 9.9 cm (3-7/8 in.), H. 9 cm (3-1/2 in.). John L. Severance Fund 1957.60

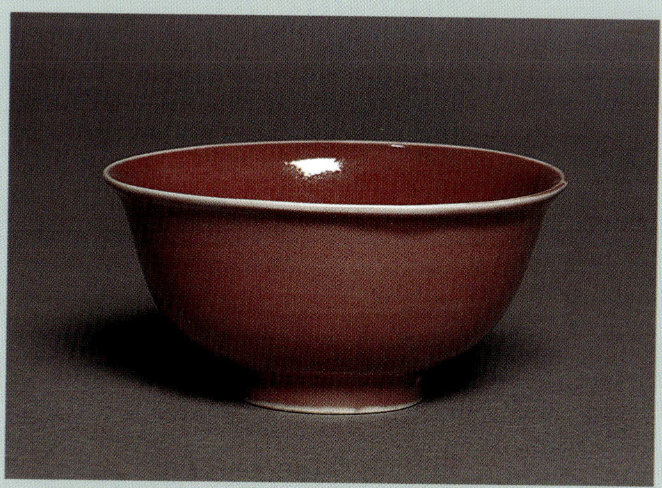

reflect the typical American collecting taste of the early 20th century. The acquisition of a large group of Cizhou ware in the 1940s under the curatorship of Howard C. Hollis enhanced the collection in the area of Tang, Song, and Yuan folk wares (see also p. 99). Even more significant was the group acquisitions made in 1957 by Sherman E. Lee that included extremely rare and precious examples of Song and Ming imperial wares that over time Chinese connoisseurs have considered exceptional (see also p. 99). With this impressive foundation, ongoing acquisitions are selective additions intended to strengthen a collection already distinguished in breadth and depth. Current notable examples are the bequests of Severance and Greta Millikin and the respective gifts of Norman Zaworski and Donna S. and James S. Reid Jr. (see also p. 92). Today, the museum's wide chronological range of superlative quality well represents the Chinese ceramic tradition from prehistory to the last imperial Qing dynasty.

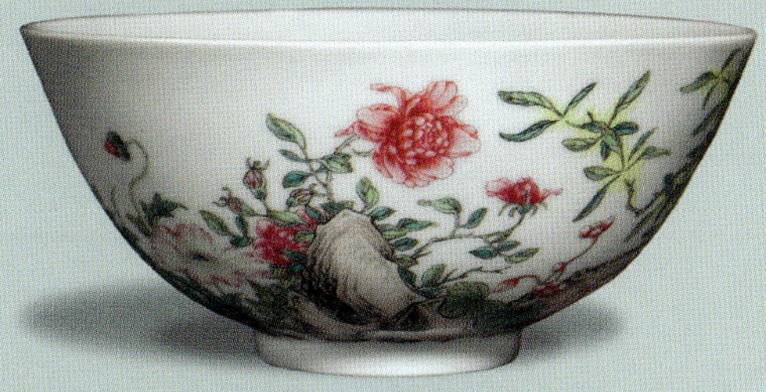

Bowl with Dragons and Clouds, late 14th century. China, Jiangxi province, Jingdezhen kilns, Ming dynasty, Hongwu period (1368–98). Porcelain with molded and incised decoration, Diam. 10 cm (4 in.). Severance A. and Greta Millikin Collection 1964.222

Bowl with Poppies, Tree Peony, and Flowering Mimosa, 1723–35. China, Jiangxi province, Jingdezhen kilns, Qing dynasty, Yongzheng mark and period (1723–35). Porcelain with *famille rose* overglaze enamel decoration, Diam. 14.1 cm (5-1/2 in.). Severance A. and Greta Millikin Collection 1964.20

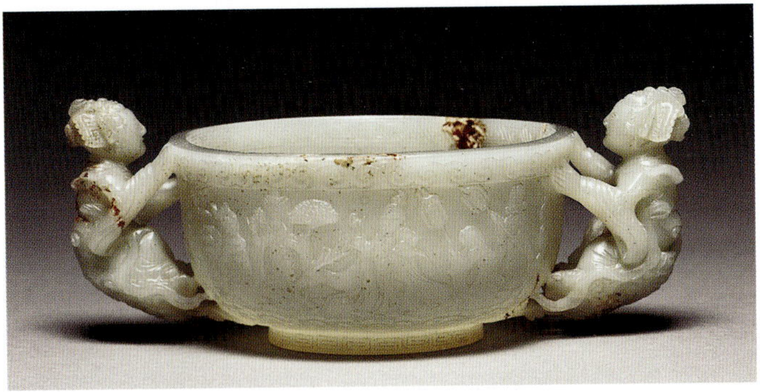

Bowl with Daoist Figures 1271–1368

CHINA, YUAN DYNASTY (1271–1368)

This exquisite jade bowl is a rare specimen of jade carving from the Yuan dynasty. It is carved with a Daoist procession scene in low relief, with images of the immortals, musicians, attendants, and emblems of immortality, such as the deer and *lingzhi* fungus. The rim of the bowl has a cloud-collar border on the exterior and a key-fret band in the interior; the root ring has another key-fret band. Two female immortals, carved in the round, flank the two sides as handles, displaying remarkable sculptural strength. This robustly carved vessel, presumably a personal item of luxury, reflects the great interest of the literati and the court in jade as a material as well as in Daoist subjects.

Jade—including nephrite and jadeite—is one of the most cherished materials in Chinese culture. Whether it was used for ceremonial implements, burial goods, personal ornaments, or decorative works of art, jade has always been of great significance to the Chinese. The light-transmitting semi-translucent or translucent stones have ritual, moral, and poetic allusions attached to them. Their radiance and purity were linked metaphorically to the virtues of the ideal Confucian man. Jade was also believed to have spiritual and magical properties and eventually became associated with Daoist beliefs and practices. The jade burial suit, for instance, was intended to preserve the corporeal body and the soul in the quest for eternity.

JADE; W. 16 CM (16-1/4 IN.) WITH HANDLES, H. 6.5 CM (2-1/2 IN.). ANONYMOUS GIFT 1952.510

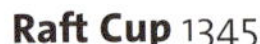

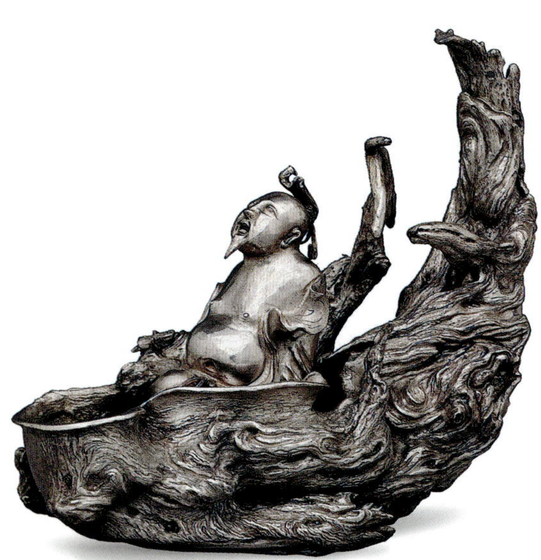

Raft Cup 1345

ATTRIBUTED TO ZHU BISHAN (CHINESE, ABOUT 1300–AFTER 1362)

The design of this silver cup is based upon the theme of Zhang Qian, a traveler and Daoist transcendent, embarking on his journey to the Milky Way. He sits comfortably in a raft in the form of a hollow tree trunk, holding a tablet in his hand. In absolute freedom he exposes his chest and raises his head, totally transfixed by the wonders of the cosmos. His fluttering sash and cloth cap, and the swirling surface patterns on the trunk enhance a sense of movement. While serving a functional purpose, this sculptural cup expresses the artist's imagination of Daoist freedom and naturalness, as well as the search for mystical oneness with the cosmos.

Four inscriptions in "seal script" appear on the bottom, attributing this silver raft cup to the celebrated Yuan silversmith Zhu Bishan and the year 1345. A long poetic inscription accompanies the image:

Wishing to visit the Milky Way, but the early
crescent-moon was on his way.
Indeed, in vain are people talking about crossing
the Silver Bay.
Why return home merely with the slab of the
loom-supporting stone,
Without searching for the brocade made by the
celestial maid?

Zhu Bishan, a Jiaxing native later residing at Suzhou, was known for his highly expressive silverwork and naturalistic subjects. Such works were much favored by scholar-gentlemen and earned him a reputation among the literati class in south China. Whether the present work is an original by Zhu Bishan or a later masterwork following the Yuan tradition requires further investigation. Its rarity and artistic excellence, nevertheless, make it a precious example of Chinese silverware.

HAMMERED SILVER SOLDERED TOGETHER, WITH CHASED DECORATION; 16 X 20.5 CM (6-1/4 X 8-1/8 IN.)
JOHN L. SEVERANCE FUND 1977.7

The Lantern Night Excursion of Zhong Kui
YAN HUI (CHINESE, LATE 13TH TO EARLY 14TH CENTURY)

This scroll begins with a small group of demons leading a procession, each performing an acrobatic trick: beating a drum, lifting a large rock, standing upside down and trying to drink, balancing a jar, and wielding a weapon. Other demons carry their master's belongings—chair, zither, brush and inkstone, book, and wine bottle—and one demon is about to present a drink. Zhong Kui, the legendary demon queller, appears after the retinue. He is carried by three demons, sheltered by a canopy, and followed by a band of musicians. The fresh, spontaneous, and humorous interpretation of the theme testifies to the artist's imagination and his interest in the grotesque.

In addition to providing delight and humor, this scroll may have presented a political angle much appreciated by scholar-gentlemen of the time. One of the demons carrying Zhong Kui wears a Mongolian hat, perhaps a spoof on those who gained power from the Mongols. Such a caricature could have been drawn around the fall of the Southern Song and the founding of the Yuan; what could be more appropriate than the wish to ward off evil spirits in the face of foreign invasion.

Yan Hui was a professional painter from Luling in Jiangxi province; another source mentions Jiangshan in Zhejiang province. Better known as a specialist of Daoist and Buddhist paintings, he had also worked on wall paintings in temples. In fact, Yan Hui was already an accomplished painter in the late years of the Southern Song dynasty, excelling in many genres, including landscape, human figure, deity, and ghost. His art gained the respect of scholar-gentlemen.

HANDSCROLL; INK AND SLIGHT COLOR ON SILK; 24.8 X 240.3 CM (9-3/4 X 94-5/8 IN.)
MR. AND MRS. WILLIAM H. MARLATT FUND 1961.206

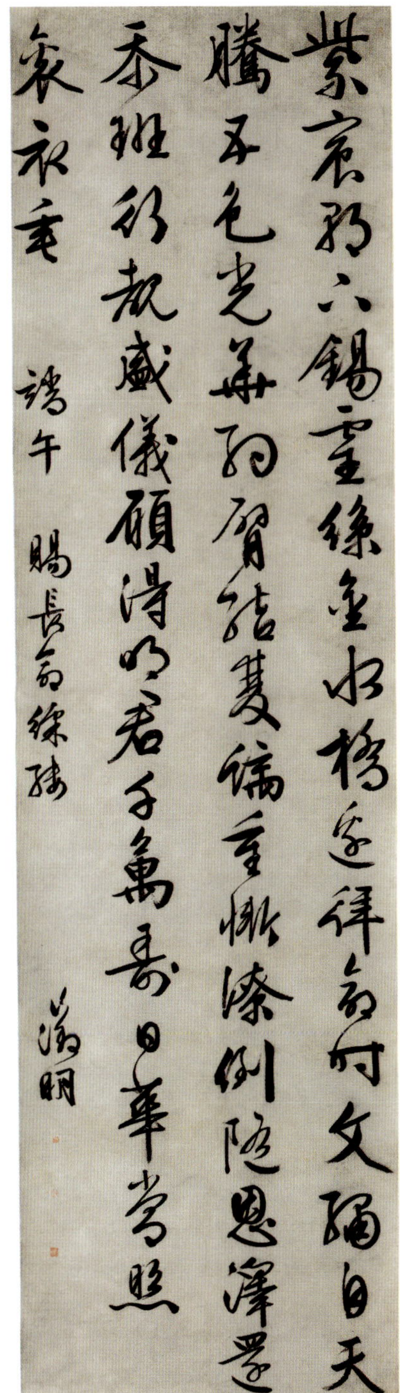

Poem on Imperial Gift of an Embroidered Silk: Calligraphy in Running Script about 1525
WEN ZHENGMING (CHINESE, 1470–1559)

Calligraphy was traditionally regarded as the most supreme of all the arts in China. Writing conveys meaning, but the art of calligraphy gives words beauty and expressive power. The abstract, linear qualities of the Chinese characters, combined with the use of the brush, open up many aesthetic possibilities. We appreciate the variations of strokes as well as the composition and spacing of characters. The traces of brush and ink represent the physical presence of the artist.

This colossal hanging scroll is a rendition of a poem by Wen Zhengming. Writing in "running script," Wen expresses his gratitude to the Jiajing emperor (r. 1522–66) for a gift, presumably bestowed in appreciation for his meritorious work. The work exhibits his mastery of the brush and an overall sophisticated grace that captures the artist's spirit. The poem reads:

From the throne, this exquisite silk was bestowed
on me,
As I expressed my gratitude to His Majesty by the
Goldwater Bridge.
This heavenly silk is embroidered with five colors.
Resplendent it is, draping over my arm with
[designs of] twin dragons.
Having received such a gift, I [bowed] in shame
over my lack of achievements.
Humbly I returned to my rank to observe the
grand ceremony.
I wish His Majesty shall live on for myriad years,
And the sun will always shine upon His trailing
robe.

Born to a family of scholar-officials in Changzhou, Jiangsu province, Wen was perhaps more accomplished in the arts than in his official life. He repeatedly failed the civil service examination and did not become a successful candidate until he reached his 50s. In 1523 he assumed an official position at the Hanlin Academy in Beijing, but he retired after three years and returned to Suzhou, where he devoted his life to artistic pursuits and dominated the local art scene.

HANGING SCROLL; INK ON PAPER; 345 X 93.5 CM (135-7/8 X 36-7/8 IN.)
JOHN L. SEVERANCE FUND 1998.169

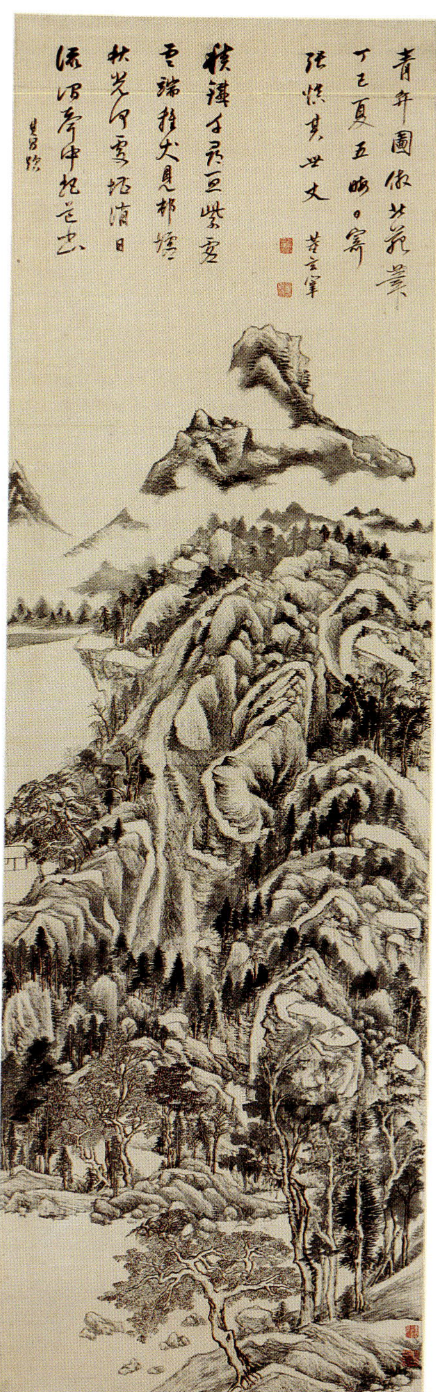

The Qingbian Mountains 1617

DONG QICHANG (CHINESE, 1555–1636)

The art of Dong Qichang was intellectual and innovative. His artistic experimentation exemplified the doctrine of "art for art's sake," yet it was not devoid of content. In this famous work, *The Qingbian Mountains,* Dong follows the brush idioms of the ancient master Dong Yuan (active 930s–960s) but radically transforms the landscape composition into a purely abstract design. He employs compositional principles such as solid and void, opening and closing to achieve an overall sense of structure. Dong's reorganization of the pictorial elements explores the equilibrium of tensions as well as the potential of brush and ink. His brushwork not only activates the flow of energy (*qi*) and the momentum of force (*shi*) in the landscape composition but also assumes life independent of the depicted forms, so much so that the painting can be appreciated for "the sheer marvels of brush and ink."

Dong Qichang adopted nature as his teacher, but he was equally concerned with the artist's mind and the creative process that transcended the experience of nature. To him, painting must involve profound understanding of the ancient methods as well as a "bloody battle" with the ancient masters. Imitation and innovation were therefore two sides of the same coin. Dong formulated a systematic reinterpretation of Chinese art history and advocated the supremacy of the literati tradition based on the notion of "legitimacy in succession" (*zhengtong*). As he turned to ancient brush methods for inspiration and synthesized the best of the literati modes of painting, he transformed them beyond recognition, creating a totally new artistic language. In this regard, his art represented the rebirth of the literati tradition and established a new order for artistic synthesis and transformation.

HANGING SCROLL; INK ON PAPER; 224.5 X 67.2 CM (88-1/2 X 26-1/2 IN.)

LEONARD C. HANNA JR. FUND 1980.10

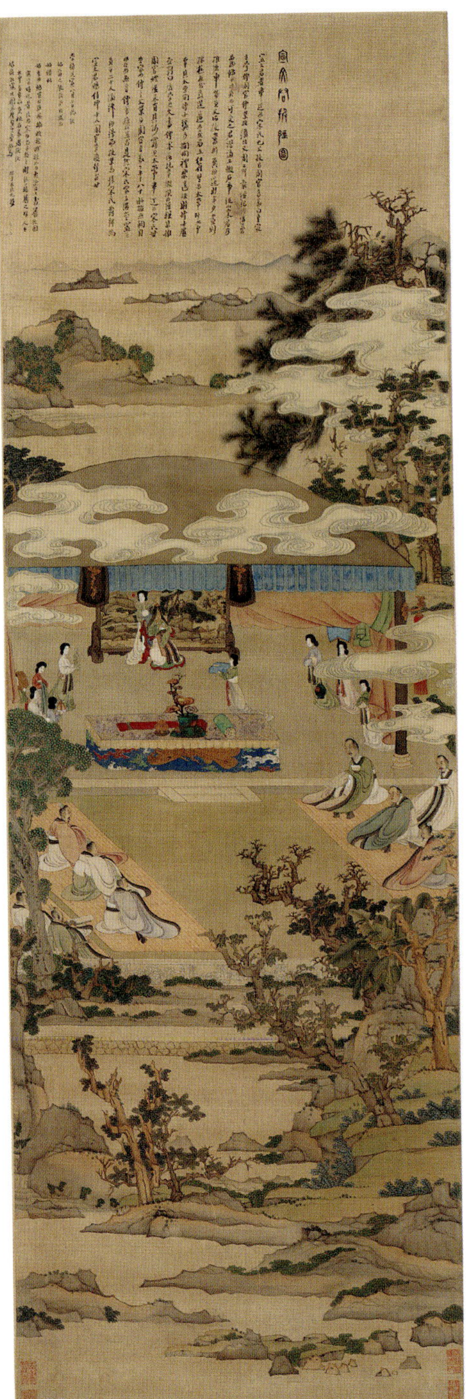

Lady Xuanwen Jun Giving Instructions on the Classics 1638

CHEN HONGSHOU (CHINESE, 1598–1652)

This extraordinary painting by Chen Hongshou depicts the story of Xuanwen Jun, or Lady of Literary Propagation, at a venerable age, instructing young scholars on the Confucian classics. It was painted for Chen's aunt on the occasion of her 60th birthday.

Xuanwen Jun, surnamed Song, came from a family of hereditary scholars and succeeded her father in the specialized study of the *Zhou guan* (*Ritual of Zhou Dynasty*), a classic text covering all standards of ritual conduct and regulations, canonical precedents, government organization, and classification of things. Her son Wei Cheng served Fu Jian, king of the former feudal state of Qin, in the Board of Rites. When Fu Jian sought an erudite scholar to teach the *Zhou guan,* Lady Song, at age 80, was the only one capable of reviving the scholarship. She was given the honorific title Xunwen Jun and 10 maids as her personal attendants.

Chen's depiction places the old lady, her attendants, and young students in a landscape setting shrouded in white clouds. A few ritual bronzes on an altar in between the instructress and the audience lend the scene an antique flavor. Chen's painting style is archaistic in the use of fine outlines and brilliant coloring with mineral pigments. In depicting the figures, he uses the "iron-wire" brush idioms with deliberate control. The faces are attenuated and exaggerated, the demeanors restrained by a sense of propriety.

HANGING SCROLL; INK AND COLOR ON SILK; 173.7 X 55.4 CM (68-1/2 X 21-7/8 IN.)

MR. AND MRS. WILLIAM H. MARLATT FUND 1961.89

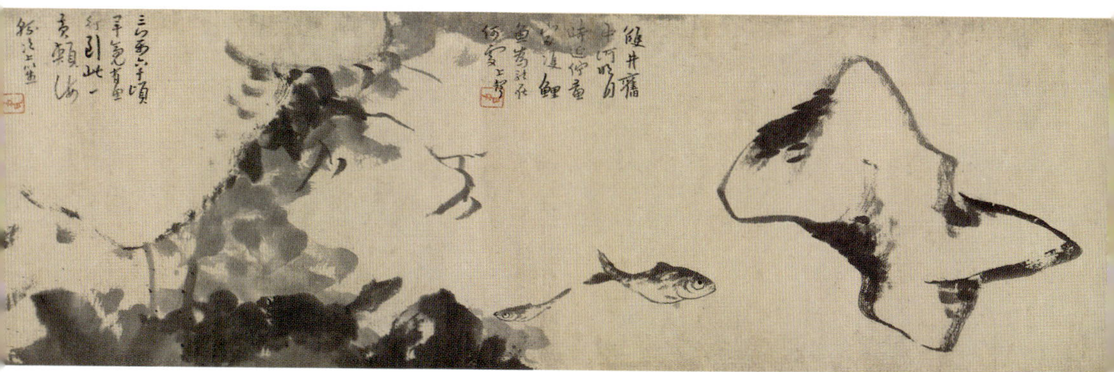

Fish and Rocks

ZHU DA (CHINESE, MID TO LATE 1600S–1705)

Zhu Da was a descendant of the Yiyang prince of Jiangxi province, a branch of the Ming (1368–1644) royal family. After the Manchu conquest and the founding of the Qing dynasty in 1644, he lost his princely status, retreated to monasteries where he sought sanctuary in Buddhist priesthood, and at times feigned insanity in public. He adopted a new name, Bada Shanren, by which he was known for the remainder of his life. He lived as a poet, painter, calligrapher, and eccentric hermit at his birthplace, Nanchang.

In this handscroll, Zhu Da juxtaposes strange, sparse images in a simple, sweeping style using few brushstrokes. The fish swim in opposite directions, and the rocks float in a void. He also includes three cryptic poems that have similarly alienated themes, referring perhaps to the marginality of Ming subjects under the Qing:

A foot and a half from heaven,
Only white clouds are moving.
Why are fellow flowers painted?
"Amid the clouds" [Yunzhong] is the "city of gold" [Jincheng].

In the Twin-wells is water formerly from midstream,
Above which the bright moon shines and lingers.
The two golden carp of the Huang family,
Where have they gone, to become dragons?

Under these thirty-six thousand acres [of lotus]
Day and night fish are swimming.
Arrived here is a single "yellow cheek,"
Ocean tide rises with the soaring notes of the flute.

HANDSCROLL; INK ON PAPER; 29.2 X 157.4 CM (11-1/2 X 62 IN.)

JOHN L. SEVERANCE FUND 1953.247

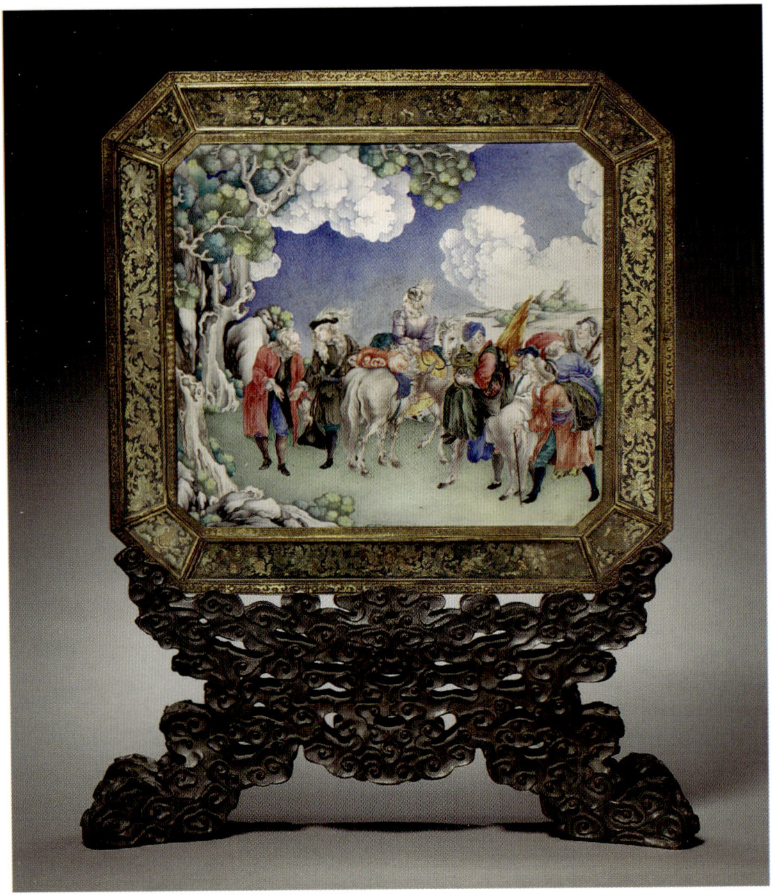

Screen with European Figures (obverse) **and Landscape** (reverse) **with Stand** 1736–95

CHINA, BEIJING PALACE WORKSHOP, QING DYNASTY, QIANLONG PERIOD (1736–95)

This two-sided table screen is a product of Sino-European contacts in the arts under Qing dynasty imperial patronage. The two sides present different artistic expressions in varied media, subjects, and styles to create a Chinese-style table screen, which, together with the cast-iron stand, is an example of an eclectic style common to imperial workshop production.

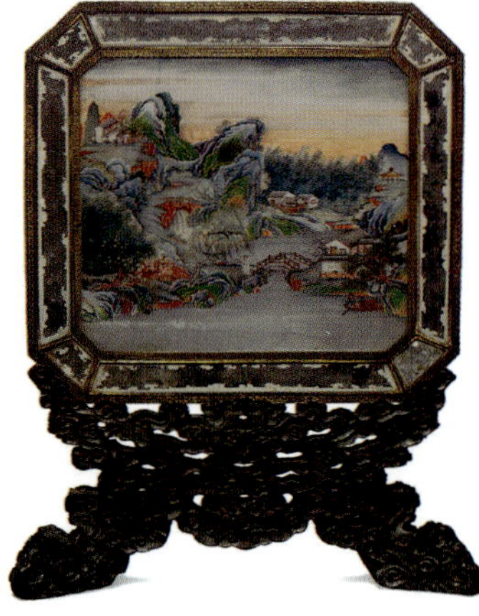

On the front is an enamel-painted copper plaque with European figures. The depictions were probably based on prints. European enamelware was introduced to China through the missionaries at the court in Beijing as well as through foreign trade in Guangzhou. The enameling technique inspired the manufacture of painted enamel on copper and porcelain, and the best pieces were produced by the imperial workshops within the palace.

On the back is an architectural landscape painted on glass. Stylistically, it follows the native Chinese traditions of figural, architectural, and blue-and-green landscape representations, thus showing contemporary styles in the different genres practiced by court painters.

At the Qing court, imperial commands made possible artistic collaboration and the incorporation of different cultural expressions in a single artwork. In the decorative arts, this directive had the effect of pushing the boundaries of possible use of each material and medium. The resultant work, though eclectic in nature, ultimately served to provide imperial pleasures or to express an all-powerful image of emperorship. The Qianlong emperor (r. 1736–95), in particular, manipulated cultural representations to foster an ideology of universal rule, centering upon him as the sole power for all artistic expression.

PAINTED ENAMEL, GLASS PAINTING, CAST-IRON STAND; 35.7 X 32.4 CM (14 X 12-3/4 IN.) PAINTING

SEVERANCE AND GRETA MILLIKIN COLLECTION 1964.243

Earth Landscape about 2004

LI HUAYI (AMERICAN, B. CHINA, 1948)

Contemporary artists no longer present Chinese ink painting as a nonproblematic continuation of old practices but are striving to reinvent this tradition. In *Earth Landscape,* Li Huayi recaptures the purity and infinity of Northern Song (960–1127) landscapes and creates a new kind of abstract configuration that offers solace and escape from "all the mess of humans" in the contemporary world. The composition is structured by using large areas of ink washes as building blocks, to which the details of rock masses, trees, waterfall, clouds, and mist are applied. While borrowing the abstract elements of Western modernism, Li ties them concretely with the traditional Chinese brush techniques of ancient masters, including the "raindrop texture-stroke" of Fan Kuan (d. after 1023), the "axe-cut texture-stroke" of Li Tang (about 1066–1150), and the "crab's claw tree" of Li Cheng (about 919–967). Juxtaposing light and dark, dense and sparse, Li's landscape offers a silent drama with stunning visual effects.

Li Huayi migrated from Shanghai to San Francisco in 1982. During the Cultural Revolution in Communist China from 1966 to 1976, he served as a "worker artist," painting in the Soviet Realistic styles for public projects and propaganda art. After the revolution, he began to react against certain Western painting styles and looked back to native Chinese traditions. The landscape subject provided him with a new sense of self and identity.

HORIZONTAL SCROLL; INK AND COLOR ON PAPER; 88.9 X 180.3 CM (35 X 71 IN.)

NORMAN O. STONE AND ELLA A. STONE MEMORIAL FUND 2006.115

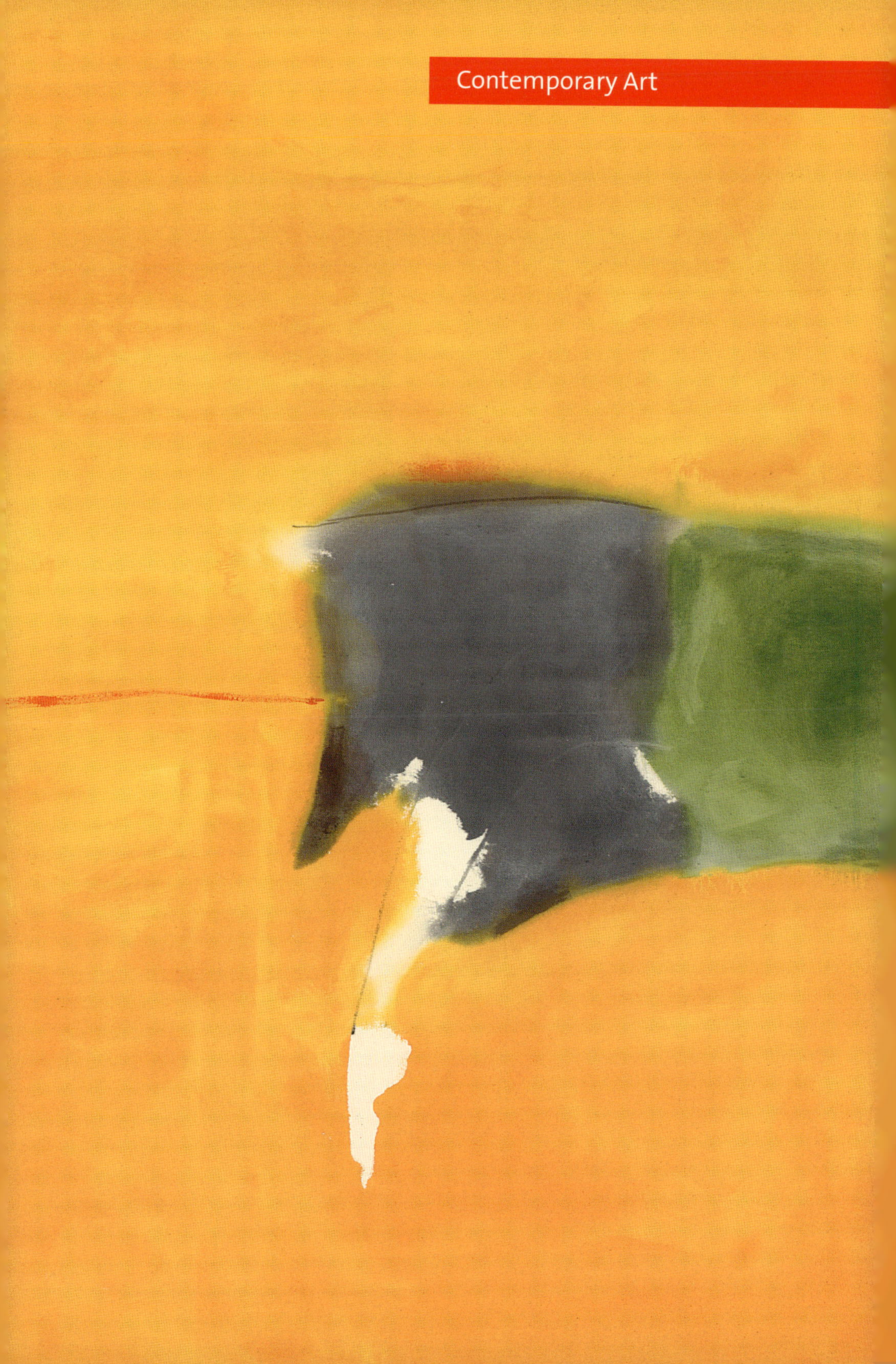

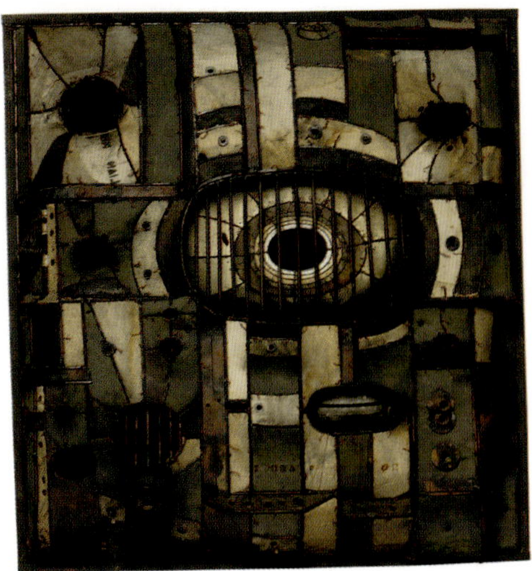

Untitled 1961

LEE BONTECOU (AMERICAN, B. 1931)

In the early 1960s, Lee Bontecou challenged artistic conventions through the creation of three-dimensional wall constructions that were neither sculpture nor painting but a hybrid of the two forms. Although raw in appearance, *Untitled* is carefully constructed using found objects including aluminum, welded steel, wire, and various types of canvas. An ambiguous form with a sporadic network of dark orifices, it evokes the human body and the savagery of war and, at the same time, alludes to a tension between the organic and the mechanical, the inside and the outside.

WELDED STEEL, CANVAS, AND WIRE; 132.1 X 121.6 X 30.5 CM (52 X 47-7/8 X 12 IN.)

CONTEMPORARY COLLECTION OF THE CLEVELAND MUSEUM OF ART 1967.77

Baby Stroller 1962

YAYOI KUSAMA (JAPANESE, B. 1929)

Yayoi Kusama created a series of three-dimensional works during the 1960s in which she transformed everyday objects by covering them with stuffed phallic protrusions. The use of repetition is typical of Kusama's work and culminates in paintings and installations in which dots form obsessive, virtually infinite patterns. In equipping a baby stroller with clearly sexual attributes, she destroys—with a violent, provocative gesture—the picture of an innocent and carefree childhood.

PRESUMABLY FOUND BABY STROLLER, PAINT, CANVAS, COTTON, AND STEEL; 89.5 X 102 X 74 CM (35-1/4 X 40-1/8 X 29-1/8 IN.)

GIFT OF HENRY H. HAWLEY IN MEMORY OF BERENICE H. KENT 2010.463

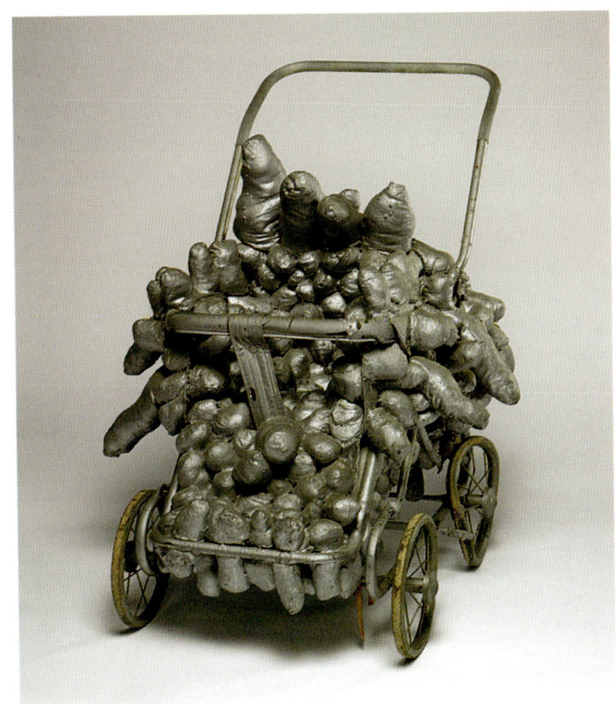

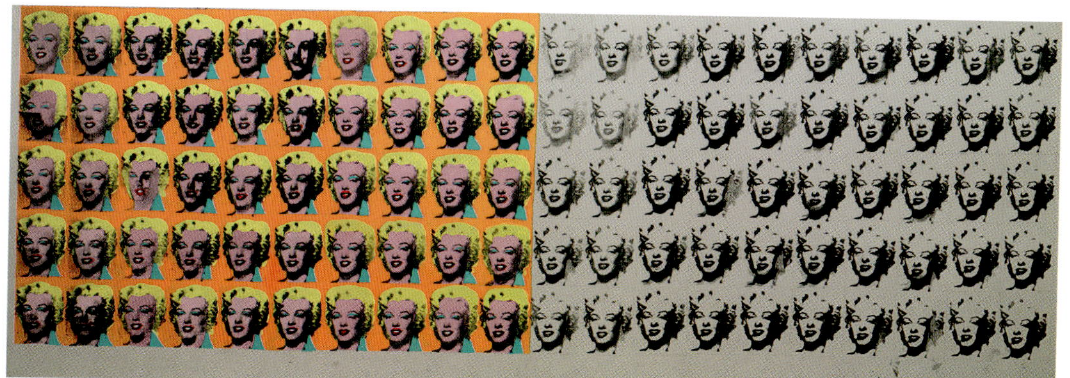

Marilyn x 100 1962

ANDY WARHOL (AMERICAN, 1928–1987)

Andy Warhol was well known in the 1960s for his works appropriated from advertisements and popular cultural icons. *Marilyn x 100* is the largest of the artist's many renderings of Marilyn Monroe, prompted by her suicide in 1962. Based on publicity photos, the painting has a strong visual duality. Astringent colors painted over the 50 silk-screened images on the left oppose the 50 black-and-white portraits that recall newspaper images of the actress. Some of the images are printed off-register, others are smudged or faded. Each print of Monroe's face is flawed, and collectively they refer to the synthetic facade of celebrity that is repeatedly mass-produced and consumed. Warhol explored Monroe's face as a sacred image—visibly damaged and deteriorated, yet celebrated as a cultural icon.

SCREENPRINT INK AND SYNTHETIC POLYMER PAINT ON CANVAS; 205.7 X 567.7 CM (81 X 223-1/2 IN.)

LEONARD C. HANNA JR. FUND AND ANONYMOUS GIFT 1997.246

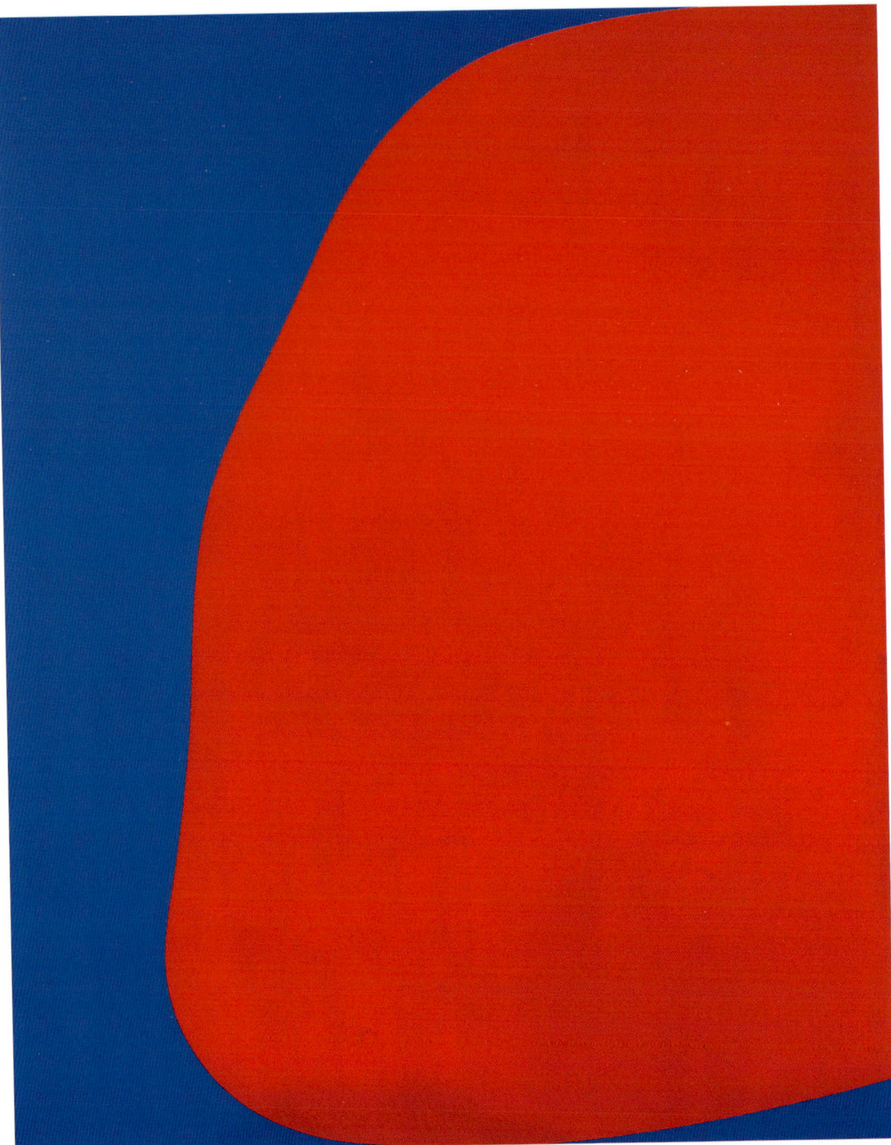

Red Blue 1964

ELLSWORTH KELLY (AMERICAN, B. 1923)

Red Blue is all about the relation of two different colors and two different, simple forms that come together, interact with each other, and affect each other's appearance. The arrangement of the two colors red and blue, which work to intensify each other, is one essential component of the work. The other is the confrontation of two different forms. The edges of one shape—the blue rectangle—are given by the limits of the canvas itself and are therefore logical and measurable, while the red color field, despite the clean, precise rendering, seems to breathe and float, activating the composition as a whole. In this way, even though there is no trace of the artist's hand, the painting refers to very natural and organic forms and ways of perception.

OIL PAINT ON CANVAS; 228.6 X 176.4 CM (90 X 69-1/2 IN.)

CONTEMPORARY COLLECTION OF THE CLEVELAND MUSEUM OF ART 1964.142

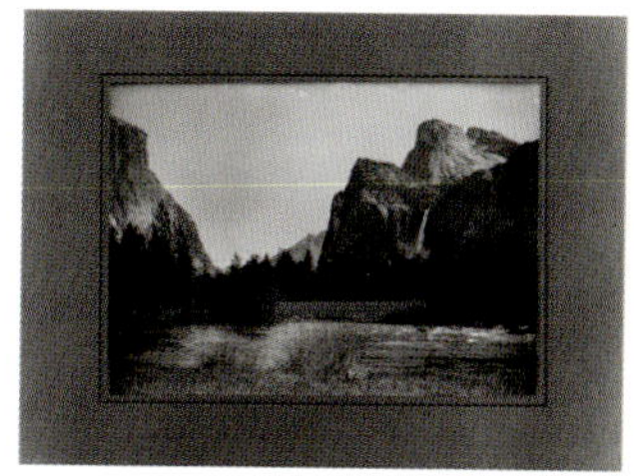

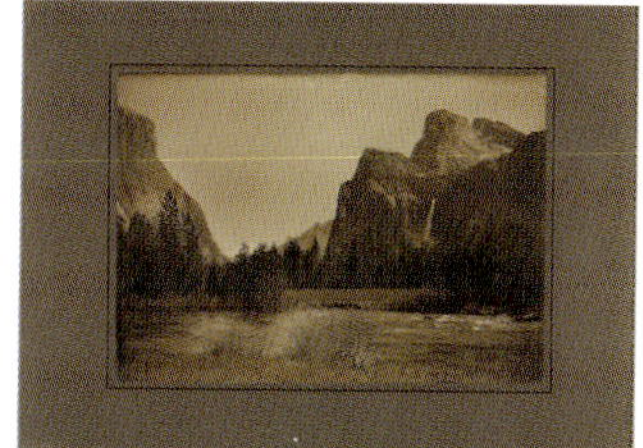

photic derives from Gr *phōt-*, o/s of *phōs*, light. The element *photo-* occurs notably in **photograph** (cf the element *-graph*), whence **photographic** and **photography** and, via the v **photograph**, the agent **photographer**.

ART © JOSEPH KOSUTH

One and Three Photographs [Ety.] 1965

JOSEPH KOSUTH (AMERICAN, B. 1945)

With *One and Three Photographs [Ety.]*, Joseph Kosuth compares different ways to represent a photograph—a dictionary definition of the word "photograph," a vintage photograph, and an identical photographic reproduction of the photograph. The artist makes a statement not about the objects but about our conventional means to register reality, implicitly asking the question: Is photography art? By focusing as much on the epistemological meaning behind a work as on its actual presence, *One and Three Photographs [Ety.]* can be regarded as an early example of a distinctively conceptually based art practice that signifies an intensification of the legacy of Marcel Duchamp.

VINTAGE PHOTOGRAPH, PHOTOGRAPH OF A PHOTOGRAPH, PHOTOGRAPHIC ENLARGEMENT OF DICTIONARY DEFINITION OF "PHOTOGRAPH," ORIGINAL PHOTO-CERTIFICATE WITH ORIGINAL CUT-OUT DEFINITION; DIMENSIONS VARIABLE. PURCHASE FROM THE J. H. WADE FUND 2009.1.1–3

Jackie Curtis and Ritta Redd 1970

ALICE NEEL (AMERICAN, 1900–1984)

While Alice Neel's work consists mostly of portraiture, there is a distinctly abstract quality in her paintings because she used simplified forms and distorted perspective. An early example of her portraits of gay couples, *Jackie Curtis and Ritta Redd* portrays two regulars from Andy Warhol's Factory. Jackie Curtis was an actor, playwright, and poet who appeared in Warhol's films *Flesh* and *Women in Revolt*. Neel plays with expectations of gender through the figures' postures and dress, which work against typical ideas of masculinity and femininity. The figure on the left is Ritta, not Jackie, as would be expected from the title.

OIL PAINT ON CANVAS; 152.4 X 106.4 CM (60 X 41-7/8 IN.)

LEONARD C. HANNA JR. FUND 2009.345

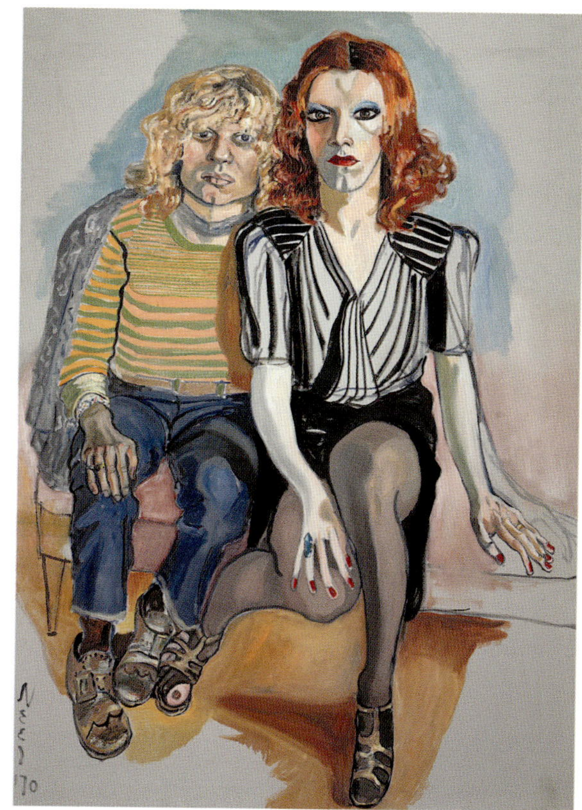

ART © ALICE NEEL

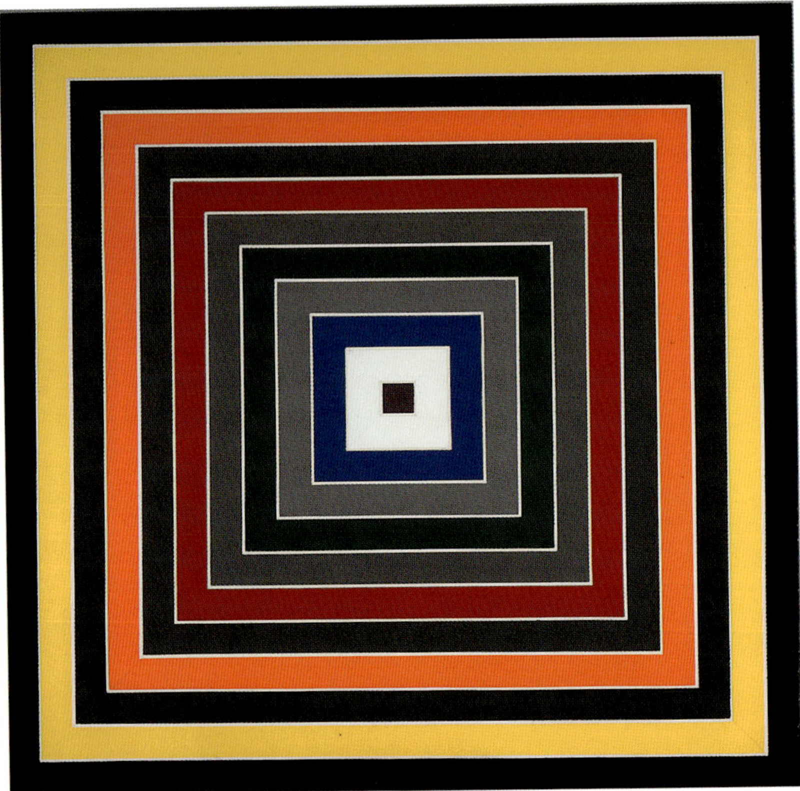

Gray Scramble (Single), VIII 1968

FRANK STELLA (AMERICAN, B. 1936)

Frank Stella's early paintings embody his reaction against the seemingly loose, gestural brushstrokes associated with Abstract Expressionism. In *Gray Scramble (Single), VIII,* Stella combines bands of sequential values and differing colors. In contrast to the depth created by the alternating light and dark bands of color, the uniformity of the paint surface emphasizes the two-dimensionality of the canvas. Using commercial paint and a house-painter's brush, Stella carefully crafted his works to create an immediate visual impression of simplicity and monumentality.

SYNTHETIC POLYMER PAINT ON CANVAS; 175.2 X 175.2 CM (69 X 69 IN.)

GIFT OF DAVID AND HELEN KANGESSER 2003.355

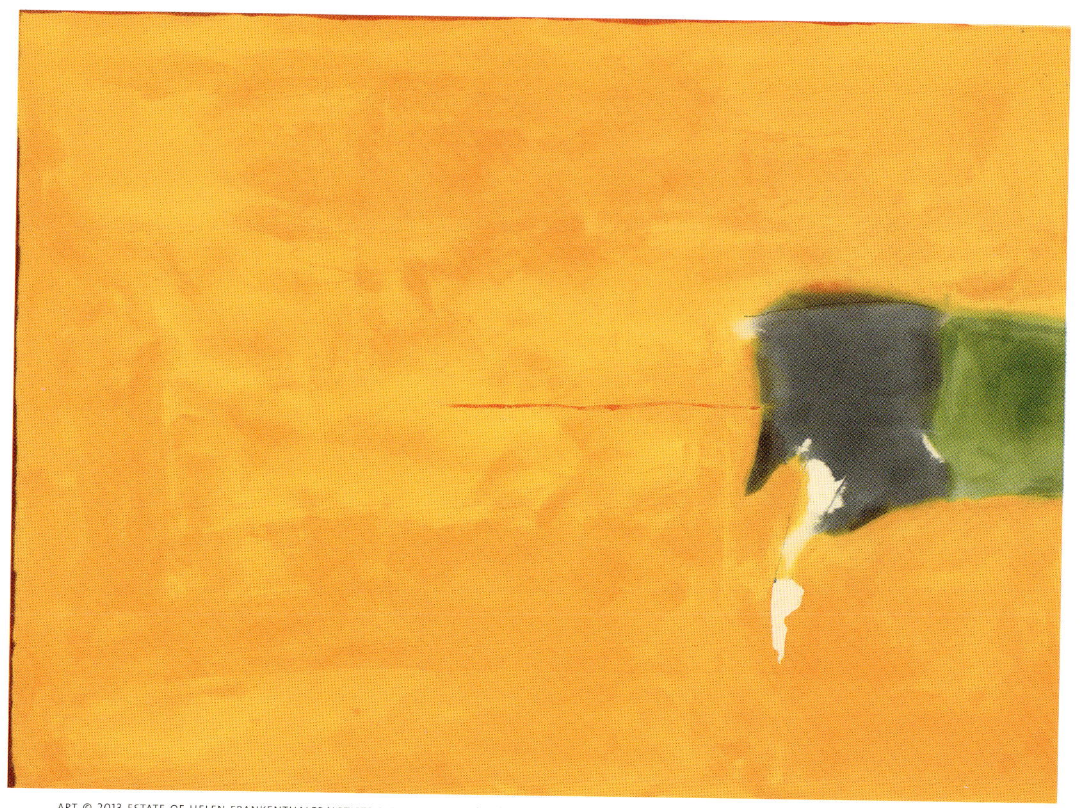

Humming Gold 1971

HELEN FRANKENTHALER (AMERICAN, 1928–2011)

Although deeply influenced by Abstract Expressionism, Helen Frankenthaler succeeded in developing a visual language that has its very own identity. Her technique of staining pigment into raw canvas helped shape an influential art movement in the mid 20th century and led to works of impressive transparency and lucidity. In circling around the recurrent themes of spatial ambiguity and landscape, Frankenthaler's paintings open up a deep, nearly infinite pictorial space. Surrounded by golden color, the dark green, gray, and white form in *Humming Gold* seems to spring back and forth on the picture plane, suspended in a space of uncertain depth. The subtle red line may evoke a horizontal line, giving the viewer an idea about his or her own scale and position in relation to the painting.

ACRYLIC PAINT ON CANVAS; 205.7 X 274.2 CM (81 X 108 IN.)

BEQUEST OF DENNIS SHERWIN 2009.294

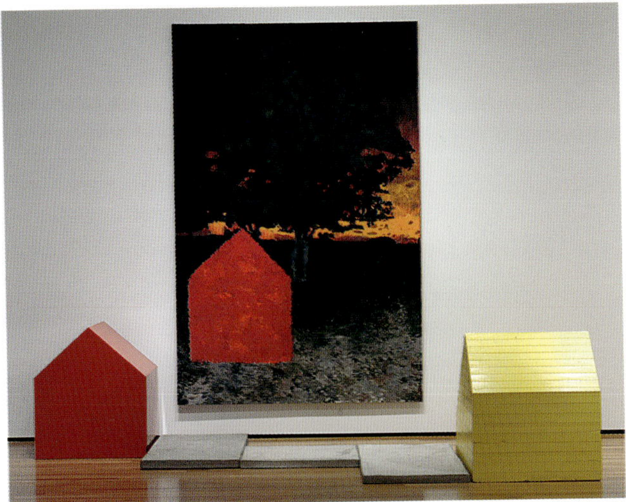

Sunset and Concrete Dock 1984

JENNIFER BARTLETT (AMERICAN, B. 1941)

In this painted, installation-based environment, Jennifer Bartlett juxtaposes a variety of images, styles, and perspectives. Since the 1980s, Bartlett has combined painting and sculptural elements to create jarring illusions: her paintings explore themes of houses, gardens, and seascapes, while her inclusion of sculpted boats, architectural structures, and other objects extends the scene into the viewer's space. In *Sunset and Concrete Dock,* the painting depicts a shallow landscape of trees and a flat geometric red house at sunset. Dense with expressive brushwork, this atmospheric scene recalls 19th-century European and American landscape painting. The painted image of the red house reappears as a three-dimensional object placed in front of the canvas, sparking a dialogue between concept and reality.

OIL ON CANVAS, PAINTED WOOD, AND CONCRETE SLABS; 335.2 X 213.3 CM (132 X 84 IN.) OVERALL

JOHN L. SEVERANCE FUND 1985.206.A–F

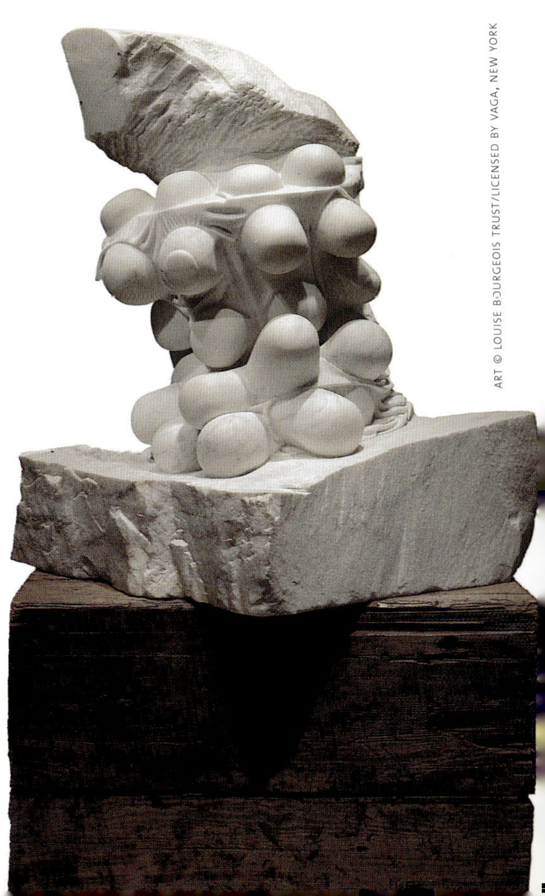

Blind Man's Buff 1984

LOUISE BOURGEOIS (AMERICAN, 1911–2010)

In *Blind Man's Buff,* ambiguous protrusions simultaneously suggest eyes, female breasts, and phallic forms, while the smooth, polished surface of the marble contrasts with the roughness of the wooden base. While feeding fantasies of attraction and violence at the same time, the sexual connotation of the work is balanced by the frivolity and playfulness of the title, which references the children's game in which a person wearing a blindfold chases the other players, guided only by their voices. The work also evokes Artemis of Ephesus, the goddess of fertility and hunting who was often depicted with a cluster of protuberances on her chest that are variously thought to represent breasts or bull testicles.

WHITE MARBLE ON WOODEN BASE; 92.7 X 88.9 X 63.5 CM (36-1/2 X 35 X 25 IN.)

LEONARD C. HANNA JR. FUND 2002.29.A–B

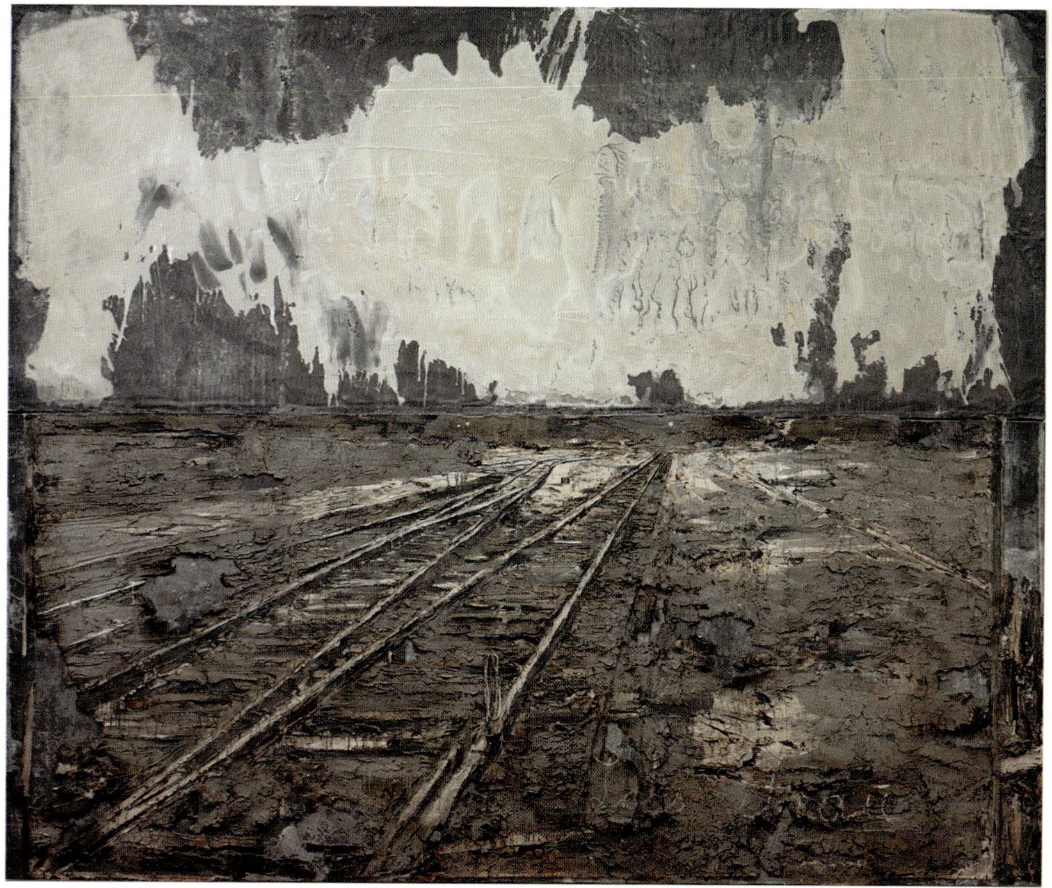

Lot's Wife 1989

ANSELM KIEFER (GERMAN, B. 1945)

A German artist, Anselm Kiefer struggles with the aftermath of the Holocaust and creates work that engages history, ethical issues of the present, and German identity through images emblematic of Nazi sites. This barren, deeply recessed landscape is based on Kiefer's photos of train tracks in France. The raw natural materials and destructive artistic process symbolize human tragedy. A substructure of lead mounted on wood, marked by footprints and tire tracks, is coated with plaster, burned, and covered with ash. Salt, applied to the upper half of the work, connects the historical event with the biblical narrative of Lot's escape from Sodom and Gomorrah. Disregarding warnings not to look back at God's destruction of those two cities, Lot's wife was turned into a pillar of salt.

OIL PAINT, ASH, STUCCO, CHALK, LINSEED OIL, POLYMER EMULSION, SALT, AND APPLIED ELEMENTS ON CANVAS, ATTACHED TO LEAD FOIL, ON PLYWOOD PANELS; 350 X 410 CM (137-3/4 X 161-3/8 IN.)

LEONARD C. HANNA JR. FUND 1990.8.A–B

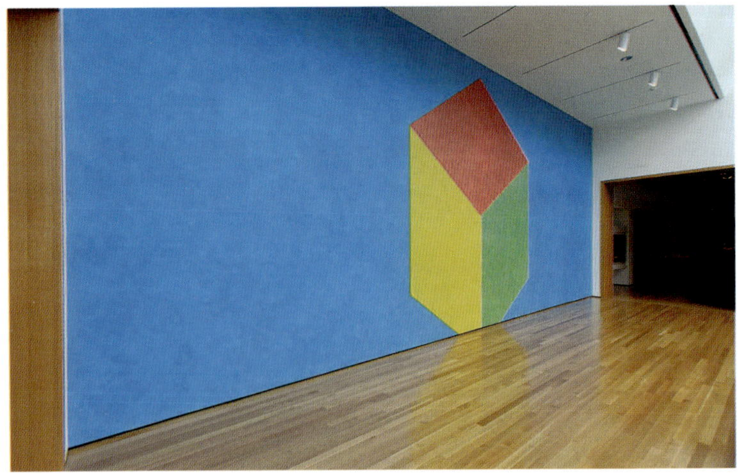

Wall Drawing 590A 1989

SOL LEWITT (AMERICAN, 1928–2007)

From the 1980s onward Sol LeWitt increasingly focused on isolated elementary shapes. By 1982 he had transformed planar figures into three-dimensional objects, playfully experimenting with repetition and the opposition between the two-dimensional plane and the drawn perspective. That same year he started to use ink washes for his wall drawings. LeWitt once said, "I would like to produce something I would not be ashamed to show Giotto." This statement clearly resounds in the luminosity and sensuality of *Wall Drawing #590A*.

COLOR INK WASH; 543.6 X 1,240.8 CM (214 X 488-1/2 IN.)

GIFT OF THE LEWITT FAMILY IN HONOR OF AGNES GUND 2012.66

Alien Huddle 1993–95

MARTIN PURYEAR (AMERICAN, B. 1941)

The freestanding sculpture *Alien Huddle* consists of three interconnected spheres. Through his craftsmanship, Martin Puryear both employs the medium (wood) in service of the form and elevates the properties of the medium itself. The arrangement of planks enveloping each sphere heightens the volumetric nature of the sculpture. Trained as a furniture maker, Puryear attached the red cedar planks to the pine core without metal fixtures that would obscure the lush, unfinished wood surface. The result is a work organic in form and medium that oscillates between intimacy and idiosyncrasy. Despite its closed totality, the surface also has a strong tactile quality.

RED CEDAR AND PINE; 134.6 X 162.5 X 134.6 CM (53 X 64 X 53 IN.)

GIFT OF AGNES GUND AND DANIEL SHAPIRO 2002.65

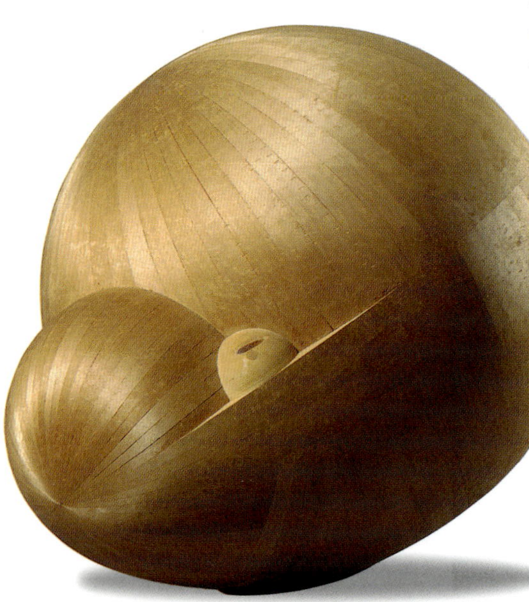

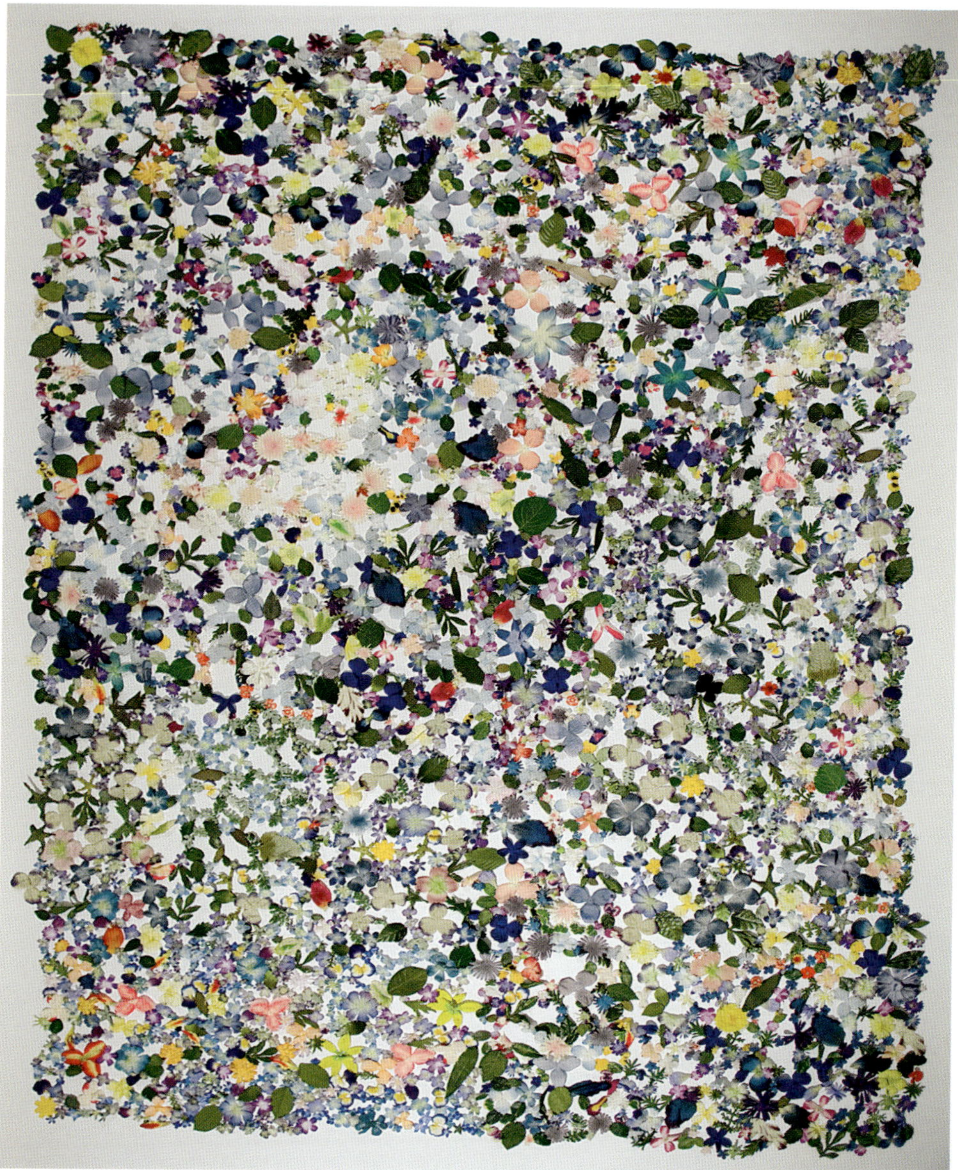

In Blue 1996

JIM HODGES (AMERICAN, B. 1957)

In his work, Jim Hodges reveals qualities of beauty and grace in the most unassuming materials. Through relatively simple acts of manipulation and reappraisal, he invests the man-made with a previously absent level of emotion and authenticity. *In Blue* is a diaphanous curtain of lush, tropical colors that is both imposing in its monumental scale and delicate in its fragility. Activated by the slightest breeze, its artificial elements ripple with the movement of life forms. To create *In Blue,* Hodges took apart hundreds of silk flowers, flattened and ironed each element, pinned the pieces together, and then carefully sewed them by hand into a scrim.

SILK FLOWERS AND THREAD; 396 X 259 CM (155-7/8 X 102 IN.)

GIFT OF AGNES GUND IN HONOR OF KATHARINE LEE REID 2005.140

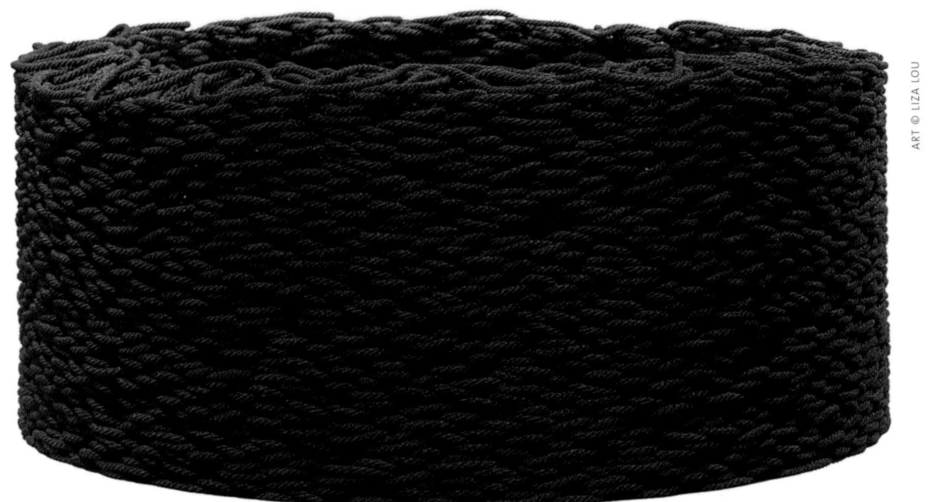

ART © LIZA LOU

Continuous Mile 2006–8

LIZA LOU (AMERICAN, B. 1969)

Liza Lou is best known for the life-size environments she painstakingly creates with colorful glass beads. For *Continuous Mile* the artist collaborated with a team of South African studio assistants from the townships of KwaZulu-Natal. The collaborative aspect is reflected in the making of the work: the mile-long length of rope is entirely woven with tiny glass beads and cotton in a traditional Zulu bead technique. "One of the things I love about sculpture," Lou has said, "is its silence. And yet the making involves a tremendous amount of noise." She has described her studio as a place where there is constant singing and sometimes dancing. "Embedded in the meaning of *Continuous Mile* is the way it was made and who made it."

LIZA LOU GRATEFULLY ACKNOWLEDGES THE ARTISANS IN KWAZULU-NATAL, SOUTH AFRICA: NOMUSA BAILEY, TRYPHINA BAILEY, SPHILILE BHENGU, MLUNGISI GUMEDE, NONHLANHLA GUMEDE, THANDAZILE GWALA, ZANELE GWALA, BANGIWE KHAWULA, NOKUTHULA LINDA, SINDI LUSHABA, SIPHO LUSHABA, NTOMBI LUTHULI, S'BONELO MADIBA, THULISILE MADIBA, PINKY MAKHOBA, BUHLE MBELE, LUBABALO MBELE, NOZIBELE MBELE, SINEKHAYA MBELE, ZANDILE MBELE, FIKILE MBHELE, LUCKY MBONGWA, MAFIKA MBONGWA, NTOMBIZODWA MLELESE, NOMASWAZI MOLAPO, THEMBISILE MOTO, PALESA MUNTU, LUCY NDLOVU, SINDI NDLOVU, NOKUTHULA NGIDI, NQOBILE NGIDI, SLINDILE NGLAMU, SHA NGOBO, NSELE, CEBISISLE NYANDA, VUYISWA NXELE, DOOI POLAKI, BUZEPHI SHANGAZE, MZI SHANGAZE, NOKUTHULA SHINGA, ZANELE SHINGA, NCAMSILE SITHOLE, PHILILE THANGO, AND PHILISILE ZWANE.

COTTON AND GLASS BEADS; 78.7 X 195.6 CM (31 X 77 IN.) AS INSTALLED

GIFT OF SCOTT C. MUELLER AND MARGARET FULTON MUELLER AND JOHN L. SEVERANCE FUND 2009.2

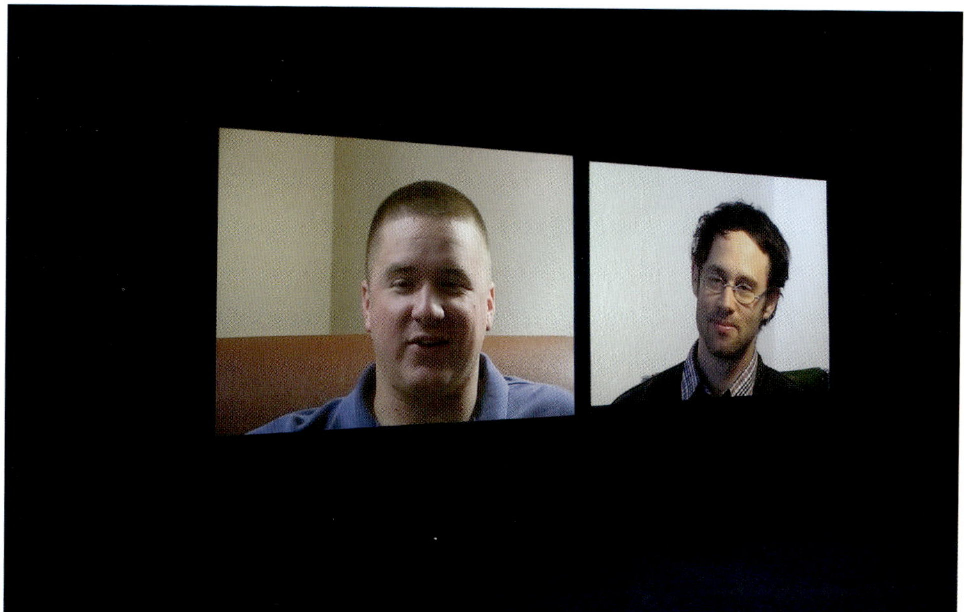

The Casting 2007

OMER FAST (AMERICAN, B. 1972)

By interweaving personal and universal experiences against the background of contemporary historical events, Omer Fast examines how mass media alters memory. *The Casting* is based on an actual interview with a U.S. Army sergeant who had been stationed in Germany and then served in Iraq. The soldier's recollections provide a unifying soundtrack to tableaux vivants re-enacting disparate moments. The seamless narration, however, has been spliced together and extended to include Fast's auditions of the actors for this work. The installation includes two projections: on the back of the screen, the interview plays the role of reality; the more theatrical images are projected on the front. While the narrator's speech remains casual, the tightly rendered film images borrow from the stereotypical language of the mass media even as the segments present an ongoing human drama. The partitioned projections encourage an open-ended experience of the video, offering a perspective on the Iraqi conflict that takes into account real lives as opposed to political content alone.

FOUR-CHANNEL VIDEO INSTALLATION; COLOR AND SOUND; 14 MINUTES; EDITION 4/6 (COMMISSIONED BY THE MUSEUM MODERNER KUNST STIFTUNG LUDWIG WIEN)

PURCHASE FROM THE J. H. WADE FUND 2009.8

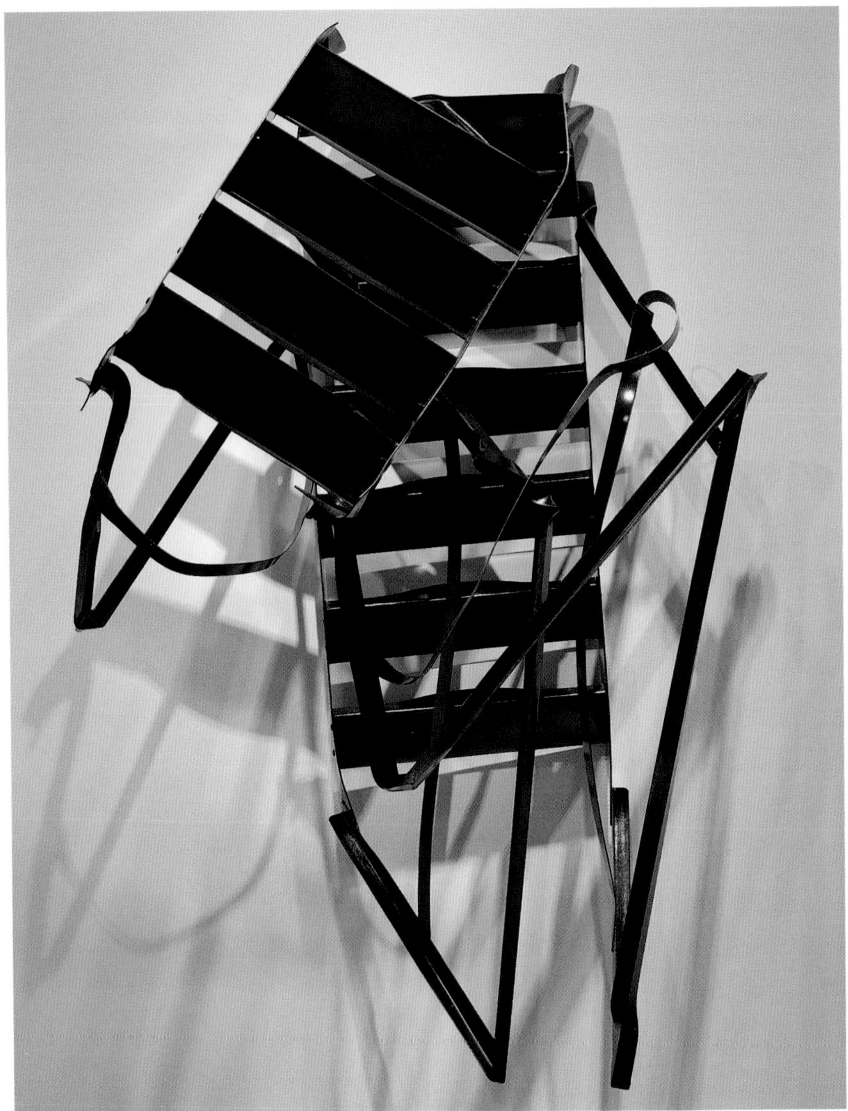

Stairs 2010

MONIKA SOSNOWSKA (POLISH, B. 1972)

Polish artist Monika Sosnowska is an active interpreter of Modernism's utopian ideals. Yet formerly idyllic places in Eastern Europe are now in ruins. *Stairs* was made during Sosnowska's first residency in the United States. Not a ready-made, it is a sculpture—an exact copy of a component of fire-escape stairs made with the assistance of metal fabricators. The newly rendered stairs were carefully bent with forklifts and then painted with enamel oil-based paint, giving the work the surreal look of a beautiful yet useless object. The artist further transformed the sculpture by hanging it on a wall where, notwithstanding its weight and factual creation, it can be read as a drawing, a cross, an oversized insect, and more. *Stairs* emphasizes architecture itself, with an image of an accessory that is usually ignored and yet is functional and lives in plain sight.

STEEL AND PAINT; 294.6 X 165.1 X 88.9 CM (116 X 65 X 35 IN.)

GIFT OF SCOTT C. MUELLER AND MARGARET FULTON MUELLER AND SUNDRY ART-CONTEMPORARY FUND 2011.1

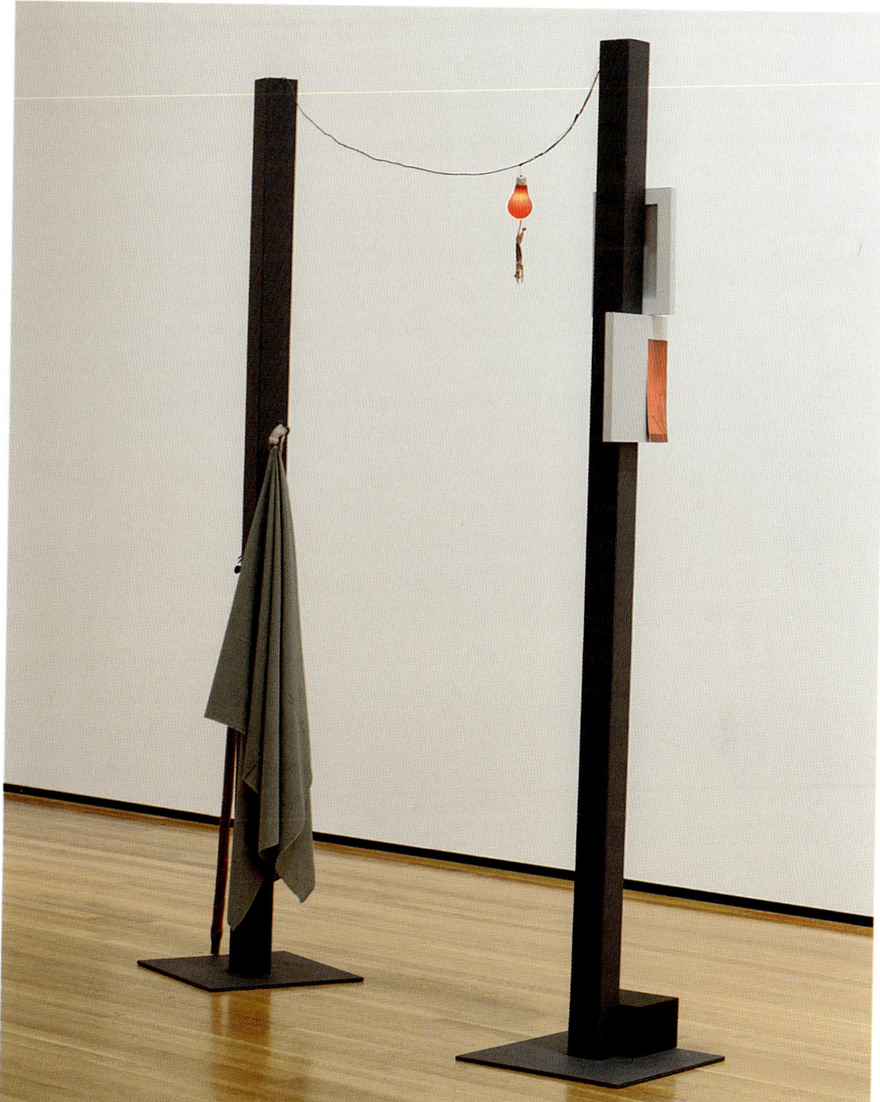

Bacon's Not the Only Thing That Is Cured by Hanging from a String 2011

GEOFFREY FARMER (CANADIAN, B. 1967)

Geoffrey Farmer equates sculpture with photography, a medium with substantial impact on the visual record of social and cultural events. In this piece, cut-out images from vintage issues of *LIFE* magazine dangle freely, like photographs hanging in a darkroom, inviting open-ended metaphors and narratives in the interplay with other found objects. In addition, subtle light effects emphasize another aspect of sculpture—its inherent theatrical nature. Illuminated lamp posts evoke an urban street corner where people connect and their lives intersect, imagined here in an intimate and magical nocturnal moment. The title also refers to photography, giving form to Susan Sontag's notion, from her popular book *On Photography,* that to hang something is to make it visible.

PRINTED MATERIAL, WOOD, METAL, PAINT, TAPE, FOAM, FABRIC, AND COMPUTER-PROGRAMMED LEDS; 245.1 X 45.7 X 58.4 CM (96-1/2 X 18 X 23 IN.) OVERALL

SUNDRY ART-CONTEMPORARY FUND 2011.33

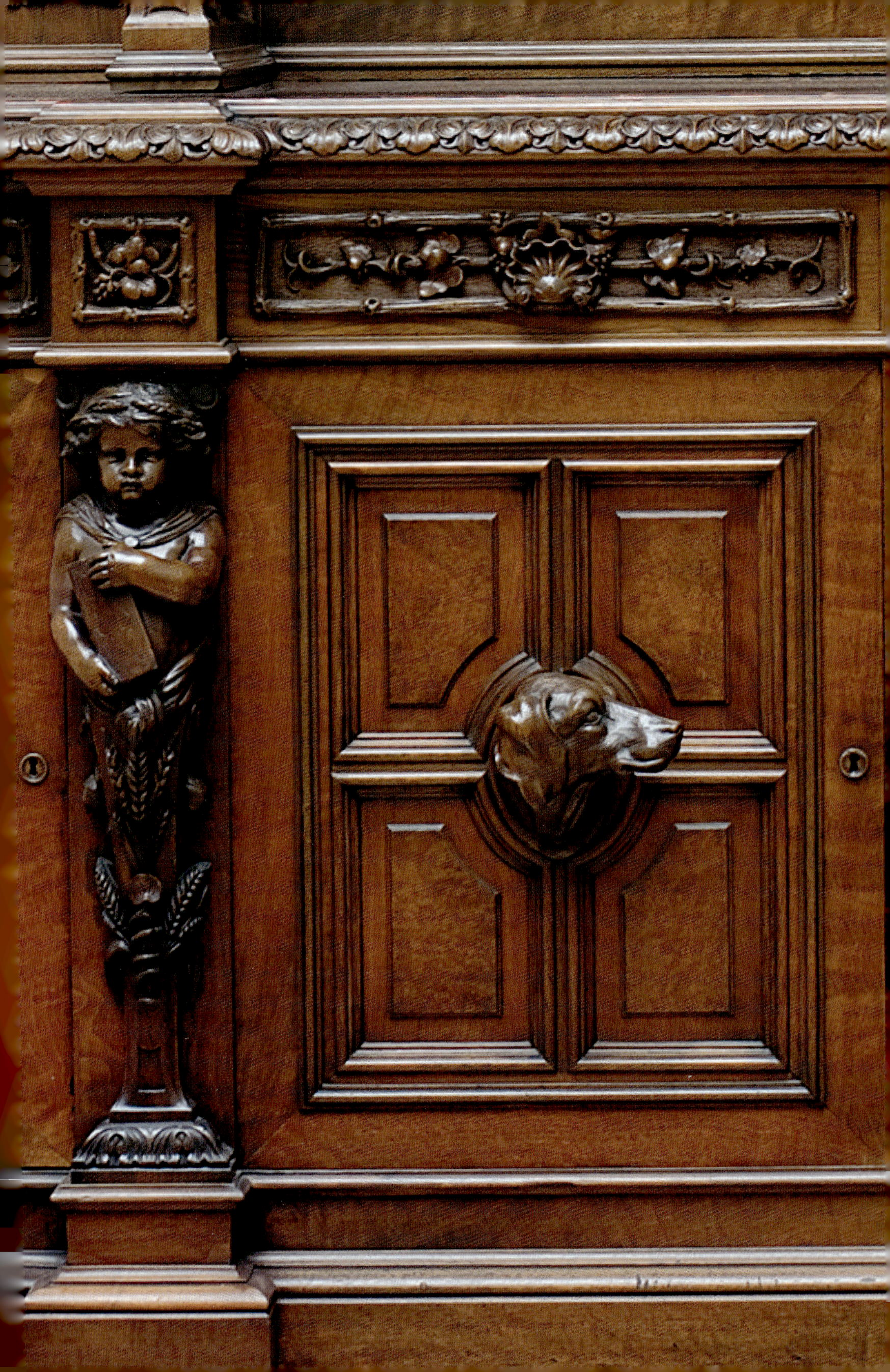

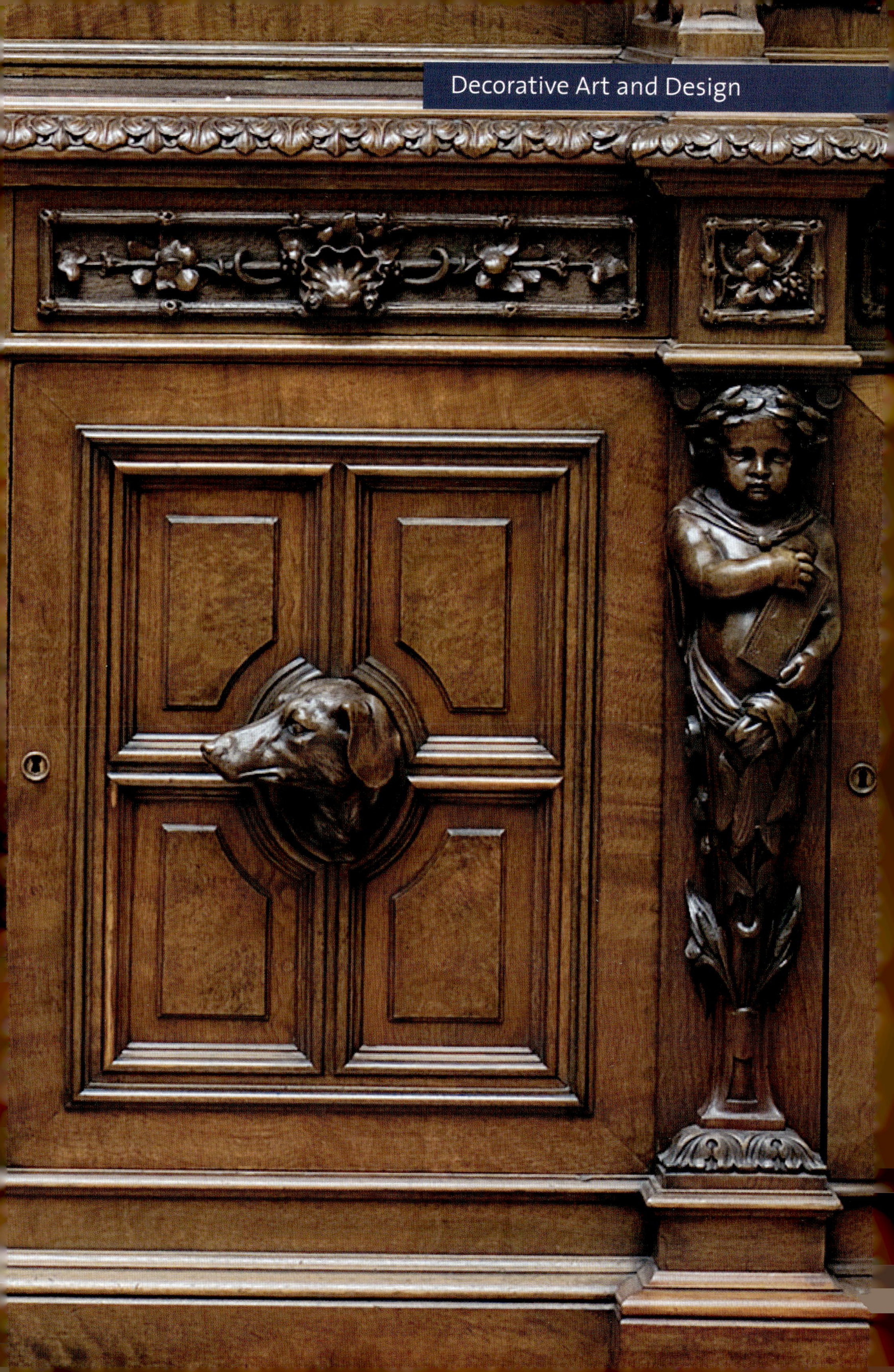
Decorative Art and Design

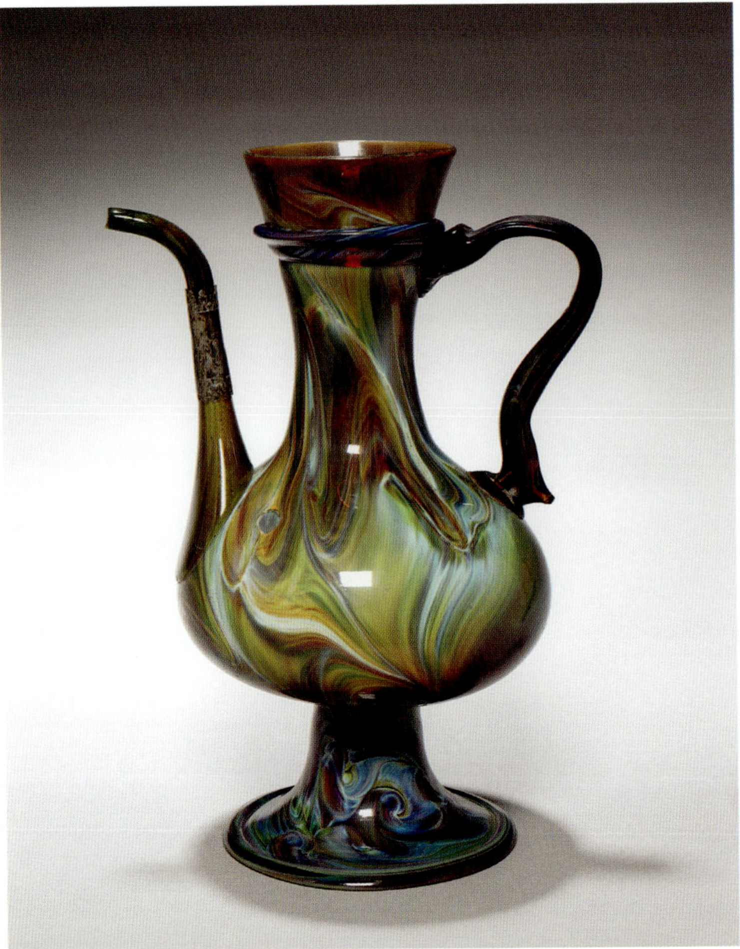

Ewer about 1500

VENICE, ITALY

The island of Murano, near Venice, has been the center of Italian glassmaking since the beginning of the 14th century. Late medieval and Renaissance production consisted mainly of utilitarian works such as tableware for wealthy households as well as presentation works of the highest quality. Early Venetian glassblowers sometimes sought to emulate rock crystal and other hardstones. This large ewer, meant to look as if it were carved from the mineral chalcedony, is called *calcedonio*.

"CHALCEDONY" INLAID GLASS; SILVER MOUNT; H. 29.6 CM (11-5/8 IN.)

JOHN L. SEVERANCE FUND 1985.141

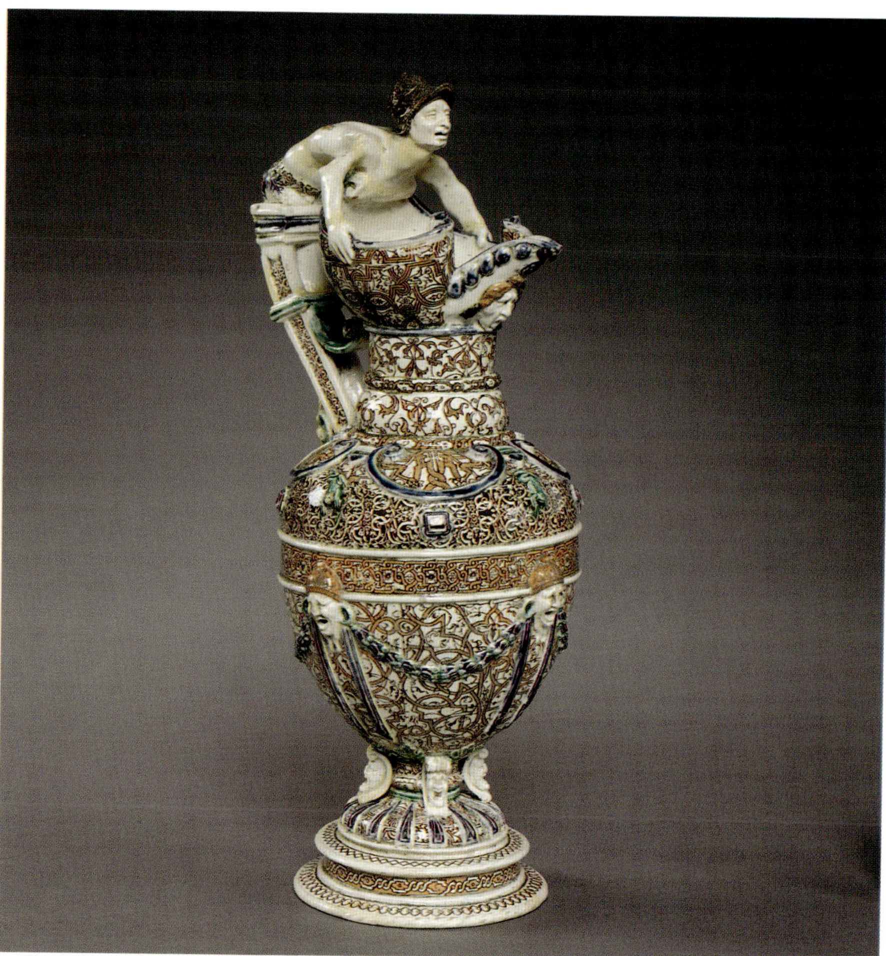

Ewer about 1540–67

SAINT-PORCHAIRE, FRANCE

Only around 60 pieces survive of the pottery (faience) attributed to Saint-Porchaire, in southwestern France. One of the most recognizable features is the method of decoration: surface patterns were achieved by impressing the clay with metal strips and then filling the voids with dark-colored watery clay, called slip. The forms directly relate to Italian Renaissance examples and represent the transfer of this style to France. Many also include references to Henri II, indicating they were probably intended for use by the French court.

LEAD-GLAZED, WHITE-PASTE EARTHENWARE WITH INLAID SLIP DECORATION; 35.6 X 13.7 CM (14 X 5-3/8 IN.) PURCHASE FROM THE J.H. WADE FUND 1953.363

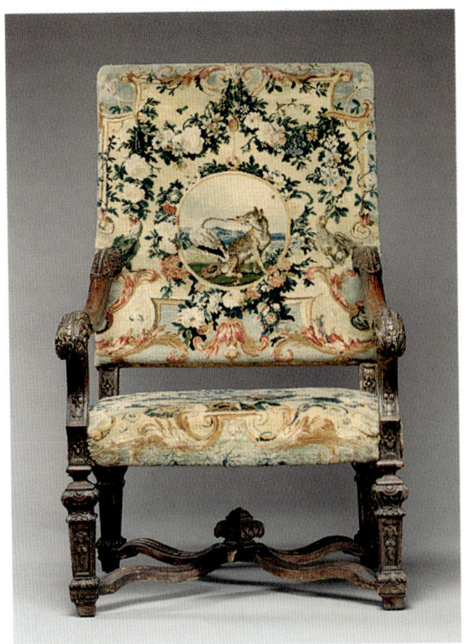

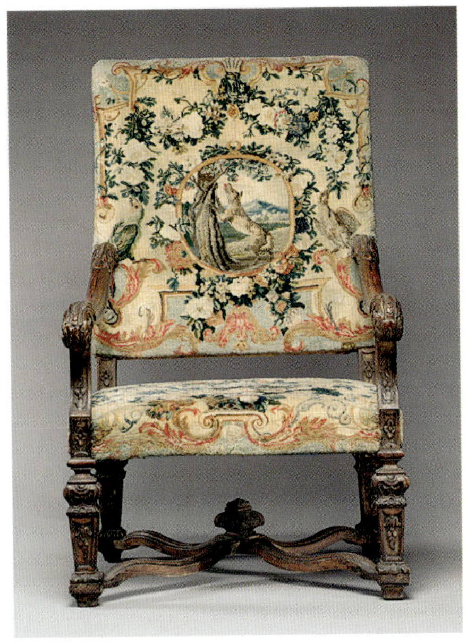

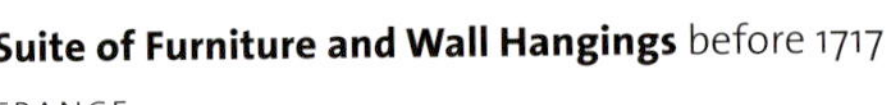

Suite of Furniture and Wall Hangings before 1717

FRANCE

Elegant furnishings upholstered in woven tapestries and made in association with wall hangings were produced for the kings of France and the royal family beginning in the 1600s. Colorful, sophisticated designs were woven in the Savonnerie factory's knotted-pile technique (144 symmetrical rug knots per square inch), adopted from Turkish carpets. Painters often created large patterns that weavers copied, with the yellow ground being the color preferred by Louis XIV (1638–1715). Suites of Savonnerie-covered furnishings filled the anterooms outside the king's chambers where courtiers waited, setting a high standard for stately furnishings

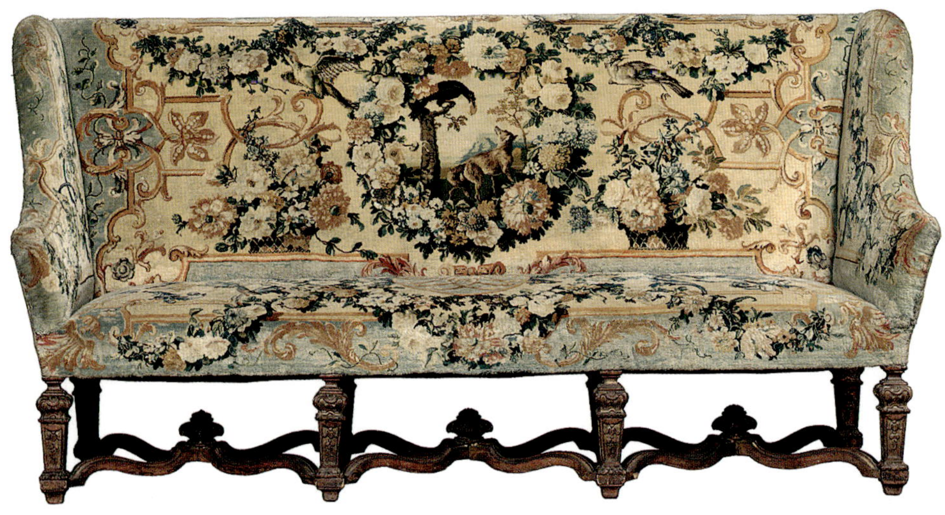

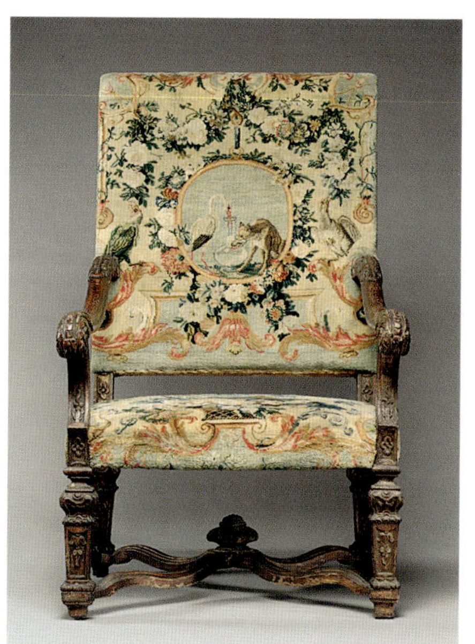

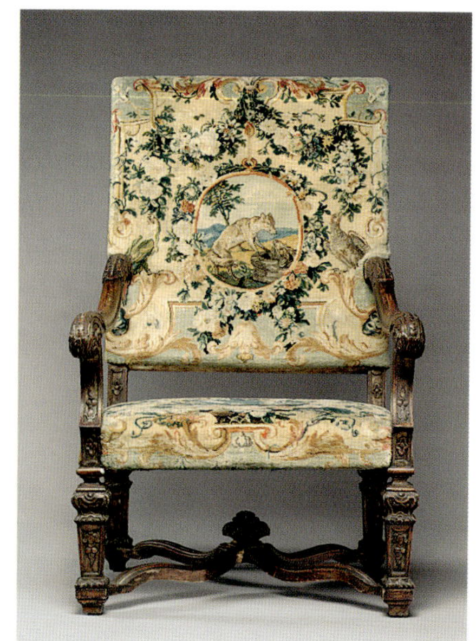

in aristocratic houses by providing luxurious comfort, sturdy construction, and protection against cold drafts.

This Savonnerie suite is thought to have been commissioned as a royal gift for the marriage of Isabella Maria de Merode to Count Francois Joseph Czernin in 1717. Their families' coats-of-arms appear within the wall panels depicting Spring and Fall, and the furniture displays themes from Aesop's Fables surrounded by architecturally inspired borders typical of the Louis XIV period. Two other wall panels from this suite, depicting Winter and Summer, are in the collection of the Toledo Museum of Art.

WOOL, HEMP; DIMENSIONS VARY

JOHN L. SEVERANCE FUND 1947.183.1–5, 1946.247, 1952.14

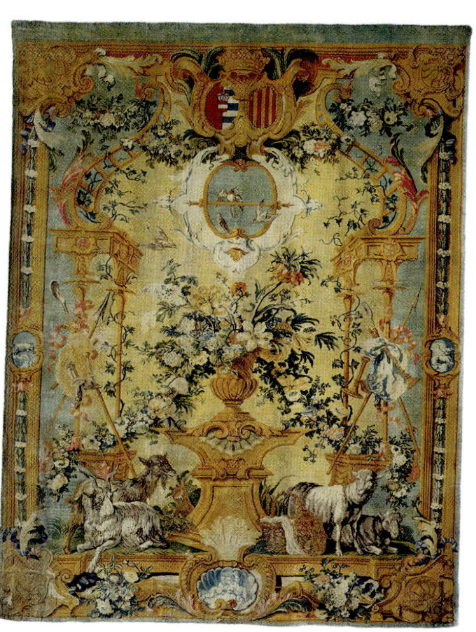

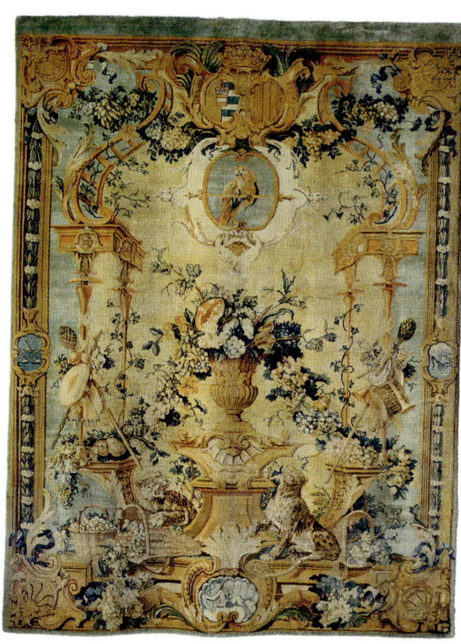

Console about 1720–21

ATTRIBUTED TO MICHEL II LANGE, PIERRE TURPIN, AND JULES-MICHEL HARDOUIN (FRENCH)

Commissioned for the Hôtel d'Évreux, the present-day Élysée Palace (official residence of the presidents of France since 1871), this gilded console reveals the interplay of politics and art that can sometimes make a splendid work even more special. The Régence period in France (1715–23) was an important transitional era in architecture and decorative arts. After the death of Louis XIV, Philippe II, the duc d'Orleans, ruled France as regent until the young Louis XV achieved his majority in 1723. Bored with the regimen of courtly life in the country, the regent and his advisors moved the seat of government from Versailles to the Palais Royale adjacent to the present-day Louvre. Paris once again became the center of activity with the aristocracy in firm control of both the social and political scenes.

One member of this displaced court was the comte d'Évreux, Henri-Louis de la Tour d'Auvergne, a wealthy career officer in the army. After the death of Louis XIV, d'Évreux commissioned a new house on the right bank of the Seine in Paris to be designed by one of the royal architects, Jules-Michel Hardouin, nephew of Jules-Hardouin Mansart, the architect for much of the building of Versailles under the late king. This console was apparently intended for the grand salon centered on the garden, created between 1720 and 1721.

With its references to antiquity—winged dragons, palm leaves, mask of Medusa, acanthus leaves, egg-and-dart molding—and its dramatic display of militaria, this console emphasizes movement and power to great effect, exactly the intention of an ambitious young army officer currying favor at court.

CARVED GILT WOOD, MARBLE TOP; 92 X 202 X 69.5 CM (36-1/4 X 79-1/2 X 27-3/8 IN.)

PURCHASE FROM THE J. H. WADE FUND 2008.6.A–B

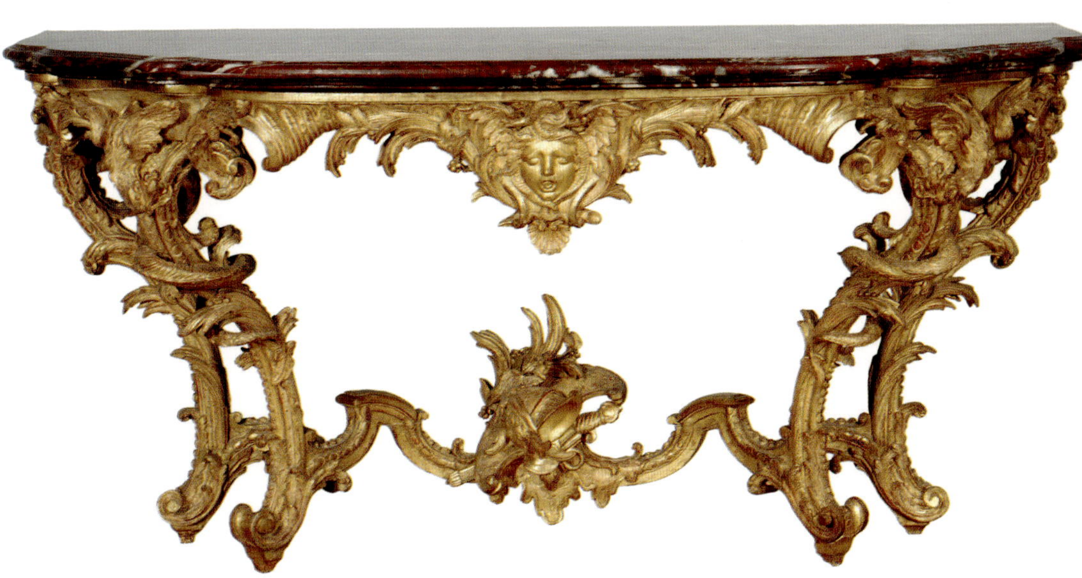

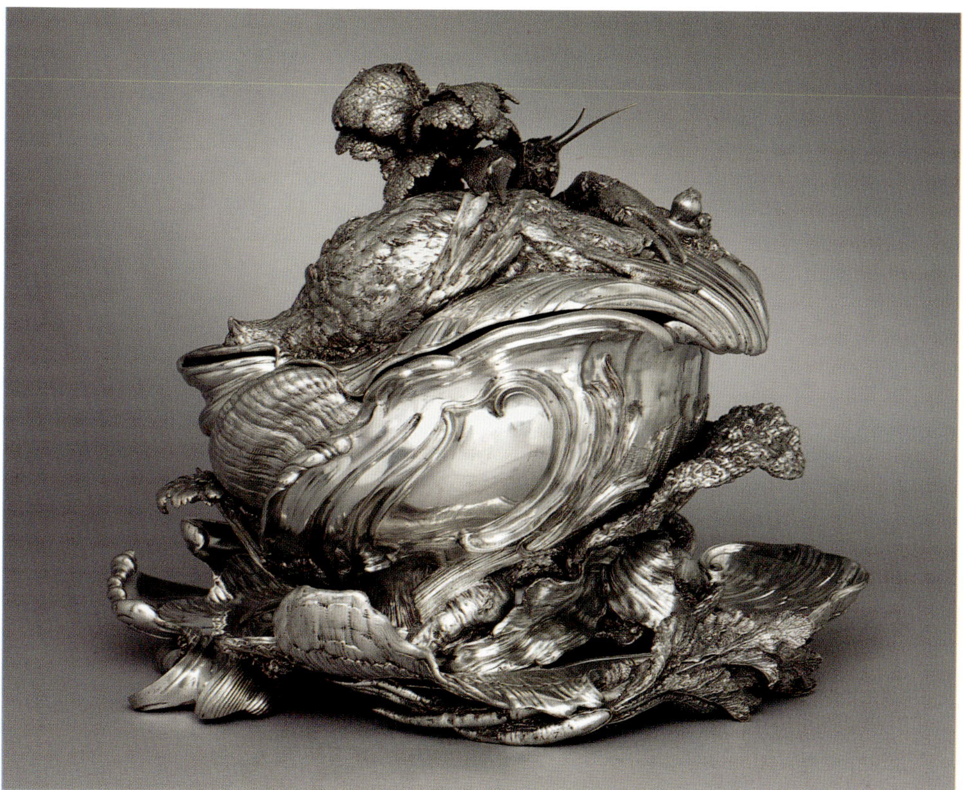

Tureen-on-Stand about 1735–40

JUSTE-AURELLE MEISSONNIER (FRENCH, 1695–1750), DESIGNER; PIERRE-FRANÇOIS BONNESTRENNE AND HENRY ADNET, PARIS, MAKERS

The most significant work in silver in the museum's collection is this elaborate tureen and stand. Often described as the quintessential work in the mature Rococo style, the tureen is a remarkable survivor of the early 18th century. Commissioned by the young English Duke of Kingston during his second visit to Paris in 1735, it is one of two nearly identical tureens that were conceived as pendants to a large centerpiece, now lost. While the actual tureens quietly resided in private collections first in England, then Russia, the engraving gives testament to the brilliance of the design and became a standard-bearer for picturesque style at the apex of the French Rococo period.

Incredibly heavy, this tureen would not have been used very often, if at all, to serve the stew of meats and seafood that its cast figures on the lid suggest. Rather, a silver tureen of this nature served a much more potent purpose: to announce the wealth and sophistication of its owner. In this case, Kingston was in Paris during a particularly vibrant period when the king and court were young and frivolous, and fashion was dominated by picturesque expressions of the exuberance of nature. Meissonnier, in conceiving this suite, pushed the limits of conventional silversmithing and demanded nothing short of sculpture from Bonnestrenne and Adnet. The swirling mass of figures and vegetation seemingly ride the crest of a silver wave, taking the eye on a journey of wonder and surprise to define not only the composition of this one piece but the spirit of the age in which it was conceived.

SILVER; 36.9 X 38.4 X 31.8 CM (14-1/2 X 15-1/8 X 12-1/2 IN.)

LEONARD C. HANNA JR. FUND 1977.182.A–C

Teapot about 1755–60

NATHANIEL HURD (AMERICAN, 1730–1778), MAKER

Nathaniel Hurd was one of several accomplished silversmiths, including Paul Revere, who worked in Boston during the Colonial period. He counted the most prominent citizens among his customers, including the Gibbs family whose coat of arms is masterfully engraved on this teapot. The inspiration for his engraved design was likely taken from the book of heraldry that can be seen in the museum's portrait of Hurd by John Singleton Copley (p. 44).

SILVER; 14.5 X 24.4 CM (5-3/4 X 9-5/8 IN.)

GIFT OF HOLLIS FRENCH 1940.228

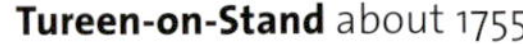

Tureen-on-Stand about 1755

CHELSEA PORCELAIN FACTORY (BRITISH)

The Chelsea Porcelain Factory, located in what is now a fashionable residential area of London but in the 18th century was dominated by commerce along the Thames River, was England's most celebrated porcelain factory in the mid 18th century. Large tureens in the form of chickens or rabbits have long been recognized as the most outstanding productions of the Chelsea factory and were modeled as adaptations of Chinese figural tureens imported into England along the vast trading routes that had been established more than a century earlier.

CERAMIC; 24.8 X 34.9 X 25.7 CM (9-3/4 X 13-3/4 X 10-1/8 IN.) TUREEN, 48.7 X 37.7 X 6.4 CM (19-1/4 X 14-7/8 X 2-1/2 IN.) STAND. PURCHASE FROM THE J. H. WADE FUND 1984.58.A–B, 2000.3

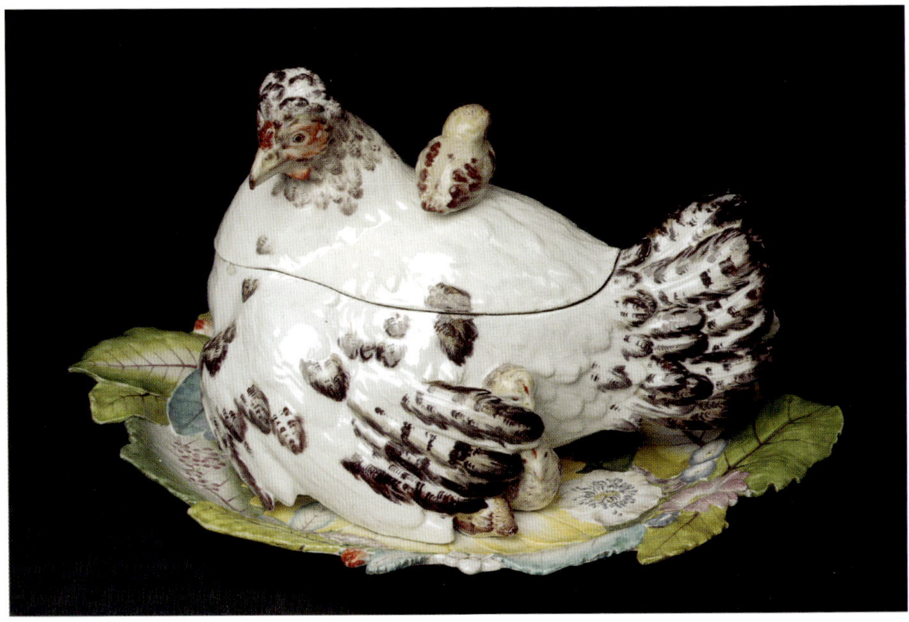

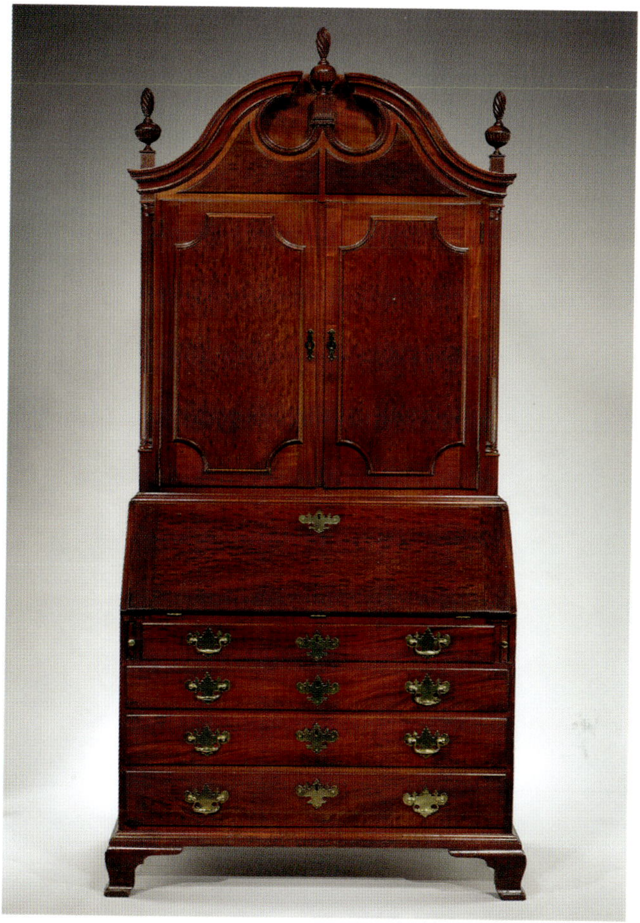

Desk and Bookcase about 1780–95

ATTRIBUTED TO THOMAS TOWNSEND (AMERICAN, 1732–1809)

In the 18th century, Newport, Rhode Island, was the fifth largest city in North America and one of the most important centers of shipping and trade along the Eastern Seaboard. Orders for furniture from its celebrated cabinetmakers came in from far and wide. This desk and bookcase was likely made for Oliver Wolcott Sr., a signer of the Declaration of Independence and later governor of the State of Connecticut. Eventually, the desk passed down through his family to Dorothy Draper, an important 20th-century interior decorator, and ultimately to her daughter, Penelope Draper Buchanan, whose husband gave it to the museum after her death—a rare, unbroken line of succession.

Large desks were designed to hold all the necessary components of a gentleman's office under lock and key: books, papers, pens and ink, and important documents. To serve such a function desks also became complicated masterworks of the cabinetmaker's art, incorporating many parts—from small drawers to large panels cut from a single tree—making them among the most expensive types of furniture available. This desk and bookcase exhibits the characteristic traits of classic Newport furniture: "plum pudding" mahogany, cupcake-like finials, and a carved shell on the inside of the desk.

MAHOGANY, RED CEDAR, CHESTNUT, WHITE PINE, BRASS;
240 X 108 X 64.8 CM (94-1/2 X 42-1/2 X 25-1/2 IN.)
GIFT OF HARVEY BUCHANAN IN MEMORY OF PENELOPE DRAPER BUCHANAN AND DOROTHY TUCKERMAN DRAPER
2012.43

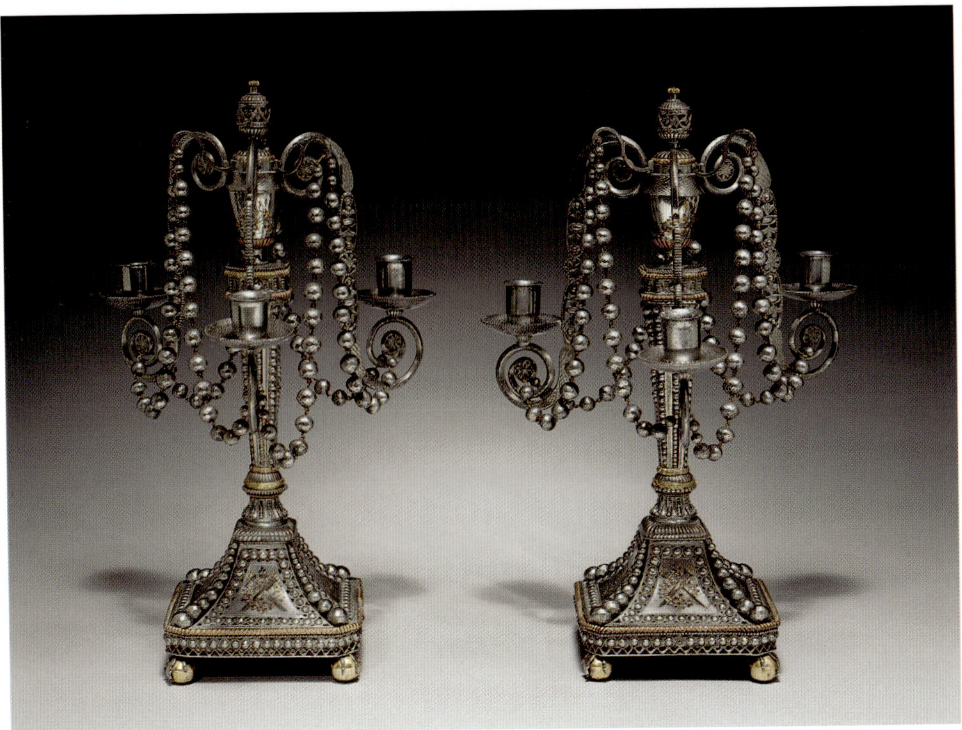

Pair of Candelabra about 1790–95

TULA, RUSSIA

Founded in 1705 by Peter the Great, the armory at Tula developed steadily over the 18th century to become one of the centers of Russian metalworking, especially in arms manufacturing. In the 1770s and 1780s, Catherine the Great took a keen interest in the work produced there, sending several of the most proficient craftsmen to England to study the decorative application of steel in armories in Sheffield and London. Subsequently, the Tula artisans surpassed the metalworkers in Britain and elsewhere on the Continent, producing decorative wares that were as precious and precise as their brilliantly embellished firearms. Catherine was so pleased that she commissioned diplomatic and royal gifts of Tula ware as well as several noted examples of furniture in the distinctive Tula style of cut steel, gilt-bronze, silver, and gold.

The most recognizable characteristic of Tula became the use of multifaceted cabochons and beads of steel that replicated faceted diamonds and crystals. No other region was able to achieve the vividness of this technique in cut steel. Most works in Tula steel were small precious works such as inkstands, bobbin holders, buttons, footstools, single candlesticks, etc. These candelabra are quintessential expressions of the Neoclassical taste in Russia during the late 18th century, a significant moment in Russian design because of the mature level of craftsmanship and style achieved by Russian workers at the time. By this point, diplomatic and cultural ties between France and Russia were strong and influential, as seen in the architecture and decoration of most major structures reflecting the French Neoclassical style.

CUT AND POLISHED STEEL WITH GOLD AND SILVERED DECORATION; 40.7 X 24.8 CM (16 X 9-3/4 IN.) EACH

LEONARD C. HANNA JR. FUND 2010.2.1–2

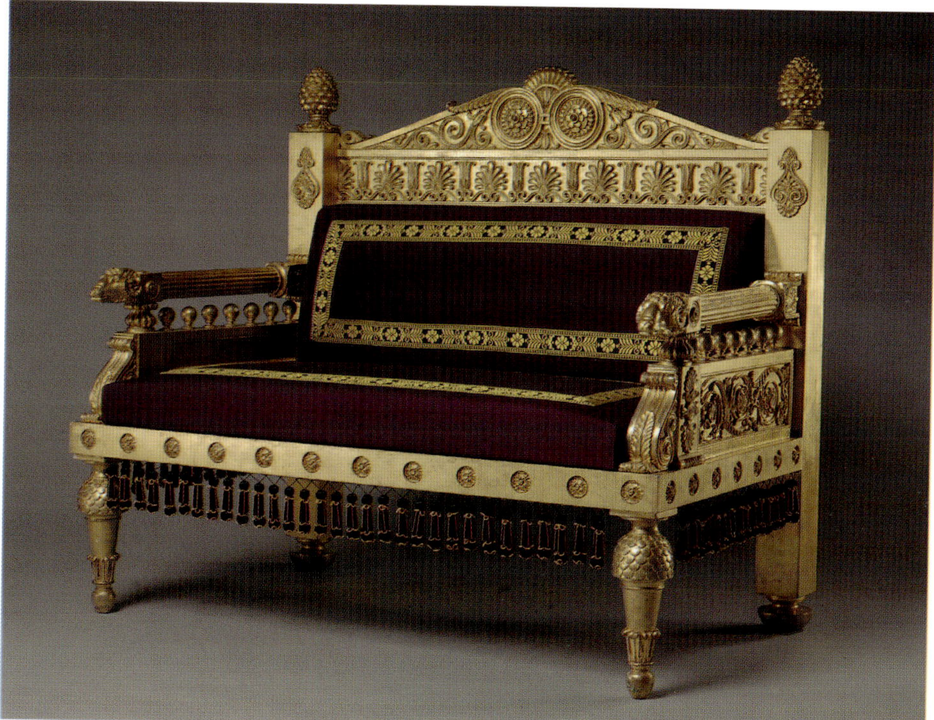

Settee about 1802–7

THOMAS HOPE (BRITISH, B. THE NETHERLANDS, 1769–1831), DESIGNER; UNKNOWN MAKER (BRITISH, LONDON)

This settee in the Neoclassical style by the English Regency designer Thomas Hope was part of the furnishings for his grand residence (Robert Adam, architect) in Duchess Street, Portland Place, London. The house featured themed rooms with suites of furniture conceived by Hope to provide a suitable background for his collection of Classical Greek and Neoclassical statuary and objets d'art. This settee was likely located on the first floor, which was intended to be opened "museum-like" to the public. With its completely gilded surface in a manner resembling gilt-bronze and numerous references to Classical carved friezes, including the elaborate reeded arms terminating in carved ram heads identical to the handles of Greek cookware or *paterae,* this settee would have served as an elegant example of "authentic" Grecian design.

Hope was born in Amsterdam in 1769 into a wealthy Dutch banking family of Scottish descent. He settled in England around 1796 after an exhaustive eight-year grand tour of the Mediterranean countries, including Egypt, Turkey, Greece, and Italy. His work in the Neoclassical style took its inspiration from various sources including his own travels and publications such as V. Denon's *Voyage dans la basse et la haute Egypte* (1802). The settee was likely part of a larger suite of furniture, although only a "large arm-chair" of identical styling was illustrated in Hope's *Household Furniture and Interior Decoration* (1807, pl. XXII), an exceptional publication that established his reputation as an influential designer of great vision.

GILT-WOOD, REPRODUCTION WOOL UPHOLSTERY; 102.2 X 113 X 71.1 CM (40-1/4 X 44-1/2 X 28 IN.)

LEONARD C. HANNA JR. FUND 2011.3

Vase Bertin about 1855

LÉOPOLD-JULES-JOSEPH GÉLY (FRENCH, 1851–1888), DECORATOR; JULES-CONSTANT PEYRE (FRENCH, B. AFTER 1811), MODELER; SÈVRES IMPERIAL PORCELAIN MANUFACTORY, FRANCE, MAKER

This monumental work is an example of what made the Sèvres porcelain factory in France one of the most celebrated in the world. Created for display at the 1855 Exposition Universelle in Paris, this vase not only featured a new form of fired clay body and slip-cast decoration, but it also displayed the artistic talent of its designer, Léopold-Jules-Joseph Gély, in its elaborate composition. This combination of innovation and artistry brought the factory acclaim and even caught the eye of the emperor, Napoleon III.

The simple form had been introduced a few years earlier in 1850 by the celebrated modeler Jules-Constant Peyre to provide a suitable surface for large-scale decoration. It was named to honor Henri Léonard Jean-Baptiste Bertin, one of the early 18th-century representatives of the king who oversaw production at the factory. The decoration was conceived by Gély, who not only designed the composition but was instrumental in developing the new method by which it was applied. Known as *pâte-sur-pâte,* this method of decoration would become a signature of the factory for the next 50 years.

PORCELAIN WITH PÂTE-SUR-PÂTE DECORATION; H. 99 CM (39 IN.), DIAM 45.8 CM (18 IN.). GIFT OF DARRELL, STEVEN, BRIAN, AND NEIL YOUNG IN MEMORY OF THEIR PARENTS, MARDELLE J. AND HOWARD S. YOUNG 2007.277

Sideboard about 1855

ATTRIBUTED TO JOSEPH ALEXIS BAILLY (AMERICAN, B. FRANCE, 1825–1883)

This Renaissance Revival sideboard is an object filled with allegory and symbolism, exhibiting some of the most elaborate carving known on a piece of American furniture of this era. Its origins are rooted in both the craze for all things French that governed taste and fashion in mid 19th-century America as well as the ambitions and pretensions of a growing wealthy class. The design conforms to that of the Parisian cabinetmaker Alexandre Fourdinois in his massive sideboard presented at the 1851 Great Exhibition in London: a tripartite division of elements reaching upward as in a great funerary monument; a carved central panel featuring a stag and other forest creatures slain in the hunt; and carved allegorical figures, referencing the Renaissance, in support. All these symbols served the central theme of Man vanquishing Nature, an easy metaphor for the real celebrated victory of Industry over Man, which provided the owner with the means to afford such a work.

While its form and composition follow closely the French example, the method of construction, style of carving, and architectural scale of this sideboard are typical of furniture made in Philadelphia in the mid 19th century. Images of the Fourdinois sideboard were reproduced with great fanfare in illustrated magazines of the period as the quintessential icon of fashion and good taste in furniture. The sideboard's maker, thought to be the Frenchman turned Philadelphian Joseph Alexis Bailly, easily adapted the Fourdinois model to his own with the use of American touchstones such as Native Americans and an American bird of prey in place of the mythological figures shown on the French example.

WALNUT; 290.4 X 211.4 X 69.4 CM (114-3/8 X 83-1/4 X 27-3/8 IN.)

PURCHASE FROM THE J. H. WADE FUND 1985.72

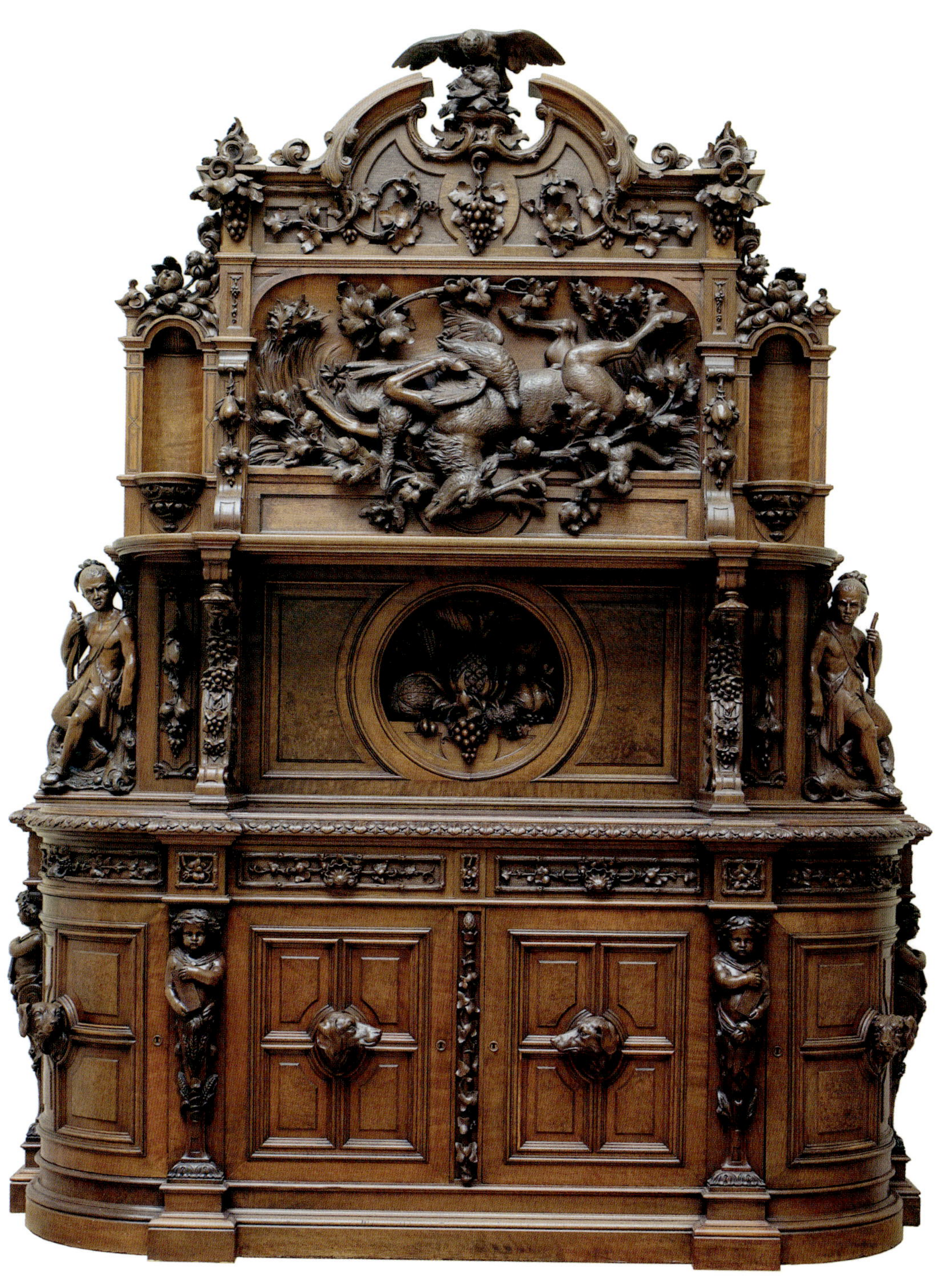

Fire Screen about 1878–80

HERTER BROTHERS, NEW YORK

Gustav and Christian Herter were among a wave of immigrant German cabinetmakers who settled in New York just before the Civil War. They brought with them superb skills in craftsmanship and quickly rose to prominence during the 1860s. Their earliest work followed the revival trend of Renaissance decoration largely influenced by European design at mid century. However, after the introduction of Japanese wares to the Western market in the 1860s, a new aesthetic emerged that incorporated Japanese sensibilities of asymmetry, naturalistic motifs, and surface patterning. Attributed to the Herter Brothers, this fire screen displays all of these motifs in abundance.

Essentially a barrier to the heat of a fireplace, a fire screen as elaborate as this one was no doubt also seen as a work of art. Here, the gilded frame contains an embossed cardboard panel, painted in colorful hues to resemble tooled leather, depicting a Japanesque landscape of cockerels feeding by a riverbank. Rather than produce an imitative design, the Herter Brothers combined Western neoclassical elements such as swags and portrait medallions with Asian floral patterning and a carved asymmetrical trellis to capture the eclectic spirit of design in the late 1870s. All these motifs speak of the artistic taste of wealthy consumers such as the San Francisco railroad baron Mark Hopkins, for whom it is thought this fire screen was commissioned. His mansion on Nob Hill, completed in 1878 and completely furnished by the Herter Brothers, is likely the screen's first home. Most of the contents of that house were removed to Menlo Park, south of San Francisco, in the 1880s before the devastating earthquake of 1906; it was from that house that the screen was sold out of the family in 1942.

GILDED WOOD, PAINTED AND GILDED WOOD PANELS, BROCADED SILK, EMBOSSED PAPER; 131.8 X 76.2 X 58.3 CM (51-7/8 X 30 X 23 IN.)

THE SEVERANCE AND GRETA MILLIKIN PURCHASE FUND 1997.58

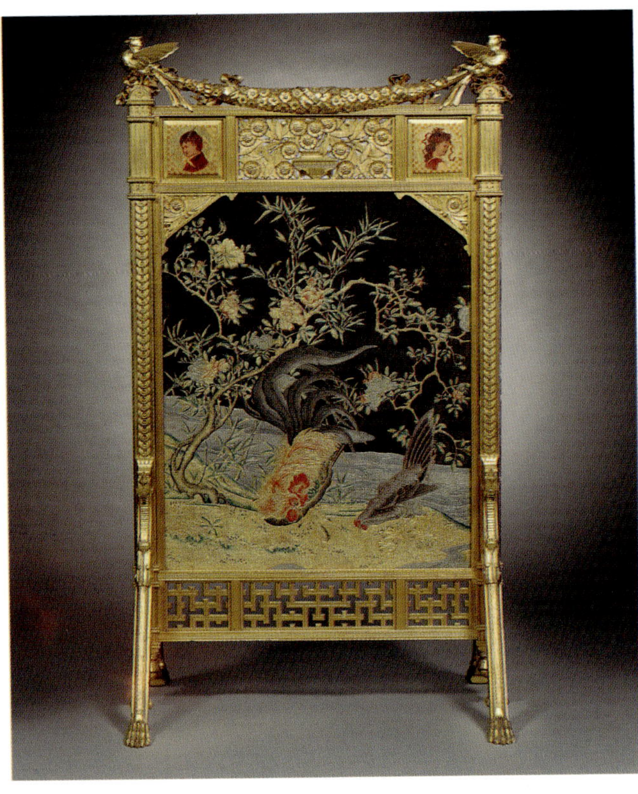

Hinds House Window about 1900

LOUIS COMFORT TIFFANY (AMERICAN, 1848–1933), DESIGNER; TIFFANY GLASS & DECORATING CO., MAKER

Louis Comfort Tiffany was the son of the founder of the famous New York jewelry firm, Tiffany & Co. Though it was Louis's vision and oversight that guided the firm in all of its creations, he employed an army of workers, mostly women, to design and fashion his celebrated stained-glass creations, from windows to lamps. His distinctive iridescent Favrile glass and painterly compositions became synonymous with a new direction in art, the Art Nouveau, which emphasized naturalistic motifs. His firm became celebrated for its ability to create three-dimensional compositions by stacking glass together rather than just painting shadow on the surface. As a result, Tiffany windows graced not only the sanctuaries of prominent religious and civic buildings but the parlors of fashionable houses as well.

Likely designed by Agnes Northrup for Louis Comfort Tiffany's firm, the Tiffany Glass & Decorating Co., this window was originally created for the Howell Hinds house, built in 1898. Located on Overlook Road in Cleveland, Ohio, the house was demolished in 1930 like other nearby estates.

STAINED GLASS; 227.3 X 114.3 CM (89-1/2 X 45 IN.)

GIFT OF MRS. ROBERT M. FALLON 1966.432

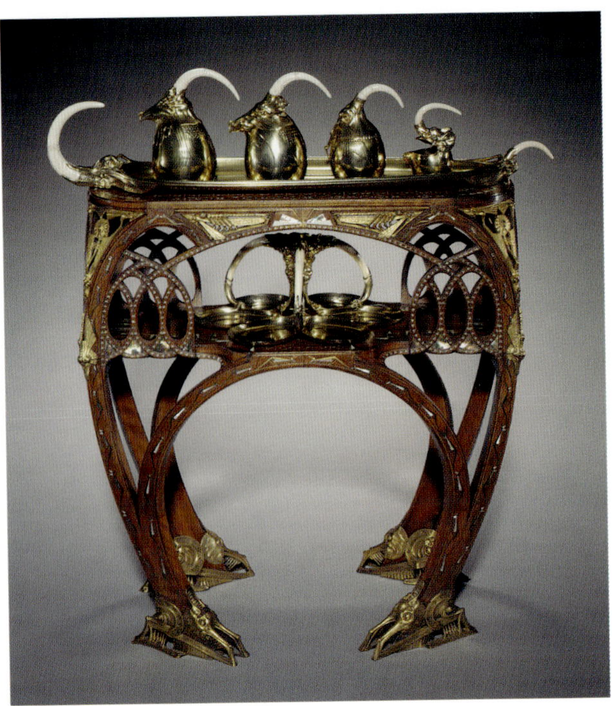

Tea Service, Salver, and Stand about 1907

CARLO BUGATTI (ITALIAN, 1856–1940), DESIGNER; ADRIEN-AURÉLIEN HÉBRARD (FRENCH, 1866–1937), MAKER

Of all the innovative artisans living and working at the turn of the 20th century, Carlo Bugatti is one of the most original. A sculptor by training, Bugatti rejected a traditional path in the fine arts for work in furniture, opening his first shop in Milan around 1880. His early exploration of exotic motifs featuring the dragonfly, beetle, and wasp so beloved by other Art Nouveau craftsmen led him to continue his work in smaller scale with increasingly abstract interpretations. In Paris, he focused on silver and jewelry design and soon attracted a small stable of patrons, including a woman from South Africa, Mrs. Anna Blake, who became fascinated by his fiercely independent spirit and unconventional designs. The critics, however, were less enthusiastic when he showed his work at the annual salons, complaining that he was going too far beyond the practical.

Mrs. Blake disagreed and became his single most devoted client, ordering first the Cleveland salver, ornamented with elephant tusks, then the tea service, and finally the stand—all reminiscent of her beloved African homeland. One of three designs Bugatti and the silversmith Hébrard created for her, this tea service was the only one completely integrated with salver and stand. The decorative scheme may have taken inspiration from elephants and warthogs, dragonflies and beetles, but it was entirely original in execution. The individual elements seemingly flow from imagination into a menagerie of fantastical creatures. The ensemble rests on a table that is even more of a confection: swirling ribbons of exotic wood highlighted with mother-of-pearl and metallic inlays in an isometric stance formed as if it were some predatory bush cat ready to pounce.

TEA SERVICE: SILVER AND IVORY; 13.5 X 76.9 X 19.9 CM (5-3/8 X 30-1/4 X 7-7/8 IN.) OVERALL; THE THOMAS L. FAWICK MEMORIAL COLLECTION 1980.74.1–5

SALVER: SILVER AND IVORY; 14.6 X 33 CM (5-3/4 X 13 IN.); LEONARD C. HANNA JR. FUND 1991.46

STAND: INLAID WOOD (MAHOGANY?), CAST AND GILDED BRONZE MOUNTS, INLAYS OF IVORY OR BONE, METAL, AND MOTHER-OF-PEARL (MARINE MUSSELS OR PEARL OYSTERS); 71.5 X 67.1 X 41.3 CM (28-1/8 X 26-3/8 X 16-1/4 IN.); LEONARD C. HANNA JR. FUND 1991.45

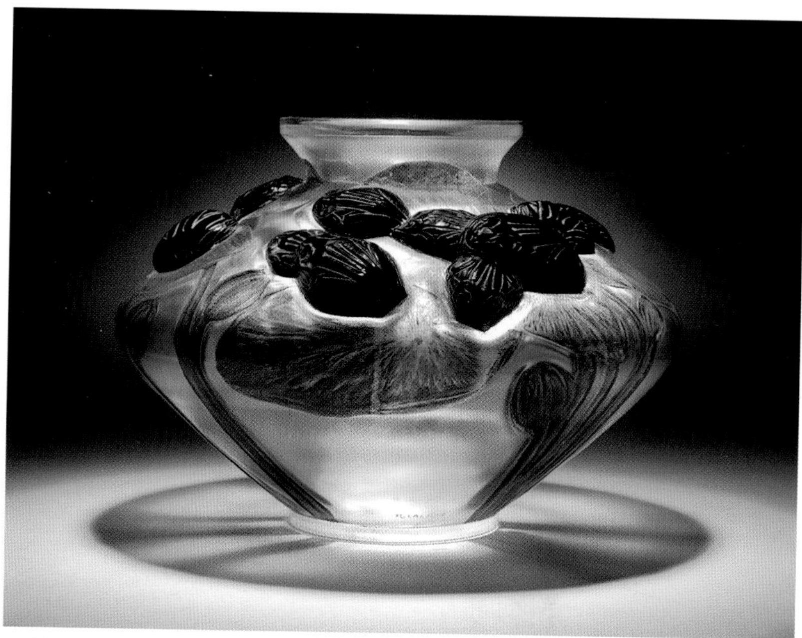

Frogs and Lilypads Vase about 1909–12

RENÉ LALIQUE (FRENCH, 1860–1945)

The *Frogs and Lilypads Vase* is a pivotal work by the recognized master of French glass in the 20th century, René Lalique. Created after he had acquired his first glassworks at Combs-la-ville (1905) and before he exhibited his first collection of glass (1912), this vase was the result of many experiments to produce artistic work that could be made in multiples. These experiments followed on from his use of carved glass, combined with gold, gems, or other materials in jewelry design after 1900. Lalique began to recognize the potential for financial success with glass, combining artistic designs that could be manufactured in multiples but still retain the aura of a unique work of art. Some scholars believe the success of Louis Comfort Tiffany, the American glass artisan, pushed Lalique in this direction. After attending the 1904 world's fair in St. Louis, Lalique visited Tiffany's glass furnaces in Corona, New York. The following year, Lalique began trying various techniques of molding glass that could achieve his goal.

While Lalique's craftsmen created a number of forms using different techniques in blown and cast glass, *Frogs and Lilypads* is one of the experiments resulting from this period, created using ceramic molds instead of the lost-wax method he began with and before using the bronze molds he eventually settled upon. Among the first glass objects Lalique exhibited at the decorative arts salon of 1912 in Paris to critical acclaim, it was then shown in New York at a small exhibition at the offices of Haviland & Co., the French ceramic manufacturer owned by the American Charles Haviland. Although a critical success, its method of production proved too labor intensive and therefore too costly and unsuitable for mass production, leaving this work as a unique example of this design.

GLASS; H. 21 CM (8-1/4 IN.), DIAM. 29.8 CM (11-3/4 IN.)

JOHN L. SEVERANCE FUND 2007.180

Kremlin Tower Clock 1913

HOUSE OF FABERGÉ, ST. PETERSBURG, RUSSIA

The revival of traditional arts and crafts among Western cultures at the end of the 19th century gave rise to a fashion among members of the imperial court in Russia for works that celebrated native Russian artistic motifs. The House of Fabergé produced many works that celebrated these traditions through the use of enamel or indigenous stones. This unique design for a table clock is an adaptation of one of the guard towers at the Kremlin in Moscow, an ancient fortress closely identified with Russian culture and history.

RHODONITE, SILVER, ENAMEL, EMERALDS, SAPPHIRES; 29 X 14.6 CM (11-3/8 X 5-3/4 IN.)

THE INDIA EARLY MINSHALL COLLECTION 1966.477

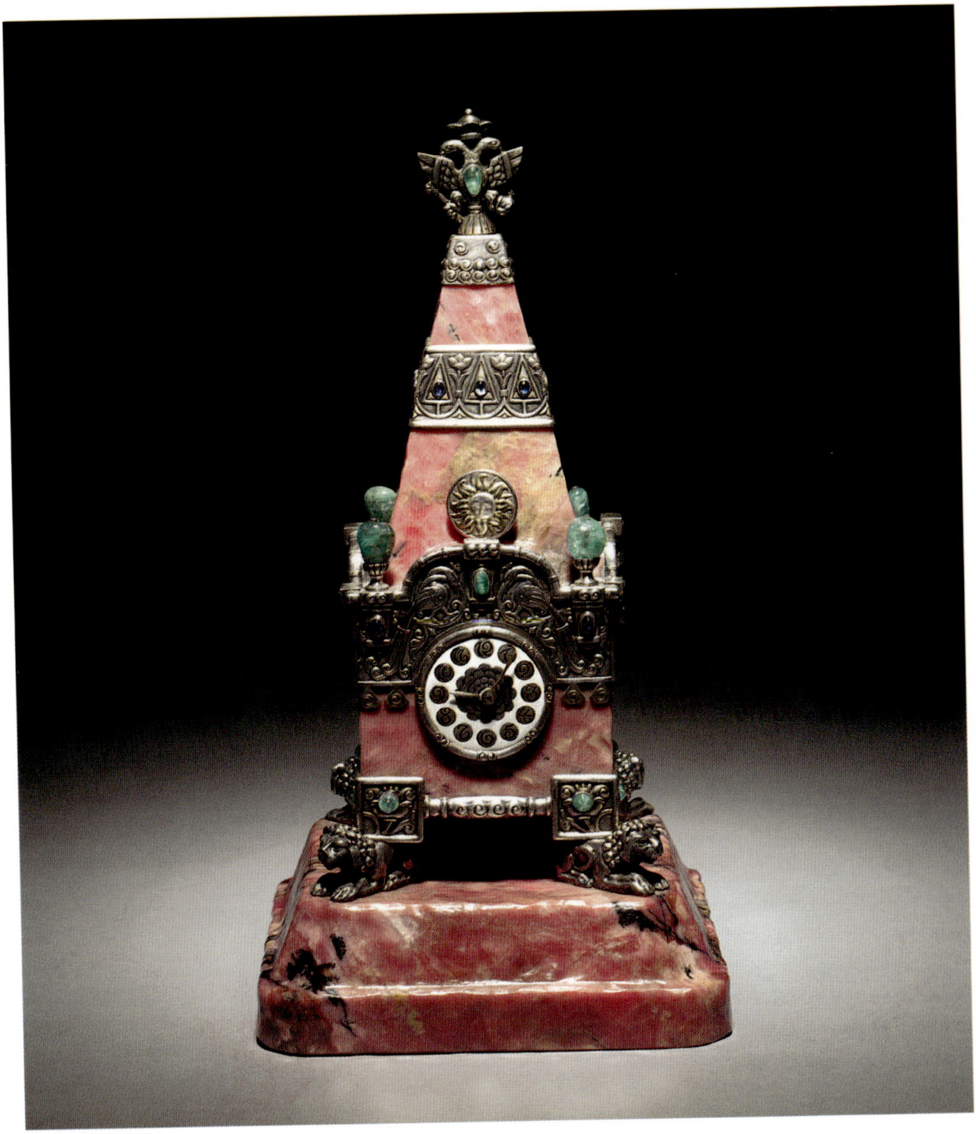

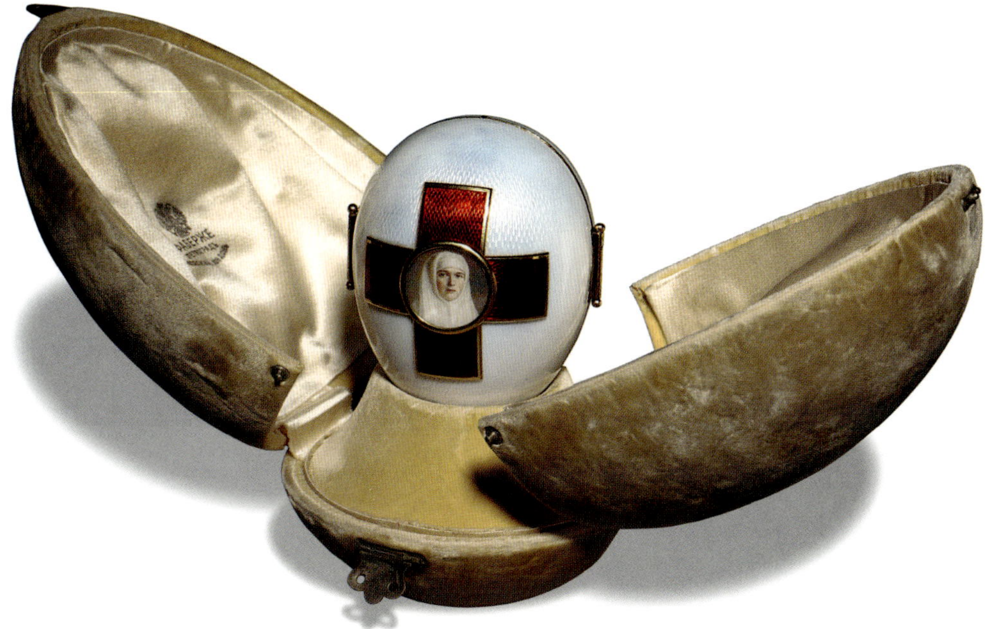

Imperial Red Cross Egg 1915

HOUSE OF FABERGÉ, ST. PETERSBURG, RUSSIA

The giving of an ornamental egg at Easter is an ancient tradition in the Russian Orthodox faith. In 1885, Tsar Alexander III first commissioned the House of Fabergé to make an egg for Tsarina Maria Fedorovna. It was to appear as a simple hen's egg, enameled in white, that opened to reveal a golden yoke containing a tiny surprise. From this relatively humble beginning, Fabergé's annual creation quickly took on a life of its own, eventually requiring teams of artisans using every technique of the goldsmith and jeweler to push the limits of creativity and material. When Nicholas II succeeded his father in 1894, he expanded the tradition by commissioning Fabergé to create an egg every year for both his wife, Alexandra Fedorovna, and his mother.

As Russia became deeply involved in World War I, the imperial family was eager to show its sympathy for the austerity and sacrifice of the Russian people. The women all joined the Red Cross and turned the state rooms of their residence into a hospital ward for wounded soldiers. Fabergé's egg of 1915 was meant to honor this service as it depicts the tsarina's two eldest daughters in their nurse's uniforms superimposed over two red crosses on a ground of luminous snow white enamel. The interior reveals a triptych icon of Saint Olga and Saint Tatiana, the daughters' patron saints, and the vanquishing of Hell by a risen Christ.

After the abdication of the tsar in 1917, this egg was confiscated by the Bolsheviks during the Russian Revolution and later sold by the Soviet government in 1930 to raise needed cash for the treasury. With its original velvet-lined case, bearing a Bolshevik inventory number duly marked in red ink, the egg eventually found its way into the collection of India Early Minshall of Cleveland, an avid devotee of Russian history and art.

GOLD, SILVER, ENAMEL, GLASS; 8.6 X 6.4 CM (3-3/8 X 2-1/2 IN.)

THE INDIA EARLY MINSHALL COLLECTION 1963.673

Viktor Schreckengost's Jazz Age Bowls

To commemorate her husband's second inauguration as governor of New York, Eleanor Roosevelt is said to have approached the Brownell-Lambertson Gallery in Manhattan to procure a suitable punch bowl for the governor's mansion. Although *New Yorker* cartoonist Peter Arno was initially considered for the task, the gallery convinced her to commission the Cowan Pottery near Cleveland instead, who then asked their young designer Viktor Schreckengost to come up with a work that reflected the dynamic nightlife of Manhattan. The result has become one of the most iconic symbols of the Art Deco movement in America.

Inspired by a Christmas Eve visit to the city, *Jazz* highlights the vibrant musical, theatrical, and social scenes swirling around the sightseer at night. The distinctive blue/black color scheme reinforces this nocturnal seduction and the cubist imagery punctuates each scene with rhythm and pulse. Even as the malaise of the Great Depression was settling in, everyone wanted to believe President Hoover's tonic that "prosperity was just around the corner." The *Jazz* bowl reflects this optimistic view, sounding in effect a nostalgic coda to the Jazz Age.

Somewhat forgotten in the shadow of the iconic *Jazz* bowl is another, arguably more important work by Schreckengost, called *Cocktails and Cigarettes*. Like its big sister, it was made at the Cowan Pottery, though in only one incarnation. *Cocktails and Cigarettes* is in the same color scheme, has the same basic shape, and treats a similar subject though not one specific to New York City. Exhibited at the 1931 May Show, an exhibition held each year by the museum to feature local artists, the bowl won

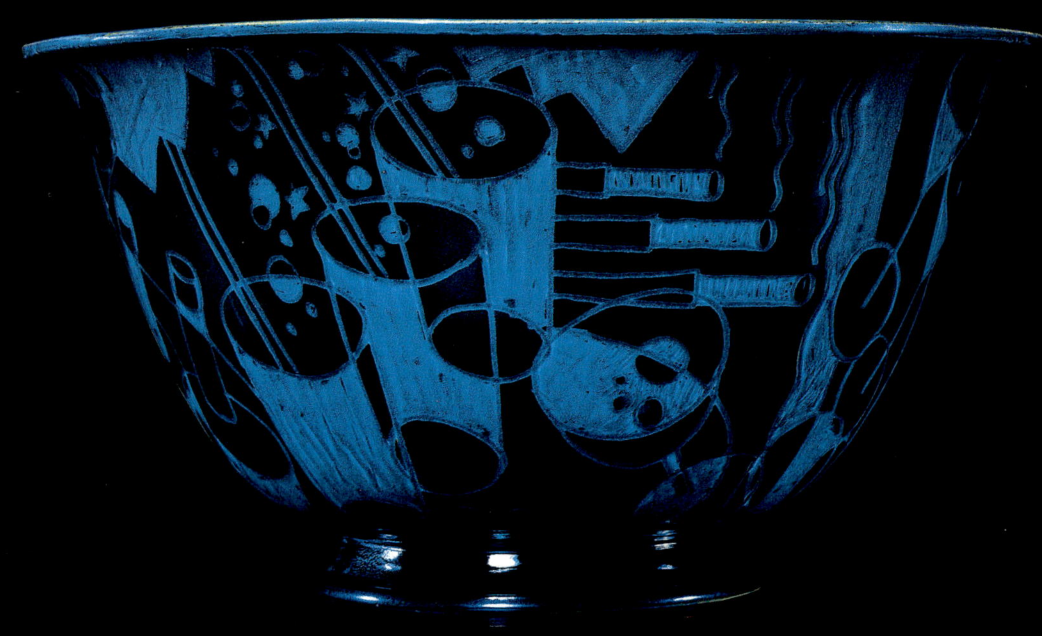

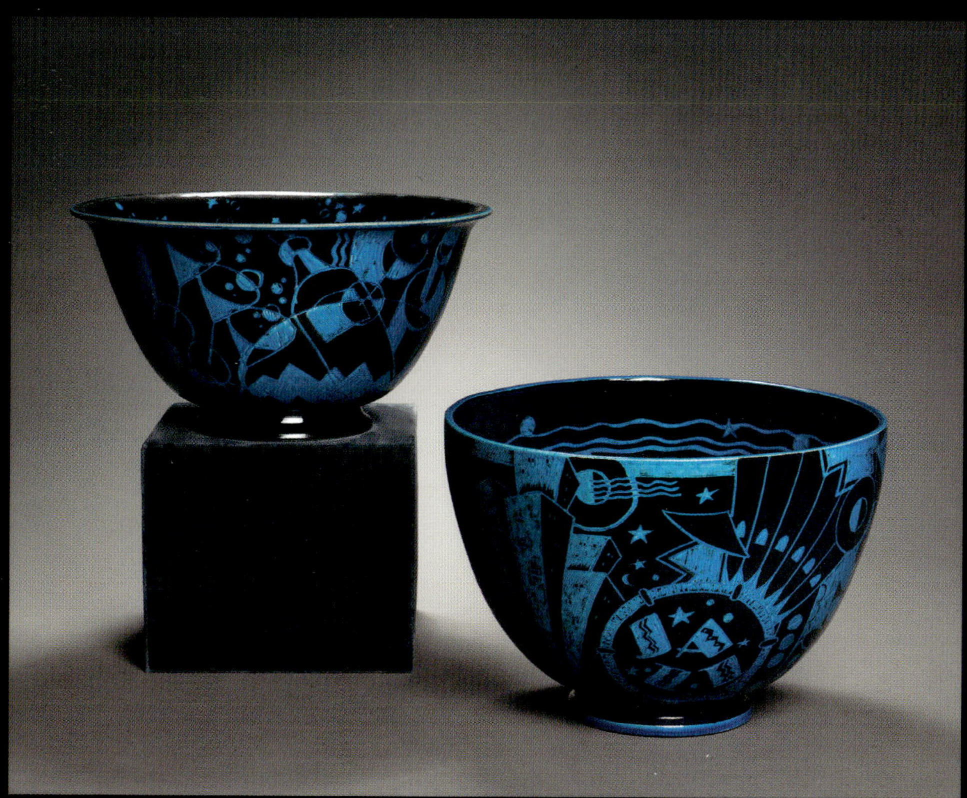

first prize in its category. In an ironic twist of fate, however, the vice-themed work caught the eye of Mrs. Sterling Mather, wife of a descendant of Cotton Mather, the famously chaste 17th-century Puritan moralist. Mrs. Mather insisted on a sum that was many times the asking price of $25 in order to provide Schreckengost with enough money to go to Europe to further his artistic career. In exchange, Schreckengost agreed not to duplicate the design. Like the *Jazz* bowl, *Cocktails and Cigarettes* challenges the impending gloom of the Depression, but in its irreverent celebration of vice, it looks back even more fervently than *Jazz* to the days before Prohibition. Both bowls became sad reminders of an era long gone and never really brought much financial success to the pottery, though Schreckengost continued to be recognized for his prescient designs.

ART © JOHN PAUL MILLER

Necklace 1953

JOHN PAUL MILLER (AMERICAN, 1918–2013)

At once an artist, teacher, and craftsman, John Paul Miller personified a lifetime of creative expression. His two greatest passions, music and art, seemingly converge in work that moves from poetic forms to intensely intricate compositions. In the post-World War II era of industrial modernism, some artists responded to the previous geometric styles of the 1930s by emphasizing biomorphic, or free-flowing, shapes and abstract compositions. His jewelry from this period recalls the expressive shapes of Alexander Calder's mobiles. Miller also introduced natural motifs in his work, including insects, in both realistic and fossilized form.

Miller's fascination with technique and process emerged in his groundbreaking rediscovery in the early 1950s of granulation, an ancient, yet forgotten, way of fusing tiny gold beads to a gold surface without solder. The fleeting creatures of earth, sea, and sky—snails, squids, crabs, moths, and flies—became his muse, inspiring a complicated palette of seductive enamels and textured forms. Historical reference and modern abstraction also infuse his designs, bringing together what he saw and what he imagined to form works that are seemingly full of curiosity and self-expression.

GOLD; H. 43.2 CM (17 IN.)

SILVER JUBILEE TREASURE FUND 1953.181

Multiple Spouted Bottle 1958

TOSHIKO TAKAEZU (AMERICAN, 1922–2011)

For well over 50 years, Toshiko Takaezu led a minor revolution in ceramic art. Her quiet shapes, with their bold decorative glazes, represent poetic studies in harnessing organic form. These ceramics have stood as totems for several generations of late 20th-century potters. Early works from the 1950s and 1960s took shape in the context of postwar biomorphic design, resulting in double, triple, sometimes multispouted "vessels" that challenge the notion of a functioning pot.

Toshiko continued this evolution in the decades that followed, first with nearly closed pots, leaving only a vestigial reminder of a functional past in the form of a tiny puckered opening. Later, she abandoned the spout altogether in her bulbous spheres, which recede to become vehicles for a mystical palette of glazes. Rising on the potter's wheel with the spirit of Nature and the alchemy of Life, Toshiko's work also reflects a disciplined approach to her quest. As she once stated, "when an artist produces a good piece, that work has mystery, an un-said quality; it is alive!"

STONEWARE; 32.5 X 38.1 CM (12-3/4 X 15 IN.)
GIFT OF THE WOMENS COUNCIL OF THE CLEVELAND MUSEUM OF ART IN HONOR OF WILLIAM MATHEWSON MILLIKEN 1958.282

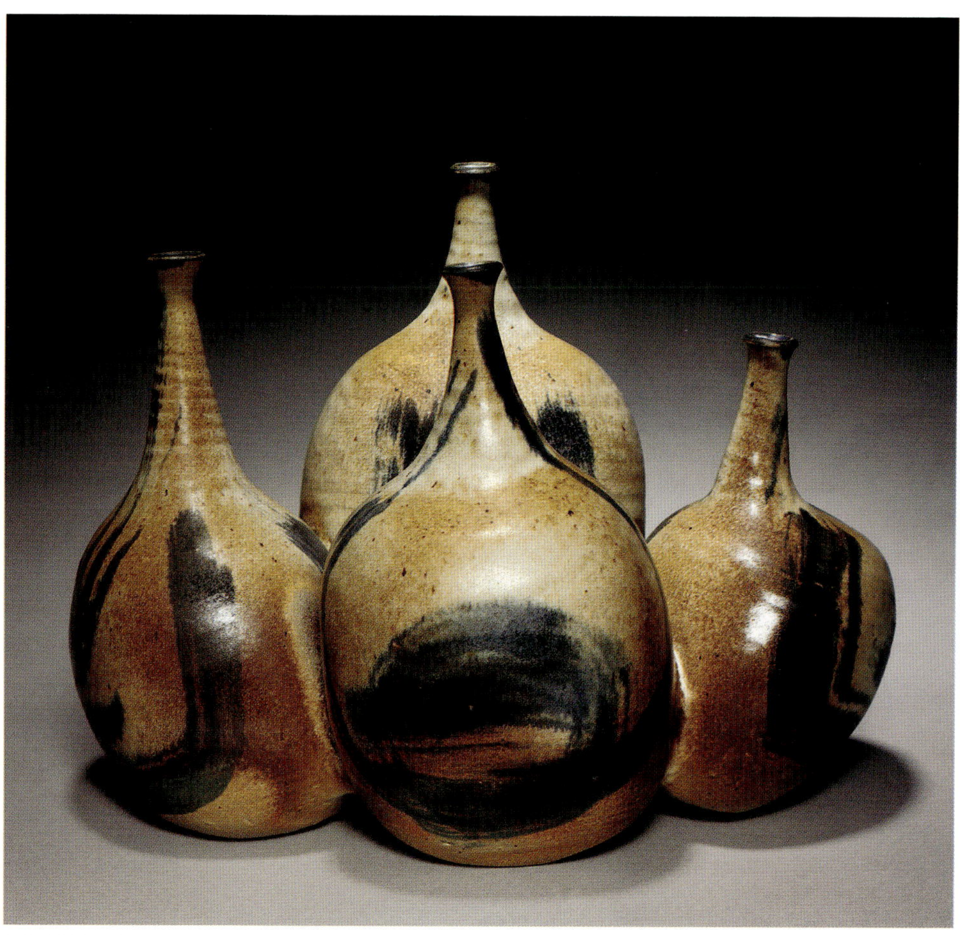

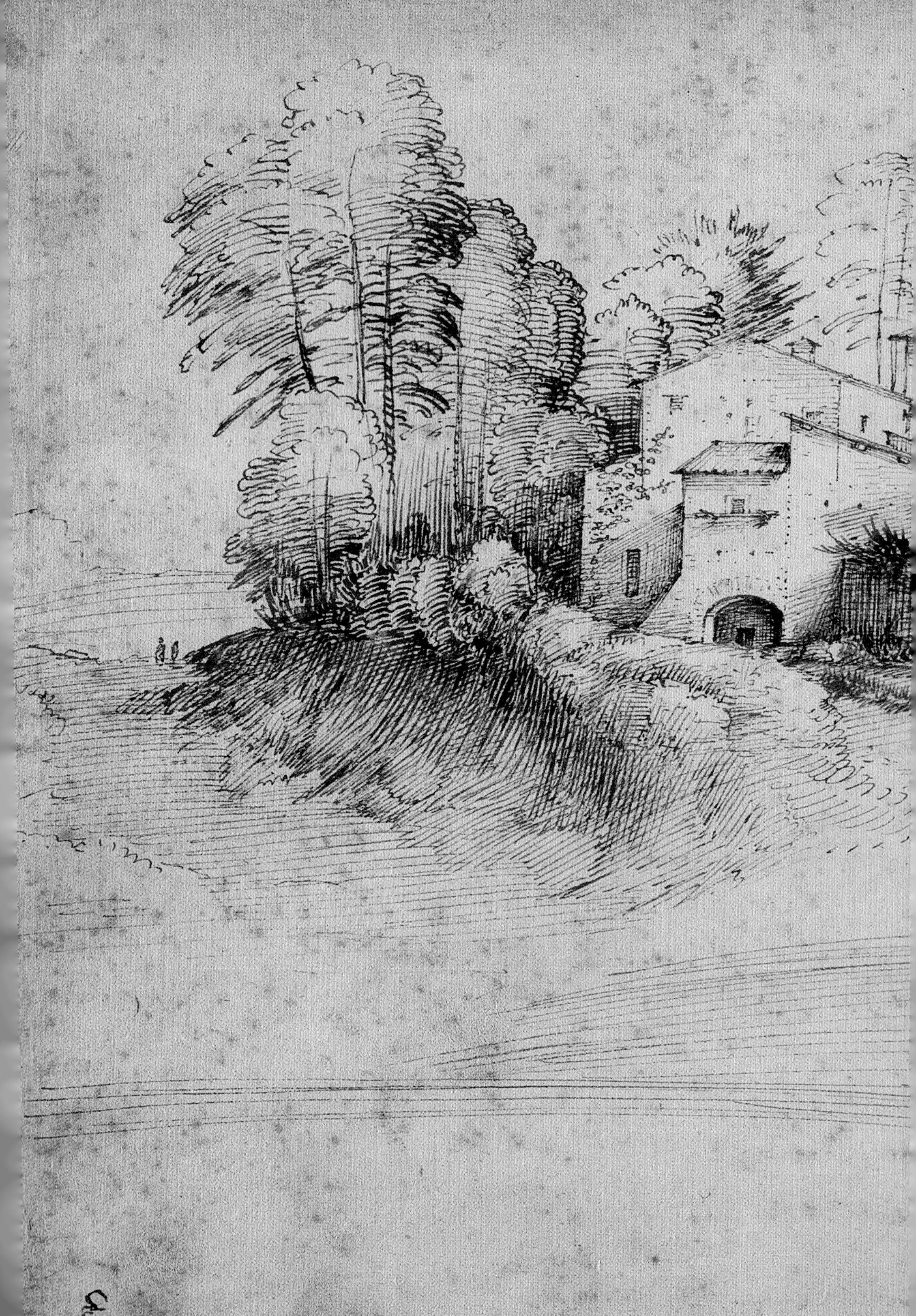

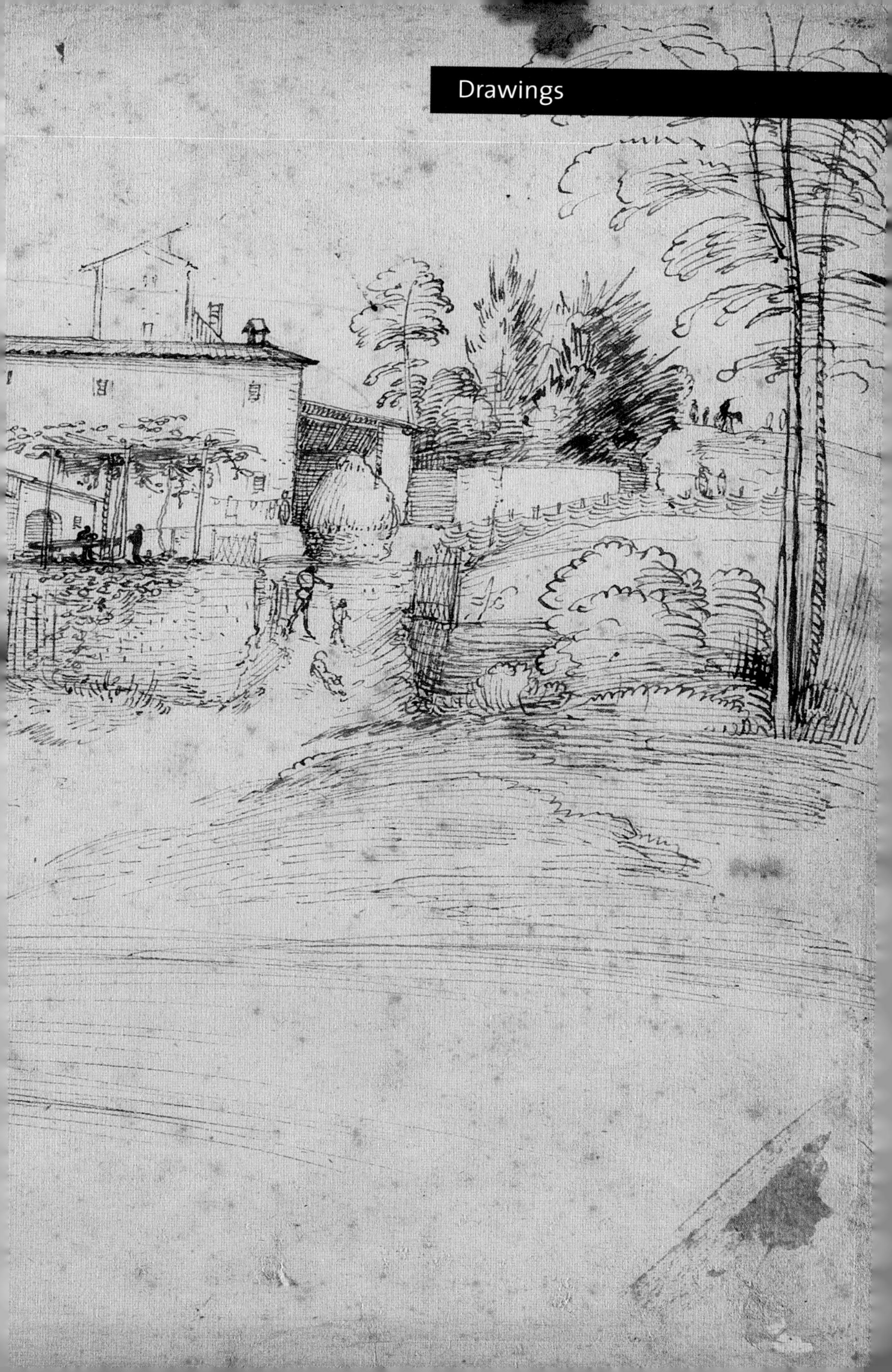

Drawings

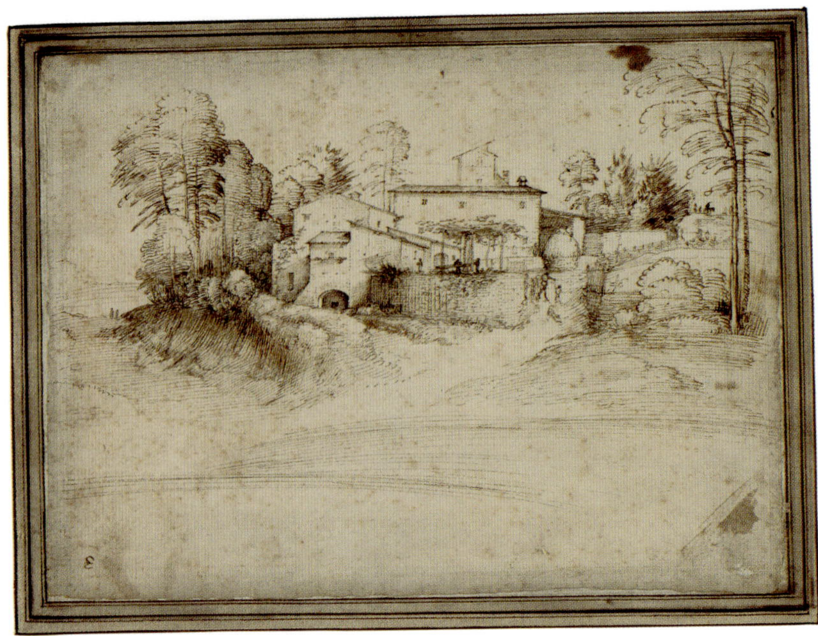

Farmhouse on the Slope of a Hill about 1508

BACCIO DELL PORTA, CALLED FRA BARTOLOMMEO (ITALIAN, 1472–1517)

One of the most influential artists of the Italian Renaissance, Fra Bartolommeo was a prolific draftsman. More than 1,000 drawings—compositional and figure studies—by his hand are known today. In 1957, a group of 41 sheets depicting landscapes appeared on the market, this drawing among them. The discovery was a dramatic one. They are among the first works of Western art dedicated completely to nature, landscapes for their own sake without suggestion of biblical or historical narrative. The rapidity and regularity of strokes used for the evergreen and deciduous trees and the sweeping lines in the foreground suggest that the landscape in *Farmhouse on the Slope of a Hill* was done directly from nature. However, the delicate shading and careful regularity with which the architecture was delineated indicate that the artist likely completed the drawing in the studio. Although the effect is one of immediacy and spontaneity, the composition is carefully balanced, the linear severity of the buildings softened by the freely drawn foliage. Among Fra Bartolommeo's known 41 landscapes, *Farmhouse on the Slope of a Hill* is the only one that can be connected with his painted oeuvre. The farmhouse in the drawing is echoed in the background of *God the Father with Sts. Mary Magdalene and Catherine* (Pinacoteca, Lucca) as well as *Holy Family with the Infant St. John the Baptist* (Rijksmuseum, Amsterdam). The other landscapes may have been drawn to stimulate the artist's imagination, or perhaps simply for the love of the natural world. The architecture in Fra Bartolommeo's landscapes was consistently humble—rural towns, convents, and farmhouses—providing the viewer with a rare glimpse into everyday life in 16th-century Italy.

PEN AND BROWN INK, ON CREAM LAID PAPER, PERIMETER MOUNTED TO CREAM LAID PAPER; 22.3 X 29.4 CM (8-3/4 X 11-9/16 IN.)

GIFT OF THE HANNA FUND; PURCHASE, DUDLEY P. ALLEN FUND; DELIA E. HOLDEN FUND; AND L. E. HOLDEN FUND 1957.498

Study for the Nude Youth over the Prophet Daniel (recto) and **Figure Studies for the Sistine Ceiling** (verso) 1510–11

MICHELANGELO BUONARROTI (ITALIAN, 1475–1564)

Michelangelo began painting the vast ceiling fresco in the Sistine Chapel in 1508, progressing from the entrance to the altar. Preparatory for one of the 20 athletic male nudes, known as *ignudi,* who act as supporting figures located at each corner of the Old Testament scenes painted down the center of the ceiling, this drawing relates to the ignudo above the prophet Daniel. Michelangelo worked out the positioning of the ignudi in red chalk drawings before painting each section of wet plaster. He likely began the study from a live model in the studio, but the degree of idealization in the figure's musculature suggests a divergence from the model. In realizing the details of the composition, the artist may have borrowed from the Belvedere torso or from one of his own wax or clay models. The energy and monumentality of the figure, whose body extends beyond the sheet, suggests the heroic athleticism of Michelangelo's sculpture. On the verso are several close studies of the foot and toes of the ignudo, as well as two studies of a head and shoulders that have not been linked to any figures on the ceiling.

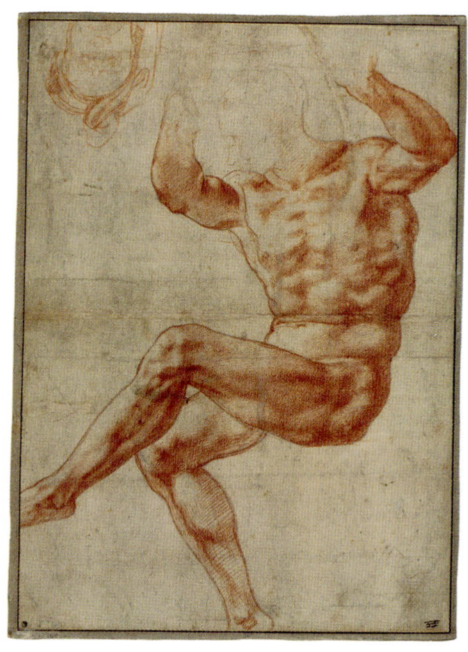

RECTO, RED CHALK AND BLACK CHALK ON BEIGE LAID PAPER; VERSO, RED CHALK HEIGHTENED WITH TRACES OF WHITE; 34.3 X 24.3 CM (13-1/4 X 9-1/4 IN.)

GIFT IN MEMORY OF HENRY G. DALTON BY HIS NEPHEWS GEORGE S. KENDRICK AND HARRY D. KENDRICK

1940.465.A–B

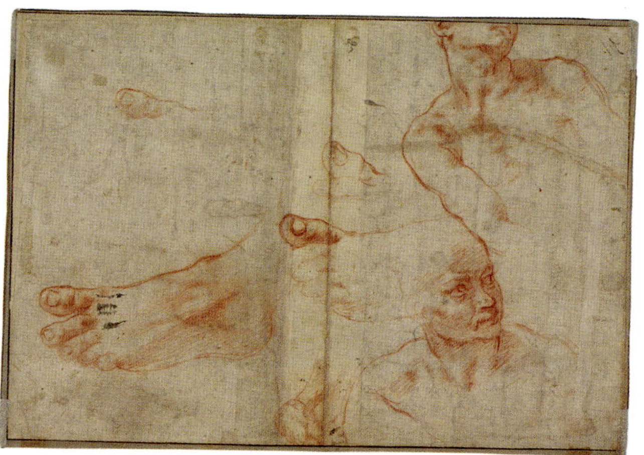

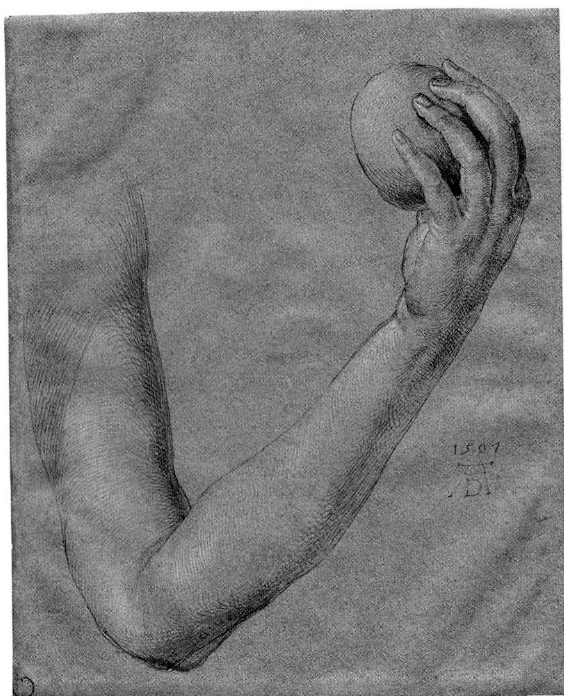

Arm of Eve 1507

ALBRECHT DÜRER (GERMAN, 1471–1528)

Arm of Eve is the only surviving preparatory drawing for Dürer's life-sized panels of Adam and Eve in the Museo del Prado, Madrid. With extraordinary economy of means—using only black and gray ink and limited wash and gouache for shading and heightening—Dürer suggested the grace and balance of the complete human form in this composition of a disembodied arm and hand. The delicacy with which Eve cradles the apple in her hand seems to suggest a mingling of interest and hesitation, indicative of a study for the action that would initiate the story of the Fall. The drawing concentrates on the details of the hand. Each of the long and slender fingers is carefully shaded; the pressure of the third and fourth fingers into the apple emphasizes tactility. The firm flesh of the figure's palm and the roundness of the curved fingers are echoed in the roundness of the fruit. Such a study of a hand in ideal proportions cannot help but suggest the hand of the artist, a self-referential nod to his own abilities.

POINT OF BRUSH AND GRAY AND BLACK WASH, BRUSH AND GRAY AND BLACK WASH, HEIGHTENED WITH WHITE GOUACHE, ON BLUE LAID PAPER; 34.4 X 26.7 CM (13-1/8 X 10-1/2 IN.)

ACCESSIONS RESERVE FUND 1965.470

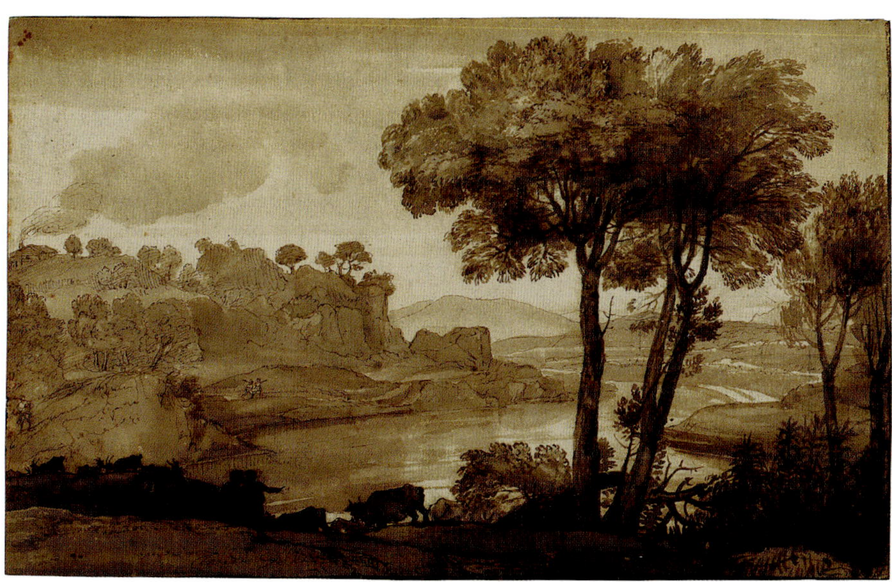

View of the Acqua Acetosa about 1645

CLAUDE GELLÉE, CALLED CLAUDE LORRAIN (FRENCH, 1604/5–1682)

This drawing represents a view of the famous Acqua Acetosa, a mineral spring that until the 19th century provided the favorite drinking water of Romans who believed in its healing powers. Although topographically accurate, this sheet is not a plein air study, but a vision of an imagined Arcadian world carefully rendered by Claude Gellée, one of the most important and original painters of the 17th century. In his youth, Claude left his birthplace in the Lorraine region of France for Italy, where he spent his career painting and drawing the Roman Campagna and the Neopolitan coastline. His sublimely beautiful pen and ink and wash drawings reveal a highly poetic response to the natural world and unparalleled sensitivity to light. The landscape throughout the Campagna, the Alban Hills, and along the Tiber is steeped in history. Even today, the classical ruins recall the legends of Roman antiquity so revered in the 17th century. This landscape of grand vistas, flickering light, and majestic trees fueled Claude's imagination. Here, with animated penwork and complex layers of wash, he described discrete planes of space leading the viewer from a shadowy foreground of trees and vegetation, to the middle distance of a curving river in full sunlight, and finally to distant hills and valleys. The drawing exemplifies Claude's vision of pastoral paradise in which mankind, the animal world, and nature are united in harmonious equilibrium.

PEN AND BROWN INK AND BRUSH AND BROWN AND GRAY WASH OVER GRAPHITE, FRAMING LINES IN BROWN INK, ON CREAM LAID PAPER; 26 X 40.5 CM (10-1/4 X 15-3/4 IN.)

GIFT OF MR. AND MRS. EDWARD B. GREENE 1928.15.A

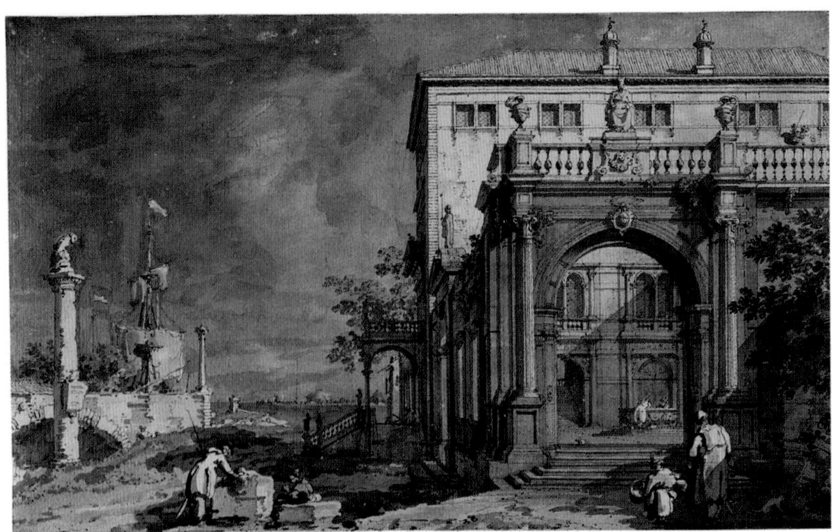

Capriccio: A Palace with a Courtyard by a Lagoon
about 1750–55
GIOVANNI ANTONIO CANAL, CALLED CANALETTO (ITALIAN, 1697–1768)

During the 18th century, Venice was a major destination for aristocrats visiting Europe's cultural sites on the Grand Tour. Travelers eagerly sought mementos of their travels; many procured paintings, drawings, and prints of this singularly picturesque Italian city. The period witnessed the rise in popularity of the *verdute* (view paintings), whose foremost practitioner was Canaletto. This drawing presents quintessential examples of the artist's *capricci*—architectural fantasies amalgamating buildings, archaeological remains, and other architectural elements into imaginary and often whimsical combinations. The palace here recalls several 16th-century Venetian buildings. The Corinthian columns on high plinths surmounted by a balustrade bring to mind the neo-Palladian portal to the Palazzo Tasca, but Canaletto accentuated its grandeur with the stairs leading up to the structure. The interior courtyard and well vaguely refer to those in the Palazzo Ducale. Canaletto made a radical departure from reality with his inclusion of the round building beyond the lagoon in the distance, reminiscent of the Pantheon in Rome. He devoted great care and skill to the combination of pen and ink to delineate the architectural framework and gray wash to provide atmosphere and shadows. The view is animated by the inclusion of peasants in the foreground going about their daily business and even more so by the effect of sunlight flickering over the city known as "La Serenissima" (The Most Serene).

PEN AND BROWN INK AND BRUSH AND GRAY WASH WITH BRUSH AND BLACK INK, OVER TRACES OF GRAPHITE, FRAMING LINES IN BROWN AND BLACK INK, ON CREAM LAID PAPER; 26.9 X 42.1 CM (10-5/8 X 16-5/8 IN.) PURCHASE FROM THE J. H. WADE FUND 1930.23

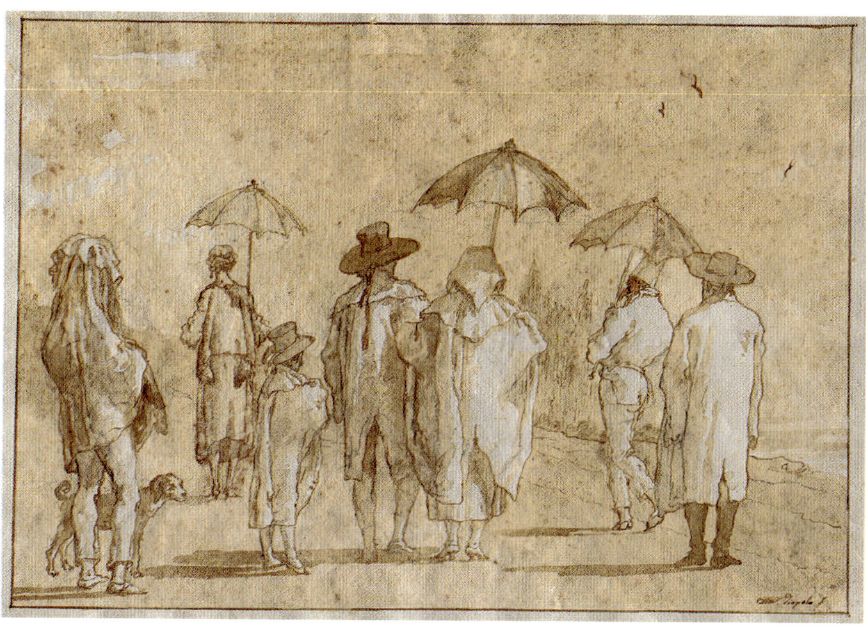

A Spring Shower about 1790s–1804

GIOVANNI DOMENICO (GIANDOMENICO) TIEPOLO (ITALIAN, 1727–1804)

Giovanni Domenico Tiepolo was the son of Giovanni Battista Tiepolo, the most renowned painter of 18th-century Italy, especially celebrated for his drawings and frescoes. Giandomenico inherited his father's studio and occupied a prominent place among Venetian painters. Although trained to be the chief assistant in the production of monumental fresco cycles and ceiling paintings, Giandomenico established his own artistic identity. Taking inspiration from the everyday, his drawings provided a panorama of 18th-century Venetian life. Among his most prized drawing series is *Divertimento per li Regazzi (Diversion for Children),* 104 drawings depicting the adventures of Punchinello, a character in the Italian Commedia dell'arte dating from the 17th century. Characterized by a hunched back, potbelly, long beaked nose, black mask, and tall cylindrical hat, Punchinello exemplified all that was clumsy, bawdy, and wicked. In the series, Giandomenico wove a tale of life, death, and regeneration, fully developing a character with a unique and complex persona. The drawings conjure a kaleidoscope of moods, ranging from the raucous, vulgar, and silly to the tender and tragic.

A more contemplative drawing than most in the series, *A Spring Shower* presents a walk in the rain. A frieze of seven figures, including two Punchinellos, is seen from behind, with each protected from the damp by an umbrella, hat, or coat. The Punchinello accompanied by a scruffy dog at the left has pulled a cloak over his head. A damp sky and clouds are indicated with pale brown wash whose puddles and rivulets accentuate the rain-soaked atmosphere. The spareness of the landscape and the anonymity of the figures imply loneliness and melancholy. No unnecessary additions detract from the composition; nothing disturbs the resonating silence.

PEN AND BROWN INK AND BRUSH AND BROWN WASH OVER BLACK CHALK, FRAMING LINES IN BROWN INK OVER GRAPHITE ON CREAM LAID PAPER; 35.5 X 47.1 CM (14 X 18-1/2 IN.)

PURCHASE FROM THE J. H. WADE FUND 1937.573

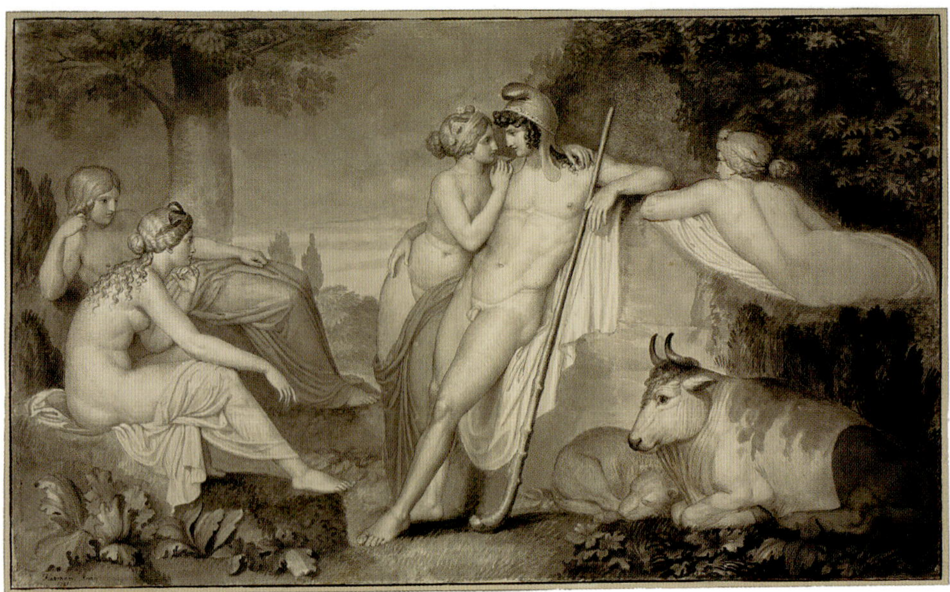

Paris and Oenone 1791

JOHN FLAXMAN (BRITISH, 1755–1826)

One of the key figures of Neoclassicism, Flaxman identified himself first and foremost as a sculptor, but his greatest fame and most lasting influence rest with his drawings. His spare designs illustrating the classical epics of Homer, Aeschylus, Dante, and Hesiod became the most celebrated work in his oeuvre, encapsulating his philosophy and spreading his stylized linearity widely. His study of Greek vase painting at the British Museum had a profound effect on his style and instilled a keen desire to work from the antique. Here, in a frieze-like arrangement, a group of female nudes surround a figure immediately recognizable as Paris with a Phrygian cap and staff. In this drawing, the figure embraced by Paris is thought to be Oenone, the daughter of the river-god Cebren. According to Quintus of Smyrna's fourth-century text *Posthomerica* (The Fall of Troy), while living in obscurity on Mount Ida the shepherd fell in love with the nymph Oenone, and together they had a son. When called upon by Zeus to judge the beauty of the goddesses Hera, Athena, and Aphrodite, Paris forsook Oenone for the love of the most beautiful of all women, Helen of Sparta, promised to him by Aphrodite, and thus initiated the Trojan War. The subject of this sheet precedes the Judgment of Paris, imagining an amorous Paris and Oenone with the nymph's handmaidens in attendance in a pastoral paradise. The singular purity, elegance of line, delicacy of washes, and degree of detail render the drawing extraordinary.

GRAY INK WASH WITH PALE BLACK-GRAY INK LINE WITH GRAPHITE AND BROWN INK ON CREAM WOVE PAPER; 30.3 X 48.8 CM (12 X 19-1/4 IN.)

PURCHASE FROM THE J. H. WADE FUND 2008.35

Prostitute Soliciting a Fat, Ugly Man (recto) and **Young Woman Wringing Her Hands over a Naked Man Lying in a Thicket** (verso) 1796–97

FRANCISCO DE GOYA (SPANISH, 1746–1828)

Among the great figures of the pictorial arts in the West, Goya is one of the few whose body of work as a graphic artist is even more important than his paintings. Goya's sets of prints, beginning with *Los Caprichos* ("Caprices") in 1799, ushered in a new aesthetic and revolutionized the range of subject matter and expressive possibilities not just of printmaking, but of European art. This double-sided sheet comes from an album of 94 drawings that the artist seems to have worked on simultaneously with *Los Caprichos*. An exponent of the Enlightenment, Goya used the sketchbook to satirize relationships between men and women, and particularly his observations of the Duchess of Alba at her estate in Sanlúcar de Barrameda. On the recto side of this drawing, the vulgar encounter between a coquette and a pot-bellied lecher reflects the bluntness of the artist's social criticism. The verso illustrates the decisive moment in the life of Saint Margaret of Cortona (1247–1297). Following a lovers' rendezvous, Margaret's paramour was murdered. His faithful dog leads her to its master, prompting her conversion and entrance into a Franciscan convent.

BRUSH AND BLACK AND GRAY WASH ON CREAM LAID PAPER (RECTO AND VERSO); 23.5 X 14.5 CM (9-1/4 X 5-3/4 IN.)

JOHN L. SEVERANCE FUND 1995.15.A–B

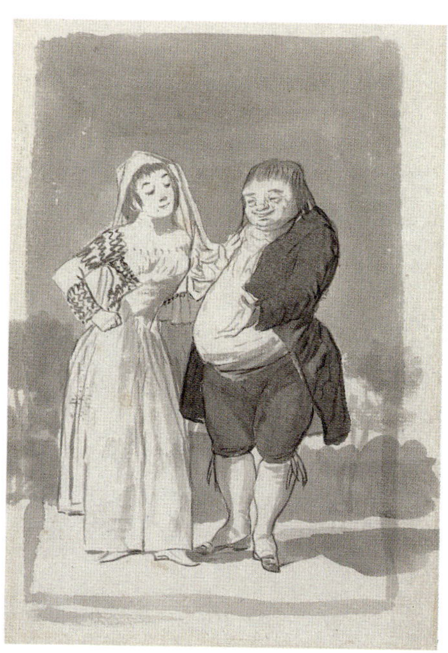

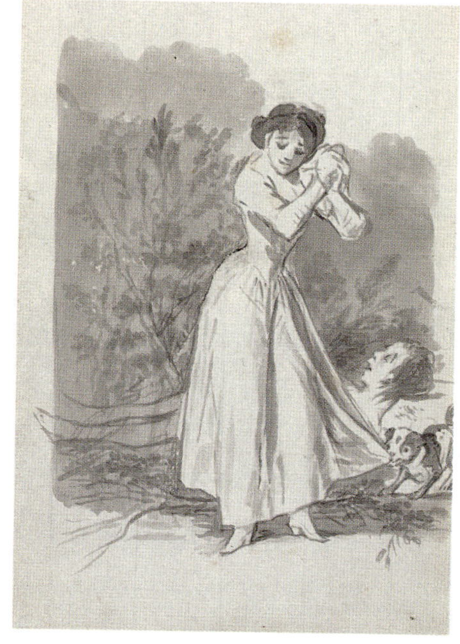

British Watercolors

A luminous group of watercolors is at the heart of the museum's collection of British drawings. The availability of commercially made watercolor from around 1775, combined with its easy portability, made it the ideal medium for plein air painting. Initially, watercolor was used for practical purposes such as surveying, cartography, and architectural drawing. The medium's character shifted, however, as the Grand Tour became popular among the British aristocracy at the end of the 18th century. Watercolors depicting the classical ruins of Greece and Rome and picturesque views of the Italian campagna were brought back to England, exponentially expanding the collecting market. Grand Tour watercolors in the collection include examples as varied as Thomas Hartley Cromek's meticulously observed *The Arch of Titus and the Coliseum, Rome* and J. M. W. Turner's diaphanous view of the Swiss Alps, *Flüelen, from the Lake of Lucerne*. The formation of exhibiting societies—the Society of Painters in Water Colours (1804) and its rival, the Associated Artists in Water Colours (1808)—provided artists with opportunities to sell their work and establish critical reputations. William Callow's *The Temple of Vesta and the Falls at Tivoli*, displayed in London in 1859, exemplifies the monumental, highly finished exhibition watercolor celebrated in mid 19th-century England and avidly collected by the emerging middle class.

A desire to transport the viewer fueled the content of many watercolor landscapes, whether by way of exotic travel, or more subtly via a spiritual connection to the English countryside. The pre-eminent Victorian critic John Ruskin encouraged young artists to "go to Nature in all singleness of heart and walk with her laboriously and trustingly." His study *Budding Sycamore*

The Arch of Titus and the Coliseum, Rome, 1846. Thomas Hartley Cromek (British, 1809–1873). Watercolor with black ink and graphite underdrawing; 52.4 x 36 cm (20 x 14 in.). Gift of the Reverend and Mrs. Danila Pascu 1975.149

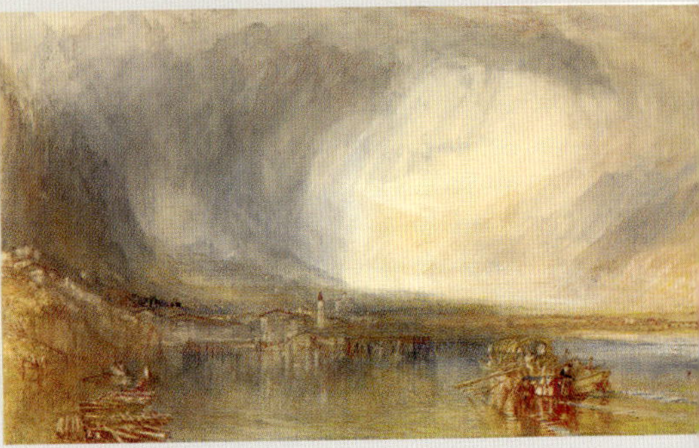

Flüelen, from the Lake of Lucerne, 1845. Joseph Mallord William Turner (British, 1775–1851). Watercolor with gouache and scratch-away; 29.2 x 47.9 cm (11-1/2 x 18-7/8 in.). Mr. and Mrs. William H. Marlatt Fund 1954.129

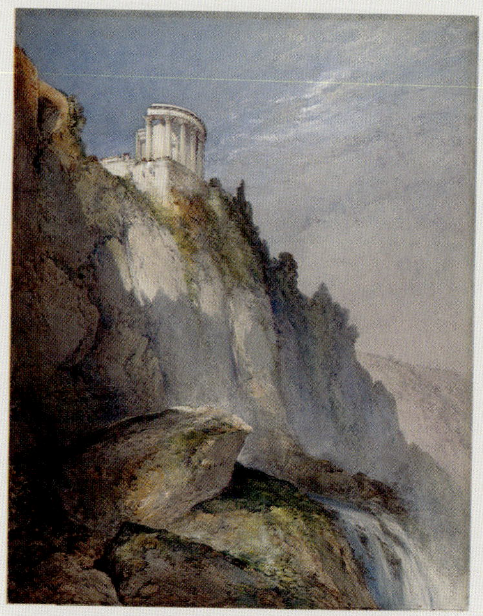

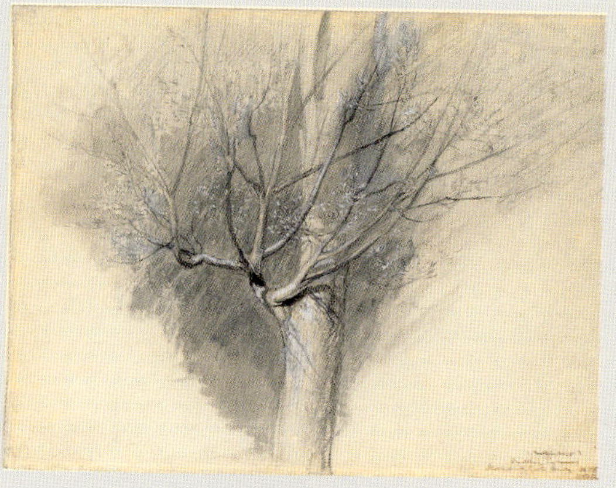

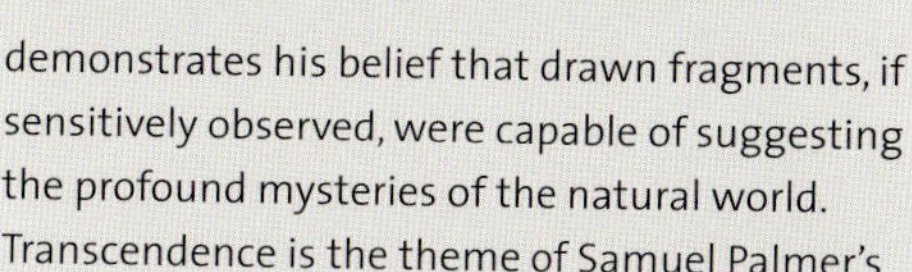

demonstrates his belief that drawn fragments, if sensitively observed, were capable of suggesting the profound mysteries of the natural world. Transcendence is the theme of Samuel Palmer's meticulously observed pastoral landscape of the hills of Surrey. The spectacularly colorful sunset in *The Golden Hour* suggests an elegy not only to a passing day, but to the brevity of life itself.

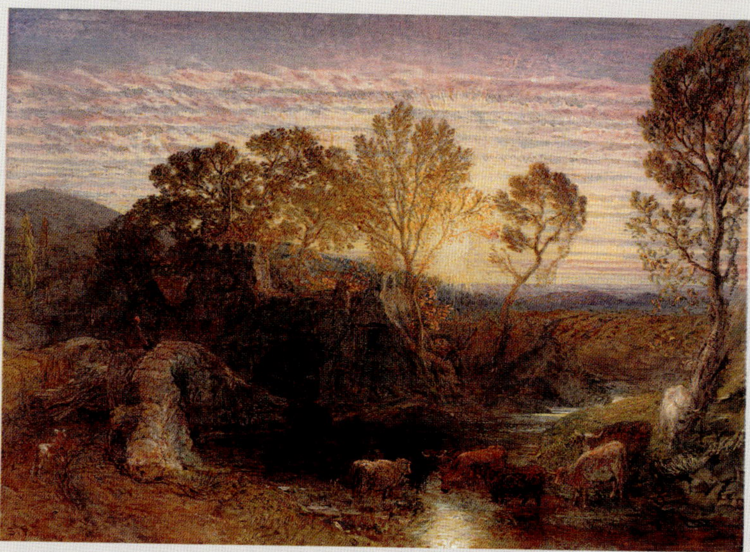

The Temple of Vesta and the Falls at Tivoli, 1859. William Callow (British, 1812–1908). Watercolor with gouache and graphite underdrawing; 75.1 x 57.8 cm (29-1/2 x 22-3/4 in.). Sundry Purchase Fund 2011.4

Budding Sycamore, about 1876. John Ruskin (British, 1819–1900). Black and gray wash, gouache, and graphite; 34.8 x 44.8 cm (13-3/4 x 17-5/8 in.). Andrew R. and Martha Holden Jennings Fund 1989.14

The Golden Hour, 1865. Samuel Palmer (British, 1805–1881). Watercolor and gouache with graphite and scraping; 25.6 x 35.4 cm (10 x 14 in.). The Severance and Greta Millikin Purchase Fund 2009.3

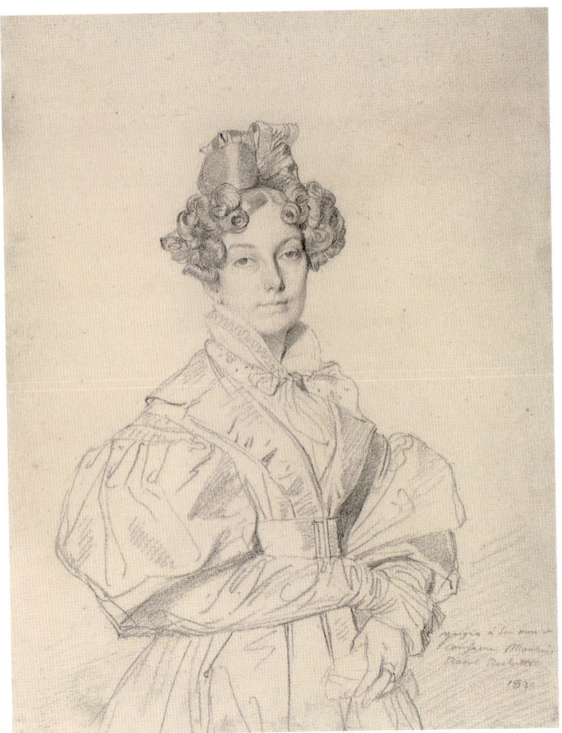

Madame Désiré Raoul-Rochette 1830

JEAN-AUGUSTE-DOMINIQUE INGRES (FRENCH, 1780–1867)

The recipient of the prestigious Prix de Rome, the young Ingres went to Italy in 1806 and remained for 18 years. While working to establish a reputation as a history painter, he supported himself by making portraits in graphite for tourists and French officials during Napoleon's rule. He resented the distraction from what he believed was his true vocation as a painter in oil of noble themes and subjects from sacred and classical literature. As a portrait draftsman, however, he was prolific, producing hundreds of portraits on paper.

After his return to Paris, Ingres achieved public success at the Salon and began to receive a steady stream of commissions. Portrait drawings were no longer a necessary source of income, but he continued to make them as gifts for friends. This drawing was made for the husband of the sitter, to whom the work is dedicated in the lower right. The wife of Désiré Raoul-Rochette, a well-known archaeologist, Antoinette-Claude Houdon (known as Claudine) was the youngest daughter of Jean-Antoine Houdon, one of the most important French sculptors of the 18th century. As was typical of Ingres, the face and head are fully elaborated, the curls in her intricate coiffure described in careful detail. Always attentive to fashion, he showed the sitter in day-wear, dressed in a redingote (a lightweight coat open down the front) and a dress with long gigot, or leg-of-mutton sleeves, stylishly full and loose at the upper arm and fitted at the lower arm and wrist.

GRAPHITE ON BEIGE WOVE PAPER; 32.1 X 24 CM (12-5/8 X 9-1/2 IN.)

PURCHASE FROM THE J. H. WADE FUND 1927.437

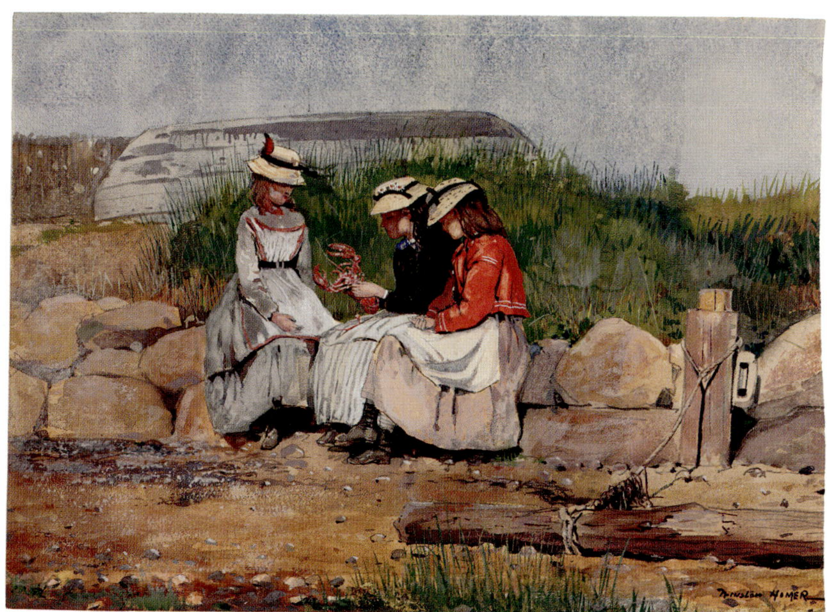

A Fisherman's Daughter 1873

WINSLOW HOMER (AMERICAN, 1836–1910)

American painter Winslow Homer created some of the most luminous and influential watercolors in the history of the medium. *A Fisherman's Daughter,* painted in Gloucester, is among a group of works that represent his first sustained use of the medium. On summer trips throughout the 1870s, Homer made a practice of exploring a single theme and locale exclusively in watercolor, which evolved into an important aspect of his artistic production alongside oil painting. There were various advantages to working in watercolor. Portable and quick drying, the medium is ideally suited to working outdoors, and he used it to capture the effects of summer light to great effect. Finished works of art made for sale could be executed quickly, providing a new source of income and broadening the appeal of his art to a wider range of collectors.

Gloucester was both the nation's busiest seaport and an increasingly popular summer resort. Rather than painting the most obvious subject of interest—the fishing fleet—Homer dedicated his early watercolors to the activities of local children playing around the docks, shipyards, and shoreline. The life of the fishermen was perilous; they often spent weeks away from home and could be lost at sea. Waiting was a central part of life for Gloucester families. In this watercolor, three girls sit on the shore of a sunlit beach and play with a lobster. There is a solemn quietude to their activity. One figure's hands are folded and all eyes are downcast and shaded by straw hats. An overturned boat on the dunes behind them suggests the ominous form of a coffin.

WATERCOLOR AND GOUACHE OVER GRAPHITE ON CREAM WOVE PAPER; 24.2 X 32.9 CM (9-1/2 X 13 IN.)

PURCHASE FROM THE J. H. WADE FUND 1943.660

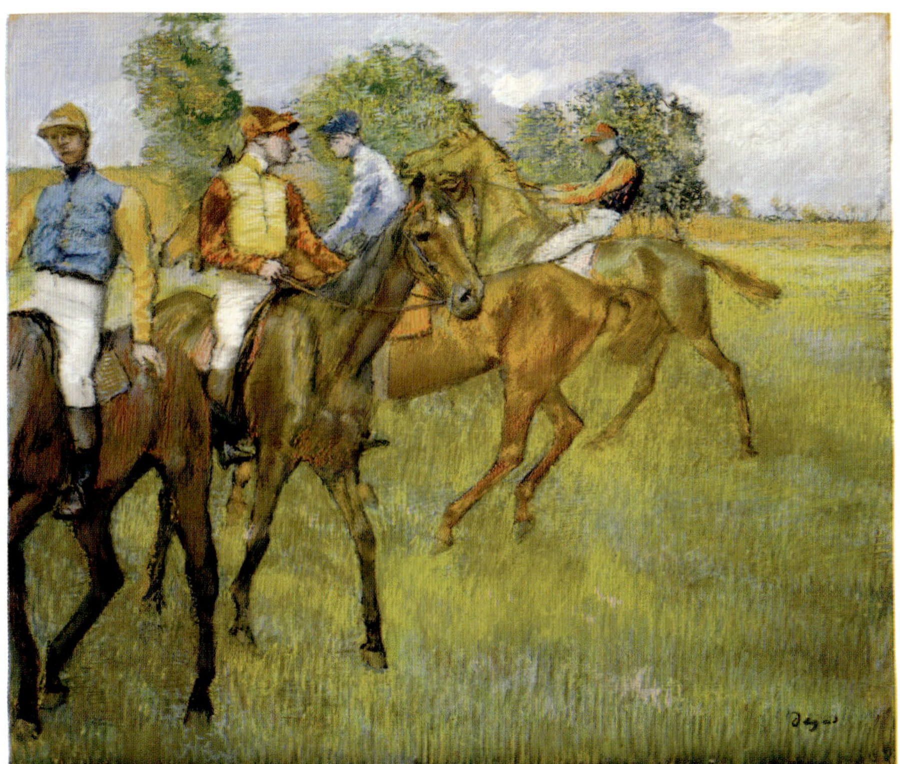

Before the Race about 1887–89

EDGAR DEGAS (FRENCH 1834–1917)

Influenced by the British interest in horse racing, which had flourished since the mid 18th century, the French developed a passion for the races about a century later. The growing number of tracks and races combined with relatively modest entrance fees and the promise of gambling attracted large crowds of spectators of all classes. While some came to enjoy the races themselves, many came to take in the spectacle of modern life.

The racetrack became a lifelong preoccupation for Edgar Degas. Like his attachments to the theater and the ballet, his enduring fascination with the races revealed his interest in addressing moments of reflection or anticipation in the midst of public, urban life. His racecourse themes display a remarkable lack of descriptive reportage; Degas seldom depicted the race itself and never the finish line. He did not commemorate a classic race or an illustrious winner. Rather, he focused on moments of rest or transition, such as the tense moments before a start, with jockeys and horses in suspended motion and often haphazardly dispersed across the canvas or page.

Degas rendered the horse and rider from about 1860 to 1900 in paintings, drawings, pastels, and sculpture. During the 1880s, he increasingly used pastel for his pictures of the track. Aside from the advantage of being able to work more rapidly and directly with sticks of pastel rather than with oil paint, the medium appealed to him for the intensity of the colors available. In *Before the Race*, the cool tones of the new green grass and the trees contrast with the shimmering coats of the horses and the vivid colors of the jockeys' silks in blue, orange, and shades of gold. With the radical cropping of the horses' bodies and the abstraction of the jockeys' faces, Degas negated any trace of sentimentality.

PASTEL ON TRACING PAPER MOUNTED TO CARDBOARD; 57.5 X 65.4 CM (22-5/8 X 25-3/4 IN.)

BEQUEST OF LEONARD C. HANNA JR. 1958.27

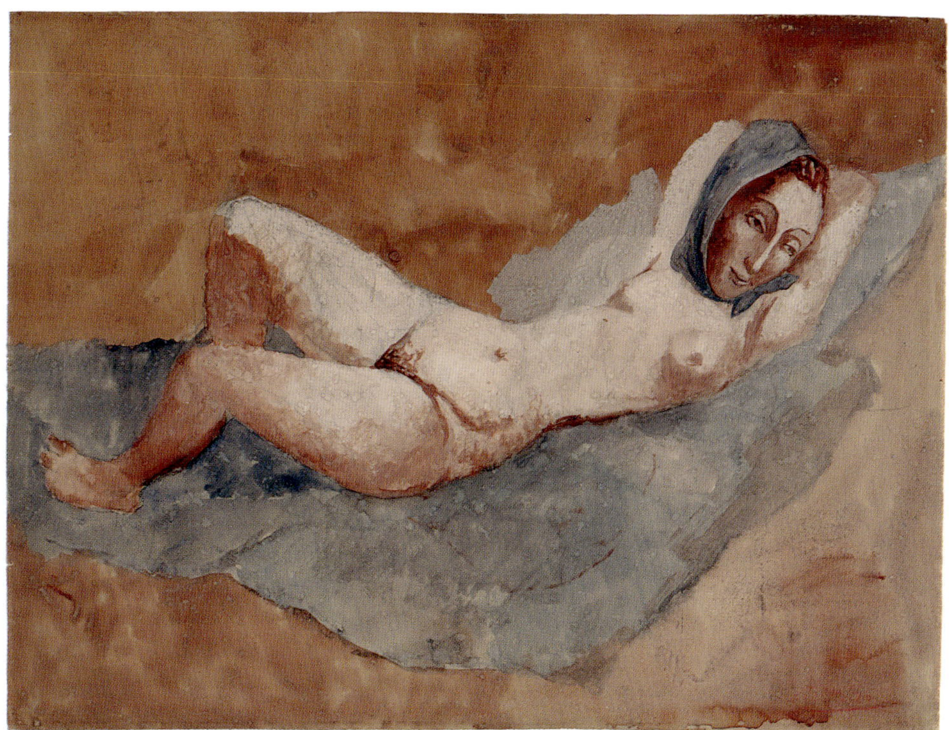

Reclining Nude (Fernande) 1906

PABLO PICASSO (SPANISH, 1881–1973)

Reclining Nude (Fernande) was painted in Gósol, a remote village in the Spanish Pyrenees where Picasso spent the summer of 1906 with his lover Fernande Olivier. Her idealized face appeared in nearly 30 drawings and paintings made that summer. In this drawing, Picasso combined the traditional with the radical. He depicted Fernande in one of the most standard poses in Western art, that of an odalisque offering her body to an unseen viewer. But he rejected classical beauty by rendering her form in an experimental style that used formal distortions and deliberate discordances. Fernande's head is wrapped in a blue regional peasant scarf, alluding to their contemporary surroundings, while her almond eyes and mask-like features were influenced by the Madonna of Gósol, a 12th-century Catalan sculpture of painted wood that Picasso encountered on their trip. The proportions of her body subvert expectation; a long slender torso appears ill-matched with a heavy lower body and short legs. Her covered head accentuates and eroticizes her nudity. Hardly modeled, her flat form floats on a swath of blue framed by a glowing, golden-orange plane, an undefined space that further disorients the viewer.

WATERCOLOR AND GOUACHE, WITH GRAPHITE AND POSSIBLY CHARCOAL ON BEIGE MODERN LAID PAPER; 47.3 X 61.3 CM (18-5/8 X 24-1/8 IN.)

GIFT OF MR. AND MRS. MICHAEL STRAIGHT 1954.865

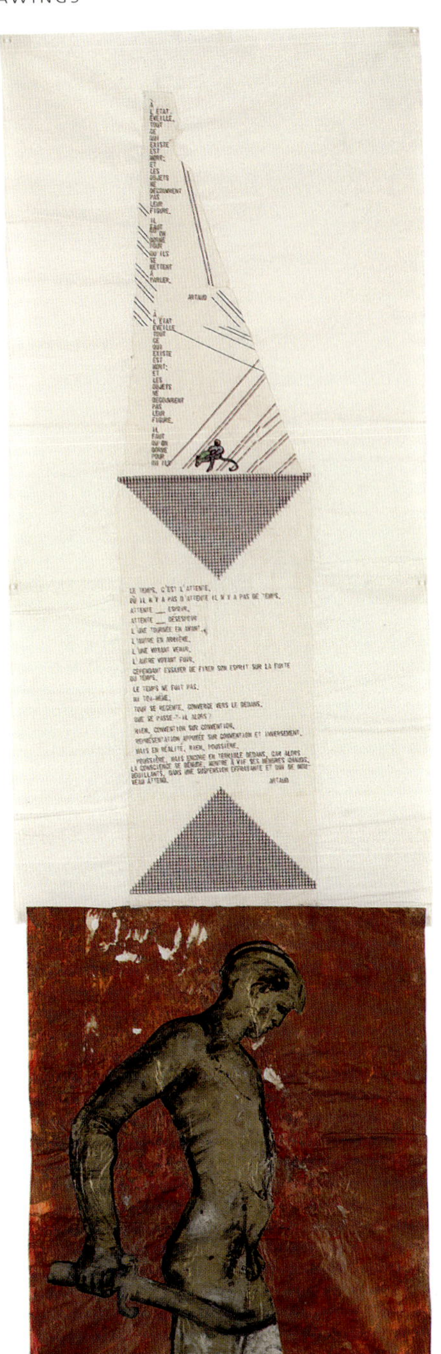

Codex Artaud XXI 1972

NANCY SPERO (AMERICAN, B. 1926)

This drawing is from Nancy Spero's most important body of work, the *Codex Artaud*. The drawings unite texts by Antoine Artaud, a revolutionary figure of the literary avant-garde of the early 20th century, with Spero's highly personal, feminist imagery. Spero found a reflection of her own state of mind and the sense of alienation she experienced as an American woman artist in the poetry of Artaud and adopted his highly sexualized, often violent language intended to shock his audience into confronting the base elements of life.

The *Codex Artaud* comprises 34 scrolls composed of sheets pasted end to end. In its debut exhibition, it was tacked directly on the walls of the first women's cooperative gallery in New York City, known as Artists in Residence. This drawing presents an extract from one of Artaud's poems arranged in a pristine array of typed capital letters. Spero's graphic additions include two converging cross-hatched triangles, a tiny woman riding a rat, and a heroic male nude holding a sword. The male figure, which occupies the bottom half of the sheet, references Benvenuto Cellini's sculpture *Perseus Beheading Medusa* (1545–54), a quintessential Renaissance subject concerned with the silencing of a powerful woman. By combining specifically female pictorial language with the writings of a poet considered an outcast and a madman, Spero created a body of work that was to inspire future generations of feminist artists.

CUT AND PASTED PAPERS, PRINTED TEXT, WATERCOLOR, METALLIC PAINTS, PEN, AND STAMPED INK ON LAID AND WOVE WHITE PAPERS; 173.4 X 52.6 CM (68-3/8 X 20-3/4 IN.)

SEVERANCE AND GRETA MILLIKIN PURCHASE FUND 2009.270

Ten Numbers: Figure 5 1960

JASPER JOHNS (AMERICAN, B. 1930)

Jasper Johns emerged as a major figure in postwar art with a landmark show at the Leo Castelli gallery in New York in 1958. Over the next decade, he established his reputation with a type of imagery that became iconic for the 20th century: flags, targets, numbers, and alphabets depicted in a variety of techniques and media, including paintings, drawings, and prints. Works of this type by Johns have had a profound impact on subsequent art because they address basic questions about perception and the nature of representation itself. In *Ten Numbers,* Johns developed the forms from commercial stencils, as he does for all of his number and alphabet imagery. The use of such "found" shapes—ones that are predetermined and widely recognizable—are meant to challenge the way the viewer looks at a type of sign normally so common as to be banal.

Ten Numbers is one work in ten parts, with the numerals "0" through "9" each represented on a separate sheet of paper. Using a soft charcoal stick as a basis, Johns heavily worked this medium with brushes, a stump (a tight roll of cloth or leather), and his own hands, developing a rich surface. His aim seems to have been to index, with each number, the different ways he could make marks using charcoal.

CHARCOAL AND GRAPHITE PENCIL ON CREAM WOVE PAPER; 34 X 27.6 CM (13-3/8 X 10-7/8 IN.)
JOHN L. SEVERANCE FUND 2001.10.F

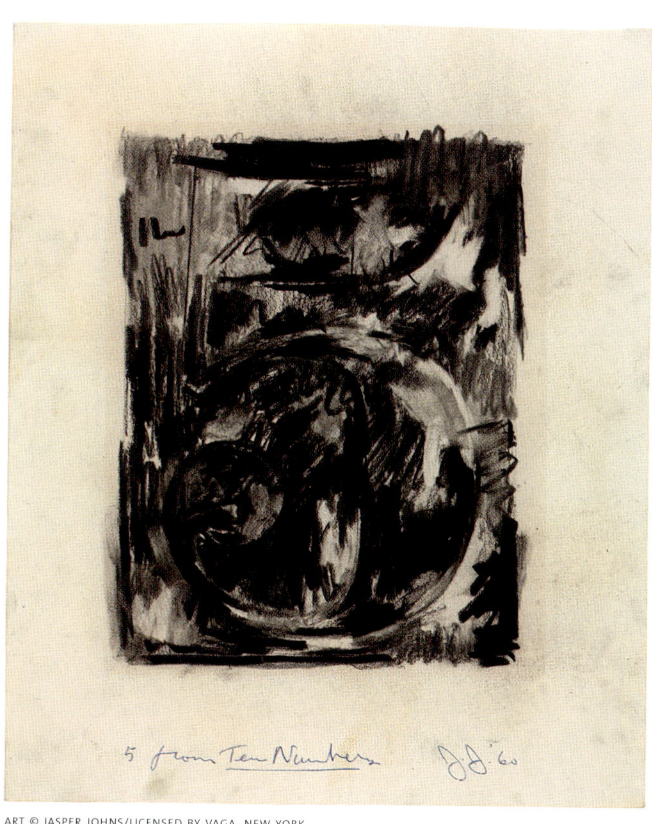

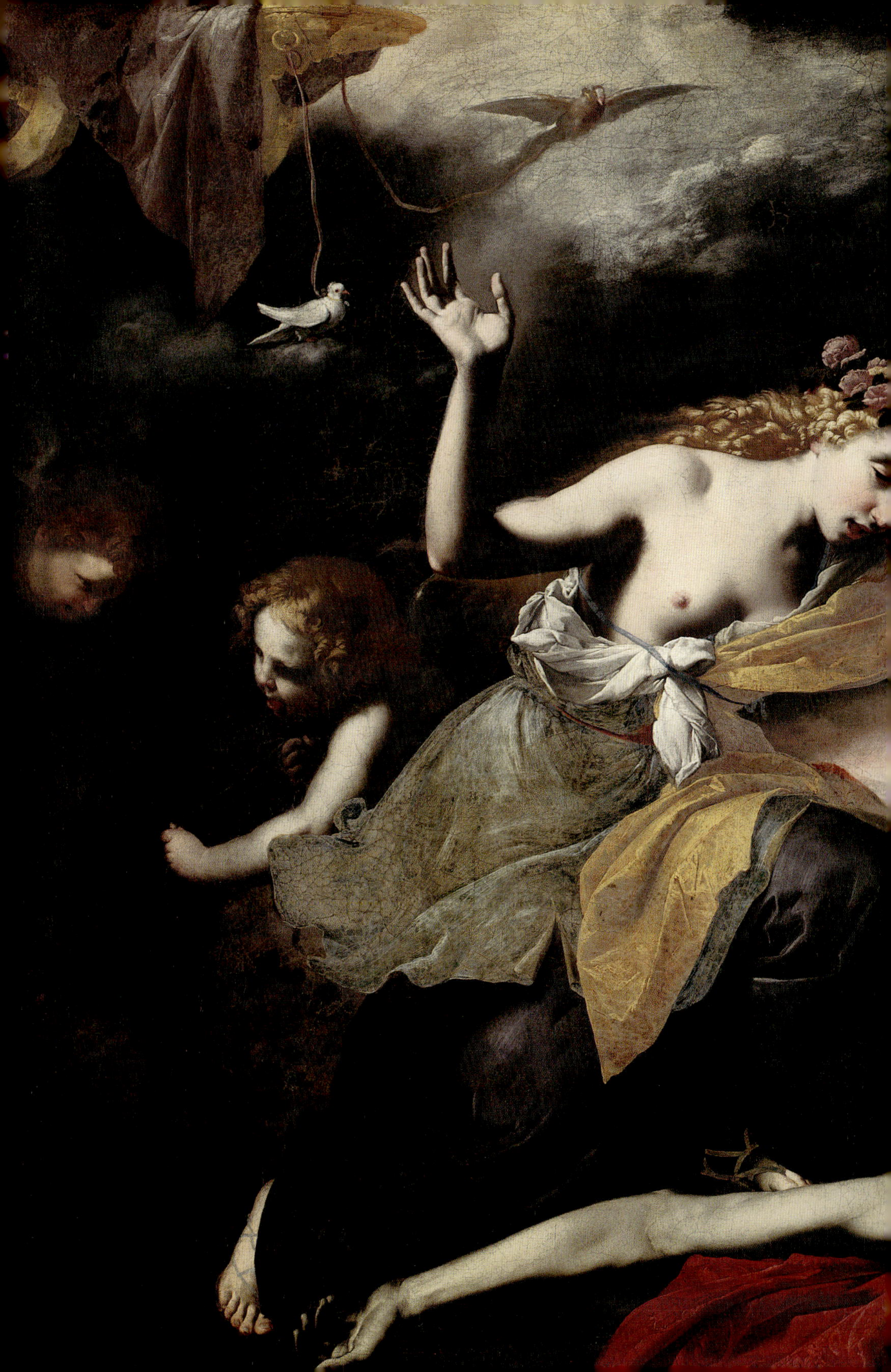

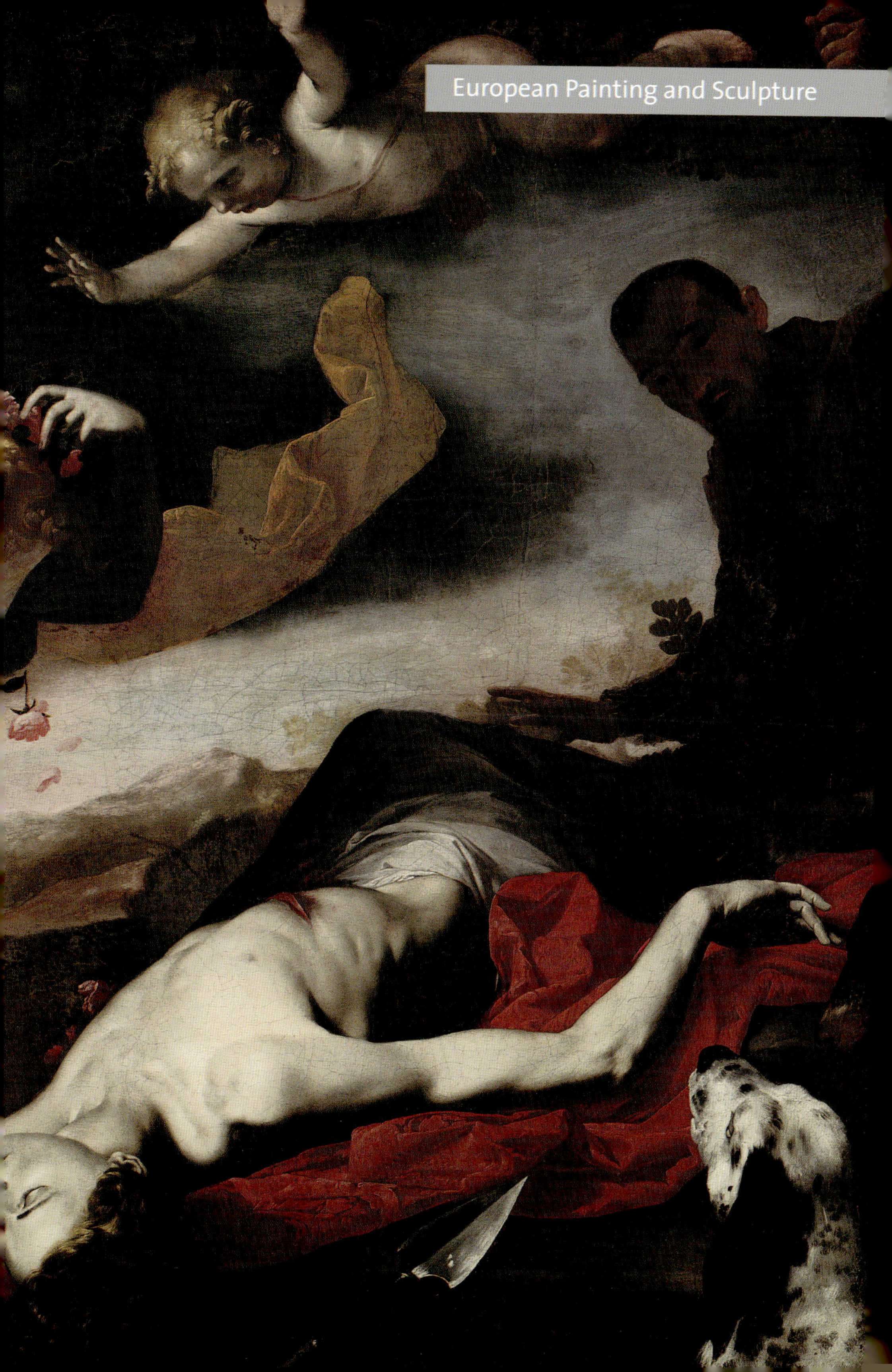

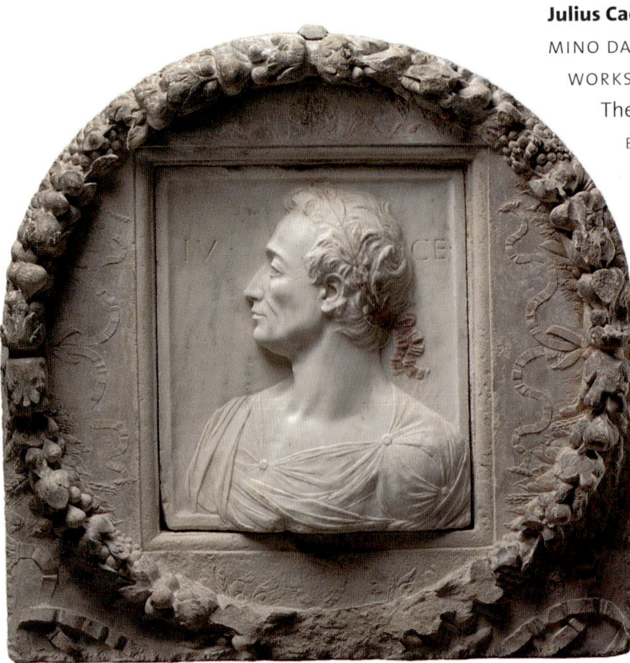

Julius Caesar about 1455–60
MINO DA FIESOLE (ITALIAN, 1429–1484) AND WORKSHOP

The Roman emperor Julius Caesar (100–44 BC) appears as a political rather than military leader, worn by the burdens of office, with carefully described signs of aging. Mino probably used ancient coins as his starting point. However, the complex carving, the clinging drapery, and the psychological intensity all characterize the inventiveness Renaissance artists brought to classical subject matter. Caesar offered elite men an important model for leadership, masculinity, and composure.

MARBLE WITH TRACES OF GILDING AND LIMESTONE WITH TRACES OF PAINT; 83 X 84 X 25 CM (32-5/8 X 33-1/8 X 9-7/8 IN.)
JOHN L. SEVERANCE FUND 2009.271

Crucified Christ about 1500
SEVERO DA RAVENNA (ITALIAN, ACTIVE ABOUT 1496–ABOUT 1543)

This sculpture may have been used for private devotion, and the holes in the hands and feet indicate that it was once mounted on a cross. But the highly finished surface, including the back, suggests that it belonged to a refined collector. Small bronzes like this one were often held to admire details such as the strands of hair streaming onto Christ's neck and shoulders, the prominent veins in his forearms and feet, and the intricate knot of patterned cloth at his side.

BRONZE; 28.6 X 23.5 X 5.5 CM (11-1/4 X 9-1/4 X 2-1/8 IN.)
JOHN L. SEVERANCE FUND 1982.127

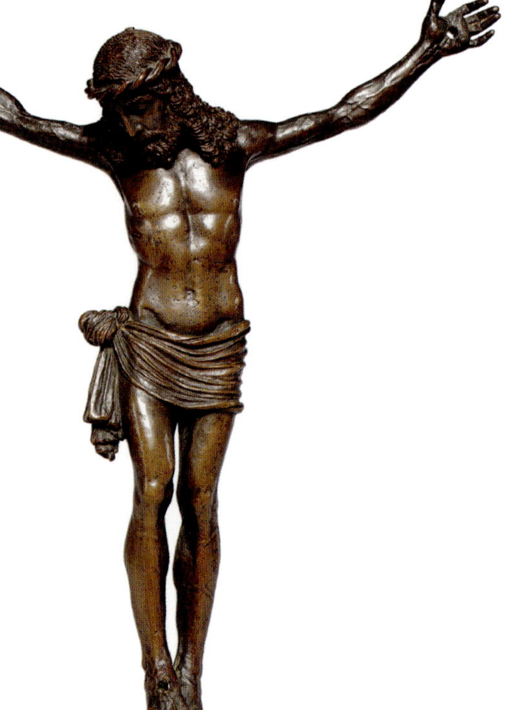

The Holy Family with Saint John the Baptist and Saint Margaret about 1495

FILIPPINO LIPPI (ITALIAN, ABOUT 1457–1504)

Lippi's sophisticated composition gracefully overlaps five figures in a round format. Oliviero Carafa, cardinal of Naples, commissioned this work, although Lippi probably painted it in Rome while working for the cardinal's family, an example of the widespread taste across Italy for the art of Florence. The meticulously detailed still-life elements on the parapet, thick with symbolic meaning, reflect Lippi's interest in the northern European painting he would have seen in Florence. Likewise the classical architecture—referring to the pagan world cast off by Christianity—demonstrates his intense engagement with ancient art and architecture in Rome. Embellished with learned references and made with expensive materials, this painting would have actively inspired religious meditation and demonstrated the patron's courtly, civilized taste.

TEMPERA AND OIL ON WOOD; DIAM. 153 CM (60-1/4 IN.)
THE DELIA E. HOLDEN FUND AND A FUND DONATED AS A MEMORIAL TO MRS. HOLDEN BY HER CHILDREN: GUERDEN S. HOLDEN, DELIA HOLDEN WHITE, ROBERTA HOLDEN BOLE, EMERY HOLDEN GREENOUGH, GERTRUDE HOLDEN MCGINLEY 1932.227

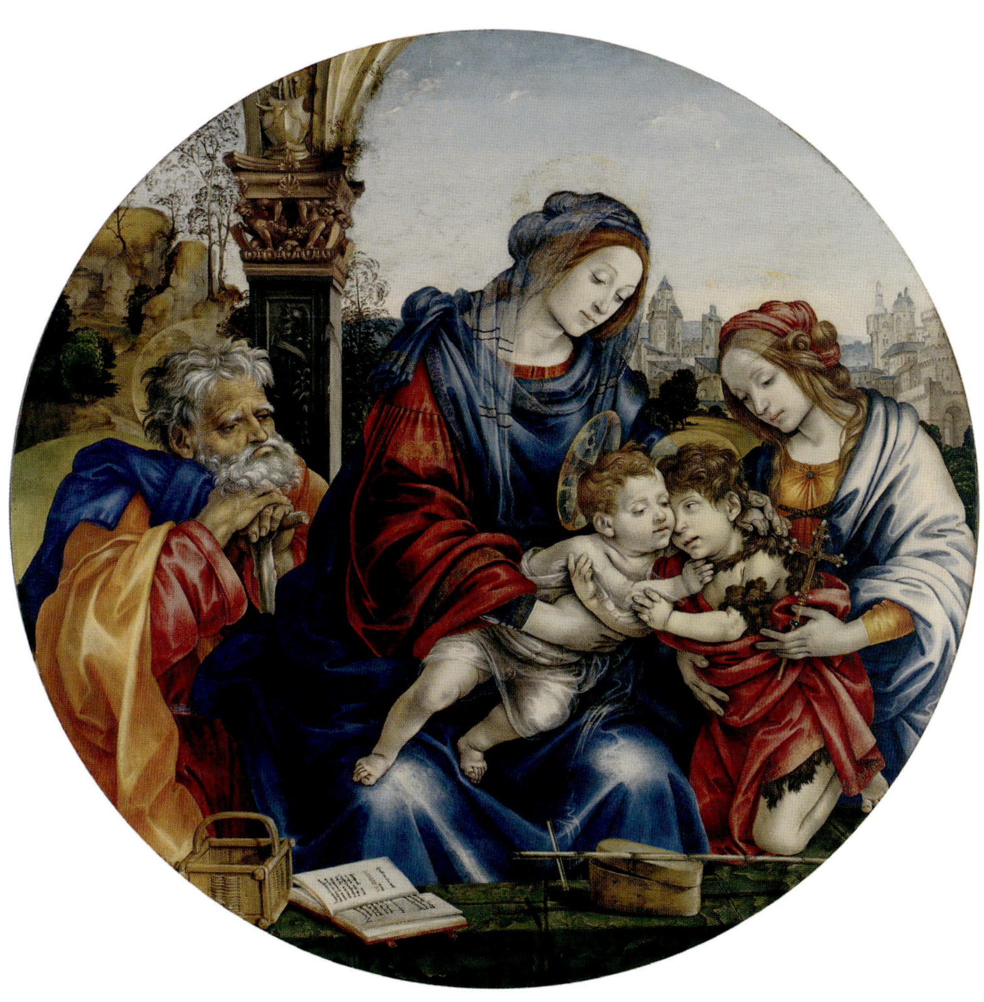

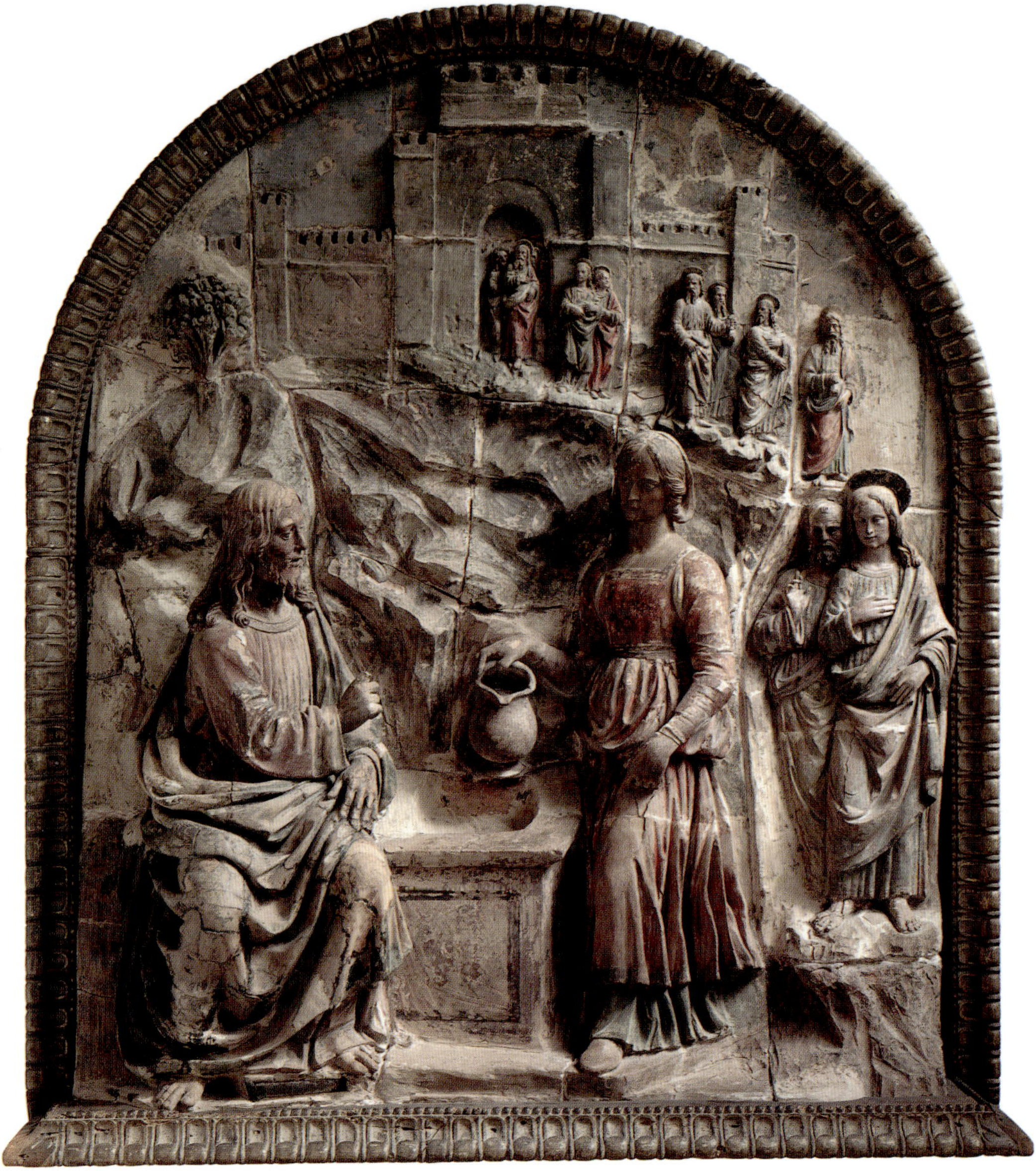

Christ and the Samaritan Woman at the Well about 1500–1530

GIOVANNI DELLA ROBBIA (ITALIAN, 1469–1529/30) AND WORKSHOP

This enormous sculpture originally came from San Vivaldo, a Franciscan friary in the Tuscan hills southwest of Florence. Between 1500 and 1530 more than 30 chapels were built there, each with a terracotta relief presenting an incident in the life of Christ. The story here stems from the Gospel of John, where Christ reveals himself as the prophet to a Samaritan woman, an important early example of conversion to Christianity. Behind the main figures presented in high relief, a path in dramatic perspective winds through a landscape, revealing the 12 disciples coming toward the viewer.

PAINTED TERRACOTTA; 221 X 177.8 X 27.9 CM (87-1/8 X 70-1/8 X 11 IN.)

GIFT OF SAMUEL MATHER 1922.210

Venus with a Burning Urn about 1500–1520

NORTHERN ITALY

Venus, the Roman goddess of love and beauty, was also linked with many virtues during the Renaissance. Here she appears as an allegory of Charity, with its associated Christian attributes. The crown refers to her place as the queen of the virtues, and the burning vessel represents Charity's two major components: the flame indicates the love of God; the urn, a sign of abundant giving, signifies the love of one's neighbor. Despite the religious symbolism, this figure's pose, hairstyle, and facial features look to ancient Roman prototypes, a common practice among Renaissance sculptors.

GILT BRONZE; 19.6 X 6.3 X 4 CM (7-3/4 X 2-1/2 X 1-3/4 IN.) WITHOUT BASE

JOHN L. SEVERANCE FUND 1948.171

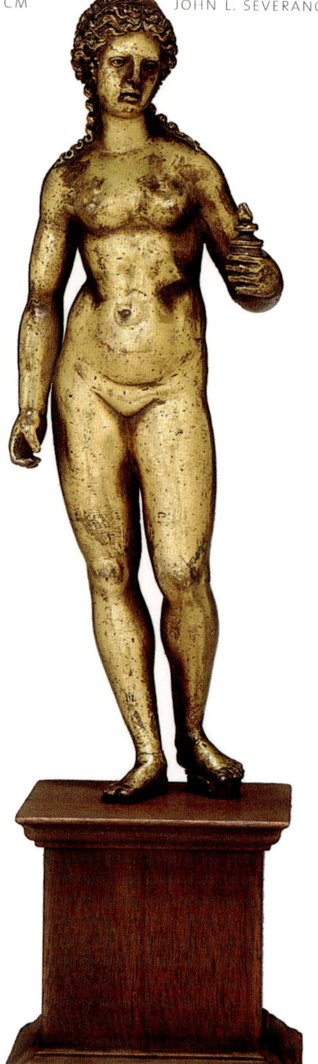

The Sacrifice of Isaac about 1527

ANDREA DEL SARTO (ITALIAN, 1486–1530)

In this test of faith from the Old Testament book of Genesis, Abraham agrees to slay his son Isaac on God's command. As Abraham raises the knife, an angel suddenly appears to halt the sacrifice. This work gains its power from the complex expressions of father and son, combining grief, strength, resignation, fear, and realization in their faces and bodies. The stance and musculature were inspired by Michelangelo's work as well as ancient sculpture. Andrea never finished this painting, and it lays bare his working methods. He transferred the design from a drawing, then reinforced the chalk with painted lines—best seen in the donkey at right. He next worked over the whole panel with thin, brushy veils of color, letting him more easily make changes to the composition, evident in the angel, Isaac's body, and Abraham's head.

OIL ON WOOD; 178 X 138 CM (70-1/8 X 54-3/8 IN.)

DELIA E. HOLDEN AND L. E. HOLDEN FUNDS 1937.577

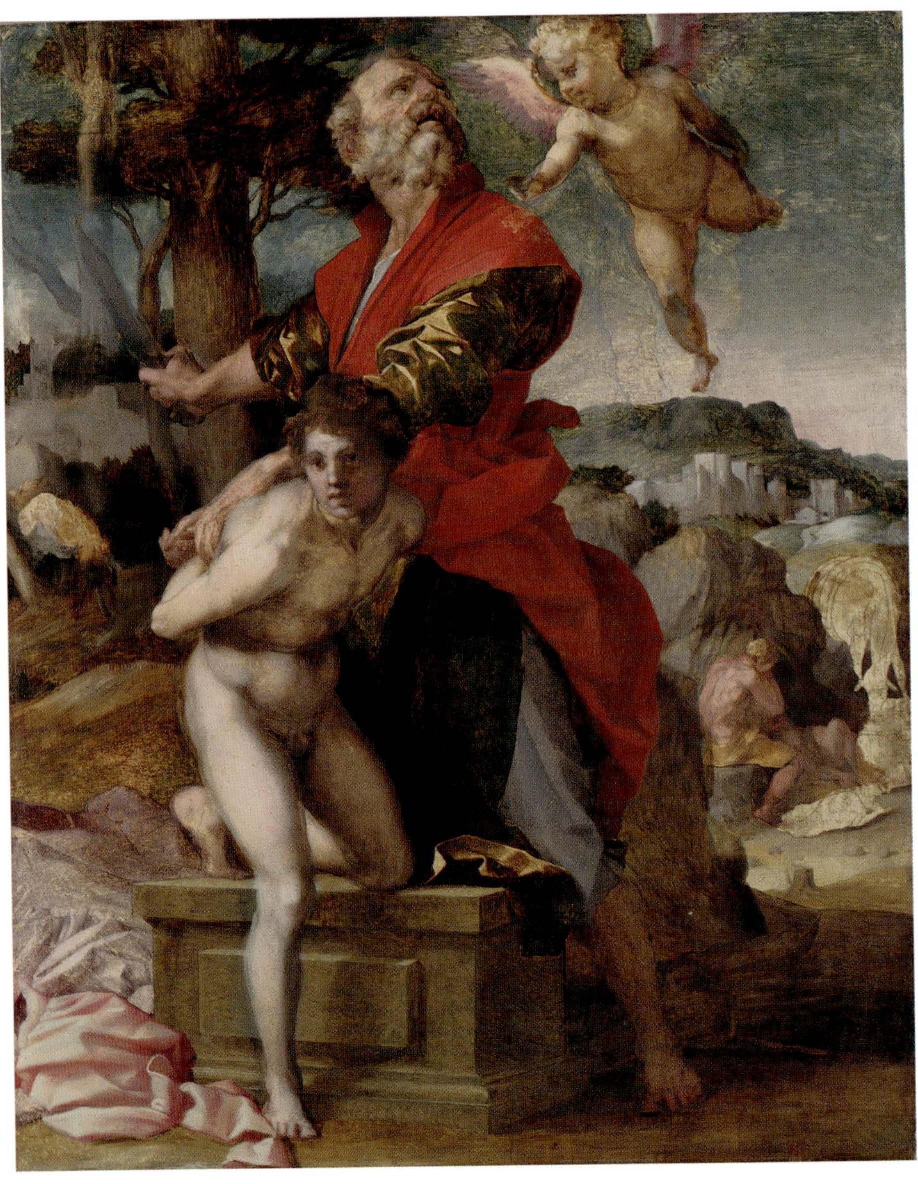

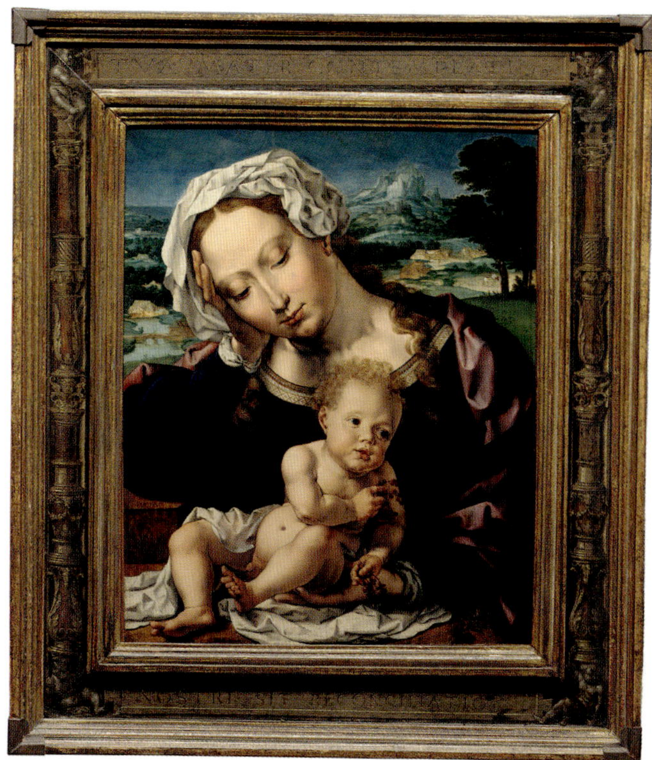

Virgin and Child in a Landscape 1531

JAN GOSSAERT (FLEMISH, ABOUT 1478–1532) AND AN ANONYMOUS LANDSCAPE PAINTER

Among the first northern European artists to study in Rome, Gossaert subsequently incorporated Italian Renaissance ideas in his work, such as the sculptural figures here. He also painted the frame, including the Latin inscription, "Mother, may your contemplation be our reconciliation." The patron is likely Mencía de Mendoza, a Spanish noblewoman, one of the most important art collectors and intellectuals of the early 1500s.

OIL ON WOOD; 47.7 X 36.6 CM (18-3/4 X 14-3/8 IN.)

JOHN L. SEVERANCE FUND 1972.47

Madonna and Child about 1530

JACOPO SANSOVINO (ITALIAN, 1486–1570)

The Virgin's classicized appearance reflects Venetian Renaissance artists' deep interest in ancient Roman art, seen in the veiled, wavy hair, the contrapposto pose, and the heavy mantle fastened to a long-sleeved chiton. The adoption of such antique ideals of beauty in depictions of the Madonna was an innovative practice during this period. As one of Sansovino's earliest bronzes, this statuette may have been made for a friend or patron, or perhaps to record a composition of which he was fond. The prominent placement of Sansovino's signature on the base indicates the cast's importance to the artist.

BRONZE; 47.6 X 17.2 X 11.5 CM (18-3/4 X 6-3/4 X 4-1/2 IN.)

JOHN L. SEVERANCE FUND 1951.316

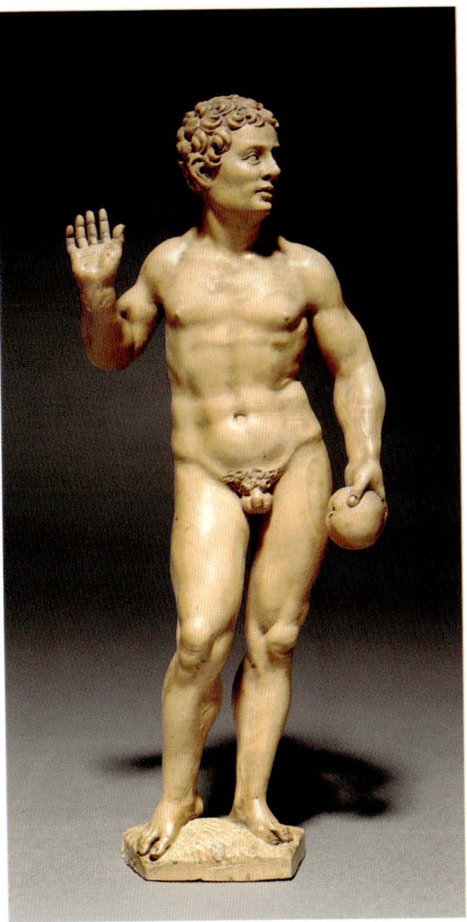

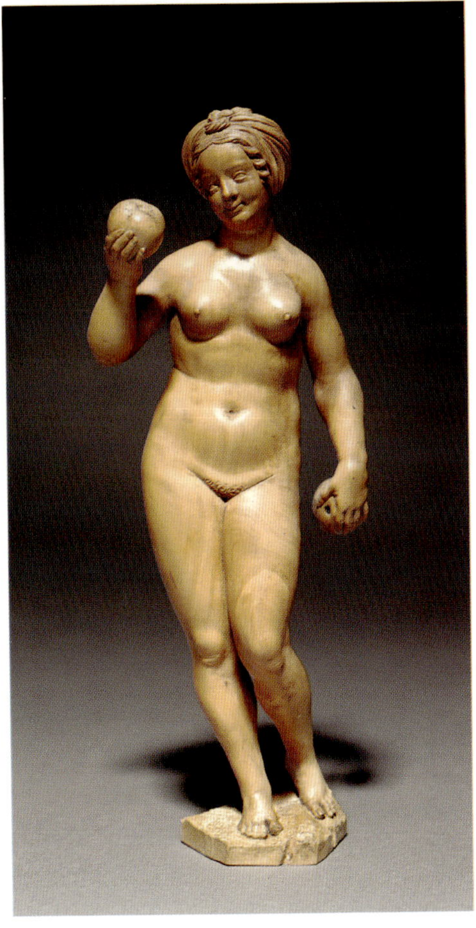

Adam and Eve about 1535

DANIEL MAUCH (GERMAN, 1477–1540)

Mauch drew upon both the late medieval and Renaissance traditions across his career. However, these small-scale statuettes—each made from a single piece of boxwood—stem from the most progressive strands of Renaissance art in southern Germany, closely connected to developments in both Italian and German bronze sculpture. The bodies reveal Mauch's careful study of human anatomy as well as an awareness of Albrecht Dürer's well-known print of the same subject.

BOXWOOD; ADAM, 18.3 X 7 X 4 CM (7-1/4 X 2-3/4 X 1-5/8 IN.); EVE, 17.5 X 6 X 4.5 CM (6-7/8 X 2-3/8 X 1-3/4 IN.)
PURCHASE FROM THE J. H. WADE FUND 1946.429.1–2

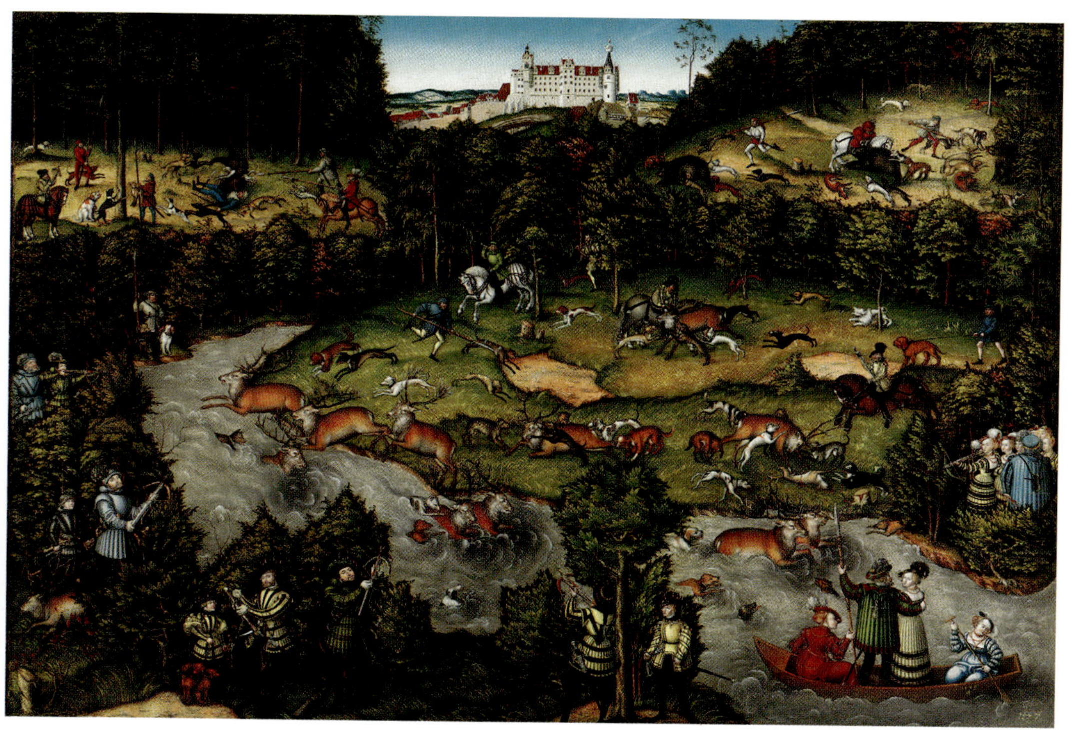

Hunting near Hartenfels Castle 1540

LUCAS CRANACH THE ELDER (GERMAN, 1472–1553)

The Protestant rulers of Saxony commissioned this animated hunt scene, set near their residence in present-day eastern Germany at Hartenfels Castle, depicted in the background. John Fredrick the Magnanimous stands in the lower left wearing dark green hunting attire; he loads his crossbow as his courtiers and dogs pursue game across the river. His wife, the Electress Sibylle, stands at right; an arrow from her weapon has pierced a nearby stag in the water. Often highly rehearsed occasions, the prince electors of Saxony were passionate practitioners of hunting with dogs and signal horns. In addition to the main stag hunt, this painting depicts two others: a bear hunt in the upper left corner and a boar hunt in the upper right.

OIL, ORIGINALLY ON WOOD, TRANSFERRED TO MASONITE; 116.8 X 170.2 CM (46 X 67 IN.)

JOHN L. SEVERANCE FUND 1958.425

Portrait of Philip II, King of Spain mid 1550s

ALESSANDRO CESATI (CYPRIOT, ACTIVE ITALY, BEFORE 1538–AFTER 1564)

Clad in armor, Philip II wears a chain with the Order of the Golden Fleece around his neck. The remarkably precise cutting describes the cloth, metal, skin, and hair while presenting the king's physiognomy with striking naturalism—complete with receding hairline and prominent chin—as well as conveying his forceful character. Carved gems were luxury arts of the highest order in the Renaissance, hotly collected and used as diplomatic gifts. The original patron is not yet known, but cameos played a prominent role at the Spanish court, where in their portraits members of the royal family often hold gems showing Philip II. The unusually clear yellow quartz, rare in the 1500s, is a marvel of both nature and craftsmanship, and is likely in its original setting.

CITRINE, MOUNTED IN A GOLD AND ENAMEL PENDANT; 4.3 X 2.8 X 0.9 CM (1-5/8 X 1-1/8 X 3/8 IN.)

BY EXCHANGE: BEQUESTS OF MRS. SEVERANCE A. MILLIKIN AND JOHN L. SEVERANCE; DUDLEY P. ALLEN FUND; GIFT OF CARRIE MOSS HALLE IN MEMORY OF SALMON PORTLAND HALLE; GIFT OF S. LIVINGSTONE MATHER, CONSTANCE MATHER BISHOP, PHILIP R. MATHER, KATHERINE HOYT CROSS 2012.53

Boy Drinking 1582–83

ANNIBALE CARRACCI (ITALIAN, ABOUT 1560–1609)

Like Caravaggio, Annibale Carracci forged a reform of the arts that returned to close observation of the natural world. The coarse surface of the canvas, the inelegant subject matter, and the striking distortion of forms from light passing through glass all speak to his naturalistic approach.

OIL ON CANVAS; 55.8 X 43.7 CM (22 X 17-1/4 IN.)

LEONARD C. HANNA JR. FUND 1994.4

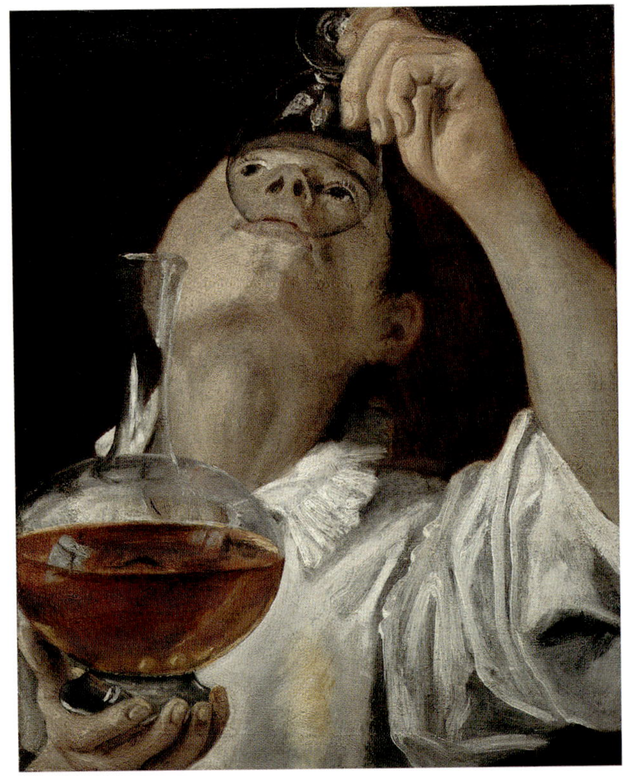

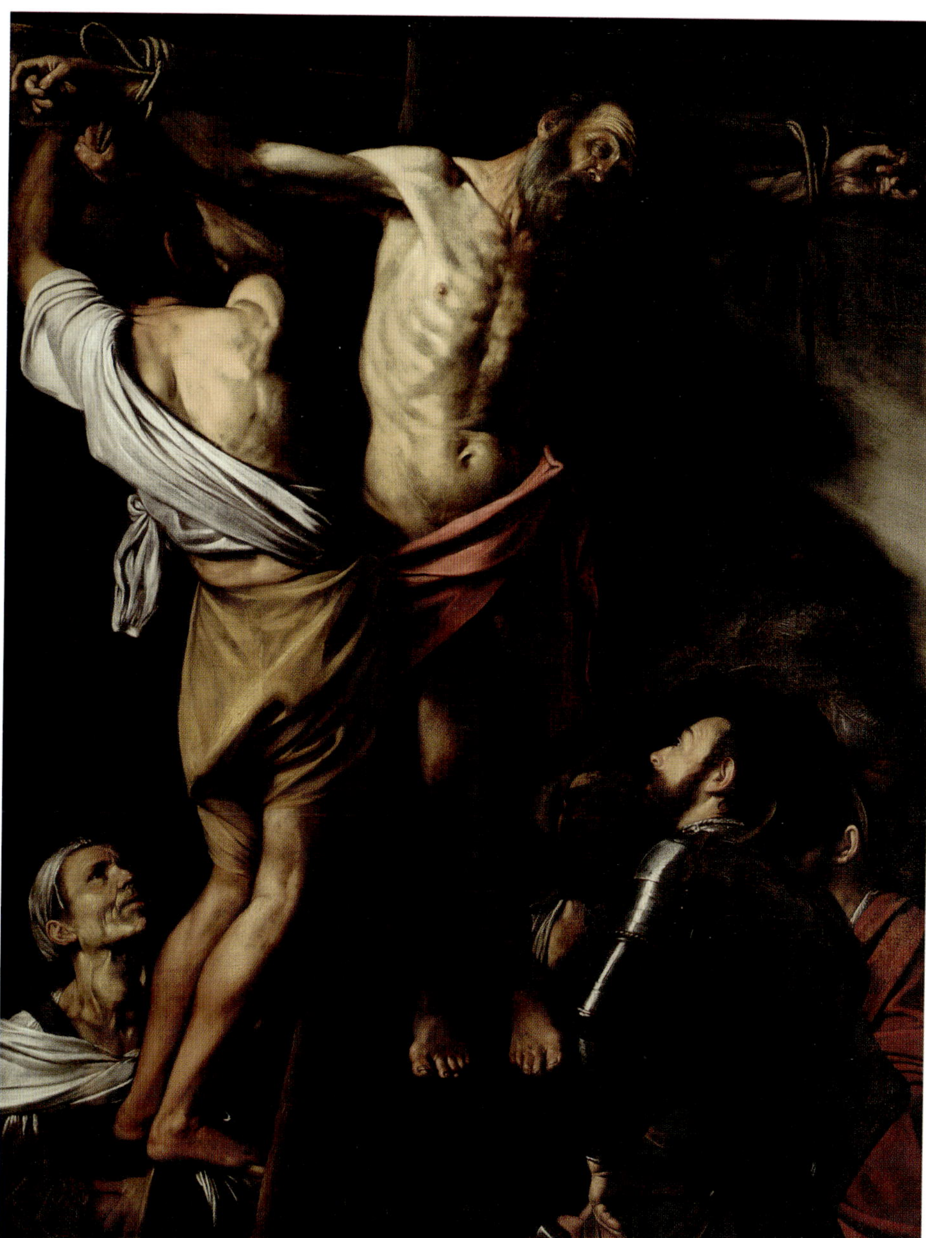

The Crucifixion of Saint Andrew 1606–7

CARAVAGGIO (ITALIAN, 1571–1610)

Sentenced to death for his missionary activity in Greece, Andrew asked to be martyred like Christ. While on the cross, Andrew preached to an enormous crowd, and when his executioners tried to remove him, a mysterious force paralyzed them. Upon his finishing a prayer, a dazzling light enveloped Andrew and he died. In an unusual interpretation, Caravaggio presents the event as intimate and private, rather than as a public spectacle, and through his innovative use of light and dark he suggests the presence of God.

OIL ON CANVAS; 202.5 X 152.7 CM (79-3/4 X 60-1/8 IN.)

LEONARD C. HANNA JR. FUND 1976.2

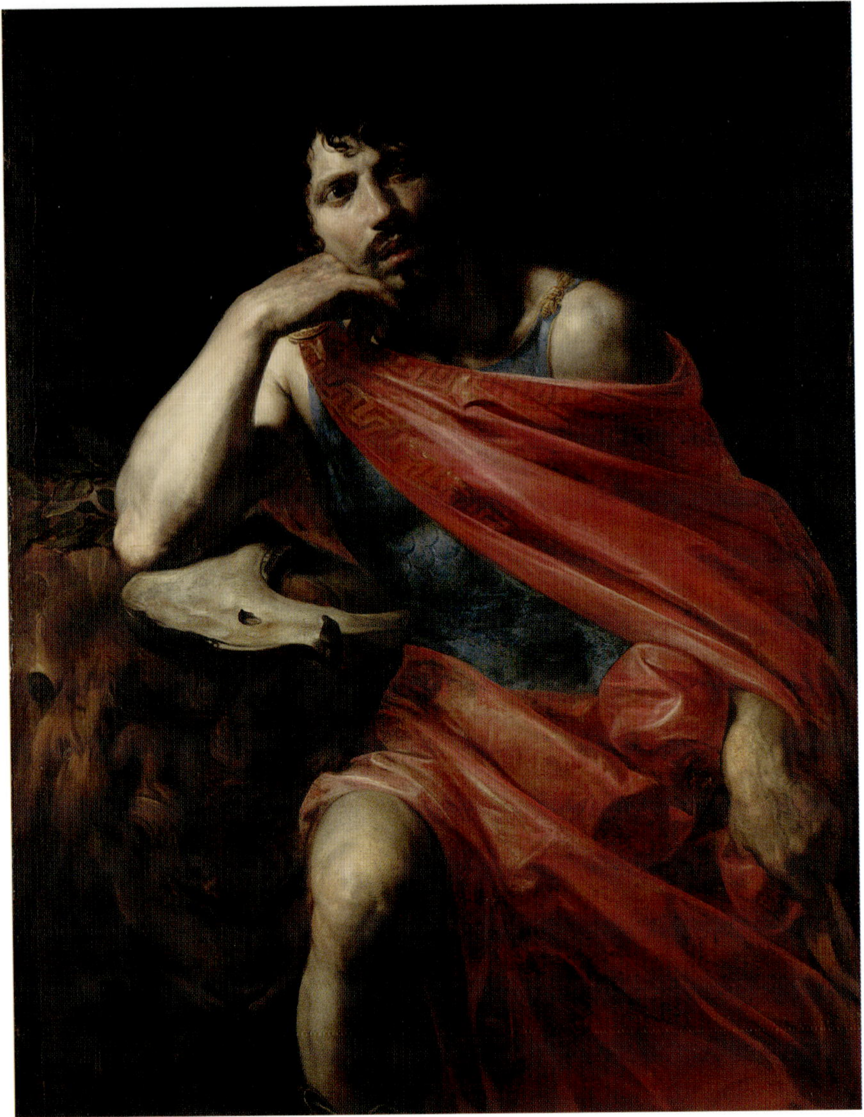

Samson about 1630

VALENTIN DE BOULOGNE (FRENCH, ACTIVE IN ITALY, 1591–1632)

The Old Testament hero Samson killed a lion with his hands and liberated the Israelites by slaughtering a thousand Philistines with a donkey's jawbone—actions represented by objects on the table. Yet Valentin, a French artist working in Rome, emphasized Samson's contemplation. Likewise, the dramatic, emotionally charged drapery contrasts with his brooding, inward expression.

OIL ON CANVAS; 135.6 X 102.8 CM (53-3/8 X 40-1/2 IN.)

MR. AND MRS. WILLIAM H. MARLATT FUND 1972.50

Portrait of the Jester Calabazas about 1631–32

DIEGO VELÁZQUEZ (SPANISH, 1599–1660)

The diminutive Calabazas was a jester serving under Philip IV of Spain. Such figures were common in the Spanish court, where they served as entertainers and playmates to the royal children. In palace performances jesters would often mime court characters, in this case a gentleman attendant, a position that someone with Calabazas's physical and developmental disabilities never would have held. His austere clothing and formal, full-length presentation, both conventions of noble portraiture, may allude to a comic routine Calabazas presented for Philip and his guests. Yet Velázquez simultaneously stresses the high esteem that the young man held in court life and thoughtfully captures his individuality.

OIL ON CANVAS; 175 X 106 CM (68-7/8 X 41-3/4 IN.)

LEONARD C. HANNA JR. FUND 1965.15

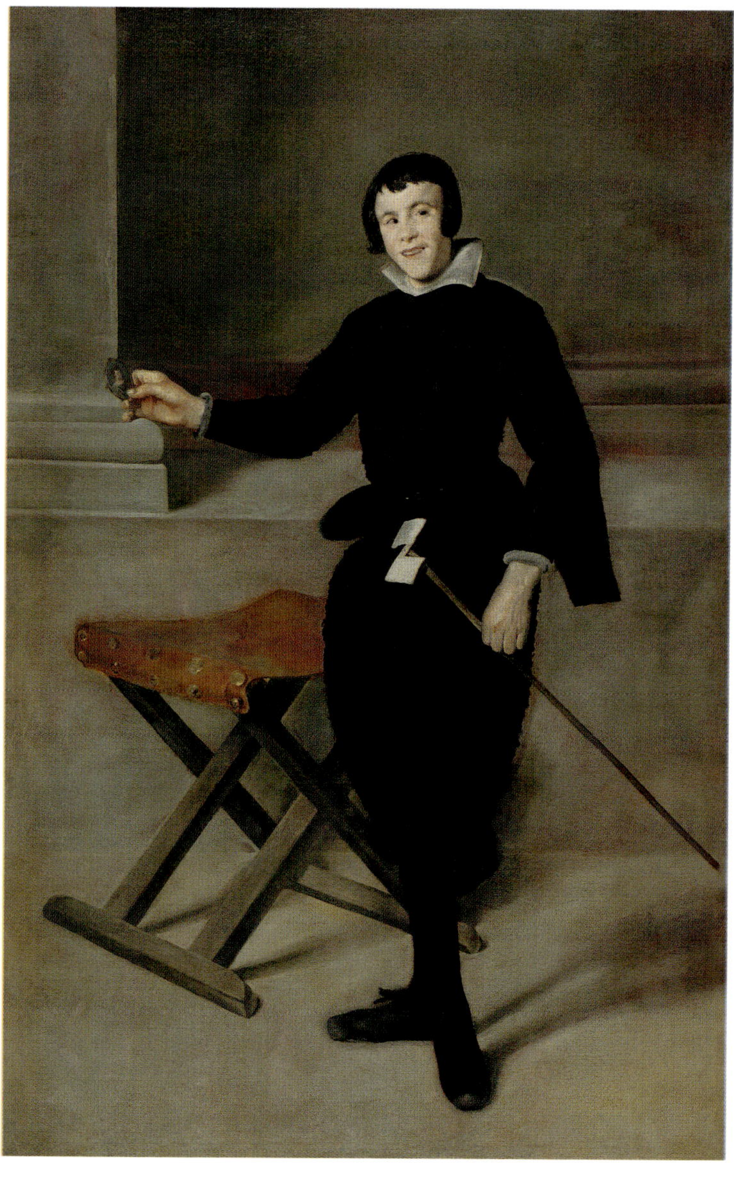

Portrait of Tieleman Roosterman 1634

FRANS HALS (DUTCH, ABOUT 1581–1666)

Roosterman's business in fine linen and silk fabrics extended as far as Flanders and France. Given his trade, it is no surprise that Hals emphasized his luxurious costume despite its sober color. Here Roosterman wears a black, beribboned doublet with slashed sleeves; a wide, folding collar; turned-back cambric cuffs, edged in bobbin lace; as well as a large beaver hat. The inscription at the upper right, painted by Hals, gives the painting's date and the sitter's age as 36.

OIL ON CANVAS; 117 X 87 CM (46-1/8 X 34-1/4 IN.)

LEONARD C. HANNA JR. FUND 1999.173

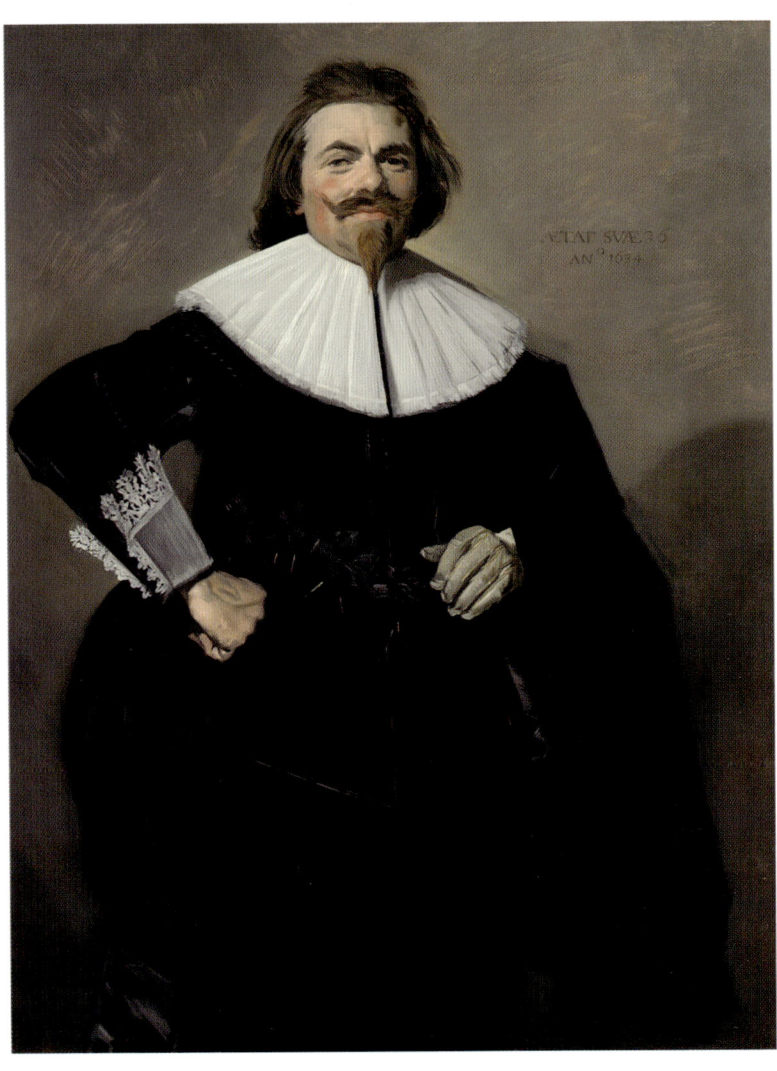

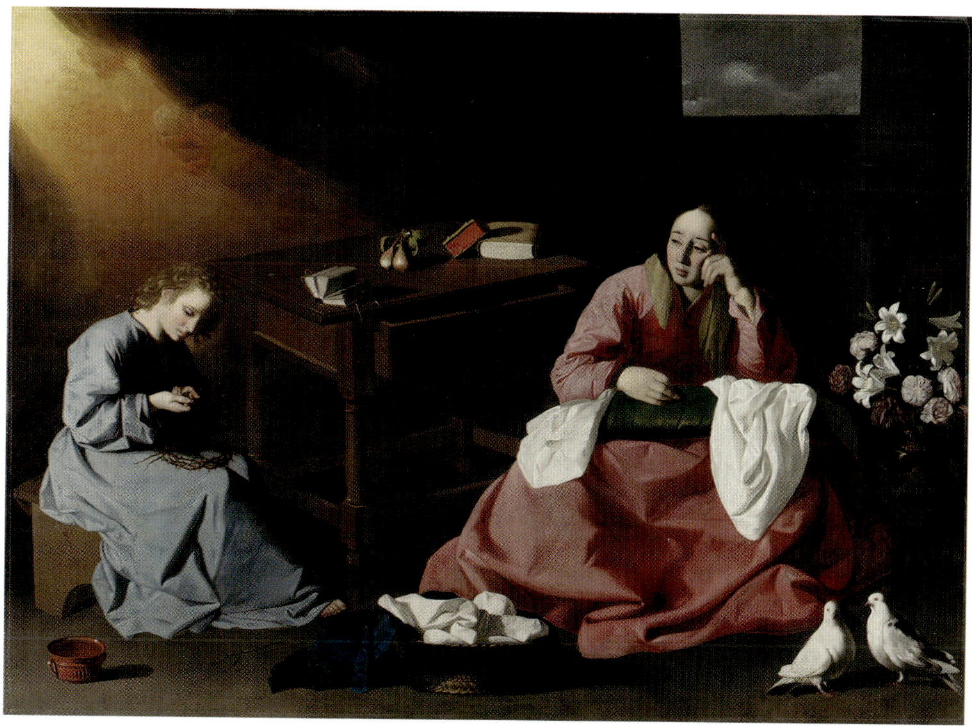

Christ and the Virgin in the House at Nazareth
about 1640
FRANCISCO DE ZURBARÁN (SPANISH, 1598–1664)
Stories of Christ's childhood and adolescence became increasingly popular during the Counter-Reformation because they were easily understood by a broad public. Rather than taking a story from the Bible, Zurbarán appears to have invented this subject, in which Jesus pricks himself on a crown of thorns he is weaving, foretelling his later torment at the Crucifixion. Despite the grand scale and monumental figures, the work has remarkable intimacy and quietness, emphasizing such details as the Virgin's tears and the numerous still-life elements.
OIL ON CANVAS; 165 X 218.2 CM (65 X 85-7/8 IN.)
LEONARD C. HANNA JR. FUND 1960.117

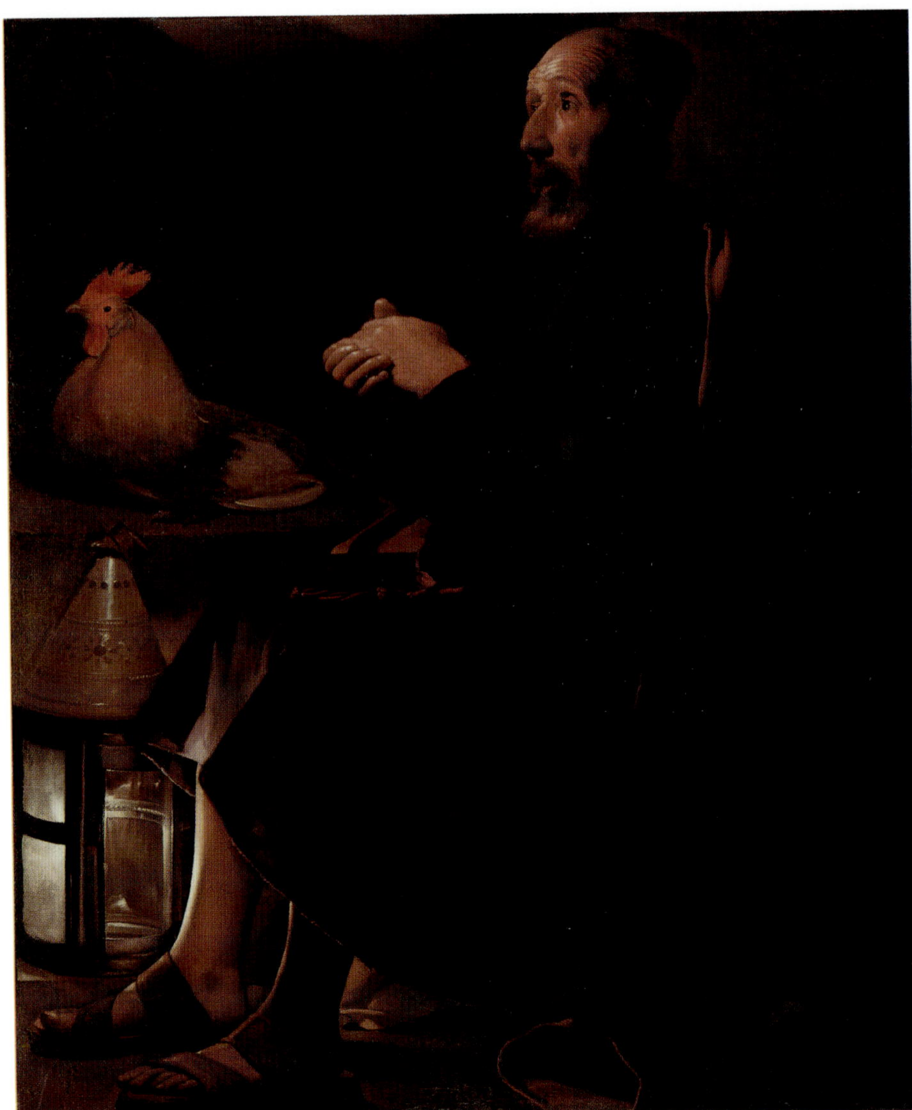

Saint Peter Repentant 1645

GEORGES DE LA TOUR (FRENCH, 1593–1652)

On the night of the Last Supper, the apostle Peter denied knowing Christ. Alone in humble surroundings, Saint Peter reflects on his betrayal with an intensity fueled by the artist's use of light and the unrelenting realism. La Tour worked in relative isolation in northeastern France, and while he is often linked to Caravaggio and his northern followers, the concentrated quietness and solitude of his figures reveal a unique voice in 17th-century painting.

OIL ON CANVAS; 114 X 95 CM (44-7/8 X 37-3/8 IN.)

GIFT OF THE HANNA FUND 1951.454

Landscape with a Windmill 1646

JACOB VAN RUISDAEL (DUTCH, 1628/29–1682)

One of Ruisdael's first signed and dated works, painted while he was a teenager, shows the artist's daring and original approach to landscape. Rather than gently easing the viewer into the composition—a more conventional approach in Dutch landscape painting at this time—Ruisdael masses dark forms in the foreground, barely penetrated by light, while opening up an expansive, sunlit plain at left.

OIL ON WOOD; 49.5 X 68.5 CM (19-1/2 X 27 IN.)

MR. AND MRS. WILLIAM H. MARLATT FUND 1967.19

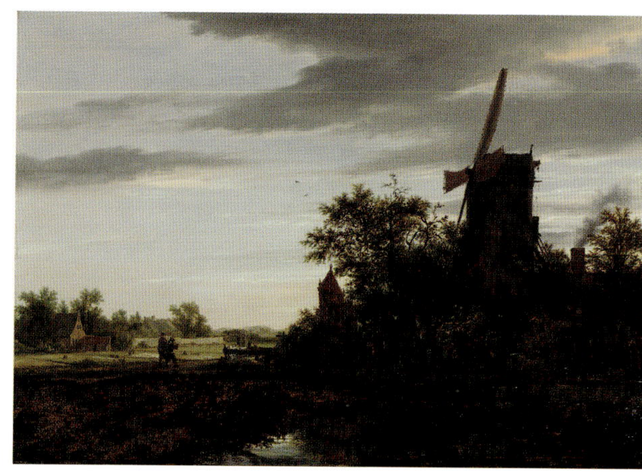

The Holy Family on the Steps 1648

NICOLAS POUSSIN (FRENCH, ACTIVE IN ITALY, 1594–1665)

The simplicity of this composition is deceptive; it is a complex meditation on the Holy Family's role in the redemption of humanity. At the center, Mary presents the Christ child to the world. At the left, Saint Elizabeth leans forward to foretell his eventual death, while her son, Saint John the Baptist, offers Jesus an apple, signifying humanity's fall from grace in the Garden of Eden. Saint Joseph, at the right, received new emphasis in the 1600s as an important model for men, especially fathers. His compass, a sign of his occupation as a carpenter, also symbolizes God the Father.

OIL ON CANVAS; 73.3 X 105.8 CM (28-7/8 X 41-5/8 IN.)

LEONARD C. HANNA JR. FUND 1981.18

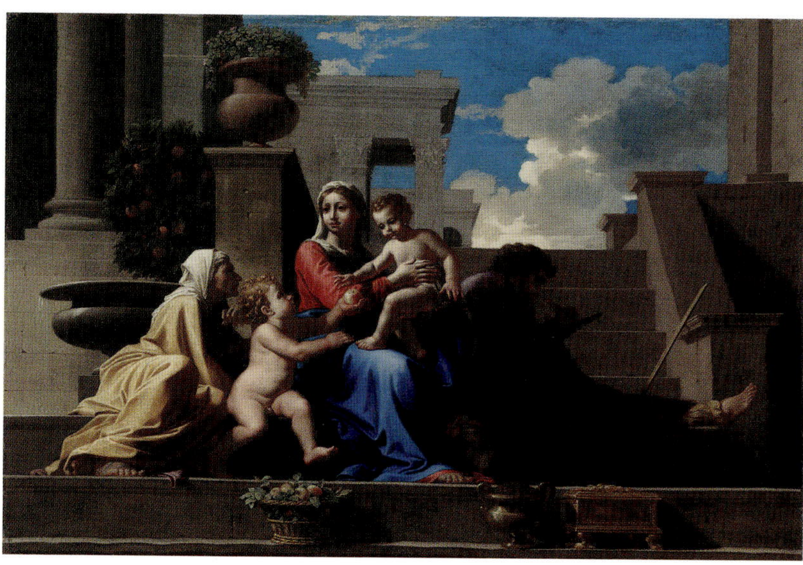

Death of Adonis about 1650

ITALY, NAPLES

Venus, the goddess of love, urged her mortal lover Adonis to hunt only the easiest game. Yet he insisted on pursuing wild boar and was eventually killed by his prey. Venus discovers the young man robbed of his life, yet the painting eternally preserves him in a state of youthful perfection. This emphasis on paradox corresponds to wordplay in Italian poetry from the 1600s, with which many artists sought visual parallels. This painting derives from a 1623 poem by Giovanni Battista Marino. The painter remains unknown, although the sophisticated literary reference, dramatic use of light, and vivid use of color demonstrate the artist's keen awareness of trends converging in Naples in the mid 1600s.

OIL ON CANVAS; 184.4 X 238.8 CM (72-5/8 X 94 IN.)

MR. AND MRS. WILLIAM H. MARLATT FUND 1965.19

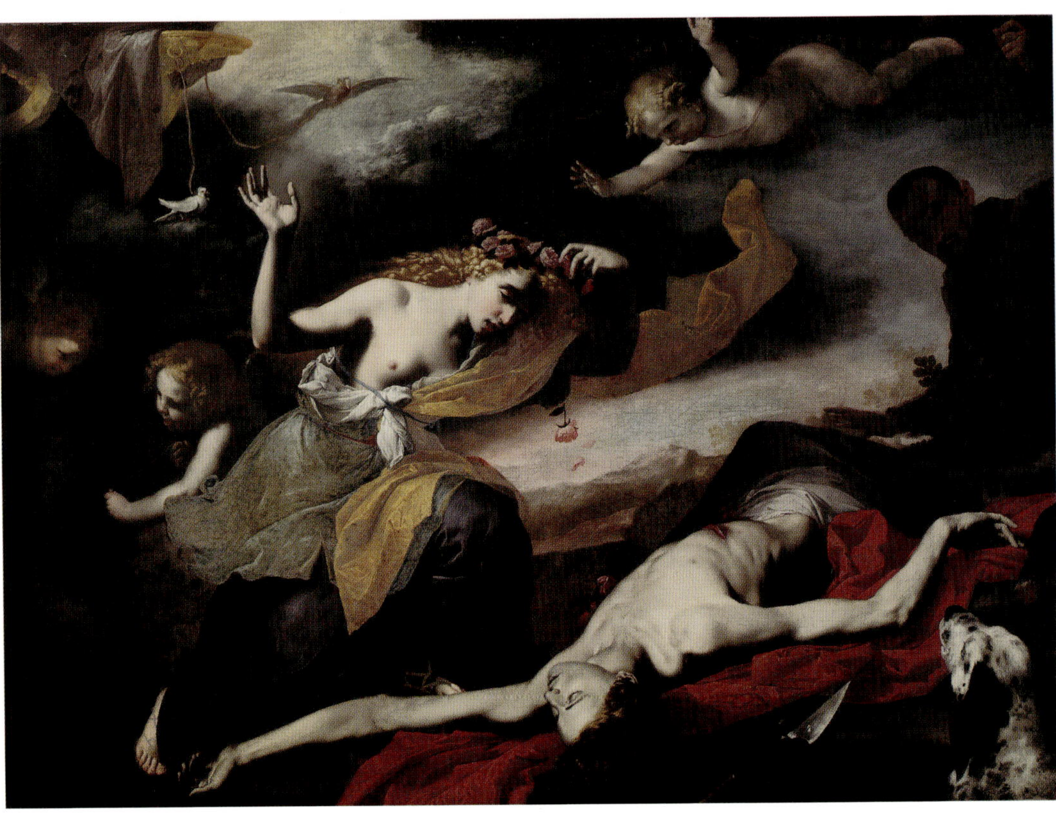

Portrait of Charles II, King of England 1653

PHILIPPE DE CHAMPAIGNE (FRENCH, 1602–1674)

Charles II fled England in 1651 during the English civil war and commissioned this portrait during his exile in France. While he never fought on the battlefield, Charles II was the last British monarch to wear a full suit of armor, which represented his rank and status. The king's gesture to the Dover cliffs, the sea, and the waiting fleet reveals his intention to return to England, which he did in 1660.

OIL ON CANVAS; 129.5 X 97.2 CM (51 X 38-1/4 IN.)

THE ELISABETH SEVERANCE PRENTISS COLLECTION

1959.38

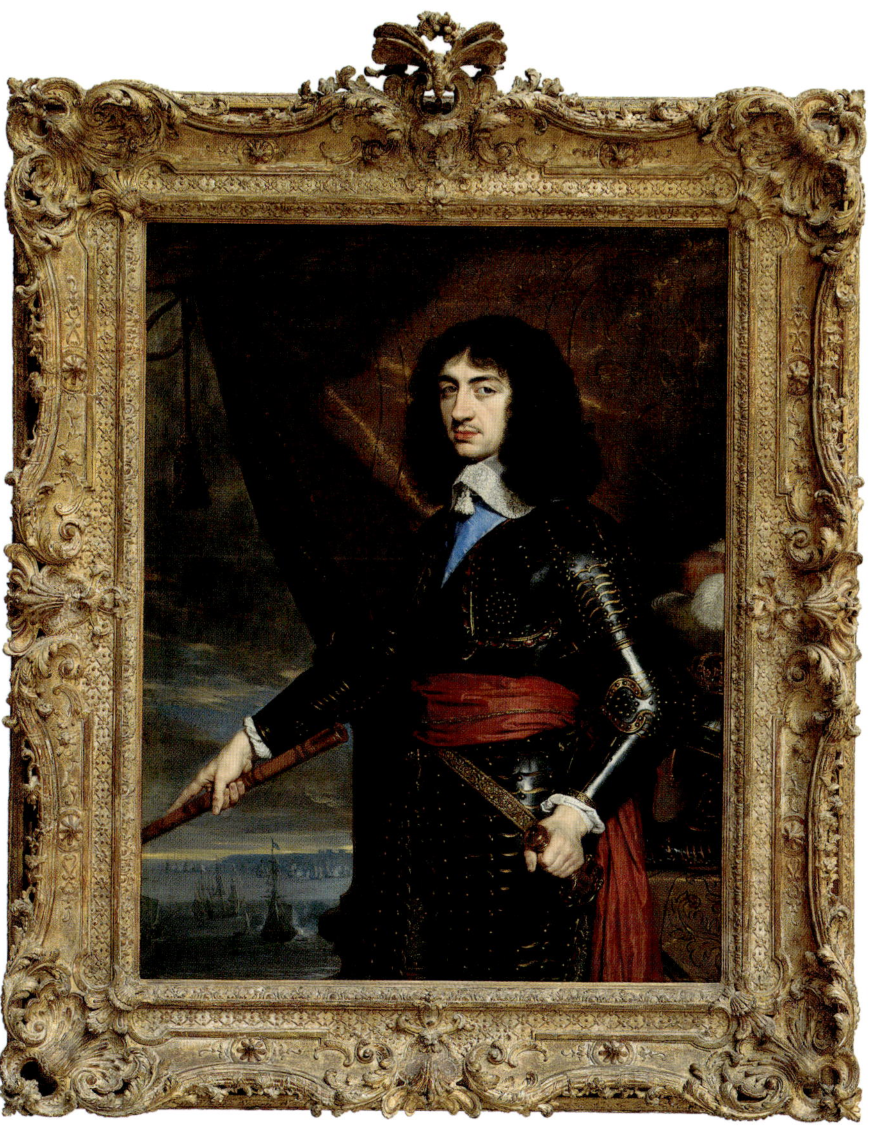

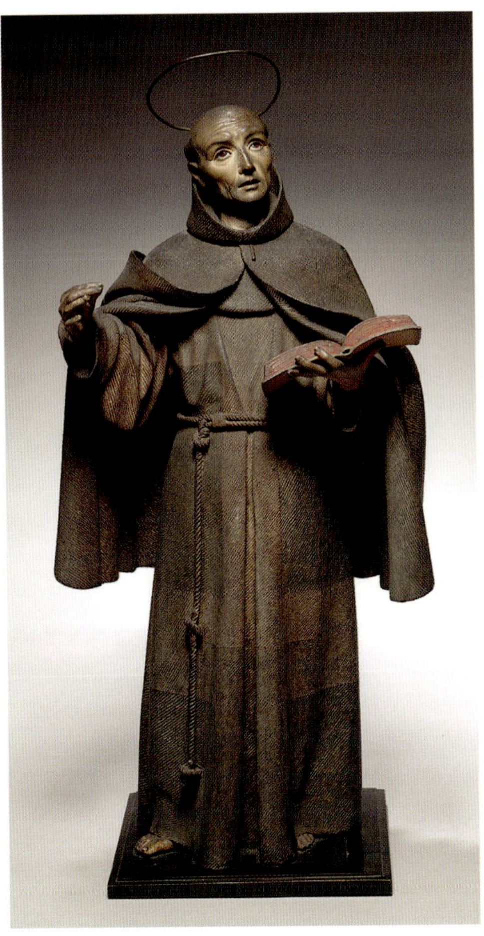

Saint Peter of Alcántara about 1663–70

PEDRO DE MENA (SPANISH, 1628–1688) AND WORKSHOP

Saint Peter of Alcántara advocated for the poor in Spain during the 1600s. He also led a reform movement within the Franciscan order and wrote many influential spiritual texts. The bare feet recall the monk's famous walk to Rome seeking approval from the pope for convents to serve Spain's destitute. According to his disciple Saint Teresa of Ávila, he received divine inspiration from God—a combination of ecstasy and pain that fueled his writing. Painted wood sculpture from Spain in the 1600s involved a team under a lead sculptor. The sculptor carved numerous pieces of wood in complex forms, then delicately covered them in gesso. The roughness of the saint's face, reflecting his age and hardships, came from texturing the surface with a brush. The glass eyes were inserted from behind the face before the wood pieces were attached. Finally, the eyelashes were added for a further touch of realism.

PAINTED WOOD, WITH IVORY AND GLASS; 72.2 X 32 X 32 CM (28-1/2 X 12-5/8 X 12-5/8 IN.)

LEONARD C. HANNA JR. FUND 2009.81

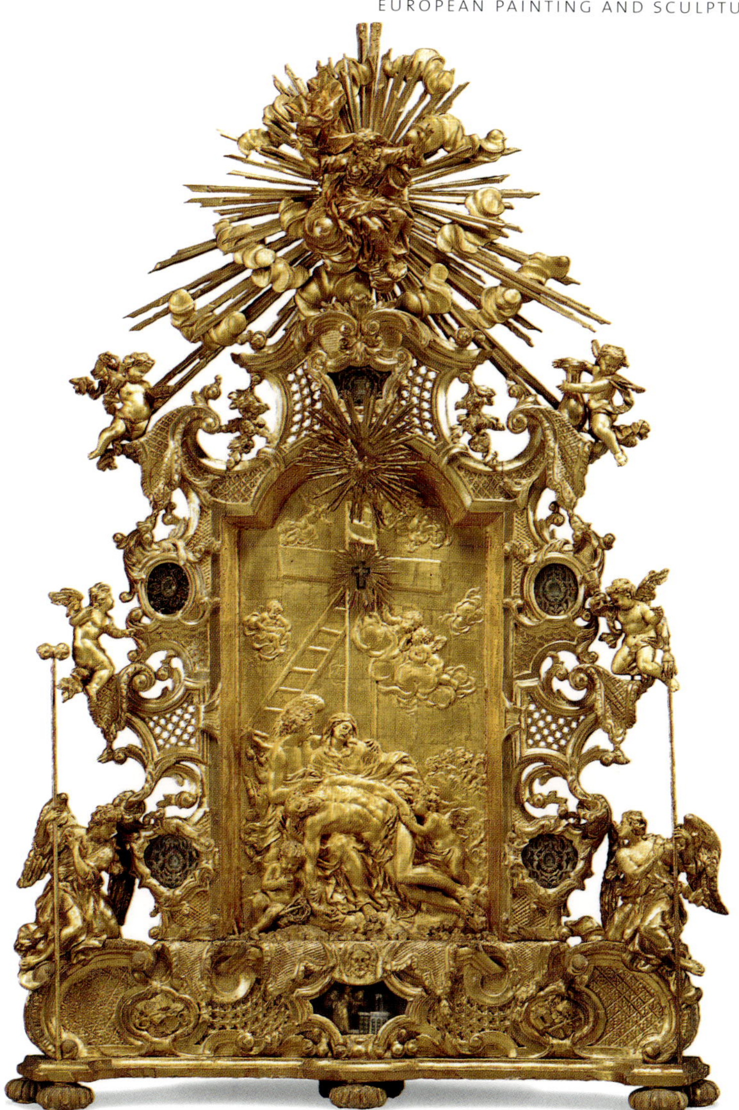

Altarpiece with Relics about 1735–40

JOSEPH MATHIAS GÖTZ (GERMAN, 1696–1760) AND WORKSHOP

Rather than simply framing a central narrative, Götz covered every surface in gold leaf, giving each part of the object equal importance. In this distinctively Central European approach, figural narrative is subordinate to the overall ensemble. Designed to rest on top of an altar, probably with a larger painted or sculpted decorative scheme behind it, this work contains relics, seen through the small windows on the perimeter. These small remains of holy figures demonstrate the persistence of a medieval Catholic tradition well into the 1700s.

GILDED WOOD, WITH RELICS IN NICHES, MOTHER-OF-PEARL, EBONY, RED SILK, GOLD WIRE, SEED PEARLS, ROCK CRYSTAL, PEN AND INK ON PAPER; 165.1 X 108 X 20 CM (65 X 42-1/2 X 7-5/8 IN.)

LEONARD C. HANNA JR. FUND 1964.357

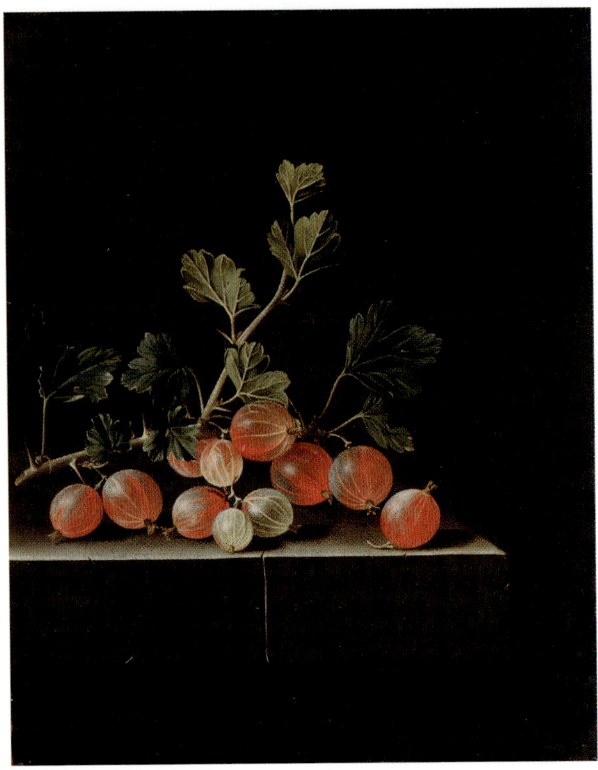

Gooseberries on a Table 1701

ADRIAEN COORTE (DUTCH, ABOUT 1660–AFTER 1707)

Coorte worked in Middelburg, a wealthy maritime city in the southern part of the Netherlands that fostered a poetic, scientific, and spiritual examination of the natural world. Gooseberries—a modest, local pleasure—could be picked in the wild, although Dutch gardeners in the 1600s were the first to cultivate the plant to improve its taste. The strong illumination gives the branch a stark grandeur, despite the small scale, and the dark background emphasizes the fruit's delicate translucency. The desiccated flower petals and waxy leaves contrast with the succulent gooseberries, with their skin on the verge of bursting.

OIL ON PAPER, MOUNTED ON WOOD; 29.7 X 22.8 CM (11-3/4 X 9 IN.)

LEONARD C. HANNA JR. FUND 1987.32

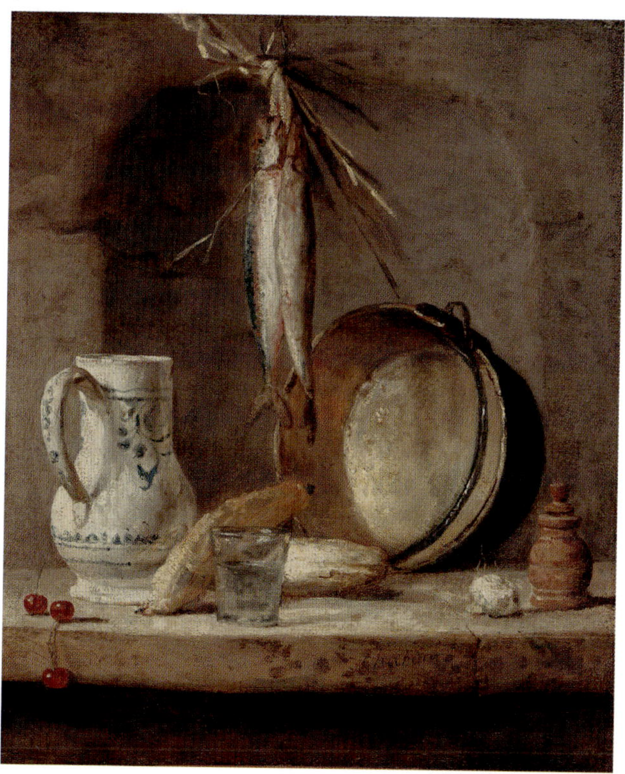

Still Life with Herrings about 1735

JEAN-SIMÉON CHARDIN (FRENCH, 1699–1779)

Chardin reflected intensely on the act of observation. Still life became a forum for sophisticated performances in paint, and his complex technique—he famously worked in private—uses a staggering combination of delicate glazes and roughly dragged thick paint to capture the varied surfaces, atmospheres, and spaces in this humble pantry shelf. Acutely aware of recent developments in optics and physics, Chardin explored ideas about light, shadow, and color, and he fully expected his work to be inspected closely.

OIL ON CANVAS; 41 X 33.6 CM (16-1/8 X 13-1/4 IN.)

LEONARD C. HANNA JR. FUND 1974.1

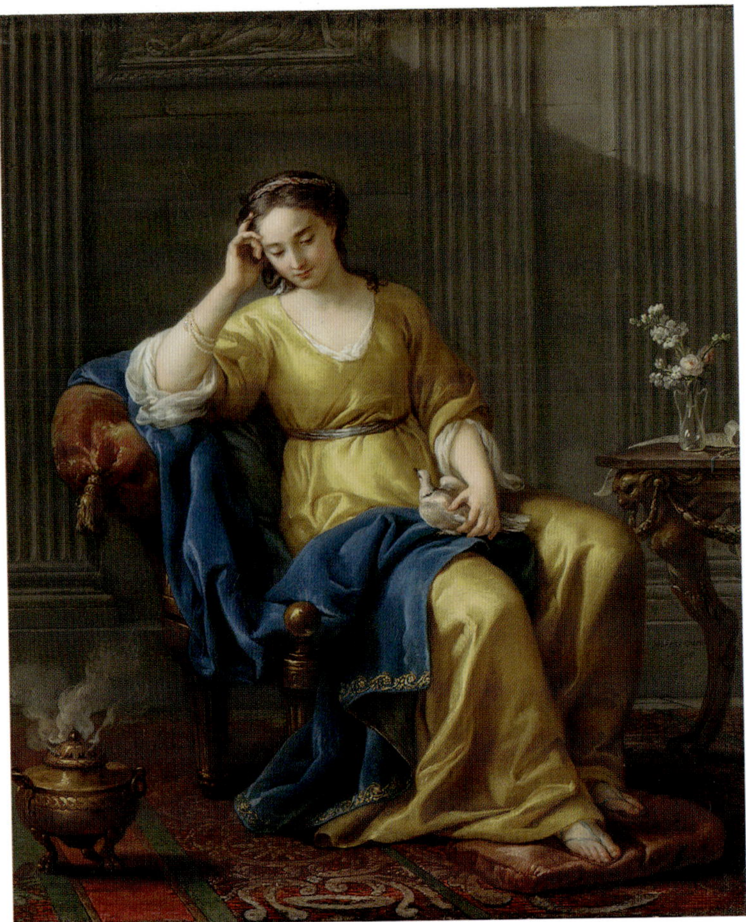

Sweet Melancholy 1756

JOSEPH-MARIE VIEN THE ELDER (FRENCH, 1716–1809)

The chair, brazier, table, and the setting all show Vien's interest in bringing archaeological accuracy to a new level of precision. His delicate handling and graceful palette derive squarely from earlier 18th-century French painting. The gesture of the melancholic figure, with her head on her hand, has roots going back to the Renaissance. However, the painting has a wistful rather than tragic tone. Images of women in interiors contemplating a letter with longing or sadness derive from earlier Dutch paintings of daily life, here transformed into an ancient context.

OIL ON CANVAS; 68 X 55 CM (26-3/4 X 21-5/8 IN.)

MR. AND MRS. WILLIAM H. MARLATT FUND 1996.1

Portrait of Catherine Rebecca Grey, Lady Manners, Later Lady Huntington 1794

THOMAS LAWRENCE (BRITISH, 1769–1830)

Born in Ireland and recently married into the aristocracy, Lady Manners had just published her first volume of verse when Lawrence painted her portrait. Despite the dazzling brushwork, the symphony of whites, and the array of classical references, the family chose not to purchase the work, which never sold and remained in Lawrence's studio for the rest of his career. The reasons for this rejection remain opaque but may relate to the peacock. The bird was associated with the goddess Juno and thus to marriage and motherhood, but it also symbolized boastful pride.

OIL ON CANVAS; 255.3 X 158 CM (100-1/2 X 62-1/4 IN.)

BEQUEST OF JOHN D. ROCKEFELLER JR. 1961.220

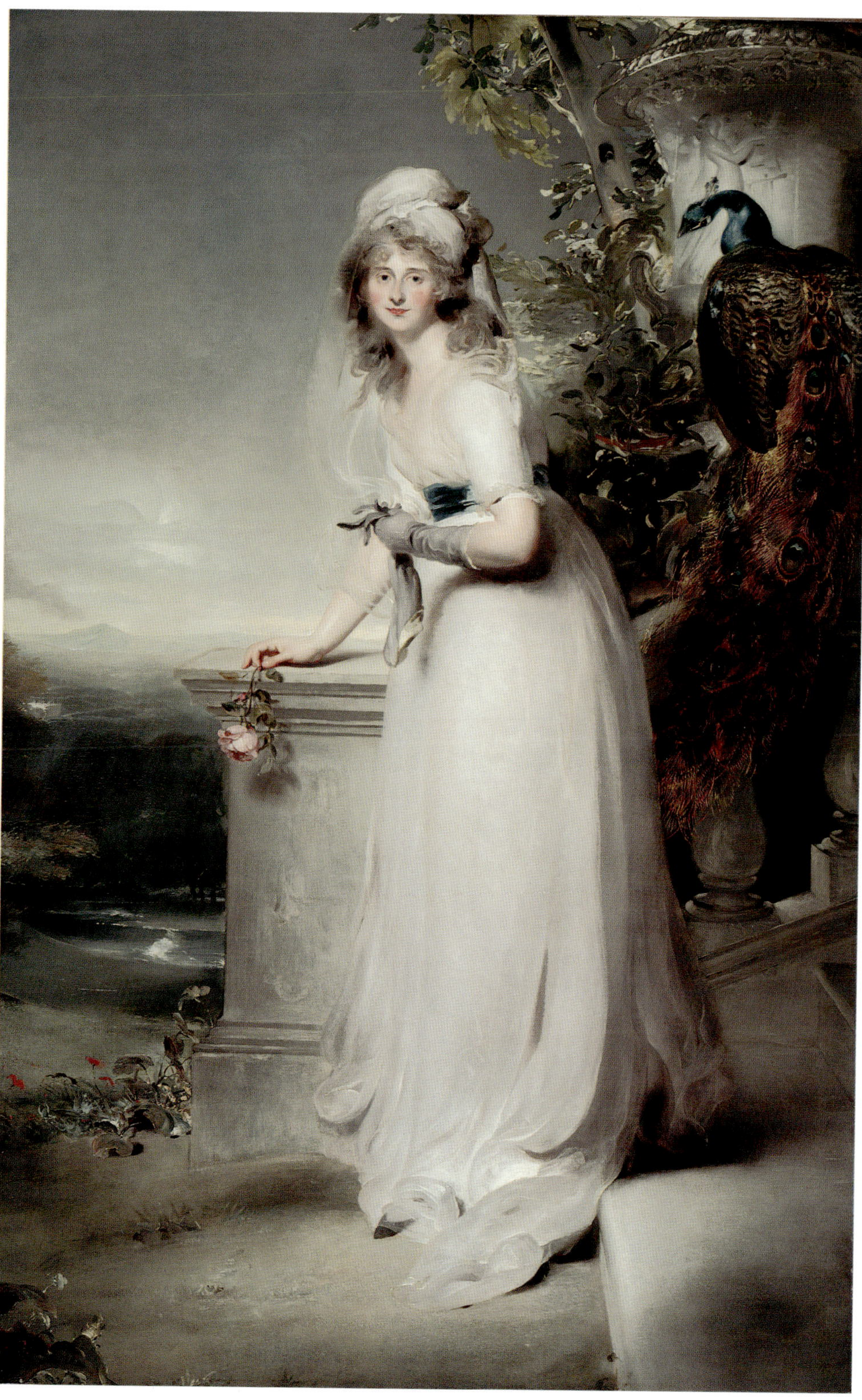

Diminutive Portraits

Miniatures were often commissioned to commemorate a departure, marriage, or death, or to reward loyalty. Tokens of affection for friends, lovers, family members, and monarchs, miniatures were painted in watercolor on delicate small-scale supports of vellum or ivory, or created in enamel. These diminutive portraits could function as relics incorporating human hair and were set in elaborate boxes or simple frames, worn on the body as jewelry, or tucked away in a pocket. The Cleveland Museum of Art's collection includes stunning miniatures spanning six centuries and representing artists from 10 countries.

The Madonna and Child in Glory is an innovative devotional painting with mysterious patronage, combining complex iconographies while presenting a tender view of the relationship between the Holy Mother and the infant Jesus. Miniatures were, however, usually portraits, and Samuel Cooper's remarkably fresh and candid representation of his friend the philosopher Thomas Hobbes is a wonderful

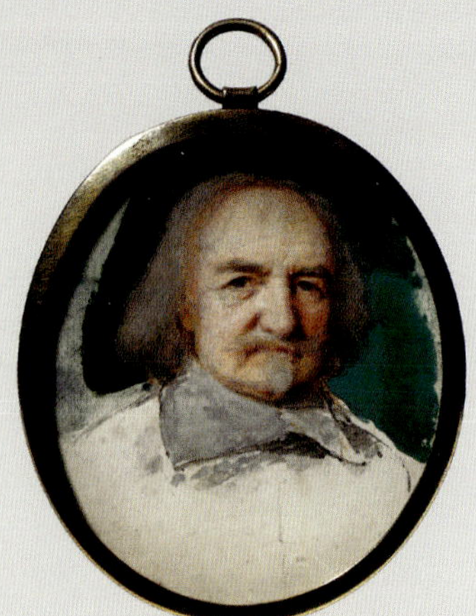

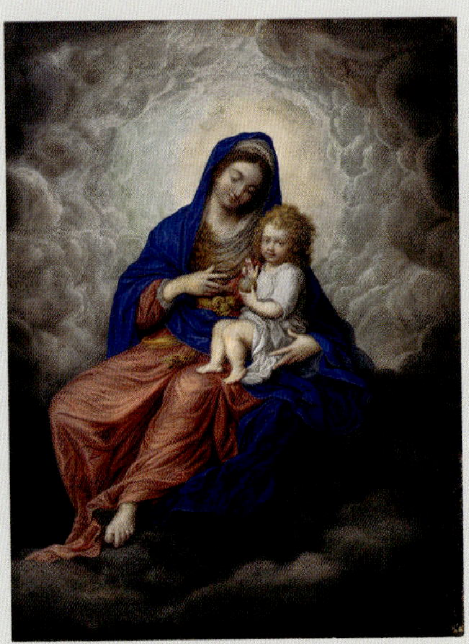

Madonna and Child in Glory, about 1605–17. Isaac Oliver I (French, active in England, about 1565–1617). Gouache and watercolor, heightened with gum arabic, with shell gold framing lines, on vellum, mounted on paper, vellum, and wood; 27.5 x 20.5 cm (10-7/8 x 8 in). Leonard C. Hanna Jr. Fund 2011.2

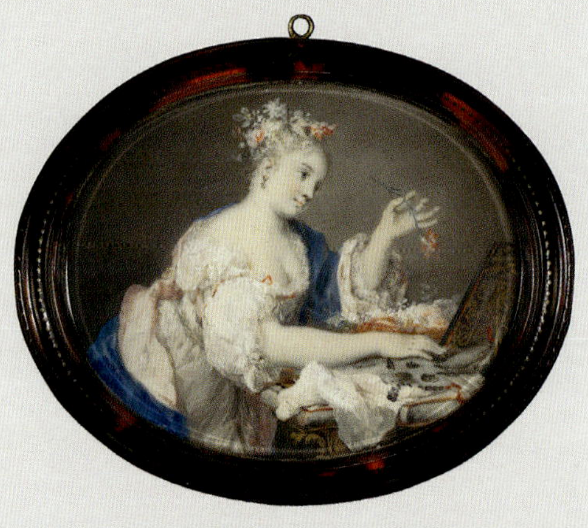

Portrait of Thomas Hobbes, about 1660. Samuel Cooper (British, 1609–1672). Watercolor on vellum; 6.7 x 5.7 cm (2-7/8 x 2-1/2 in.). The Edward B. Greene Collection 1949.548

Woman Putting Flowers in Her Hair, about 1710. Rosalba Carriera (Italian, 1675–1757). Watercolor on ivory; 8.6 x 10.5 cm (3-3/8 x 4-1/8 in.) unframed. The Edward B. Greene Collection 1940.1203

example. Cooper executed a handful of these deliberately unfinished miniatures of the celebrated men and women he found most interesting.

Rosalba Carriera pioneered the tradition of painting in watercolor on ivory in the early 18th century in Venice, creating portraits and decorative scenes on the lids of snuff boxes that were popular among tourists. The translucent ivory surface enabled artists to achieve a degree of refinement and fluidity beautifully conveyed in Richard Cosway's *Portrait of Catherine Clemens and Her Son, John Marcus Clemens*. While Cosway's depictions flattered his sitters, John Smart was known for the frankness and good humor of his portraits. His *Self-Portrait* conveys his skill at communicating the smallest details of physiognomy and individual character.

Among the most famous French miniaturists was François Dumont, whose portrait of the still-life painter Anne Vallayer-Coster sensitively represents the woman as a professional artist engaged in the act of painting. The characteristically round format and heavy frame distinguishes this French miniature from the British style seen in examples by Cosway and Smart.

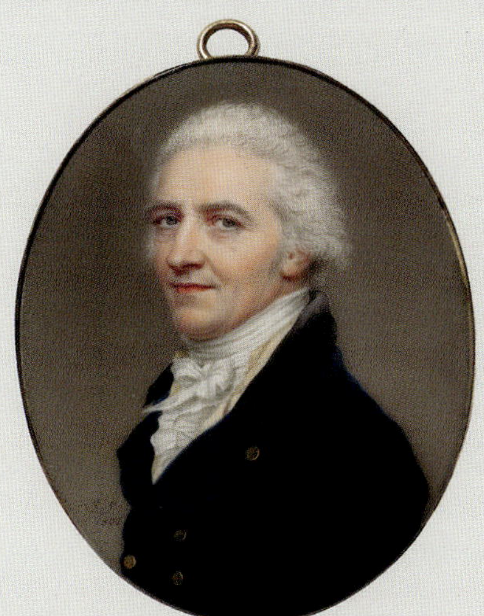

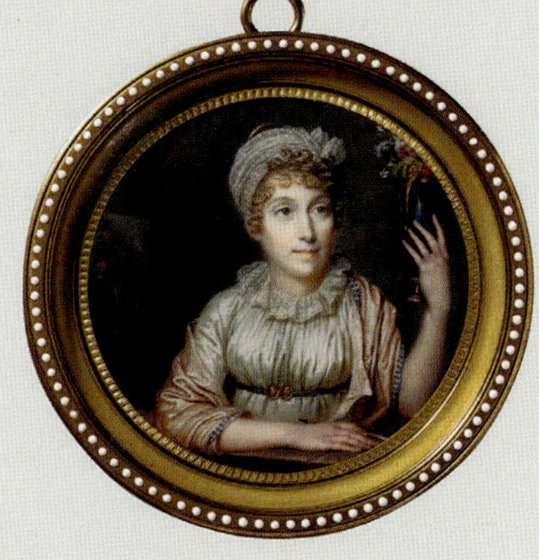

Portrait of Catherine Clemens and Her Son, John Marcus Clemens, about 1800. Richard Cosway (British, 1742–1821). Watercolor on ivory; 9.5 x 7.3 cm (3-1/2 x 2-7/8 in.) framed. The Edward B. Greene Collection 1941.552

Self-Portrait, 1802. John Smart (British, 1741–1811). Watercolor on ivory; 7 x 5.7 cm (2-3/4 x 2-1/4 in.) framed. The Edward B. Greene Collection 1952.95

Portrait of Anne Vallayer-Coster, 1804. François Dumont (French, 1751–1831). Watercolor on ivory; Diam. 7.3 cm (2-7/8 in.) unframed. The Edward B. Greene Collection 1943.639

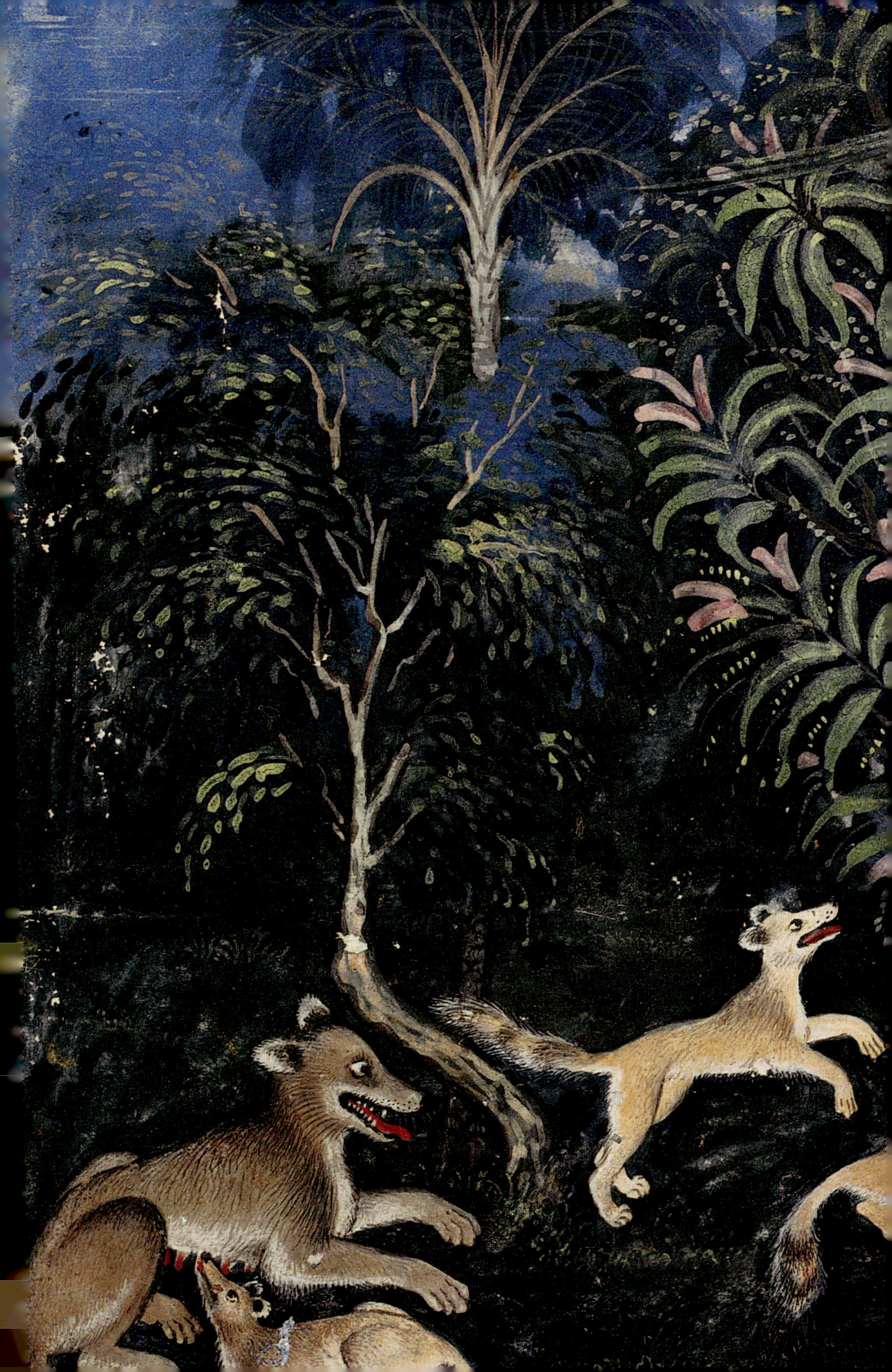

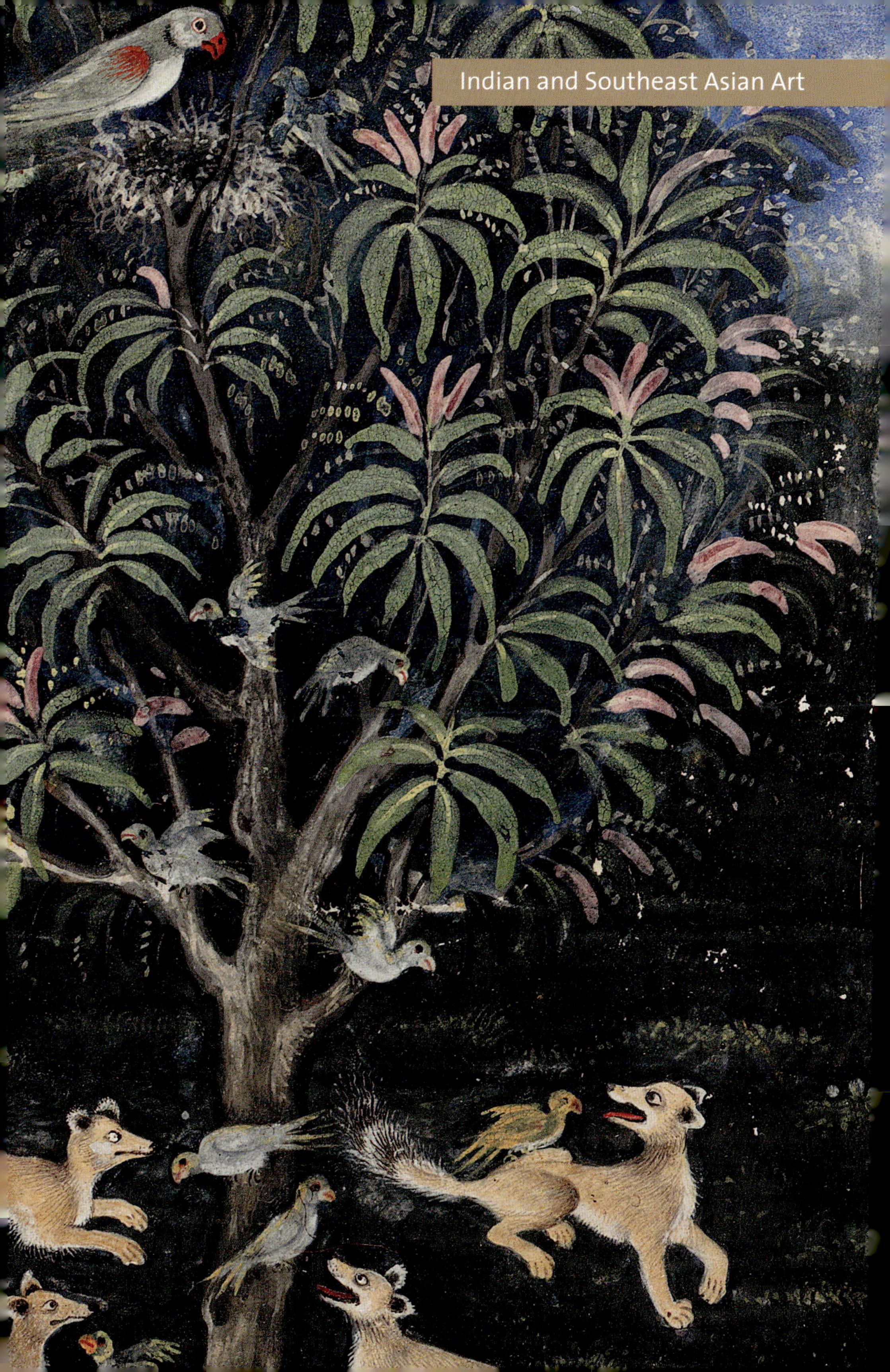
Indian and Southeast Asian Art

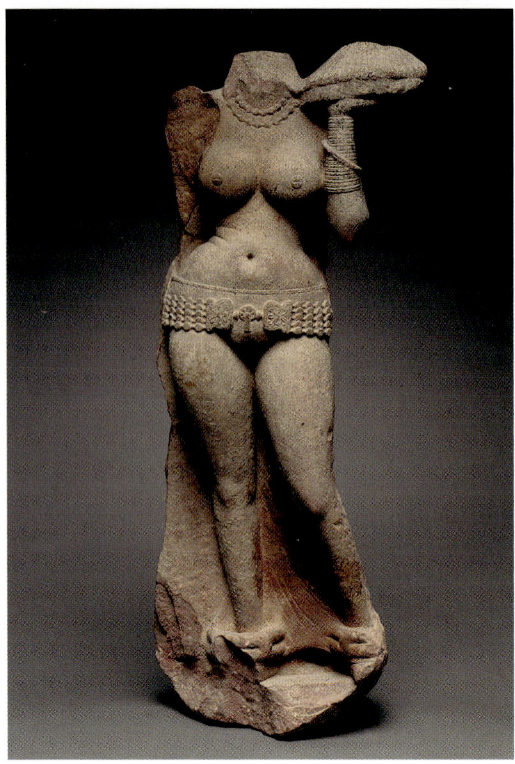

Female Devotee early 2nd century AD
NORTHERN INDIA, MATHURA, KUSHAN PERIOD (1ST CENTURY–320 AD)

During the early centuries of art in India, sculpted railings demarcated places of worship from ordinary spaces. This female devotee, most probably from such a railing, is shown in the process of approaching the place of worship carrying a covered wicker tray that would have been filled with fresh flower garlands. Whether she is a depiction of a nature goddess or an idealized laywoman is unclear. Her form exemplifies the ideal of the young mother with breasts full of milk and broad hips; a beaded girdle secures her lower garment. The skirt is indicated only by the top and bottom hems and by the incised pleat lines between her legs. The clasps of the girdle have a vegetal ornament called the *srivatsa*, or "child of the goddess of good fortune." The pearl strings dangling from the center of the rosette point directly to her genitalia, lending further emphasis to her nature as a fertile mother capable of generating life. Life-affirming imagery dominated the sculptural programs of gateways and exterior railposts of early Buddhist sites, for such imagery was considered cleansing, purifying, and auspicious. As they passed these images on entering the sacred space, devotees were metaphorically cleansed, as though they had passed through pure water to wash away the dust of the ordinary world in preparation for their devotions in the sanctuary.

The sense of dynamism and power in the stance, the masterful transformation of stone into the suppleness of youthful voluptuous flesh barely interrupted by clothing, and the touches of naturalism as in the slipping of the large bangle down the spiral cuff are all stylistic characteristics of female figures made during the early second century.

SANDSTONE; 74.5 X 30 X 15 CM (29-3/8 X 11-3/4 X 5-7/8 IN.)

BEQUEST OF JEPTHA H. WADE III IN HONOR OF EMILY V. WADE 2012.19

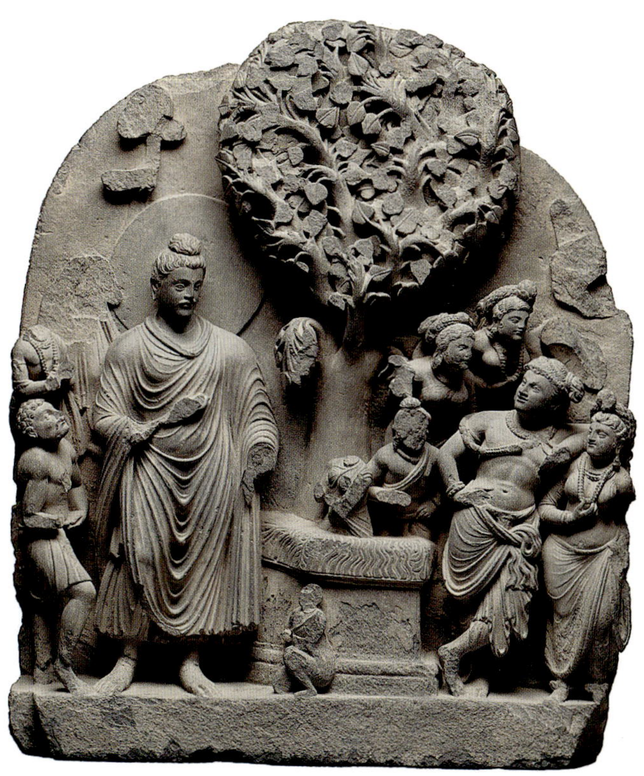

Approaching the Bodhi Tree 2nd century AD
PAKISTAN, GANDHARA

Narrative scenes from the life of the historical Buddha Shakyamuni (about 563–483 BC) are among the most popular objects recovered from Buddhist sites in Gandhara, a region that straddles the Indus River and the Hindu Kush in present-day eastern Pakistan and Afghanistan. During the Roman Empire, especially the first through third centuries, when this sculpture was carved, trade along the silk routes from Rome to China flourished, and a continuous stream of Roman merchants traveled through Gandhara, which had a history of extended contact with the Mediterranean world in the wake of the conquests of the Hellenistic ruler Alexander of Macedon (356–323 BC). Indian artists in this region developed a Greco-Roman hybrid style for the works of art that adorned Buddhist monuments in profusion.

In the center of the composition is a ficus tree with its distinctive heart-shaped leaves. Known as the Bodhi tree, it was under this tree that the Buddha achieved enlightenment or "awakening" (*bodhi*). An altar had already been set up under the tree because the local villagers worshiped the nature divinity who resided in the tree. The nature divinity is depicted here emerging from the altar to worship the Buddha. Under normal circumstances the divinity is invisible, but this relief shows her in human form to honor the Buddha as he is about to achieve his ultimate goal. The goddess of the earth, who will witness the moment of his enlightenment, kneels on the ground at the base of the altar. The figures at the right are the overconfident Mara and his daughters, personifications of obstacles to enlightenment, who will fruitlessly attempt to seduce and frighten the Buddha away from reaching enlightenment.

SCHIST; 73.7 X 57.2 CM (29 X 22-1/2 IN.)
LEONARD C. HANNA JR. FUND 1997.151

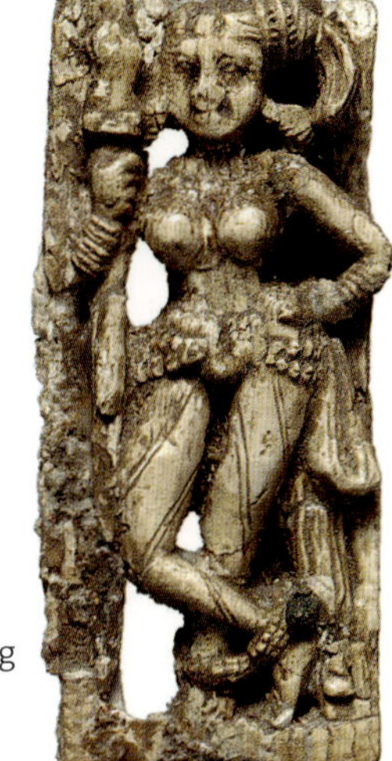

Young Woman with a Spear 1st–2nd century AD

AFGHANISTAN, BEGRAM, KUSHAN PERIOD (1ST CENTURY–320 AD)

This ivory carving, a rarity in American collections, is a work of decorative art that faced a piece of wooden furniture. Indian ivory-faced furnishings were found in an extraordinary deposit of items being traded along the Silk Road, which stretched from Rome to China. Also found in this deposit from Begram were lacquer boxes from China dating to the Han dynasty (206 BC–AD 220) and, from Rome, works of painted glassware, decorative terracottas, and bronze figurines of popular Greco-Roman deities such as Serapis and Harpocrates. Roman histories describe how sought-after Indian ivories, textiles, and spices were among the elite of the empire. The wood on which the ivory and lacquer were affixed has long disintegrated, with only small pieces of the veneers remaining.

This smiling female guardian figure has her hair tied up to one side, wound around with an embroidered strip of cloth. She stands akimbo with her upper garment removed and tied in a loose looped knot at her side. A broad girdle holds up her clinging, diaphanous skirt. This work may have been made in the southern or central regions of India and then exported to Afghanistan, where it would be distributed for sale on the international market of domestic luxury items.

IVORY; 9 X 3.8 CM (3-1/2 X 1-1/2 IN.)

LEONARD C. HANNA JR. FUND 1985.106

Head of a Buddha 5th century

INDIA, MATHURA, GUPTA PERIOD (320–647)

Sculptures of the Buddha made during the fifth century in India are characterized by a sense of introspection, peace, and meditative concentration. Linear qualities—the arc of the eyebrows, outlines of the lips, and sharp delineation of the eyes—are balanced by the smooth planes of the face with its gently swelling volumes. Historians of Indian art consider the sculptures from this period to have achieved a level of classical idealism and to embody the spiritual qualities associated with the prevailing notions of an enlightened being. While some of the most celebrated and high-quality works of art were produced at this time, it was also a period of political instability, when the Gupta Empire was struggling to maintain power in northern India.

The identifying marks of the Buddha became codified by the fifth century. The cranial protuberance at the crown of his head ultimately derived from the coiled topknot of hair worn by members of the upper classes of Hindu society, into which the Buddha was born as a prince. Artists of Mathura transformed the wavy locks of hair into stylized curls, which eventually took the appearance of an expanded cranium that was then interpreted as a mark of an enlightened being, whose consciousness has expanded beyond the limits of an ordinary person. His elongated earlobes are a vestige of his life as a prince, when he wore massive earrings, as was the custom among the wealthy in ancient India. Texts also state that the Buddha had three rolls of flesh at his neck, a mark of physical beauty.

SANDSTONE; 30.6 X 16.6 CM (12 X 6-1/2 IN.)

JOHN L. SEVERANCE FUND 1963.504

Standing Buddha 591

INDIA OR NEPAL, GUPTA PERIOD (320–647)

Few bronze images of the Buddha dating to this early period in the history of Indian art survive, since the material lends itself to being melted down and reused. This example is also exceptional because the inscription on its base is a rare record of a pious donation made by a Buddhist nun of the sculpture along with the funds to provide food for a particular monk in a local monastery, and it is dated to the year AD 591.

This monk's robes are plain, without pleat lines to obscure the beauty of the contours of the body. Only the rippling scalloped clusters of the hem lend some sense of energy and subtle ornament to the composition. The Buddha's right hand is held up in the gesture that assures the viewer he can promise freedom from fear. His lowered left hand holds the end of his garment. He stands on a lotus flower, indicating his status as greater than human. A full-body halo, now missing, would have underscored his nature as an enlightened being.

BRONZE; 46 X 14.5 X 11 CM (18-1/8 X 5-6/8 X 4-1/2 IN.)

PURCHASE FROM THE J. H. WADE FUND 1968.40

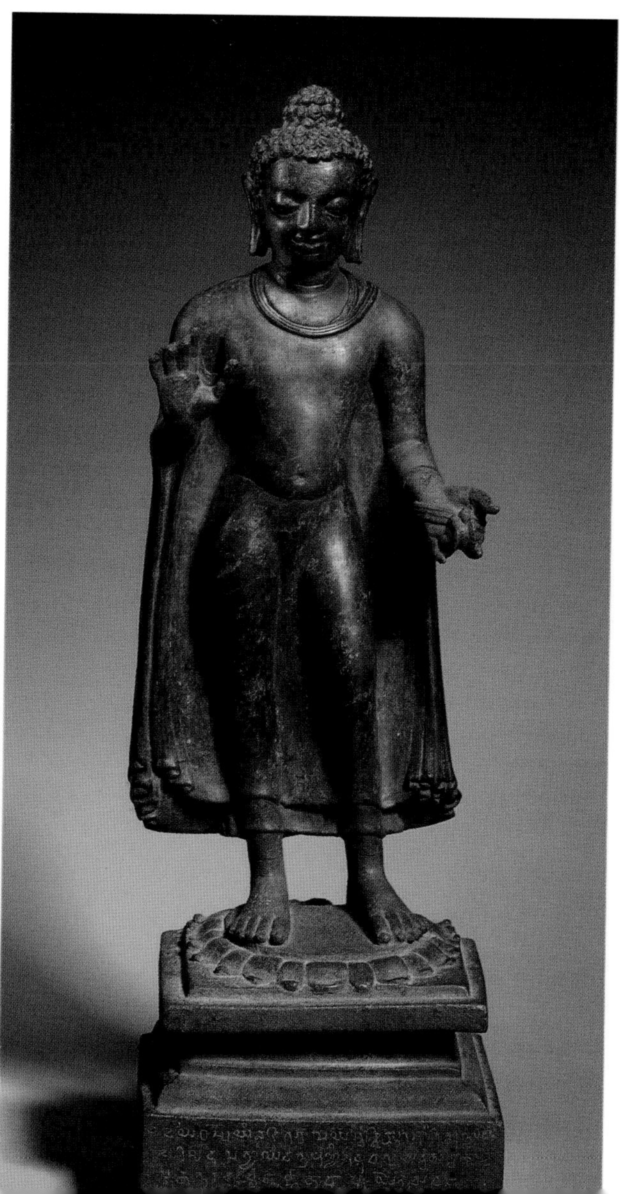

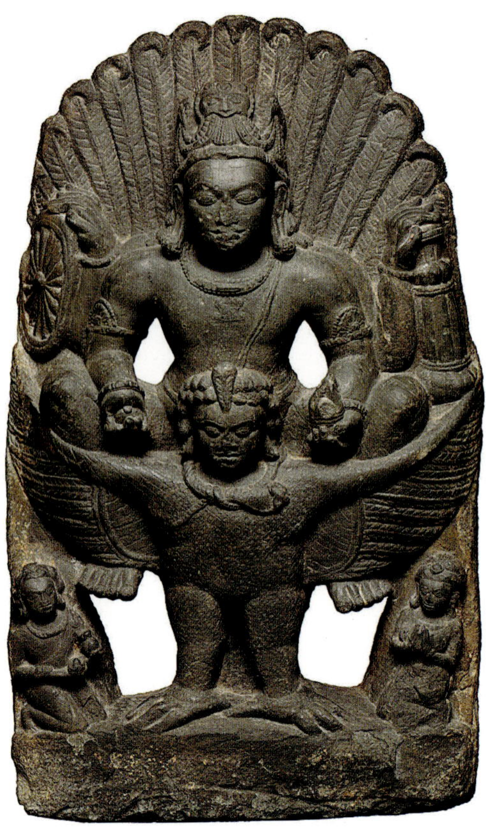

Vishnu Riding on Garuda 6th–7th century

EASTERN INDIA, EARLY PALA PERIOD (ABOUT 750–ABOUT 1200)

This sculpture is a significant early iconic depiction of Vishnu, one of the major gods of medieval Hinduism. He has a royal mien and, like a king, wears a crown with pearl festoons issuing from the mouth of a mythical leonine figure. His four arms indicate his status as a god whose powers exceed those of ordinary human beings. Each of his hands holds an implement: the discus, the club, the conch, and the citron fruit. In the middle of his chest is an auspicious symbol, the *srivatsa* or "child" (*vatsa*) of Sri, the goddess of good fortune and Vishnu's wife. His broad shoulders and short torso are stylistic characteristics of sculptures made during the sixth century.

Vishnu's vehicle is the man-eagle called Garuda, here shown with a human head, wings outstretched, and tail feathers expanding like a fan behind the god's head. He is the enemy of serpents, and a subjugated serpent is tied around his neck. Garuda's determined expression lends confidence that he will do anything in his power to support Vishnu in his accomplishments. Tiny worshipers kneel in veneration on either side of the imposing figures.

CHLORITE; 81.3 X 47 CM (32 X 18-1/2 IN.)

PURCHASE FROM THE J. H. WADE FUND 1961.46

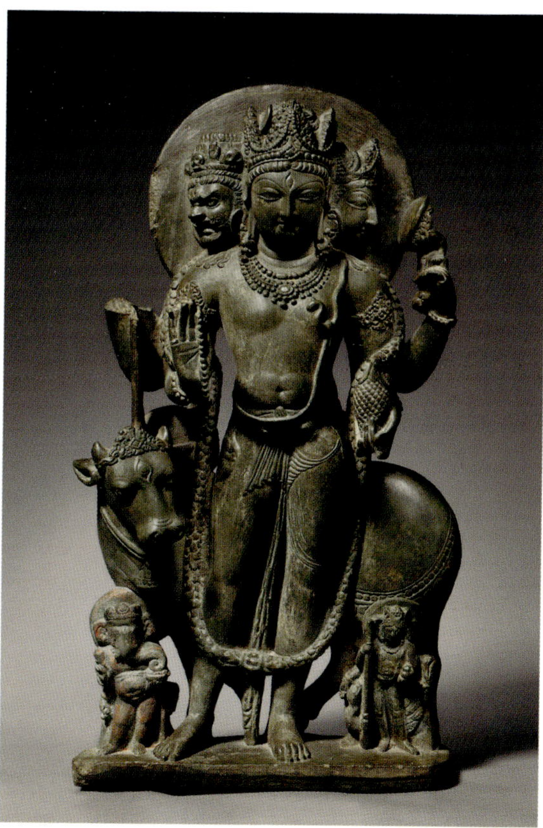

Standing Shiva Mahadeva 8th century

INDIA, KASHMIR

Shiva, along with Vishnu, is one of the most prominent and powerful among the gods of medieval Hinduism. This early iconic form embodies his contradictory aspects in equal measure. Shiva is both a yogi who lives outside of society and a king who rules the world. His countercultural yogic qualities can be seen in the matted locks of hair piled up behind his crown, his erect phallus, referencing the physical discipline of maintaining erection without ejaculation, and the cobra that girds his torso, its tail hooked gracefully behind its rearing head. He also wears the crown and jewels of a king.

The face of Shiva that looks forward embodies his sovereignty. He grants freedom from fear with the gesture of his upraised right hand, and his lowered left hand holds a citrus fruit, used in temple worship. His feminine aspect, implying creation and nurturing preservation, emerges as a face from his left side, which gazes into a mirror held in the upper of his two left hands. The head at his right side, suggesting his powers of destruction, has fangs, a furrowed brow, and a fearsome crown of skulls. He would have held a long-handled trident in his upraised right hand.

Shiva's two sons, the elephant-headed Ganesha indulging in a bowl of sweets and the warrior Skanda holding a spear with his peacock mount behind him, stand at his feet. Shiva's vehicle, the bull Nandi, turns his head protectively around the side of his master, with a determined expression in all three of his eyes, which mirror the three eyes of Shiva.

The plain areas of the bull's haunch and Shiva's body offset the elegant areas of ornament and patterning, as seen especially in the pleated end of his lower garment, tucked at the waist and stretched at his pelvis.

SCHIST; H. 53 CM (20-7/8 IN.)

BEQUEST OF MRS. SEVERANCE A. MILLIKIN 1989.369

Parshva, the 23rd Jina 9th century

CENTRAL INDIA

The Jain religion arose in India around the same time as Buddhism; its founder was a senior contemporary of the Buddha. Unlike Buddhism, which was no longer practiced in India after the 13th century, Jainism has continued to flourish to the present day. The goal for Jains is the attainment of liberation from cycles of birth and death by following strict practices of nonviolence and meditation. According to Jain tradition, 24 people have achieved liberation during this world cycle; this sculpture depicts the 23rd, named Parshva. Liberated beings of the Jain tradition are called Jinas, which means "conquerors" in the spiritual sense.

Parshva is identified by the serpent whose body coils behind his body, his seven-headed hood spreading out like a halo behind Parshva's head. This sculpture was made for followers of the branch of Jainism called Digambara who enforce the regulations of total nudity among those seeking liberation. The only adornment of his figure is the auspicious symbol on his chest and the wheels of righteousness on his palms. The stark form of the nude body standing in a posture of meditation is masterfully set off from the array of gods and serpent divinities who venerate him. He stands with his feet on a lotus pedestal, but his hierarchically tall form reaches to the heavens, where gods fly to honor him with flower garlands. Three umbrellas over his head indicate his status as a liberated being worthy of worship.

SANDSTONE; 160.7 X 67 CM (63-1/4 X 26-3/8 IN.)

JOHN L. SEVERANCE FUND 1961.419

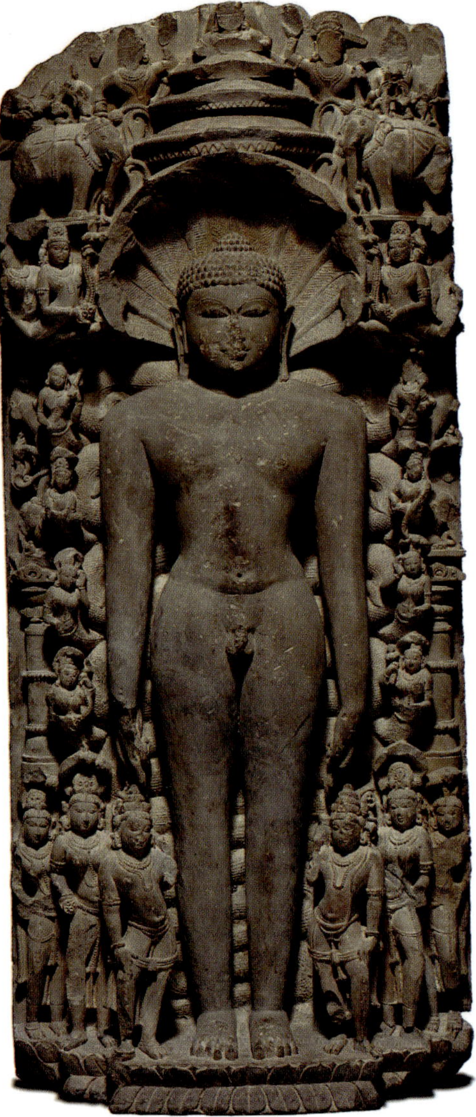

Brahma late 10th–early 11th century

SOUTH INDIA, CHOLA PERIOD (900–13TH CENTURY)

This life-size tour-de-force of South Indian sculpture carved in the round depicts the form of the creator god Brahma as emanated from Shiva, whom many Hindus regard as the ultimate omniscient deity. This sculpture was made for placement in a niche on the north exterior wall of a temple sanctum. According to Shaivism—the branch of Hinduism that upholds Shiva as the single omnipotent originator of the universe, including all the other gods—Shiva manifested himself in the form of Brahma to complete the task of creating the world under Shiva's direction.

Brahma is considered to be the paradigmatic Hindu priest, and his images typically have the attributes of a priest. Hindu priests are called Brahmins because of their association with Brahma, and they form the highest class of orthodox Hindu society. In this sculpture, his priestly aspects are seen in the

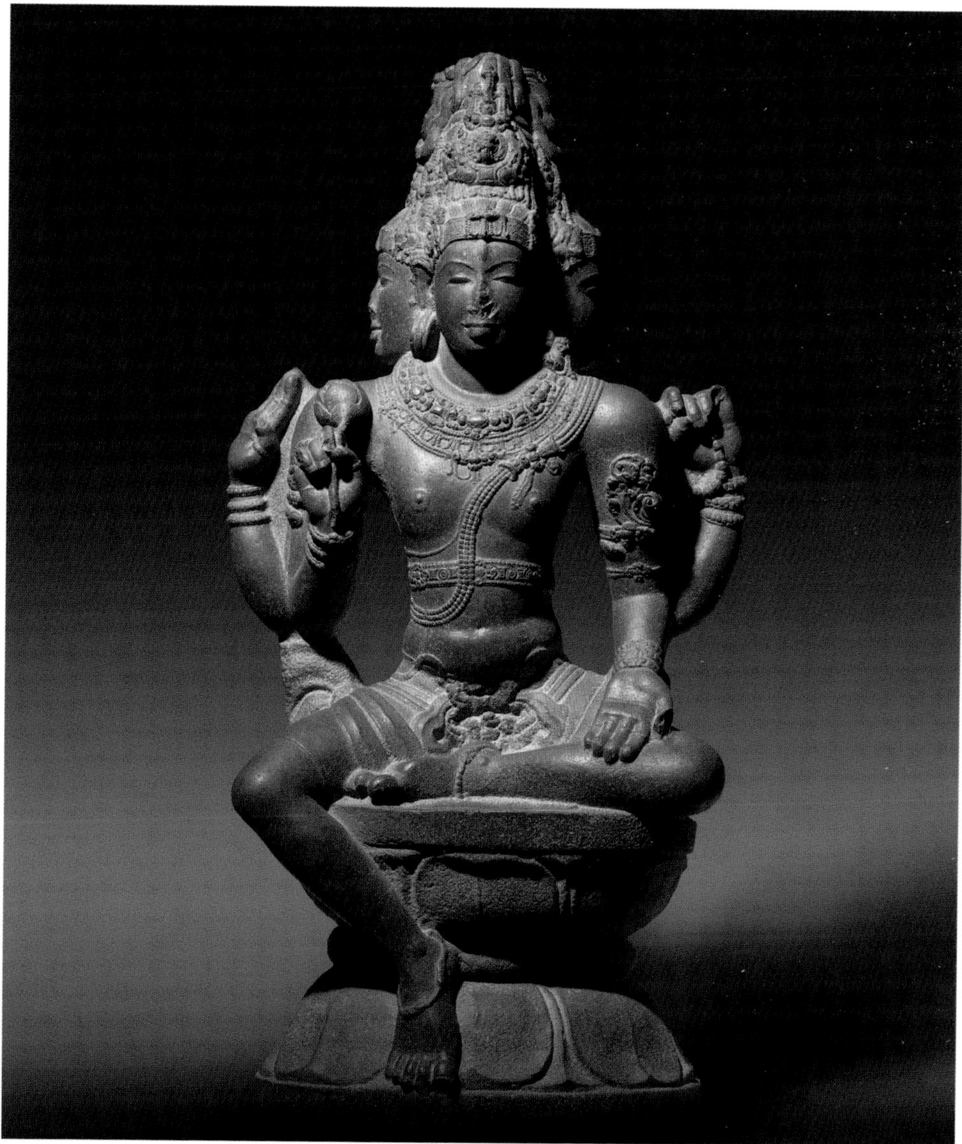

prayer beads he grasps in his upraised left hand, the matted dreadlocks piled on his head, and the sacred thread in the form of a triple strand of pearls draped over his left shoulder and across his body. He is also shown here in a special regal aspect, with crowns and jewels, seated with one leg up in the posture known as "royal ease." Indicating his status as a divinity are the lotus pedestal, four arms connoting superhuman power, and four heads that convey the idea that his creative activities spread in all four directions. His upper right hand enjoins freedom from fear, and his lower right hand holds the lotus bud associated with birth and the process of creation. His lowered left hand is held in the gift-giving gesture, suggesting the gift of creation he will bestow upon the world.

GRANITE; 162.6 X 48 X 80 CM (64 X 18-7/8 X 31-1/2 IN.)
LEONARD C. HANNA JR. FUND, THIS WORK WAS ACCEPTED IN HONOR OF STANISLAW CZUMA IN RECOGNITION OF HIS LONG SERVICE TO THE CMA
2007.155

Nataraja, Shiva as Lord of Dance 11th century
SOUTH INDIA, CHOLA PERIOD (900–13TH CENTURY)

One of the most celebrated sculptural forms in the history of Indian art, this elegant and dynamic figure embodies some of Hinduism's most fundamental tenets. According to Hindu thought, time is cyclical; the world is created, maintained, and preserved for a time, then destroyed only to be created again. For Hindus who view Shiva as the one omnipotent creator divinity, he is responsible for all creation and destruction. The ring of fire and the tongue of flame he holds in his left hand refer to destruction, and the drum in his raised right hand refers to the relentless beat of time as it moves forward inevitably to the next phase of the cycle. His lower right hand, which is held up with the palm facing out, signals to his devotees not to be afraid of all this impending destruction. He indicates by pointing to his right foot that one can be liberated from the cycles of birth

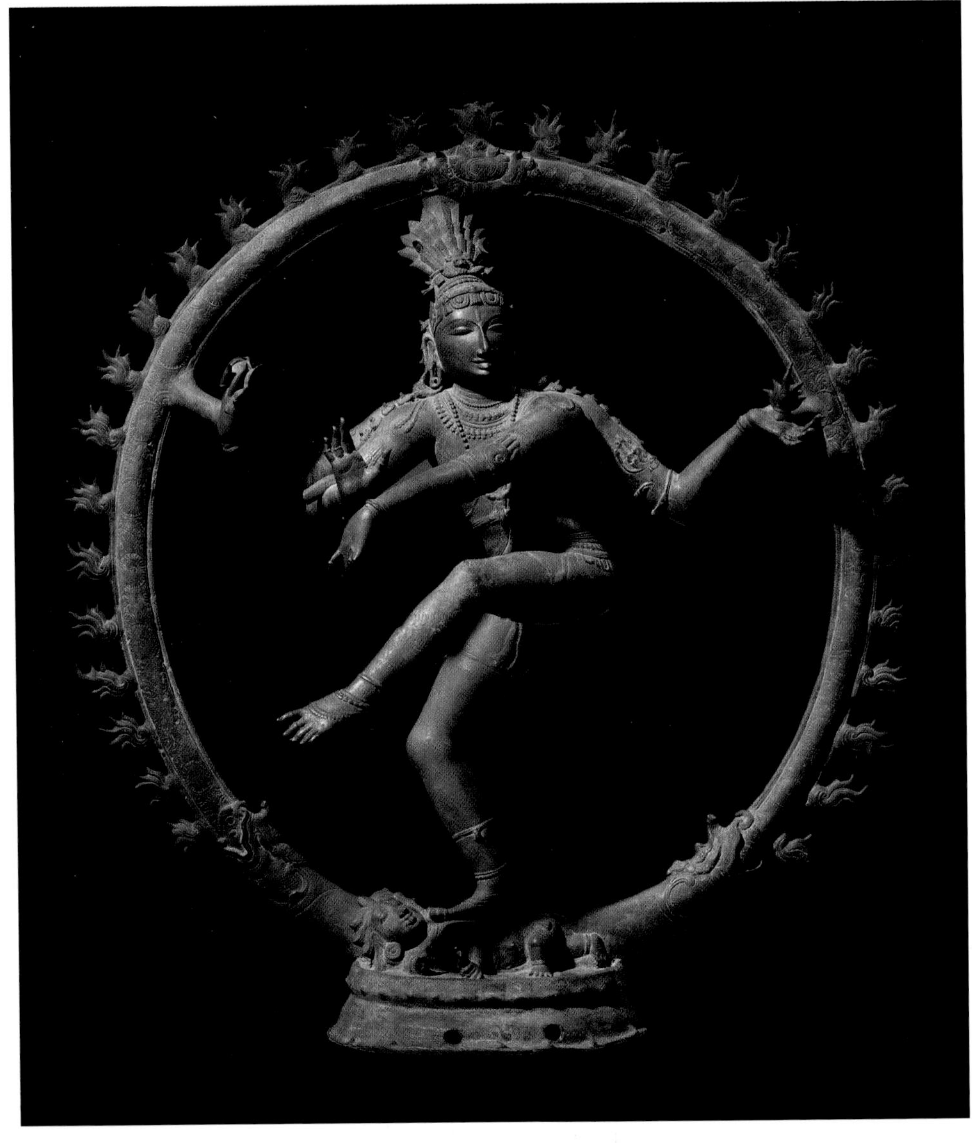

and death through devotion to him. With every step in his dance, he lands on a dwarfish figure personifying ignorance.

Bronzes, solid cast using the lost-wax technique, were kept in the treasuries of temples and brought out on festival days when Brahmin priests ritually transferred the presence of god from the icon in the temple sanctum into the portable bronze image. The image was then dressed in splendid textiles and bedecked with flower garlands and oversized eyes that can be seen from afar. Dowels inserted through the two holes in the base were affixed to a large chariot that would parade the image through the streets for the multitudes to see. When people came to see the image of god on these special festival days, god could see the devotees coming to see him. This act of mutual seeing between god and devotee is an important way for Hindus to receive blessings from the day.

BRONZE; 111.5 X 101.7 CM (43-7/8 X 40 IN.)

PURCHASE FROM THE J. H. WADE FUND 1930.331

Shiva Bhairava 13th century

SOUTHWESTERN INDIA, MYSORE, HOYSHALA PERIOD (1022–1346)

The Hoyshala style of sculpture is unmatched in its exuberant embellishment. Temples and sculptures are covered with baroque ornamentation, all in a chloritic schist that lends itself to finely detailed carving.

In the midst of all the carvings are the smooth planes of the face of the main figure, the Hindu god Shiva in his wrathful form as Bhairava. Close examination of the face reveals the fangs and the third eye of wisdom. His two lower arms have broken off, but the lower part of a mace that was held in his lower right hand remains by his foot. His upper right hand holds the drum that keeps the rhythm of the march of time moving inexorably forward, and in his upper left hand he grips a staff, entwined with a cobra, the top of which has a decomposing head. This head refers to a scene of Shiva's mythology when he cut off the fifth head of Brahma, who was being arrogant and challenging the superiority of Shiva.

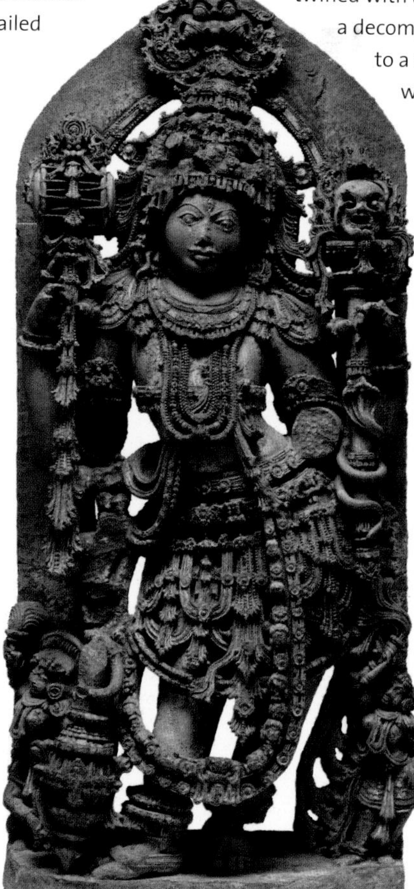

CHLORITIC SCHIST; 113.4 X 49.2 CM (44-5/8 X 19-3/8 IN.)

JOHN L. SEVERANCE FUND 1964.369

Tale V: The Parrot Mother Cautions Her Young on the Danger of Playing with Foxes from the *Tales of a Parrot*, about 1560

DASWANTH (INDIAN, ACTIVE 16TH CENTURY)

This page is from the nearly complete illustrated manuscript *Tales of a Parrot*, one of the most important documents of early imperial Mughal painting. The Mughal Empire was established in 1526 by Babur (r. 1526–30), a warrior of Turkic and Mongol descent from the Central Asian valley of Ferghana, in present-day Uzbekistan.

Babur's grandson Akbar (r. 1556–1605) became emperor at age 13 following the sudden and untimely death of his father. Together with accomplishing the work of stabilizing and expanding Mughal territories across northern India, Akbar took a keen interest in increasing the number of artists and projects of the imperial painting atelier. Fond of adventure stories, the young emperor selected the *Tales of a Parrot* as one of his first commissions. It contains stories told on successive nights by a pet parrot to keep his mistress entertained so she would not rendezvous with her lover while her husband was away. Each story is an engaging fable unto itself.

The illustrations were painted by several dozen local Indian artists assembled by Akbar under the guidance of seven Persian masters brought from the capital of the Safavid kingdom of Iran to India by his father in 1555. The paintings throughout the manuscript show the formation of a Mughal style that combines elements of Persian and Indian traditions in relatively realistic compositions that accorded with Akbar's personal taste. Daswanth, who produced the painting on this page, was an eccentric Indian artist from Delhi whom Akbar saw painting murals on the street and selected on the spot to join the court atelier.

OPAQUE WATERCOLOR, INK, AND GOLD ON PAPER; 20.3 X 14 CM (8 X 5-1/2 IN.)

GIFT OF MRS. A. DEAN PERRY 1962.279.32.A

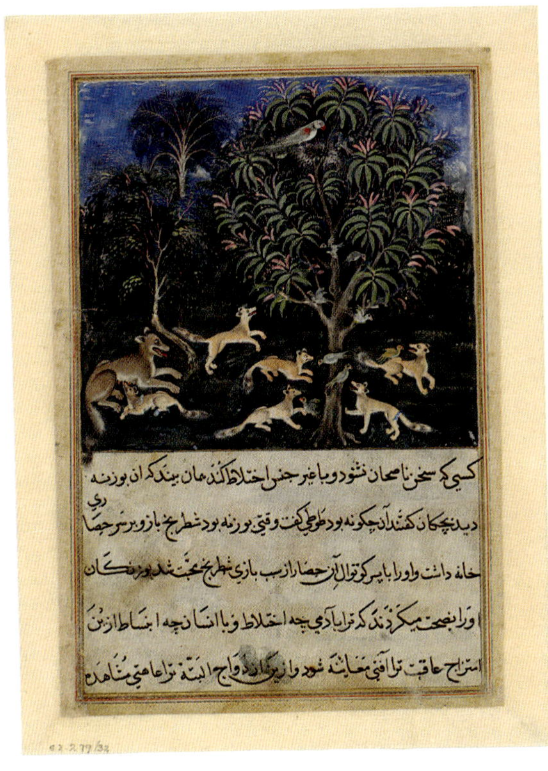

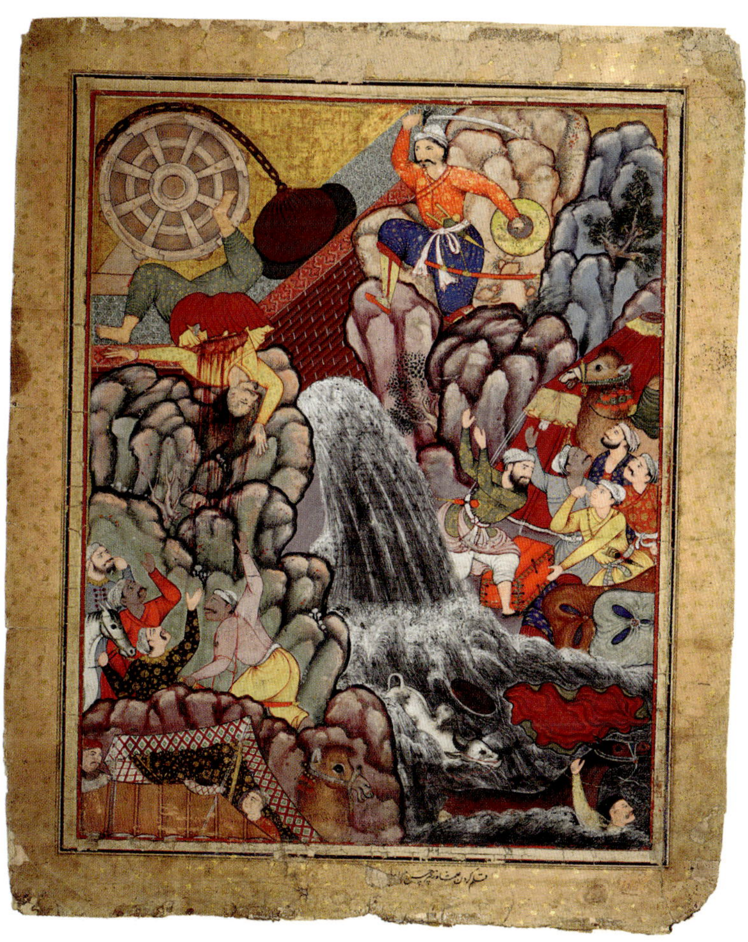

Alam Shah Closing the Dam at Shishan Pass
from the *Adventures of Hamza,* about 1570
INDIA, MUGHAL PERIOD (1526–1858)

One of the grandest accomplishments in the history of Mughal painting, the *Adventures of Hamza* was an ambitious commission early in the reign of emperor Akbar (r. 1556–1605). After 14 years of intense labor in the imperial painting workshop at Delhi, 14 volumes, each with about one hundred full-scale paintings measuring nearly three feet in height, were completed.

The swashbuckling stories filled with violence and intrigue were thinly veiled pious Muslim texts about the early years of Islam, when Hamza, uncle of the Prophet Muhammad, was obliged to defend against murderers and infidels such as the one who lies slain at the upper left corner. Figures gesticulate wildly as Alamshah, son of Hamza, is about to slice the chain that will drop the massive bronze ball and stop the torrent of water flooding Hamza's camp and drowning his heroes. The dam had been built by demons working under the command of King Solomon at a mountain pass that Hamza and his army of Islam needed to traverse.

The golden sky and colorful rocks derive from Persian painting traditions, but the Indian artist, possibly Shravana (active 1500s), provided them with strong modeling to give them a heavy, three-dimensional quality, unique to the Mughal idiom. The splashes of bright red and yellow, angularity of the figures' gestures, and preference for profile presentations reveal ties to indigenous Indian traditions. The penchant for gore and the choice of the climactic moment underscored by the dramatic diagonal composition seem to have been inspired by Akbar himself. This consistent hybrid style was formulated in a relatively short period of time, largely because the emperor took personal interest in reviewing the work of his artists. Every Friday, he examined the week's progress and awarded financial bonuses to those whose work he most admired.

OPAQUE WATERCOLOR, INK, AND GOLD ON PAPER; 83.7 X 67 CM (33 X 26-3/8 IN.)

GIFT OF GEORGE P. BICKFORD 1976.74

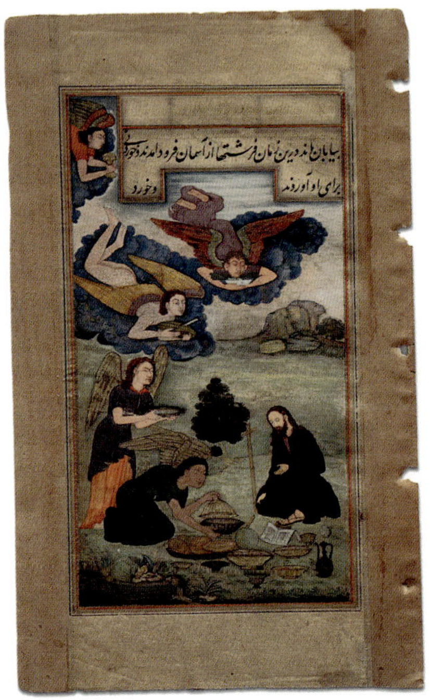

Angels Bring Food to Jesus in the Desert from the *Mirror of Holiness*, 1602–4

INDIA, ALLAHABAD; MUGHAL PERIOD (1526–1858)

The *Mirror of Holiness,* an account of the life of Christ, was commissioned by the Mughal emperor Akbar (r. 1556–1605) near the end of his illustrious reign, during which he had expanded the boundaries of the empire to include most of northern and western India and present-day Pakistan and southern Afghanistan. Known for his ecumenism and interest in other religions, especially Christianity, Akbar asked the Spanish Jesuit missionary Father Jerome Xavier (1549–1617) to write Christ's life story in the Persian language. In the hopes of converting the emperor—and hence the country of India—to Christianity, Jerome lived as the emperor's guest at the Mughal court from 1595 until 1614. Jerome completed the text in 1602 at the capital city of Agra.

Multiple copies of the text were made, and Cleveland's version is the most complete, with 27 surviving illustrations. This illustrated manuscript of Jerome's text was commissioned by the son of Akbar, Prince Salim (1569–1627), who would become the emperor Jahangir in 1605. Prince Salim had rebelled against Akbar in 1600 and in defiance established his own court and atelier in Allahabad, about three hundred miles east of Akbar's capital at Agra; this manuscript was written and illustrated there between 1602 and 1604, when the prince relented and returned to Agra.

The illustrations do not follow any pre-existing European model. The artist interpreted the scenes directly from the Persian text of Father Jerome, which includes standard scenes from the Gospels as well as apocryphal passages.

OPAQUE WATERCOLOR, INK, COLOR, AND GOLD ON PAPER; 26.2 X 15.7 CM (10-3/8 X 6-1/8 IN.)

JOHN L. SEVERANCE FUND 2005.145.15

Buddha about 7th century

THAILAND, PROBABLY SHRI THEP

This elegant, monumentally scaled sculpture is the earliest type of Buddha image to be made in Southeast Asia. It comes from a site in north-central Thailand that was part of the Dvaravati kingdom, which lasted from the sixth until the thirteenth century.

The body shows direct links with the sculptural traditions at Sarnath, in northern India, on the banks of the Ganges River. At Sarnath, the site of the Buddha's first teaching, a prolific school of sculpture developed that reached an apogee in quality during the fifth century. The style of Buddha image distinctive to Sarnath is characterized by an attenuated, idealized form of the Buddha's body beneath a plain robe uninterrupted by pleat lines. The face has the peaceful introspection that became canonical during the Gupta period of the fifth century in India. Unlike Indian prototypes are the shape of the head and facial features, which

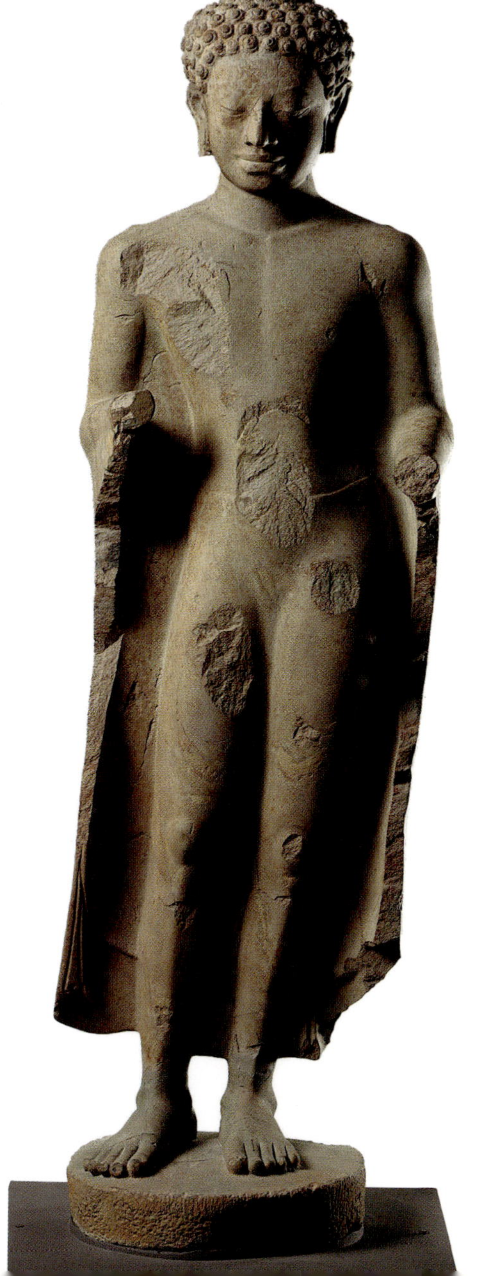

suggests that the artists and patrons of Dvaravati chose to make the Buddha resemble the local Mon population.

The figure's stance has been rendered with remarkable fluidity, and the abstracted caps of the knees and minimalist modeling of the pelvis lend the figure an otherworldly, transcendent demeanor, balanced by the approachability of the gently smiling countenance. Noteworthy too are the delicately modeled neck and shoulders; the back of the figure is fully finished, which is rare among sculptures from this time and region. Fortuitously, the feet were located in Thailand one year after this Buddha entered the collection, and they have been restituted to the sculpture.

SANDSTONE; 132.7 X 114.2 CM (52-1/4 X 45 IN.)

LEONARD C. HANNA JR. FUND 1973.15

Krishna Govardhana 6th–7th century

CAMBODIA, PRE-ANGKOREAN PERIOD (600–802)

This remarkable colossal sculpture depicts Krishna, an incarnation of the Hindu god Vishnu, in one of the earliest sculptural representations known from Cambodia. He is shown performing the miracle of raising Govardhana Hill in order to shelter the villagers and cows from the torrential downpours sent by Indra, king of the gods, who was angry at Krishna for having suggested that the villagers no longer give him sacrificial offerings.

Krishna was only seven years old when he performed this superhuman feat, so this sculpture depicts him with bare head, youthful features, and short lower garment called a *sampot*. Nonetheless, the extreme power of this child god is elegantly conveyed, for he appears to raise the mountain almost effortlessly, his right leg only slightly bent under the weight, as though he were holding an umbrella rather than a mountain.

The eight sculptures excavated from the southern Cambodian site of Phnom Da represent the earliest phase of stone sculptural production in the region, and all but two—one in the Musée Guimet in Paris and this Krishna—are still in Phnom Penh. In the early 1970s when this sculpture first came to the attention of then director Sherman Lee, it had been in the collection of Adolphe Stoclet in Brussels since 1912, and only the head and torso were known. In a dramatic conclusion to the efforts of Stanislaw Czuma, Cleveland's emeritus curator of Indian and Southeast Asian art, to recover the remaining pieces of the lower body, which had been buried in the garden of Stoclet's neighbor decades earlier, this imposing masterpiece was reconstructed by Cleveland's conservators to its present condition.

LIMESTONE; H. 244 CM (96-1/8 IN.), W. 200.8 CM (79 IN.) WITHOUT BASE

JOHN L. SEVERANCE FUND 1973.106

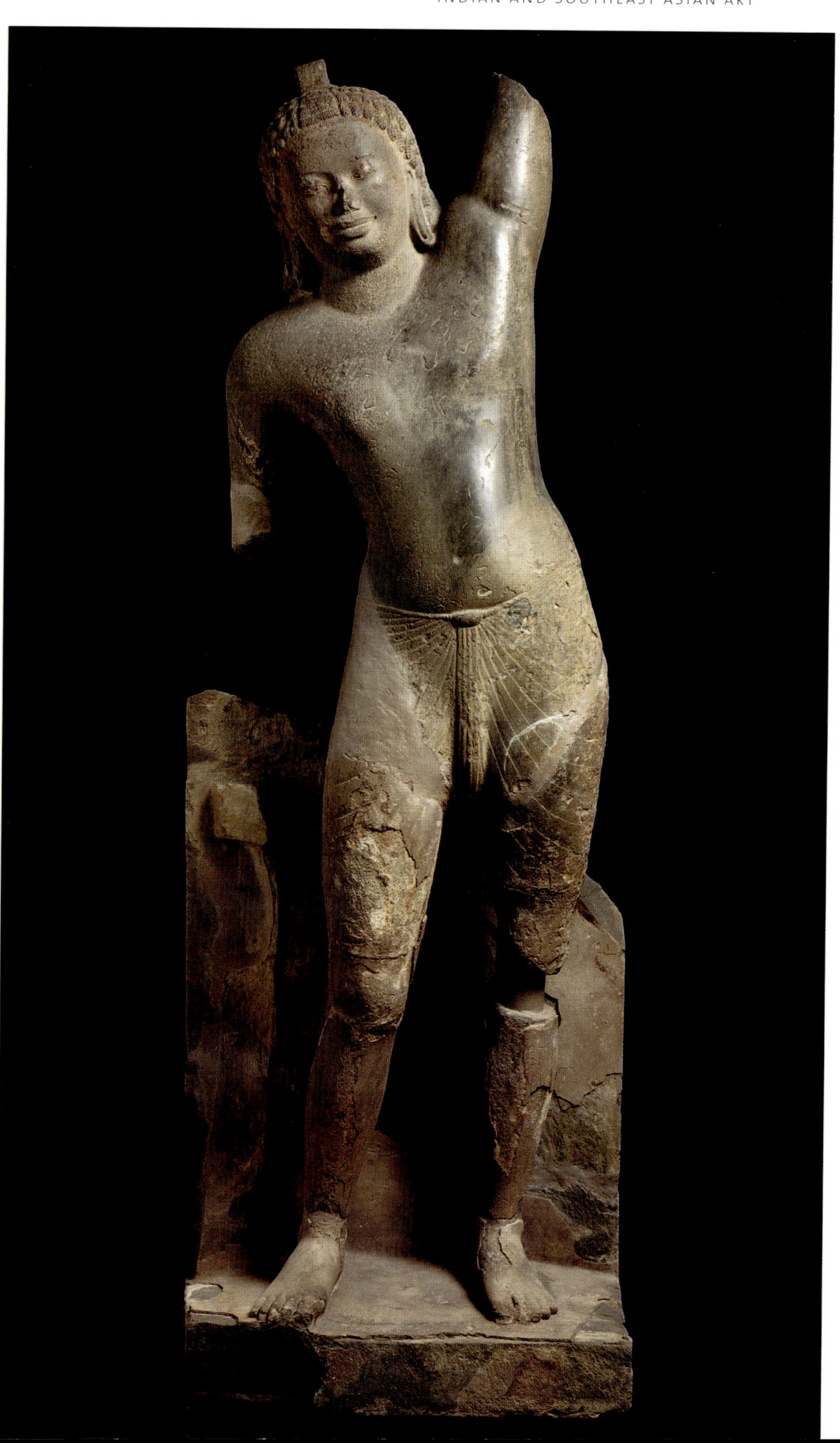

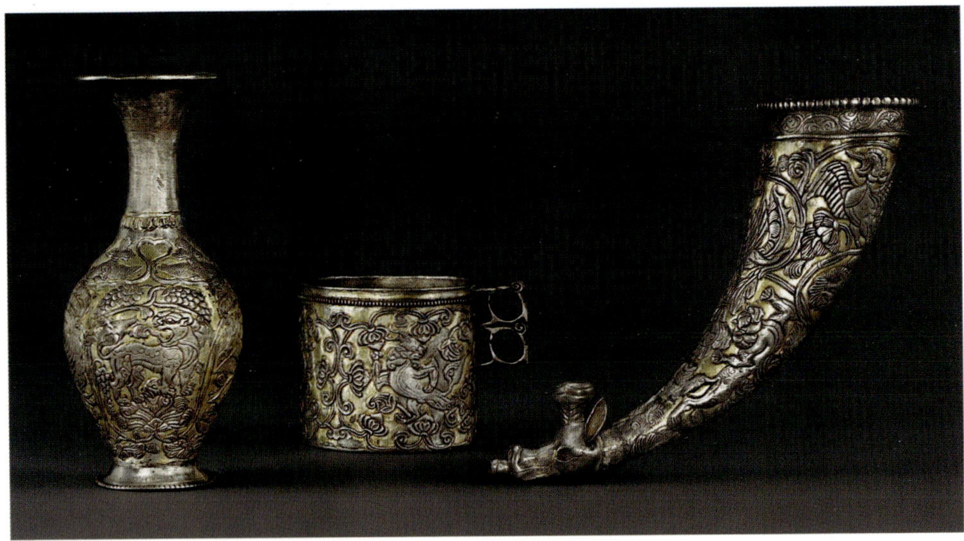

Vase, Beaker, and Rhyton mid 7th century

TIBET OR CENTRAL ASIA

These three vessels are of remarkable historical importance. An inscription on the base of the beaker states that they were the property of the Chinese queen, probably the wife of Tibet's first historical king, Songtsen Gampo (r. 627–50). He instituted Buddhism as the state religion of Tibet and expanded and consolidated his territories through marital alliances with princesses from the neighboring countries of Nepal and China. Wen-cheng, a Chinese princess of the Tang dynasty (618–907), moved to Lhasa to be the wife of the Tibetan king. Songtsen Gampo was also responsible for instituting the Tibetan script, still in use today. The ownership inscription at the base of the handled cup may be the earliest surviving text written in Tibetan.

The vessels reveal an amalgamation of Chinese and Central Asian elements, which is characteristic of art made during the expansionist Tang dynasty when contacts with the West were cultivated. Imagery associated with regions along the Silk Road—grapevines, beaded borders, and heart-shaped motifs—appear on these vessels. The form of the rhyton as a drinking vessel and the use of silver derive from Persian sources. The lush, luxurious quality of the design and the form of the lions and curling dragon on one side of the vase, however, suggest familiarity with Chinese forms. Offsetting the repoussé silver design work is a background of gilded silver foil that has been skillfully hammered into place.

SILVER WITH GILDING; H. 2.9 CM (9 IN.) VASE, H. 10.2 CM (4 IN.) BEAKER, L. 30.5 CM (12 IN.) RHYTON
PURCHASE FROM THE J. H. WADE FUND 1988.67.1–3

Cosmic Buddha Vairochana last half 12th century

CENTRAL TIBET

Iconic paintings on cloth used for religious purposes in the Himalayan regions are called *tangkas*. This extraordinary example, which is in remarkably good condition, is from one of the earliest groups that survive from central Tibet, near the location of the capital in Lhasa. The form of Buddhism associated with this painting is called tantric or esoteric Buddhism.

Tantric Buddhist texts posit the existence of a primordial Buddha, who generated all other Buddhas, and Cosmic Buddhas, who preside over various quadrants of the universe. These theoretical Buddhas are distinguished visually from earthly Buddhas by their crown and jewels, as seen in this example of the Cosmic Buddha of the Center. Here, Vairochana's hands are held in the teaching mudra, and he grasps a tiny *vajra* between thumb and forefinger. The presence of the vajra, the symbol for a lightning bolt, further associates this figure with tantric practices, which were developed to assist practitioners in achieving their spiritual goals with the "speed of lightning."

Flanking the central figure are two standing and four seated bodhisattvas, beings close to attaining Buddhahood. Along the top row are images of the founders and transmitters of tantric teachings. Starting at the upper left, Vajradhara, the embodiment of the essence of all Buddhas, is shown as the source of the teachings received in visions during yogic meditations by Indian masters, two of whom, Tilopa and Naropa, are adjacent to the image of Vajradhara. At the upper right, from left to right, are Marpa, his student Milarepa, and his disciple Gampopa, tantric masters who developed the teachings in Tibet. Remarkably, the figure of Gampopa's disciple Phagmo Drupa (1110–1170), who founded an important branch of the Kagyu order of Tibetan monastic Buddhism, is in Vairochana's crown. At the bottom, guardians and protectors flank a central image of the white, 11-headed Bodhisattva of Compassion.

OPAQUE WATERCOLOR AND GOLD ON SIZED COTTON; 111 X 73 CM (43-3/4 X 28-3/4 IN.)

MR. AND MRS. WILLIAM H. MARLATT FUND 1989.104

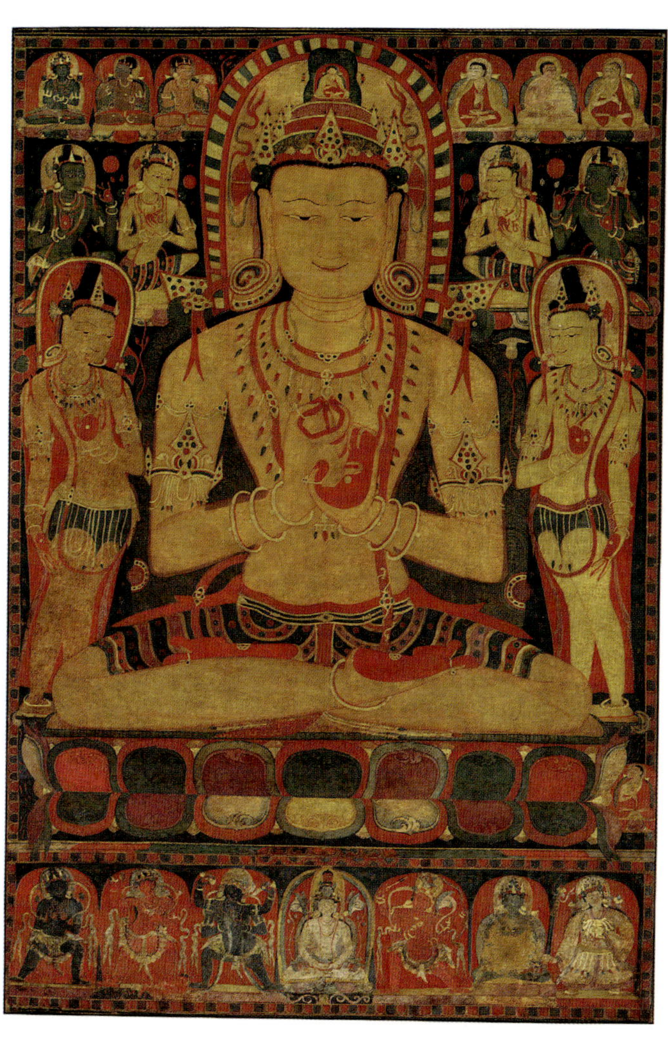

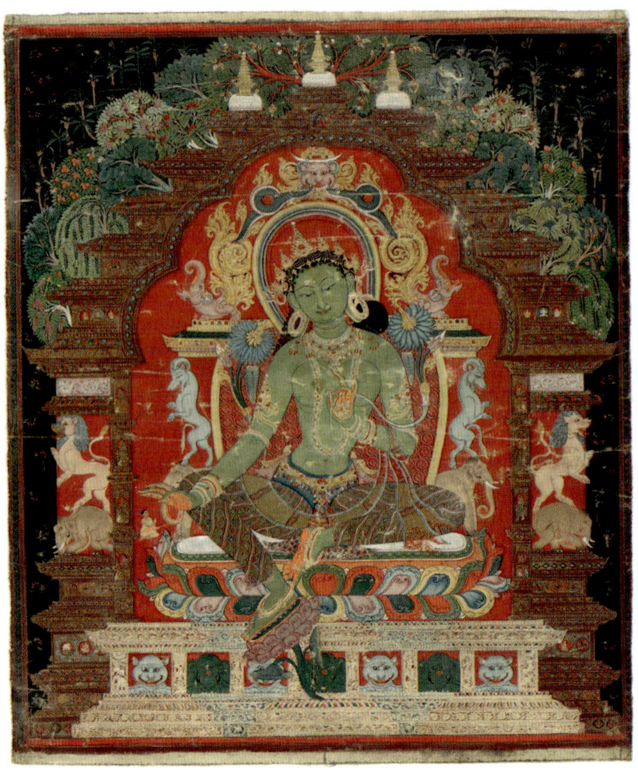

Green Tara about 1260s

TIBET

This work of stunning refinement is in the Nepalese style of the early central Tibetan painting tradition. It is distinguished by its jewel-like use of color, delicate shading, exquisite detailing, and, most of all a lilting, confident quality of line that imparts an unparalleled elegance and clarity to the composition.

The central figure is a popular female form of a Buddha who developed in the medieval Indian tantric Buddhist tradition, which spread to Nepal and Tibet. The Buddha from which Green Tara emanated is Amoghasiddhi, one of the so-called Five Cosmic Buddhas, each of whom presides over a direction (center, north, south, east, west) and is identified by a color and symbolic hand gesture. Amoghasiddhi presides over the north, he is green in color, and his mudra means "fear not"; Green Tara shares those attributes.

In accordance with the standard iconography of Green Tara, she sits with one leg drawn up on her multicolored lotus seat; her other foot rests on a smaller lotus footstool. Her left hand is held up in the gesture indicating that she is a source for transmitting Buddhist teachings, and the stem of a blue lotus winds gracefully through her fingers. Her hair is arranged asymmetrically with a big bun over her left shoulder and long loose curls falling behind her right. Delicate curls of hair are arranged over her forehead.

A small monk sits beneath her right hand, perhaps a practitioner who receives her teachings through visualization and meditation. Green Tara is surrounded by an elaborate throne supported by animals and mythical creatures. A forest of trees can be seen behind the jewel-studded architectural structure in which she sits, each one referencing the tree under which a Buddha reached enlightenment.

INK AND COLOR ON SIZED COTTON; 52.4 X 43.2 CM (20-5/8 X 17 IN.)

PURCHASE FROM THE J. H. WADE FUND BY EXCHANGE, FROM THE DORIS WIENER GALLERY 1970.156

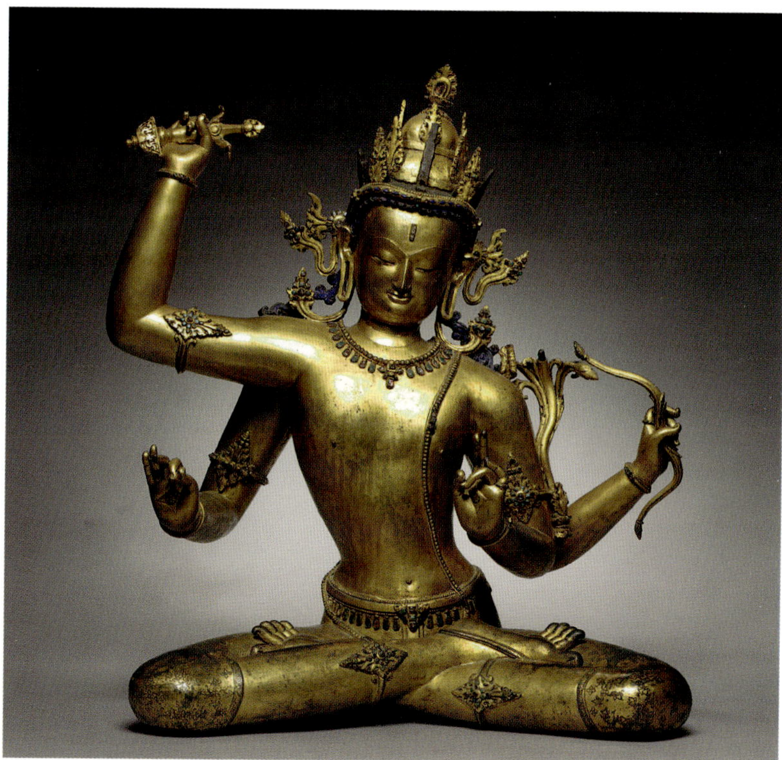

Bodhisattva Manjushri 15th century

NEPAL

The imposing scale of this sculpture is furthered by the active placement of the astonishing four arms and the bright gilding. This image depicts one of the main bodhisattvas, beings who are only one stage away from full enlightenment in the Buddhist tradition. As such, they are depicted with the appearance of a royal prince since the historical Buddha was a prince prior to his renunciation and life as a wandering ascetic. This example has the sharp features, sweet expression, and crisp ornamental details characteristic of images made in Nepal during the 15th century.

Manjushri is the Bodhisattva of Wisdom. He holds in his upraised right hand the hilt of a sword that, like wisdom itself, metaphorically cuts through and defeats ignorance. His lower, rear left hand grasps a bow that was probably strung with a wire that is now missing. Also missing is the arrow that he likely held in his lowered right hand. Arrows were often symbols for mantras, strings of syllables thought to have the power to focus the mind and work like missiles to destroy negativity and affliction. The gesture of his lowered left hand indicates the transmission of Buddhist wisdom teachings. The lotus stem that rises at the left elbows originally probably held another attribute of Manjushri, a book of sutras that contains Buddhist expositions.

The legs of this figure are crossed in the yogic posture of meditation with the big toe flexed in concentration. Yoga is of central importance in tantric Buddhism, because high-level practitioners are able to discipline the body to such an extent that the mind can also be controlled. Consequently, they become able to engage in meditative visualizations in which enlightened beings and bodhisattvas can appear and transmit the methods and techniques for reaching enlightenment quickly.

GILT BRONZE; 78.1 X 67.6 CM (30-3/4 X 26-5/8 IN.)

LEONARD C. HANNA JR. FUND 1964.370

Tantra in Buddhist Art

Tantra literally refers to the weft of a fabric, the threads that run in the opposite direction from the warp. This literal meaning reveals that the tantric system of practices runs counter to conventional ways of reaching enlightenment. In order to achieve enlightenment within a single lifetime, tantric practices harness the power of visualization and the aid of beings who have already achieved enlightenment and can appear in powerful forms to help a practitioner overcome obstacles. The Buddha Akshobhya, for example, takes on a tantric form called Hevajra.

Dancing Hevajra is one of the most stunning examples of tantric art in the collection. Here he is surrounded by a circle of dancing female beings of enlightenment called *dakinis,* each raising a particular implement in her right hand. *Vajravarahi* is a larger scale Tibetan version of an important dakini who is an embodiment of the wisdom of enlightened beings.

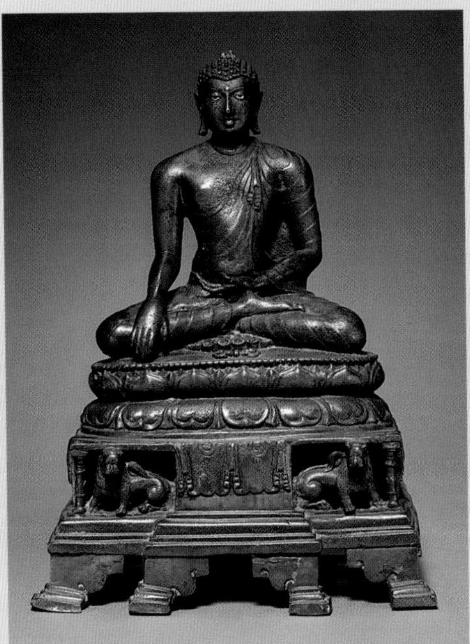

Akshobhya, 9th century. Northeastern India, Bihar, Kurkihar, Pala period (8th–12th centuries). Bronze with silver and copper inlay, 38.8 x 26.3 cm (15-1/4 x 10-3/8 in.). Purchase from the J. H. Wade Fund 1970.10

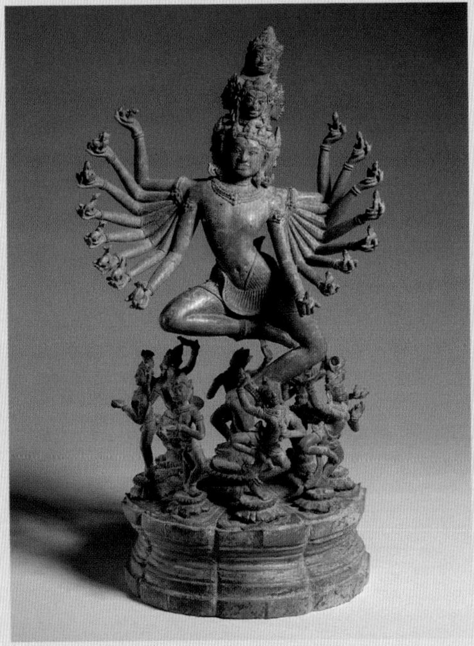

Dancing Hevajra, around 1200. Northern Thailand, Khmer Empire, Angkorean period (9th–early 15th century). Bronze, 46 x 23.9 cm (18-1/8 x 9-3/8 in.). Gift of Maxeen and John Flower in honor of Dr. Stanislaw Czuma 2011.143

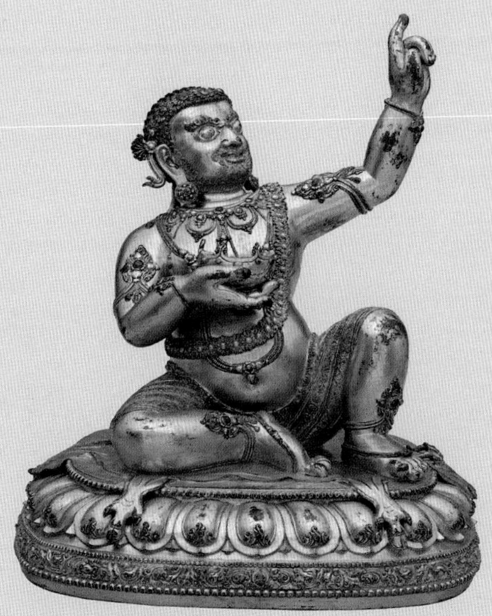

The Indian yogi Virupa, who lived during the ninth century, was the main exponent of the *Hevajra Tantra,* which was explained to him by Hevajra's consort in a meditative vision.

Vajravarahi is identified by the head of a female boar (*varahi*). Lithe and beautiful, she is often shown in the midst of an ecstatic dance wielding a flaying knife, her weapon used to defeat out-of-control lustful passions.

The arrangement of Hevajra's 16 arms vividly implies the multifarious energies that emanate from his core as he dances with two pairs of legs. His eight heads have a variety of expressions, from the benign to semi-fierce, and they, like his multiple limbs, convey the sense of his superhuman power. A favorite image among tantric Buddhists in the Khmer kingdom under Jayavarman VII (1125–1218), Hevajra references the contents of the text called *Hevajra Tantra,* which contains a method for achieving enlightenment more quickly than by conventional means.

Scientific analyses have revealed that this depiction of *Dancing Hevajra* survived in such good condition because it apparently was buried in a pot filled with water. X-ray, metallurgical analyses, and thermoluminescence testing of the clay core have yielded evidence that indicates all the sections of this assemblage were cast at the same time, well before tantric practices were replaced by mainstream Buddhism in Southeast Asia around 1400.

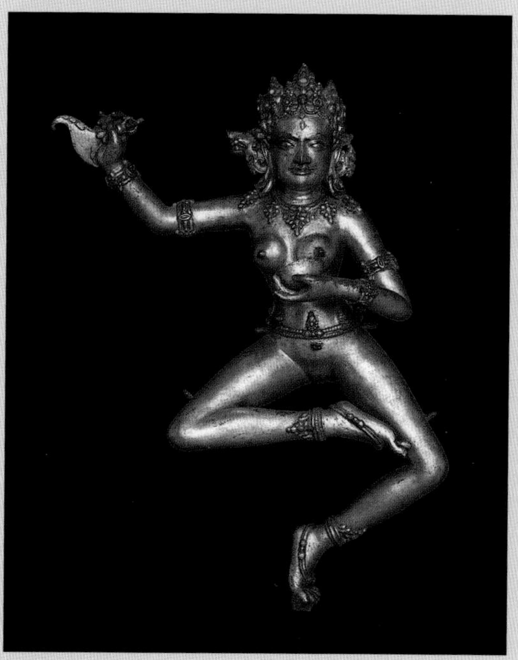

Virupa, 1407–10. China, Ming dynasty, Yongle reign (1402–24). Gilt bronze, H. 43.6 cm (17-1/8 in.). Gift of Mary B. Lee, C. Bingham Blossom, Dudley S. Blossom III, Laurel B. Kovacik, and Elizabeth B. Blossom in memory of Elizabeth B. Blossom 1972.96

Vajravarahi, 14th century. Tibet. Gilt bronze, H. 36 cm (14-1/8 in.). Leonard C. Hanna Jr. Fund 1982.50

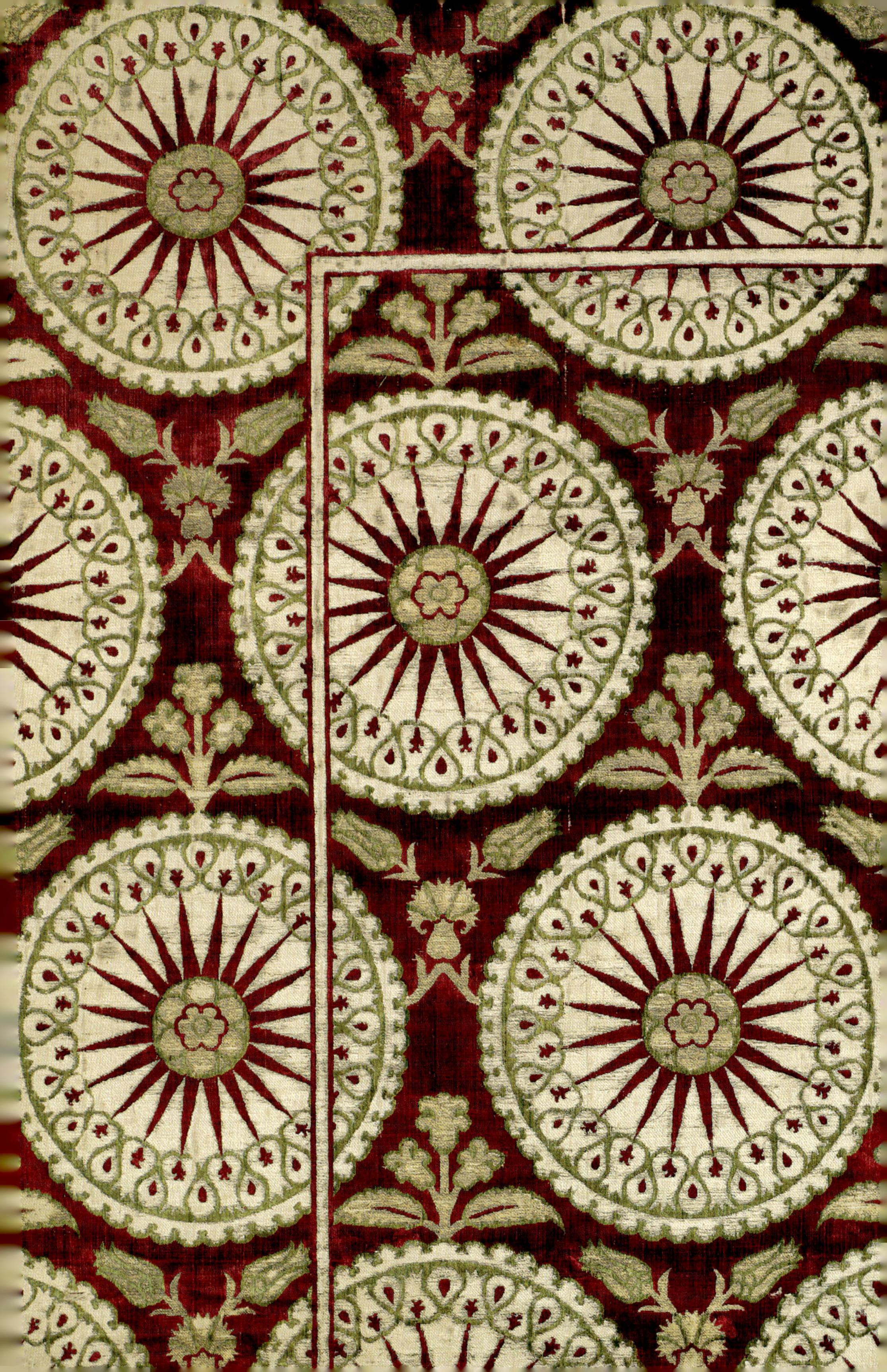

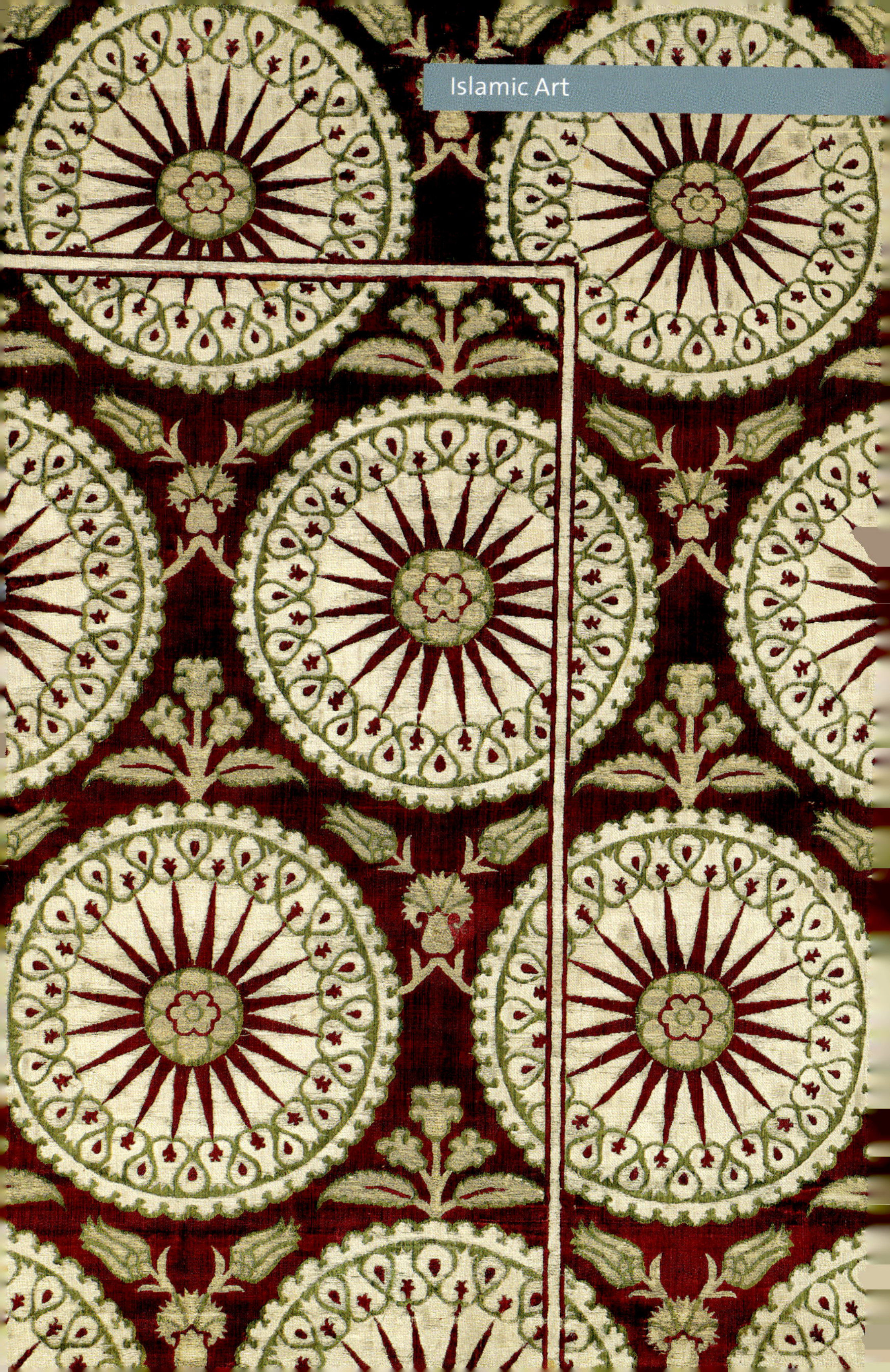
Islamic Art

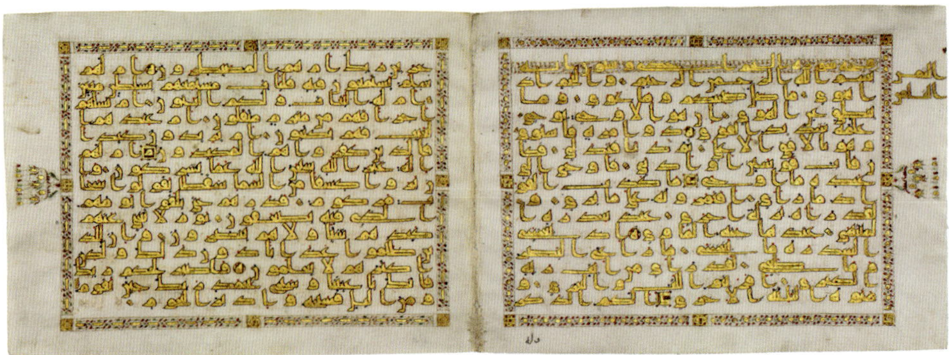

Two Folios from a Qur'an, with Gold Text Outlined in Ink 800s

NORTH AFRICA, IRAQ, OR IRAN, AGHLABID DYNASTY (800–909) OR ABBASID PERIOD (750–1258)

Calligraphy, the art of beautiful writing, was elevated above all other art forms in the Islamic world because Allah, God, revealed the divine word of Islam to the Prophet Muhammad in the Arabic language. Arabic script evolved gradually until the 800s when Muslim scribes produced copies of the Qur'an that were calligraphic masterpieces. This Qur'an, written entirely in gold, exemplifies the angular form of writing known as kufic at its finest. Distinctive markings—short ink strokes, colored dots—identify the vocalization of the text. Each folio is framed by an interlacing border and displays a leafy motif in the outer margin.

The text on the right folio is the opening of the Chapter of the Star (53:1–21) with a section heading in the margin and an illuminated foliate band for the chapter heading at the top of the page. It begins: "By the star when it plunges, your comrade is not astray, neither errs, nor speaks he out of caprice. This is naught but a revelation revealed." The text on the left folio is from the Chapter of the Moon (54:13-27).

GOLD, INK, AND COLORS ON PARCHMENT; 26.7 X 73 CM (10-1/2 X 28-3/4 IN.)

SEVERANCE AND GRETA MILLIKIN PURCHASE FUND 1993.39.1.A–B

Pillow Cover with Arabic Inscription 800s

EGYPT, AL-BAHNASÁ, ABBASID PERIOD (750–1258) OR TULUNID PERIOD (868–905)

This rare complete pillow cover is a masterpiece of contrasting colors. Crimson and blue-green wool form alternate areas in the field pattern of bird-inhabited roundels, supported by mustard-colored wool and undyed linen. Each primary color forms half of the ground color while the alternate color forms the ground color of the pearl roundels, and contrasts again with mustard-color on the checkered bodies of the flying birds holding leaves in their beaks. On each half, the four birds face one another in distinct units. The colors in the end borders, however, are consistent, with large pearls, foliate vines, and rosettes in the plain outer band. Across the top of the field, the Arabic text written in angular kufic script with foliate terminals reads: "In the name of God. Blessing from God to its owner. Of what was made in the tiraz." The word "tiraz," meaning factory, was probably in al-Bahnasá, which was renowned for colorful wool textiles with figures from a "gnat to the elephant." Similar pillow covers have been found in third- through fifth-century Egyptian burials. As a funerary pillow cover folded down the center, the birds are appropriately ascending in flight.

TAPESTRY WEAVE; WOOL AND LINEN; 80 X 83.2 CM (31-1/2 X 32-3/4 IN.)

PURCHASE FROM THE J. H. WADE FUND 1959.48

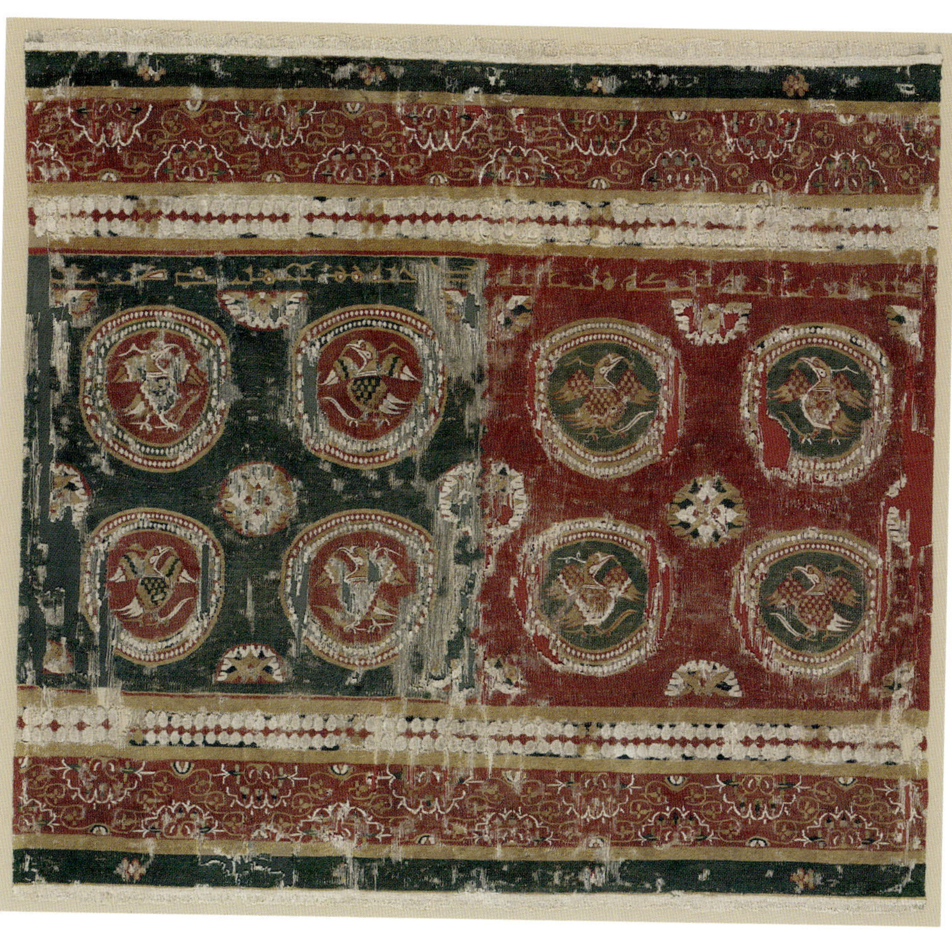

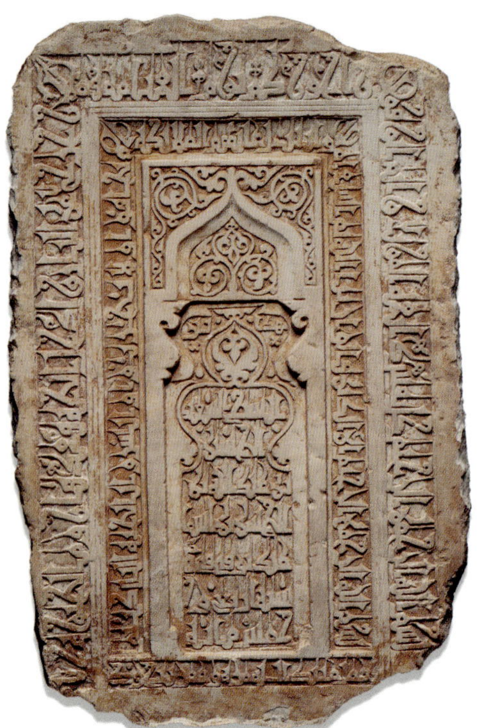

Inscribed Tombstone of Shaikh al-Husain ibn Abdallah ibn al-Hasan 1110

IRAN, YAZD, SELJUK PERIOD (1040–1194)

Monumental simplicity characterizes the composition and elegant Arabic calligraphy on this Iranian tombstone. The center is carved with a *mihrab,* the arched prayer niche in a mosque wall that is oriented toward Mecca. It is inscribed with the name of the deceased and his death date, AH 504/AD 1110. The names of its two master carvers appear across the bottom: "The work of Ubaidallah Murra[?] and Umar[?]." The arrangement of palmette leaf scrolls in the mihrab bordered by multiple inscription bands is more complex than in tombstones from other Muslim countries.

The Arabic Qur'anic inscriptions bordering the niche are written with great elegance in angular kufic script in which verticals end in half or full palmette leaves. The outer border reads: "In the name of God, the Merciful, the Compassionate. Every soul shall taste of death, and ye shall only receive your recompenses on the Day of Resurrection. And who so shall escape the fire, and be brought into Paradise, shall be happy. And the life [of this world is but a cheating fruition]" (3:185). The inner border reads: "In the name of God, the Merciful, the Compassionate. But as for those who say, 'Our Lord is God,' and who go straight to Him, the Angels shall descend to them and say 'Fear ye not, neither be ye grieved, but rejoice ye in the Paradise which ye have been [promised]' " (41:30).

LIMESTONE, CARVED; 65 X 42.6 CM (25-5/8 X 16-3/4 IN.)

EDWARD L. WHITTEMORE FUND 1950.9

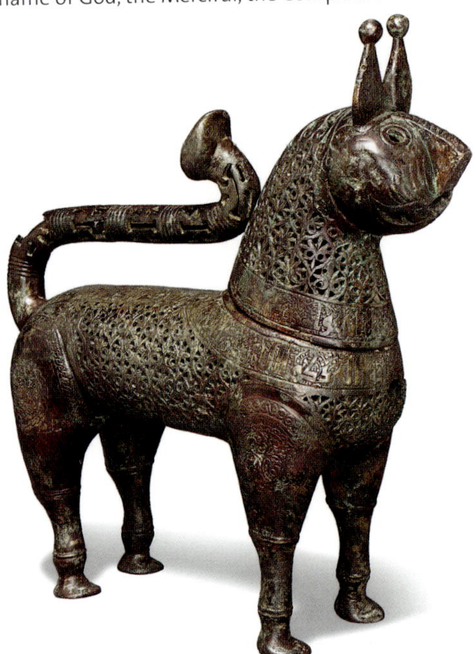

Lion Incense Burner 1150–1200

IRAN, KHURASAN, SELJUK PERIOD (1040–1194)

This robust lion was cast in several pieces with a removable head, enabling hot coals and incense to burn inside the body and scented smoke to rise through the pierced decoration to perfume the air. Openwork designs of palmette leaves in curved lattices enrich the body and neck, and an Arabic inscription is visible around the neck, shoulders, and along the spine. The expressive face has a decorated nose, curved whiskers, alert ears with a palmette motif, curly mane, and open eyes and mouth for wafting incense. Foliate scrolls in scalloped roundels decorate the legs, and an interlacing knot adorns the end of the more angular tail. This spirited lion is one of the larger zoomorphic incense burners that were popular, most likely in secular settings, in Iran during the 11th and 12th centuries.

The inscription written in angular kufic script is from the Qur'an: "O believers, when proclamation is made for prayer on the Day of Congregation, hasten to God's remembrance and leave trafficking aside; that is better for you, did you but know. Then, when the prayer is finished, disperse through the land and seek God's bounty, and remember God frequently that you may prosper" (62: 9–10).

COPPER ALLOY, CAST, ENGRAVED, CHASED, AND PIERCED; 35.5 X 11 X 32.5 CM (14 X 4-3/8 X 12-7/8 IN.)

JOHN L. SEVERANCE FUND 1948.308.A–B

Luster Dish with Polo Player 1170–1200

IRAN, KASHAN, SELJUK PERIOD (1040–1194)

Polo was an ancient sport of kings in Iran. The mounted polo player on this masterful dish represents the Iranian ideal of beauty, with a round moon-like face and fine features reserved in white against the luster ground. Painted in the monumental style with bold fluid strokes, he is dressed in a dotted knee-length robe and tall boots and riding a sprightly dappled horse. Curving vines with plump palmettes enrich the ground.

Luster, a golden sheen imitating pure gold, transformed base materials into expensive luxury ware. Potters most likely invented the technique in Iraq, which migrated to Egypt and then to Iran where it reached its greatest height in Kashan from the 1170s until about 1220. Lusterware, a major Islamic contribution to world ceramics, is an overglaze technique that requires two firings, one for the glaze and a second reduction firing at a lower temperature for the luster. Designs were painted on the cold glaze surface with a mixture of metallic oxides, sulfur, and ocher suspended in vinegar; after firing, this mixture formed a thin metallic layer that was polished to reveal the cherished glistening luster.

FRITWARE WITH LUSTER-PAINTED DESIGN; DIAM. 35.5 CM (14 IN.), H. 7.2 CM (2-7/8 IN.)

PURCHASE FROM THE J. H. WADE FUND 1944.74

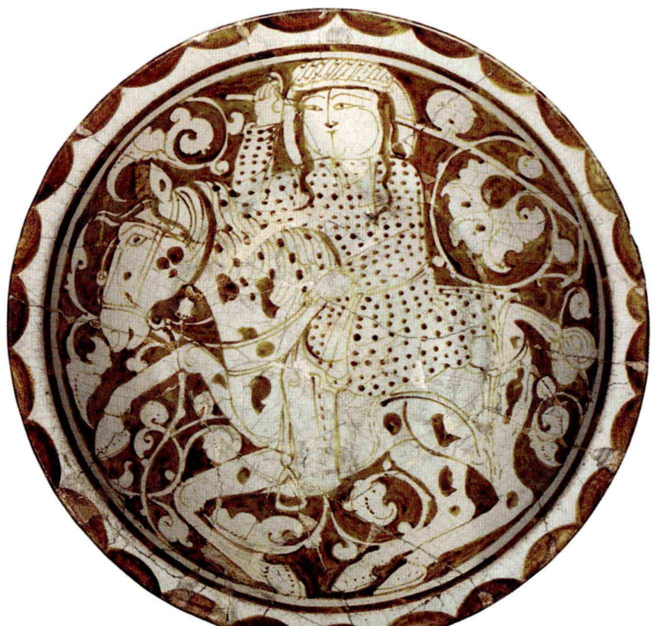

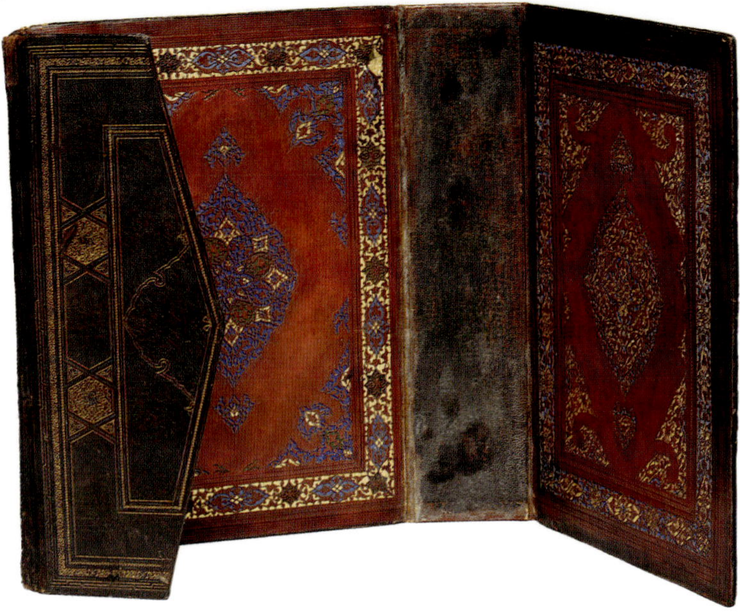

Bookbinding for a Qur'an about 1435–60

IRAN, POSSIBLY SHIRAZ, TIMURID PERIOD (1370–1507)

This exquisite bookbinding illustrates the exemplary artistic and technical refinement created by master craftsmen in Iran during the 15th century. The tooled, stamped, and gilded decoration on the front and back covers displays a similar border, lobed central medallion enriched with vines, palmette leaves, and strapwork, plus indented and embellished corner pieces. The border on the front cover incorporates verses from the Qur'an in the four corner units that alternate with hexagons enriched with elaborate gilded interlacing knots. A Qur'anic verse also appears on the spine. The decorated triangular flap, a distinctive feature of Islamic bookbindings, is attached to the back cover of the binding and tucked under the front cover to protect the outer edge of the pages. This elaborate binding, a labor-intensive process that took an estimated two years, required 550,000 blind stamps and 43,000 gold stamps.

The more protected inner covers are elaborately decorated in delicate openwork, or filigree, with tiny motifs in brown leather silhouetted on blue and ivory grounds in different refined medallion patterns. Under royal patronage in Herat, in modern-day Afghanistan, artists were trained and dispersed what they had learned in Iran, Ottoman Turkey, and Mughal India.

LEATHER OVER PAPER PASTEBOARDS; OUTER COVERS TOOLED, STAMPED, GILDED; INNER COVERS OPENWORK OVER COLORED PAPER; 36 X 81.6 CM (14-1/8 X 32-1/8 IN.) PURCHASE FROM THE J. H. WADE FUND 1944.495

A Princely Banquet in a Garden double-page frontispiece from a *Shahnama* by Firdausi, 1444

IRAN, SHIRAZ, TIMURID PERIOD (1370–1507)

This exuberant Iranian double-page frontispiece of Firdausi's *Shahnama* (Book of Kings) illustrates the most elaborate version of a garden feast in a newly developed format. Although unidentified, the scene may be a celebration of a marriage, with elements of diplomacy and a courtly hunt. A prince and princess, dressed in a luxurious ermine-lined blue surcoat, are seated on a medallion carpet under an elaborate canopy accompanied by several young ladies and a musician in the foreground. The prince appears to be offering a pomegranate on a gold dish to the princess while servers transport food and drink in gold and ceramic vessels, some possibly cherished Chinese blue-and-white porcelain.

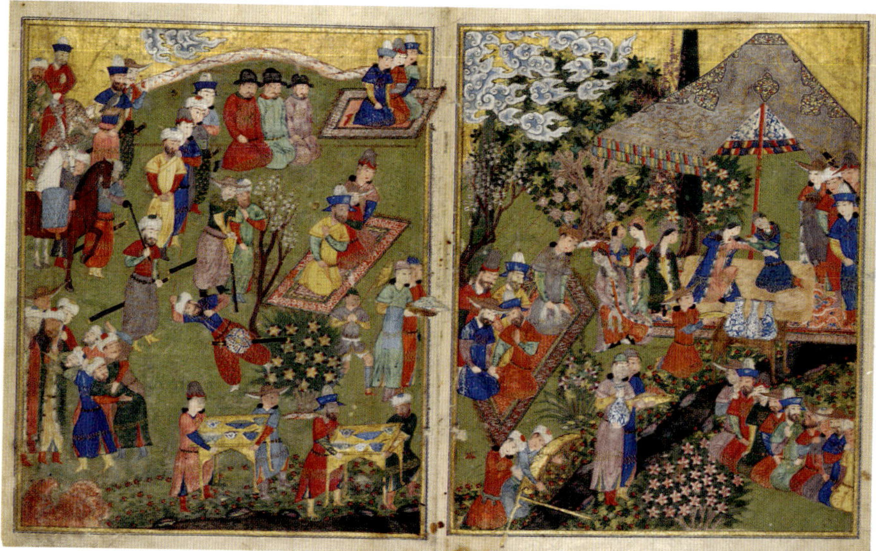

Chinese men with black headgear imply a diplomatic occasion; however, they are not kneeling on carpets as are most of the Iranians in a popular banquet tradition. In the upper left the figures of a falconer, horses, attendants, and two cheetahs (highly coveted for hunting) suggest that this banquet may have been offered after a courtly hunt, a prestigious symbol of power and wealth.

OPAQUE WATERCOLOR, GOLD, AND SILVER ON PAPER; 32.7 X 22 CM (12-7/8 X 8-5/8 IN.) (LEFT), 32.5 X 22.1 CM (12-3/4 X 8-3/4 IN.) (RIGHT)

JOHN L. SEVERANCE FUND 1956.10 AND PURCHASE FROM THE J. H. WADE FUND 1945.169

Rustam's Seventh Course: He Kills the White Div from Shah Tahmasp's *Shahnama* by Firdausi, 1522–37

ATTRIBUTED TO MIR MUSAVVIR (IRANIAN, ABOUT 1510–1555)

This spectacular jewel-like painting of violence in a lyrical setting was made to illustrate the greatest Iranian manuscript ever produced: a sumptuous royal copy of Firdausi's national Iranian epic, the *Shahnama* (Book of Kings) made for Shah Tahmasp during the 1520s and 1530s. The splendor of the "coloring and the portraiture" of 258 large paintings on gold-flecked paper in the manuscript with 742 folios was acclaimed even in its own day. In this spectacular landscape, blossoming trees and brilliantly colored rocks in astonishing hues of lavender, blue, and pink lean toward the action like

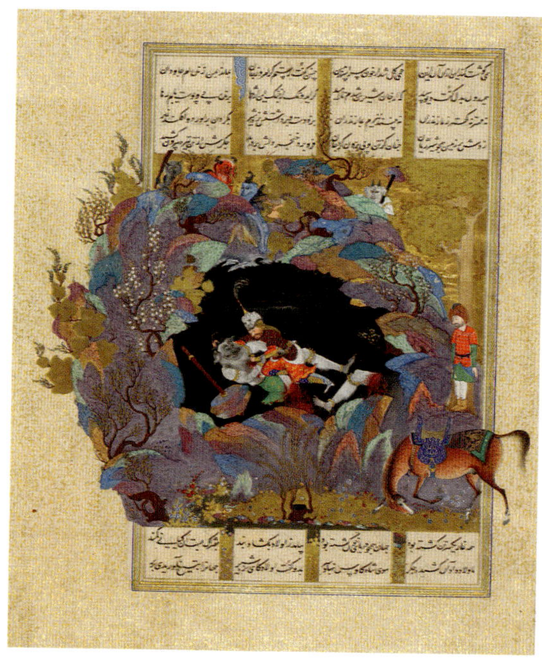

spectators. The legendary hero Rustam, identified by his tiger-skin clothing, kills the savage chief of the demons, the White Div, in an immense cave as distressed demons watch from above. Completing this last of seven trials, Rustam uses the White Div's blood to cure the Iranian king Kay Kaus of his blindness. The painting integrates a refined classical style with exuberant vitality and is attributed to Mir Musavvir.

This resplendent manuscript had an impeccable pedigree until the 1970s. It was originally in the collection of Shah Tahmasp, then of Ottoman Sultan Selim II (gift from Shah Tahmasp in 1567), and then Baron Edmond de Rothschild. Its last owner, Arthur A. Houghton Jr., regrettably disassembled and dispersed it in the 1970s.

OPAQUE WATERCOLOR, GOLD, SILVER, AND INK ON PAPER; 47.5 X 32.2 CM (18-3/4 X 12-5/8 IN.)

LEONARD C. HANNA JR. FUND 1988.96.A–B

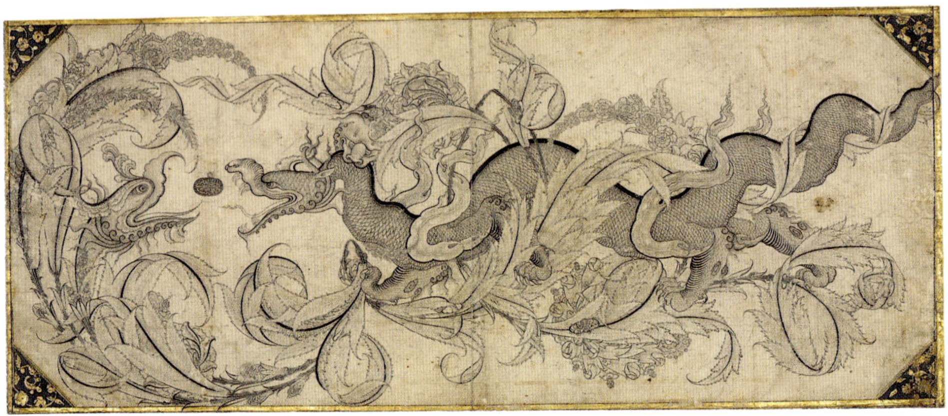

A Dragon, Lion, and Phoenix amid Foliage mid 1500s

TURKEY, ISTANBUL, OTTOMAN PERIOD (1516–1918)

ATTRIBUTED TO ŞAHKULU (IRANIAN, ACTIVE IN ISTANBUL, 1520/21–1555/56)

This exquisite drawing is the finest of a small group known as "dragon drawings" with fanciful curving flora and foliation in the epitome of the saz style that blossomed during the mid 16th century in Ottoman court art in Istanbul. As a single page without literary texts, this large drawing differs from the dominant historical painting style. A fierce undulating dragon entangled in swirling foliage is under attack from a lion above while assaulting a phoenix whose body dissolves into floral and foliate forms. Richly layered vegetation sways, twists, bends, and pierces itself. The fierce image is executed with spontaneity and sensitivity, drawn with pen and brush in many shades of black without added color. Strong black calligraphic lines define the primary motifs, while soft feathery lines provide details and washes produce volume enriched with texture. This magnificent drawing is attributed to Şahkulu, an Iranian-trained artist who joined the Ottoman imperial painting atelier in Istanbul in 1526 and became its head in 1545. The stamp is inscribed with a verse from the Qur'an, "And I commit my case unto God" (40:44).

INK, GOLD, AND WASHES ON PAPER; 17.3 X 40.2 CM (6-3/4 X 15-7/8 IN.)

PURCHASE FROM THE J. H. WADE FUND 1944.492

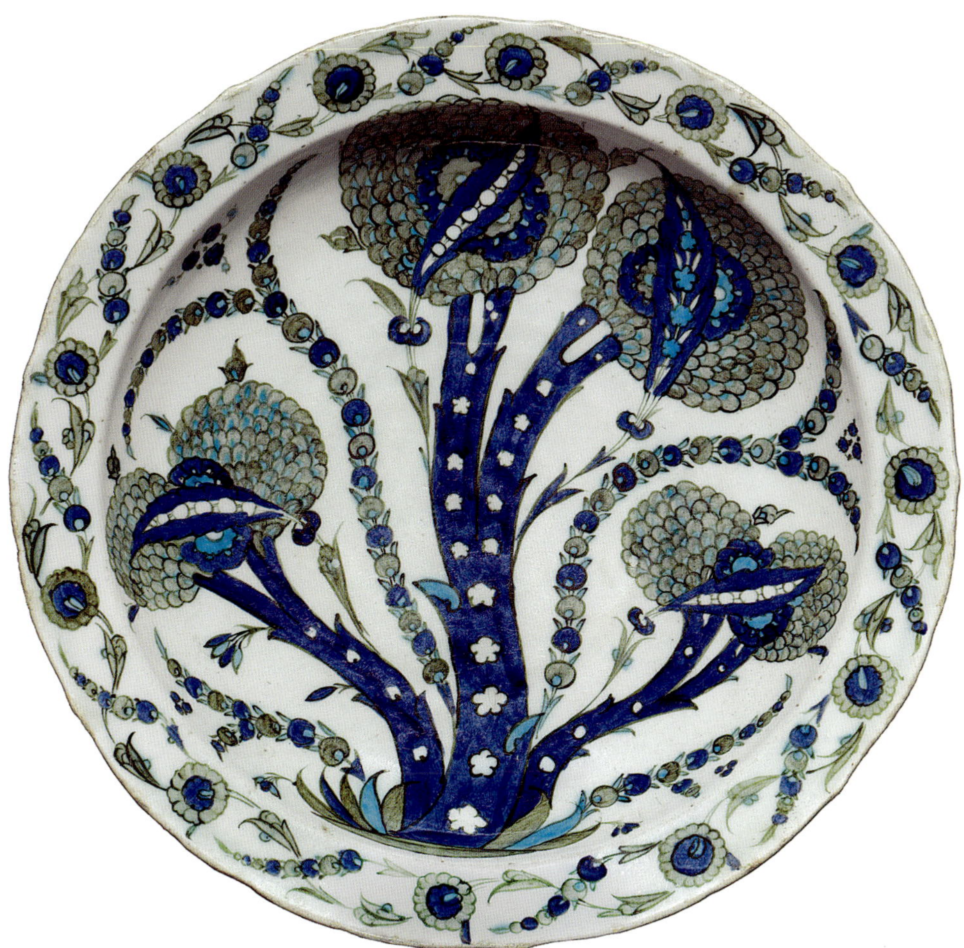

Large Dish with Artichokes 1535–45

TURKEY, IZNIK, OTTOMAN PERIOD (1453–1924)

With its exuberant and confident design of surging artichokes, this large dish is a spectacular example of the finest and most inventive period of underglaze painted ceramics produced at Iznik under the patronage of the Ottoman court. Its distinct color palette and new spirit of painterly spontaneity, instead of more calculated stenciled patterns, characterize Iznik's revolutionary production during 1530–60, decades that mark the high point of Ottoman art during the reign of Sultan Suleyman the Magnificent. In this vigorous freehand tree design lightly outlined in black, swaying trunks sprout artichoke-like crowns of leafy plumage, intersected by flowering fronds and curving leaves; undulating floral designs enrich the rim. The colors—cobalt blue, turquoise, and sage-green—are beautiful and original. A technical triumph during the 1550s introduced a brilliant intense red, applied in a thick slip, along with a new floral aesthetic that created the mature style for which Iznik is renowned as one of the world's great ceramic traditions.

FRITWARE WITH UNDERGLAZE-PAINTED DESIGN; DIAM. 36.4 CM (14-3/8 IN.)

PURCHASE FROM THE J. H. WADE FUND 1995.17

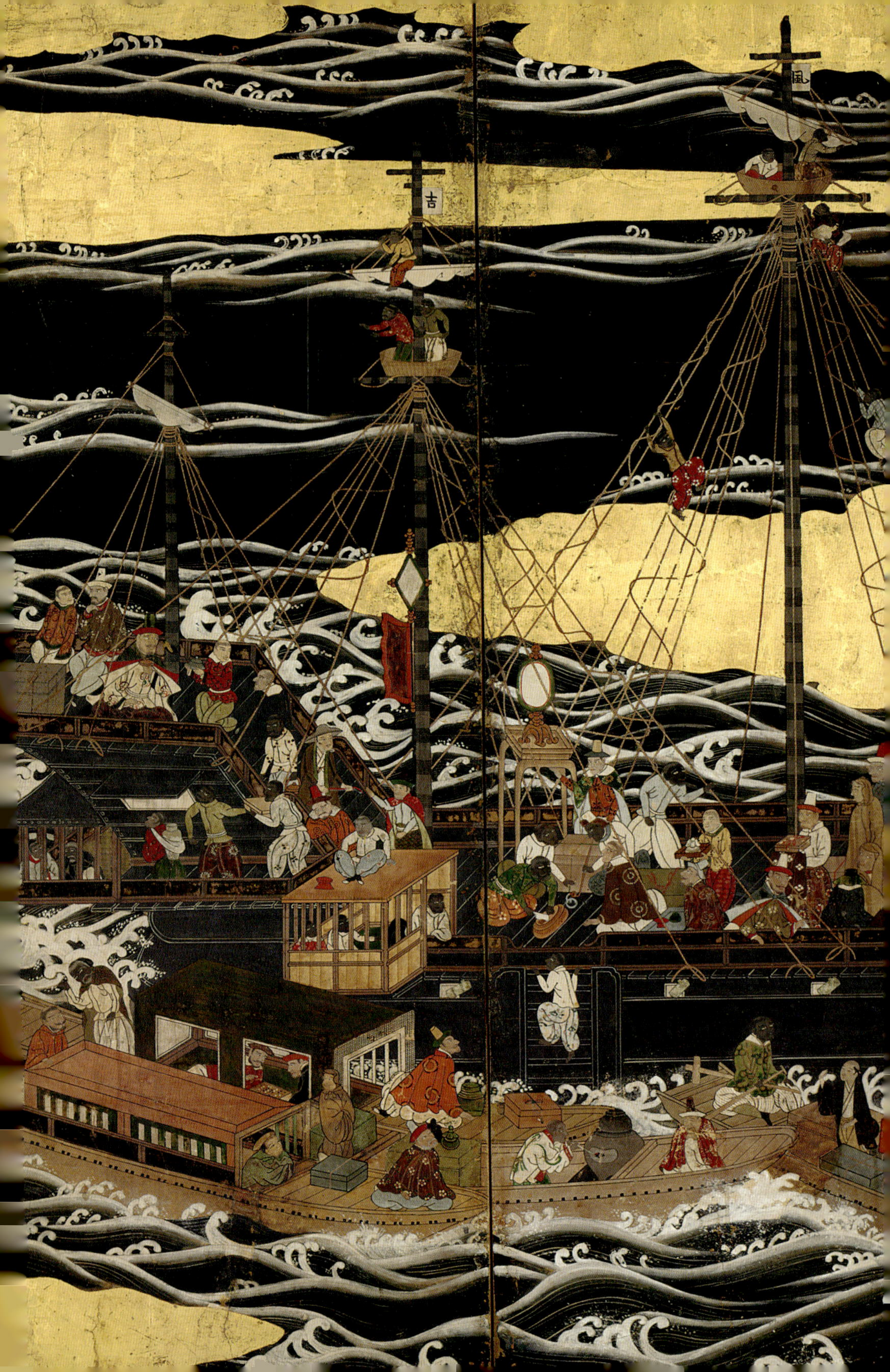
風
吉

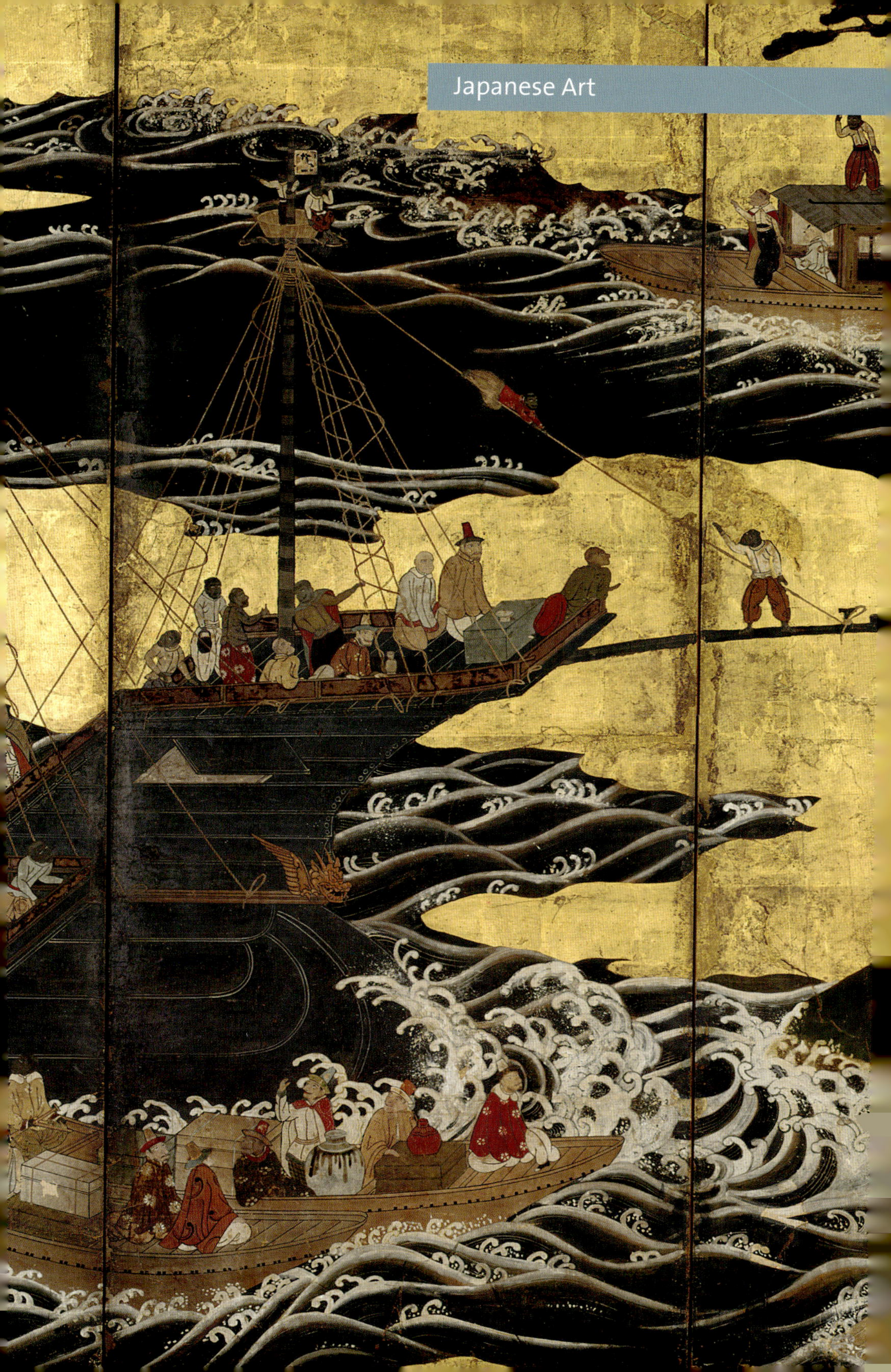
Japanese Art

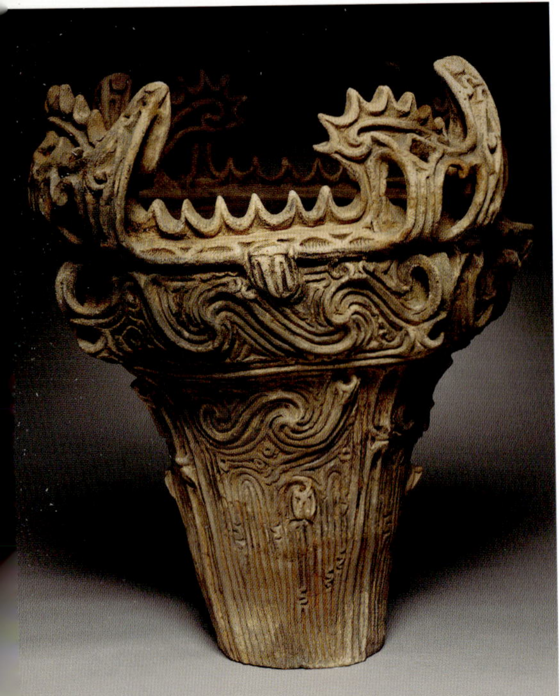

Flame-Style Storage Vessel about 2500 BC

JAPAN, JOMON PERIOD (ABOUT 10,500–300 BC)

The Jomon, or early Japanese people, excelled at ceramic production, particularly of utilitarian vessels. This vessel, for example, might have been used to cook food. Regional artistic differences existed in prehistoric Japan, and vessels of this particular scale and type, called "flame-style" by art historians for the coil-built decorations on the rim, were found around the present-day city of Niigata in northeastern Japan. This vessel is extraordinary, taller than most of the known surviving examples.

EARTHENWARE WITH CARVED AND APPLIED DECORATION; H. 61 CM (24 IN.), DIAM. 55.8 CM (22 IN.)

JOHN L. SEVERANCE FUND 1984.68

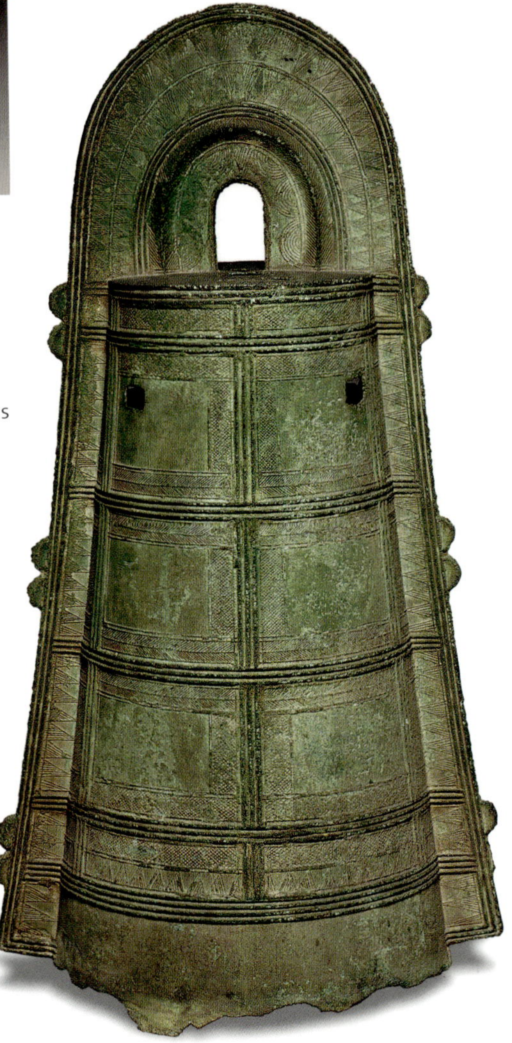

Dotaku A D 100–200

JAPAN, YAYOI PERIOD (400 BC–A D 300)

The flow of new peoples from Korea to Japan during the Yayoi period brought new technologies of bronze and iron casting. Similarly, the form of the *dotaku,* or bronze bell, is thought to have originated in Korea. The Korean prototypes—thickly cast, stout bells—were transformed in Japan into sculptural forms with sophisticated surface decoration. These dotaku are often uncovered near burial sites paired with a metal spear or sword nearby, suggesting ceremonial importance.

CAST BRONZE; 97.8 X 48.9 CM (38-1/2 X 19-1/4 IN.)

GIFT OF MRS. ARTHUR ST. JOHN NEWBERRY 1916.1102

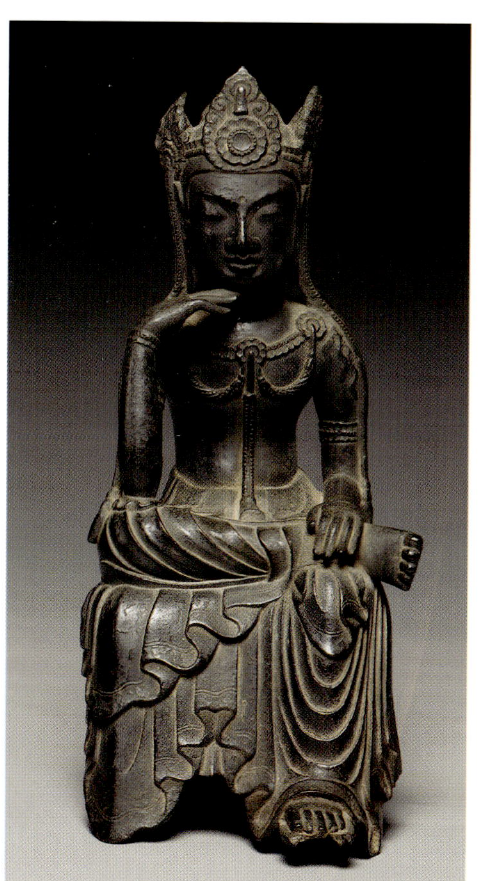

Buddha of the Future, Maitreya late AD 600s

JAPAN, LATE ASUKA TO EARLY NARA PERIOD (600–710)

Buddhism was introduced to Japan in the sixth century. For early Japanese devotees, Buddhism offered the promise of salvation through faith in the Buddha of the Future, who would appear at the end of the world. The concept of eternal salvation held particular resonance with the Japanese aristocracy, who became the staunchest supporters of this new faith. Small sculptures like this one, with its gentle grace and powerful presence, were popular devotional objects.

CAST BRONZE, INCISED, WITH TRACES OF GILDING; H. 45.8 CM (18 IN.)

JOHN L. SEVERANCE FUND 1950.86

Mirror with Incised Design of Bishamonten 1000s–1100s

JAPAN, HEIAN PERIOD (794–1185)

This mirror may have served as a votive plaque, suspended above an altar or against a temple wall. Worshipers would have appealed to the fiercely protective Bishamonten, guardian of the northern quadrant of the universe, to provide for their safety and well-being. The incised decoration shows Bishamonten with sword in hand standing on a demon while two fierce attendants look on. The Goddess of Wealth, Kichojoten, stands at Bishamonten's proper left and one of the guardian's sons, possibly Saisho or Naja, is on his right.

SILVERED BRONZE; DIAM. 15.3 CM (6 IN.)

THE SEVERANCE AND GRETA MILLIKIN PURCHASE FUND 1977.32

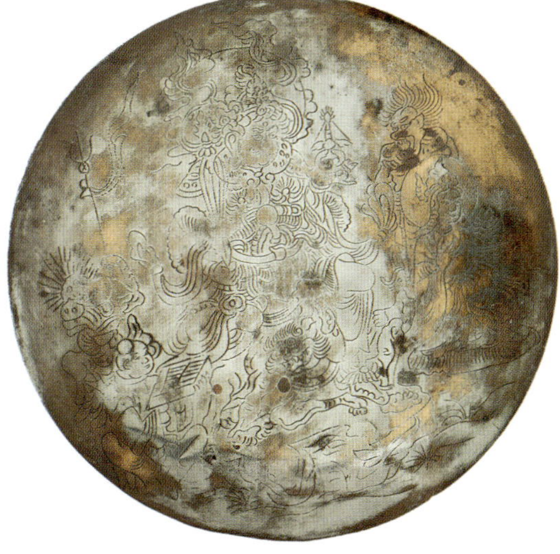

Buddhist Tabernacle late 1100s

JAPAN, HEIAN PERIOD (794–1185)

This tabernacle was created to house nearly three hundred sutras, or religious scrolls. On the inside of the doors, fierce figures dressed in elaborate armor and decorated with gold and silver foil served as guardians for the scrolls. On the back wall are two stylized Sanskrit names: Shaka, the Historical Buddha, on the left, and Amida, the Buddha of the Western Paradise, on the right. The whole structure is housed on a base of two lotuses, symbols of purity. One of a pair of known surviving tabernacles, these incredibly fine luxury objects might have been commissioned as a way of gaining religious merit during uncertain times.

BLACK LACQUER OVER A WOOD CORE WITH HEMP CLOTH COVERING, GOLD PAINT, CUT GOLD LEAF, INK, MINERAL PIGMENTS, AND METALWORK; H. 160 CM (63 IN.) OVERALL

JOHN L. SEVERANCE FUND 1969.130

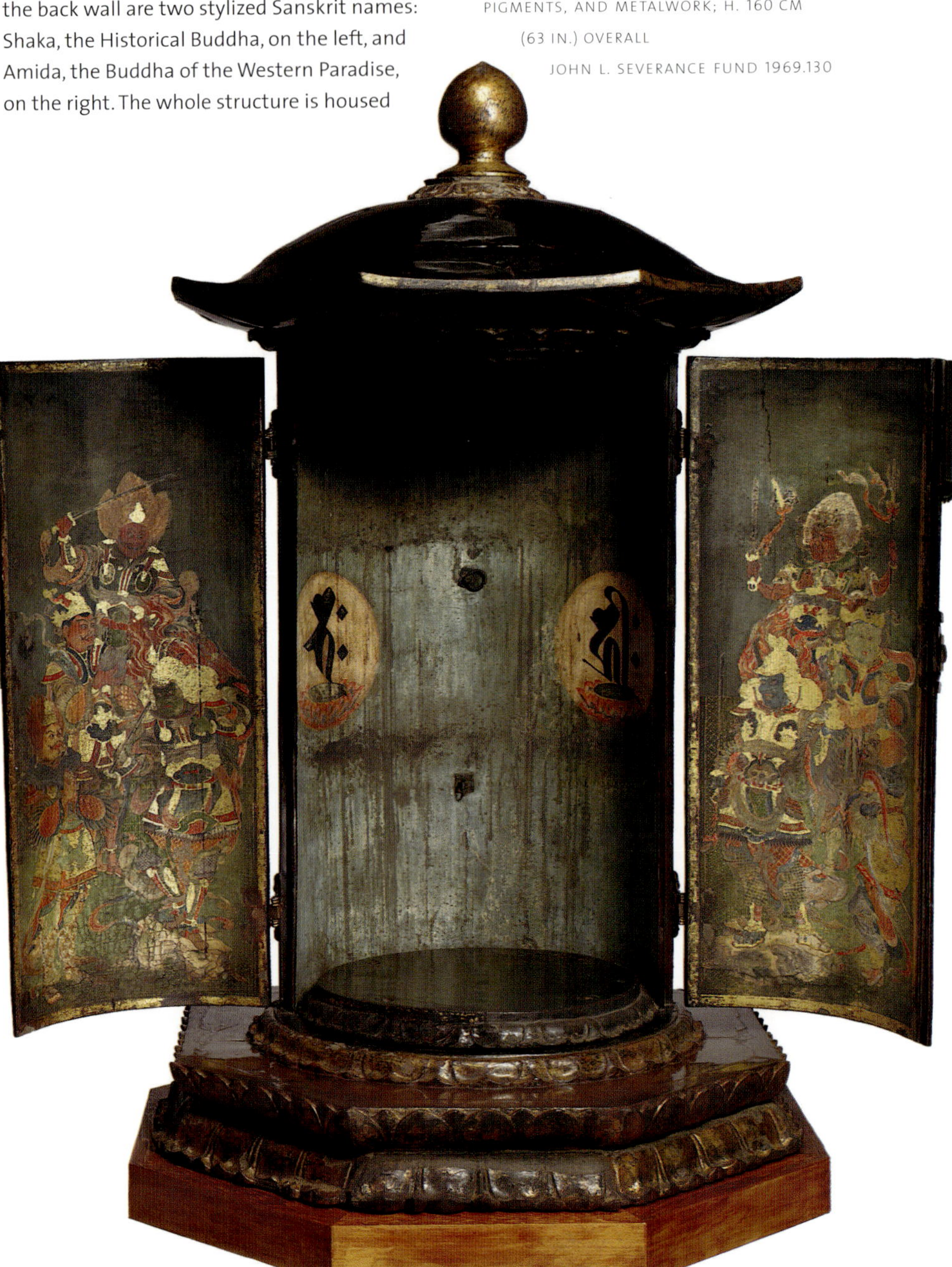

The Buddha of the Western Paradise, Amida Nyorai 1269

KOSHUN, WITH ASSISTANTS KOSHIN AND JOSHU (JAPANESE, ACTIVE 1200S)

The Amida Buddha stands in a posture of welcome, greeting the souls of the recently deceased into the Western Paradise. Documents found in the figure's hollow core confirm that this work was commissioned by high-ranking political and religious authorities in 1269. During this period, sympathetic, welcoming depictions of the Buddha became increasingly prized by the faithful. This figure's dynamic form and dramatic presentation were achieved through technical prowess. Multiple pieces of wood were assembled, covered with lacquered hemp, and then decorated with minute pieces of gold leaf.

WOOD WITH CUT GOLD LEAF AND POLYCHROMY; H. 94.6 CM (37-1/4 IN.)

JOHN L. SEVERANCE FUND 1960.197

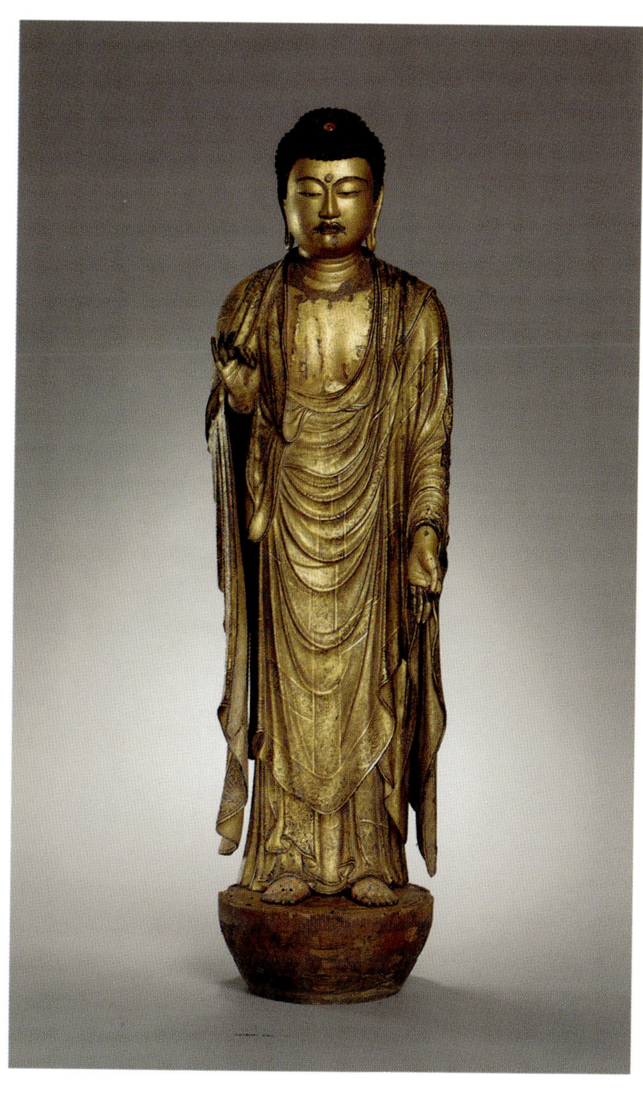

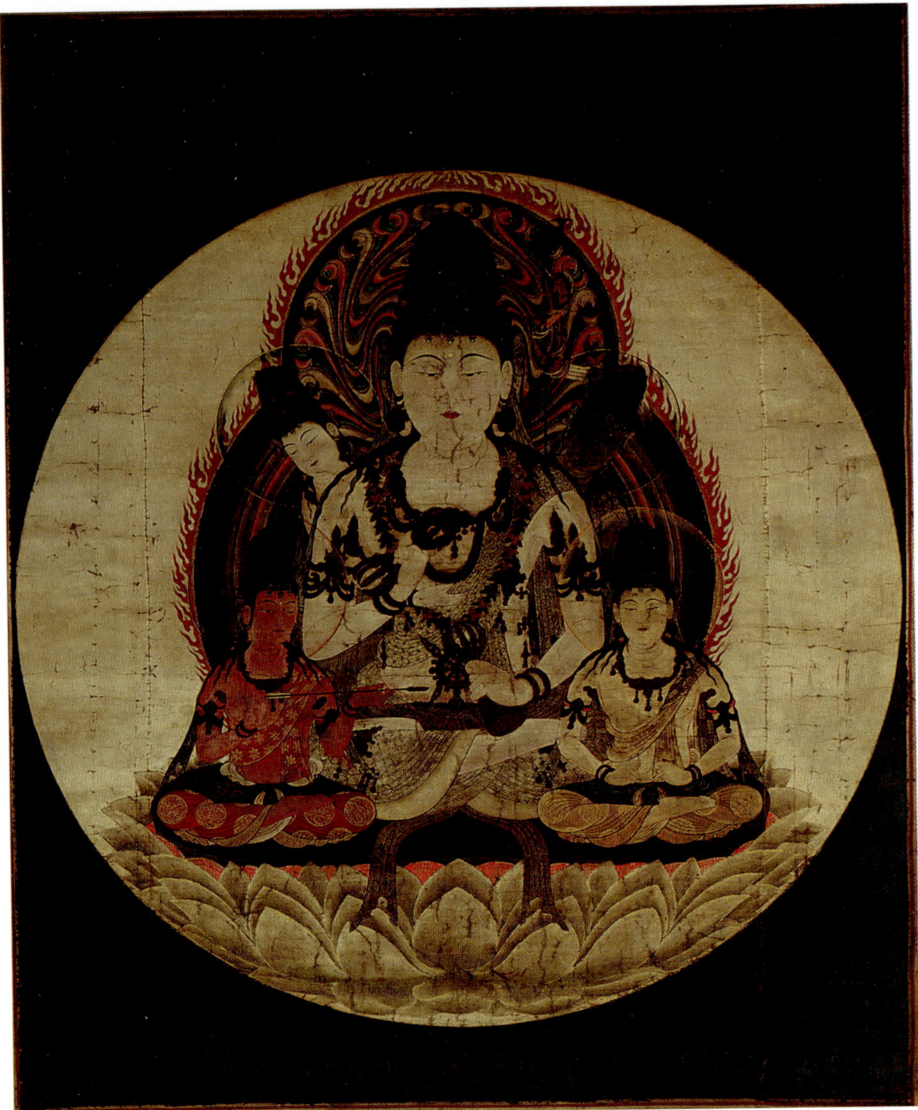

The "Secret Five" Bodhisattva: Gohimitsu Bosatsu 1200s

JAPAN, KAMAKURA PERIOD (1185–1333)

Devotees of the Shingon sect of Buddhism believe enlightenment is possible for the faithful within this very lifetime. Images of the Buddha served an important instructional role in understanding the mysteries of faith and for honing one's buddha nature toward enlightenment. While Buddhism was founded by the historical Buddha, many sects venerate additional buddhas, or enlightened ones—bodhisattvas, or bosatsu. In this painting, the large, central image represents the Supreme Buddha. Surrounding him are depictions of the four "human illusions," each distinguished by color and attributes (clockwise): passion, pride, desire, and sensory delight. For Shingon followers, awareness and control of these four human illusions are essential to achieving enlightenment.

HANGING SCROLL; INK, COLOR, GOLD, AND SILVER ON SILK; 63.5 X 78.1 CM (25 X 30-3/4 IN.)

MR. AND MRS. WILLIAM H. MARLATT FUND 1961.423

Legends of the Yuzu Nembutsu Sect: Yuzu Nembutsu Engi 1300s

JAPAN, KAMAKURA PERIOD (1185–1333)

After 24 years of intense study, contemplation, and self-denial, the Buddhist priest Ryonin (1072–1132) was visited in a dream by the Amida Buddha. The priest learned that no amount of human effort can release one from the cycle of birth and death; only true faith in Amida will allow one to reach nirvana. The deity promised salvation in the Western Paradise to those who practiced *nembutsu,* the repeated recitation of Amida's name. Ryonin abandoned his previous practices to teach the mantra and to preach *yuzu,* the interconnectedness of all things in the natural and spirit worlds.

Subsequent leaders of Yuzu Nembutsu, the sect of Pure Land Buddhism that Ryonin founded, commissioned illustrated handscrolls to popularize the faith, using them to introduce complex religious concepts even to the illiterate. The many scenes in this scroll depict his death and the subsequent miracles that occurred among practitioners of Yuzu Nembutsu. It originally was paired with a scroll, now in the collection of the Art Institute of Chicago, showing scenes from Ryonin's life. Despite the popularity of the religious narrative tradition, relatively few early handscrolls have survived.

HANDSCROLL; INK, COLOR, AND GOLD ON PAPER; 29.8 X 1,232.4 CM (11-3/4 X 485-5/8 IN.)

MR. AND MRS. WILLIAM H. MARLATT, JOHN L. SEVERANCE, AND EDWARD L. WHITTEMORE FUNDS 1956.87

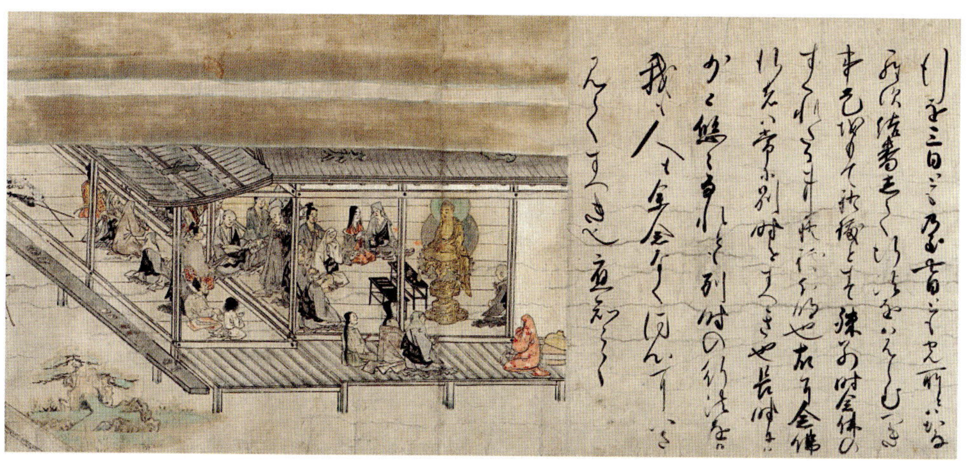

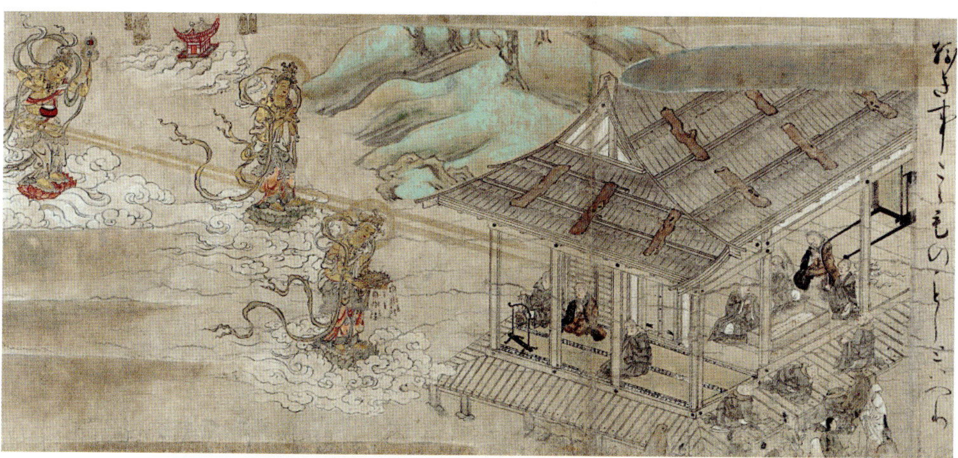

Jar with Scenes of Frolicking Monkeys 1302

JAPAN, KAMAKURA PERIOD (1185–1333)

To make this vessel, a wooden form was covered with successive layers of lacquer, the clear sap of the highly toxic *Rhus verniciflua* tree. In this time-consuming process, each layer must dry before another is added. Lacquer was, therefore, an expensive status symbol; aristocrats prized lacquered architectural features, furniture, musical instruments, and serving vessels. This jar is particularly noteworthy as the only surviving lacquer jar with a narrative scene from the period, showing a family of monkeys trying to cross a river at the bottom.

WOOD, COVERED WITH HEMP CLOTH AND COLORED LACQUER; H. 49.4 CM (19-1/2 IN.), DIAM. 47.2 CM (18-5/8 IN.)

LEONARD C. HANNA JR. FUND 1984.8

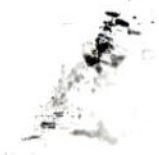

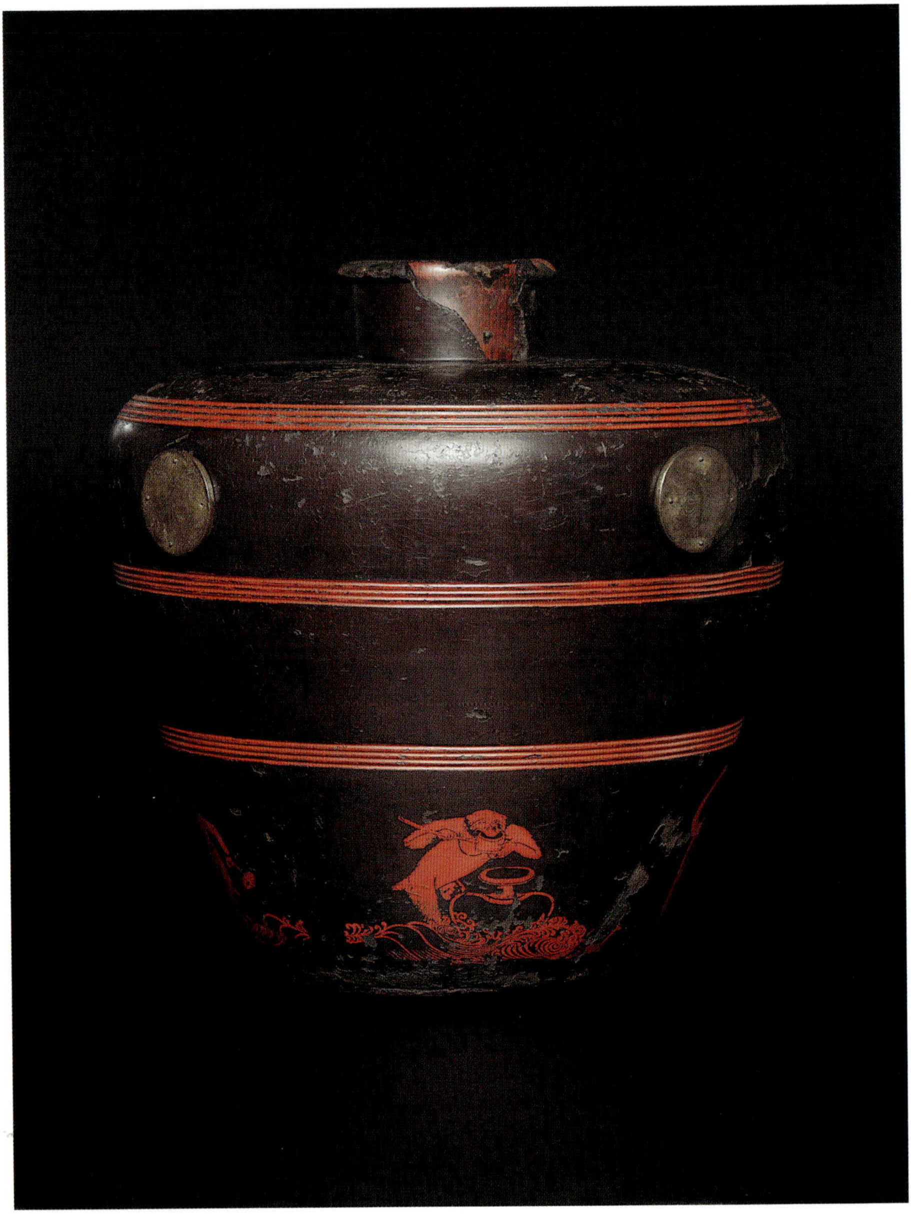

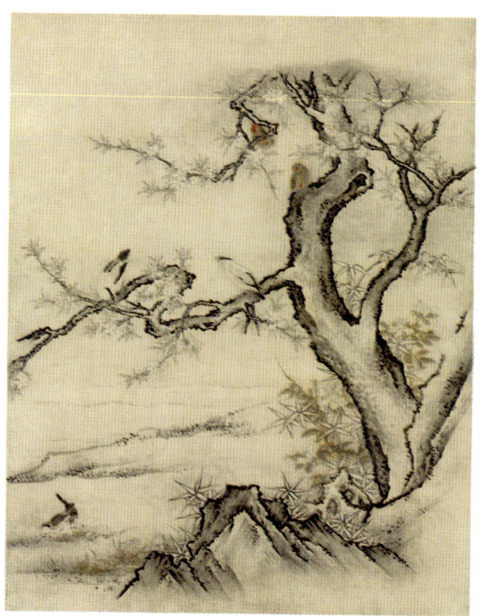

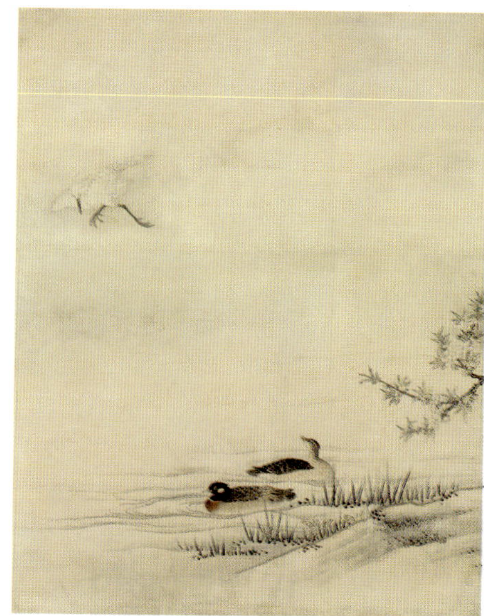

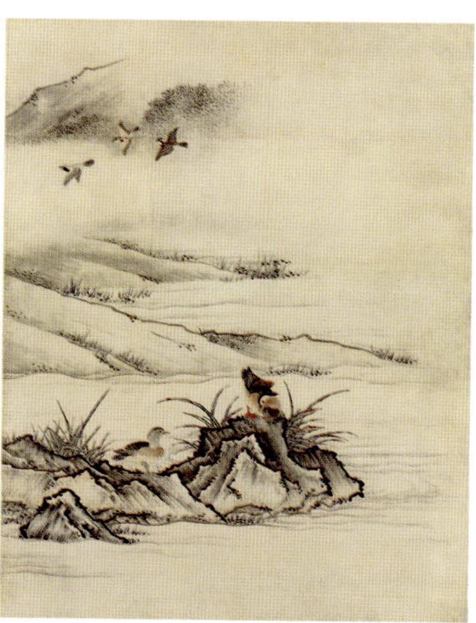

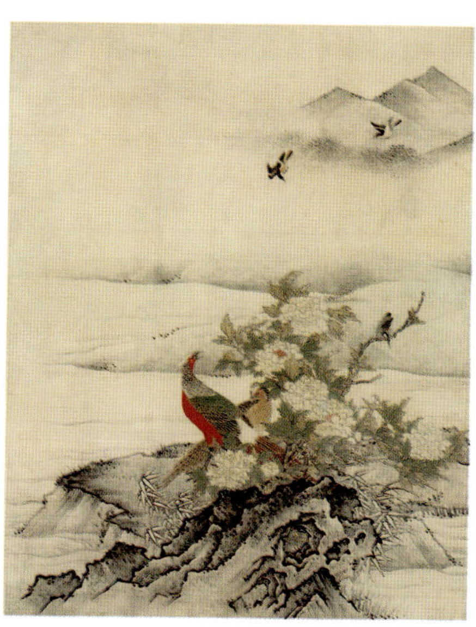

Flowers and Birds in a Spring Landscape 1500s

ATTRIBUTED TO KANO MOTONOBU (JAPANESE, 1476–1559)

These four paintings originally decorated sliding doors (*fusuma*) that partitioned the interior of a Japanese building. Painters from the Kano School, named after the artist Kano Motonobu, were major forces in the production of screens and architectural interiors in Kyoto. When he headed the workshop, his work was prized by the upper strata of society. Kano is credited with combining the subtlety of Chinese black ink painting, as seen in the rocks and hills, with the color and realism of Japanese painting, seen in the birds and flowers. Landscape scenes like this were prized by the elite of Kyoto, both for their contemplative aesthetic and for their patrons' refined taste.

FOUR FUSUMA PANELS MOUNTED AS HANGING SCROLLS; INK AND COLOR ON PAPER; 177.1 X 137.1 CM (69-3/4 X 54 IN.) EACH

LEONARD C. HANNA JR. FUND 1970.6.1–4

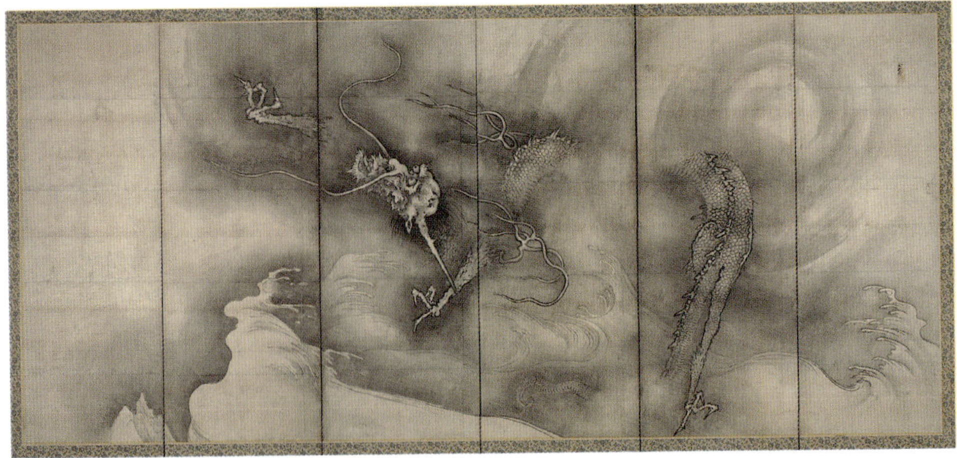

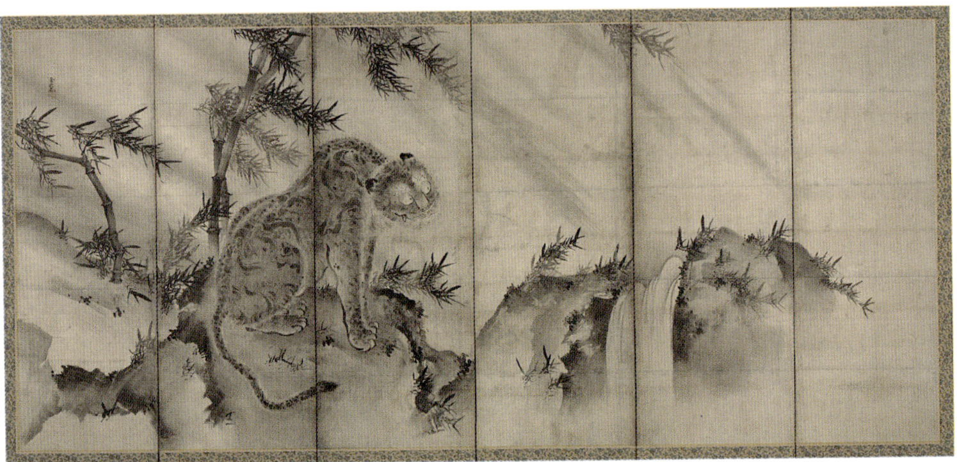

Dragon and Tiger 1500s

SHUKEI SESSON (JAPANESE, 1504–1589)

The Zen monk and self-taught ink painter Shukei Sesson lived in the relatively remote provinces near present-day Tokyo, rather than in Kyoto, the cultural center. His outsider status seems to have allowed him to develop his own painting style featuring energetic brushwork, innovative settings, and an extraordinary command of dry and wet ink. His native Japanese decorative approach to the water and rocks breaks with Chinese precedents.

A three-clawed dragon emerges from the clouds and flies above the waves on the top six-paneled screen. The screen below features a meek tiger gazing at a small waterfall while bamboo sways in the breeze. The mythological creature soars between the elements of sea and sky; the real animal sits immobile on land with nature moving around him. In East Asia, the pairing of a dragon in the clouds and a tiger in the wind has a long tradition and multiple layers of meaning. Sesson, however, took an unorthodox approach by adding psychological depth and humor to his animals. Instead of inspiring fear, this dragon has an oddly bemused expression, and the tiger resembles a slightly goofy housecat rather than a powerful predator. These monochromatic compositions are masterpieces of Sesson's style.

PAIR OF SIX-FOLD SCREENS, INK ON PAPER; 157.2 X 339 CM (61-7/8 X 133-1/2 IN.) EACH

PURCHASE FROM THE J. H. WADE FUND 1959.136.1–2

Arrival of the "Southern Barbarians" about 1600

JAPAN, MOMOYAMA PERIOD (1573–1615)

In this pair of screens a formidable Portuguese ship with fanciful rigging arrives in a Japanese port, much to the delight of the locals. The anonymous artist's attention to detail in the depiction of the people, often grouped in vignettes, makes for a compelling scene, heightened by the billowing gold clouds that lead the eye through the composition. Near the top of the top screen, rich women, sequestered in their homes, enjoy the dockside scene. In the scene on the bottom, townspeople and shop owners watch as the Portuguese walk down the street, obvious in their cartoonish, balloon-shaped pants. At the right in both screens are Jesuit priests, identified by their long black robes. Japanese patrons were curious about the outside world, and scenes of foreigners were particularly popular.

PAIR OF SIX-FOLD SCREENS; INK, COLOR, AND GOLD ON PAPER; 146.7 X 337.2 CM (57-3/4 X 132-3/4 IN.) EACH

LEONARD C. HANNA JR. FUND 1960.193.1–2

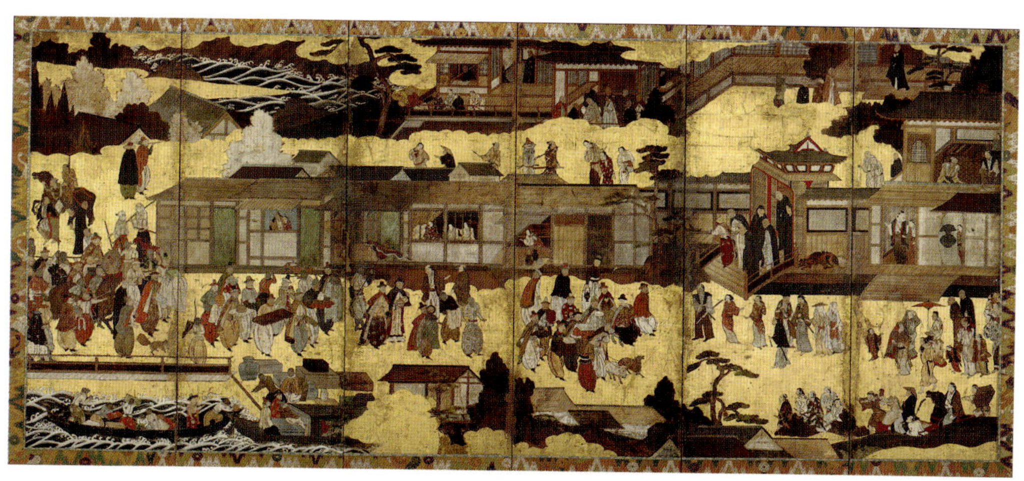

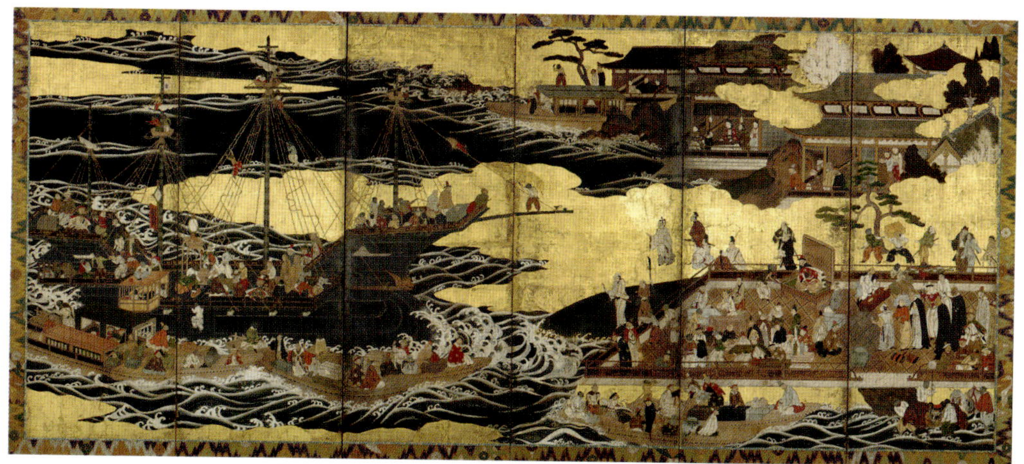

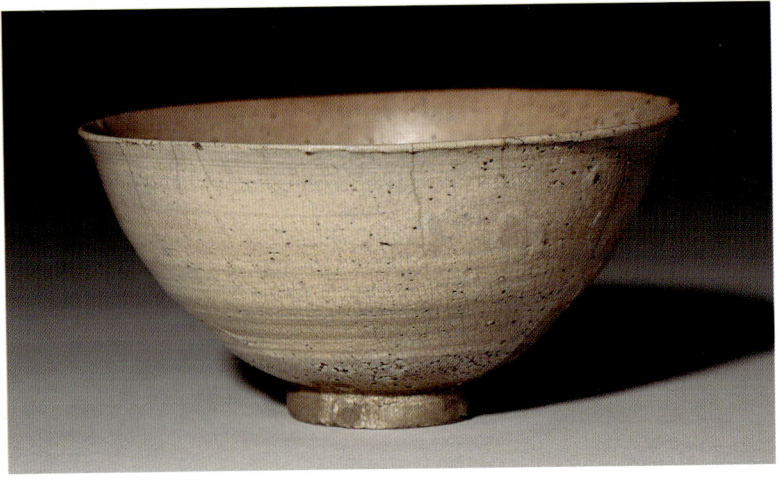

Tea Bowl about 1600

JAPAN, MOMOYAMA PERIOD (1573–1615)

Wide-mouthed bowls were used for whipped tea, such as that consumed during the tea ceremony, and Karatsu ware like this bowl was among the most prized. The port city of Karatsu, Saga Prefecture, was known for kilns that produced glazed, high-fired, Korean-style pottery. The Japanese ruler Toyotomi Hideyoshi had invaded Korea in 1592 and 1597, returning with families of Korean potters as spoils of war. This region was one of the sites where those potters were resettled.

STONEWARE, KARATSU WARE; H. 9.5 CM (3-3/4 IN.), DIAM. 18.4 CM (7-1/4 IN.)

GIFT OF IWAO AND TAKAKO SETSU IN HONOR OF DR. AND MRS. SHERMAN E. LEE 1983.158

Standing Figure of a Beauty about 1690

JAPAN, SAGA PREFECTURE, ARITA VILLAGE, EDO PERIOD (1615–1867)

Red lips, white skin, black hair, and sash were considered the height of beauty in this woman's time. Her fashionable, brightly colored garment was created by brushing enamel on prefired porcelain. This colorful, floral aesthetic is characteristic of Kakiemon ware, a type of ceramic produced in Arita, a village near the port of Imari. Ceramics from Arita were exported to Europe via Dutch traders but were also popular among Japanese collectors.

KAKIEMON WARE, PORCELAIN WITH OVERGLAZE ENAMEL DECORATION; H. 38 CM (15 IN.)

JOHN L. SEVERANCE FUND 1964.366

Ivy Lane 1700s

FUKAE ROSHU (JAPANESE, 1699–1757)

This 18th-century screen illustrates a poem from *Ise Monogatari,* or *Tales of Ise,* a 10th-century anthology. The setting gives the painting its name: "Ivy Lane" or "The Pass through Mount Utsu." While traveling to exile in the remote northern provinces, Ariwara no Narihara (about 824–880) happened on an itinerant monk along a mountainous ivy lane. The aristocrat in blue entrusted the monk with a love poem to be delivered to his beloved, left behind in the capital, Kyoto. This theme seems to have resonated for Fukae Roshu since, at age 16, he had been exiled because of a scandal involving his father.

The elegant Rimpa school of painting flourished in the Edo period (1615–1867), when the new middle class had the leisure and financial resources to patronize and appreciate art. Rimpa artists were inspired by Heian period (794–1185) literature, like the *Tale of Ise,* and reinterpreted earlier Japanese motifs to appeal to contemporary audiences, rather than drawing inspiration from imported Chinese classics. Roshu created a poetic landscape with decorative shapes and colors instead of accurately depicting nature. He used the Rimpa school's diffused ink technique, *tarashikomi,* to give texture to the rocks and mountains, while creating a stage-like setting for this poignant scene.

SIX-FOLD SCREEN; INK AND COLOR ON GILDED PAPER; 132.5 X 267.2 CM (52-1/8 X 105-1/4 IN.)

JOHN L. SEVERANCE FUND 1954.127

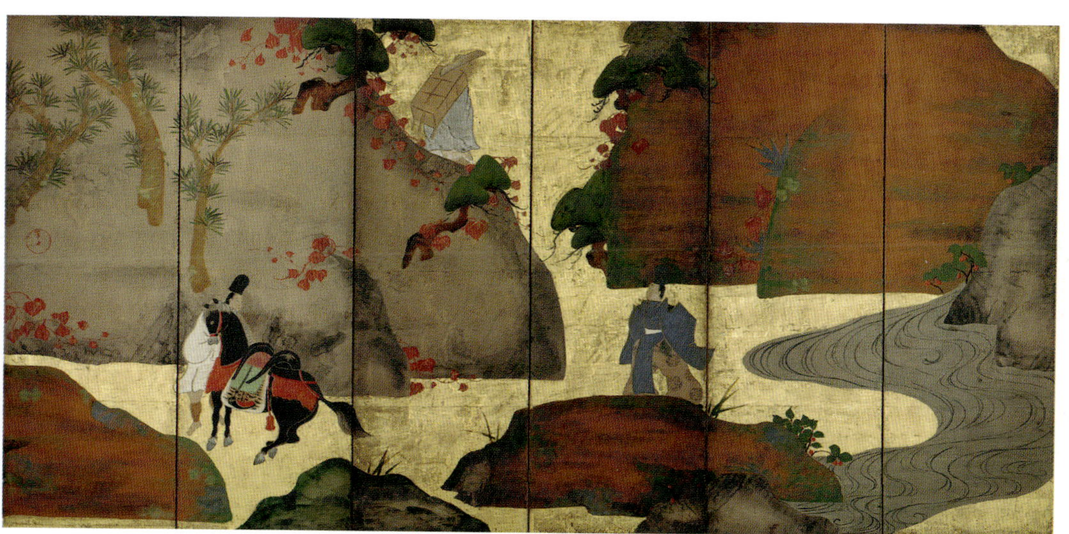

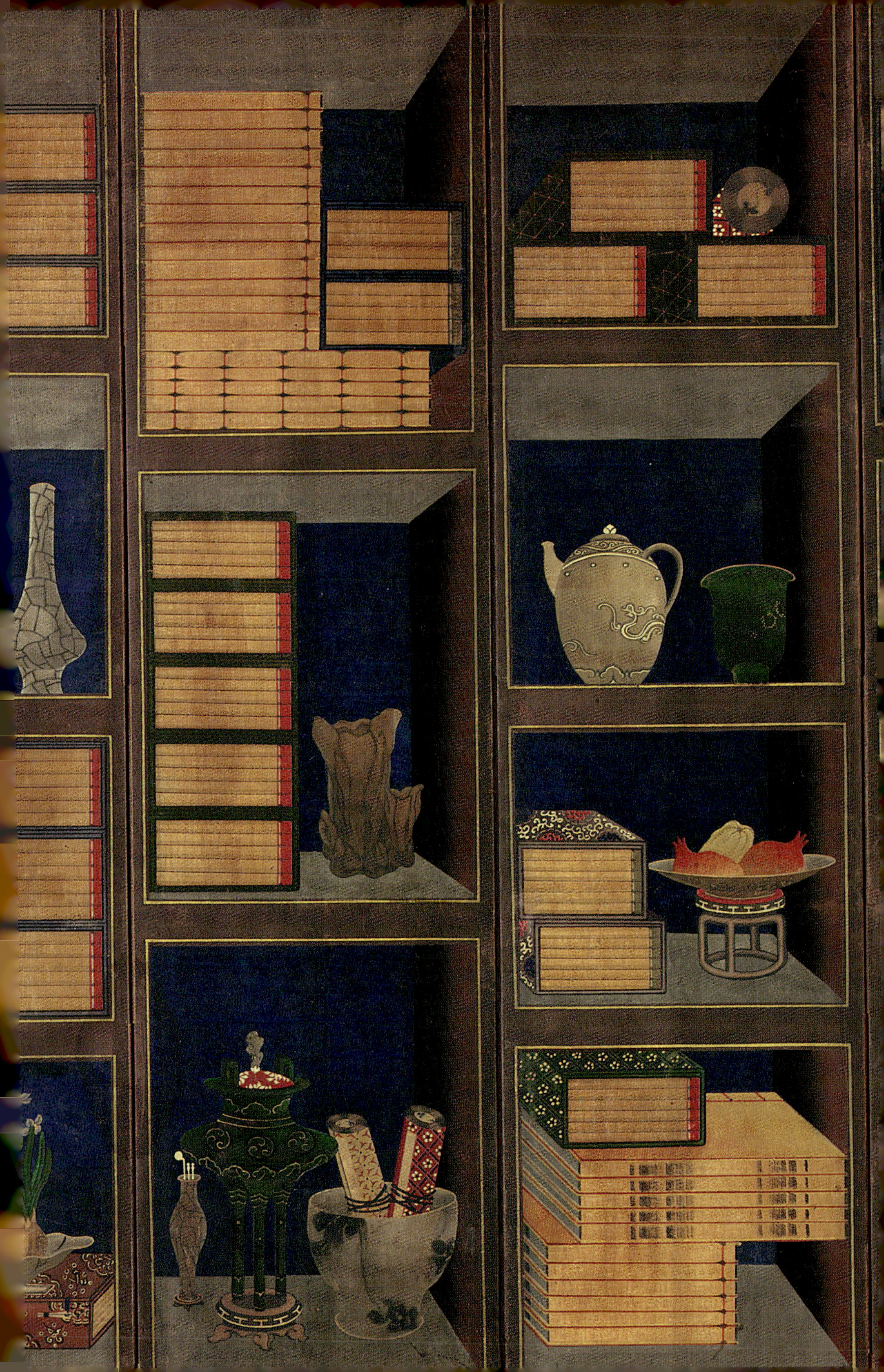

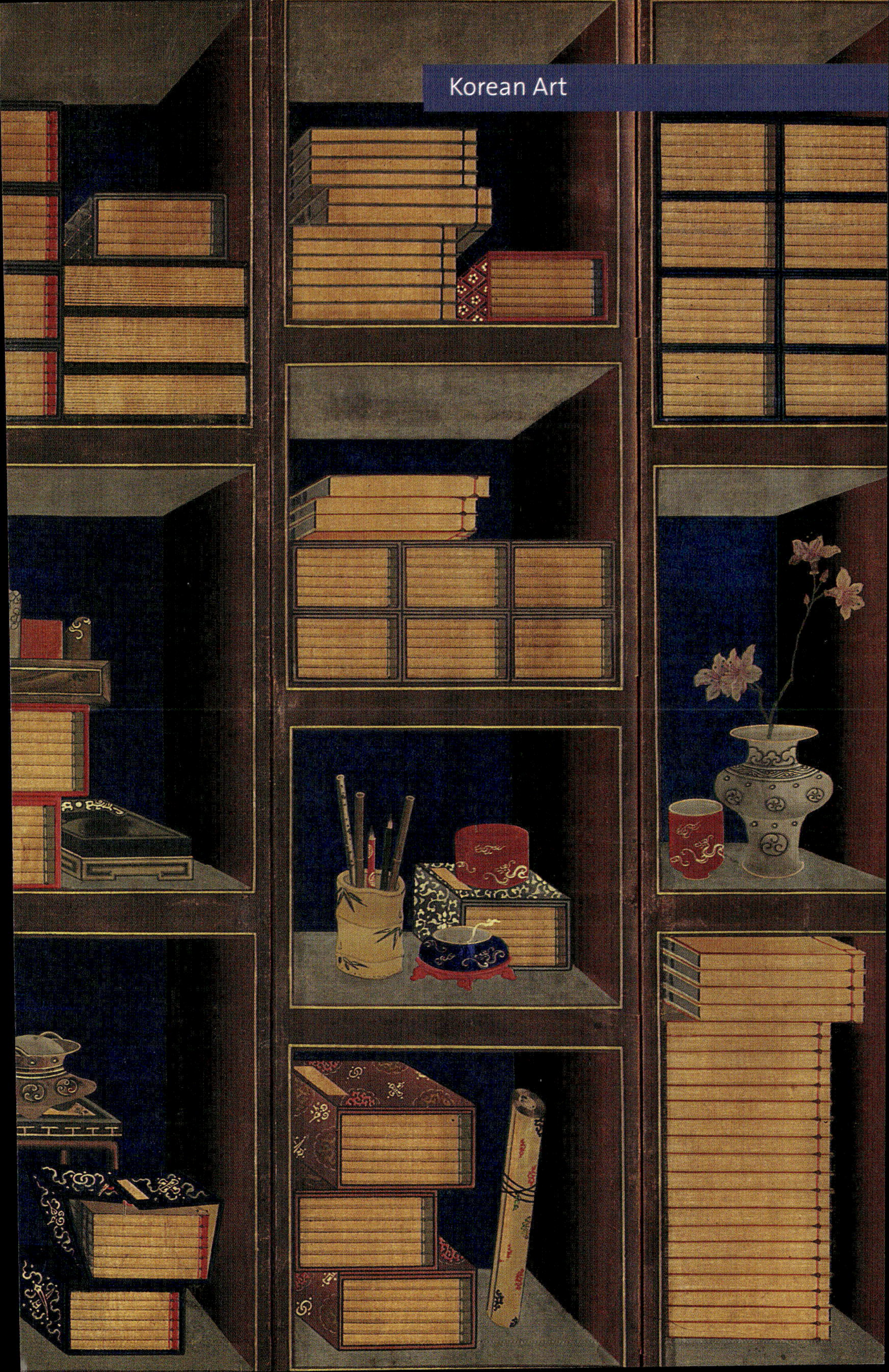

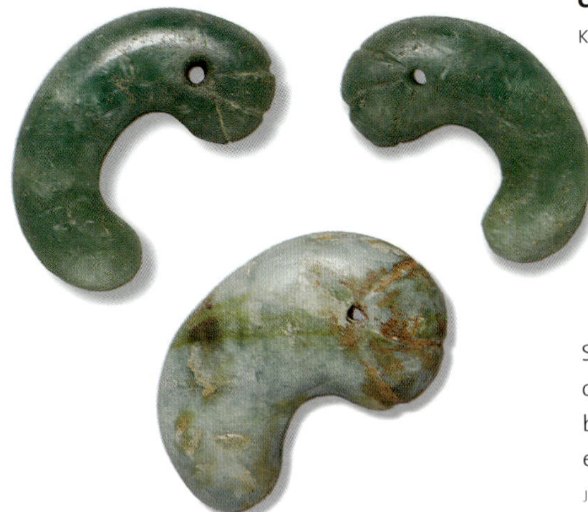

Comma-Shaped Jades 57 BC–AD 668

KOREA, OLD SHILLA PERIOD (57 BC–AD 668)

Historically associated with power in Korea, jade was used to make objects and decorations for the aristocracy. During the Old Shilla Period, comma-shaped jades such as these examples were the most essential decorative element of the gold crowns and ornaments used for the burials of kings, queens, and other nobles. After the state of Shilla united the Korean Peninsula in 668, the use of jade in prestigious mortuary objects declined, brought on by the arrival of Buddhism and the ebbing of shamanism.

JADE; L. 7.2 CM (2-7/8 IN.) AVERAGE

GIFT OF THE JOHN HUNTINGTON ART AND POLYTECHNIC TRUST 1917.1057, 1917.1060–61

Amita (Amitabha) 800s

KOREA, UNIFIED SHILLA PERIOD (668–935)

The Pure Land sect of Buddhism originated in India and spread across Asia, gaining particular status in China, Korea, and Japan. With the sect's proliferation, images of Amita, who is the focus of Pure Land practice, gained in popularity in Korea during the Unified Shilla period. This figure's gestures of reassurance and wish fulfillment indicate that it is likely an image of Amita. The broad shoulders and voluptuous body of this Buddha illustrate the stylistic influence from the Chinese Tang dynasty (618–907), whose aesthetics extended throughout East Asia in the eighth and ninth centuries.

GILT BRONZE; H. 26 CM (10-1/4 IN.)

LEONARD C. HANNA JR. FUND 1988.34

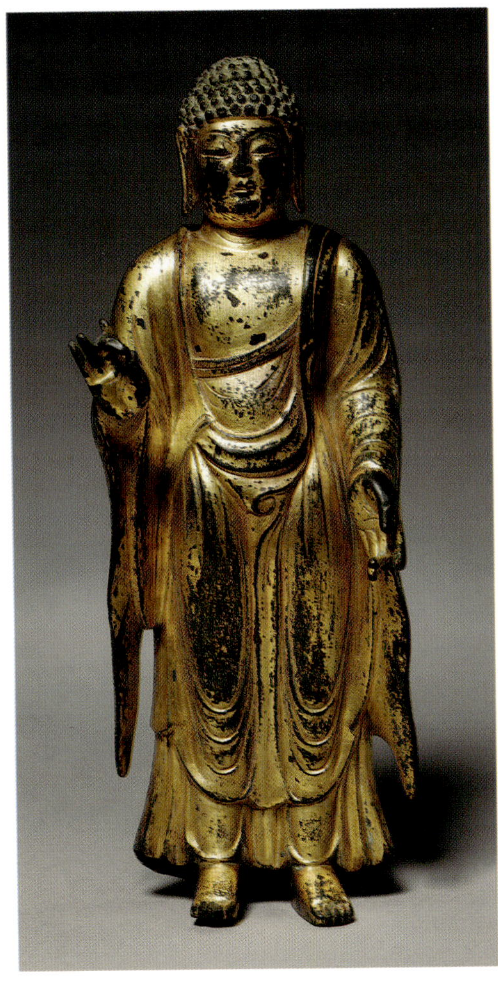

Kundika: Water Ewer 1100s

KOREA, GORYEO PERIOD (936–1392)

The kundika evolved from a water bottle, which Indian monks carried with their eating bowls during their travels, into an offering vessel containing purified water for the Buddhist altar. The typical kundika consists of a long, thin, straw-like mouth at the top, an egg-shaped body, and a pouring mouth. Kundikas were originally made in bronze inlaid with silver; gradually celadon became the medium of choice for economical reasons as well as to fill broader needs.

Celadon wares, which have a special glaze designed to mimic the milky, light green shades of jade, are among the most important of the various types of ceramics produced throughout the Goryeo period. Diverse decorative techniques were employed with such wares, including monochrome celadon glazing, patterns incised in the body of the pot under the glaze, and inlaid celadon, which is unique to Korean celadon wares. Goryeo potters cut designs into the pots and filled the voids with different colored clay. The technique is similar to the process of inlay used in metalwork.

CELADON WARE WITH INCISED AND CARVED DECORATION; 36.2 X 14 CM (14-1/4 X 5-1/2 IN.)
GIFT OF JOHN L. SEVERANCE 1921.631.A–B

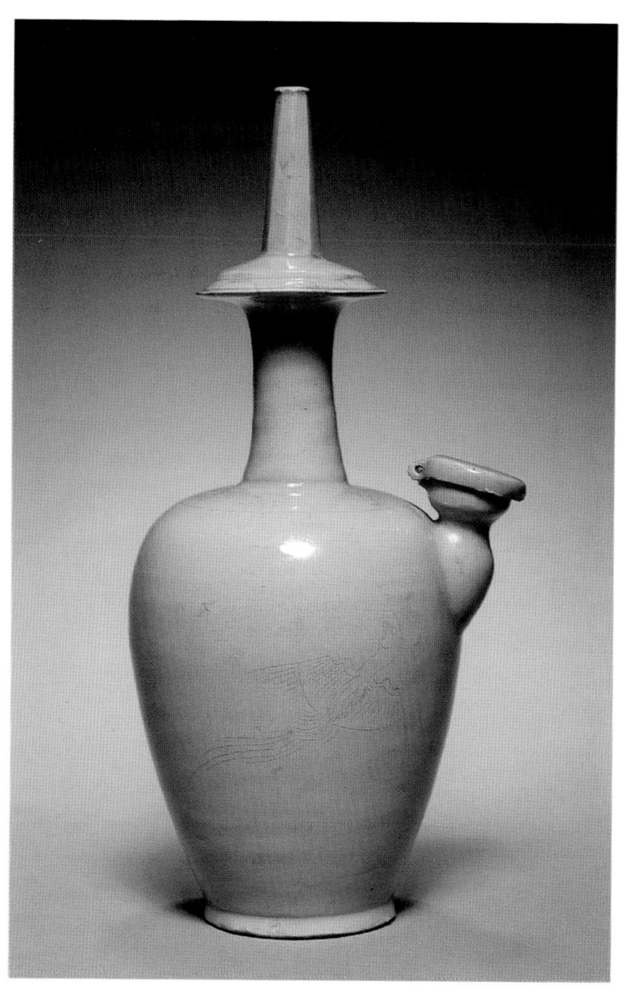

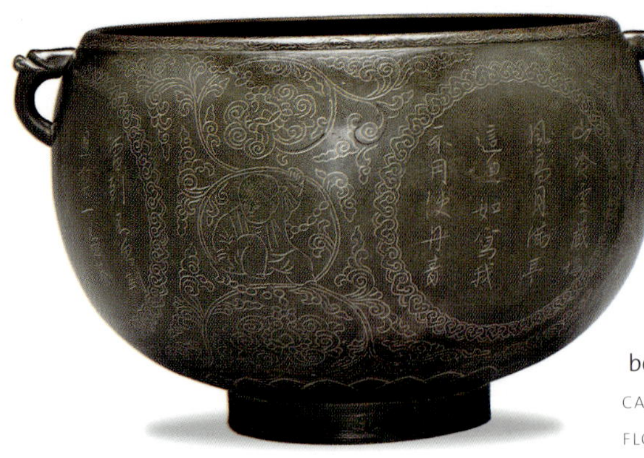

Basin with Inscribed Figures and Calligraphy
1300s

KOREA, GORYEO PERIOD (936–1392)

Inlay, a technique of cutting designs into a form and filling the voids with a contrasting material (in this case, silver), became popular in Korea during the Goryeo period. While the technique was very fashionable then, this example shows rare decorative motifs, including roundels containing four-line poems interspersed between images of a child holding a flower.

CAST BRONZE WITH INLAID SILVER INSCRIPTIONS, FLORAL DÉCOR, AND FIGURAL DESIGNS; H. 17 CM (6-3/4 IN.), DIAM. 28.3 CM (11-1/8 IN.) AT RIM

LEONARD C. HANNA JR. FUND 1985.112

Arhat (Nahan) 1235

KOREA, GORYEO PERIOD (936–1392)

An *arhat,* an advanced disciple of the Buddha, is represented here in profile with a halo encircling his head. Now remounted in the hanging-scroll format, this fragment comes from a handscroll that once depicted 500 arhats. He sits on a woven bamboo stool, offering an alms bowl to a small flaming dragon. This hanging scroll is one of only about 10 known fragments that survive today, all of which (except for this piece) are currently preserved in Korea or Japan.

HANGING SCROLL; INK AND SLIGHT COLOR ON SILK; 54.3 X 40.6 CM (21-3/8 X 16 IN.)

PURCHASE FROM THE J. H. WADE FUND 1979.71

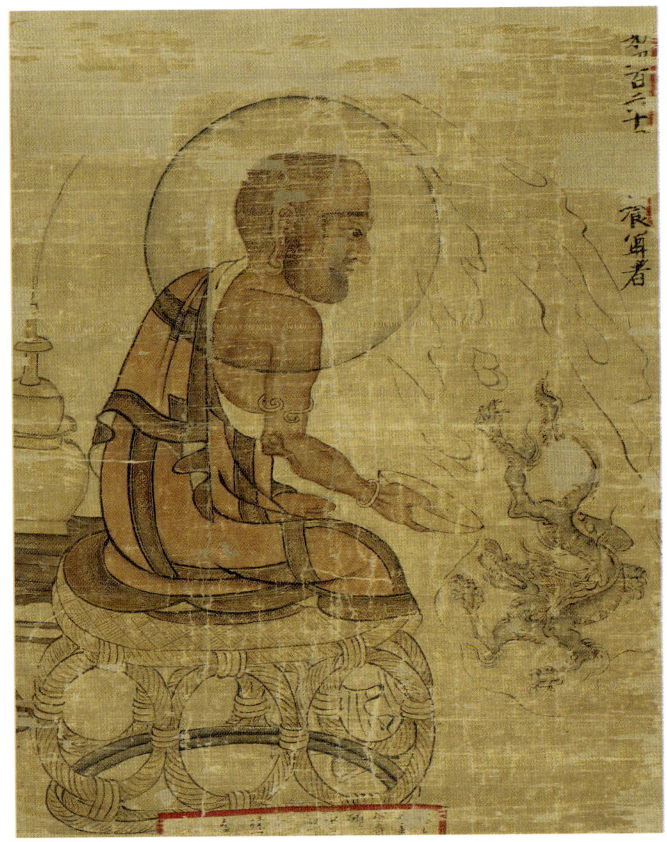

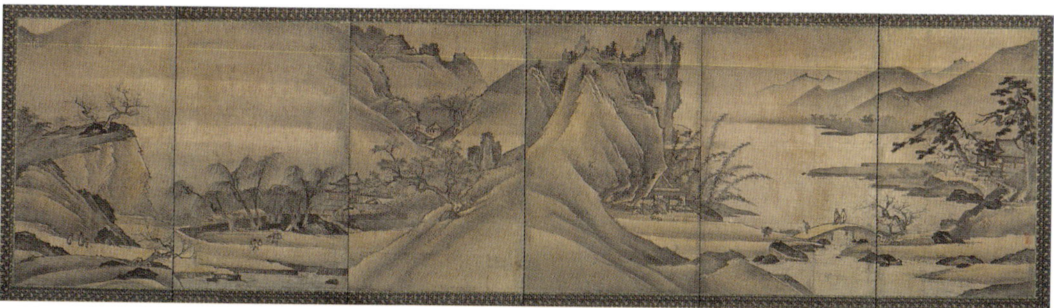

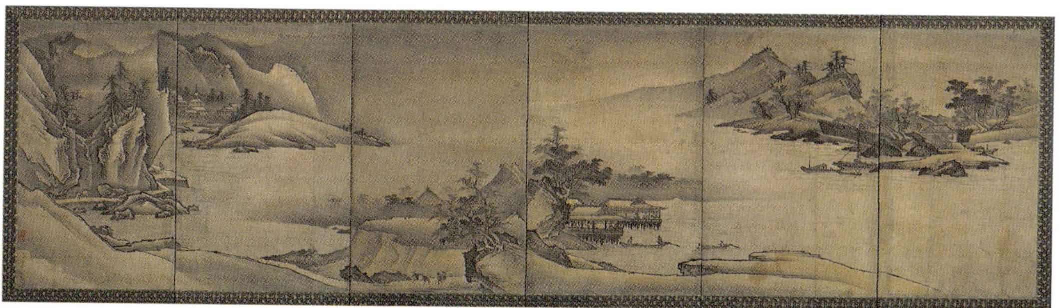

Landscape of the Four Seasons about 1424

YI SUMUN (KOREAN, B. 1404)

In the 15th century, diplomats, missionaries, and merchants traveled between Ming China, Joseon Korea, and Muromachi Japan, exchanging ideas, artistic theories, and material goods. The Korean painter Yi Sumun immigrated to Japan in 1424 at the age of 20. His youthful training in Korea and his experiences in Japan allowed him to blend Korean, Chinese, and Japanese elements in his paintings. His rough brushwork and solid, dark ink washes resemble Korean painting techniques of the period. He also used the "axe-cut" texture strokes and bold landscape forms common in Chinese Ming period (1368–1644) court painting. The four seasons was a popular theme among medieval Japanese ink painters because the changing seasons alluded to Buddhist teachings about the transitory nature of life.

The seasons are depicted beginning at the top right with gentlemen in a spring landscape. The composition moves through summer and autumn to end with a wintry scene on the far left side of the bottom screen. Yi Sumun, whose seals are at the lower outer edge of each screen, planned the composition to create a dynamic, idealized landscape. Each screen has a central mass in the foreground, balanced by other scenes set in the middle distance.

PAIR OF SIX-FOLD SCREENS; INK AND SLIGHT COLOR ON PAPER; 92.7 X 348.7 CM (36-1/2 X 137-3/8 IN.) EACH

JOHN L. SEVERANCE FUND 1976.92.1–2

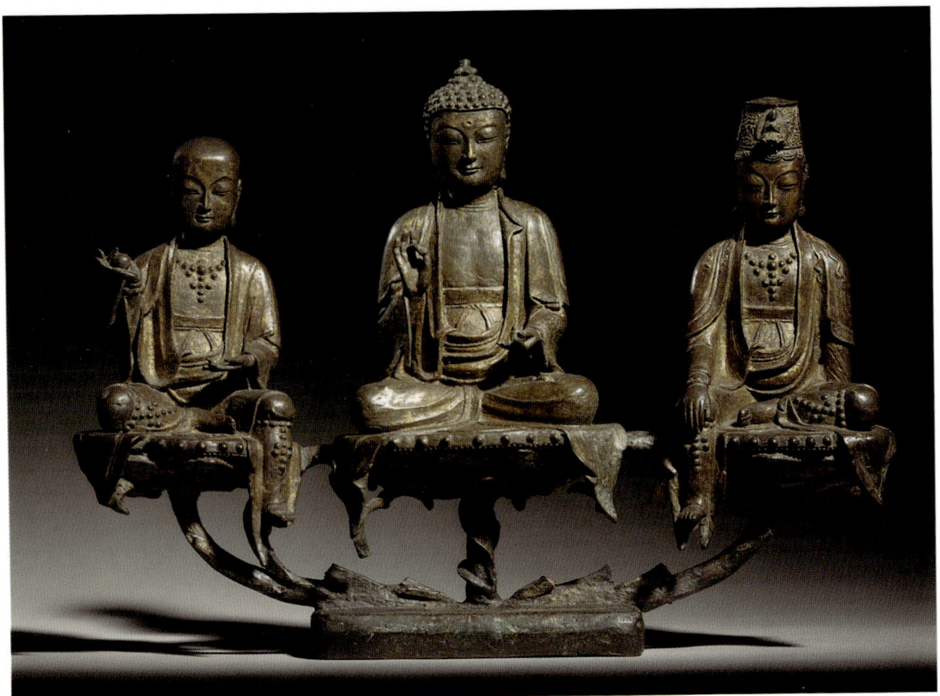

Amita (Amitabha) Triad 1400s

KOREA, JOSEON PERIOD (1392–1910)

This rare 15th-century bronze triad shows Amitabha, the Celestial Buddha (Amita in Korean), in the center. He is flanked by two attendants, Ksitigarbha (Jijang Bosal in Korean) on his left and Avalokitesvara (Kuaneum Bosal in Korean) on his right. Jijang is responsible for the instruction of all beings until the appearance of the Maitreya Buddha, the Buddha of the Future. Kuaneum is Amita's most compassionate agent, aiding those on their journey toward the Western Paradise of the Pure Land Buddhist sect. The three figures are shown on lotus seats with their hands in a gesture of blessing. This sculpture would have likely been placed in front of a large mural depicting the Western Paradise.

BRONZE WITH TRACES OF GILDING; 40.6 X 16.5 X 54.6 CM (16 X 6-1/2 X 21-1/2 IN.)

WORCESTER R. WARNER COLLECTION 1918.501

Snowscape with Figures 1584

KIM SI (KOREAN, 1524–1593)

This scroll is a rare surviving example of early Joseon period painting. The names of the painter and patron, the date, and the title of the painting are all inscribed. Kim Si was a member of the literati, high-ranking or aristocratic men who eschewed court life to focus on literary and artistic pursuits. This decision was often made in response to political strife at court, and Kim Si was no exception. His father, Kim Anro (1481–1537), was at one time the highest ranking court official in Korea but was executed after years of political struggles. Kim Si pulled away from the court and spent his life doing calligraphy, painting, and reading. This image of a solitary scholar in his studio surrounded by trees and snow-covered mountains reflects the literati desire for a life devoted to art and poetry. In the painting, a scholar watches a visitor approaching by boat, while travelers leave his studio on foot by the back gate.

HANGING SCROLL; INK ON SILK; 52.3 X 67.2 CM (20-5/8 X 26-1/2 IN.)

MR. AND MRS. WILLIAM H. MARLATT FUND 1987.187

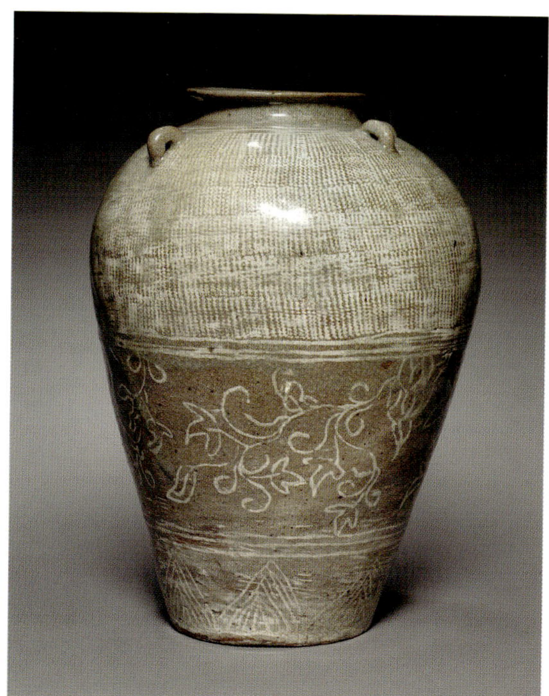

Storage Jar 1400s

KOREA, JOSEON PERIOD (1392–1910)

The surface of this jar is divided into three concentric bands of decoration using a combination of inlaid and stamped techniques. Inlaid lotus petals, a motif associated with Buddhism, rise up from the bottom of the vessel; inlaid grape vines embellish the middle register; at the top, an impressed rope-curtain adorns the shoulders, on which four loop handles secure a lid. This vessel, like others of its type, may have originally been used to bury a placenta. Aristocratic families practiced this custom in the belief that it would bring good health and future prosperity to the child.

STONEWARE, BUNCHEONG WARE WITH INCISED, STAMPED, AND SLIP-INLAID DECORATION; H. 37.5 CM (14-3/4 IN.)
JOHN L. SEVERANCE FUND 1963.505

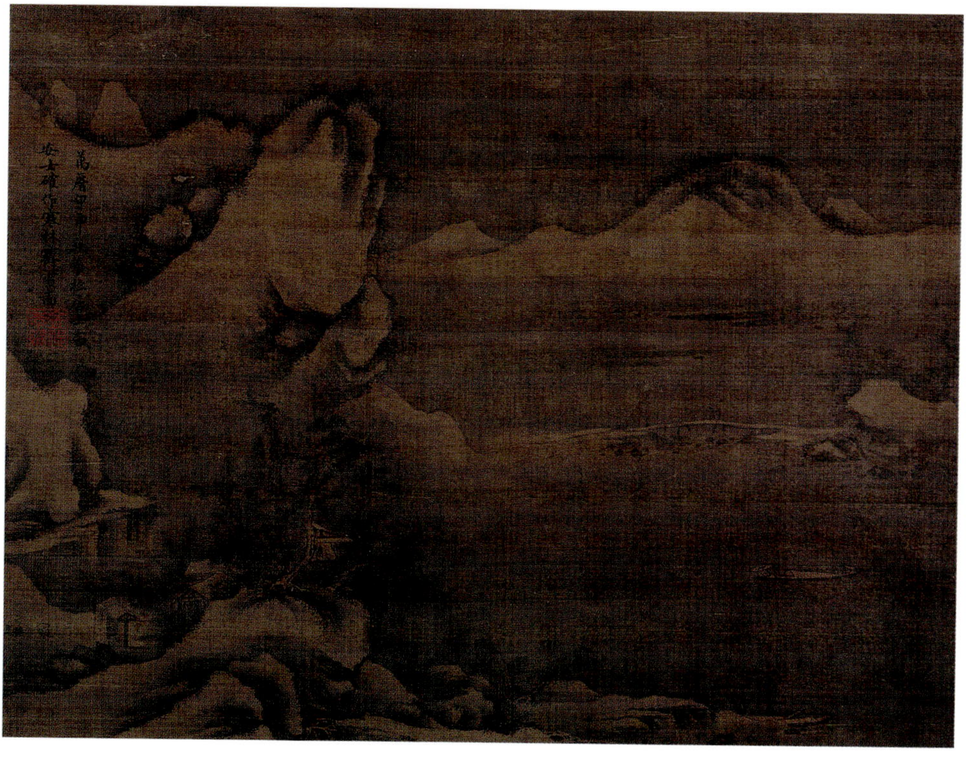

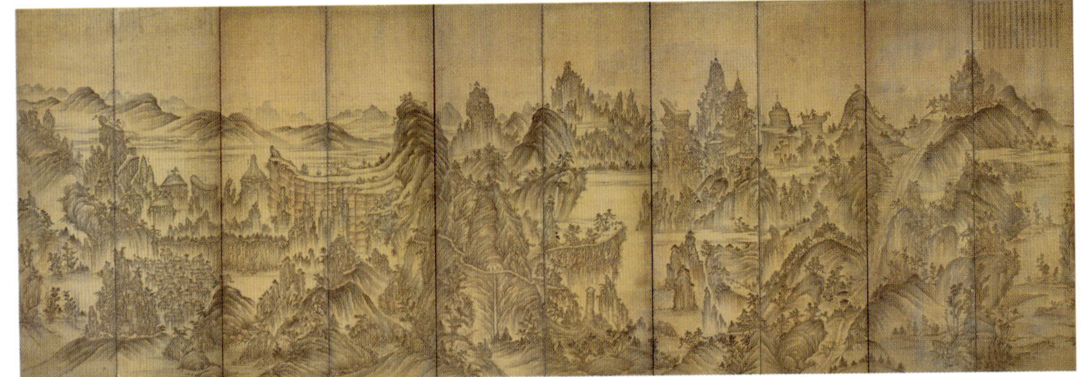

The Seven Jeweled Peaks: Chilbo Mountains
1700s
KOREA, JOSEON PERIOD (1392–1910)
This panoramic scene shows the Chilbo Mountains with their needle-pointed and rounded pinnacles. This area was formed ages ago from a volcanic eruption in Hangyeong-bukdo province in northeast Korea. The inscription in the upper right-hand corner and labels throughout the painting identify various peaks, temples, and shrines, such as Gaesim-sa Buddhist Temple. Small figures, dwellings, and trails are placed throughout the landscape, depicted using a bird's-eye view. This painting was regarded as a Jingyeong, or true-view landscape. The style follows the orthodox literati school of the Chinese Qing dynasty (1644–1911), a style imported to Joseon period Korea. Viewers can imagine following the small figures in the scene on pilgrimages to sacred regions to express their Buddhist faith.

TEN-PANEL SCREEN; INK AND COLOR ON CLOTH; 158.1 X 438.2 CM (62-1/4 X 172-5/8 IN.)
MR. AND MRS. WILLIAM H. MARLATT FUND 1989.6

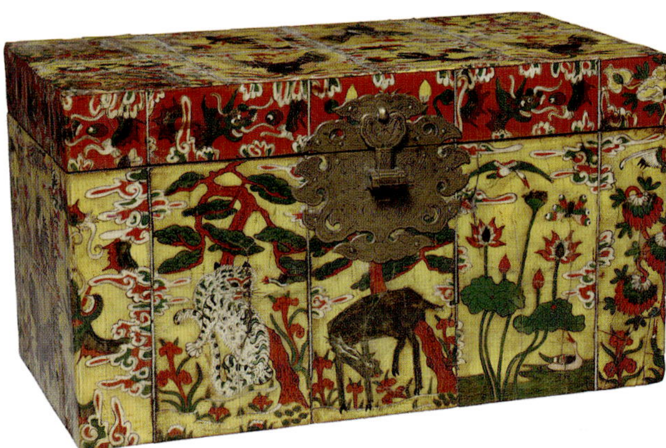

Box: "Hwagak" Type 1800s
KOREA, JOSEON PERIOD (1392–1910)
This box is decorated with the technique of ox-horn painting *(hwagak)*. The ox horn was cut, soaked in water, boiled, and then pressed into thin flat sheets. The sheets were painted with popular motifs of Korean paintings, such as tigers under pine trees, ducks in a lotus pond, and deer. The painted surfaces were attached to wooden boxes, and finally, the boxes were coated with varnish for protection. The translucent quality of the ox horn offers both a lively surface for the painting and a contrast to the color of the wood.

PAINTED WOOD WITH FLATTENED OX-HORN INLAY; 29.9 X 16.5 X 16.2 CM (11-3/4 X 6-1/2 X 6-3/8 IN.)
SUNDRY PURCHASE FUND 1920.37

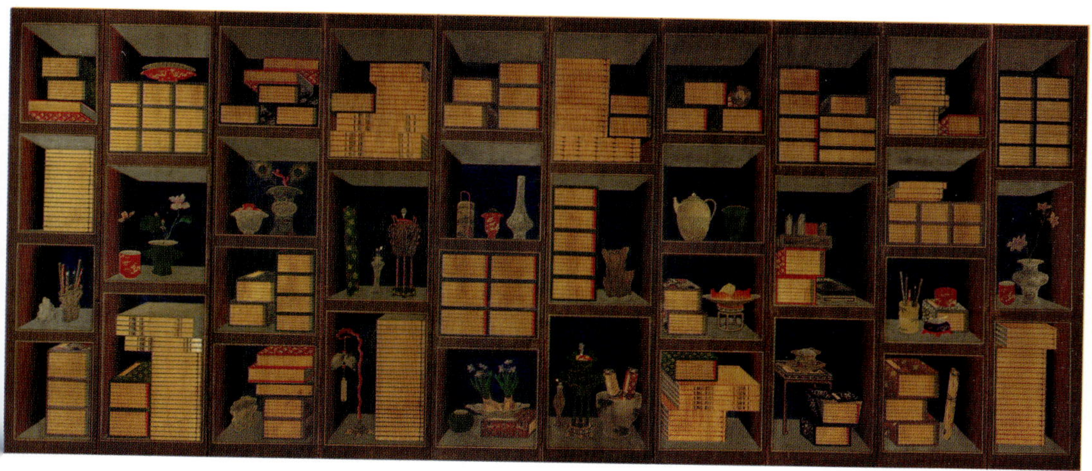

Scholar's Accouterments (Chaekgori) late 1800s

KOREA, JOSEON PERIOD (1392–1910)

This screen presents a Korean Confucian scholar's collection displayed on a bookcase. The tradition of *chaekgori*, or books and things, dates from at least the late 18th century, after King Jeongjo (r. 1776–1800) placed a screen behind his desk in his palace. Soon every nobleman acquired a similar status symbol to fill his studio with auspicious messages and cultural allusions.

The shelves are lined with books and scholars' tools: brushes, ink sticks, and ink stones. Other items include expensive imports such as peacock feathers and red coral, and Chinese antiques prized by Joseon period collectors such as elegant ceramics and a bronze for Confucian ancestor worship. These accouterments symbolize an ideal gentleman's sophistication and education.

The chaekgori theme was rendered using a mixture of Eastern and Western systems of perspective. Western linear perspective and modeling create the illusion of deep shelves, rounded ceramics, and weighty books. Yet this screen has the multiple vanishing points typical of East Asian painting. Since it is more than 12 feet wide, a Western-style single vanishing point would result in distortion of the image, and the shelves on the end panels would tilt at dramatic angles. The painter solved this perspective problem by drawing upon both Asian and European traditions.

TEN-PANEL FOLDING SCREEN; INK AND COLOR ON SILK;
139 X 29 CM (54-3/4 X 11-3/8 IN.) EACH PANEL
LEONARD C. HANNA JR. FUND 2011.37

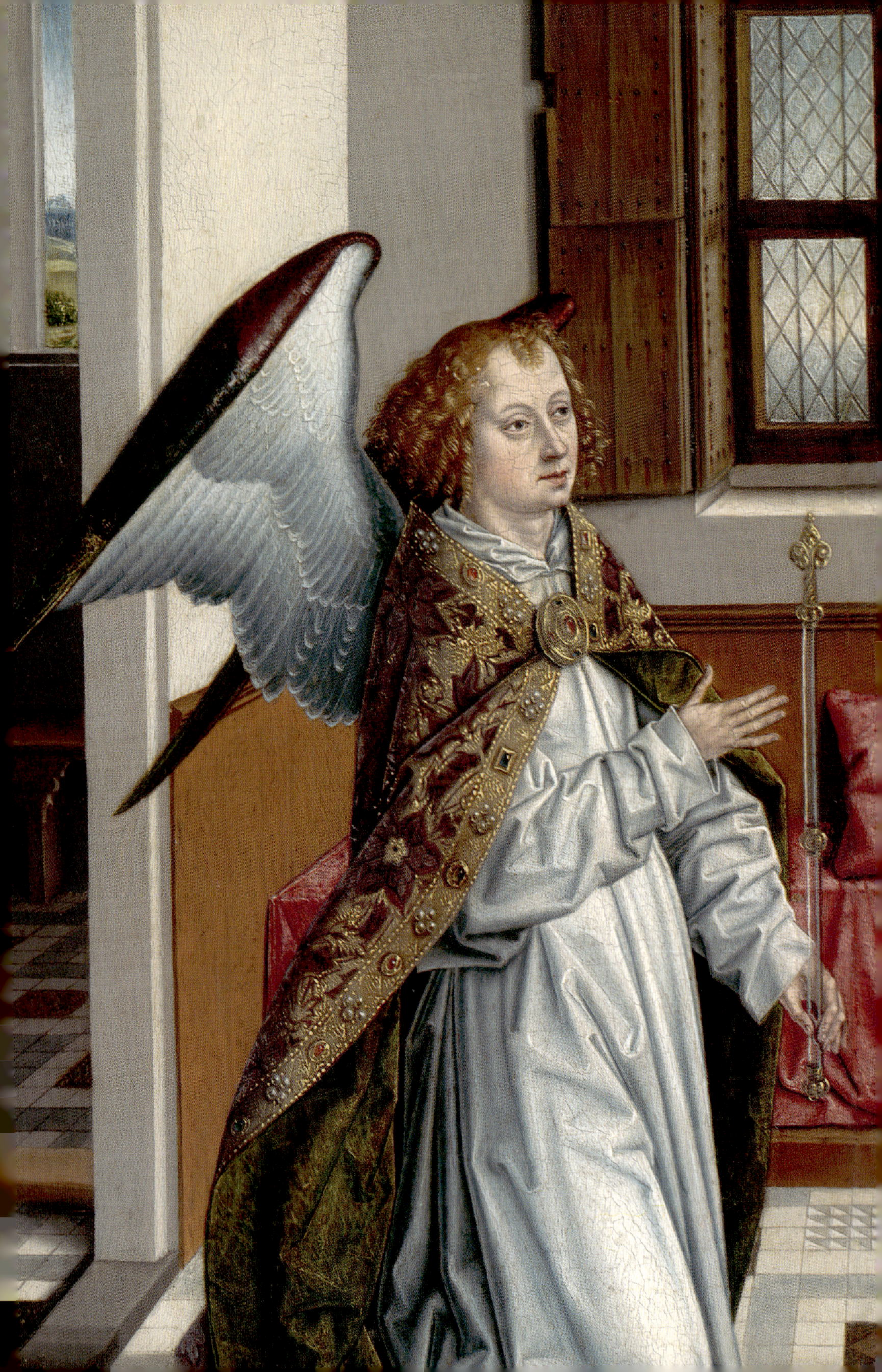

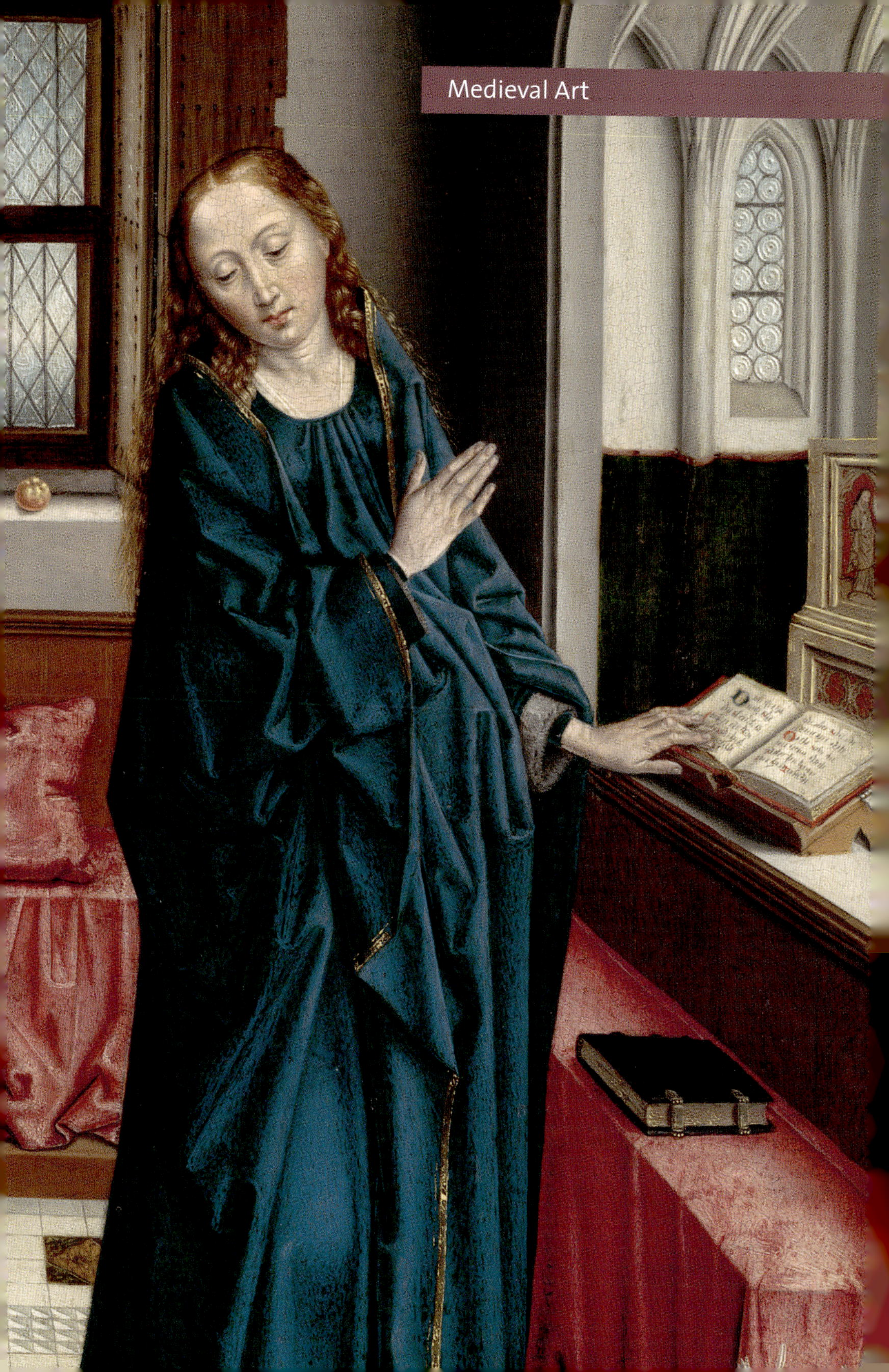
Medieval Art

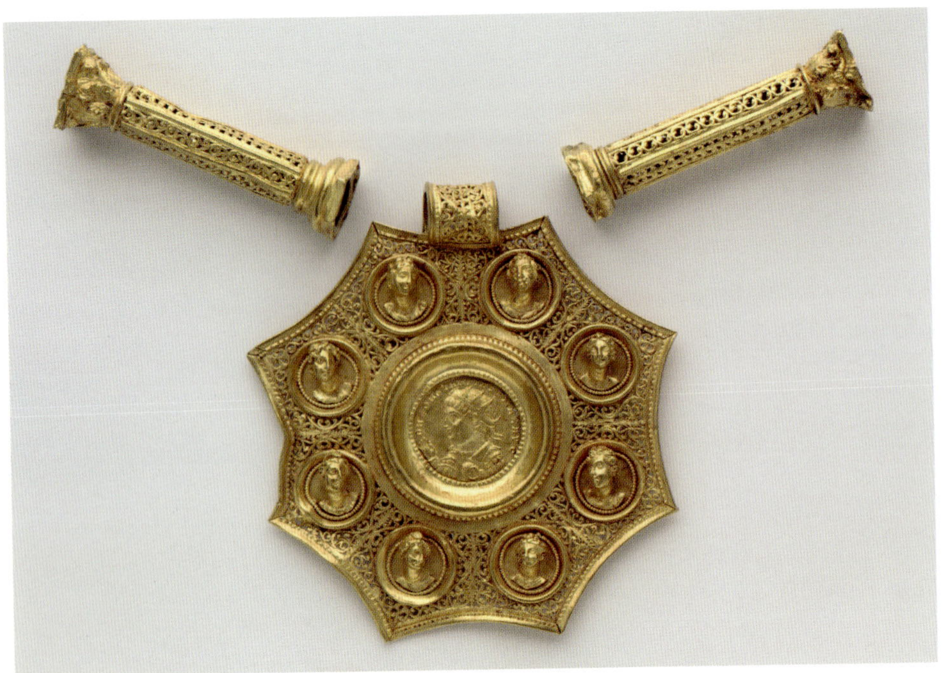

Constantinian Pendant and Spacers AD 324–26
EASTERN MEDITERRANEAN (PROBABLY SIRMIUM OR NICOMEDIA), LATE ROMAN, BYZANTINE
Mounted at the center of the octagonal pendant is a rare coin issued by Constantine the Great, the Roman Empire's first Christian emperor. His portrait appears on the front of the coin and those of two of his sons on the back. Constantine's image is surrounded by male and female busts, some of which are mythological figures. The pendant once formed the centerpiece of a sumptuous gold necklace, likely a gift for a high-ranking court official or member of the imperial family. The spacers are in the form of Corinthian columns.

OPUS INTERASSILE; GOLD; 9.7 X 9.4 CM (3-7/8 X 3-3/4 IN.) PENDANT; 6.5 X 1.9 CM (2-1/2 X 3/4 IN.) SPACERS
LEONARD C. HANNA JR. FUND 1994.98.1–4

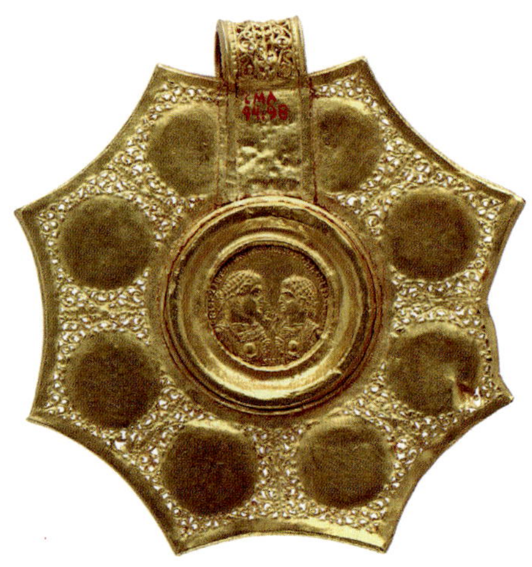

Brooch in the Form of a Six-Pointed Star late 700s–early 800s

FRANKISH, EARLY CAROLINGIAN

This gold brooch originally functioned as a garment clasp. Archaeological and pictorial evidence associates its design with women, who used such ornaments to fasten their veils or mantles just beneath the chin. Its rare form, a hexagram (six-pointed star), suggests it also functioned as a talisman or amulet both to attract good luck for the wearer and to ward off evil. The Franks were likely introduced to the hexagram and its apotropaic effects through the Romans.

GOLD WITH REPOUSSÉ AND FILIGREE DECORATION, COPPER BACKPLATE; H. 7.7 CM (3 IN.)

SEVERANCE AND GRETA MILLIKIN PURCHASE FUND 2009.344

Enthroned Mother of God and the Infant Christ ("The Stroganoff Ivory") 950–1025

CONSTANTINOPLE, BYZANTINE

The Virgin Mary is seated on a lavishly carved, high-backed throne; the two angels hovering above draw attention to the Christ child poised in her lap. Representations of the enthroned Virgin and Child have a long tradition in Byzantine art, stretching back as far as the sixth century. With one hand raised in blessing and the other holding a scroll, Jesus is portrayed as an emotionless and supernatural child, visualizing for the pious beholder the mystery of his incarnation. The ivory has been identified as belonging to a distinct group of Middle Byzantine ivories named the "Nikephoros group" after an ivory cross reliquary with an inscription mentioning Emperor Nikephoros II (r. 963–69).

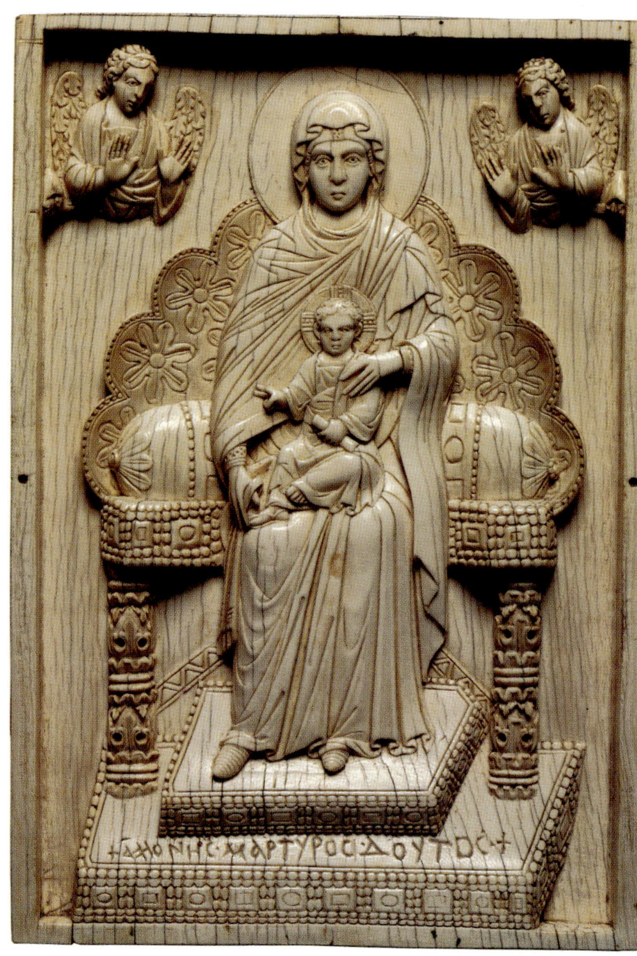

IVORY; 25.3 X 17.2 CM (10 X 6-3/4 IN.)

GIFT OF J. H. WADE 1925.1293

The Jonah Marbles

These five sculptures illustrate a language of symbols developed by the early Christians. They make reference to resurrection, life after death, and salvation. The four figures of Jonah depict incidents from the biblical story. After disobeying the Lord's command to proclaim judgment on the city of Nineveh, the Old Testament prophet Jonah was cast into the sea and swallowed by a sea monster. He spent three days praying inside the beast before being disgorged, unharmed. When asked a second time, Jonah obeyed the Lord but was displeased when the city was spared. After pleading for Nineveh's destruction, Jonah left the city and rested in the shadow of a large gourd vine. The Lord, however, made the vine wither,

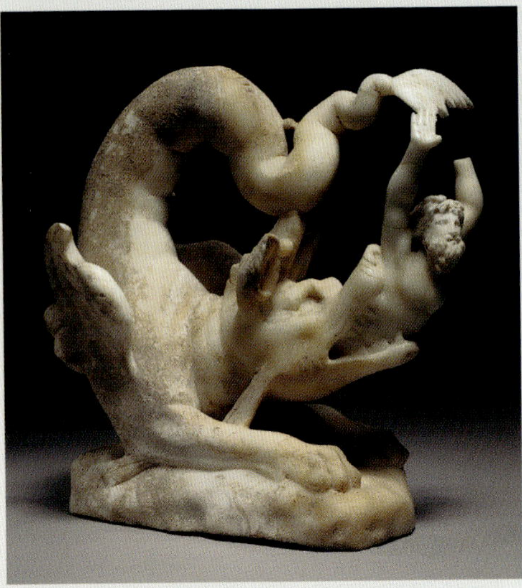

exposing Jonah to the burning sun. The moment in the biblical story describing Jonah standing with arms raised, the fourth figure, is unclear.

Jonah Swallowed and *Jonah Cast Up* were understood by early Christians to represent the death and resurrection of Christ. The story of the gourd vine suggests it is a symbol of the resurrection. Iconographically, *Jonah under the Gourd Vine* evolved from pagan mythological figures who, on waking, arose to everlasting life in paradise. The figure of *Jonah Praying* with arms extended has been interpreted to represent either the moment of his repentance within the whale's belly or else giving thanks after his deliverance.

Jonah Swallowed, about AD 280. Eastern Mediterranean, Late Roman/Early Christian. Marble; H. 50.4 cm (19-7/8 in.). John L. Severance Fund 1965.237

Jonah Cast Up, about AD 280. Eastern Mediterranean, Late Roman/Early Christian. Marble; H. 41.5 cm (16-3/8 in.). John L. Severance Fund 1965.238

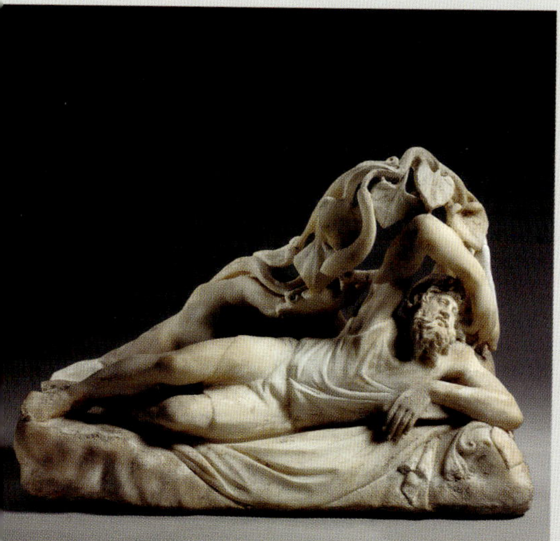

Images of a youthful shepherd carrying a sheep over his shoulders were popular with Romans of traditional faith as well as Christians living in the Late Roman Empire. Painted on the walls or the ceiling of a burial chamber or carved on a marble sarcophagus, such images could invoke the deceased's hope for a peaceful afterlife spent in a pastoral setting. For Christians, this image took on a more specific meaning, referring to the passage in the Gospel according to John in which Christ called himself as a good shepherd who lays down his life for his sheep. Allegedly found together with the Jonah statuettes, this figure likely represents Christ as the Good Shepherd.

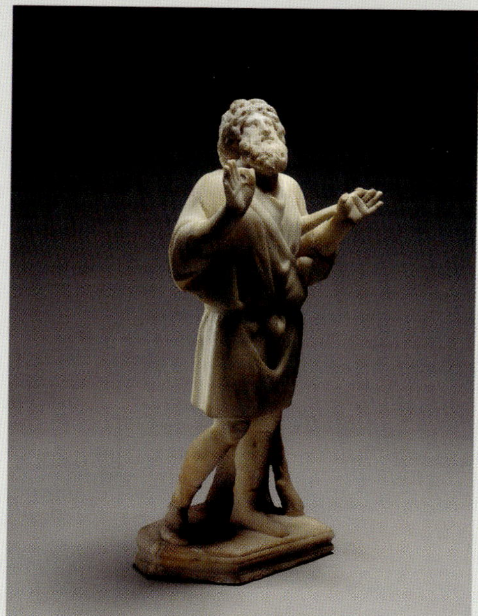

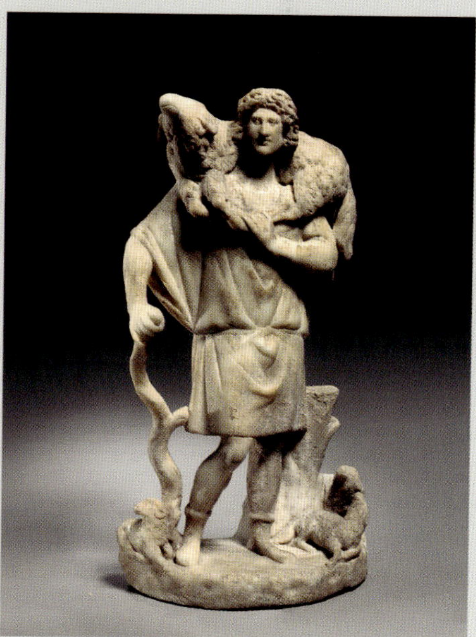

Jonah under the Gourd Vine, about AD 280. Eastern Mediterranean, Late Roman/Early Christian. Marble; L. 46.3 cm (18-1/4 in.). John L. Severance Fund 1965.239

Jonah Praying, about AD 280. Eastern Mediterranean, Late Roman/Early Christian. Marble; H. 47.5 cm (18-3/4 in.). John L. Severance Fund 1965.240

The Good Shepherd, about AD 280. Eastern Mediterranean, Late Roman/Early Christian. Marble; H. 49.5 cm (19-1/2 in.). John L. Severance Fund 1965.241

Icon of the Mother of God and Infant Christ

about 1425–50

ATTRIBUTED TO ANGELOS AKOTANTOS (CRETAN)

The touching cheeks of mother and child in a loving moment characterize this type of icon, known as a "Virgin Eleousa" (Virgin of Tenderness). It signifies Christ's incarnation, suffering, and death for the sake of humankind. Three ornamental stars on the Virgin's cloak are traditional symbols of her chastity; a blue cap covers her hair and protects her modesty. Wearing a pale green tunic and deep orange cloak, both highlighted in gold, the child holds a scroll tied with a ribbon, a symbol of the Gospels. Angelos Akotantos was the pre-eminent artistic personality on Crete during the 1400s. This icon is from his period of greatest activity and predates the collapse of Constantinople in 1453. The treatment of the faces and draperies is handled with fluency and skill and reveals Akotantos to be a painter of great talent. Given its large scale, the icon was intended for use within an orthodox church, possibly a monastery, not for a private home.

TEMPERA AND GOLD ON WOOD; 96 X 70 CM (37-3/4 X 27-1/2 IN.)

LEONARD C. HANNA JR. FUND 2010.154

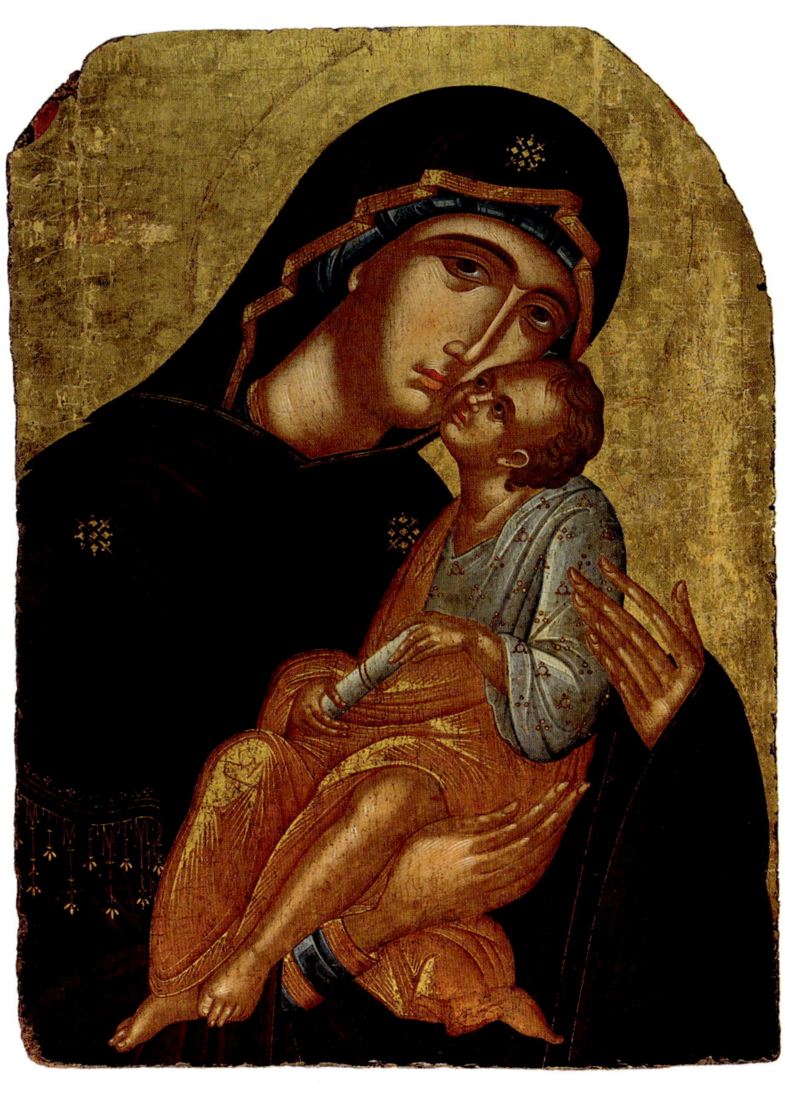

The Spitzer Cross about 1190

MASTER OF THE ROYAL PLANTAGENET WORKSHOP (FRANCE)

This cross was likely made around 1190 for the Royal Abbey of Grandmont, just outside Limoges, then under the patronage of King Henry II of England, where it would likely have served in liturgical processions in the abbey. The largest known cross to survive from Limoges in the champlevé technique, it received its name from its former owner, Frederic Spitzer, an important Parisian 19th-century collector of medieval objects. It has justly been hailed as the finest Limoges enameled cross known. The work's coloration exemplifies its refined craftsmanship. Christ's body, rendered in white enamel with fine lines defining the rib cage, abdomen, and muscles, provides striking contrast with the vibrant yellow, green, blue, and gold of the cross and his halo and loincloth.

GILT-COPPER AND CHAMPLEVÉ ENAMEL; 67.4 X 41.9 CM (26-1/2 X 16-1/2 IN.)

GIFT OF J. H. WADE 1923.1051

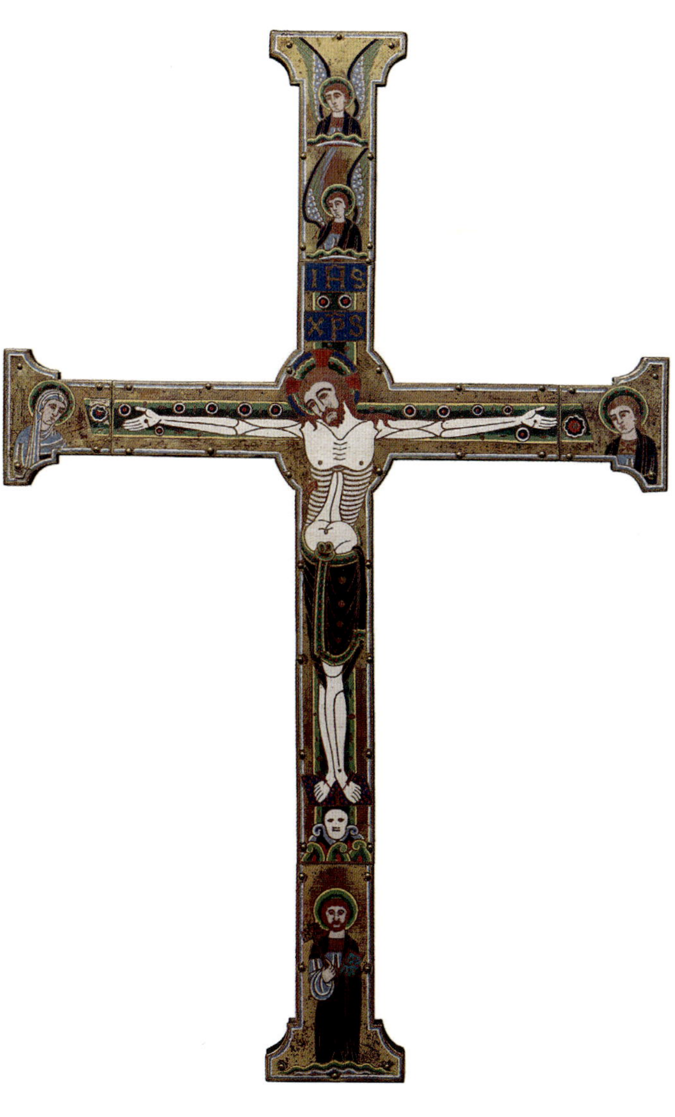

The Guelph Treasure

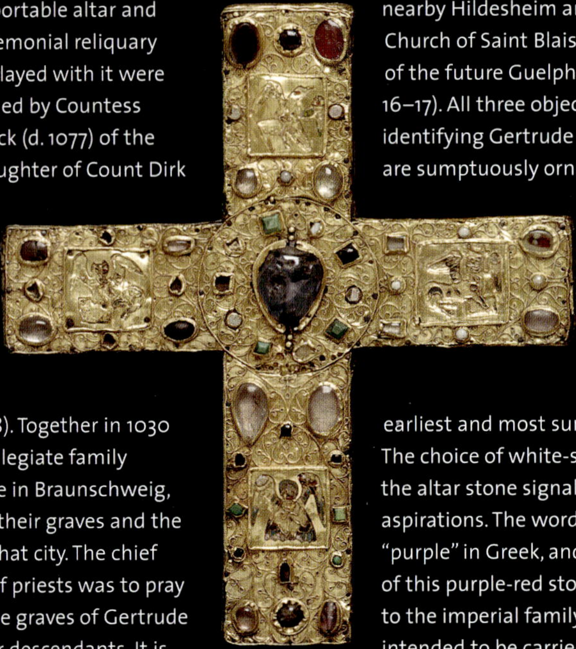

This golden portable altar and the two ceremonial reliquary crosses displayed with it were commissioned by Countess Gertrude of Brunswick (d. 1077) of the House of Guelph, daughter of Count Dirk III of Holland. Related to the imperial family, Gertrude was married to the powerful Liudolf Brunon, Count of Brunswick (d. 1038). Together in 1030 they founded the collegiate family chapel of Saint Blaise in Braunschweig, the intended site of their graves and the future cathedral of that city. The chief duty of the college of priests was to pray in perpetuity over the graves of Gertrude and Liudolf and their descendants. It is believed that this group of objects was ordered by Countess Gertrude within the period 1038–45, shortly after the death of her husband. They were made by goldsmiths working in nearby Hildesheim and presented to the Church of Saint Blaise, forming the basis of the future Guelph Treasure (see pp. 16–17). All three objects bear inscriptions identifying Gertrude as the patron. They are sumptuously ornamented with precious and semi-precious stones, pearls, and enamels.

The portable altar is one of the Guelph Treasure's earliest and most sumptuous objects. The choice of white-speckled porphyry as the altar stone signals Gertrude's worldly aspirations. The word "porphyry" means "purple" in Greek, and in antiquity the use of this purple-red stone was restricted to the imperial family. The crosses were intended to be carried in liturgical processions or placed on a church altar. The inclusion of relics within the crosses endowed them with an additional role as devotional objects.

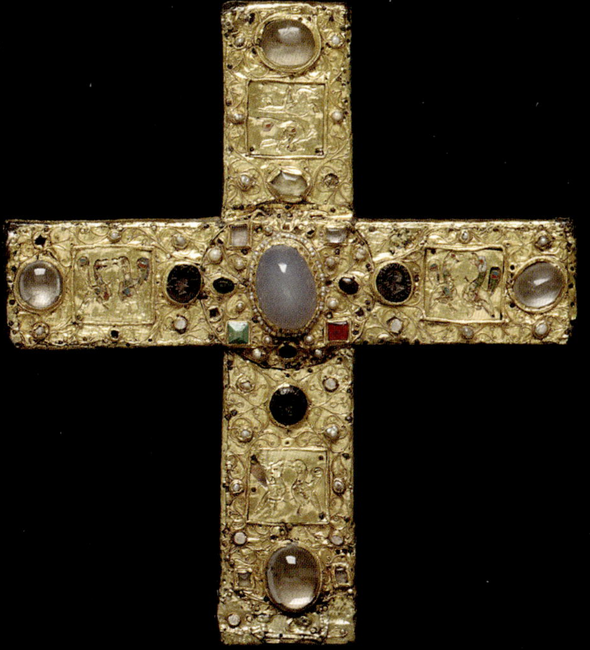

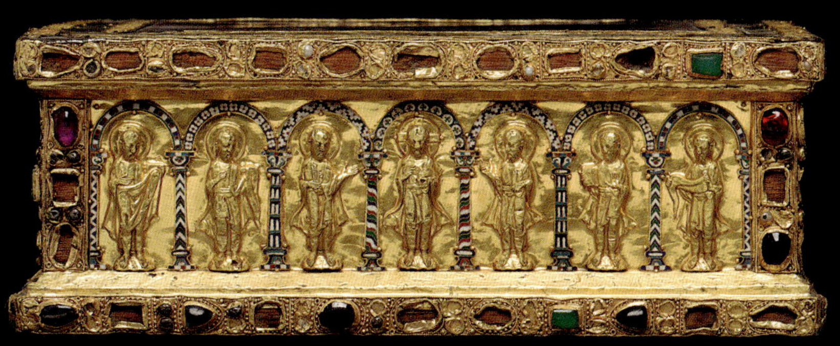

Ceremonial Cross of Count Liudolf, about 1038–45. Germany, Hildesheim. Gold worked in repoussé, cloisonné enamel, intaglio gems, pearls, wood core; 24.2 x 21.6 cm (9-1/2 x 8-1/2 in.). Gift of the John Huntington Art and Polytechnic Trust 1931.461

Portable Altar of Countess Gertrude, about 1038–45. Germany, Hildesheim. Gold, cloisonné enamel, porphyry, gems, pearls, niello, wood core; 10.5 x 27.5 x 21 cm (4-1/8 x 10-7/8 x 8-1/4 in.). Gift of the John Huntington Art and Polytechnic Trust 1931.462

Virgin and Child in Majesty (Sedes Sapientiae)

about 1150–1200

FRANCE, AUVERGNE

This sculpture belongs to a group of early representations of the Virgin and Child known as the "Sedes Sapientiae" (Throne of Wisdom). The subject embodies a complex and core Christian doctrine of the Virgin's role in the Incarnation (the moment in which Christ became flesh) and ultimately in the redemption of humankind. Mary is seated frontally, gazing toward the beholder. Sitting on a throne, she in turn becomes the throne to the Christ child, thus symbolizing her role in giving birth not only to the human Jesus, but also to the divine Christ. The Incarnation gave Mary a unique role

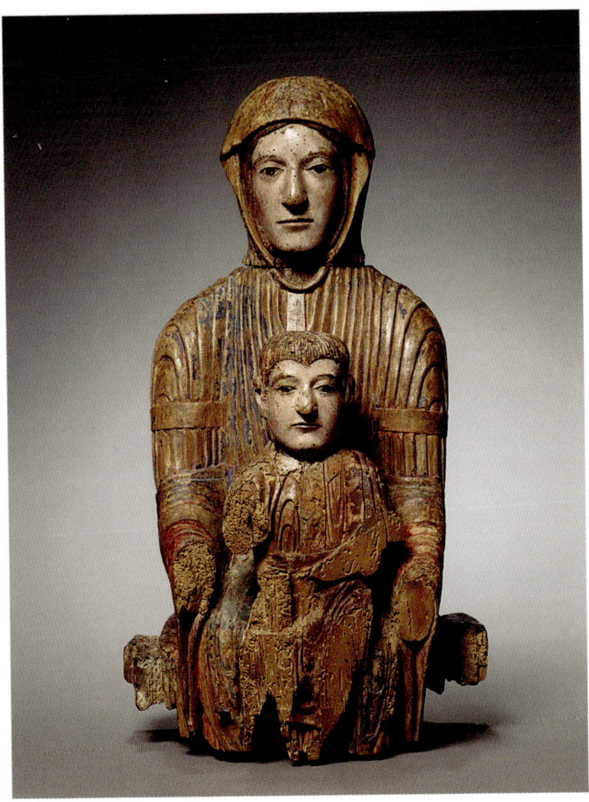

as principal mediator between heaven and earth, between God and humankind. As a result, her image proliferated in art, especially after the 12th century, a period in which there was surging interest in Mary's life and increasing devotion to her person and images.

One in a rare group of surviving figures produced in the Auvergne region of central France during the second half of the 12th century, this sculpture shows the characteristic linear, calligraphic draperies forming beautiful swirls and contours. These Auvergne Virgins are estimated to number fewer than 30. All are made of wood and smaller than life-size in order to make them portable. Evidence suggests that they were moved from altar to altar or church to church and were frequently carried in procession within churches and town streets on Marian feast days. The heads were intentionally removable in order to "dress" them in costumes for such processions.

WALNUT WITH POLYCHROMY; 40 X 22 X 24 CM (15-3/4 X 8-5/8 X 9-1/2 IN.)

SEVERANCE AND GRETA MILLIKIN PURCHASE FUND

2012.52

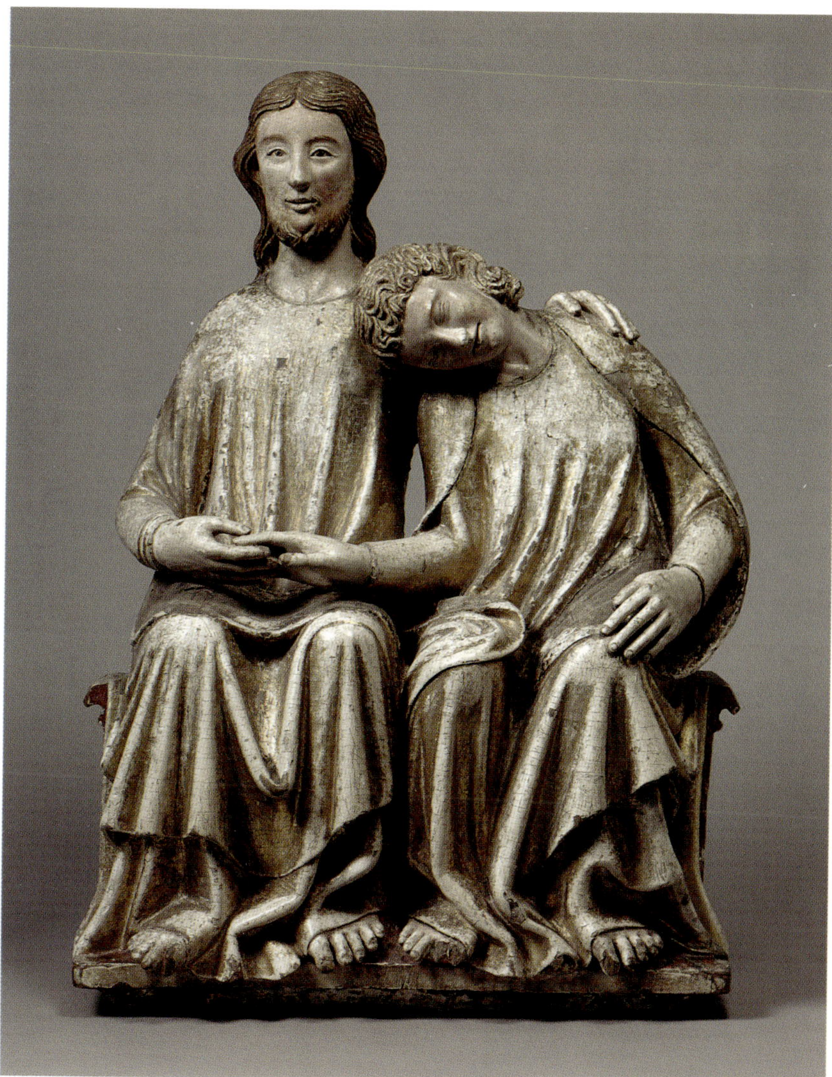

Christ and Saint John 1300–1320

GERMANY, SWABIA (LAKE CONSTANCE REGION)

The subject here was a fertile one for devotional sculpture in Swabia, a region on Germany's border with Switzerland. Some 28 examples of the so-called Christ and Saint John groups have been documented by recent scholarship, and the subject appears to be unique to this region, where the sculptures' popularity increased in the years shortly after 1300. Many such works adorned the chapels of Dominican convents. As a focus of devotion, the sculpture reflects the fundamental religious beliefs rooted in mysticism that dominated the period. It would have had special appeal to female viewers in convent settings in that it reflects the mystical union of the soul with God through the divine heart of Christ. Sensitively modeled to capture the pathos of the moment, this sculpture is artistically among the finest to survive.

OAK WITH POLYCHROMY; 92.7 X 64.5 X 28.8 CM (36-1/2 X 25-3/8 X 11-3/8 IN.)

PURCHASE FROM THE J. H. WADE FUND 1928.753

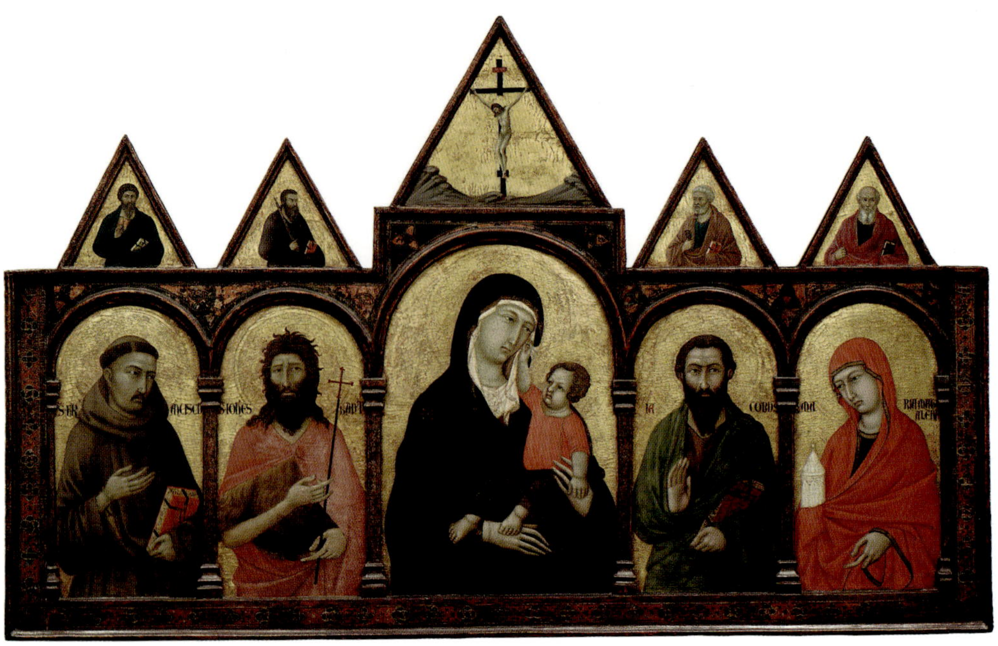

Virgin and Child with Saints about 1320

UGOLINO DI NERIO DA SIENA (ITALIAN, ACTIVE 1317–ABOUT 1327)

In this remarkably complete altarpiece, the Virgin and Christ child are surrounded by saints: Francis, displaying his stigmata, and John the Baptist to the left; James and Mary Magdalene to the right. In the pinnacles above, flanking the Crucifixion, are four other saints including Peter and Paul. The saints depicted here are particularly relevant to the Franciscans, strongly suggesting the altarpiece was commissioned for a Franciscan church. The Sienese painter Ugolino di Nerio, the most accomplished follower and possible pupil of Duccio, is known to have made a career providing Franciscan communities with similar altarpieces for their churches in late medieval Italy.

TEMPERA AND GOLD ON WOOD; 122.5 X 192.5 CM (48-1/4 X 75-3/4 IN.)

LEONARD C. HANNA JR. FUND 1961.40

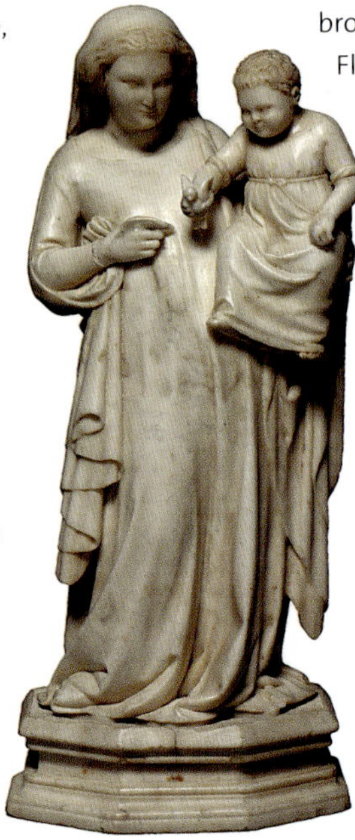

Madonna and Child about 1330–40

ATTRIBUTED TO ANDREA PISANO (ITALIAN, ABOUT 1290–1348/49)

One of the most important and beautiful of such sculptures by Andrea Pisano in existence, this is his only sculpture in the United States. The attribution is based on a comparison with his bronze reliefs for the Baptistry doors in Florence, fully documented examples of his work. A large body of other statues and reliefs survive that were unquestionably produced in his workshop. While his style is based on sculpture typical to Pisa, with its bulk and sense of drama, he was much influenced by the art of the Florentine painter Giotto and by French Gothic metalwork. Andrea became master of works at Orvieto Cathedral in 1347.

MARBLE WITH TRACES OF GILDING; 5 X 15.9 X 15.1 CM (2 X 6-1/4 X 6 IN.)

LEONARD C. HANNA JR. FUND 1972.51

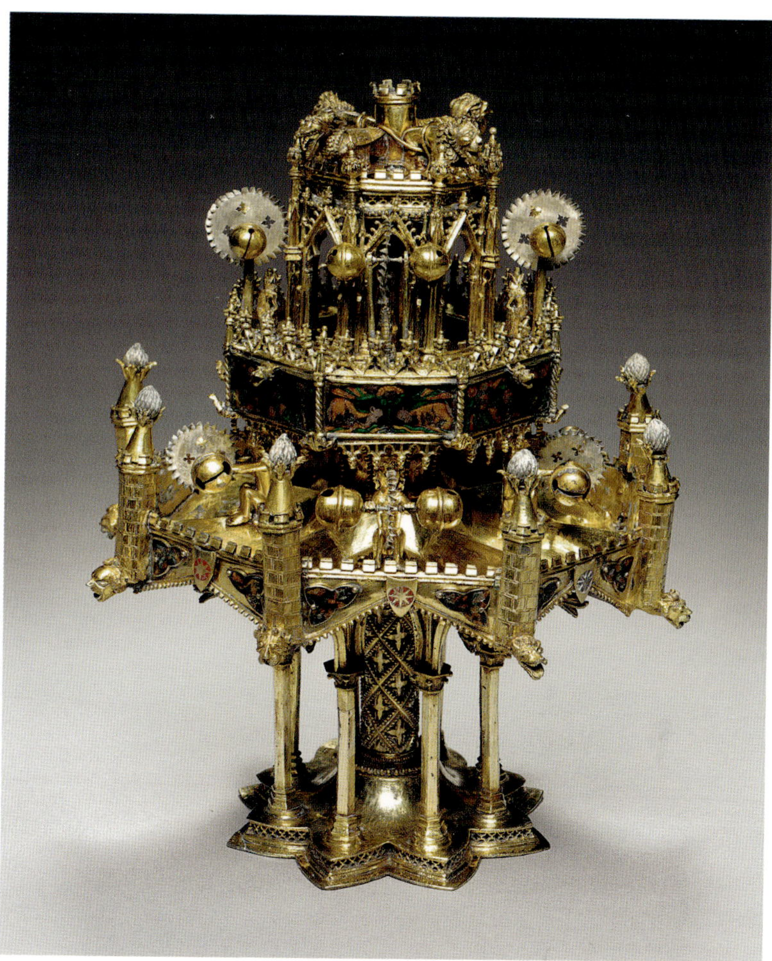

Table Fountain about 1320–40

FRANCE, PARIS(?)

This unusual object is the most complete example of its type known to have survived from the Middle Ages. Medieval inventories indicate that such small fountains, generally made from precious metals, once existed in large numbers. Some must have been made for temporary use and linked to a great ceremonial or social event. An exquisite piece of Gothic architecture in miniature, this table fountain originally stood in a large catch basin. Scented water, pumped through a central tube, would have emerged at the top through a series of nozzles creating water jets that, in turn, forced the rotation of the water wheels and rang the tiny bells. Such objects were likely mounted on tripods or small side tables to be admired for the beauty of their craftsmanship. They were clearly feats of technical ingenuity intended to entertain guests through the motion of cascading water and the accompanying sound of ringing bells.

Possessions like this table fountain were much loved by the Valois princes of France, including the dukes of Burgundy, for they embodied aristocratic values: magnificence in appearance, ceremony, and surroundings. Objects of gold, illuminated manuscripts, tapestries, music, and pageants were emblematic of status, wealth, and power.

GILT-SILVER AND TRANSLUCENT ENAMEL; 33.8 X 25.4 X 26 CM (13-1/4 X 10 X 10-1/4 IN.)

PURCHASE FROM THE J. H. WADE FUND 1924.859

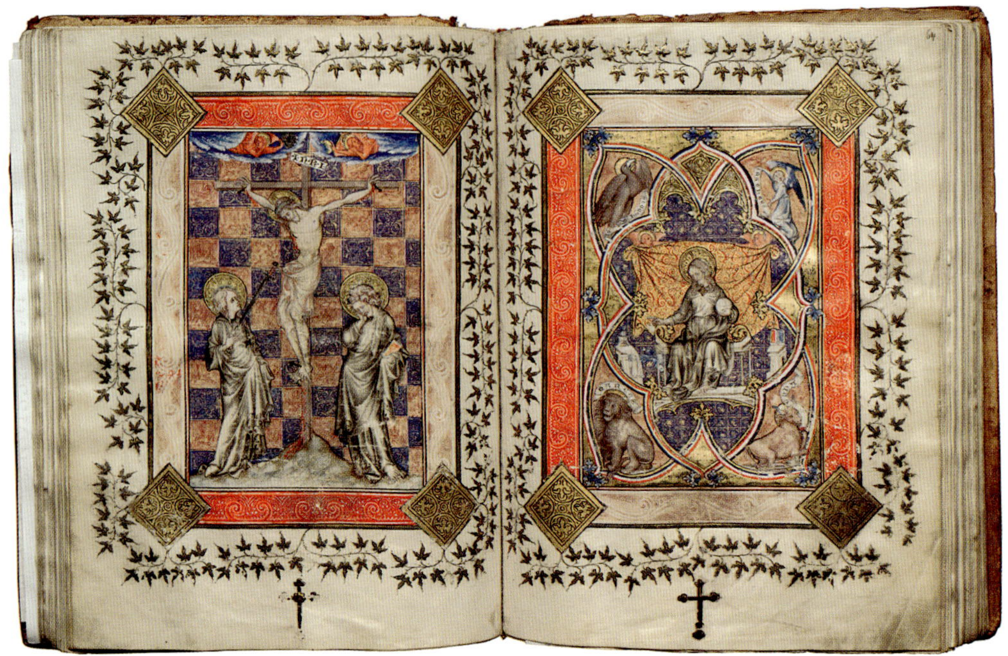

The Gotha Missal about 1370–72

MASTER OF THE BOQUETEAUX (FRENCH, ACTIVE ABOUT 1350–80) AND WORKSHOP

The style and quality of the decoration of this manuscript are typical of deluxe Parisian books made for aristocratic or royal patrons. Most of the book's decoration appears to be the work of the Master of the Boqueteaux, an artist active at the court of Charles V. His style was apparently shared by a number of book illuminators working in and around Paris at the time. It is very possible that the Gotha Missal belonged to Charles V, but that cannot be proved since the manuscript has no royal portraits and lacks a colophon. Given the book's magnificent decoration, however, it would seem that it was produced for a Valois prince, if not for the king himself. The manuscript receives its name from the German dukes of Gotha, its later owners.

INK, TEMPERA, AND GOLD ON VELLUM; 27.1 X 19.5 CM (10-5/8 X 7-5/8 IN.) FOLIO

MR. AND MRS. WILLIAM H. MARLATT FUND 1962.287

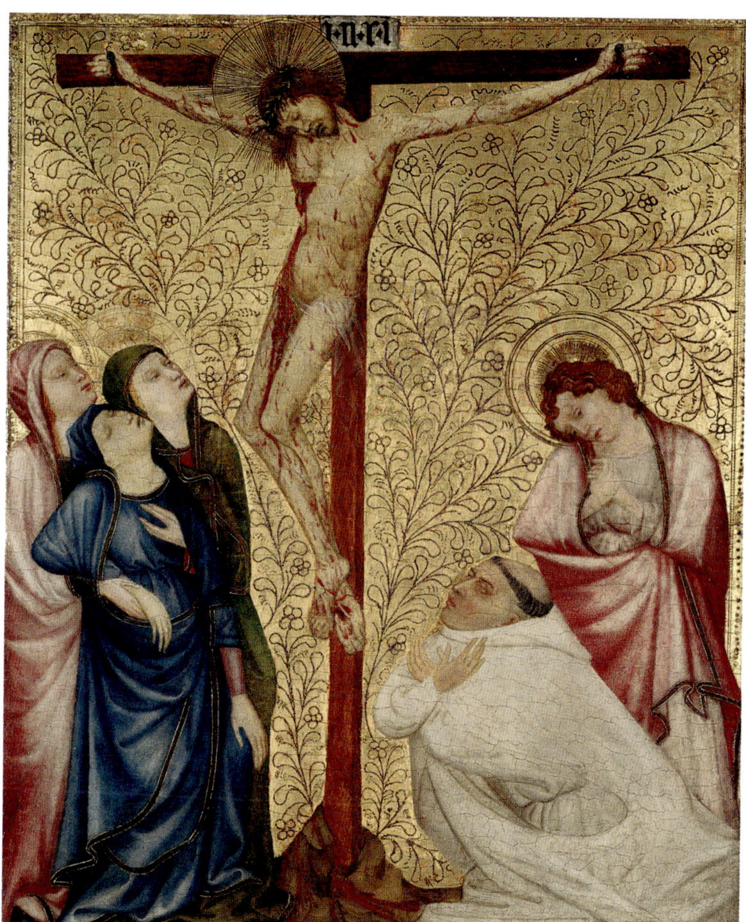

Calvary with a Carthusian Monk 1389–95

JEAN DE BEAUMETZ (FRANCO-FLEMISH, ABOUT 1335–1396)

Appointed the official court painter to the Burgundian duke Philip the Bold in 1376, Jean de Beaumetz created devotional paintings for the monks' cells at the Chartreuse de Champmol between 1389 and 1395. Philip and his wife, Margaret, founded that monastery to house the ducal tombs. This panel is only one of two of the original 26 that have survived; the second is preserved in the Louvre in Paris. The Carthusians were intensely devoted to the Passion of Christ, and particularly bloody images of the Crucifixion often decorated their cells. Isolated from one another, the monks contemplated the sacrifice of Christ (emphasized here by the presence of a Carthusian monk at the foot of the cross), creating an empathetic connection with the suffering of the Virgin, who faints in the arms of the two Marys. Saint John the Evangelist, on the right, bows his head in sorrow. The punched decoration in the gold background represents the Trees of Life and Knowledge, emphasizing the biblical connection between Adam and Christ.

OIL ON OAK; 56.6 X 45.7 CM (22-1/4 X 18 IN.)

LEONARD C. HANNA JR. BEQUEST 1964.454

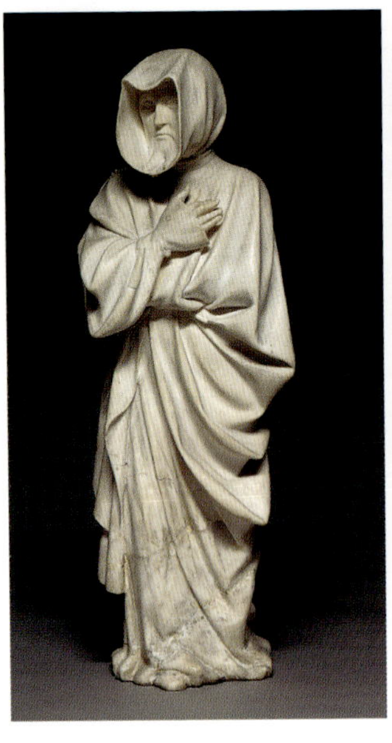
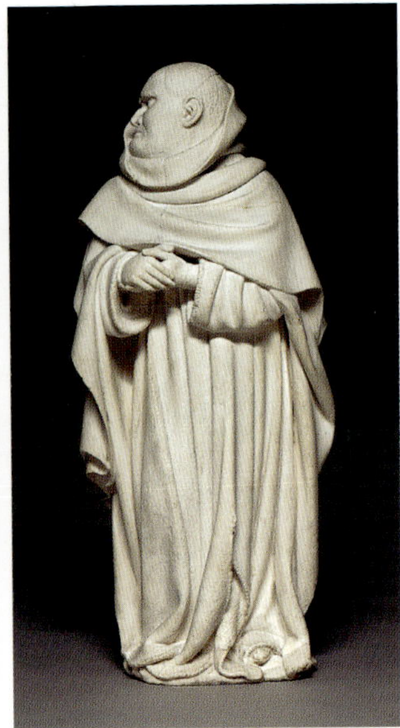
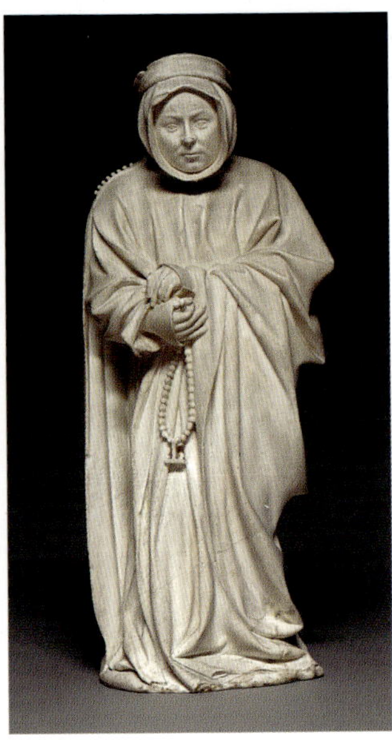

Three Mourners from the Tomb of Philip the Bold, Duke of Burgundy about 1404–10

CLAUS DE WERVE (FRANCO-FLEMISH, ABOUT 1380–1439)

Throughout most of their history the alabaster mourners from the tomb of Philip the Bold have evoked a sense of awe and mystery as well as curiosity and admiration. Originally arranged in processional order around the sides of the ducal tomb within a marble arcade, these realistically carved figures remain the most famous elements from Philip the Bold's tomb in the Chartreuse de Champmol. Carved by Claus de Werve, no two are alike. They retain minute details of costume and features; some are nearly portrait-like in their depiction of facial creases and expression, suggesting actual individuals, while the faces of others are partly obscured by their cowls.

The tomb of Philip the Bold is celebrated as one of the most sumptuous and innovative of the Middle Ages. Planning early, Philip commissioned it in 1384 from his court sculptor, Jean de Marville. The design featured two large slabs of black marble. The upper slab supported a prominent effigy of the duke lying in state, flanked by figures of angels; between the slabs was an intricate open arcade with 41 remarkable alabaster statuettes arranged in processional rank. Although its design and initial construction was the work of Marville, responsibility passed to Claus Sluter after Marville's death in 1389. After Sluter's death in 1406, his nephew Claus de Werve continued work on the tomb. The project was completed in 1410. Philip's son John the Fearless (d. 1419) copied the design for his tomb, as did many others throughout the century. The tomb was destroyed during the French Revolution, though the mourners and other fragments have been preserved.

VIZILLE ALABASTER; H. 41.7 CM (16-3/8 IN.) OVERALL

PURCHASE FROM THE J. H. WADE FUND 1940.128 AND BEQUEST OF LEONARD C. HANNA JR. 1958.66–67

Saint John the Baptist about 1410

ROBERT CAMPIN (FLEMISH, ABOUT 1375–1444)

According to tradition, John the Baptist wears a hair shirt under a white cloth, associated with newly baptized Christians. The flag bearing a red cross symbolizes resurrection. In marked contrast, the background features a lavish gold-patterned silk. The display of such luxurious fabrics continues an ancient tradition of using the finest objects in the worship of God. This painting has been cut down along the lower edge and would originally have shown a full-length image of the saint. It was probably the right wing of a triptych, with John the Baptist gazing at a central image of the Virgin and Christ child.

Campin first settled in Tournai around 1405–6 as a free master of the guild of painters, and he bought citizenship there in 1410, which suggests he was born elsewhere. Although heavily indebted to contemporary masters of manuscript illumination, Campin displayed greater powers of realistic observation than any other painter before him. He was one of the first artists to experiment with the use of oil-based colors in lieu of egg-based tempera to achieve the brilliant color typical of this period.

OIL AND TEMPERA ON OAK; 17.3 X 11.6 CM (6-3/4 X 4-5/8 IN.)

GIFT OF THE JOHN HUNTINGTON ART AND POLYTECHNIC TRUST 1966.238

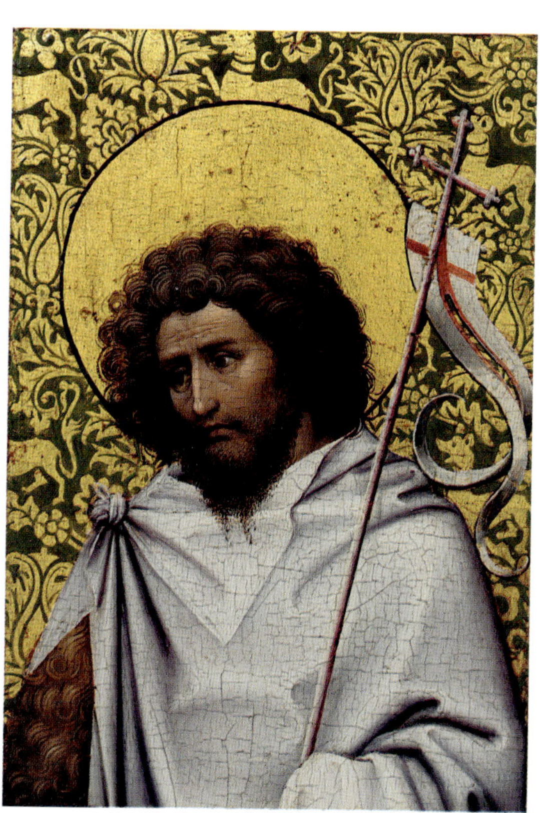

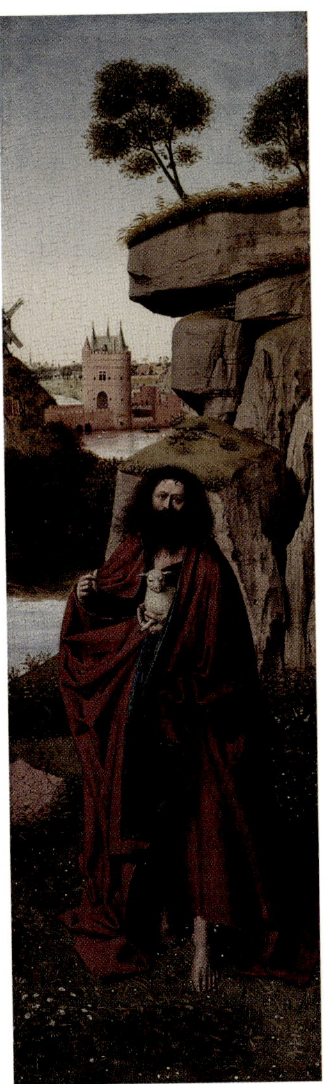

Saint John the Baptist in a Landscape about 1440

ATTRIBUTED TO PETRUS CHRISTUS

(NETHERLANDISH, ABOUT 1410/20–1475/76)

The overall style of this painting suggests that it was painted by an artist closely associated with the Netherlandish painter Jan van Eyck. The saint's facial structure and the treatment of his cloak are typical of Petrus Christus, who was active in the city of Bruges. He was a probable pupil of and successor to Jan van Eyck, with whom his paintings have often been confused. Here, Christus depicts John the Baptist as an isolated, monumental figure without his typical hair shirt or other references to his life. This approach is derived from Claus Sluter's monumental image of Saint John from the portal at the Chartreuse de Champmol and from manuscript illuminators for Philip the Bold and his brother Jean de Berry. Here, John holds the Lamb of God, a symbol of Christ's sacrifice and a reference to John's proclamation of Christ's redemption of humankind.

Hans Memling succeeded Christus as the next great painter in Bruges.

OIL ON WOOD; 39.6 X 11.5 CM (15-5/8 X 4-1/2 IN.)

LEONARD C. HANNA JR. FUND 1979.80

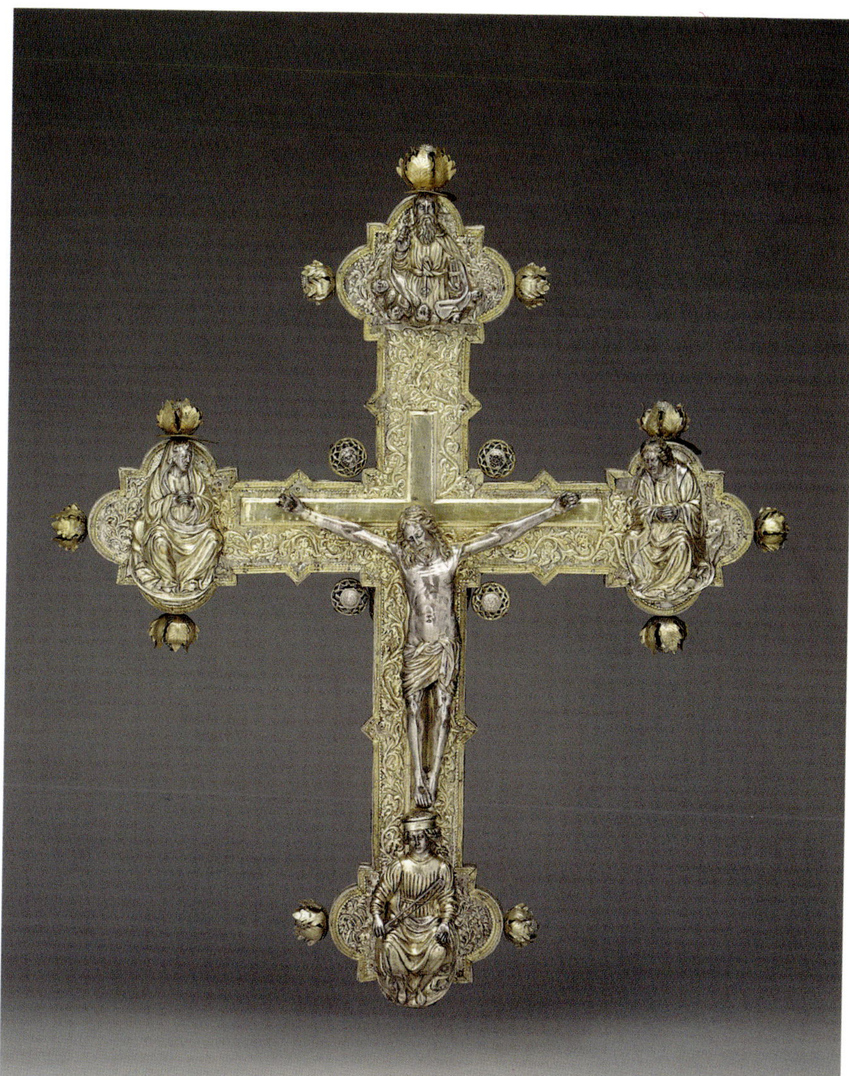

Processional Cross about 1440–50

PIETRO VANNINI (ITALIAN, 1413/14–1495/96)

This extraordinary object, meant to be carried in religious processions within a great church, is an example of the high level of skill achieved by 15th-century Italian silversmiths. The cross was made from hammered, chased, and gilded sheets of silver attached to a wood core. The figures are made in repoussé, a technique of hammering the silver from the back to create a design. On the front of the cross is the figure of Christ with the seated Virgin on one side, Saint John on the other, and God the Father blessing from above. The back of the cross includes the figure of Christ in Majesty at the center, with an evangelist at the end of each arm.

SILVER, GILT-SILVER, AND REPOUSSÉ OVER WOOD; 72.7 X 61 X 12.7 CM (28-5/8 X 24 X 5 IN.)

PURCHASE FROM THE J. H. WADE FUND 1926.243

Saint Anthony Abbot and the Archangel Michael

1458

FILIPPO LIPPI (ITALIAN, ABOUT 1406–1469)

These panels depicting Saint Anthony Abbot and Saint Michael (right) originally flanked a central scene of the adoration of the Christ child, now lost. Saint Michael's sword and shield refer to his role as heaven's defender against evil. Saint Anthony Abbot rejected all earthly possessions in pursuit of a contemplative life in the desert. Generally regarded as the founder of monasticism, he wears a monk's habit. Giovanni di Cosimo de' Medici of Florence commissioned the ensemble as a gift to Alfonso V of Aragon. Fra Filippo Lippi, one of the masters of the early Renaissance in Florence, depicted realistic, weighty figures in a three-dimensional space established using a perspective system of converging diagonals, which was inspired partly by Masaccio's Brancacci Chapel.

TEMPERA ON WOOD; *SAINT ANTHONY ABBOT*, 81.3 X 40 CM (37 X 15-3/4 IN.); *THE ARCHANGEL MICHAEL*, 94 X 40 CM (37 X 15-3/4 IN.)

LEONARD C. HANNA JR. FUND 1964.150.1–2

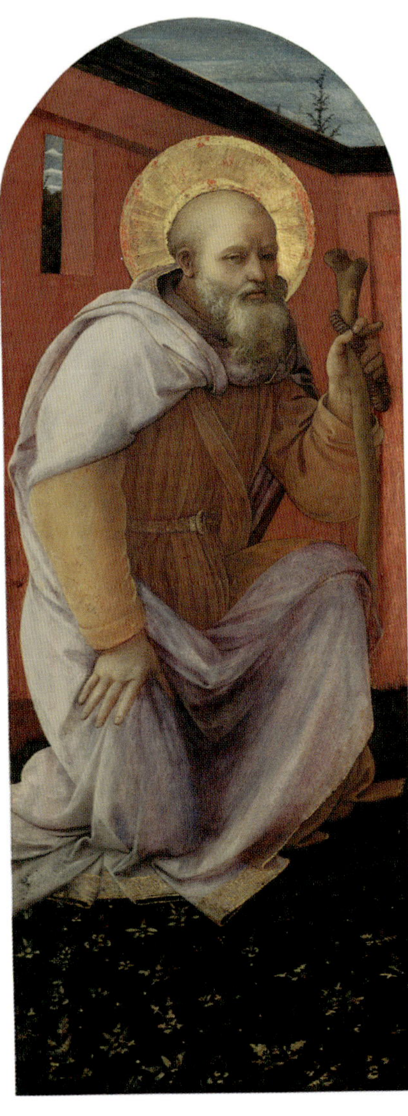

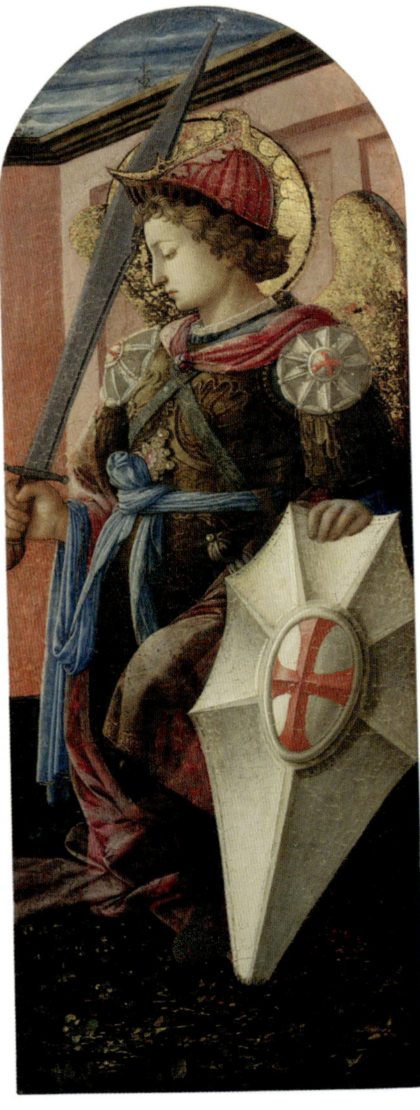

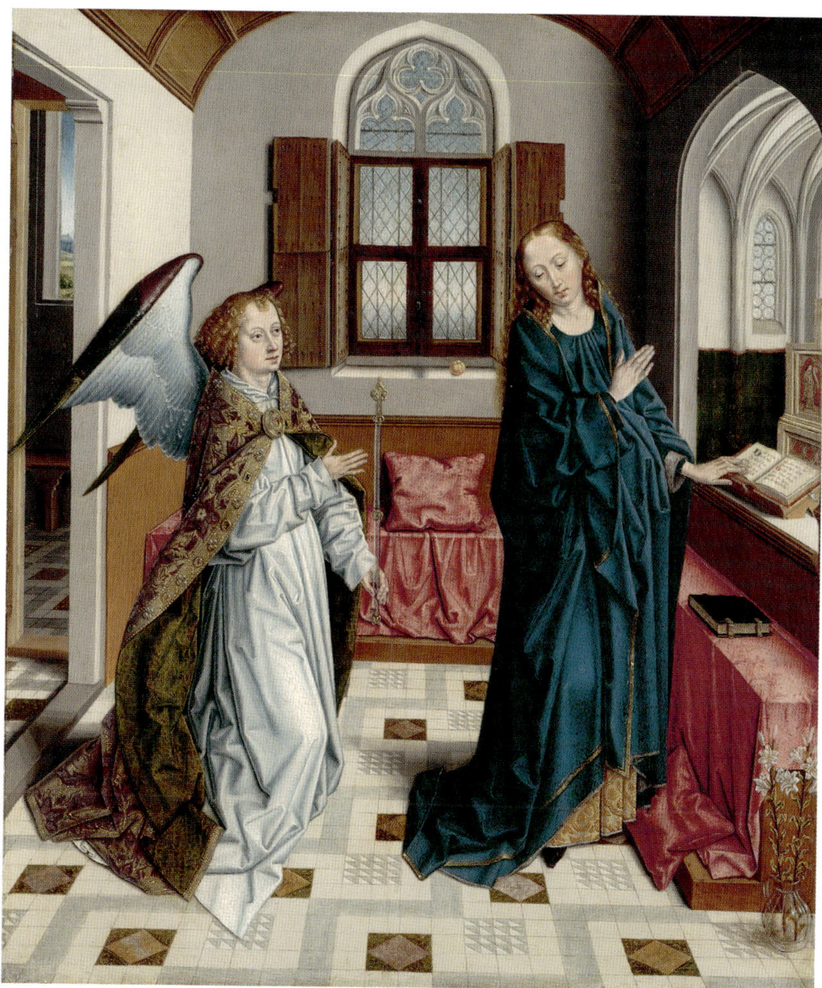

The Annunciation about 1480

ALBRECHT BOUTS (NETHERLANDISH, 1451/55–1549)

The son of the painter Dieric Bouts, Albrecht Bouts was from a family of painters in Leuven. He specialized in small devotional paintings for a ready market in Antwerp and other Flemish cities. This painting depicts an important event in the life of Mary—the Annunciation by the angel Gabriel that she will conceive and bear a son. The Incarnation of Christ is believed to have taken place at precisely this moment. The prevalence of this scene in medieval Christian art reflects its doctrinal importance and its role as a meditative event. The Virgin is represented here in a luxurious private chapel. The vase with lilies on the floor symbolizes her purity. The orange on the window sill is a symbol of chastity and generosity, and the closed book suggests that Old Testament prophecies have now been fulfilled.

OIL ON WOOD; 50.2 X 41.5 CM (19-3/4 X 16-3/8 IN.)

BEQUEST OF JOHN L. SEVERANCE 1942.635

Enthroned Virgin and Child about 1480s

GIL DE SILOÉ (SPANISH, D. ABOUT 1501) OR WORKSHOP

This impressively carved and distinctively conceived Virgin and Child is, on stylistic grounds, probably by Gil de Siloé or a member of his important workshop. A sculptor of northern origin, Siloé was employed by Queen Isabella to undertake several large-scale sculptural projects in Burgos, including the production of important royal tombs at the Carthusian monastery of Miraflores. Regarded as the most important Spanish sculptor of the late 15th century and the leading exponent of the Burgos school of sculpture, Siloé worked in both wood and stone. The scale and the design of this sculpture strongly suggest it was self-contained, not part of a larger architectural context. It was likely intended to be an independent devotional image, probably viewed from slightly below. The material, its quality, and the superiority of the carving also indicate a discerning patron, which Queen Isabella was known to be. While an association between this Virgin and Child and Isabella cannot be proved, this beautifully and distinctively carved sculpture may be a private object made for her or a member of her household.

ALABASTER WITH TRACES OF GILDING AND POLYCHROMY; 31.5 X 22.5 X 16 CM (12-3/8 X 8-7/8 X 6-1/4 IN.)

JOHN L. SEVERANCE FUND 2008.145

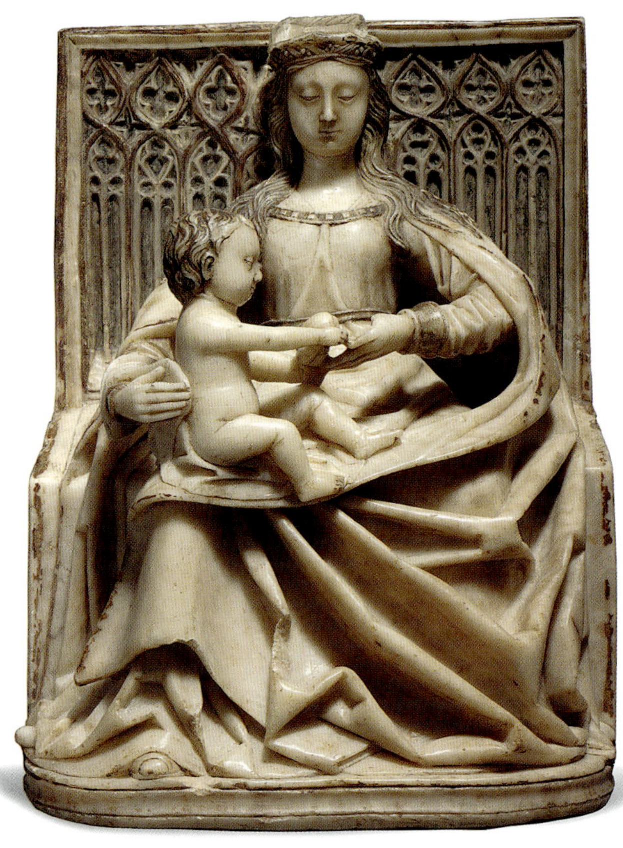

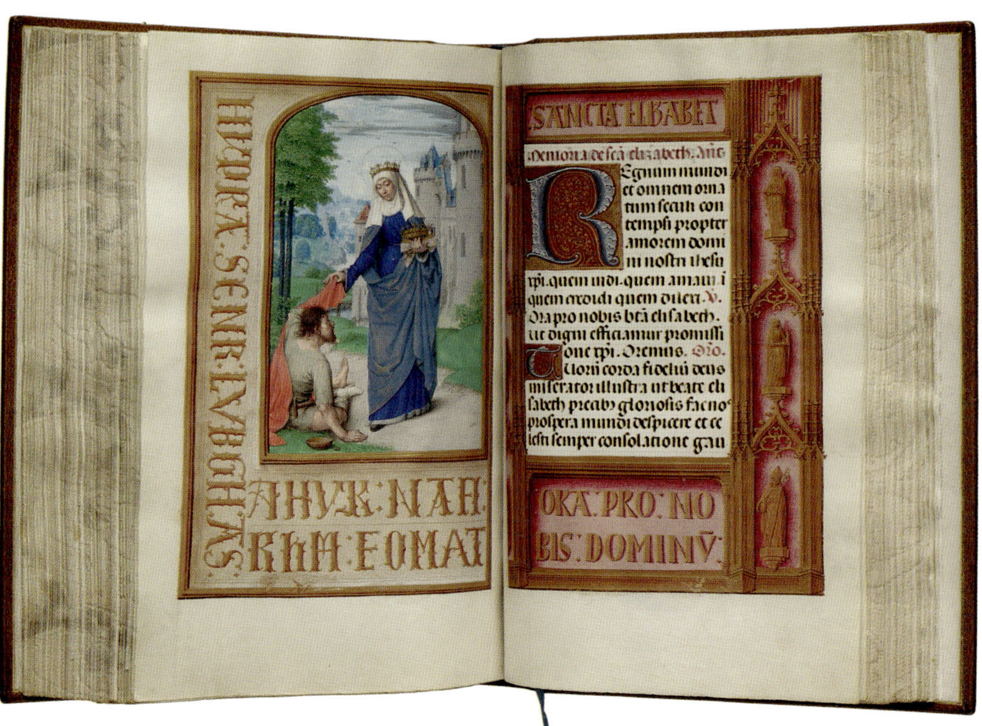

Book of Hours of Isabella the Catholic Queen of Spain (1451–1504), about 1495–1500

ALEXANDER BENING (FLEMISH, ABOUT 1444–1519) AND ASSOCIATES

A great lover of Flemish art, Queen Isabella treasured her many devotional books. This deluxe manuscript, undoubtedly a gift for her private devotions, was probably by highly organized and distinctly talented manuscript painters active in Ghent and Bruges. The Ghent-Bruges school represents the culmination of Flemish book painting, whose main features were the use of rich colors, illusionistic effects, a love of landscape, and a strong sense of visual narrative. Manuscripts produced by this circle of artists are renowned for their border decoration featuring a rich variety of realistically painted flowers, scrolling acanthus leaves, birds, and butterflies.

INK, TEMPERA, AND GOLD ON VELLUM; 23.5 X 17.3 CM (9-1/4 X 6-3/4 IN.) FOLIO

LEONARD C. HANNA JR. FUND 1963.256

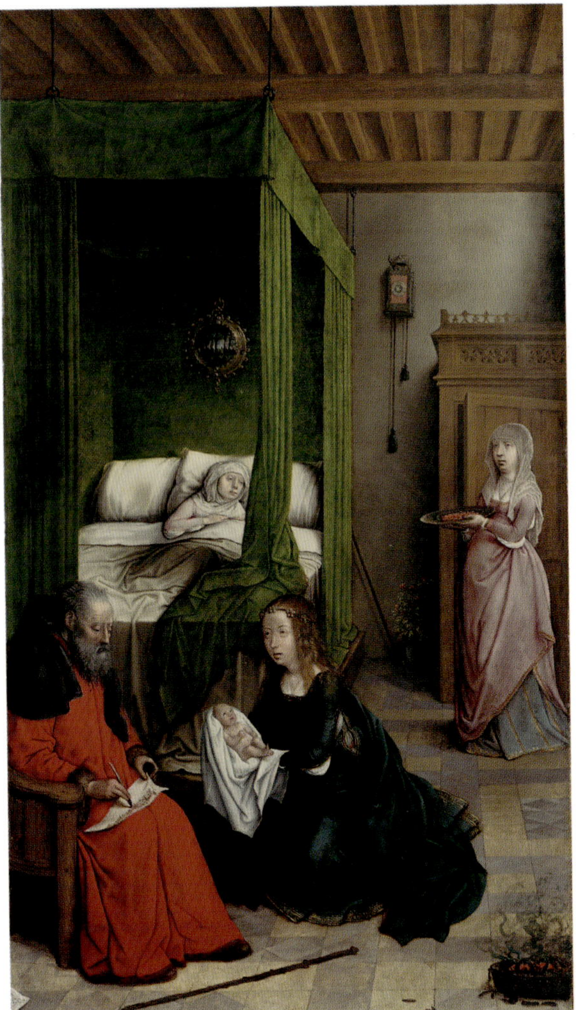

The Birth and Naming of John the Baptist

1496–99

JUAN DE FLANDES (FLEMISH, 1460–1519)

This painting is a panel from the important five-panel altarpiece commissioned by Queen Isabella of Spain for the Carthusian monastery of Miraflores near Burgos, site of the royal tombs of her parents and brother. All five panels were likely painted during the artist's early employment at the royal court.

Typical of Flemish art of the period, with its love of naturalistic detail and almost photographic depiction of a domestic interior, this scene suggests a comfortable burgher's home in 15th-century Ghent or Bruges. The artist transformed a contemporary setting to frame the story of the birth of John the Baptist. Having just given birth, Elizabeth lies in bed. Nearby, her cousin, the Virgin Mary, presents the newborn child to his elderly father, Zacharias. Having lost his ability to speak when he doubted an angel's prophecy of the child's birth, Zacharias writes the chosen name for his son. At that moment his speech was restored.

OIL ON WOOD; 88.4 X 49.9 CM (34-3/4 X 19-5/8 IN.)

JOHN L. SEVERANCE FUND 1975.3

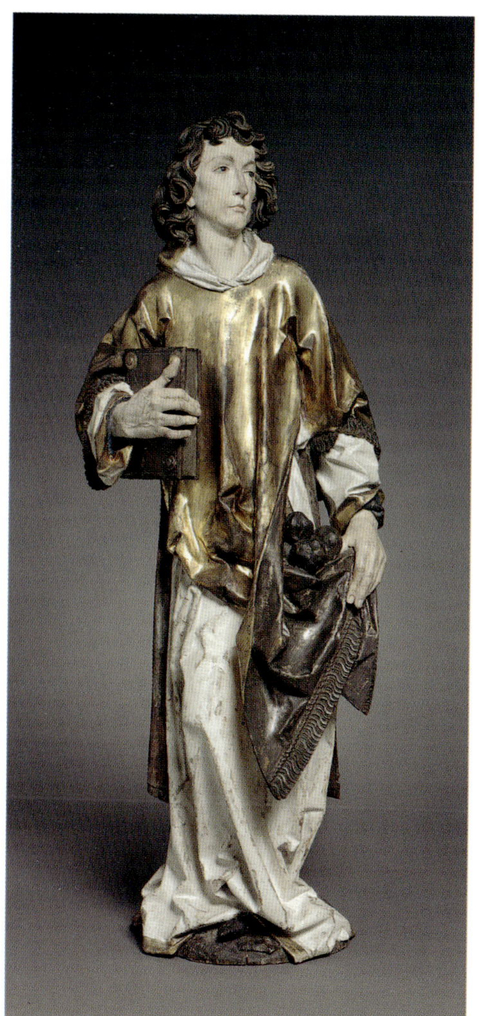

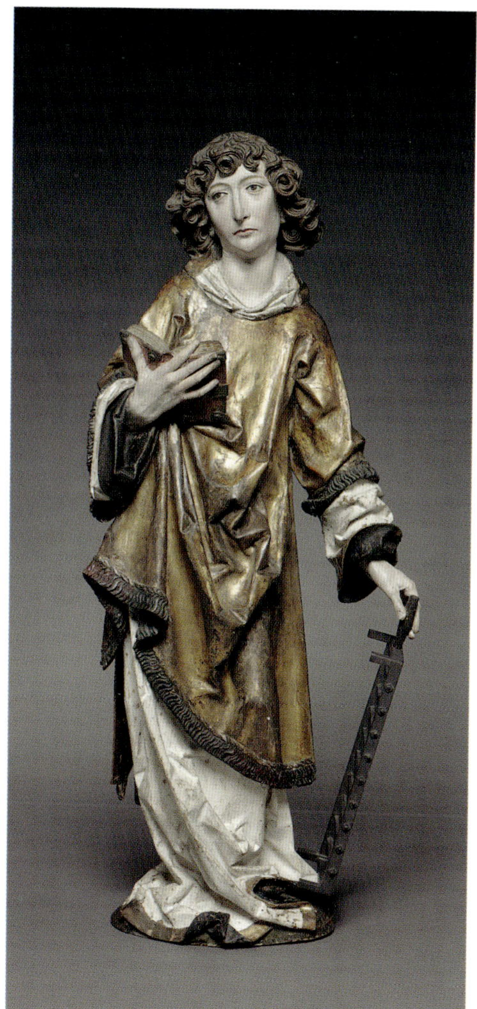

Saint Stephen and Saint Lawrence about 1502–10

TILMAN RIEMENSCHNEIDER (GERMAN, ABOUT 1460–1531)

These sculptures, along with two female saints preserved in the Historisches Museum in Frankfurt, are believed to be the remaining fragments of a large altarpiece carved by Riemenschneider for the Dominican convent in Rothenburg in Franconia (demolished in 1813). Each saint wears a dalmatic to indicate his status as a deacon in the early church, and each holds the instrument of his martyrdom: Saint Lawrence a grill and Saint Stephen stones. Art in Germany through the early 1500s remained firmly anchored in the Gothic style with its associated interests in realism. Riemenschneider was one of the most prolific and versatile sculptors of this style. He was a recognized master in both stone and wood. His flourishing workshop employed as many as 40 apprentices in sculpting, woodcarving, and painting. He became a wealthy landowner in Würzburg, eventually rising to councilman and mayor. His sculptures are noted for the dreamy, melancholy, introspective quality in their expressions, as well as a remarkable attention to detail.

POLYCHROMED AND GILDED LINDENWOOD; 93.5 X 35 X 23.5 CM (36-3/4 X 13-3/4 X 9-1/4 IN.) AND 93.8 X 38.5 X 21.8 CM (36-7/8 X 15-1/8 X 8-5/8 IN.)

LEONARD C. HANNA JR. FUND 1959.42–43

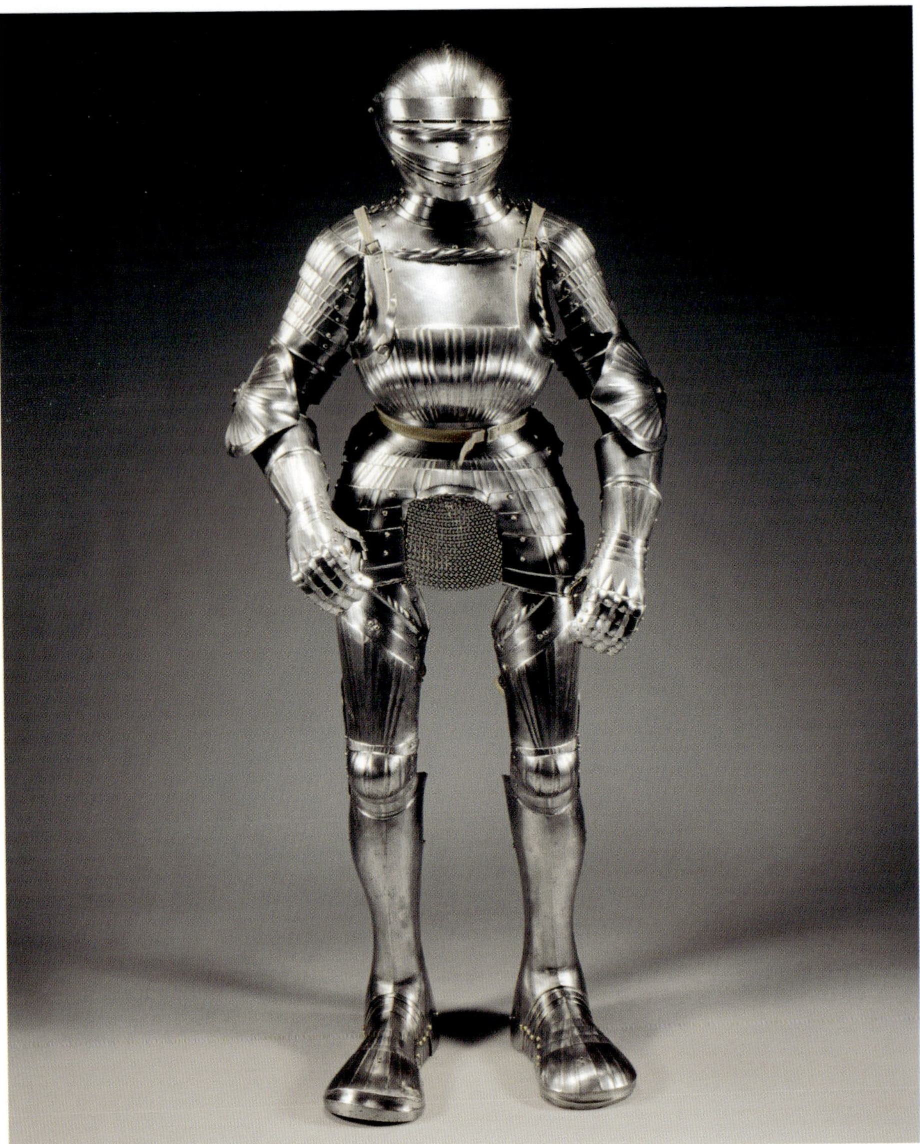

Field Armor in Maximilian Style about 1510–15
GERMANY, AUGSBURG(?)
Most of the elements of this armor were made together, forming a single suit. The lower legs contain some modern restorations. The helmet is believed to be the work of the esteemed Augsburg armorer Lorenz Helmschmied, who was active at the Hapsburg, Mantua, and Urbino courts between 1467 and his death in 1515. Intended for field (battle) use, the armor is complete, with helmet, cuirass, gorget, pauldrons, upper and lower arm canons, fauld, upper and lower leg elements, and sabatons. It is of a style known as "Maximilian" distinguished by its regularly fluted surfaces and so-named since it coincided with the reign of Emperor Maximilian I (d. 1519), whose workshops produced armor in this style. The style was fashionable in South Germany and Austria during the early decades of the century. Production centers included Nuremberg, Augsburg, and Innsbruck. The flutings of the armor may have originated as a

means of imitating the pleats of male apparel of the time. It quickly became apparent that the flutes also served as a strengthening device similar to corrugated metal, which enabled the armorer to use thinner and therefore lighter plates of steel. Such suits of armor demanded time-consuming and highly precise work from their makers, which in turn quickly drove the production costs so high that the fashion disappeared by 1540. Armor of this style is prized today for its sculptural linearity.

STEEL AND LEATHER, BRASS RIVETS; H. 170.2 CM (67 IN.) OVERALL

PURCHASE FROM THE J. H. WADE FUND 2012.38

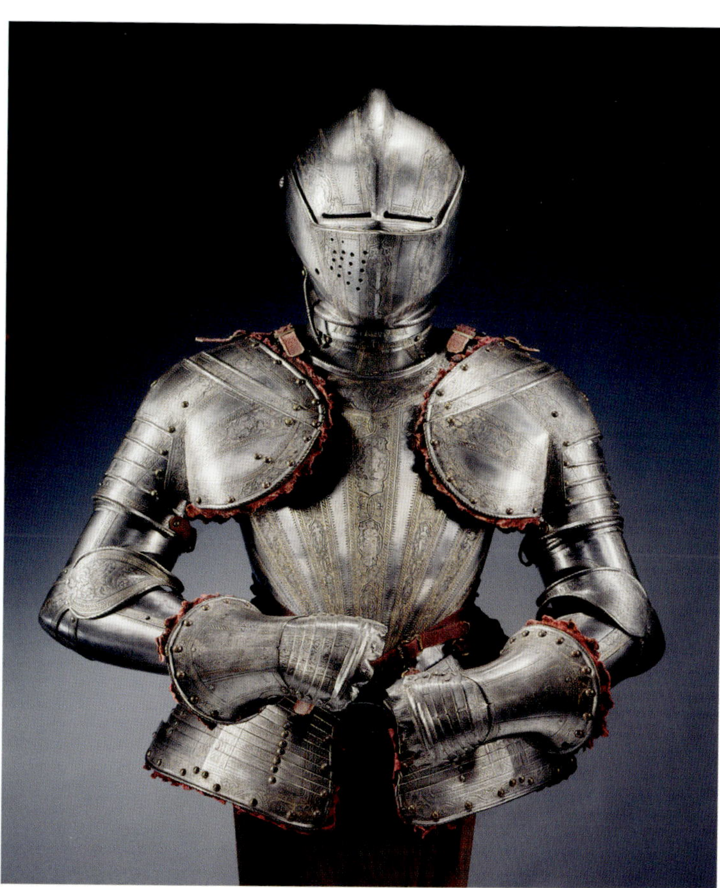

Half-Armor for the Foot Tournament about 1590

POMPEO DELLA CESA (ITALIAN)

This armor was designed for the foot tournament, an event that was separate from the equestrian jousts popular during the Middle Ages and still favored by aristocrats throughout Europe during the Renaissance. Foot tournaments were commonly fought over a barrier that separated the combatants and gave protection to their legs, so a half-armor such as this one would have offered sufficient protection. The original owner of this suit would have worn it with colorful puffed and slashed britches and hose. The use of outlandish accessories, such as a large ostrich feather plume (a brass plume holder may be seen on the back of the helmet) and red velvet pickadils between the steel plates, provided additional splendor.

STEEL, ETCHED AND GILDED; 31.7 X 27.7 X 21.6 CM (12-1/2 X 10-7/8 X 8-1/2 IN.) OVERALL

JOHN L. SEVERANCE FUND 1996.299

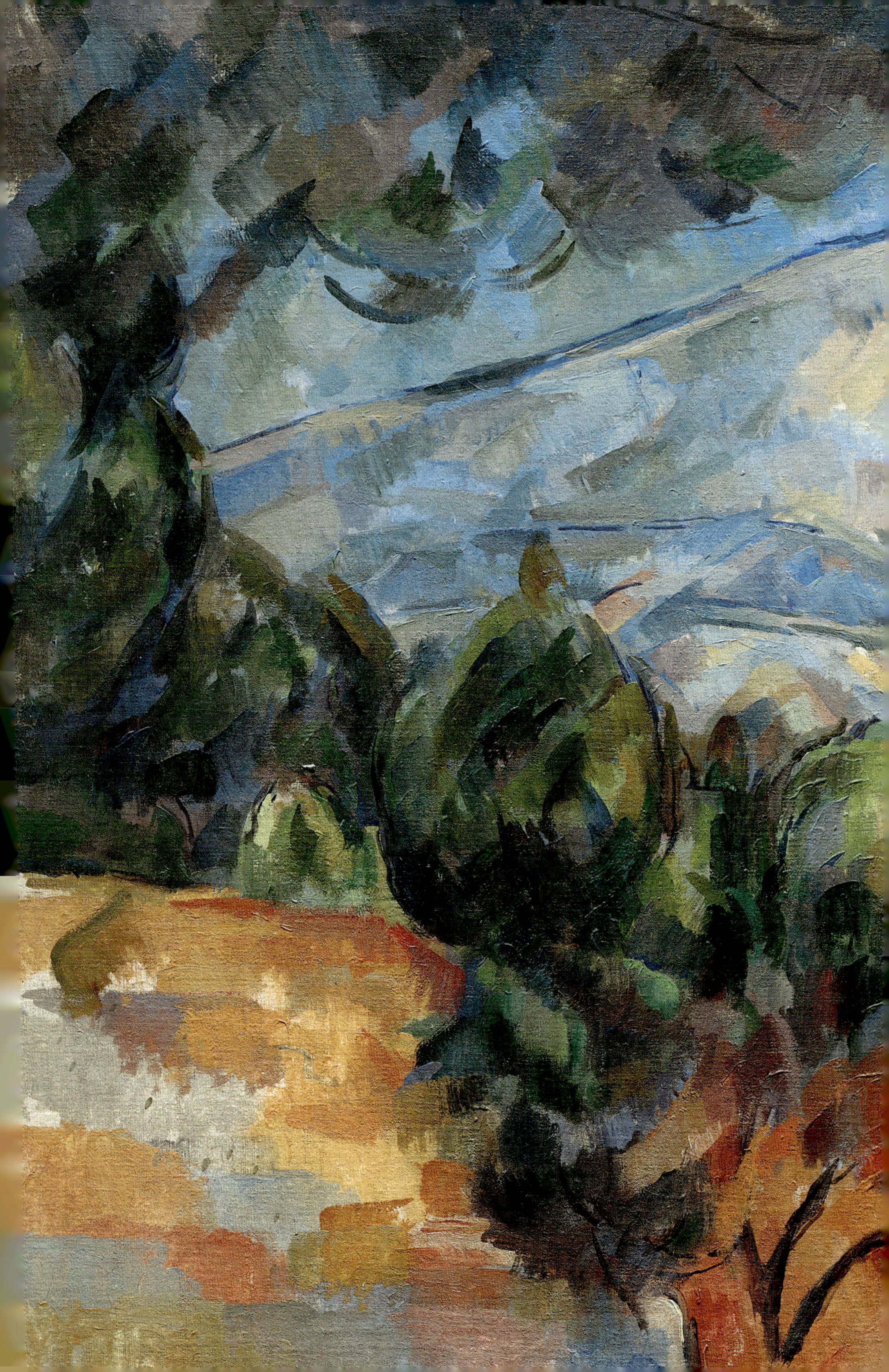

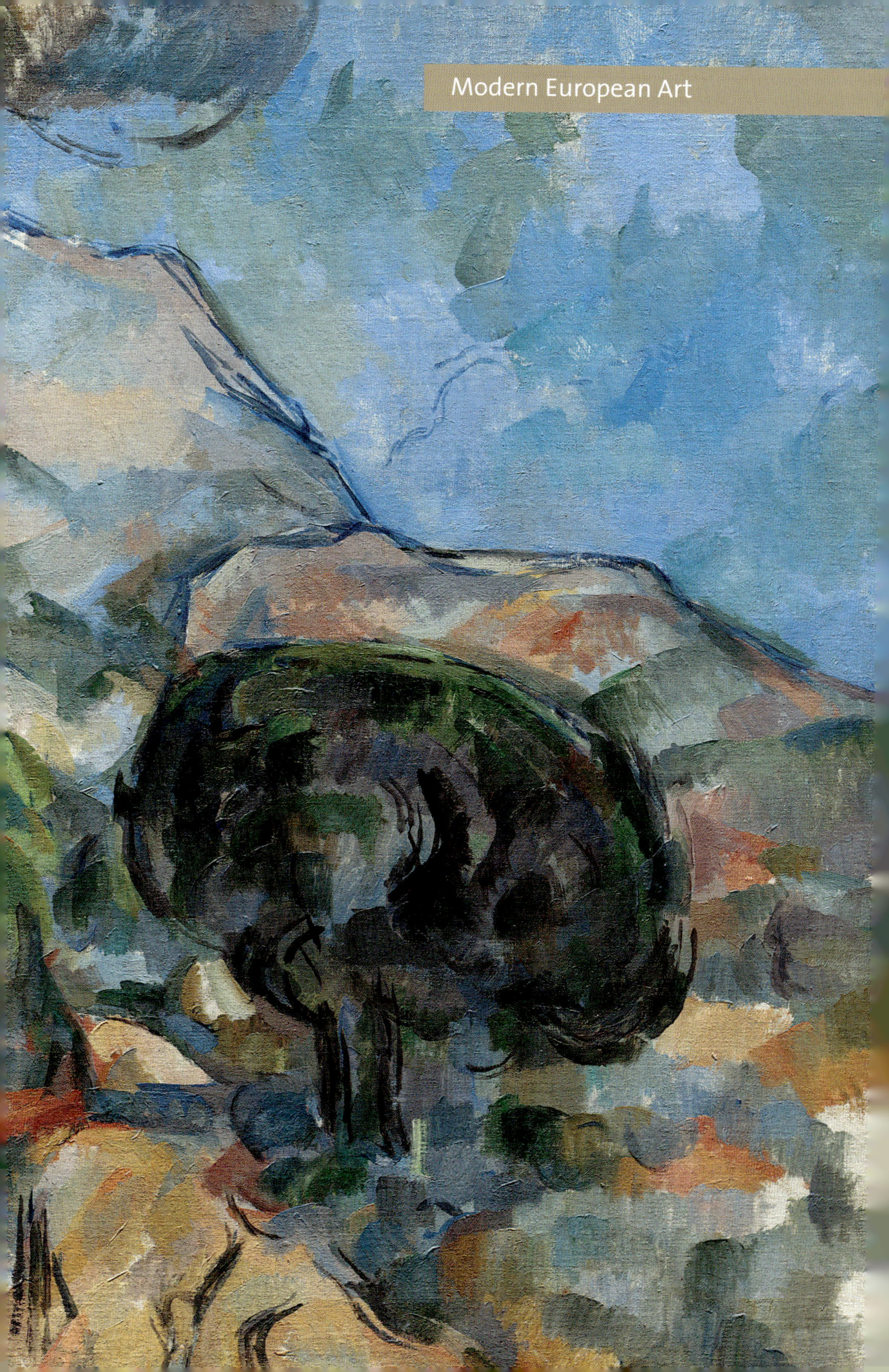
Modern European Art

Terpsichore Lyran (Muse of Lyric Poetry) 1816

ANTONIO CANOVA (ITALIAN, 1757–1822)

In Greek mythology, Terpsichore was one of the nine Muses, or goddesses of creative inspiration. The lyre, the Greek inscription below on the short column, and the caduceus (entwined snakes) on the side identify the figure as Terpsichore Lyran, muse of lyric poetry. The Muses are also the subject of a series of large paintings by Charles Meynier on view in gallery 201. The idea for the sculpture originated with a commission from Napoleon's brother, Lucien, for an idealized portrait of his wife, Alexandrine. Canova made this version for a British aristocrat and exhibited it in 1817 at the Royal Academy in London to great acclaim.

MARBLE; 177.5 X 78.1 X 61 CM (69-7/8 X 30-3/4 X 24 IN.)

LEONARD C. HANNA JR. FUND 1968.212

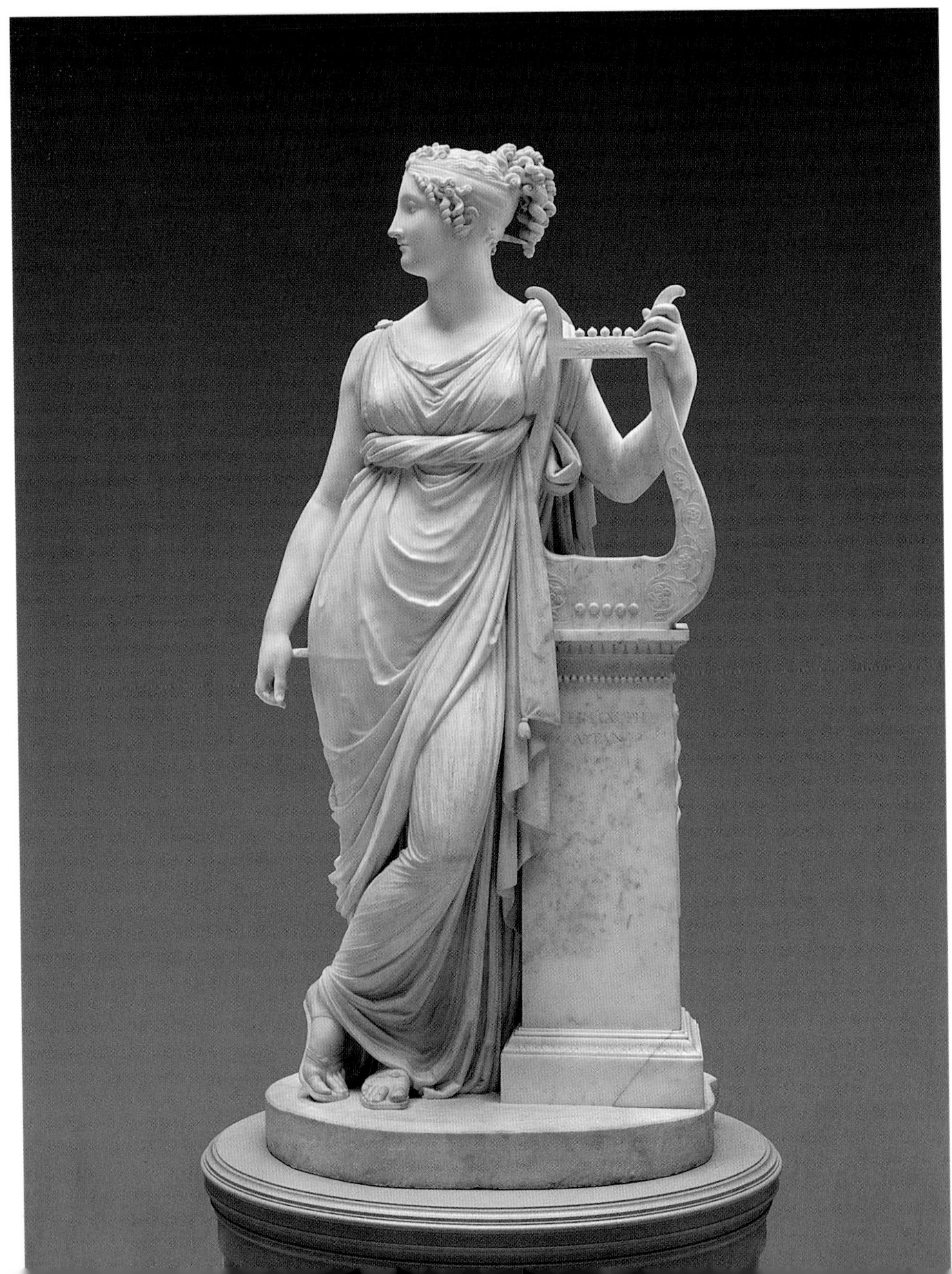

Cupid and Psyche 1817

JACQUES-LOUIS DAVID (FRENCH, 1748–1825)

David used the story of Cupid and Psyche to explore the conflict between idealized love and physical reality. Cupid, lover of the beautiful mortal Psyche, visited her nightly on the condition that she not know his identity. Cupid was usually depicted as an ideal adolescent, but here David presents him as an ungainly teenager smirking at his sexual conquest. David took inspiration from a number of ancient texts, including an obscure, recently published Greek poem by Moschus that describes Cupid as a mean-spirited brat with dark skin, flashing eyes, and curly hair.

OIL ON CANVAS; 184.2 X 241.6 CM (72-1/2 X 95 IN.)

LEONARD C. HANNA JR. FUND 1962.37

La Cervara, the Roman Campagna about 1830–31

CAMILLE COROT (FRENCH, 1796–1875)

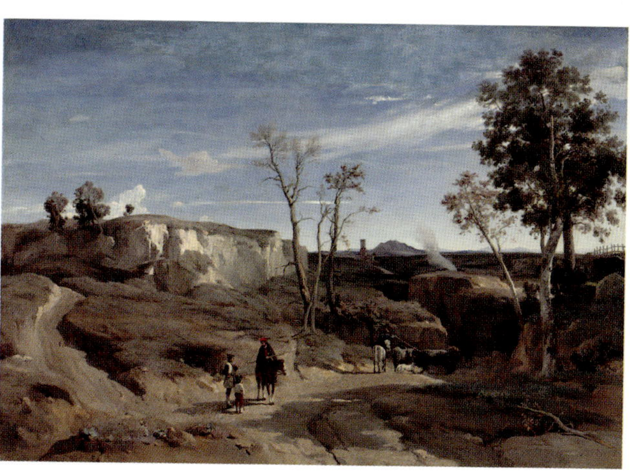

Corot recorded form and tonal qualities in outdoor drawings and oil sketches, then executed his paintings in the studio. Attracted to the beauty of the Italian countryside, he often sketched around Rome, where he lived from 1825 to 1828. This painting's highly structured composition, based on forms moving into the distance along a series of diagonals, is characteristic of Corot's early style and recalls the classical landscapes of the 17th-century painter Nicholas Poussin.

OIL ON CANVAS; 97.6 X 135.8 CM (38-3/8 X 53-1/2 IN.)

LEONARD C. HANNA JR. FUND 1963.91

The Burning of the Houses of Lords and Commons, 16 October, 1834 1835

JOSEPH MALLORD WILLIAM TURNER (BRITISH, 1775–1851)

On the night of October 16, 1834, fire consumed the Houses of Parliament in London. Londoners gathered along the banks of the river Thames to gaze in awe at the horrifying spectacle. A low tide made it difficult to pump water to fire-fighting equipment on land, just as it hampered steamers towing fire-fighting equipment up the river. Although the tide eventually shifted, the effort was futile, and the fire burned uncontrollably for hours.

Although Turner based the painting on an actual event, he used the disaster as the starting point to express man's helplessness when confronted with the destructive powers of nature, here dissolved in brilliant swaths of color and variable atmospheric effects that border on abstraction.

OIL ON CANVAS; 92.7 X 123.2 CM (36-1/4 X 48-1/2 IN.)

BEQUEST OF JOHN L. SEVERANCE 1942.647

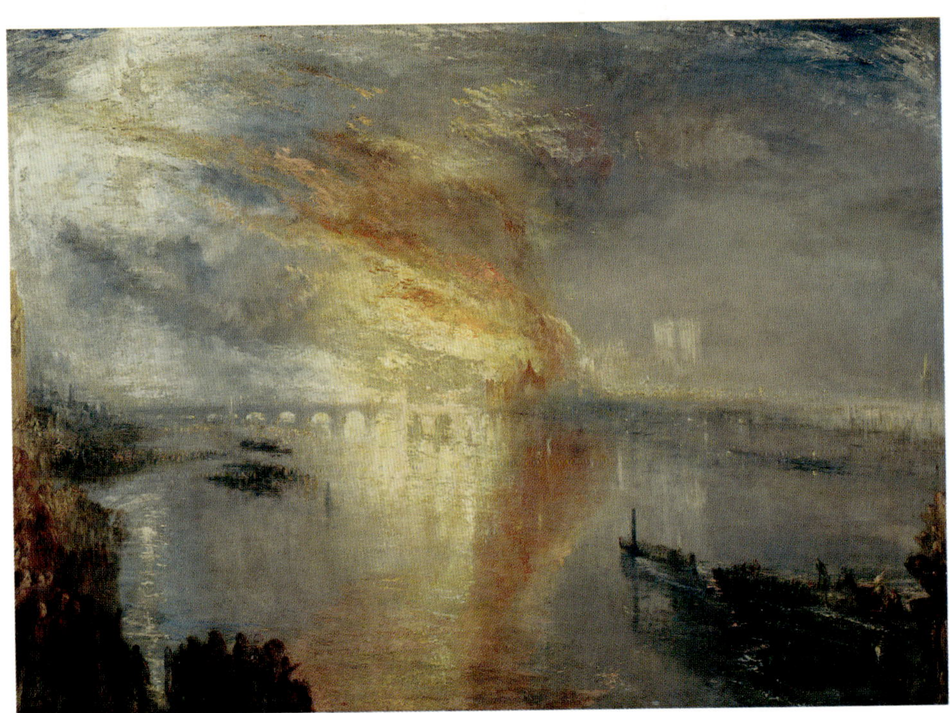

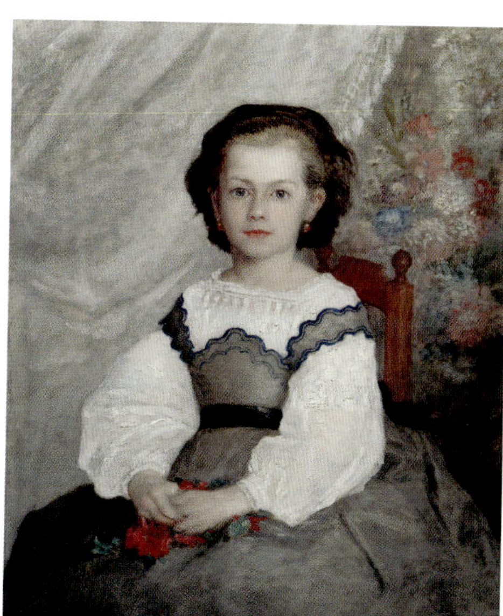

Romaine Lacaux 1864

PIERRE-AUGUSTE RENOIR (FRENCH, 1841–1919)

Commissioned by the Lacaux family, Renoir probably painted this portrait while living at an artist's colony in the village of Barbizon. Possibly his earliest signed canvas, this painting is among the first in which he explored a new, more luminous palette after abandoning the dark tones of his academic studies. The delicate treatment of the girl's face and hair reflects Renoir's early training as a porcelain painter in Limoges.

OIL ON CANVAS; 81.3 X 65 CM (32 X 25-5/8 IN.)

GIFT OF THE HANNA FUND 1942.1065

The Red Kerchief about 1868–73

CLAUDE MONET (FRENCH, 1840–1926)

This painting initially depicted two figures seated inside the room, each flanking the French doors. Monet eventually replaced them with the woman wearing a red kerchief. Walking by quickly in the snowy landscape, she throws a momentary glance at the viewer, her facial features suggested only by summary dabs of paint. Monet's daring technique and attempt to capture a fleeting moment represents a radical departure from accepted painting conventions of the time.

OIL ON CANVAS; 99 X 79.8 CM (39 X 31-3/8 IN.)

BEQUEST OF LEONARD C. HANNA JR. 1958.39

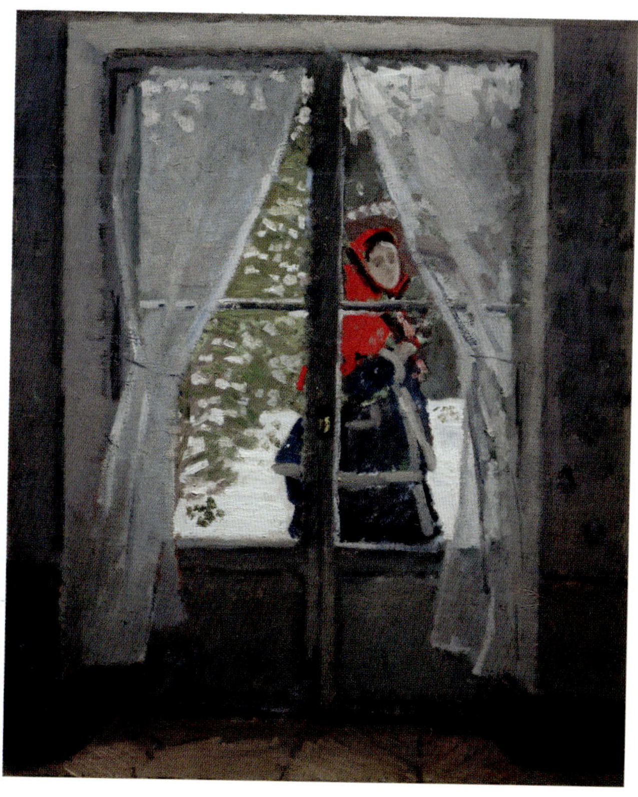

The Age of Bronze 1875–76, cast 1916–17
AUGUSTE RODIN (FRENCH, 1840–1917)
Rodin produced the original version of this crucial, breakthrough sculpture while living in Brussels (1871–77). Hoping to establish his reputation, he sent the sculpture to an exhibition in Paris, where it provoked a tremendous scandal based on accusations that its stunning realism was achieved by direct casting from a live model. The controversy was only resolved when Rodin's model was brought to Paris and casts of his body were compared with the sculpture. This version was cast during the artist's lifetime and donated to the museum in 1918. Its expressive surfaces are enlivened by a rich, warm, translucent patina that Rodin specifically selected for this cast and referred to as "crushed grape."
BRONZE; 182.2 X 66.4 X 47 CM (71-3/4 X 26-1/8 X 18-1/2 IN.)
GIFT OF MR. AND MRS. RALPH KING 1918.328

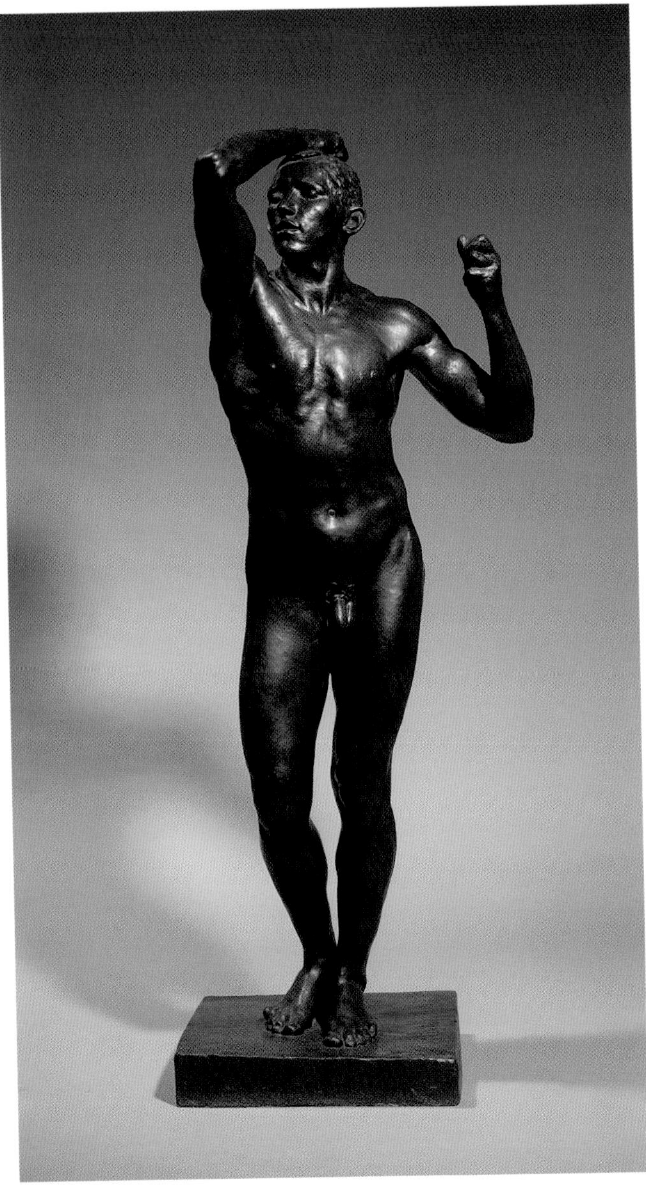

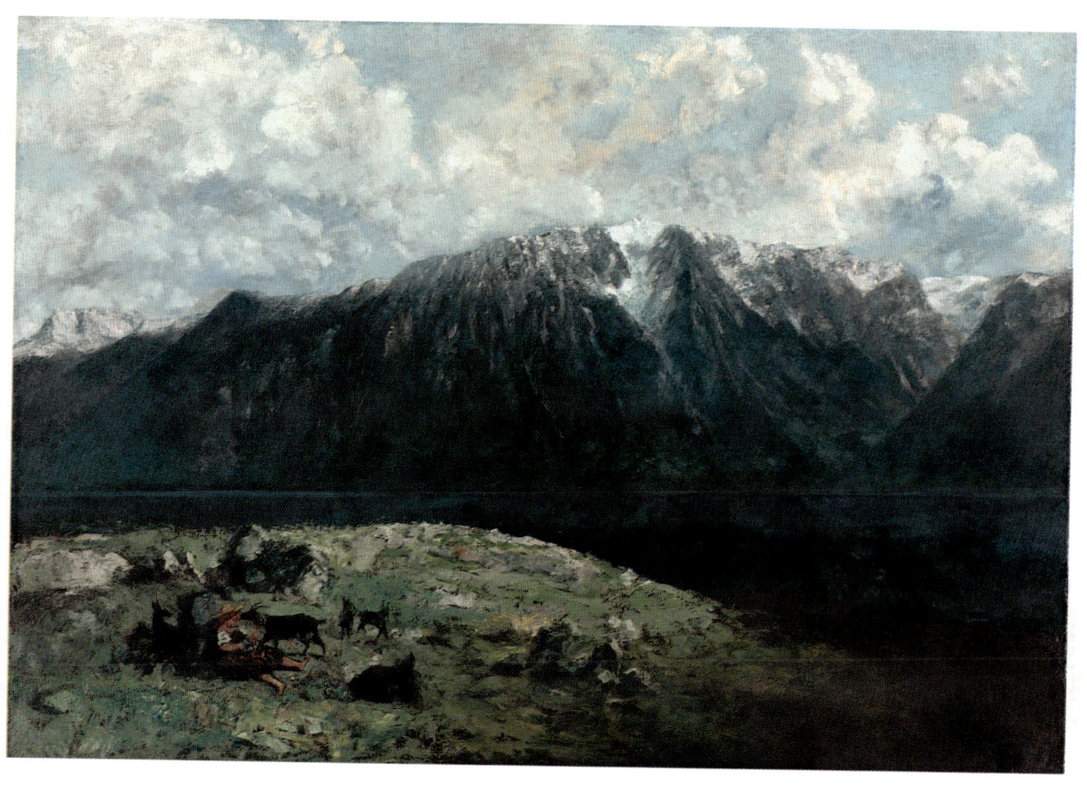

Panoramic View of the Alps 1877

GUSTAVE COURBET (FRENCH, 1819–1877)

Courbet was still working on this large landscape, intended for the Paris Universal Exposition of 1879, when he died in December 1877. He painted it during his exile in Switzerland, where he sought refuge after being condemned for subversive activities in the Paris Commune of 1871. While some areas are heavily worked with a palette knife, the lower right remains unfinished.

OIL ON CANVAS; 151.2 X 210.2 CM (59-1/2 X 82-3/4 IN.)

JOHN L. SEVERANCE FUND AND VARIOUS DONORS BY EXCHANGE 1964.420

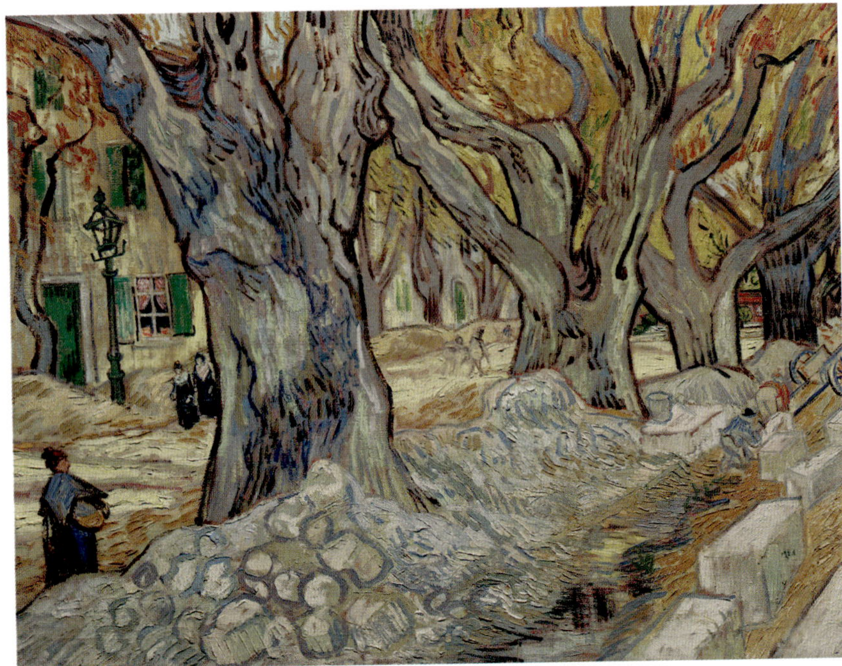

The Large Plane Trees (Road Menders at Saint-Rémy) 1889

VINCENT VAN GOGH (DUTCH, 1853–1890)

In 1889, after suffering a severe hallucinatory seizure, Van Gogh committed himself to an asylum near Saint-Rémy. While walking through the town that fall, he was impressed by the sight of men repairing a road beneath immense plane trees. Rushing to capture the yellowing leaves, he painted this composition on an unusual cloth with a pattern of small red diamonds, visible in the picture's many unpainted areas. "In spite of the cold," he wrote to his brother, "I have gone on working outside till now, and I think it is doing me good and the work too." After painting this composition directly from nature, Van Gogh used it to produce a second, more restrained, version in the studio that is now in the Phillips Collection in Washington, DC.

OIL ON CANVAS; 73.4 X 91.8 CM (28-7/8 X 36-1/8 IN.)

GIFT OF THE HANNA FUND 1947.209

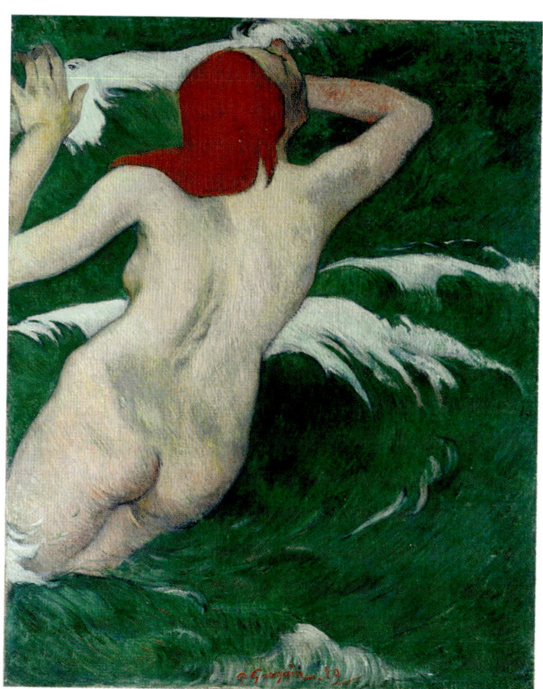

In the Waves 1889

PAUL GAUGUIN (FRENCH, 1848–1903)

Painted at Pont-Aven in northwest France, this depiction of a nude figure throwing herself into the sea suggests a metaphor for a woman forsaking civilization and abandoning herself to her natural, primitive instincts. The simplified lines and exaggerated colors, especially the contrasting green and orange, seem invented rather than observed from life. Gauguin exhibited the painting at the Café Volpini in Paris in 1889, a seminal event in his emergence as a leader of the Symbolist movement.

OIL ON CANVAS; 92.5 X 72.4 CM (36-3/8 X 28-1/2 IN.)

GIFT OF MR. AND MRS. WILLIAM POWELL JONES 1978.63

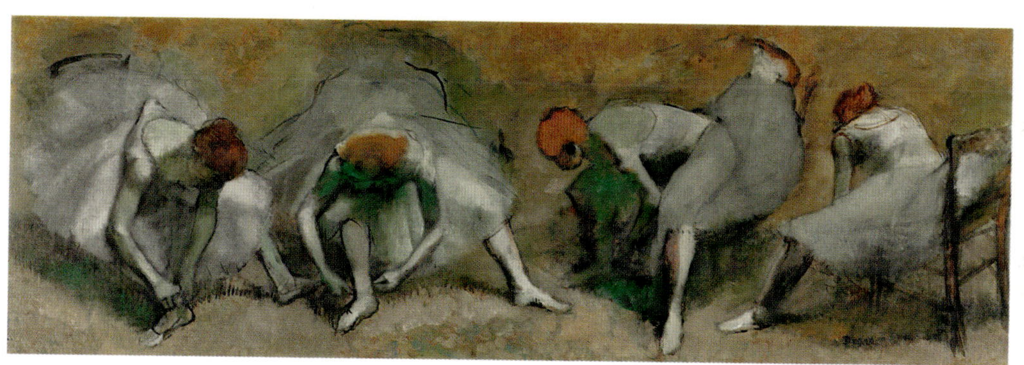

Frieze of Dancers about 1895

EDGAR DEGAS (FRENCH, 1834–1917)

This painting may have been inspired by a single dancer seen from different viewpoints, comparable to the stop-motion photographs of Eadweard Muybridge. Presented in an unusually wide format, and originally in a white frame designed by Degas himself, the figures are surrounded by washes of color applied so spontaneously that the paint ran and dripped. Degas even applied paint with his thumb, seen in the small oval shapes in the foreground.

OIL ON CANVAS; 70 X 200.5 CM (27-1/2 X 78-7/8 IN.)

GIFT OF THE HANNA FUND 1946.83

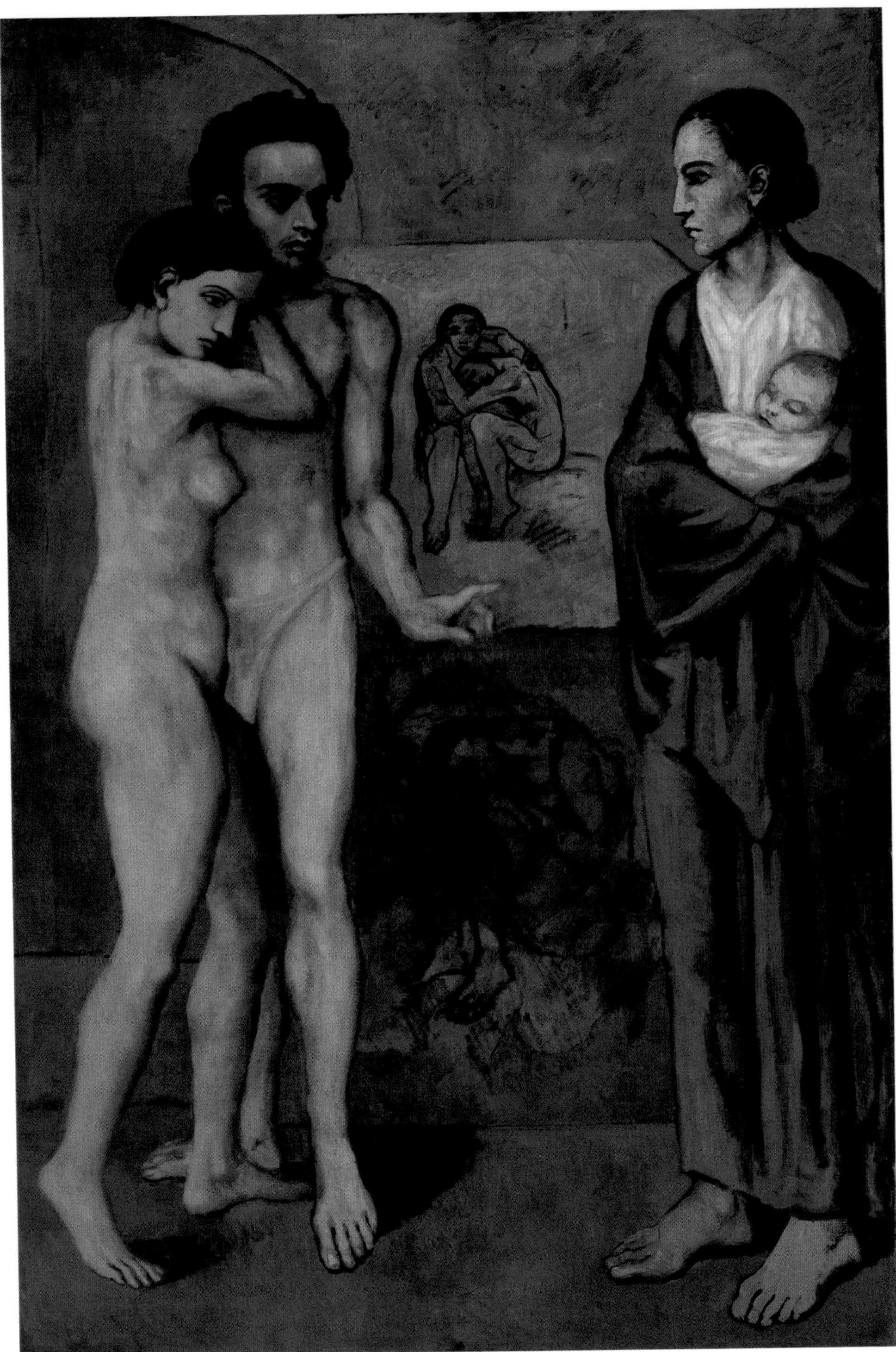

La Vie (Life) 1903

PABLO PICASSO (SPANISH, 1881–1973)

In 1901, depressed over the suicide of a close friend, Picasso launched into the melancholic paintings of his Blue Period. Only 20 years old and desperately poor, he restricted his palette to cold colors suggestive of night, mystery, dreams, and death. His obsession with themes of human misery and social alienation reached its climax with *La Vie,* a complex and enigmatic painting, the artist's culminating masterpiece of the Blue Period (1901–4). The subject has been variously interpreted as an allegory of sacred and profane love, a symbolic representation of the cycle of life, and a working-class couple facing the hazards of real life.

OIL ON CANVAS; 196.5 X 129.2 CM (77-3/4 X 50-7/8 IN.)

GIFT OF THE HANNA FUND 1945.24

Mont Sainte-Victoire about 1904

PAUL CÉZANNE (FRENCH, 1839–1906)

During the last 20 years of his life, Cézanne repeatedly painted the towering mountain of Sainte-Victoire near his home in Aix-en-Provence. Aiming to reform Impressionism by bringing order and structure to the study of nature, he created tightly integrated compositions of merging, intersecting planes. Here, a rising tree branch echoes the distant mountain slope, thereby relating foreground to background. Sensations of space are created through rhythmic patterns of warm and cool color.

OIL ON CANVAS; 72.2 X 92.4 CM (28-3/8 X 36-3/8 IN.)

BEQUEST OF LEONARD C. HANNA JR. 1958.21

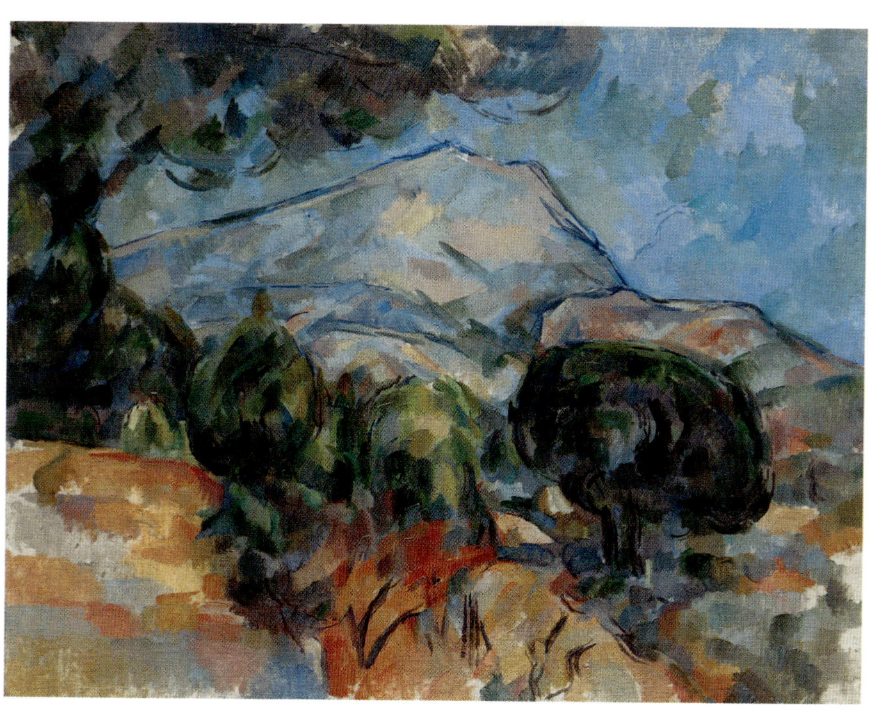

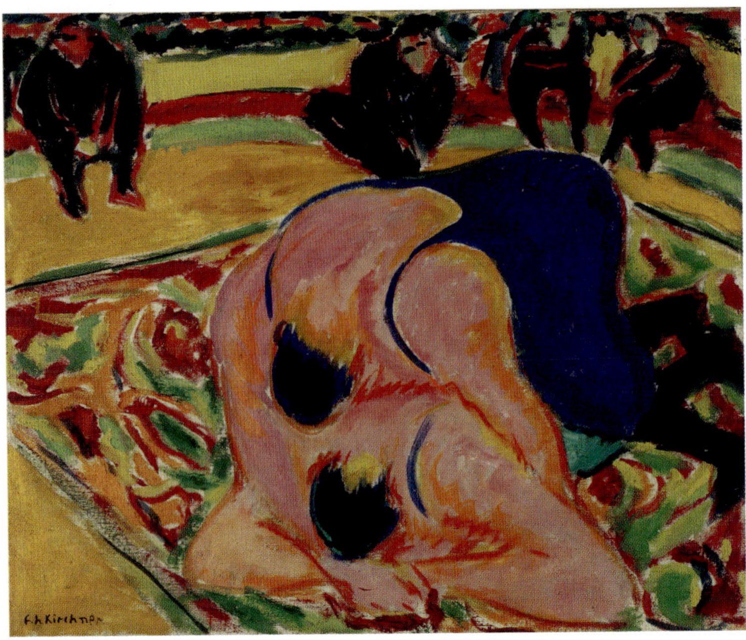

Wrestlers in a Circus 1909

ERNST LUDWIG KIRCHNER (GERMAN, 1880–1938)

A leading painter of Die Brücke (The Bridge), a German Expressionist group formed in Dresden in 1905, Kirchner pursued an art of pure, raw emotion, while advocating a revolutionary approach based on complete freedom from social and aesthetic norms. Focusing on the psychology of modern life, he began painting street scenes, cabarets, and circus performers. He enhanced this painting's deliberately crude appearance by painting on coarse canvas and leaving the surface unvarnished. Despite serving in the German army during World War I, Kirchner became a principal target of the Nazis' systematic assault against so-called "degenerate art." During the 1930s, 639 works by Kirchner were removed from German museums and either destroyed or sold to foreign collectors and museums. The year after the Nazis organized the Degenerate Art exhibition in Munich, Kirchner committed suicide.

OIL ON CANVAS; 80.5 X 94 CM (31-3/4 X 37 IN.)
CONTEMPORARY COLLECTION OF THE CLEVELAND MUSEUM OF ART AND BEQUEST OF WILLIAM R. VALENTINER 1966.49

Detachable Figure (Dancer) 1915

JACQUES LIPCHITZ (LITHUANIAN-FRENCH, 1891–1973)

Lipchitz began making Cubist sculptures in 1915, the year he produced this rare assemblage of oak and ebony blocks. The interlocking blocks suggest abstract patterns of light and shadow, while multiple views of a single figure appear at the top. One face is delicately carved into a block near the raised arm, while two ebony blocks on the adjacent side suggest an abstract face with the elongated features of an African mask.

EBONY AND OAK; 97 X 21.5 X 21.4 CM (38-1/4 X 8-1/2 X 8-1/2 IN.)
GIFT OF MRS. AYE SIMON 1972.367

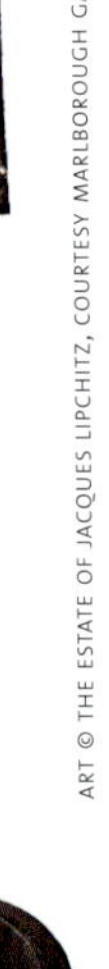

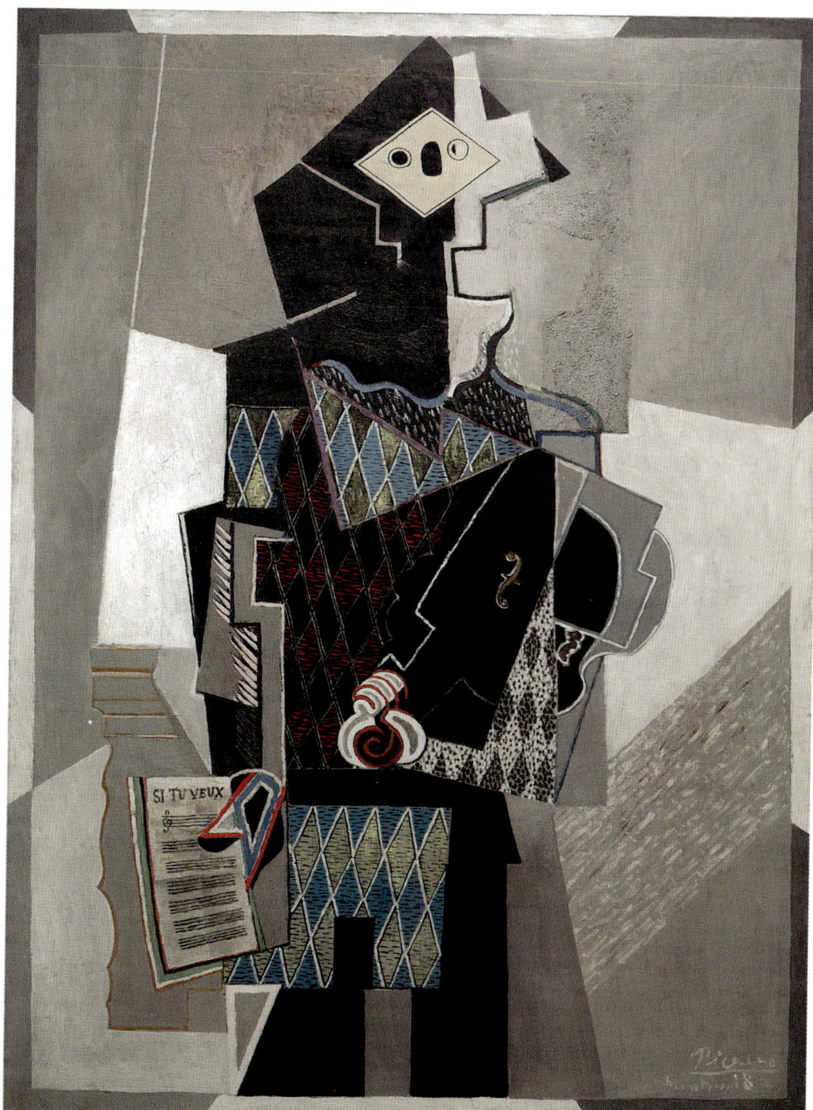

Harlequin with Violin: Si tu veux 1918

PABLO PICASSO (SPANISH, 1881–1973)

The diamond-patterned costume and triangular hat identify the musician in this painting as one of Picasso's alter egos, Harlequin, a jokester from the popular Commedia dell' arte. The white-brimmed portion of the hat indicates that Picasso combined Harlequin with Pierrot, another figure from the Commedia. The phrase "Si tu veux" on the sheet of music may refer to a popular song that begins, "If you wish, Marguerite, make me happy by giving me your heart." This lyric may refer to Picasso's marriage to Russian ballerina Olga Koklova in 1918.

OIL ON CANVAS; 142.2 X 100.3 CM (56 X 39-1/2 IN.)

LEONARD C. HANNA JR. FUND 1975.2

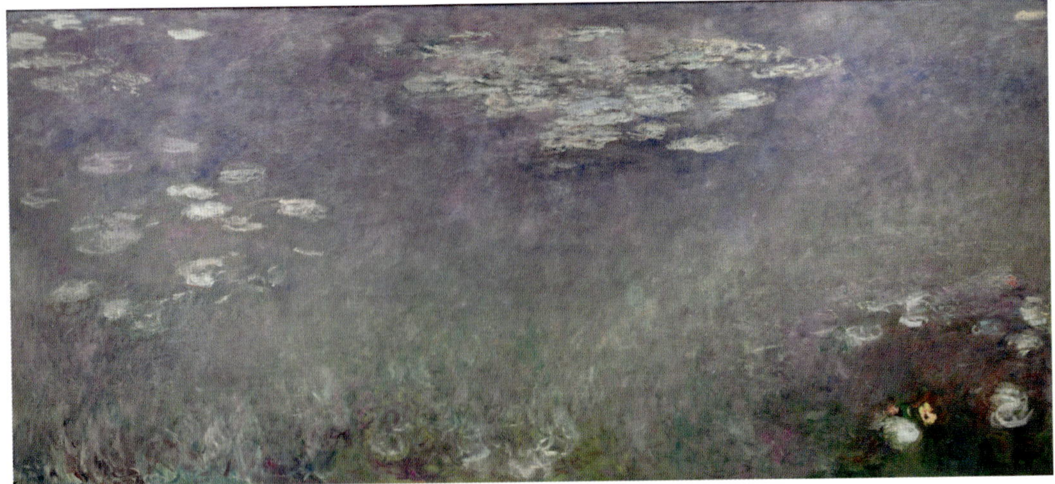

Water Lilies (Agapanthus) about 1919–26

CLAUDE MONET (FRENCH, 1840–1926)

Monet spent the last 30 years of his life painting the lily pond at his home in Giverny, a small town on the Seine River, just north of Paris. This expansive composition focuses on the momentary effect of sunlight both penetrating and reflecting off the shimmering water. While reflections of passing clouds dance across the illusive watery surface, plant fronds sway underneath. Around 1914, Monet conceived an ambitious plan—called his "Grande Décoration"—of arranging a series of such paintings in a continuous panorama that would surround and enclose the viewer in an environment of pure color. The plan was realized in the 1920s with the installation of two such rooms at the Musée de l'Orangerie in Paris. Cleveland's painting is the left panel of a three-part variation on the water lily theme. Its companions are at the Saint Louis Art Museum and the Nelson-Atkins Museum of Art in Kansas City.

OIL ON CANVAS; 201.3 X 425.8 CM (79-1/4 X 167-1/2 IN.)
JOHN L. SEVERANCE FUND 1960.81

Male Torso 1917

CONSTANTIN BRANCUSI (ROMANIAN, 1876–1957)

Hoping to reveal the "true sense of things," Brancusi mused, "What can sculpture do without?" This sculpture reduces the human form to a timeless, universal essence. The smooth, highly polished brass surface was unusual at a time when most metal sculptures were cast in bronze. Not only does the reflective surface unify the parts into one continuous form, but it also

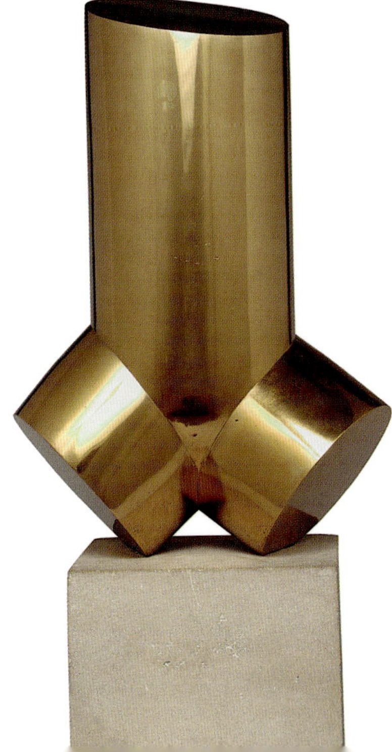

dematerializes the sculpture's mass, transforming the figure into a spiritual lightness. Brancusi made three versions of this sculpture: a wood version (Philadelphia Museum of Art) and two in brass (CMA and the Hirshhorn Museum and Sculpture Garden, Smithsonian Institution).

BRASS; 63.8 X 30.5 X 19.1 CM (25-1/8 X 12 X 7-1/2 IN.)

HINMAN B. HURLBUT COLLECTION 3205.1937

The Dessert about 1921

PIERRE BONNARD (FRENCH, 1867–1947)

One of the great colorists of the 20th century, Bonnard painted this scene either at his home at Vernon, just north of Paris, or at his summer home near Cannes in southern France. The woman leaning on her elbows is the artist's wife, Marthe. The boy smoking has been identified as Ari Redon, son of the artist Odilon Redon. The painting explores the simple pleasures of daily life, enriched through Bonnard's application of glowing, sensual color.

OIL ON CANVAS; 76.2 X 80 CM (30 X 31-1/2 IN.)

GIFT OF THE HANNA FUND 1949.18

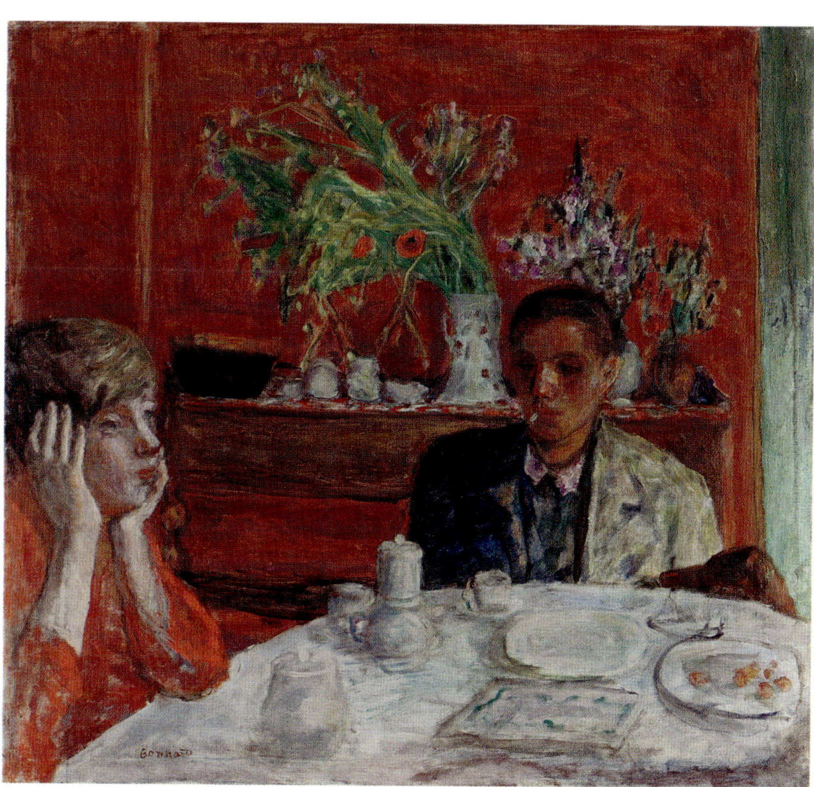

The Dream 1931

SALVADOR DALÍ (SPANISH, 1904–1989)

The Dream gives visual form to the strange, often disturbing world of dreams and hallucinations. Ants cluster over the face of the central figure, obscuring the mouth, while the sealed, bulging eyelids almost seem to be moving. The man at the far left—with a bleeding face and amputated left foot—refers to the classical myth of Oedipus, who unwittingly killed his father and married his mother. The column that grows from the man's back and sprouts into a bust of a bearded man refers to the Freudian father, the punishing superego who suppresses the son's sexual fantasies. In the distance, two men embrace, one holding a golden key or scepter symbolizing access to the unconscious. Behind them, a naked man reaches into a permeable red form, as if trying to enter it.

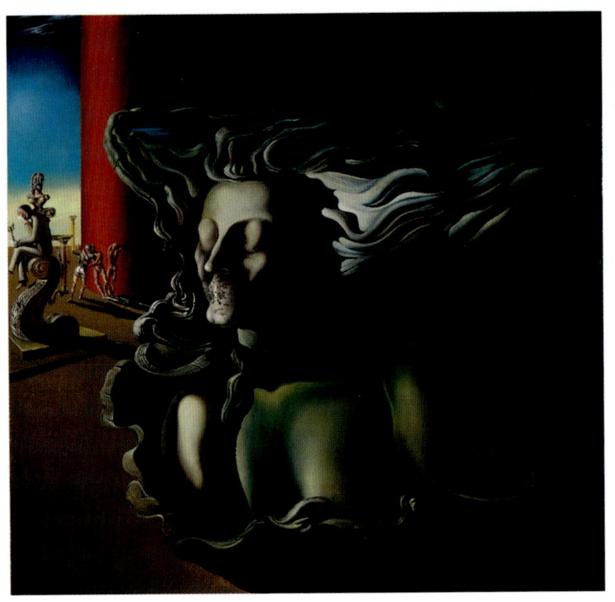

OIL ON CANVAS; 96 X 96 CM (37-3/4 X 37-3/4 IN.)

THE CLEVELAND MUSEUM OF ART, JOHN L. SEVERANCE FUND 2001.34

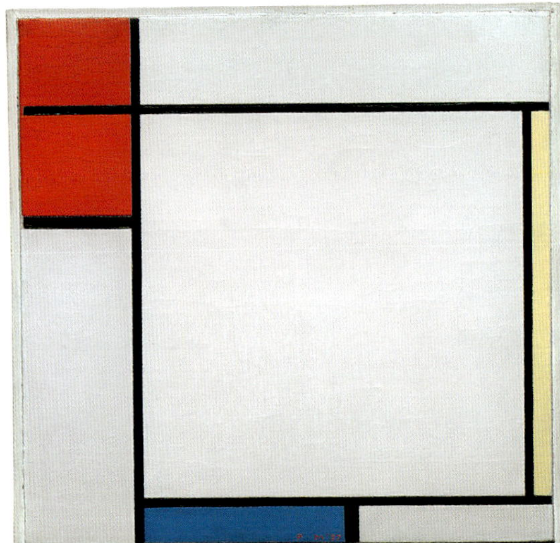

Composition with Red, Yellow, and Blue 1927

PIET MONDRIAN (DUTCH, 1872–1944)

Mondrian was one of the first artists to produce completely abstract or "non-objective" paintings. By 1917, he had reduced his paintings to vertical and horizontal lines, primary colors, and flat, geometric shapes. Reacting against the carnage of World War I, he aspired to create an art of utopian balance, harmony, and spiritual essence. He also developed a unique method of framing his paintings by attaching small strips of painted wood around the sides or tacking edge.

OIL ON CANVAS; 49.5 X 49.5 CM (19-1/2 X 19-1/2 IN.)

CONTEMPORARY COLLECTION OF THE CLEVELAND MUSEUM OF ART 1967.215

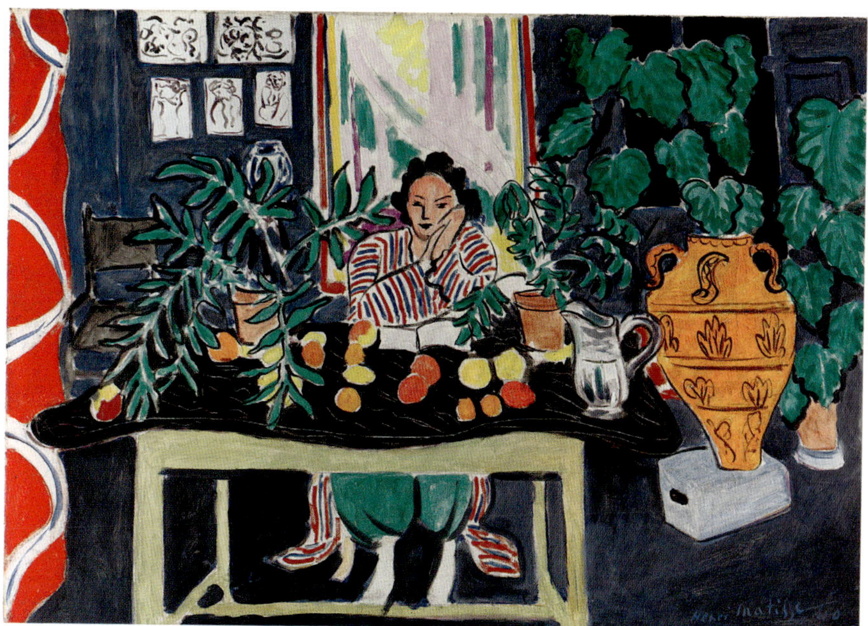

Interior with Etruscan Vase 1940

HENRI MATISSE (FRENCH, 1869–1954)

"I have always tried," wrote Matisse, "to hide my own efforts and wished my works to have the lightness and joyousness of springtime." He achieved that aim in this canvas, painted in Nice during the early months of World War II. A tapestry design hangs behind the woman, while the window to the right is covered in black. The oak table, a light wood with a natural finish in real life, is painted black and green, thereby transforming it into a decorative shape that anchors the center of the composition.

OIL ON CANVAS; 73.7 X 108 CM (29 X 42-1/2 IN.)

GIFT OF THE HANNA FUND 1952.153

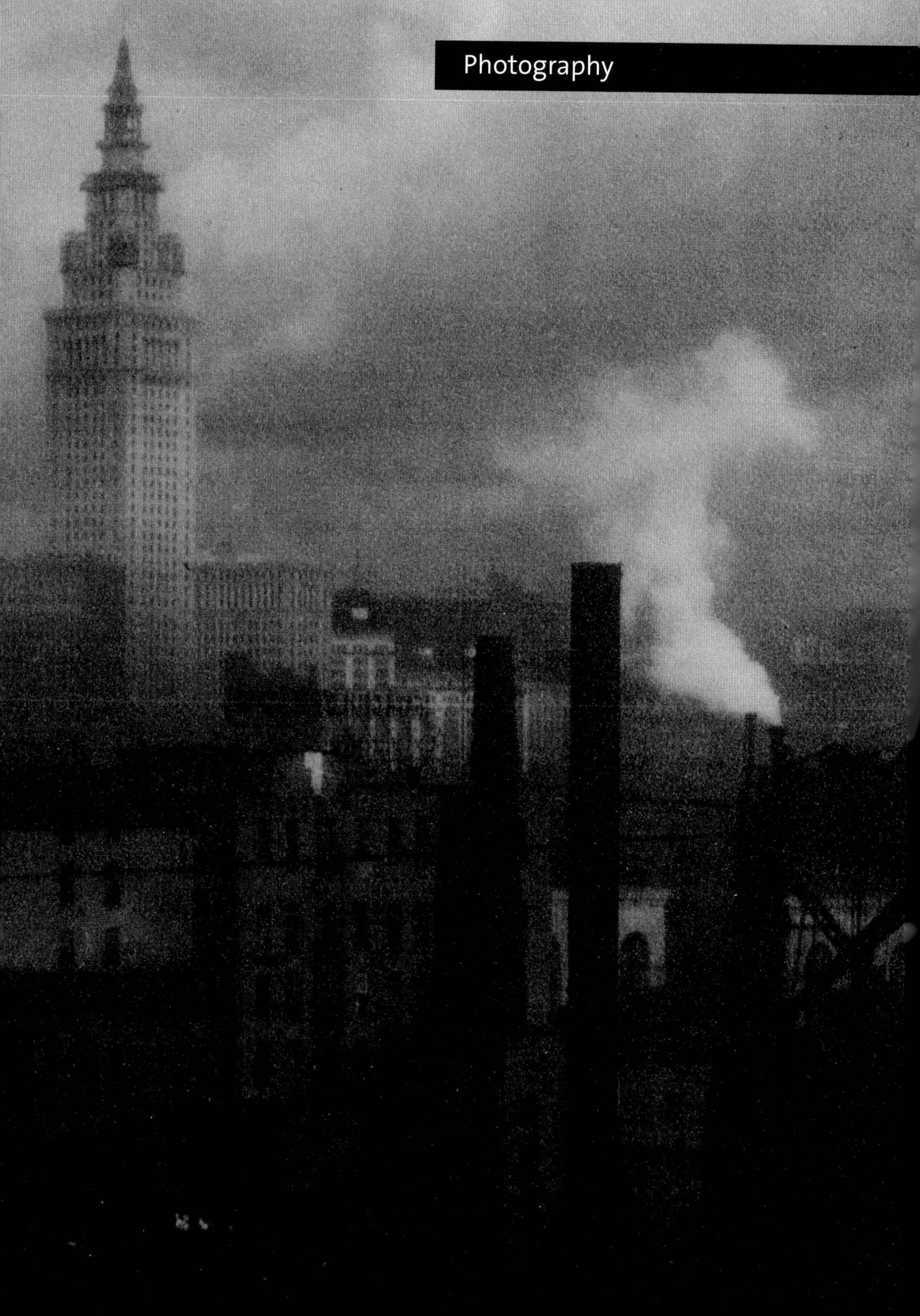

Photography

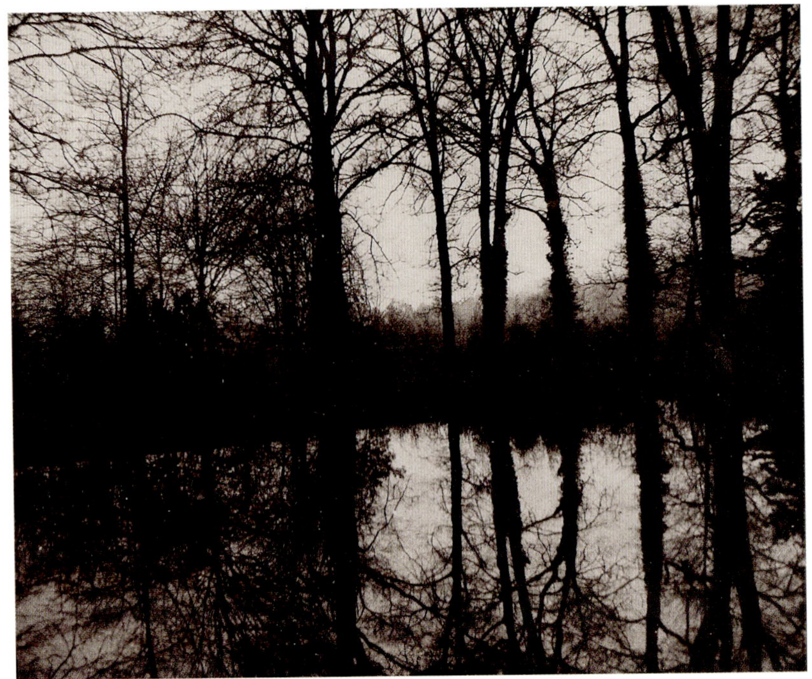

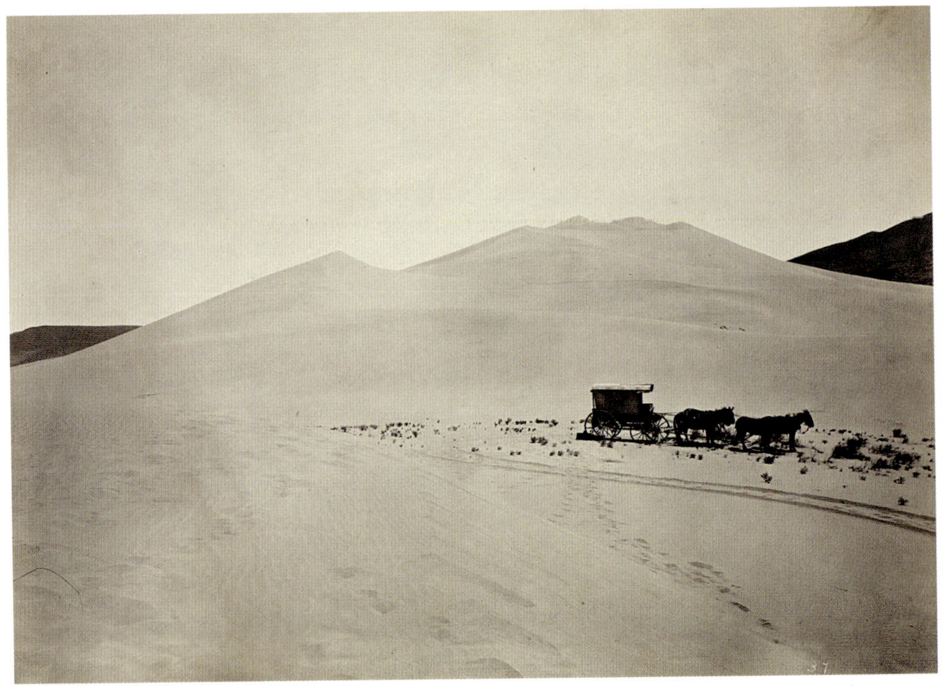

Winter Trees Reflected in a Pond 1841–42

WILLIAM HENRY FOX TALBOT (BRITISH, 1800–1877)

William Henry Fox Talbot made *Winter Trees Reflected in a Pond* a few years after he invented the calotype process, a precursor of modern photography. This masterfully composed landscape attests that, from the very beginning of the medium, a photograph could indeed be a work of art.

Talbot captured the lacy branches of trees mirrored on the glassy surface of the pond at the picturesque 13th-century Lacock Abbey in Wiltshire. The result is a radically abstract composition for its time. Talbot framed the image so the top edges cut off the treetops and the bottom their reflection. The trunks become rhythmic dark verticals separating strips of light. The shoreline is set at a slight angle and somewhat below the visual center, subtly disrupting a nascent grid. This geometric foundation emphasizes the graphic qualities of the image and downplays the camera's faculty for reportage. The color of the print was also an aesthetic choice. Talbot could produce calotypes in many hues, including some that would provide more contrast, but he preferred soft, warm browns. Here, they add to the somber tenor of the scene.

The impetus for Talbot's invention of photography was art: he wanted an apparatus that would create art directly from nature. Looking back from the era of digital photography, it is evident that artistry resides in the photographer, not the camera. Talbot was indeed a talented artist and *Winter Trees* a starkly beautiful landscape, as expressive and personal as any painting.

SALTED PAPER PRINT FROM CALOTYPE NEGATIVE; 16.4 X 19.1 CM (6-1/2 X 7-1/2 IN.)

PURCHASE FROM THE J. H. WADE FUND 2006.4

Sand Dunes, Carson Desert, Nevada 1867

TIMOTHY H. O'SULLIVAN (AMERICAN, 1840–1882)

One of O'Sullivan's best-known images, this noontime scene is one of hundreds of photographs he took for the 40th Parallel Survey, or King Survey. This three-year government expedition analyzed the geology and natural resources of uncharted regions of Nevada, Utah, Colorado, Idaho, and Wyoming, the future path of the transcontinental railroad. Because he was one of only a few with the technical prowess to produce exquisite photographs in the field, O'Sullivan was given a great deal of freedom about what and how to photograph. More significant in terms of photographic history was his willingness to discard the formal conventions that practitioners had borrowed from European landscape painting.

Most mid 19th-century depictions of the West are inviting landscapes meant to lure Easterners to civilize the wilderness and harvest its abundant resources. O'Sullivan produced a composition as spare as this desert landscape. The value scale is reduced to a contrast of light and dark: the sand and sky versus the mules, mountains, and wagon (a Civil War ambulance that he converted into a portable darkroom). Sand, mountain, and sky become flattened forms that suggest, to modern eyes, a tension between three-dimensional space and the flat plane of the paper. Even the mood feels modern, emphasizing isolation and suggesting that humans are at the mercy of uncaring nature.

ALBUMEN PRINT FROM WET COLLODION NEGATIVE; 19.7 X 27 CM (7-3/4 X 10-5/8 IN.)

JOHN L. SEVERANCE FUND 2002.45

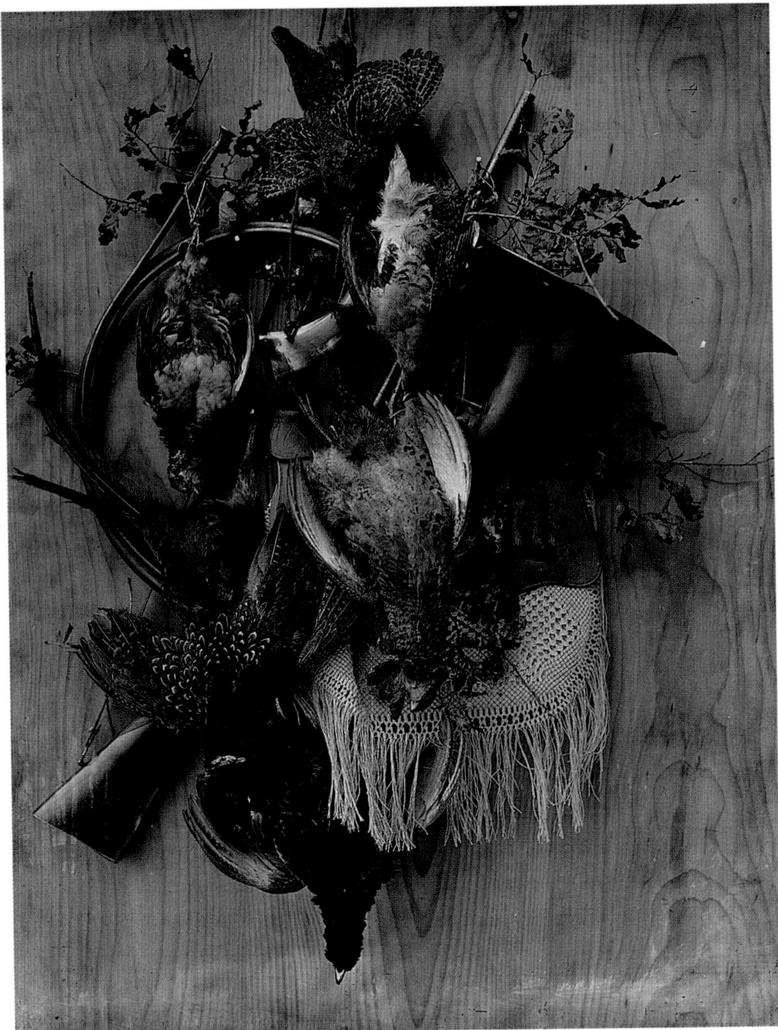

Trophy of the Hunt about 1867

ADOLPHE BRAUN (FRENCH, 1812–1877)

Adolphe Braun's *Trophy of the Hunt* is one of a series of eight hunt-trophy images. Such photographs were affordable alternatives to the costly painted hunt scenes adorning the country houses of the European upper classes and aristocrats. Here Braun shows an array of game birds prized for their flavor and the hunting challenge they offer. Framed and hanging in a dimly lit dining room, this large photograph might indeed be mistaken for a painting. Braun's artful arrangements continue a tradition of hunt still lifes that was popular in the artist's native region of Alsace and in northern Germany from the 17th century on. The 19th-century versions, created by photographers and even a few Impressionist painters, evoke a leisurely rural pastime that was becoming rare in an increasingly urban, industrialized France.

Braun's photography firm, one of the world's largest at the time, was an entrepreneurial endeavor. To remain competitive, he experimented with the latest technical innovations. The hunt-trophy prints were made from glass-plate negatives measuring 78.7 x 70 cm (31 x 24 in.). Virtuoso technical productions, they offer exquisite detail and subtle tonal range, in large part because Braun used a new carbon printing process. This series, unlike many of his other endeavors, seems not to have met with commercial or critical success. Fewer than 20 of the prints survive, suggesting that a limited quantity was produced. Nonetheless, the images remained in the firm's sales catalogue for two decades, suggesting that Braun held these photographs among his artistic, if not his commercial, triumphs.

CARBON PRINT; 78 X 59.8 CM (30-3/4 X 23-1/2 IN.)
ANDREW R. AND MARTHA HOLDEN JENNINGS FUND
1985.144

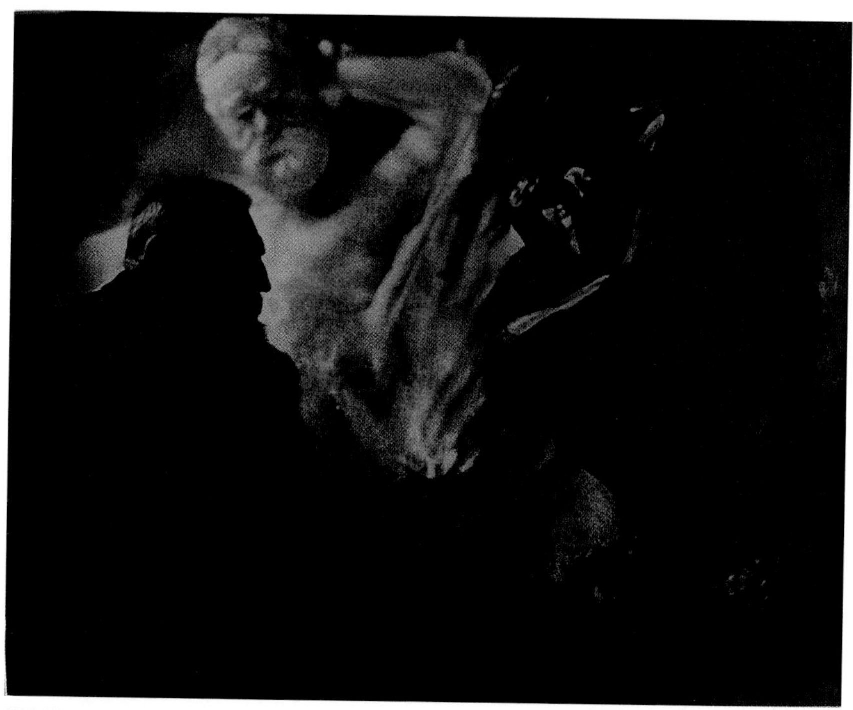

Rodin—The Thinker 1902

EDWARD STEICHEN (AMERICAN, 1879–1973)

Edward Steichen visited Auguste Rodin's studio weekly for a year before asking to photograph the celebrated sculptor. The young American's goal was to create a portrait of genius, not just a physical likeness. Steichen silhouetted Rodin's massive head and shoulders against his monument to French author Victor Hugo, which glows with light from a skylight. A darker creation, perhaps Rodin's alter ego, perches across from him as if in conversation: a bronze of *The Thinker*.

Rodin's studio was crowded and Steichen did not have a lens with a wide enough angle to capture both sculptures and their creator in a single shot. He made two negatives, one of Rodin and Victor Hugo and the other of *The Thinker*, and printed them together. In this composite print, the negative with Rodin is reversed, setting the artist opposite his creation. A year later, Steichen wrote that "every photograph is a fake from start to finish," proudly proclaiming the overwhelmingly subjective, expressive nature of his supposedly impartial, mechanical medium. Photography was art, not merely documentation.

CARBON PRINT, TONED; 36.2 X 43.8 CM (14-1/4 X 17-1/4 IN.)
GIFT OF MR. AND MRS. THOMAS A. MANN 1989.399

Triangle Composition (Harry Losée) 1922

JANE REECE (AMERICAN, 1869–1961)

This depiction of dancer Harry Losée is one of a handful of experimental portraits of him produced in the Dayton, Ohio, studio and darkroom of Jane Reece. Reece was an acolyte of the Pictorialist movement, which argued that photography could be more than documentation, it could be a vehicle for personal artistic expression.

Dayton native Losée was studying and performing with Denishawn, a modern dance company, in 1922. Reece's portraits of him communicate the avant-garde character of modern dance through extreme, angular poses and abstract geometric backgrounds. Pictorialists commonly experimented with different papers, printing techniques, and handwork on both negative and print, but Reece blazed new trails in these images. She used tissue or celluloid overlays during the printing process to create a purely photographic background that varied slightly in each print. Relatives to Reece's technique are the photograms (cameraless photographs) made by Man Ray in Paris, starting around the same time.

Reece's flirtation with modernism and abstraction seems to have been limited to her depictions of Losée. Perhaps she was inspired by Cubist painting or the Vorticist photographs of Alvin Langdon Coburn. Or perhaps this body of work was collaborative, with Losée striving to recreate through photography the modernist sets and lighting designs he had seen in New York or Los Angeles. Whatever its inspiration, the result is a set of thrilling theatrical portraits unique for their time.

GELATIN SILVER PRINT; 24 X 19 CM (9-1/2 X 7-1/2 IN.)

JOHN L. SEVERANCE FUND 1996.358

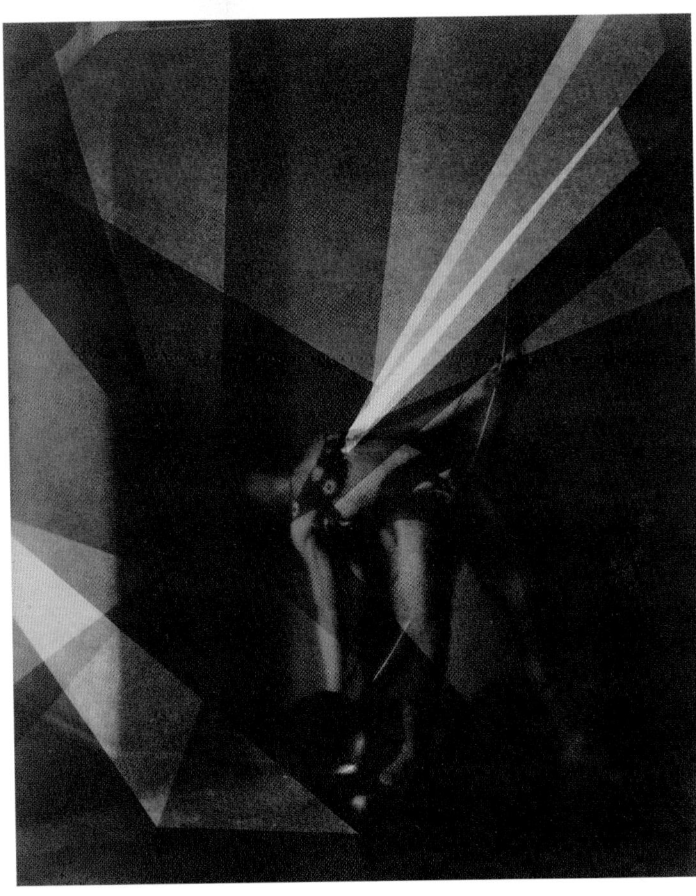

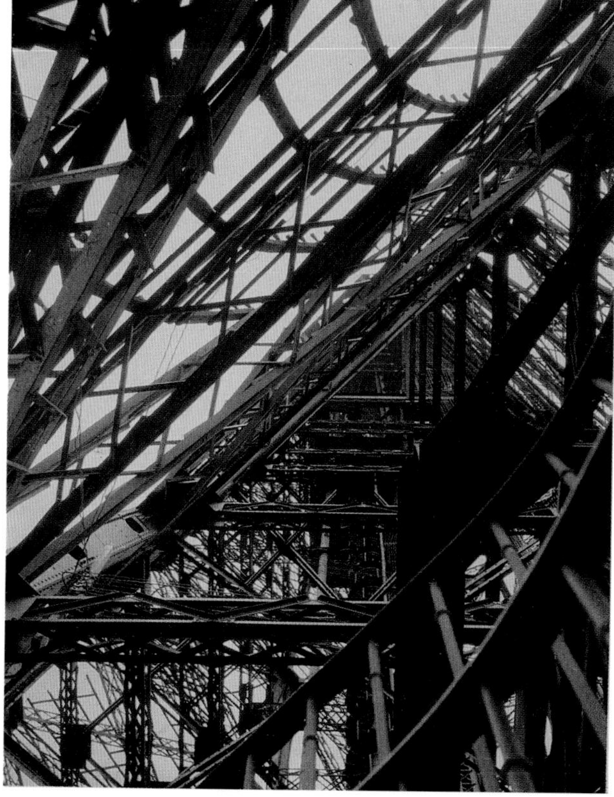

Eiffel Tower, Paris 1925

LÁSZLÓ MOHOLY-NAGY (AMERICAN, B. HUNGARY, 1895–1946)

Artist, theorist, and teacher László Moholy-Nagy became an advocate for photography in the 1920s, just as many avant-garde artists began employing the medium. He acquired a camera in 1919, but seems to have made no artful images with it until 1925, the year of *Eiffel Tower*. One of the earliest avant-garde photographs of this much-photographed edifice, this print emphasizes abstraction and formalism rather than representation. Its grid of diagonal and vertical lines, slightly askew, evokes Analytical Cubism, Robert Delaunay's paintings of the tower, and the thrusting diagonals of Russian Constructivist abstractions.

Despite its connections with painting, camera vision shaped *Eiffel Tower*. Sharp focus, distortion, and the extreme close-up are at its core. It is framed to eliminate any horizon line or context, which disorients the viewer. The smaller, lighter cameras that appeared in the 1910s and 1920s encouraged odd vantage points such as bird's- and worm's-eye views. Moholy and others used them to shock viewers out of visual complacency and into understanding the new relationship between man and space that resulted from the advent of the airplane and skyscraping structures like the Eiffel Tower. *Eiffel Tower* presents what the camera lens saw, unfettered by intellectual understanding or memories. Moholy believed that, by presenting "an unprejudiced optical view," photography offered modern man an entirely new way of seeing.

GELATIN SILVER PRINT; 28.1 X 21.1 CM (11-1/8 X 8-3/8 IN.)

DUDLEY P. ALLEN FUND 1997.144

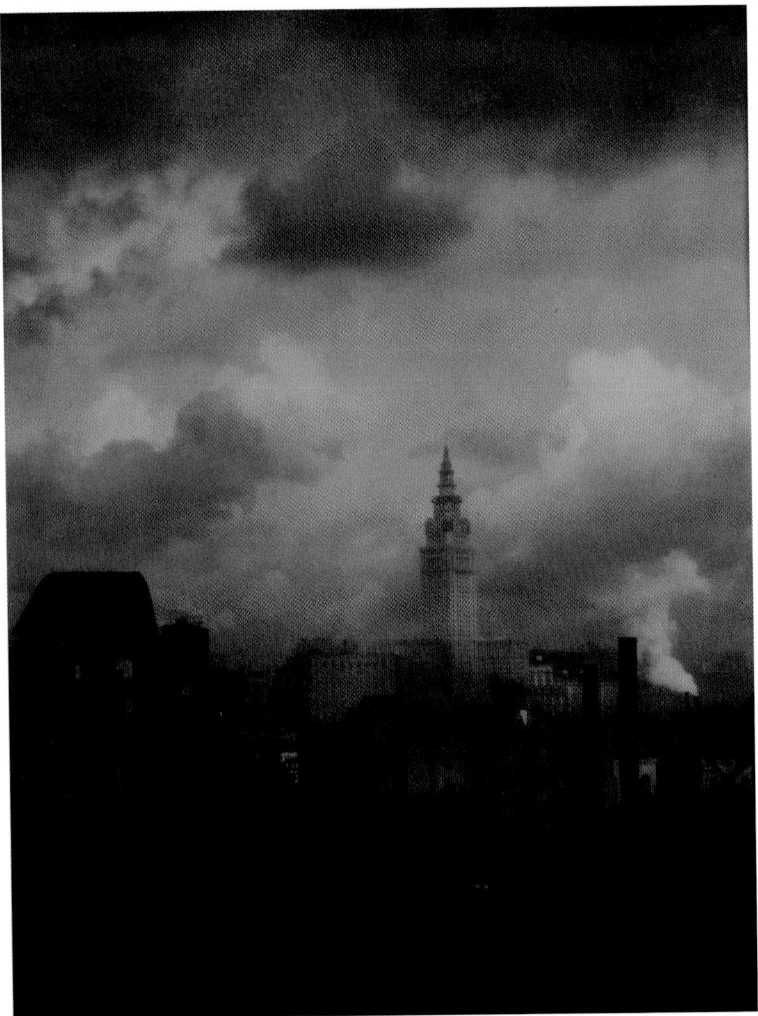

Terminal Tower 1928

MARGARET BOURKE-WHITE (AMERICAN, 1904–1971)

This spectacular vintage print is the largest known version of Margaret Bourke-White's iconic photograph of Cleveland. The 52-story Terminal Tower, a cathedral of commerce and capitalism, was an apt symbol for a city literally and financially on the rise in the 1920s. The building was still under construction when 23-year-old Bourke-White arrived in Cleveland in 1927. She was fascinated by city's smoky, gritty factories—especially the steel mills—and spent every free moment photographing in the Flats, the industrial area between downtown and Lake Erie. Instead of employing the new angular modernist style, Bourke-White applied the soft focus and atmospheric effects of the older Pictorialist movement to produce romantic images of industrialism.

This view of the tower was shot from the west side of the Cuyahoga River, at a high vantage point, looking across the Flats toward downtown. Looming at the picture's left edge is the massive Detroit-Superior Bridge. Isolated near the middle of the frame, the tower's delicately ornamented spire floats above the city. Yet even this soaring structure seems small compared to the billowing clouds that fill the top of the frame.

Bourke-White masterfully contrasts light

and dark, engineering and architecture, to attest that Cleveland, built on shipping and manufacturing, was now achieving loftier goals. The image also reminds us that human ambitions can fall victim to more powerful forces. This was a lesson well worth remembering in 1928, the year before the onset of the Great Depression.

GELATIN SILVER PRINT; 49.4 X 37.2 CM (19-1/2 X 14-5/8 IN.)

GIFT OF HUNTINGTON BANK 2003.361

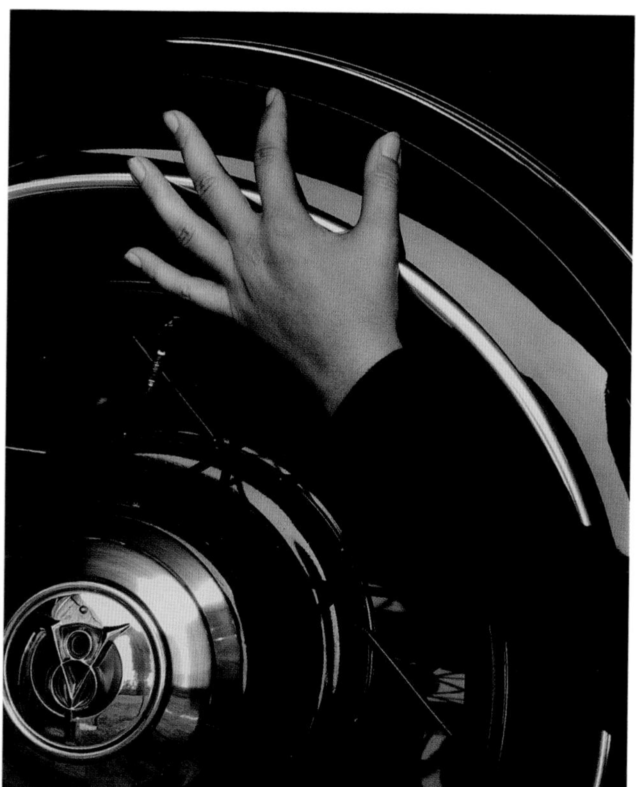

Georgia O'Keeffe—Hand and Wheel 1933

ALFRED STIEGLITZ (AMERICAN, 1864–1946)

In 1934, the Cleveland Museum of Art invited Alfred Stieglitz to participate in a photography exhibition. One of the century's most influential photographers, Stieglitz sent 10 prints including two of his wife, the painter Georgia O'Keeffe. Close-ups of her with her car, they belong to an extended series of portraits he made of her between 1917 and 1937.

O'Keeffe had devoted the proceeds from the sale of one of her paintings to purchase the car. In this image, her elegantly long fingers caress the spare tire. The new Ford V-8 convertible coupe was not just a glossy object of consumer desire. For O'Keeffe it symbolized her independence, the freedom to go off and paint wherever she liked. The occasion for these photographs was her reunion with her husband, and with the car, after weeks of hospitalization and months of convalescence from a nervous breakdown.

At the end of the Cleveland exhibition, all 10 photographs were donated to the museum. They were the first photographs to enter the collection.

GELATIN SILVER PRINT; 24.2 X 19.2 CM (9-1/2 X 7-1/2 IN.)

GIFT OF CARY ROSS, KNOXVILLE, TENNESSEE 1935.99

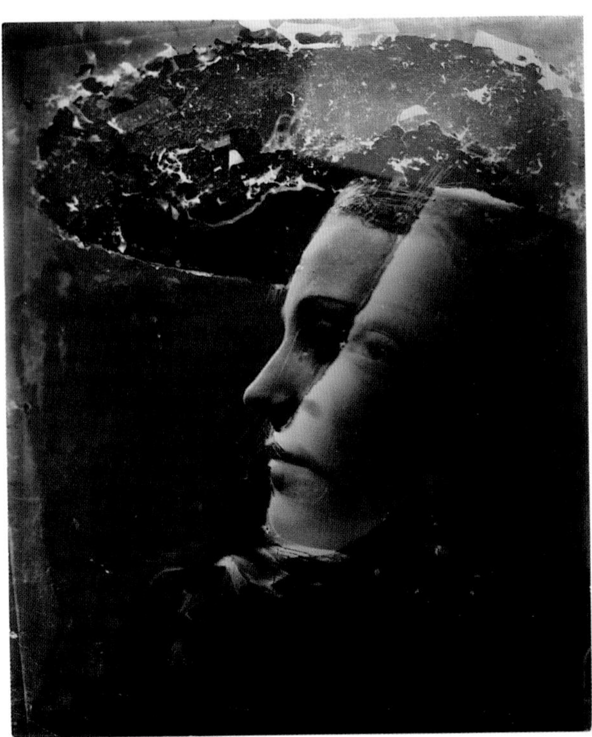

Double Portrait with Hat about 1936–37

DORA MAAR (FRENCH, 1907–1997)

Dora Maar was a Parisian photographer whose fashion, advertising, and portrait commissions helped subsidize her artistic experiments in the medium. In 1934 she began making Surrealist photographs that soon graced the avant-garde movement's publications and exhibitions.

Double Portrait reveals its Surrealist origins in its rupture with reality, dream-like mood, post-Freudian evocation of a divided consciousness, and adventurous combination of techniques. Maar sandwiched together two negatives of the same model, both possibly cannibalized from a 1936 fashion assignment on spring hats. The painted gray background and hat (or disintegrating halo?) were created on the negative rather than through the lens. Maar softened and manipulated the photographic emulsion, lifting off pieces and scraping into areas, techniques more akin to printmaking than photography. *Double Portrait* is the high point of a series of 10 prints created with the same faces, hat, and background.

In 1936, Maar met Pablo Picasso and quickly become his lover and muse. By 1938 Picasso had convinced her to abandon photography and devote herself to painting, a medium in which she could never outshine him. Although the face in *Double Portrait* is not Maar's, it is tempting to interpret the dualities presented in the image as reflections of her emotional state at the time, torn between her career and independence and Picasso's demands and potent personality.

GELATIN SILVER PRINT; MONTAGE WITH HANDWORK ON NEGATIVE; 29.8 X 23.8 CM (11-3/4 X 9-3/8 IN.)

GIFT OF DAVID RAYMOND 2008.172

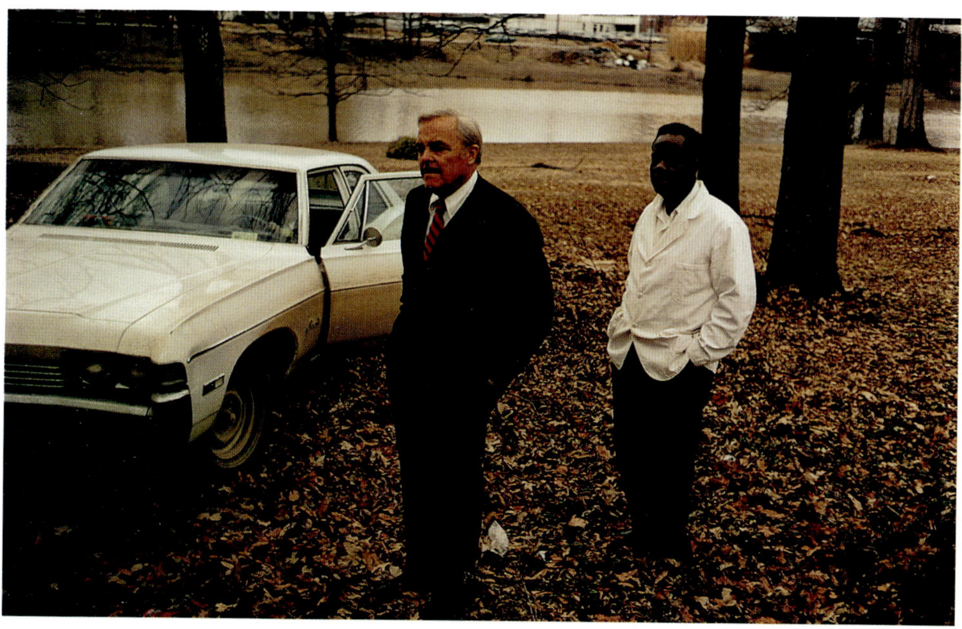

Sumner, Mississippi, Cassidy Bayou in Background 1972 (printed 1986)

WILLIAM EGGLESTON (AMERICAN, B. 1937)

William Eggleston has often denied that his work is about the American South, but it is hard not to see *Sumner, Mississippi,* one of his key works, as a view of a vanishing way of life. This terse summary of racial relations in the early 1970s was captured in Eggleston's hometown. He shot the image after attending a family funeral.

The photograph's compositional structure hangs on the rhythmic relationship between two figures who are clearly boss and servant. Leading the way is a white man in a dark suit; following him and echoing his pose is a dark man in a white jacket. Next to the white man is a car, an emblem of wealth and personal freedom in mid 20th-century America. The photograph reveals neither Eggleston's personal connection to the event nor the social changes being wrought by the civil rights movement at this time.

In an era dominated by black-and-white photography, Eggleston was an early champion of color work. The appearance of *Sumner, Mississippi* on the cover of the avant-garde art journal *Artforum* in 1983 signaled another change for photography: the medium was now considered equal in importance to painting and sculpture.

DYE TRANSFER PRINT; 28 X 43.2 CM (11 X 17 IN.)

GIFT OF MUSEUM MEMBERS IN 1989 1989.421

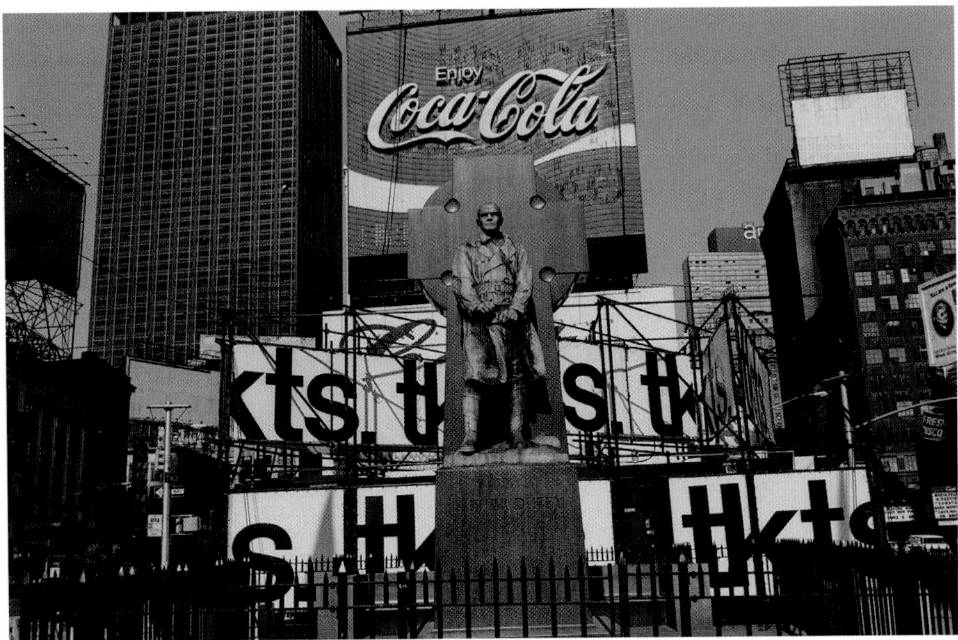

New York City, Father Duffy 1974 (printed late 1970s or early 1980s)

LEE FRIEDLANDER (AMERICAN, B. 1934)

Lee Friedlander has produced extraordinary photographs addressing many genres—from portraits and nudes to the beauties and banalities of the urban landscape. His photograph of Duffy Square, the northern triangle of New York's Times Square, conveys the congestion and layered archaeology of midtown Manhattan while commenting on the fate of the American monument. The image is jam-packed with billboards and signage. Occupying its center is another type of ad, a 1937 statue of Father Francis P. Duffy in his army uniform, protected from admirers and the curious by a wickedly barbed fence. This Roman Catholic priest, the most decorated U.S. Army chaplain of World War I, returned to New York at war's end to become pastor of the nearby Holy Cross Church, also known as the actors' church. The monument celebrating Duffy's life of service harks back to a patriotic ideal that had been tarnished for many by the Vietnam War era of the 1970s.

GELATIN SILVER PRINT; 18.8 X 28.1 CM (7-3/8 X 11-1/8 IN.)

JOHN L. SEVERANCE FUND 1993.151

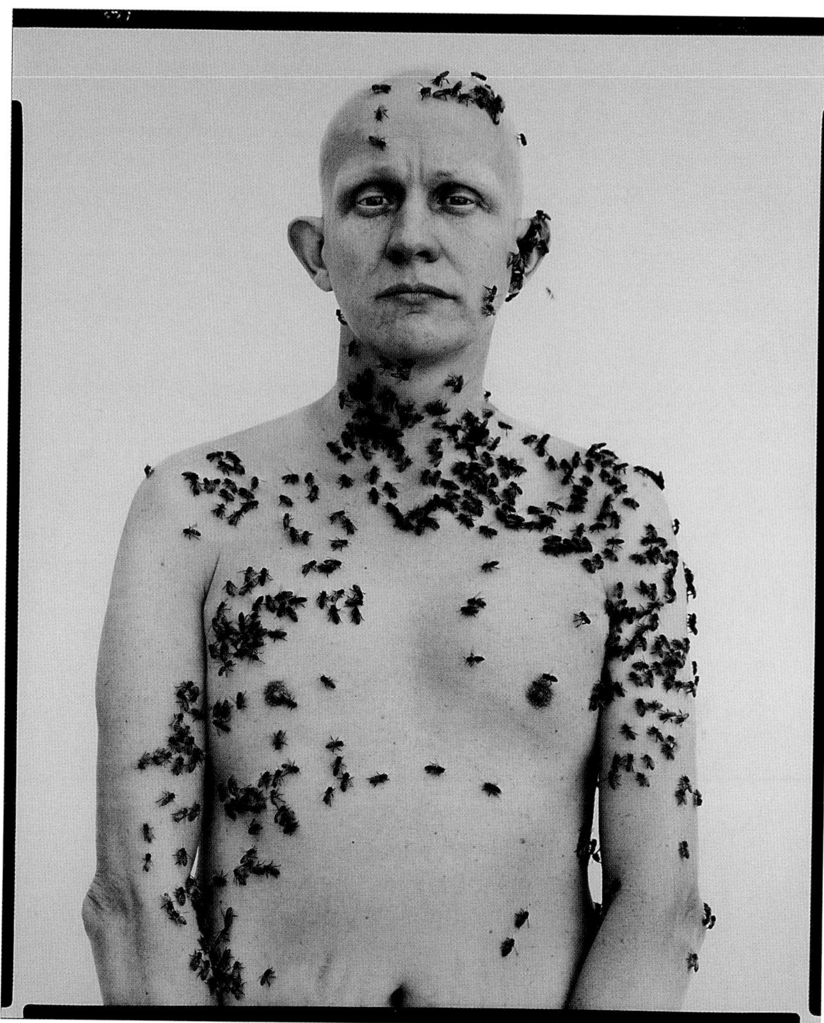

Ronald Fischer, beekeeper, Davis, California, May 9, 1981 1981 (printed 1985)

RICHARD AVEDON (AMERICAN, 1923–2004)

Richard Avedon, one of America's most celebrated portrait and fashion photographers, was commissioned by the Amon Carter Museum in Fort Worth to photograph the American West. Traveling throughout the region each summer for six years, Avedon sought out ordinary working people who were "surprising—heartbreaking—or beautiful in a terrifying way."

Avedon found Ronald Fischer by posting a notice in a beekeepers' magazine soliciting snapshots of people willing to be photographed with bees on their body. He posed Fischer, as he had all the sitters for *In the American West,* outdoors against a large white sheet of seamless paper that eliminated any sense of location. An entomologist brought 120,000 bees and rubbed scent from the hive's queen bee on Fischer's chest, which attracted the insects and lessened their desire to sting. After shooting 121 sheets of film in two days, Avedon chose this image, in which the beekeeper "removes himself in a Buddhist way" and seems oblivious to the pain. It was closer to Avedon's own understanding of how best to endure and prevail.

GELATIN SILVER PRINT; 143.1 X 114.5 CM (56-3/8 X 45-1/8 IN.)

LEONARD C. HANNA JR. FUND 2005.143

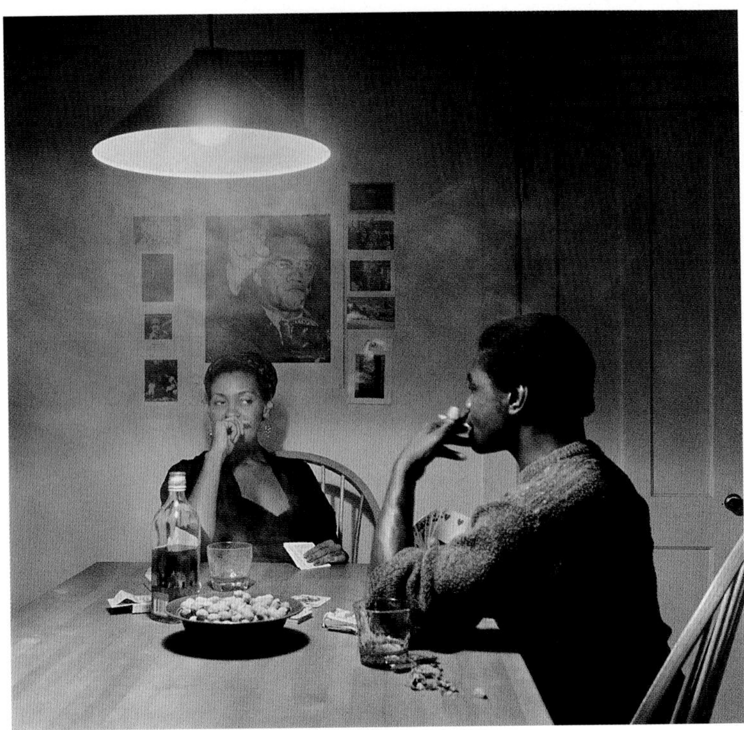

Man Smoking from *The Kitchen Table Series,* 1990 (portfolio printed 2003)

CARRIE MAE WEEMS (AMERICAN, B. 1953)

This print is part of *The Kitchen Table Series,* a cinematic narrative of a woman's relationships with her lover, child, and friends in photographs and text panels. Carrie Mae Weems—author, director, photographer, and subject—also portrays the protagonist, a flirtatious, vulnerable, and eventually fiercely independent Everywoman. Weems's early photographs were documentary images, but in the mid 1980s she began combining staged images with text to comment on societal and political aspects of racism. This remained her theme until *The Kitchen Table Series*.

In this work, it is neither incidental nor central that the main characters are black. The politics of desire and issues of intimacy and power occupy center stage. Battles between the sexes and the generations all occur at a table in Weems's kitchen. The camera, and thus the viewer, is inside the room, observing the action across the table. The text panels, written in the third person, rarely synchronize with the pictures but instead present internal monologues that riff on popular songs and clichés. The final text reveals that the woman is "in her solitude, so it wasn't nobody's business what she did."

Weems produced *The Kitchen Table Series* in 1990 as individual gelatin silver prints and in 2003 as a portfolio of platinum prints accompanied by text panels. Perhaps she chose platinum's softer, more delicate palette for this later version to better reflect what she describes as "the subtle and ephemeral qualities of love: its power to embrace and to destroy."

SERIES: 20 PLATINUM PRINTS, 38.1 X 38.1 CM (15 X 15 IN.) EACH; 14 LETTERPRESS TEXT SHEETS, 35.5 X 35.5 CM (14 X 14 IN.) EACH

PURCHASE FROM THE J. H. WADE FUND 2008.116.1–34

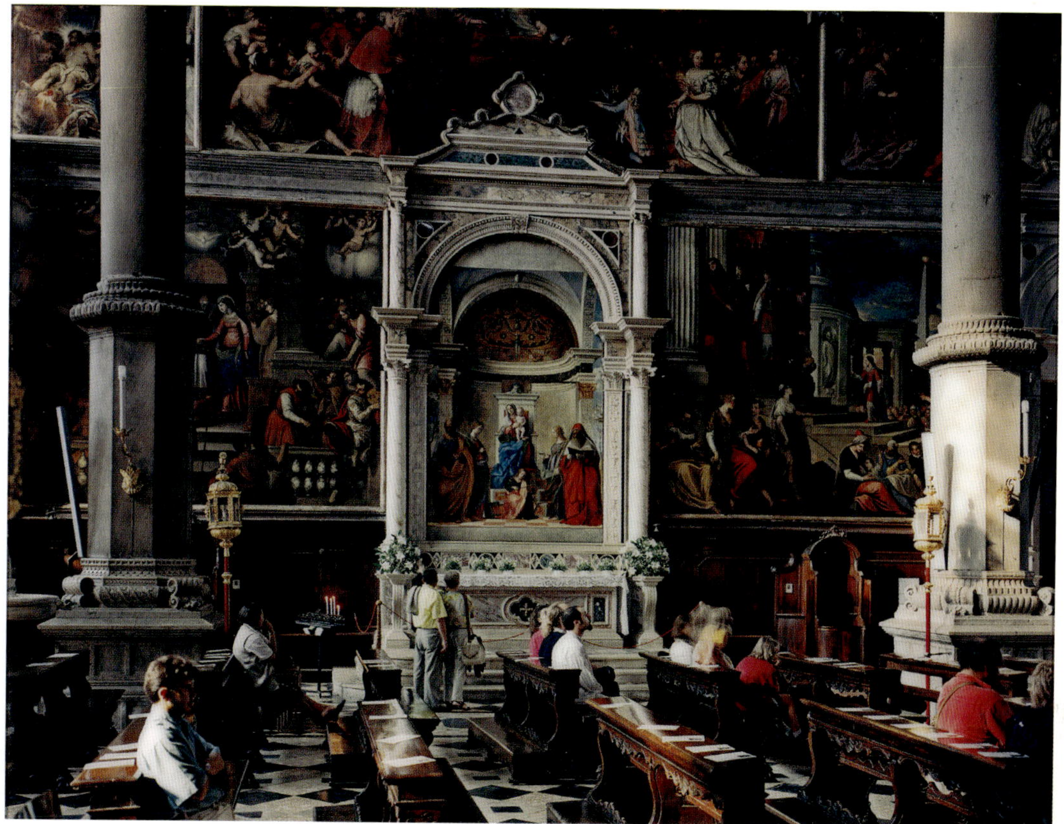

San Zaccaria, Venice 1995

THOMAS STRUTH (GERMAN, B. 1954)

What impact does viewing great art have, wondered Thomas Struth. Did "being confronted with your own imagination, with the fictive personification in . . . paintings, and with the artist's vision of the world at the same time" change you? He sought to answer those questions by photographing visitors contemplating historic art in museums and religious sites.

Struth's photograph of the interior of the Venetian church of San Zaccaria, with its altarpiece by Giovanni Bellini, echoes the symmetry of that painted scene of benediction and adoration. A blur (the record of someone in the front pews moving) raises the issue of photography's relationship to time. Struth's exposure lasted two seconds but his image spans 490 years, linking the year of the altarpiece's creation, 1505, with the lives of people in 1995.

The blur also invokes a snapshot's informality and verity. While Struth's image is neither posed nor fabricated, it is definitely not casual. It took the photographer four days and 60 exposures to find a moment when real life reflected the harmony of Bellini's idealized scene.

In person the scale of this photograph communicates an authority that cannot be understood from reproductions. In addition, Struth employed a new mounting technique that makes the colors appear extraordinarily vivid, comparable to the liquid brilliance obtained from varnishing an oil painting.

Did making these images answer Struth's question? One would expect an artist to believe in art's transformative powers, but Struth's photographs on the topic remain tantalizingly ambiguous.

CHROMOGENIC PRINT FACE-MOUNTED TO ACRYLIC; 182 X 230.5 CM (71-5/8 X 90-7/8 IN.)

LOUIS D. KACALIEFF, M.D., FUND 1996.13

Meat and Text from the *1/2* series, 1998

ZHANG HUAN (CHINESE, B. 1966)

Toward the end of his studies in classical Chinese ink painting, Western drawing and painting techniques, and art history, Zhang Huan began to make "concept photos," performances created just for the camera without an audience present. He focused the camera on his body, which he realized was "the only direct way through which I come to know society and society comes to know me. The body is the proof of identity. The body is language."

The *1/2* series was inspired by the Beijing market where Zhang ate breakfast every morning. In this photograph, the artist's body is covered with Chinese characters—symbolizing words, thoughts, and culture—and two sets of animal ribs. At the market, recalled Zhang, "I could see rows and rows of ribs on sale at different stalls. When I saw the ribs, I saw myself. Half of a person is his body and the other half is his soul."

CHROMOGENIC PRINT; 119.4 X 104.1 CM (47 X 41 IN.)
PURCHASE FROM THE J. H. WADE FUND 2012.100.2

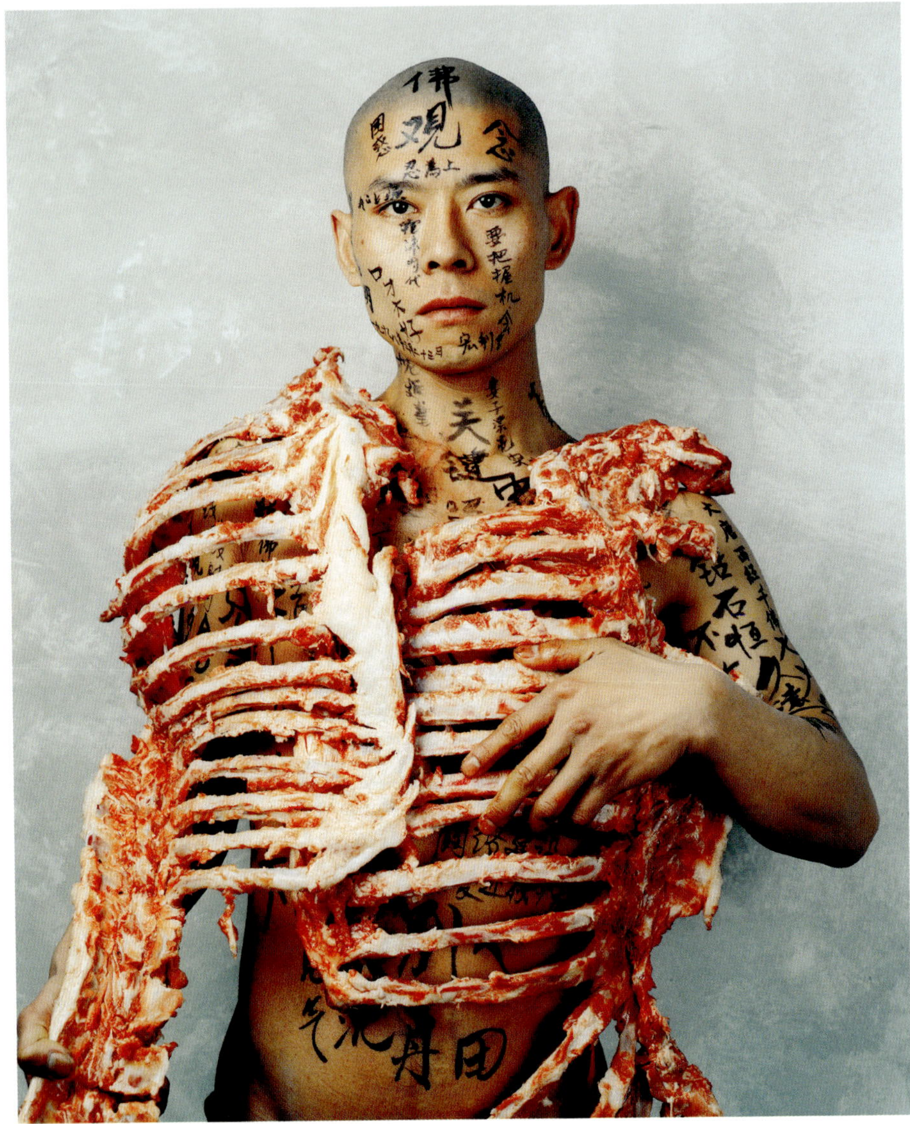

Winter in America 2005

HANK WILLIS THOMAS (AMERICAN, B. 1976) AND KAMBUI OLUJIMI (AMERICAN, B. 1976)

Winter in America uses stop-action animation and G.I. Joe figures to act out the shooting and death of Hank Willis Thomas's cousin Songha Willis outside a Philadelphia nightclub during a robbery. As children, Thomas and his collaborator, Kambui Olujimi, used similar figures to create violent, although in that case imaginary, scenarios. Underlying the video is Thomas's suggestion that such toys breed "a culture of violent thoughts for young boys who are invited to author violent scenarios before they can even read."

Thomas employs numerous media including photography, video, and installation to examine how history and culture are framed, who is doing the framing, and how these factors affect our interpretation of reality. His imagery is usually appropriated, most often borrowed from the language of popular culture and advertising. The accessibility and familiarity of these visual languages, from Nike and Absolut Vodka ads to action figures and stop-action cartoons, draw in the viewer and amplify the impact of the content.

VIDEO ACCOMPANIED BY PHOTOGRAPH AND BOOK; DIMENSIONS VARIABLE

PURCHASE FROM THE J. H. WADE FUND 2012.60

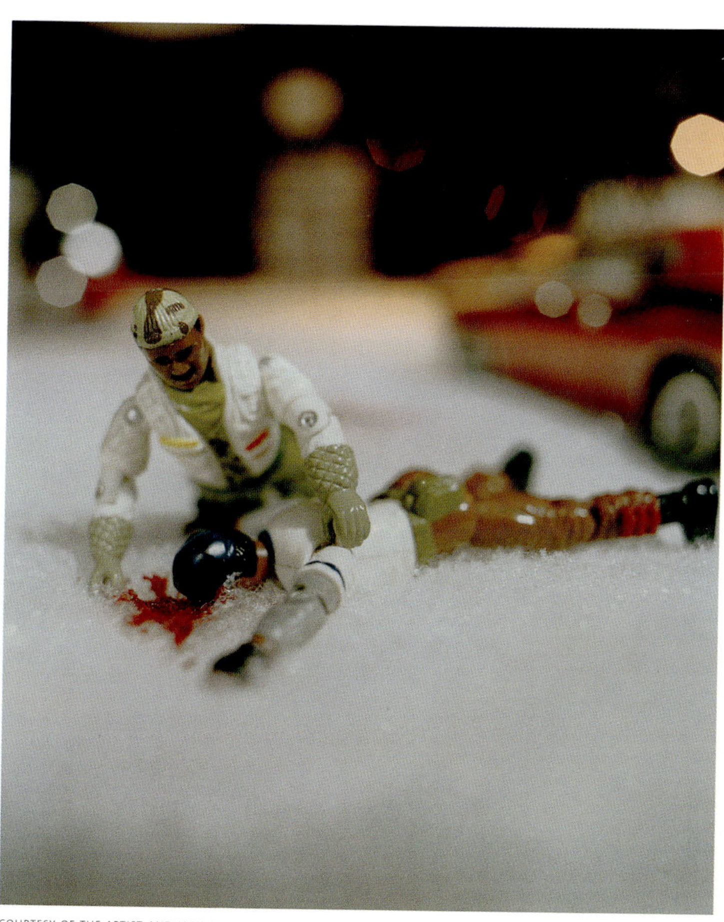

COURTESY OF THE ARTIST AND JACK SHAINMAN GALLERY, NEW YORK

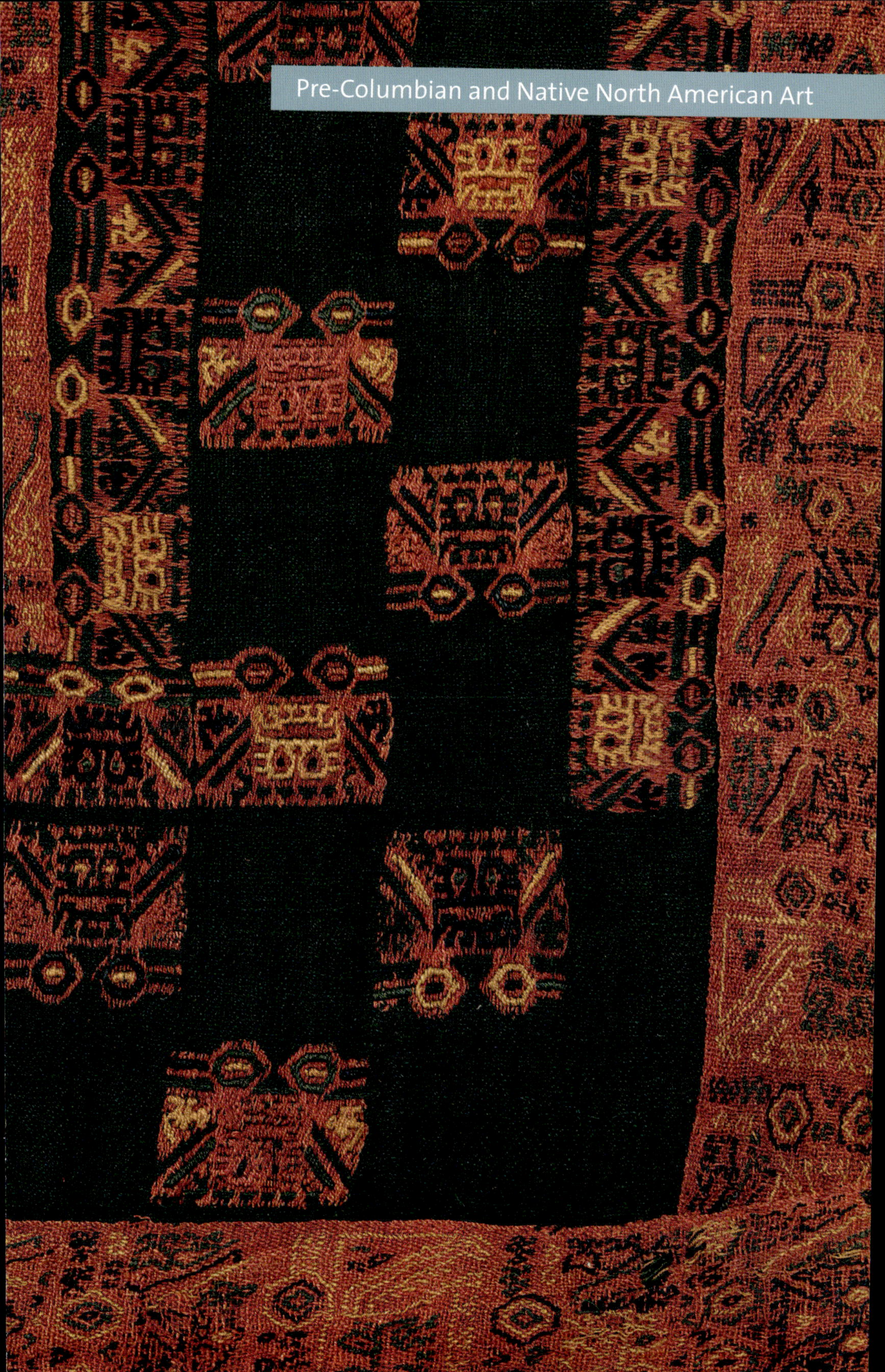

Pre-Columbian and Native North American Art

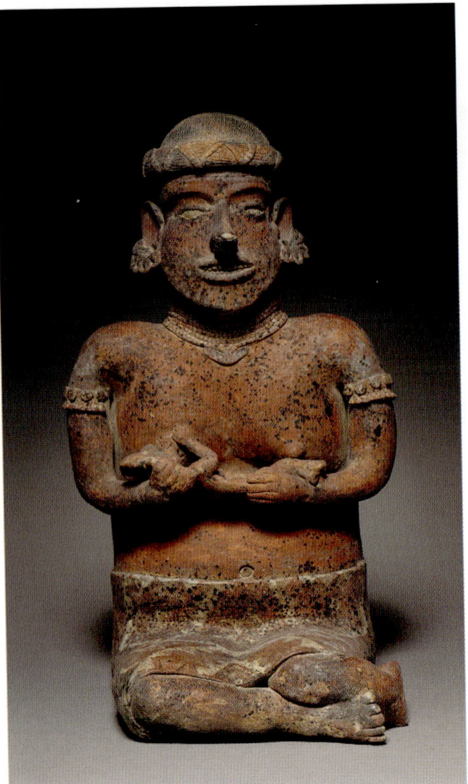

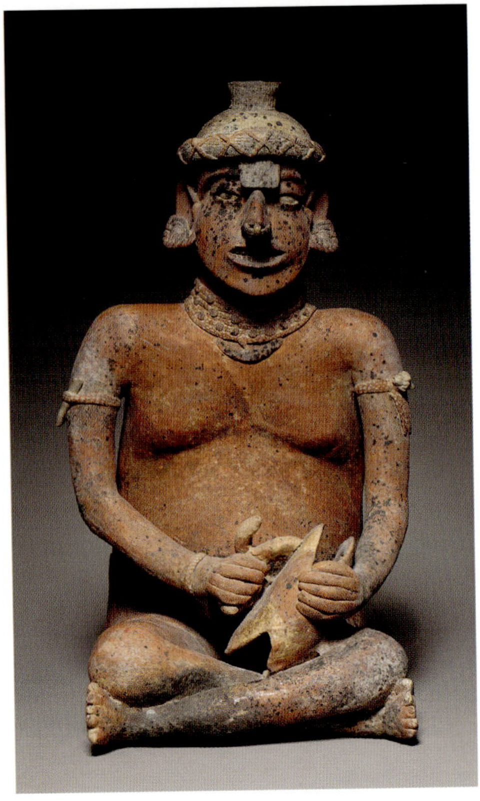

Seated Couple 200 BC–AD 300

MESOAMERICA, NAYARIT, IXTLÁN DEL RÍO STYLE

Between 200 BC and AD 300 in Mesoamerica, the powerhouse cultures of the Classic period, including Teotihuacán and Maya, began to take shape. At the same time, West Mexican chieftains gained power, their new glory reflected in the elaborate shaft tombs that shelter both their remains and those of family members along with many offerings, including handsome sculptural ceramics like these two. Many of these ceramics may refer to the crucial stages and activities of a chief's life, such as marriage, feasts, and war.

Extremely fine examples of their kind, this couple may commemorate the marriage of an important person such as a chief but could also represent siblings of a chiefly family. Whatever their relationship, unity is conveyed by their physical similarities, including the jewelry, which marks high social station. The female is unusual in nursing an infant, likely a reference to generational renewal and the continuation of noble bloodlines. The significance of the male's activity—beating a turtle-shell drum—is not understood.

CERAMIC, SLIP; 52.3 X 30.5 X 29.5 CM (20-5/8 X 12 X 11-5/8 IN.) AND 56 X 31.8 X 30.5 CM (22 X 12-1/2 X 12 IN.)

GIFT OF CLARA TAPLIN RANKIN 1998.83.1–2

Head Fragment 1600–300 BC
MESOAMERICA, OLMEC STYLE

The Olmec style, Mesoamerica's earliest complex art style, saw its most monumental and refined expression on the Gulf Coast of Mexico, where the Olmec built several important centers filled with ceremonial architecture and stone monuments famous for their size and precocious realism. Most famous are enormous, life-like heads that probably represent Olmec rulers. The identities of smaller human figures like the one from which this exquisite, sensual fragment comes are less certain, but their connection to rulership is suggested by their fineness and material, often jadeite, the most precious medium that ancient Mesoamerican artists worked.

The figure to which the fragment belonged was unusually large and either stood upright or sat on something, such as a throne. The pillowy flesh beneath the eyes, the carefully delineated teeth, and the fleshiness of the lips, which are parted as though in speech, help to convey a remarkable sense of vitality. The profile face of a supernatural being is incised just in front of each ear, perhaps indicating that the subject had special power.

JADEITE; 7.4 X 6.2 X 5 CM (2-7/8 X 2-1/2 X 2 IN.)
PURCHASE FROM THE J. H. WADE FUND 1961.31

Vessel with Battle Scene 600–900
MESOAMERICA, MAYA STYLE

Maya art is above all a courtly art that chronicles the lives of the royalty who governed cities scattered from Guatemala's rainforests to the Yucatán Peninsula. Though independent, these cities were intertwined through political alliances, war, and trade. Together their fortunes rose and fell, blossoming into an extraordinary period of expansion and artistic achievement between AD 600 and 900. During this period, the Maya lived in a crowded political landscape torn by rivalries in which elites scrambled to gain advantage. The scene on this vessel commemorates the importance of such power struggles.

Likely used as a gift to cement a political relationship, the vessel depicts a battle's aftermath: the presentation of prisoners. A front-facing lord, who wears

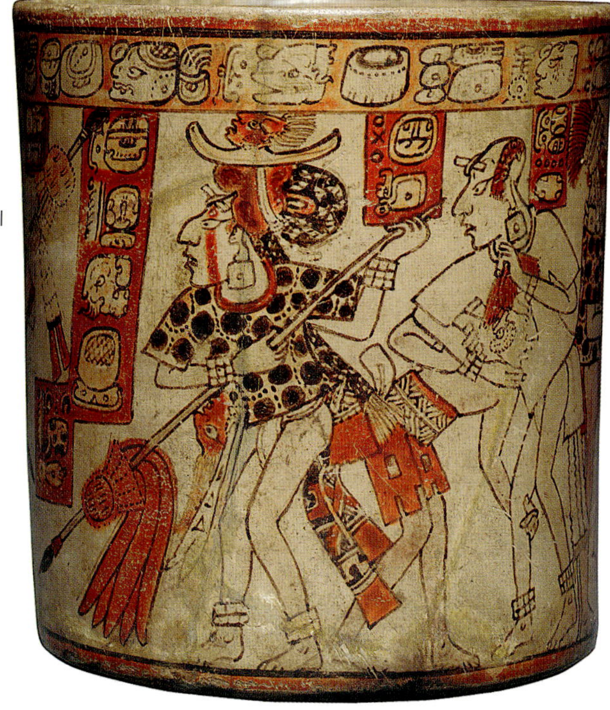

a loincloth and straw hat, turns to review 10 elegantly drawn warriors, some humiliated and stripped of battle regalia and others dressed in elaborate headgear and garments sometimes made of jaguar pelts. The hieroglyphs encircling the rim dedicate the vessel, used to drink an elite beverage made of cacao (chocolate) beans. The vessel belongs to a group of seven similar vases painted by the same master artist in the Nebaj region of Guatemala.

CERAMIC, SLIP; H. 16.9 CM (6-5/8 IN.)

JOHN L. SEVERANCE FUND 2012.32

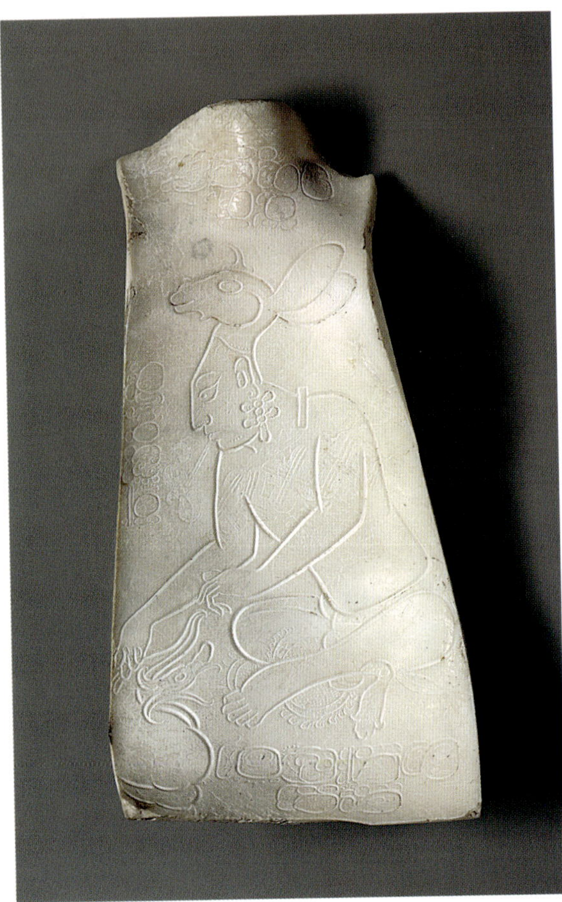

Shell with Seated Noble 600–900

MESOAMERICA, MAYA STYLE

This beautiful plaque, perhaps meant to be held for close viewing, is incised with the image of a nobleman who wears a loincloth and a deer headdress as he gestures toward a serpent-headed conch shell, perhaps the same type of conch from which the plaque is made. The deeply carved lines that define the figure contrast with the lighter, more delicate incising used to detail the loincloth, a thin cigar with its wisps of smoke, and a patterned band across the chest that could represent body paint or tattooing. The hieroglyphs scattered across the surface give the name of the male depicted—Jewel Jaguar—and mention a locale known as Sun Water (*k'ina'*), which may have been located in the Usumacinta River region of Guatemala or Mexico.

CONCH SHELL; 16.6 X 7.9 X 3.5 CM (6-1/2 X 3-1/8 X 1-3/8 IN.)

THE NORWEB COLLECTION 1965.550

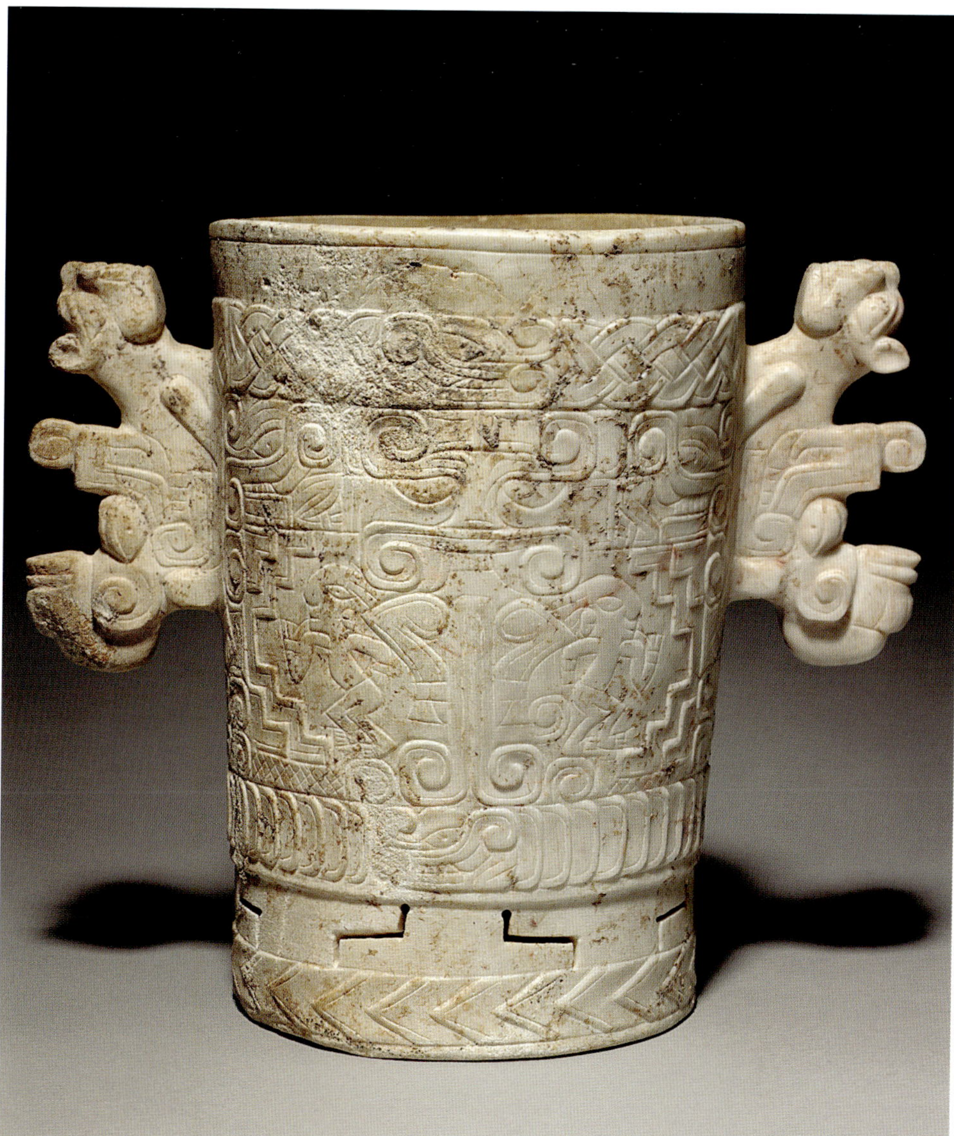

Vessel 700–1000

MESOAMERICA, ULÚA VALLEY

Made by eastern neighbors of the Maya, this marble vessel is one of the finest and largest of its kind. On the exterior are several typical motifs that combine to create a design of unusual complexity, a visual puzzle. Key is a grotesque head, either in profile or front-facing, with a leg near its mouth. For instance, in the main panel a frontal version of the head hovers over two disembodied legs, the knees pointed sharply outward. Beside each leg is a lively (and rare) human. The vessel's handles play out the same theme: the grotesque head, here with clearly upturned snout, disgorges (or ingests) a feline with splayed front legs that are lightly incised on the vessel's surface. Little is known about the meanings of the motifs or the uses these vessels served. A few have been found in tombs.

MARBLE; 27 X 30.3 X 17.4 CM (10-5/8 X 11-7/8 X 6-7/8 IN.)

JOHN L. SEVERANCE FUND 1990.9

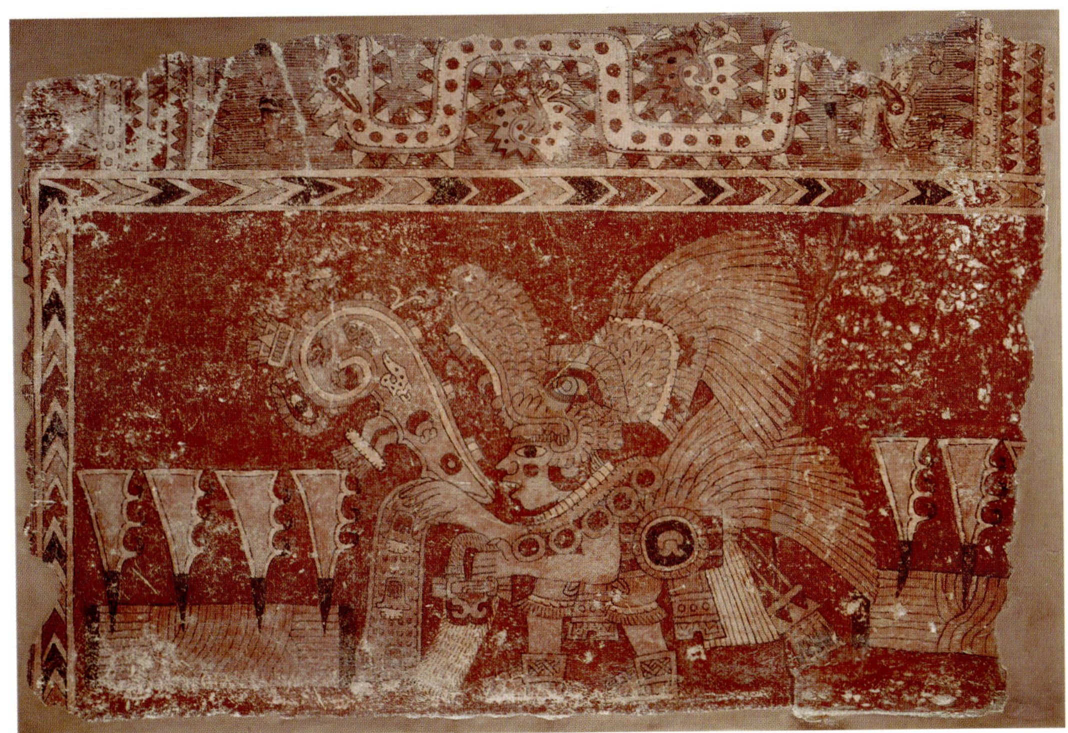

Mural Fragment with Elite Male 650–750

MESOAMERICA, TEOTIHUÁCAN, TLACUILAPAXCO APARTMENT COMPOUND, TEOTIHUACÁN STYLE

In the first century BC, Teotihuacán exploded into being and went on to establish itself as Mesoamerica's premier city. Contemporary with the Maya, Teotihuacán wielded far greater influence through trade and diplomatic networks. So exalted was its reputation that, five centuries after its fall, the Aztecs called it "The Place of the Gods." The name has some reality: Teotihuacán's monumental architecture implies that the city was viewed as the seat of creation, and the city's mural art—much of it found in the apartment complexes of wealthy elites—shows an earthly paradise populated by deities and humans whose hands pour forth streams of riches.

This well-dressed male belonged to a row of identical figures who processed along the walls of a patio in an apartment compound near one of the city's most important temples. He utters a chant or prayer, materialized in the scroll that emerges from his mouth, and a flower-filled libation cascades from one hand. In the other hand, he carries an incense bag. The thorny, triangular leaves of the maguey (agave) cactus, in front and behind, may allude to the offering of precious blood and a ritual beverage made from the cactus's sap (pulque, a less refined form of tequila). The leaves are thrust into objects that may represent bundles or plots of land.

FRESCO; 83.2 X 116.2 CM (32-3/4 X 45-3/4 IN.)
PURCHASE FROM THE J. H. WADE FUND 1963.252

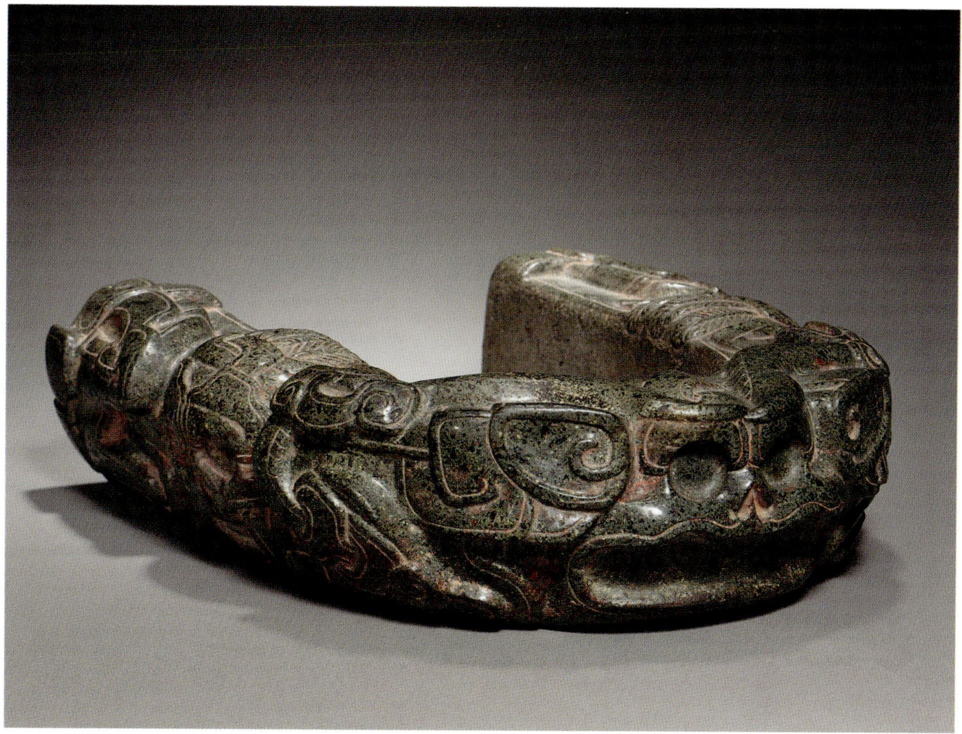

Ballgame Hip Protector (Yoke) 600–900

MESOAMERICA, CLASSIC VERACRUZ STYLE

The ancient ballgame played on Mexico's Gulf Coast seems to have had profound purpose: to assure the cycles of planetary bodies that control seasonal alternation and agricultural fertility. These cycles were likely viewed as contests between cosmic forces for which the ballgame served as earthly expression. Testimony to the struggle's violence lay in the sacrifice of ballplayers, whose deaths may have assured rebirth of the sun from darkness. Players apparently could not use their hands to return the solid rubber ball during play, bouncing it instead from their hips and perhaps their knees and elbows.

U-shaped ballgame sculptures like this one imitate the shape of belt-like protectors, perhaps made of wood and padding, worn to shield ballplayers from injury during play. This fine example embodies a major theme of the ballgame: the connection between fertility and death. It is made of greenstone, a precious material that through its color symbolizes the lush burgeoning of nature after the rainy season. The imagery, however, is menacing: a monstrous head snarls from the curve, and human skulls appear on the sides.

GREENSTONE, PIGMENT; 41.5 X 37.5 X 11 CM (16-3/8 X 14-3/4 X 4-3/8 IN.)

LEONARD C. HANNA JR. FUND 1973.213

Ballgame Thin Stone Head (Hacha) 600–900

MESOAMERICA, CLASSIC VERACRUZ STYLE

In contrast to other small-scale ballgame sculptures, such as the U-shaped hip protector (p. 327), it seems unlikely that thin stone heads, known as *hachas,* are renditions of actual ballgame gear. Their function, which may have determined the peculiar wedge shape they have when viewed from the front, remains unclear. The notch at the back of most examples, however, suggests they might have served as architectural ornaments during ceremonies concerning the game. Also, in a few artistic depictions of game activities, such heads rest on U-shaped hip protectors.

In this elegant example, a tapering headdress, its base formed by a grotesque head with upturned snout, soars above a serene human face of obscure identity. It could represent a heroic, idealized player, a ballgame patron, or a character from the game's lore. The large area of red pigment on one side may have been sprinkled onto the head after it was buried in an offering or a tomb.

STONE, PIGMENT; 61.6 X 20 X 8.8 CM (24-1/4 X 7-7/8 X 3-1/2 IN.)

SEVERANCE AND GRETA MILLIKIN PURCHASE FUND 2001.89

Seated Male Carrying Maize 1325–1521

MESOAMERICA, AZTEC STYLE

In the few centuries before the Spaniards arrived in the Americas, the Aztecs built an empire that spanned most of central Mexico. Today the Aztecs are often imagined as savages fond of human sacrifice—a reputation they cultivated to intimidate their enemies. But they were also talented engineers, religious philosophers convinced of the sacredness of all existence, keen historians, and artists who created a unique, distinctive style.

An unusual example of that style, this appealing figure probably represents an Aztec deity, either Macuilxochitl ("Five Flower") or Xochipilli ("Flower Prince"), whose domain was beauty, the arts, and such pleasures as game playing, dancing, and sex. Both names include the Aztec word for "flower," and in one hand the figure holds a cone of flowers, perhaps the blossoming crown of a cactus. For the Aztecs, flowers were richly metaphoric, signifying beauty and refinement as well as fertility in general and sexuality in particular. The burden of maize cobs on his back also may allude to this deity's creative, positive energies.

STONE, PIGMENT; 31.1 X 24.1 X 30.5 CM (12-1/4 X 9-1/2 X 12 IN.)

THE NORWEB COLLECTION 1949.555

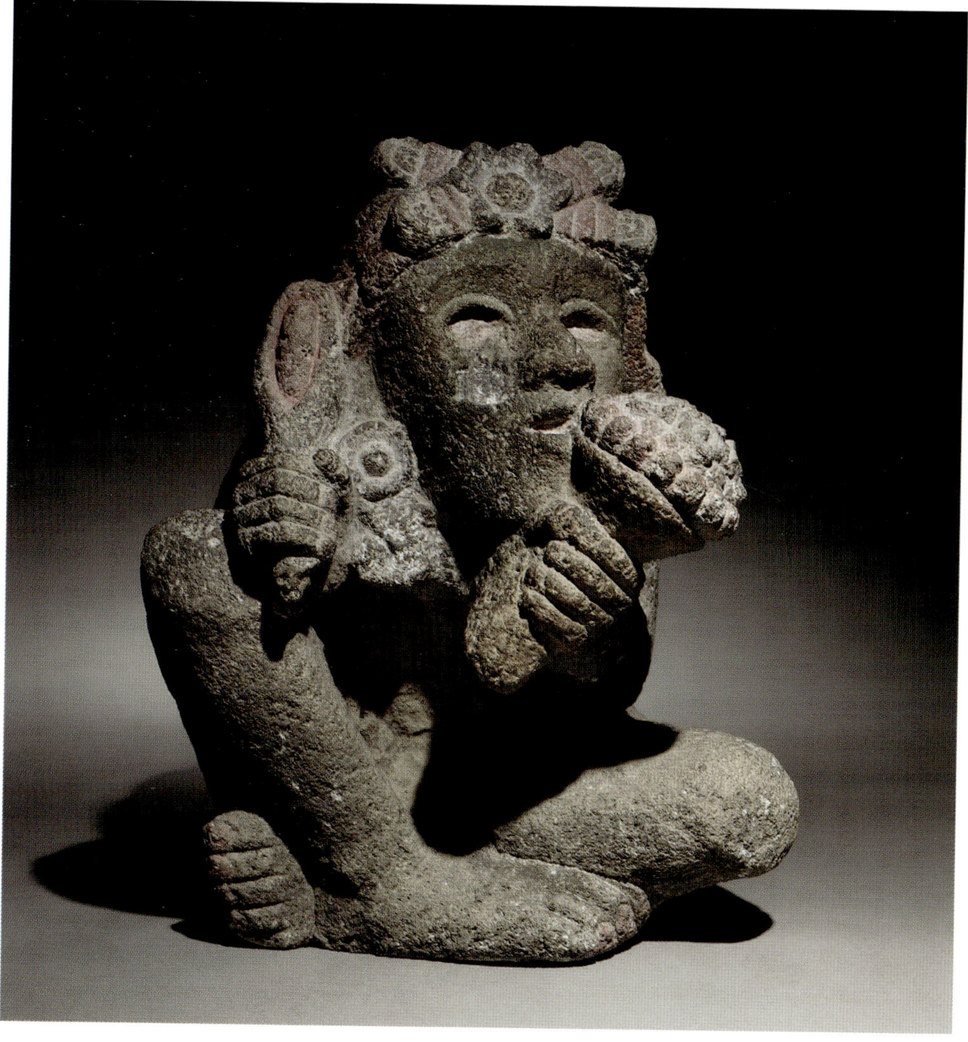

Animal Effigy Vessel 1000–1550

COSTA RICA OR NICARAGUA, NICOYA REGION, PATAKY POLYCHROME STYLE

By the time this high-status vessel was made, people had been living for more than two thousand years in the territory occupied by Costa Rica, which in antiquity comprised three cultural regions: the northwestern Nicoya area, which extended into Nicaragua; Diquís in the southwest; and the Atlantic Watershed, east of the continental divide. This vessel, executed in the Pataky polychrome style, comes from the northwest, famous for imaginative ceramics whose vivid colors, fluid line, and abstraction have contemporary appeal.

The Pataky style excels in animal portrayals that combine a modeled head—commonly a feline's but in this case perhaps that of a fox or coatimundi—with a pear-shaped chamber that doubles as the animal's body. The meanings of these animals are not well understood but it may be important that, as here, many strike distinctly human poses; creatures that combine the human and animal often have mythic or supernatural import, and some Pataky examples have been interpreted as representations of shamans. The two-dimensional motifs painted beneath the vessel's rim are thought to be inspired by central Mexican art, although the exact nature and extent of Mesoamerican influence in Costa Rica is still under investigation. Many Pataky polychrome vessels show no evidence of wear and for this reason are thought to have been created specifically for funerary purposes.

CERAMIC, SLIP; 29.5 X 22.1 X 29.8 CM (11-5/8 X 8-3/4 X 11-3/4 IN.)

LEONARD C. HANNA JR. FUND 1997.3

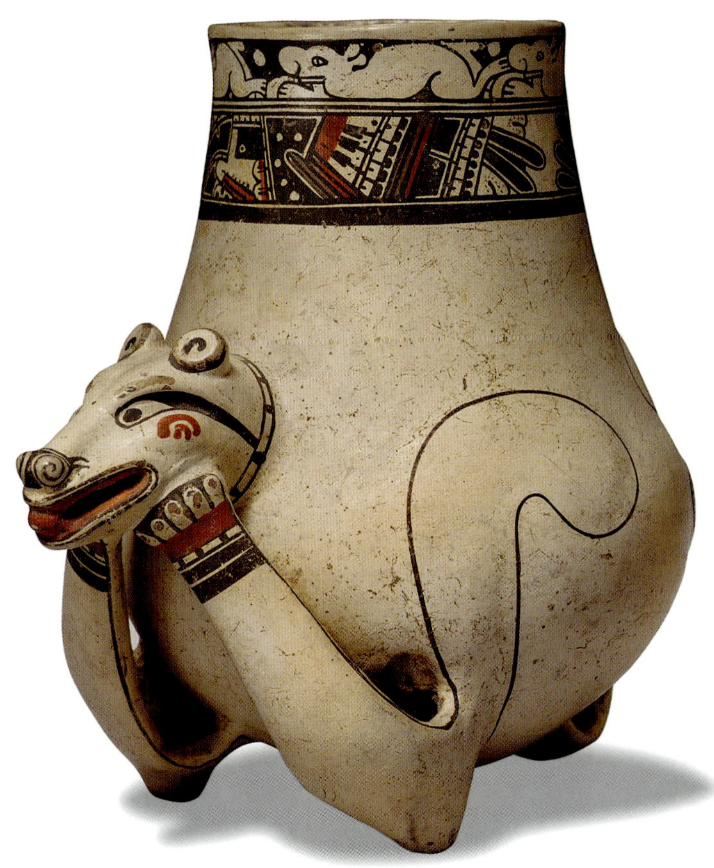

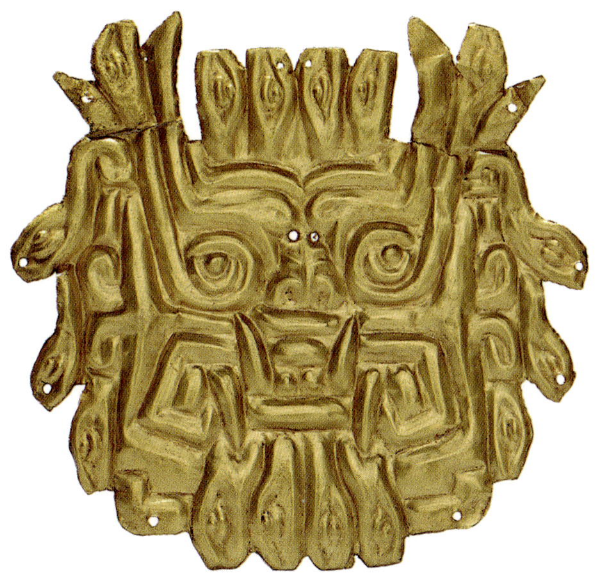

Head-Shaped Plaque 1200–500 BC

CENTRAL ANDES, CHONGOYAPE?, CHAVÍN STYLE

One of the Andean region's most complex early art styles developed at the temples of Chavín de Huántar. Chavín art was devoted to expressing a religion that people in far-flung regions found appealing; the site became a pilgrimage center and arts depicting Chavín deities spread to many areas of the Andes, where they co-existed with local art styles and religious cults. Many of these objects portray the supernatural creatures that were central to Chavín religion and draw their features from fearsome predators: felines, raptors, and the caiman.

This impressive gold ornament depicts the head of one of the most important of these divine beings—the so-called Staff Deity, its mouth bristling with fangs and its hair or fur transformed into writhing serpents. When turned upside-down, the head recomposes into a second face that might represent an aspect of the Staff Deity or a creature related to the deity. The plaque, which apparently was stitched to a backing via the holes that pierce the edges, may belong to a large group of Chavín-style gold objects found in a very wealthy tomb (or tombs) in the late 1920s near Chongoyape, a town on Peru's north coast.

GOLD; 12.5 X 13.8 CM (4-7/8 X 5-3/8 IN.)

DUDLEY P. ALLEN FUND 1938.431

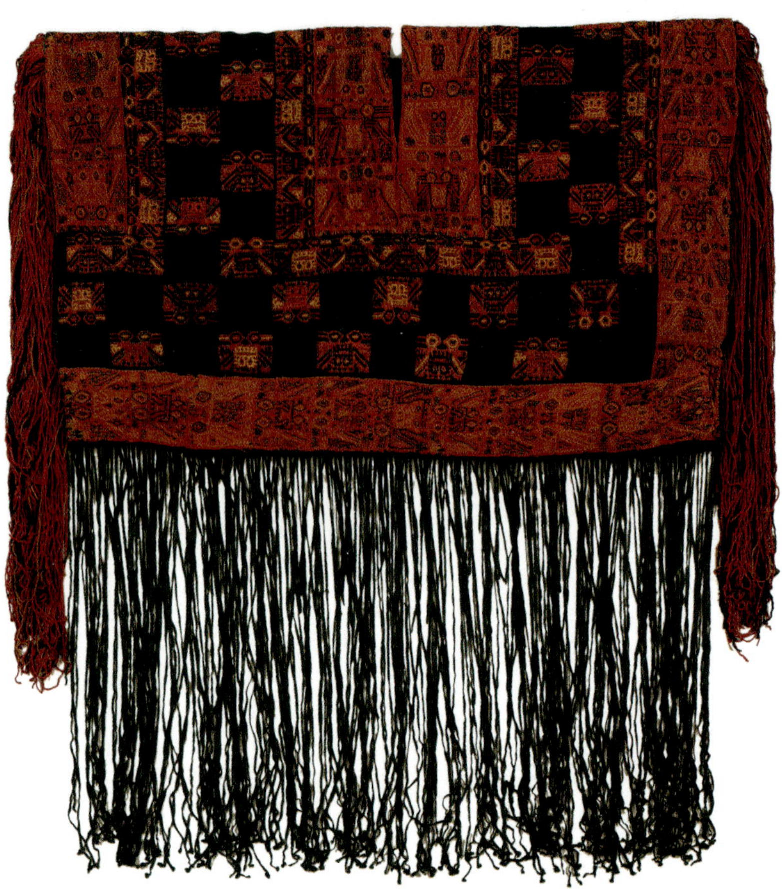

Tunic 300 BC–AD 100

CENTRAL ANDES, PROBABLY PARACAS PENINSULA, PARACAS STYLE

Around 700 BC, the Paracas culture began to take form on Peru's south coast, a desert watered unpredictably by rivers that flow down from the eastern Andes Mountains. Living in modest farming villages in these river valleys, the Paracas poured their artistic energies into creating one of the New World's most famous textile traditions. This lavishly fringed tunic—together with a matching mantle (shawl-like garment) and headband in the museum's collection—is similar to textiles recovered from a renowned cemetery known as the Paracas Necropolis, located on the Paracas Peninsula.

In use between about 300 BC and AD 100, the cemetery contained more than four hundred mummy bundles of varying sizes, each created by wrapping a human body in cloth. (In one instance, 45 pounds of beans replaced the corpse, suggesting that ancestors were tied to fertility.) In small bundles, the cloth was plain; in the less common larger bundles, some nearly five feet tall, plain shrouds alternated with colorful, elaborately decorated garments like the museum's tunic, mantle, and headband, all of which are embroidered with the image of a two-headed bird rendered in different color combinations and orientations. It is not clear whether the textiles formed a set that an important Paracas man wore as an ensemble.

CAMELID FIBER; 147.3 X 73.7 CM (58 X 29 IN.)

THE NORWEB COLLECTION 1946.227

Shell with Feline 100 BC–AD 650

CENTRAL ANDES, NASCA STYLE

Between about 100 BC and AD 650, the Nasca occupied a cluster of neighboring valleys on Peru's desert south coast, where, scattered in small communities and hamlets, they patiently coaxed the parched, austere land into bloom using scarce water from rivers that too often slowed to a trickle. Existence was precarious, and the Nasca seem to have devoted much of their ceremonial life to anxious attempts to assure the seasonal flow of water, the renewal of the land, and the endurance of those who lived on it.

This inlaid ornament likely relates to those concerns since it is made of one valve of a reddish-orange *Spondylus* shell, a thorny oyster here scraped clean of its characteristic spines. Many ancient Andean people attributed the power of fecundity to *Spondylus* and used it either whole or ground into powder as a crucial component of rain-making rites. The little feline that appears on the shell seems to confirm these associations. It represents a pampas cat, a wild predator not much larger than a domestic cat that preys on small agricultural pests and in art is often associated with beans and other crops, here the golden fruit or vegetable that it clutches in one paw. The cat may have been regarded as a guardian of ripening fields.

SPONDYLUS SHELL, SHELL, STONE, GOLD; 7.5 X 7.4 CM (3 X 2-7/8 IN.)

IN MEMORY OF MR. AND MRS. HENRY HUMPHREYS, GIFT OF THEIR DAUGHTER HELEN 1950.567

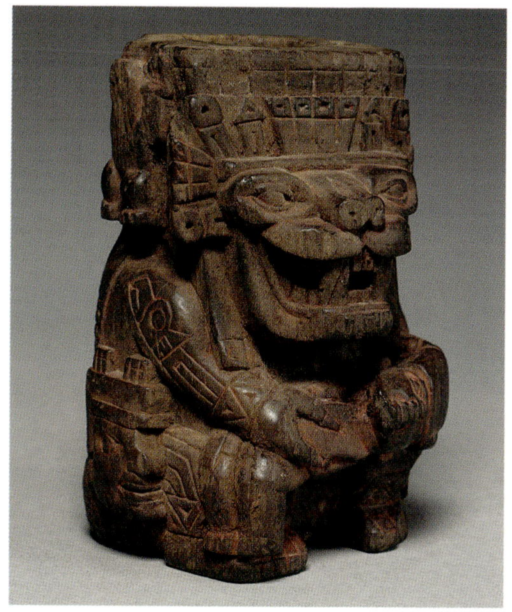

Sacrificer Container 769–887

CENTRAL ANDES, WARI STYLE

Between 600 and 1000, the Wari created a cosmopolitan polity that many today regard as Peru's first empire. The legacy that the Wari left includes a number of impressive urban centers in the highlands, along with a corpus of finely made elite arts buried in offerings and in tombs both in the highlands and in Pacific coastal regions to the west of the Andes mountain range. This wood container, now missing its upper stopper, was likely found on the Peruvian coast, where arid desert conditions encouraged its preservation.

The container is carved in the shape of a magnificent, feline-headed supernatural creature who draws a broad knife across the throat of the human victim it holds in its lap; severed human heads hang from the feline's belt and dangle by the trachea at the back of its headdress. As the container suggests, the Wari seem to have practiced human sacrifice, probably as an unusual and exceptionally precious offering made to entice the benevolence of cosmic forces. The container's function is unknown. Its inner surface retains invisible traces of cinnabar, the red-orange pigment that is more apparent on the exterior.

WOOD, CINNABAR; 10.8 X 7 X 7.5 CM (4-1/4 X 2-3/4 X 3 IN.)

JOHN L. SEVERANCE FUND 2007.193.A–B

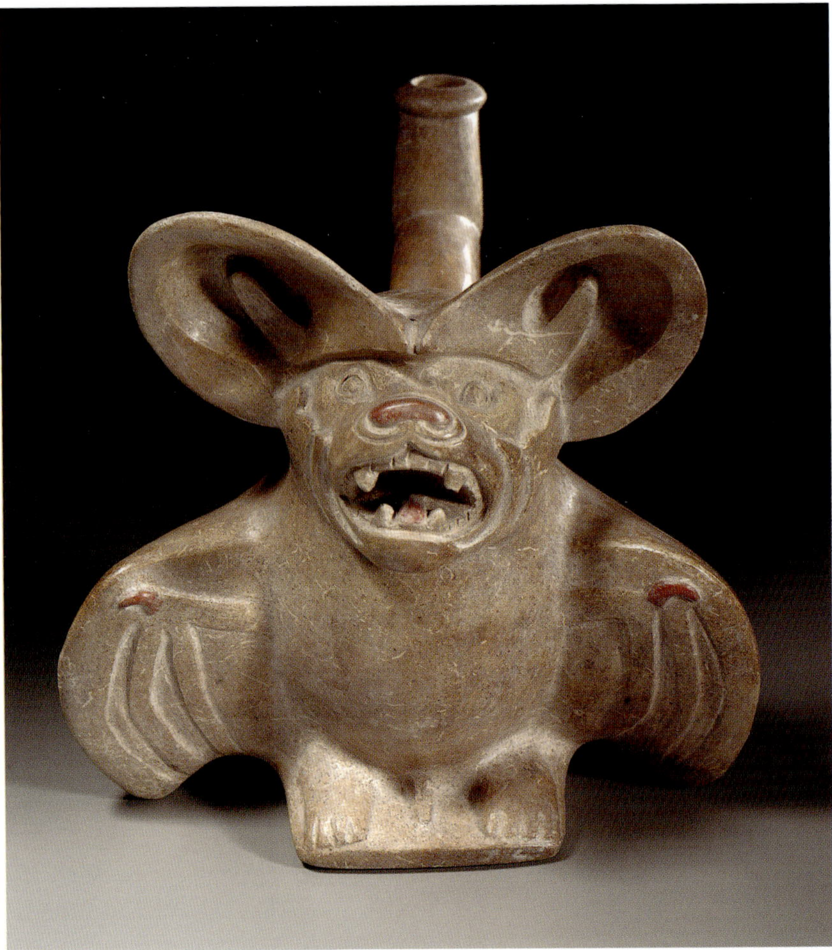

Mastiff (Dog-Faced) Bat Vessel 200–850

CENTRAL ANDES, MOCHE STYLE

Moche territory on Peru's north coast was divided into northern and southern spheres, each of which had somewhat different artistic emphases. This vessel may be from northern Moche territory, which is noted for the exceptionally fine sculptural ceramics made there in early Moche times.

The vessel illustrates two principles of the Moche art style. First is its keen interest in realism: the bat's head is depicted with great fidelity, including the folds on the face, the architecture of the ear, and the small, indistinct eyes. Second is its focus on capturing activity at its peak: the bat seems to be portrayed as though dropping from its roost, just before spreading its wings to take flight. Though the significance of bats in Moche art is not well studied, they seem to carry complex symbolism that, in this instance, may be linked to the Peruvian hairless dog, which in Moche art appears in ritual scenes and also has large, rounded ears.

CERAMIC, SLIP; 18.4 X 17.7 X 15.8 CM (7-1/4 X 7 X 6-1/4 IN.)

JOHN L. SEVERANCE FUND 2005.6

Nose Ornament 200–850

CENTRAL ANDES, MOCHE STYLE

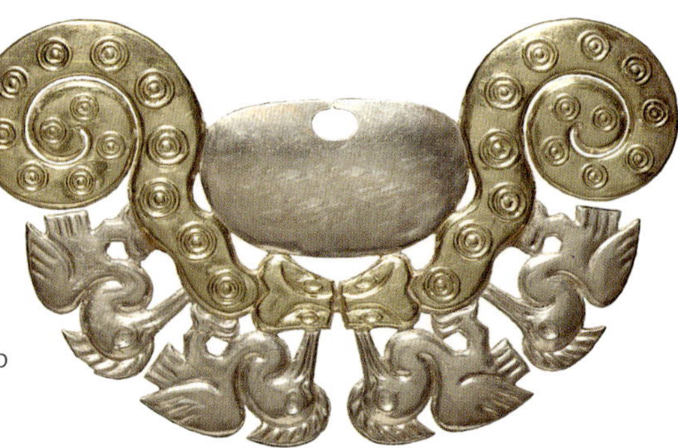

At its height, the Moche realm spanned a 400-mile swath of Peru's north coast, a desert made habitable by fertile river valleys that sheltered administrative-religious centers. Although the Moche shared features of culture, including a realistic art style, the centers were independent of one another. The largest has two enormous structures, together built of some 193 million adobe bricks, that attest the power of Moche lords, who were buried in tombs filled with fine ceramics as well as gold and silver ornaments. This example, which hung from the septum of the nose to cover the wearer's mouth, combines serpents and long-necked birds in an elegant composition whose symbolism may have lodged as much in the color of the metals as in the imagery.

The Moche were among the most inventive metalsmiths in the Andes, and they developed many complex techniques for joining and enriching the surfaces of metals, which they usually worked by hammering rather than casting. This ornament was made by first joining gold and silver sheets through heating and hammering. Then came the relief decoration, followed by the selective removal of metal along the joins. Finally, the ornament was trimmed and polished.

GOLD AND SILVER; 7.6 X 13.9 CM (3 X 5-1/2 IN.)

SEVERANCE AND GRETA MILLIKIN PURCHASE FUND 2005.177

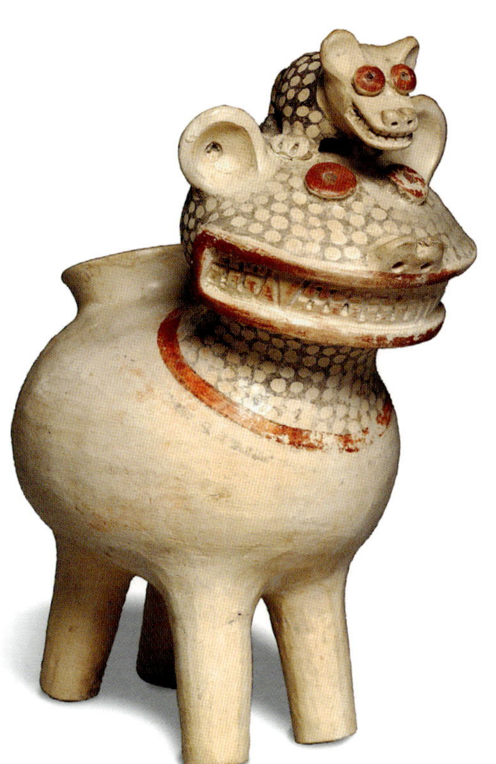

Feline Vessel 1–700

CENTRAL ANDES, RECUAY STYLE

Contemporaries of the north coast Moche, the chiefdoms of the Recuay culture flourished in the Callejón de Huaylas, a large basin between mountain ranges in Peru's north highlands. There, between about AD 1 and 700, the Recuay developed a distinctive art style in stone sculpture, textiles, and ceramics, the last unusual in their occasional use of white rather than terracotta colored clay for either the vessel or the slip used to paint it.

Recuay art is understudied and it is difficult to know the meaning of this wonderfully stylized feline on whose head perches a small passenger that may be a coatimundi, a nosy, busy, raccoon-like animal. Elsewhere in Recuay art, felines are shown as virile predators, making it likely that in general they were symbols of leadership. The feline is painted with white and red slips; after firing, a resist application of black pigment was used to create the dotted pattern.

CERAMIC, SLIP, PIGMENT; 20.3 X 10.1 X 15.2 CM (8 X 4 X 6 IN.)

THE CHARLOTTE EKKER AND CHARLOTTE VAN DER VEER MEMORIAL FUND 2009.9

Gold Ornaments from Sitio Conte

In the 1930s, archaeologists from Harvard University excavated at a famous cemetery at Sitio Conte in the Coclé Province of central Panama. They uncovered a total of 59 graves and classified them as small, intermediate, and large, the last each containing many bodies and hundreds of objects, including multitudes of gold ornaments ranging from helmets to necklaces, pectorals, arm bands, ear ornaments, and the like.

The largest of the large tombs was Grave 26, the origin of the museum's chest plaque and rod-shaped ear ornament; the plaque was one of many objects deposited near the tomb's main occupant while the ear ornament was found with the remains of one of the more than 20 other individuals buried in the tomb. Specialists usually interpret Grave 26 and others like it as the resting places of chiefs and the retainers who accompanied them in death. According to Spanish sources, the region's most powerful chiefs were interred in the 16th century in this way—armored in gold, the supreme symbol of power and rank, and with many companions.

The impressive, front-facing creature on the chest plaque merges the body of a human with the claws of a reptile and streaming head appendages that may be inspired by

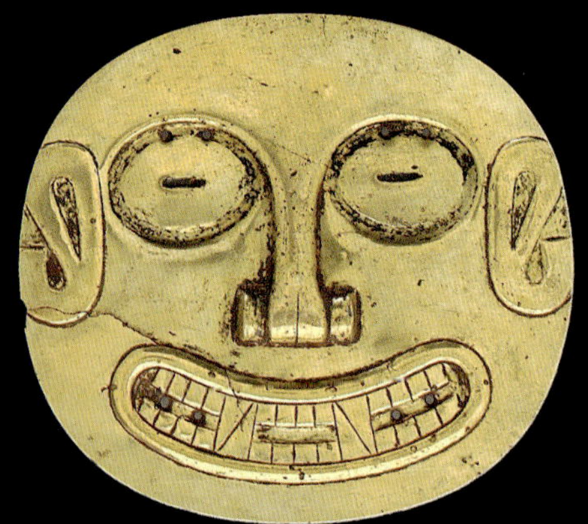

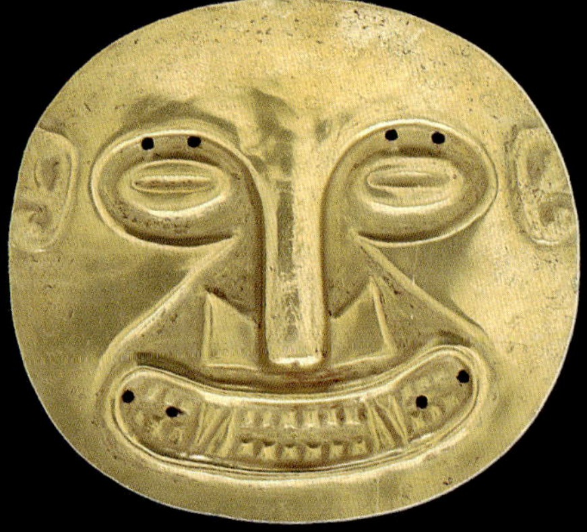

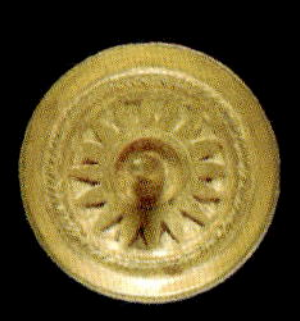

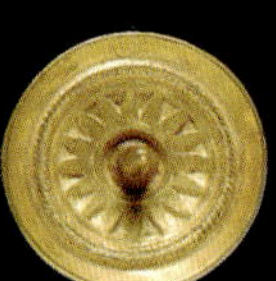

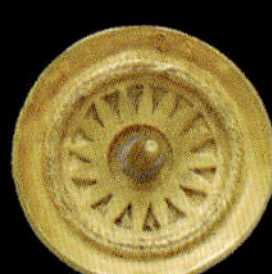

Rod-Shaped Ear Ornament, 400–900. Panama, Conte style. Gold with greenstone; L. 15.5 cm (6-1/4 in.), Diam. 2 cm (3/4 in.). John L. Severance Fund 1951.547

Two Plaques, 400–900. Panama, Conte style. Gold; 9.3 x 10 cm (3-5/8 x 3-7/8 in.) and 10.5 x 11.3 cm (4-1/8 x 4-1/2 in.). The Norweb Collection 1951.155 and John L. Severance Fund 1954.390

Three Ear Ornaments, 400–900. Panama, Conte style. Gold; 3.1 x 3.2 cm (1-1/8 x 1-1/4 in.) each. Robert Holden Bole Fund 1958.191.1–2 and 1958.192

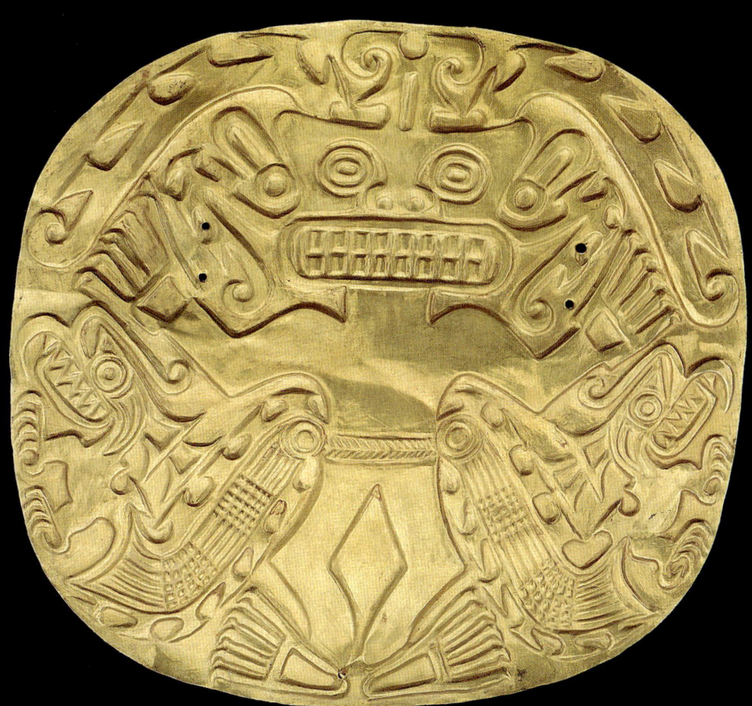

an iguana's head crest. The meaning of this composite being is unknown but perhaps, as in later periods, reptilian imagery and the warm gleam of gold linked the chiefly wearer with the sun's creative force. If so, chiefs may have been esteemed as mediators between the human community and the cosmic realm, perhaps explaining their association with iguanas, which today are regarded as powerful mediators among the layers of the universe and as symbols of cosmic creative energy. Modern natives in the isthmus region also associate iguanas with knowledge, power, and correct social behavior—all traits of effective chiefs.

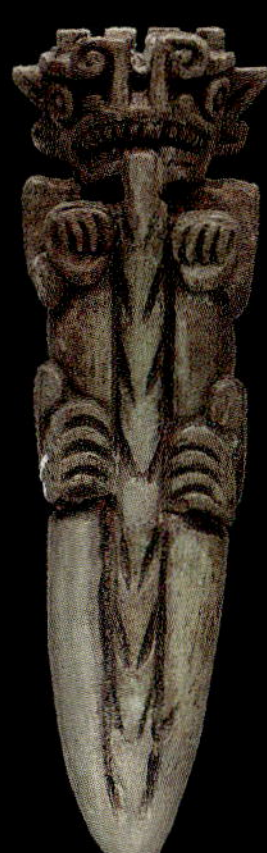

Chest Plaque, 400–900. Panama, Conte style. Gold; 25.1 x 26.7 cm (9-7/8 x 10-1/2 in.). Gift of Mrs. R. Henry Norweb, Mrs. Albert S. Ingalls, with additions from the John L. Severance Fund 1952.459

Animal-Shaped Ornament, 400–900. Panama, Conte style. Gold; 4.3 x 5.5 x 14 cm (1-3/4 x 2-1/8 x 5-1/2 in.). John L. Severance Fund 1951.318

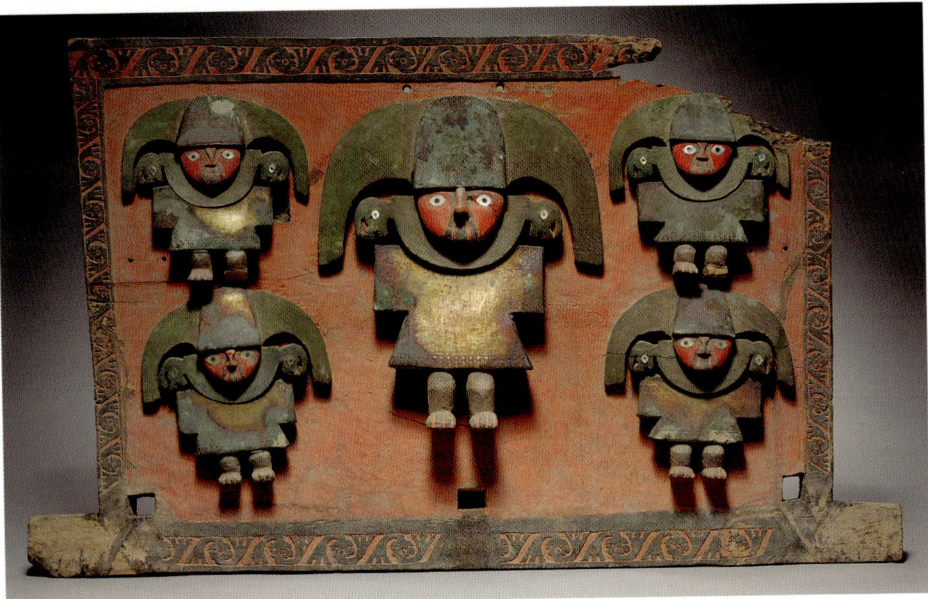

Backrest of a Litter 900–1460s

CENTRAL ANDES, CHIMÚ STYLE

The Chimú grew out of the Moche, their north coast predecessors, and went on to build the only empire to develop on the Andean coast. At Chan Chan, their capital, Chimú rulers lived in palaces that were the centers of art production so vast it may have occupied 10,000 artists at the empire's height. Chimú kings presumably distributed these objects to cultivate alliances, and many fine examples were buried in royal tombs so rich that, after the conquest, the Spaniards issued permits to mine them.

This rare, dramatic Chimú object served as the back support of a litter carried by human porters, a mode of transport reserved for honored members of many societies without draft animals or wheeled vehicles. The simple, bold figures—perhaps a Chimú lord and four officials of his domain—all wear wide collars, tunics, and crescent headdresses that are either brightly painted or covered with golden but now-corroded sheet metal. The holes at the bottom served as lashing points for beams that supported the litter's seat; while riding in the litter, the occupant leaned against the undecorated side of the backrest.

WOOD, PIGMENT, GOLD ALLOY, SHELL; 60.4 X 95 CM (23-3/4 X 37-3/8 IN.)

JOHN L. SEVERANCE FUND 1952.233

Tunic 900–1460s

CENTRAL ANDES, CHIMÚ STYLE

This tunic, an article of men's wear, belongs to a relatively small group of Chimú garments described as the "Pelican style" after the type of bird that often appears in the textiles' imagery. Here, the difficult-to-see birds are confined to narrow borders on the tunic's edges while the body is given over to horizontal registers of geometric stepped motifs. Another trait that unifies the style is the masterfully hand-spun yarns used to fabricate the garments; made entirely of undyed white cotton, the yarns are extremely fine, each measuring a mere 0.1 to 0.2 millimeters in diameter. Other kinds of Pelican-style garments in the museum's collection include a large mantle (or hanging), a huge loincloth, a turban, a padded hat, and two narrow, tasseled bands.

The garments express an important aspect of the Chimú textile aesthetic: a penchant for combining different, structurally achieved textures and surfaces, some heavy and sculptural and others so airy and fine they are nearly invisible. In the tunic, for instance, the fabric varies from areas of sheer, filmy transparency on the body to dense, more three-dimensional regions in the borders. Pelican-style garments are also an especially elegant articulation of the reduced, spare, and minimal visual vocabulary characteristic of the period.

COTTON; 57.2 X 151.1 CM (22-1/2 X 59-1/2 IN.)

SEVERANCE AND GRETA MILLIKIN PURCHASE FUND

2011.111.1

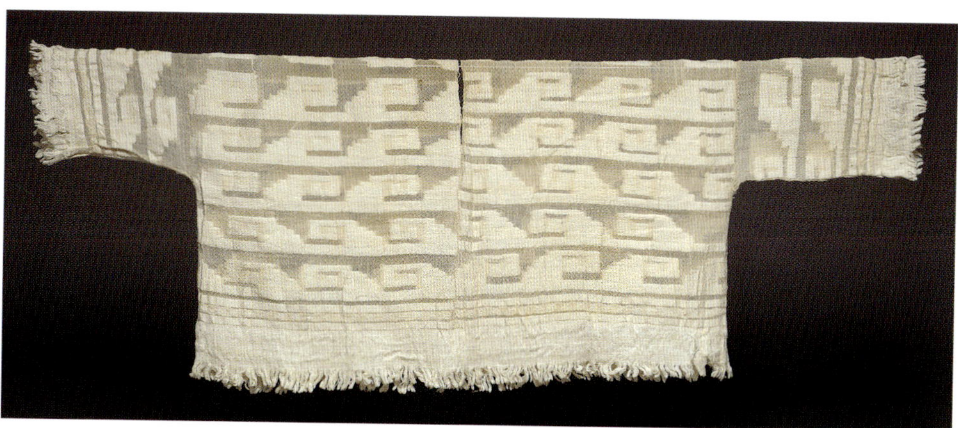

Feast Ladle late 1800s–early 1900s

NORTH AMERICA, NORTHWEST COAST, TLINGIT STYLE

At the time this feast ladle was made, many Northwest Coast societies devoted their art and ceremony to maintaining the social hierarchies of important families, and formal feasting occasions were important to these efforts. Such feasts occurred during potlatches and other ritual celebrations held during the winter ceremonial season, a time of renewal when people were free of the work of gathering food. Families organized these events to claim the right to inherit power and wealth, proving their worthiness to do so not only by hosting feasts but also by giving lavish gifts and exhibiting objects emblazoned with crests (treasured human and animal images that explain how families received many kinds of privileges from other-than-human beings). Unfortunately, the specific story behind the creatures portrayed on this impressive serving ladle—an imposing eagle and, on the underside of the bowl, a bear's head—has been lost. Such elaborate utensils, which included smaller spoons for eating, were the "family silver" of Northwest Coast noble clans.

MOUNTAIN SHEEP HORN, COW HORN, COPPER, SHELL; W. 13 CM (5-1/8 IN.), L. 44.2 CM (17-3/8 IN.)

THE HAROLD T. CLARK EDUCATIONAL EXTENSION FUND

1953.386

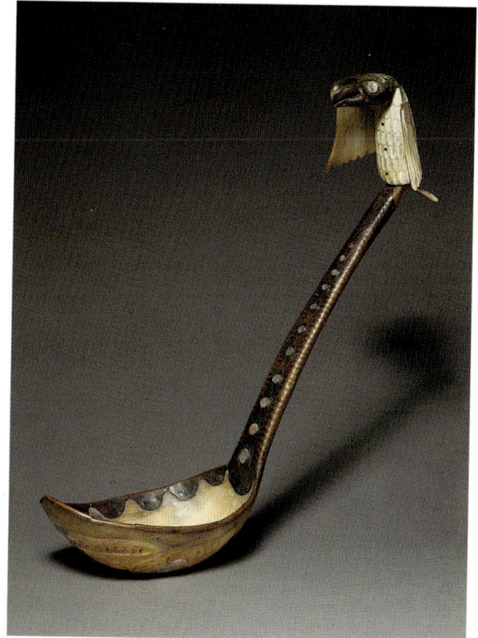

The Norweb Collection of Pre-Columbian Art

From the 1940s through the 1960s, Emery May Holden Norweb played a crucial role in developing the museum's Pre-Columbian collection, which today, as a partial result of her efforts and support, is one of the finest of its size in the country. Mrs. Norweb's interest in Pre-Columbian art probably stemmed from her experience of it in Latin America; her husband, R. Henry Norweb, served in high-level diplomatic positions, including ambassador, at the U.S. Embassies in Peru, Bolivia, Chile, and other Latin American countries. She was named a museum trustee in 1941, during the directorship of William M. Milliken, and was elected president of the board of trustees in 1962. She later acerbically remarked of that august event: "When I was asked to become president, I thought the foundation of the museum had probably collapsed. We were really moving with the times then—abstraction, French impressionism, and a woman president!"

During a chance meeting, Milliken introduced Mrs. Norweb to John Wise, one of the best-known and most active Pre-Columbian art dealers of his time. Milliken thought this encounter marked the beginning of her interest in developing the ancient American part of the museum's collection, although she had already amassed a private collection, including elaborate textiles said to come from the Paracas Necropolis on Peru's south coast. Mrs. Norweb donated these textiles to the museum in the 1940s, a gift that still forms the core of the Paracas holdings (see p. 332).

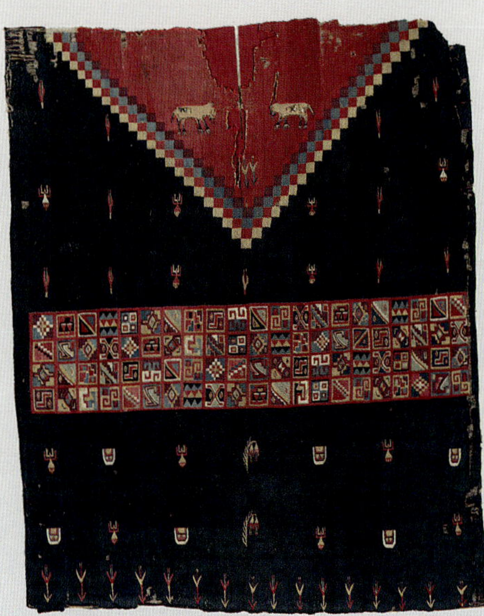

Half Tunic, after 1532. Central Andes, Colonial Inca style. Interlocked tapestry; camelid fiber and cotton; 95.3 x 72.4 cm (37-1/2 x 28-1/2 in.). The Norweb Collection 1951.393

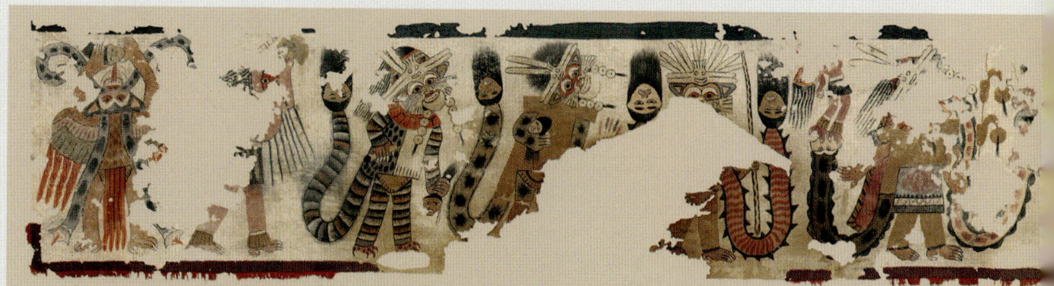

In all, the Pre-Columbian portion of the Norweb Collection (she also collected in several other areas, focusing her greatest attention on coins) contains more than 80 objects and textiles, some of which, like the Paracas textiles, are among the museum's finest representatives of their regions' artistic achievements. Among other Norweb works that serve as collection "signatures" are the three shown here (see also pp. 324 and 329). During her time on the board of trustees, she also supported the acquisition from other sources of about three hundred Pre-Columbian works of art, including a large Panamanian gold pectoral offered by John Wise for which she donated acquisition funds (see pp. 336–37).

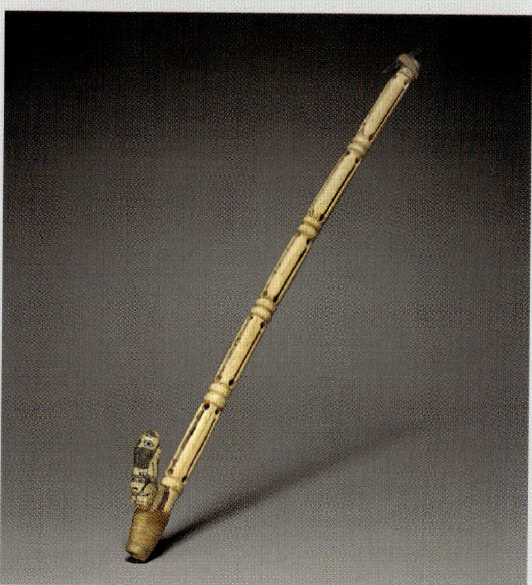

Cloth with Procession of Figures, 100 BC–AD 200. Central Andes, Nasca style. Cotton and pigment; 69.8 x 280.7 cm (27-1/2 x 110-1/2 in.). The Norweb Collection 1940.530

Spear Thrower, 200 BC–AD 200. Central Andes, late Paracas or early Nasca style. Bone, hematite, cotton thread, sinew; 5.8 x 2 x 48.3 cm (2-1/4 x 3/4 x 19 in.). The Norweb Collection 1940.507

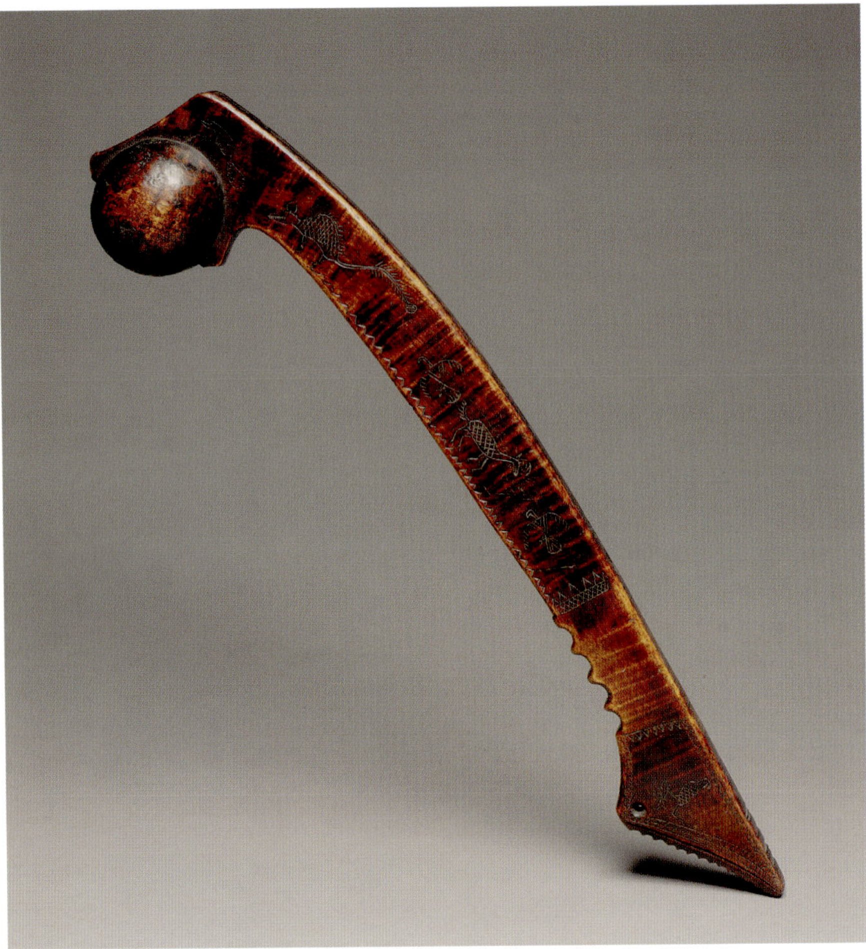

Ball-Headed War Club late 1700s–early 1800s
NORTH AMERICA, NORTHEAST WOODLANDS, GREAT LAKES

This well-designed weapon carries one of the richest, most beautiful known records of Great Lakes *nindoodem* (clan) images. These animal representations, incised on two sides of the shaft, represent clan ancestors that existed at the time of creation in the mythic past. Included is an antlered animal that may be a caribou along with other mammals (perhaps beavers, otters, or martens) and birds. Also present are the thunderbird, shown from above with wings outspread, and perhaps the long-tailed underwater panther, both powerful spirit beings. It is not known why the club refers so lavishly to clans, whose relationships shaped native politics through the 1800s.

The ball at the striking end is held within a jaws-like form that probably refers to an animal's muzzle. This abstract animal imagery invoked a protector being that endowed the club's owner with power.

WOOD (MAPLE?); 58.6 X 7.8 X 13.1 CM (23-1/8 X 3-1/8 X 5-1/8 IN.)

ANDREW R. AND MARTHA HOLDEN JENNINGS FUND 1991.21

Water Jar (Olla) 1850–60

NORTH AMERICA, SOUTHWEST, NEW MEXICO, ZUNI

The millennia-long heritage of ancient Southwest civilizations is alive today in the region's native cultures, which remain strong despite centuries of destructive colonization. Among Pueblo people, ceramic art is one of the most famous testaments of this continuity and each modern pueblo (village) has developed distinctive pottery styles, in part through creative dialogue with the past.

This ceramic—a jar that, balanced atop the head, was used to carry water—represents a painting style popular at New Mexico's Zuni pueblo in the later 19th century. The water well was a gathering place in villages across the southwest, and the public visibility of water-carrying vessels explains their elaborate decoration. The body of this example is painted with a beautifully abstracted rainbird whose black beak spirals between two stylized wings. The wings' stepped shape and hachure represent rain-filled clouds. The head of a bird, now without its body, also appears beneath the rim. The vessel apparently was well used; it shows signs of wear, especially at the rim.

CERAMIC, SLIP; 25.5 X 33 CM (10 X 13 IN.)

GIFT OF AMELIA ELIZABETH WHITE 1937.898

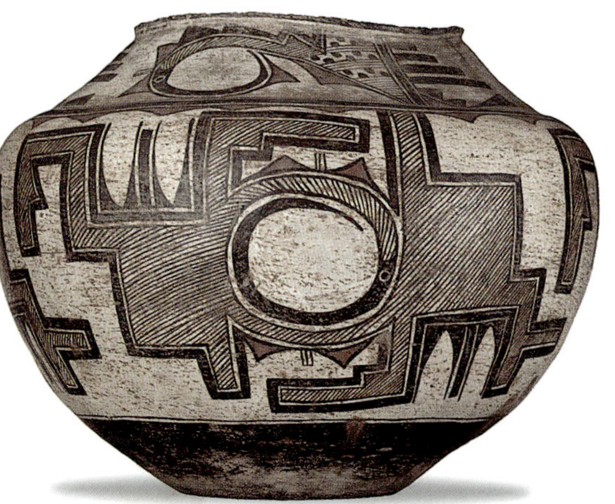

Tobacco Basket late 1800s

NORTH AMERICA, CALIFORNIA, YUROK

At the time of European contact, the principal native art of California was basketry, which depends aesthetically on contrasts of dark and light and geometric patterns with complex symmetries. In native communities before 1890, baskets served both ceremonial and practical purposes, the latter including food gathering, preparation, service, and storage. The 1892 Chicago World's Fair acquainted European Americans with baskets and stimulated a collecting craze that transformed native basket weaving and its economy.

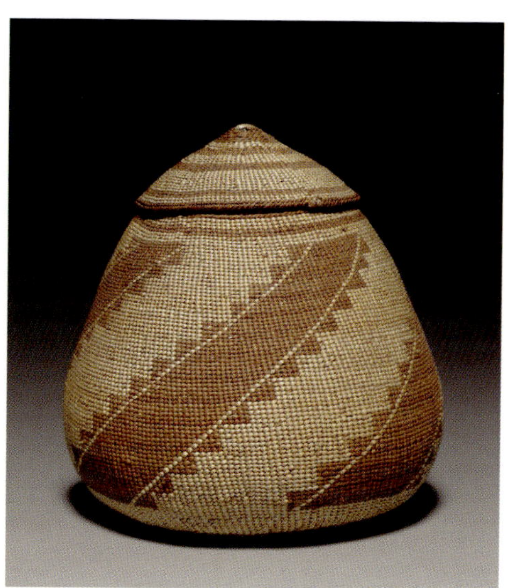

This exceptional Yurok basket is a document of that period: although made for the curio market at the turn of the 20th century, it has roots in native practice and belief concerning tobacco, which grew indigenously in California and sometimes was stored in lidded baskets made specifically for the purpose. The Yurok, for instance, believe that tobacco is a gift from a creator spirit. During World Renewal ceremonies, both in the past and today, they use it as a symbol of the yearly rebirth of the cosmos. They also smoke tobacco recreationally.

PLANT MATERIALS; H. 19 CM (7-1/2 IN.), W. 17 CM (6-3/4 IN.)

PRESENTED BY WILLIAM ALBERT PRICE IN MEMORY OF MRS. WILLIAM ALBERT PRICE 1917.498

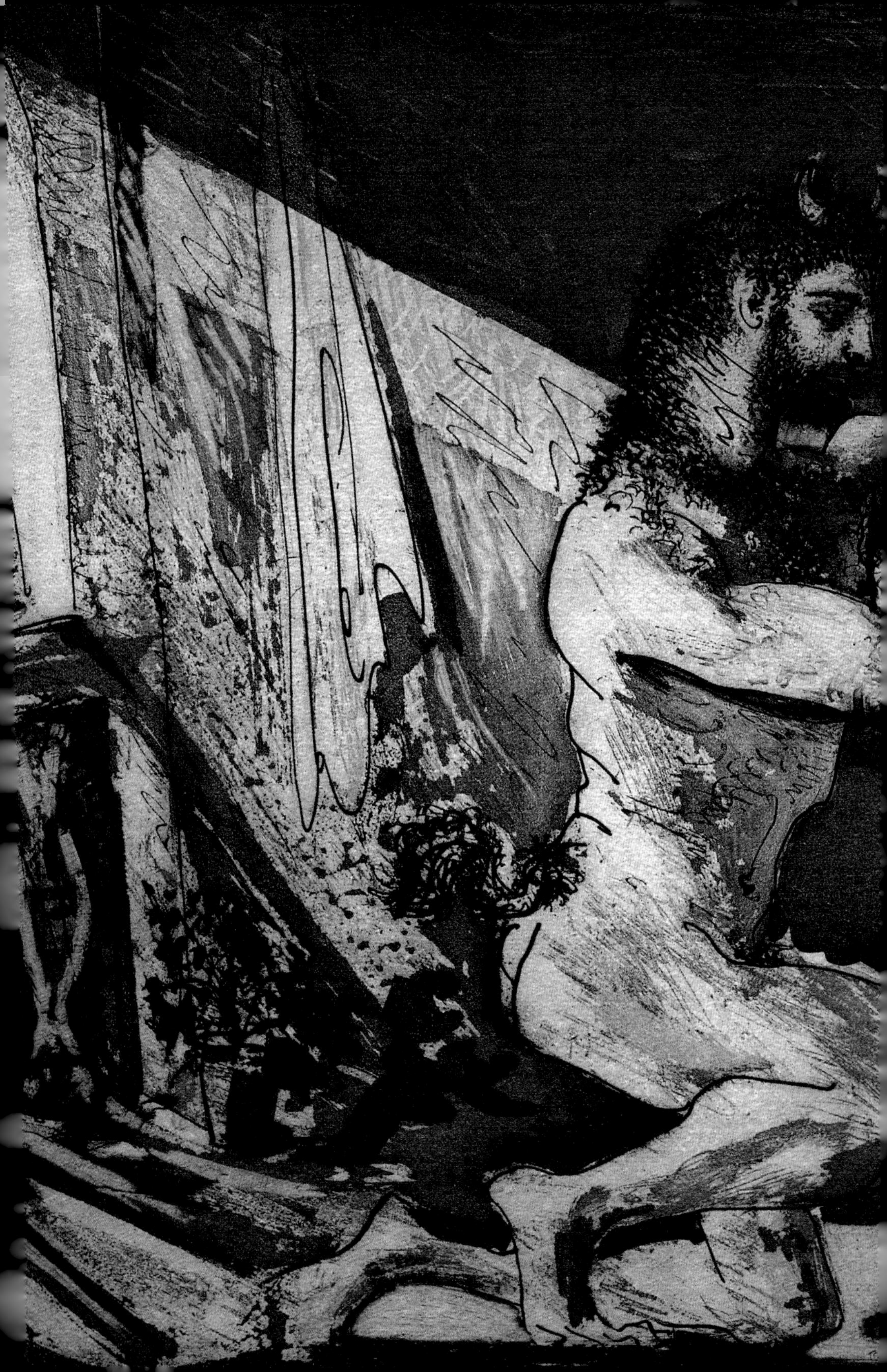

Prints

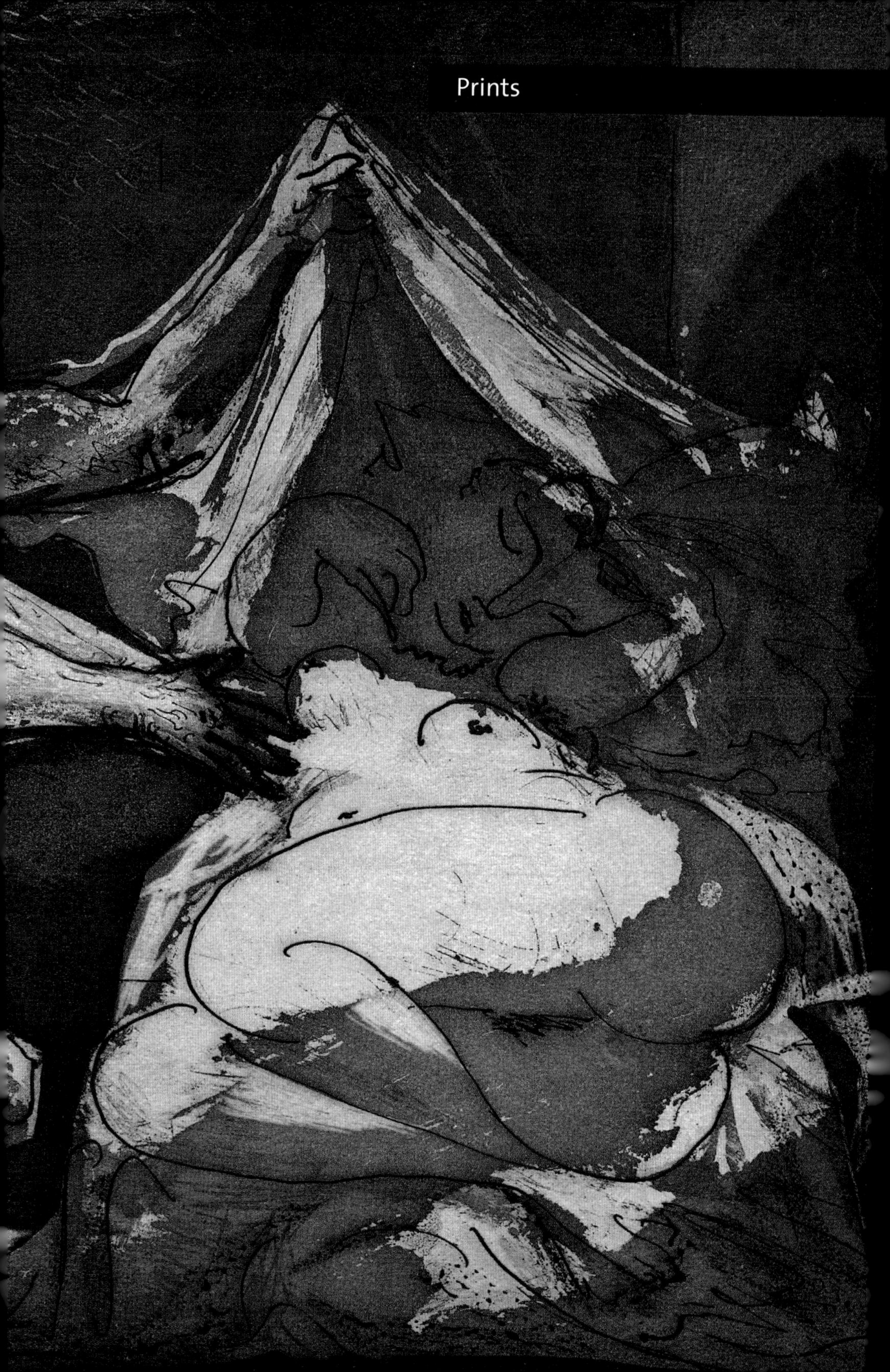

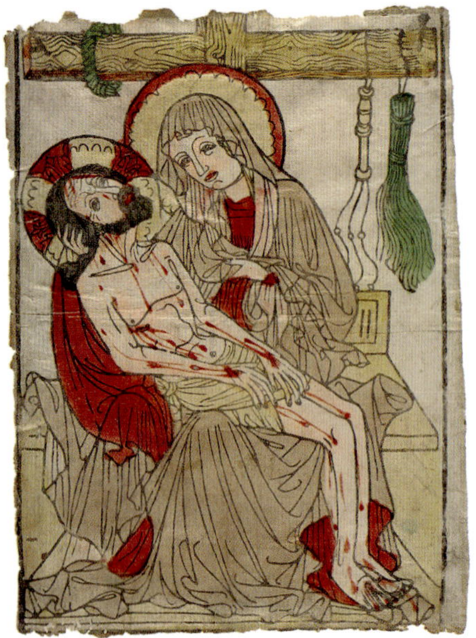

Only about 20 single-sheet, single-image woodcuts hand colored with watercolor and printed on a full sheet of paper from northern Europe have survived. Remnants of adhesive on the back suggest that this one was pasted inside the cover of a book, which protected it. Extraordinary in its large size, fresh color, and good state of preservation, this is the only known impression of the image, a rare treasure.

WOODCUT, HAND COLORED WITH WATERCOLOR; 38.7 X 28.8 CM (15-1/4 X 11-3/8 IN.)

SEVERANCE AND GRETA MILLIKIN TRUST 2002.4

Pietà about 1450

ANONYMOUS (GERMAN)

The first carved woodblocks were printed on textiles or vellum until about 1400, when a steady supply of paper was available. Early woodcuts illustrate mostly religious subjects, translating the stories of Christ, the Virgin Mary, and the saints into pictorial form for a mostly illiterate public. These simple, direct images provided a means for an intimate dialogue between the individual and the holy figure depicted. Inexpensive woodcuts were sold at pilgrimage sites and fairs, and pasted on altarpieces and walls to be used for personal devotion. As they were also invested with near-magical powers, woodcuts were sewn into clothing and placed in books and other personal objects to protect against sickness, famine, and war.

Fifteenth-century German woodcuts were produced by anonymous artisans, making them difficult to date securely until 1460, when they began to be used as book illustrations. This print retains certain characteristics of early examples, such as lines that taper and end in slightly curved hooks or widen into loops like the eyes of large needles, although its elaborate composition and technical sophistication make it similar to examples dated about 1450.

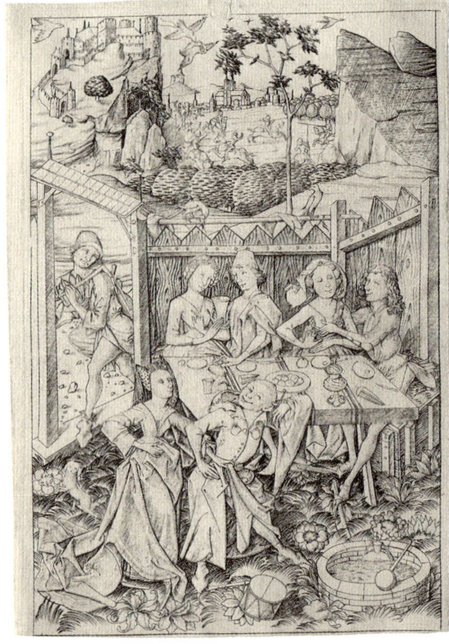

The Garden of Love (Large Plate) about 1465

MASTER ES (GERMAN, ACTIVE ABOUT 1450–67)

Goldsmiths ornamented their works with engraved images or decorative patterns throughout the Middle Ages. During the 1430s in the Rhine valley, goldsmiths realized that the incised designs on metal objects could be filled with ink and impressed on paper, which was finally available in some quantity.

The Master ES, who has not been identified, probably trained as a goldsmith. He was the most significant engraver active in northern Germany about the middle of the 15th century when, for the first time, printmakers signed their work. Of the some three hundred engravings attributed to this artist, 18 are signed with the initials "E" and "S" and 16 of the plates are dated between 1461 and 1467. The Master ES, an imaginative and creative artist, was the first printmaker to use the technique of crosshatching to create areas of shadow to model figures. He was very innovative and used various burin effects like stippling to achieve subtleties of shading and texture.

This representation of the Garden of Love, one of the most frequently illustrated secular subjects of the late 14th and 15th centuries, departs from pictorial tradition. The scene was usually depicted as an idyllic realm of music, feasting, and games where women inspired dedicated service from their admirers. The Master ES, however, satirizes the ideals of courtly love and warns against the immoral behavior forbidden by the Church and local authorities. The woman in the foreground who is opening the man's coat represents temptation and sin; her companion, the fool, symbolizes lust. *The Garden of Love (Large Plate)* is known in only five impressions.

ENGRAVING; 23.2 X 15.1 CM (9-1/8 X 6 IN.)
JOHN L. SEVERANCE FUND 1993.161

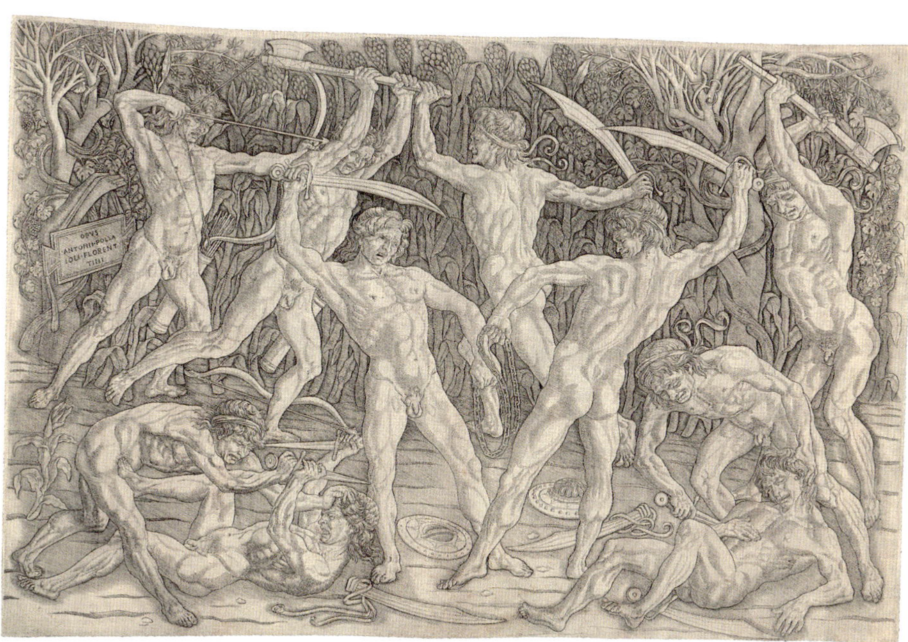

Battle of the Nudes 1470s–80s

ANTONIO DEL POLLAIUOLO (ITALIAN, 1431–1498)

Antonio del Pollaiuolo was a renowned Florentine painter, sculptor, draftsman, and goldsmith. Since only a small number of his works survive, the artist is celebrated for his printed masterpiece *Battle of the Nudes,* a monumental, complex composition. Among the largest of all 15th-century Italian engravings, this print is perhaps the earliest to be signed with the full name of the artist who designed and executed it. Although one of the earliest works of Renaissance art to convincingly portray the figure in motion, it is not accurate since all visible muscles are shown flexed simultaneously. Pollaiuolo's bronze sculpture *Hercules and Antaeus* features two struggling figures twisted in space, requiring the viewer to encircle it to appreciate the entire composition. In the same way, the *Battle of the Nudes*—10 men in a variety of poses including paired opposites—provides multiple viewpoints of the human form in action, the two-dimensional equivalent of moving around a three-dimensional form.

Battle of the Nudes is typical of 15th-century Florentine art in the flowing line that outlines form and in the importance of antiquity; some poses are reminiscent of ancient sculpture, and the shallow space echoes carved classical reliefs. Although works of the time usually tell a story or illustrate a classical text or historical event, the meaning of this engraving remains elusive. Yet its artistic and intellectual intricacy would have appealed to educated viewers.

Pollaiuolo developed an unusually refined technique of zigzag strokes. This style is particularly beautiful in this silvery example, which is the only known impression of the engraving's first state, before the plate was re-engraved and printed with a more densely pigmented and blacker ink. It is a masterwork of European art.

ENGRAVING; 42.4 X 60.9 CM (16-3/4 X 24 IN.)
PURCHASE FROM THE J. H. WADE FUND 1967.127

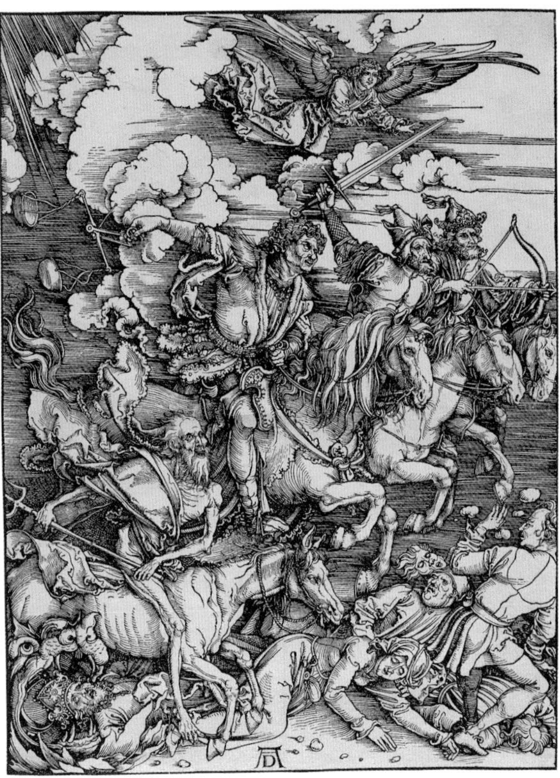

The Four Horsemen of the Apocalypse about 1498

ALBRECHT DÜRER (GERMAN, 1471–1528)

Shortly after Dürer returned to Nuremberg from Italy in 1495, he began work on woodcuts to illustrate the last book of the New Testament, the Revelation of St. John the Divine, or the Apocalypse. The Revelation was generally believed to foretell the events that would take place at the Second Coming of Christ.

In 1498, Dürer published both Latin and German editions comprising a title page and 15 full-sheet woodcuts, with text printed on the verso of all the sheets except the last one. The woodcuts were designed to be looked at independently, however, and do not illustrate the text on the facing page. The finest impressions, when the blocks were in the best condition, were most often printed without text like this one of the Four Horsemen. Although the Apocalypse had been depicted many times in the 15th century, Dürer's version was remarkable. The woodcuts were unique in their large scale, breadth of concept, and unity of design, and it was the first book in Western art to be published and illustrated by the artist.

In Revelation, a lamb with seven horns and seven eyes takes a scroll from an enthroned figure of Christ and breaks its seven seals. The first four seals reveal the four apocalyptic riders. The first horseman, with a bow and a crown, has the power to conquer; the second, with a sword, can take peace from the earth; the third, with scales, represents justice; and the fourth, on a sickly pale horse, is Death followed by Hell. In this powerful image, the riders' wind-blown clothing, the racing clouds, and the figures trampled under the hooves of the approaching horses suggest vigorous movement.

WOODCUT; 39 X 28.1 CM (15-3/8 X 11-1/8 IN.)

GIFT OF THE PRINT CLUB OF CLEVELAND 1932.313

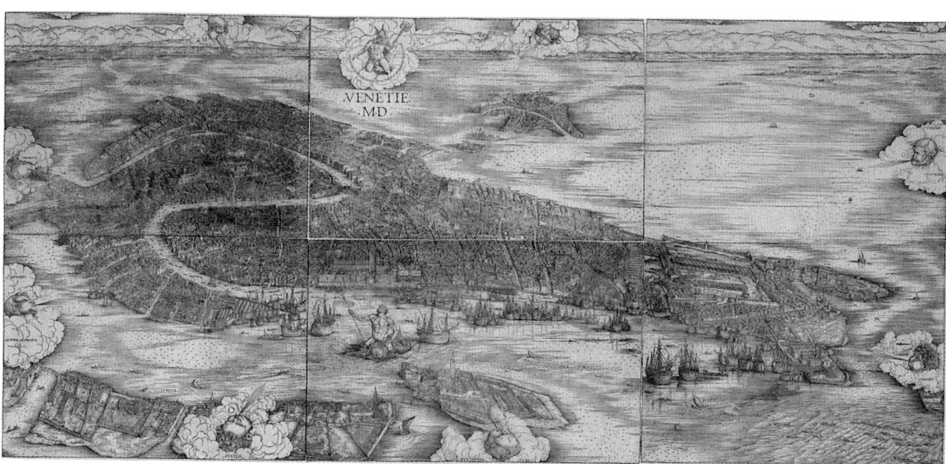

View of Venice 1500

JACOPO DE'BARBARI (ITALIAN, ABOUT 1460/70–BEFORE 1516)

By the end of the 15th century Venice, a great emporium for the production of books and prints, had emerged as the major printing center in Europe. The woodcut developed beyond its humble origins as a popular art for simple pious imagery, playing cards, and book illustration. Following the tradition of large maps executed on several sheets of paper, woodcuts began to be printed from multiple blocks, greatly increasing their size and impact.

One of the first known large bird's-eye views produced in woodcut, *View of Venice* is perhaps the first ever made of this city. A monumental print, it measures some four by nine feet, comparable in scale but a less expensive alternative to tapestries and mural decorations. The six sheets making up this print would have been pasted directly to a wall or a canvas so that few fine early impressions in prime condition, like this one, have survived.

View of Venice was revolutionary in its great size, wealth of detail, and the sheer beauty of its design and execution. More than just a topographical record, however, the map champions Venice as the premier trading and maritime power of Europe. While a figure of Mercury, the patron of commerce, hovers above the city, Neptune, the lord of the seas, rides astride a giant fish directly below.

WOODCUT ON SIX SHEETS OF PAPER; 134 X 281 CM (52-3/4 X 110-5/8 IN.)

PURCHASE FROM THE J. H. WADE FUND 1949.565.1–6

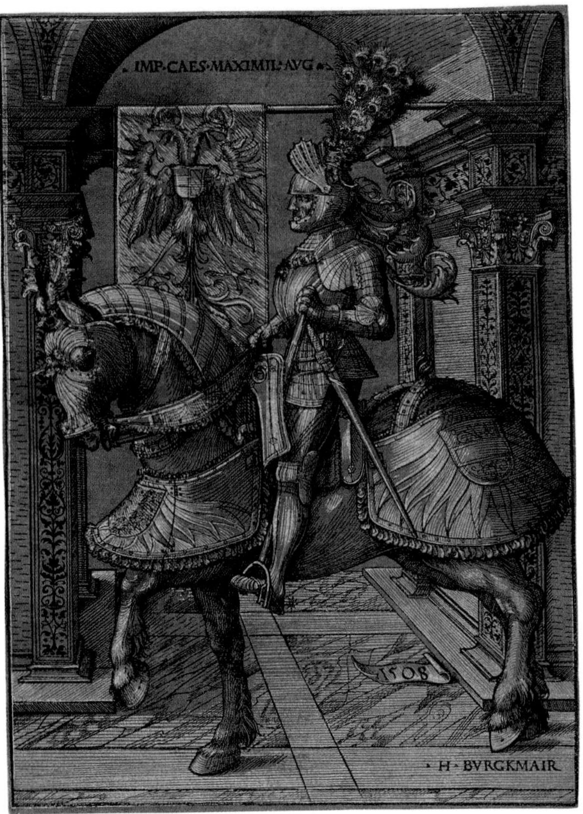

Maximilian I 1508

HANS BURGKMAIR (GERMAN, 1473–1531)

In the early 15th century the first woodcuts were printed in black and color was added by hand with watercolor. By the end of the century, however, artists were experimenting with ways to print in color. Chiaroscuro drawings were very popular, and ways were sought to duplicate the same effect by printing from wood blocks. Chiaroscuro drawings create the illusion of three dimensions by delineating the image with a pen and brown or black ink on paper tinted with wash in a middle tone; shadows are added with a brush and brown or black wash, and white heightening establishes highlights.

In 1507, Lucas Cranach took the first step toward producing a chiaroscuro woodcut when he printed *St. George and the Dragon* on a tinted paper using two blocks—one for the black outline and the other for the highlights, printing an adhesive that was flocked with gold. In 1508, Hans Burgkmair produced *Maximilian I,* which is also on tinted paper but the black-line block and the highlights were printed in black and white, respectively. One of only three surviving impressions printed in this manner, this striking and rare treasure illuminates the development of the chiaroscuro woodcut. By 1509 printmakers had streamlined the process; the line block was still printed in black, but a second block printed the background color, and unprinted areas of white paper formed the highlights.

WOODCUT PRINTED ON BLUE HAND-TINTED PAPER; 32.3 X 22.7 CM (12-3/4 X 8-7/8 IN.)

JOHN L. SEVERANCE FUND 1950.72

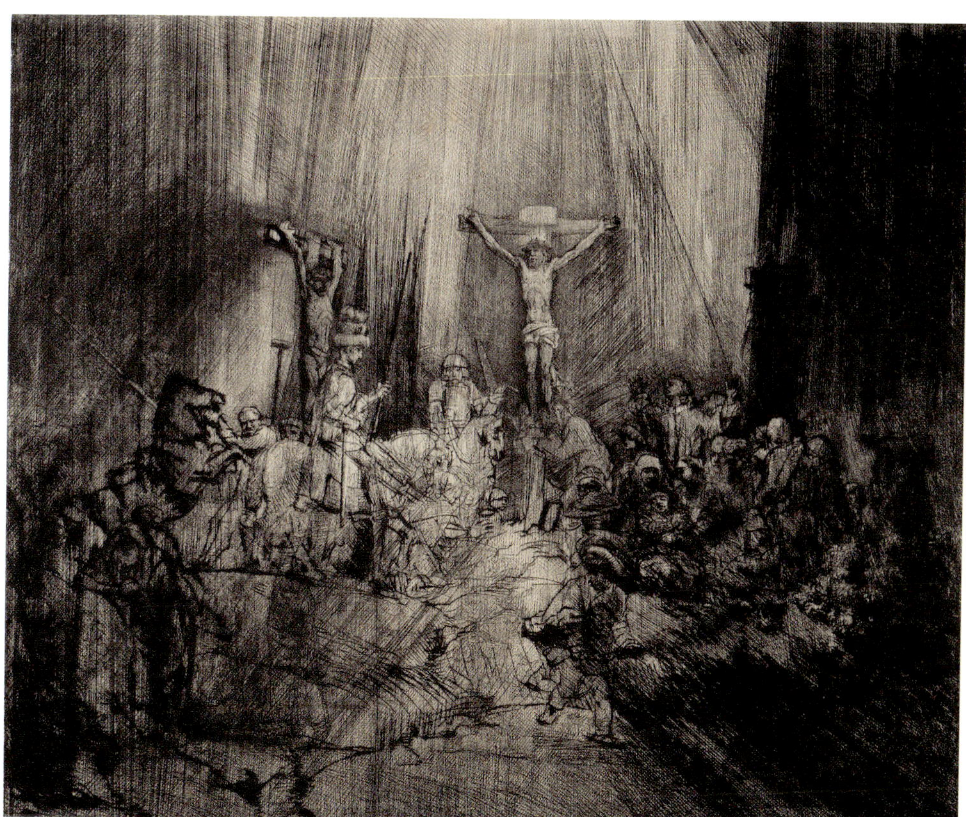

Christ Crucified between Two Thieves 1653–55

REMBRANDT VAN RIJN (DUTCH, 1606–1669)

Not only a gifted painter and superb draftsman, Rembrandt was also an experimental and original printmaker. *Christ Crucified between Two Thieves,* one of his largest and most significant prints, was executed entirely in drypoint, which produces blurred lines and rich, velvety shadows. Although earlier artists had occasionally made drypoints, he used the technique extensively and was the first to execute prints in pure drypoint on this monumental scale.

Rembrandt redefined the expressive potential of printmaking. Using drypoint, he achieved the density of color and breadth of line produced by black chalk or black ink applied with brush or broad-nib pen, as in his drawings. Drypoint lines are ephemeral, however, because the burr created by the drypoint tool wears down quickly, altering the lines after only about 40 impressions. In order to continue printing the plate, Rembrandt reworked it, changing the image somewhat.

Although drypoint is an inherently linear medium, Rembrandt also used it to obtain tonal qualities associated with painting. In this state of *Christ Crucified between Two Thieves* slashing strokes obscure the spectators and create a tenebrous setting, focusing attention on Christ bathed in celestial light. A literal illustration of Luke's description of the cataclysmic event, "and there was a darkness over all the earth," the gloom becomes an active force that threatens to extinguish the light of Christ. The museum's fine impression of the fourth state powerfully illustrates the pathos of Christ's sacrifice and demonstrates Rembrandt's passionate intensity and genius as a printmaker.

DRYPOINT; 37.5 X 44 CM (14-3/4 X 17-3/8 IN.)

BEQUEST OF RALPH KING AND PURCHASE FROM THE J. H. WADE FUND 1959.241

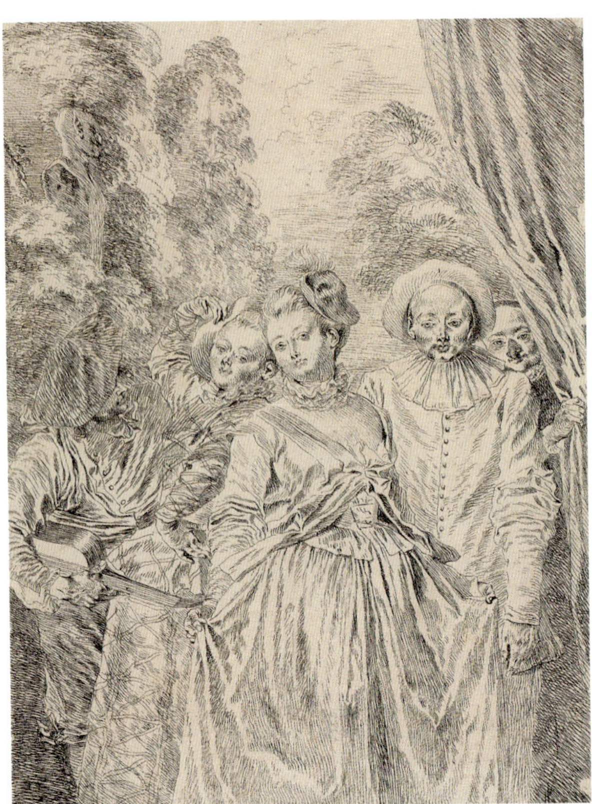

The Clothes Are Italian 1715–16

JEAN ANTOINE WATTEAU (FRENCH, 1684–1721)

The Clothes Are Italian is the most distinguished of the 14 etchings executed by Watteau, one of the principal painters of 18th-century France. The scene depicts actors probably taking a bow at the end of a performance, an effect reinforced by the curtain at right being pulled aside for them. Identified by their costumes, Columbine and Harlequin are characters from the Italian Commedia dell'arte, while Pierrot could be found at French fair theaters. Because it is unlikely that characters from both French and Italian comedies would have appeared together, the composition is probably an invention of the artist rather than a record of a specific troupe or performance. The title of the print is the opening line of a short poem that appears at the bottom of the plate.

Watteau drew on the etching plate with a light touch, executing *Clothes Are Italian* in a sketchy manner. His nervous, flickering strokes effectively evoke form and light, giving the figures a wonderful liveliness and spontaneity. Since the plate was lightly bitten in an acid bath, it was not possible to print many impressions and only three examples, including this one, have survived.

The plate was then reworked by Charles Simonneau, a professional printmaker, who added a multitude of detail that suited contemporary 18th-century taste, as did the regularity of the engraved lines. Watteau's freely executed etched drawing was replaced by a mechanical and stultifying style that ruined the charming scene.

ETCHING; 27.5 X 20 CM (10-7/8 X 7-7/8 IN.)

SEVERANCE AND GRETA MILLIKIN PURCHASE FUND

2008.3

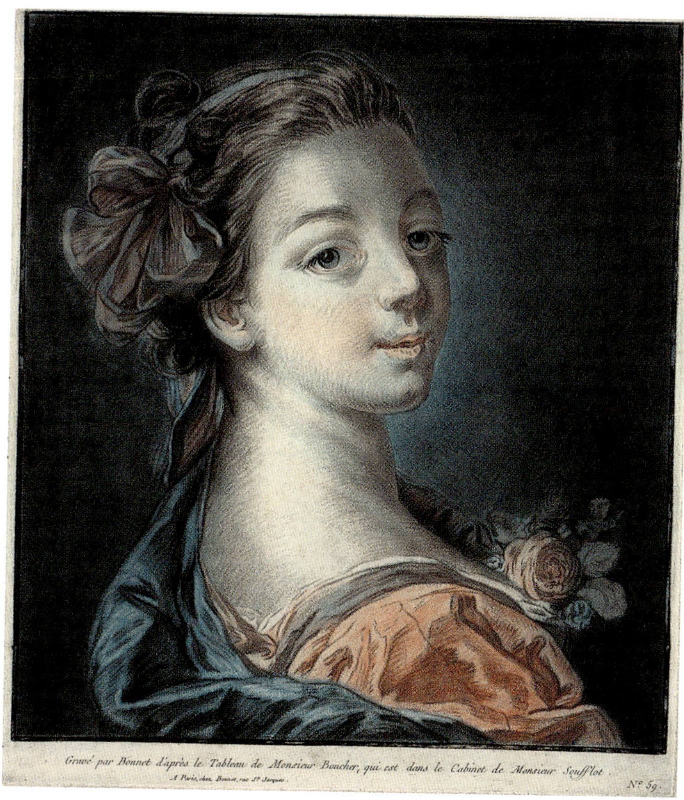

Head of a Woman (after François Boucher) about 1771

LOUIS-MARIN BONNET (FRENCH, 1736–1793)

The 18th century in France, the Age of Enlightenment, was a period of enormous technical invention in many fields, including printmaking. The desire to emulate drawing media spurred innovation as printmakers developed new ways to create tone.

Chalk drawings by artists such as François Boucher and Jean-Honoré Fragonard were so popular that serious collectors amassed them in portfolios and framed them to display on walls. Alert to the potential market for printed facsimiles of chalk drawings, printmaker Jean-Charles François developed a technique to imitate the grainy texture of chalk on a copper plate in 1757. To emulate the haphazard character of marks made with chalk, he modified the *mattoir,* a blunt printmaking tool ending in clusters of teeth, so that the toothed points were of varying thicknesses and set at irregular intervals and angles. François printed in one color, sanguine, but in 1765 his rival Bonnet devised a method to use multiple plates to print in several colors in order to reproduce Boucher's two- and three-color chalk drawings. By 1769 Bonnet was able to print a range of colors from several plates, replicating multicolored pastels in a print medium.

The best of the chalk-manner etching and engravings remain among the supreme examples of color printing, unrivaled in their technical sophistication and sensitive interpretation of their models. The museum's example, *Head of a Woman,* reproduces a pastel portrait by Boucher that is thought to portray his daughter Jean-Elisabeth Victoire, who married the artist's favorite pupil, Jean-Baptiste Henri Deshays.

CHALK-MANNER ETCHING AND ENGRAVING; 41.5 X 35.7 CM (16-3/8 X 14 IN.)

DUDLEY P. ALLEN FUND 1996.6

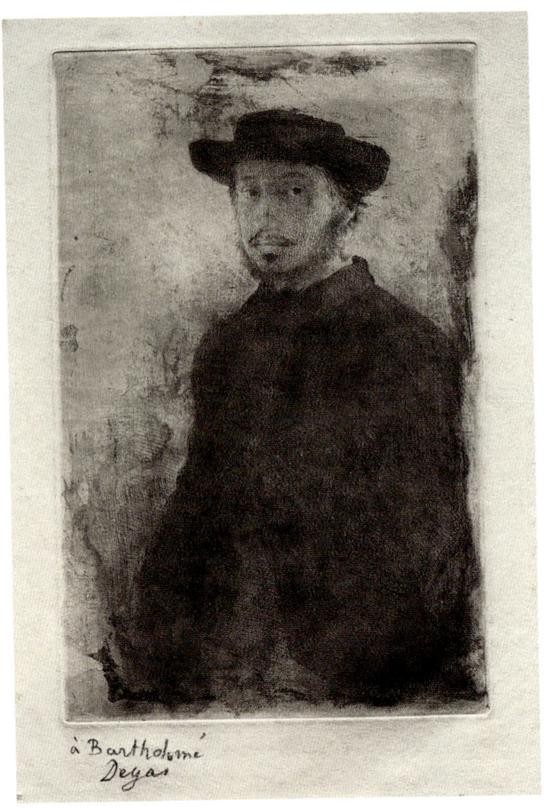

Self-Portrait 1857

EDGAS DEGAS (FRENCH, 1834–1917)

Degas frequently used himself as a model for portrait drawings and oil paintings in the 1850s. This etching, his only self-portrait in a print medium, follows very closely, in reverse, a drawing in the Metropolitan Museum of Art in New York that may have served as the model. There are also affinities with an oil painting on paper dated 1857–58 at the Clark Art Institute in Williamstown, Massachusetts.

Through successive stages of biting the plate, Degas built up the darks gradually, using layers of crosshatching to copy the chiaroscuro effects of the Metropolitan drawing where black crayon produces large areas of tone. He began the print by lightly drawing the figure on the plate. Although accidental biting is visible in the second state on the figure and background where the etching ground was permeated by acid, the figure has more substance because of an experimental but intentional bitten tone on areas like the coat and hands. The third and most successful state, like this impression, is more dramatic because of additional tone and etched lines on the face, hat, and coat. The artist compensated for the false biting by wiping the plate carefully yet differently for each impression, modeling the figure in light and shade and creating a dark, shadowy background.

This impression—there are only 10 known of the first three states—is inscribed to the artist's friend, the painter and sculptor Paul-Albert Bartholomé (1848–1928). An especially beautiful sheet, it was printed from a plate carefully wiped to create atmospheric, chiaroscuro effects yet allow the clearly drawn eyes to look directly at the viewer. The result is a psychologically powerful, intense portrait of the artist at age 23.

ETCHING AND DRYPOINT; 23 X 14.5 CM (9 X 5-3/4 IN.)

JOHN L. SEVERANCE FUND 2004.87

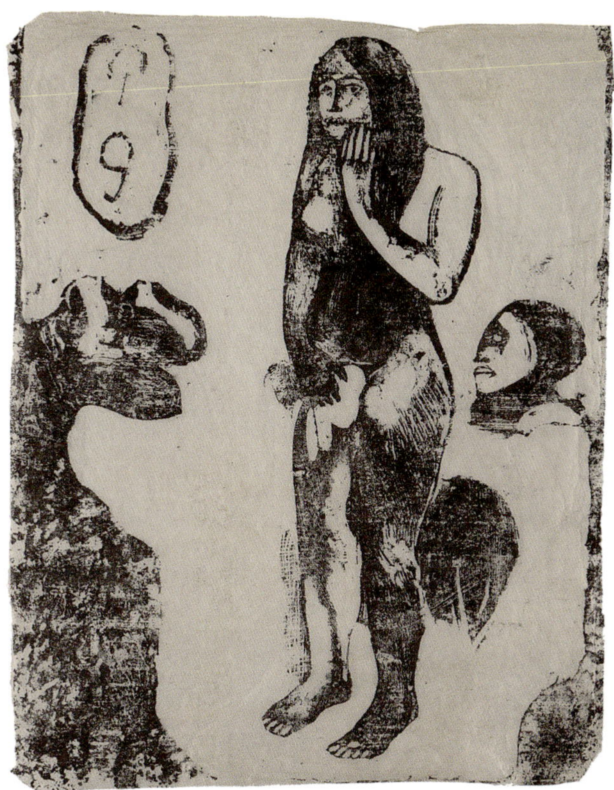

Eve 1898–99

PAUL GAUGUIN (FRENCH, 1848–1903)

While in Tahiti, between 1896 and 1900 Gauguin worked on a text, *L'Esprit moderne et le catholicisme,* that attempts to reconcile the Gospels of the New Testament with the spirit of modern science. Gauguin had extensive knowledge of spiritual practices and wanted to create an ideal universe where ancient and modern traditions of the East, West, and Oceania merge. Since he believed in the power of images as carriers of ideas, he created 14 woodcuts during 1898–99 that are the visual equivalents of parables or fables. In his understanding of Christian, Buddhist, Hindu, and Egyptian teaching, such elementary modes of instruction begin the process of enlightenment.

In his quest for a universal religion, Gauguin mixed Christian and Polynesian imagery. While Eve's gesture of modesty recalls earlier representations of the Expulsion from Eden, the disembodied hooded head (the *tupapau,* an evil spirit that haunts Tahitians), and the rat (the shadow of a ghost), are Polynesian symbols. Combining Eve, an image of guilt and violation, with Tahitian symbols of death increases the potency of the scene.

Gauguin, an innovative printmaker, experimented endlessly with carving and printing woodblocks, varying the ink, paper, colors, and modes of printing each impression. His woodcuts have a naive or archaizing quality as well as a handmade, crude power that influenced the next generation of European printmakers.

This impression of *Eve* is the only known example of the first state. Gauguin then changed the block so that the black shape in the lower right is blank and additional white lines appear on Eve and the rat.

WOODCUT; 27 X 20.5 CM (10-5/8 X 8-1/8 IN.)

JOHN L. SEVERANCE FUND 1991.158

Monotypes

A monotype is a unique work of art. An artist creates a design with ink or paint on a nonabsorbent flat and smooth surface, covers it with a sheet of paper, and runs it through a press or prints it by hand. Because the media dries quickly, monotypes must be spontaneously executed and reflect the artist's first impulse. There is also an element of chance since the pressure of transferring the design blurs it to some degree, creating softened edges.

The first monotypes were made in the 17th century by Giovanni Benedetto Castiglione. Probably unaware of those prints, Degas reinvented the technique about 1874. This master of monotype used the medium to construct forms with shadow and light by building broad tonal areas without reliance on line. Inspired by a trip through the Burgundy countryside in 1890, Degas produced a group of relatively large monotypes, for the first time using colored inks. Manipulating oil color with a rag, he fabricated vague landscape designs from his imagination, letting colored masses represent earth, vegetation, and sky, and creating an almost abstract visionary and evocative scene in *Esteral Village*.

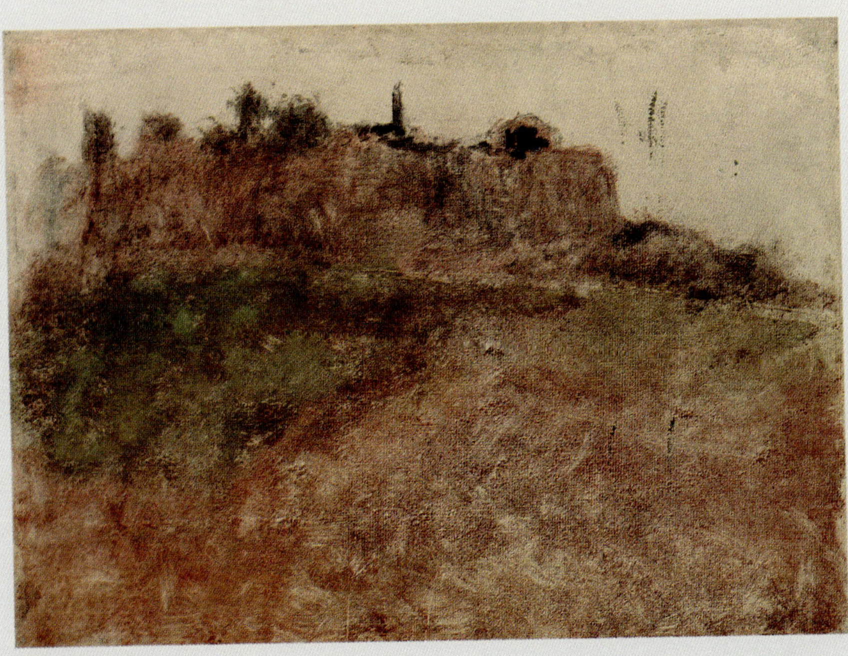

Esteral Village, about 1890. Edgar Degas (French, 1834–1917). Monotype; 30 x 39.9 cm (11-7/8 x 15-3/4 in.). Fiftieth Anniversary Gift of the Print Club of Cleveland 1966.177

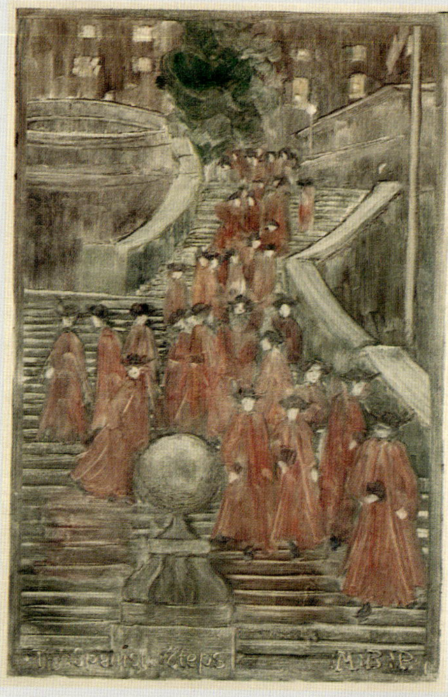

John Sloan, a committed printmaker, began to make monotypes in the early years of the 20th century. *The Theatre* reflects his first experience with opera. Although he and his wife, Dolly, enjoyed attending the theater and music halls, the well-dressed people in the audience of this monotype probably reflect the two operas he attended in February 1909. Sloan exploited the inherent luminosity of monotype to record the darkened interior during a performance. He used green ink to delineate the brilliantly lit stage and created the effect of the light reflected across the space by covering the plate with ink and then wiping it away to construct highlights.

The technique was introduced in America in 1880, and Maurice Prendergast became a devoted and skilled practitioner. Belying its modest size, *The Spanish Steps* is Prendergast's supreme achievement among his Italian monotypes. Selecting a classic Roman tourist site, theatrical with its sweeping curves, he depicted three dozen red-robed Catholic seminarians flowing down the carefully delineated monumental staircase.

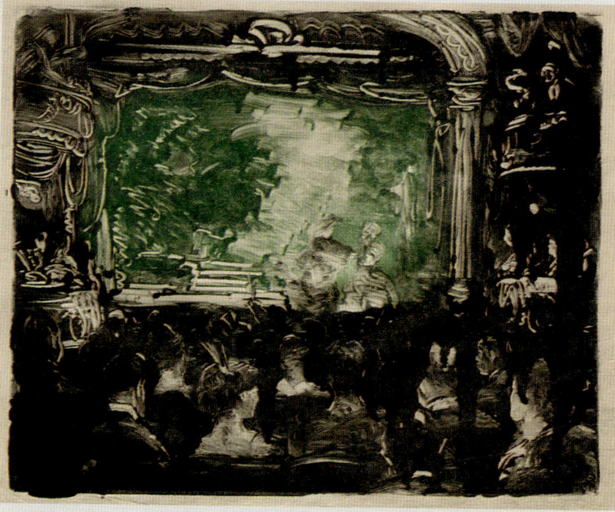

The Spanish Steps, about 1898–99. Maurice Prendergast (American, 1858–1924). Monotype; 29.7 x 19 cm (11-3/4 x 7-1/4 in.). Mr. and Mrs. Charles G. Prasse Collection 1982.167

The Theatre, 1909. John Sloan (American, 1871–1951). Monotype; 19.1 x 22.8 cm (7-1/2 x 9 in.). Gift of Mr. and Mrs. Ralph L. Wilson in memory of Anna Elizabeth Wilson 1961.162

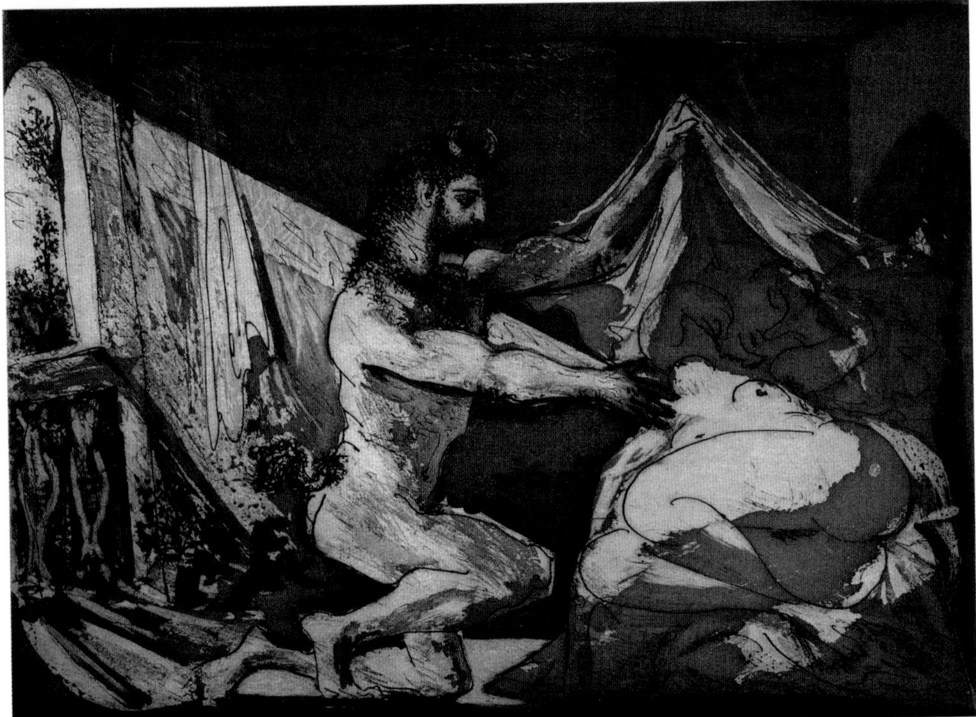

Faun Revealing a Sleeping Woman 1936

PABLO PICASSO (SPANISH, 1881–1973)

In 1937, the art dealer and print publisher Ambroise Vollard obtained 97 unpublished plates executed between 1930 and 1936 from Picasso, the greatest printmaker of the first half of the 20th century. Three etched portraits of Vollard were added to the group and these one hundred plates, known as the *Vollard Suite*, were printed in 1939.

Picasso did not create the prints in the *Vollard Suite* as a unified set. Instead, they address several themes: the sculptor's studio, the Minotaur, the battle of love, and the influence of Rembrandt. All have personal meaning for Picasso, whose work is often autobiographical. For instance, *Faun Revealing a Sleeping Woman* depicts his mistress Marie-Therèse Walter. Unhappy with his wife, the Russian dancer Olga Koklova, the artist, then in his 40s, met the beautiful 17-year-old Marie-Therèse in 1925. From that point the voluptuous Marie-Therèse appears repeatedly in his work.

Familiar with Rembrandt's prints, Picasso was thinking of the Dutch artist's scene of a leering Jupiter uncovering the sleeping Antiope when he executed *Faun Revealing a Sleeping Woman*. Picasso's personal relationship with his model is reflected in the tenderness of the faun's gesture and his contemplation of the supine beauty. This lustful yet loving ambience is reinforced by the light flooding the room and illuminating the figures. While the outlines of the scene are etched, aquatint (a printmaking technique that creates a wash-like effect) is used to achieve large areas of tone.

This impression is a special proof made before the edition. Usually, unworked areas of the plate are cleanly wiped and there is a strong contrast of black ink and white paper. For this impression, however, a thin layer of ink was left to create an overall wash of pale gray. This tone acts like a veil, adding to the warm sensuality of the scene.

ETCHING AND AQUATINT; 31.7 X 41.9 CM
(12-1/2 X 16-1/2 IN.)
LEONARD C. HANNA JR. FUND 2006.113

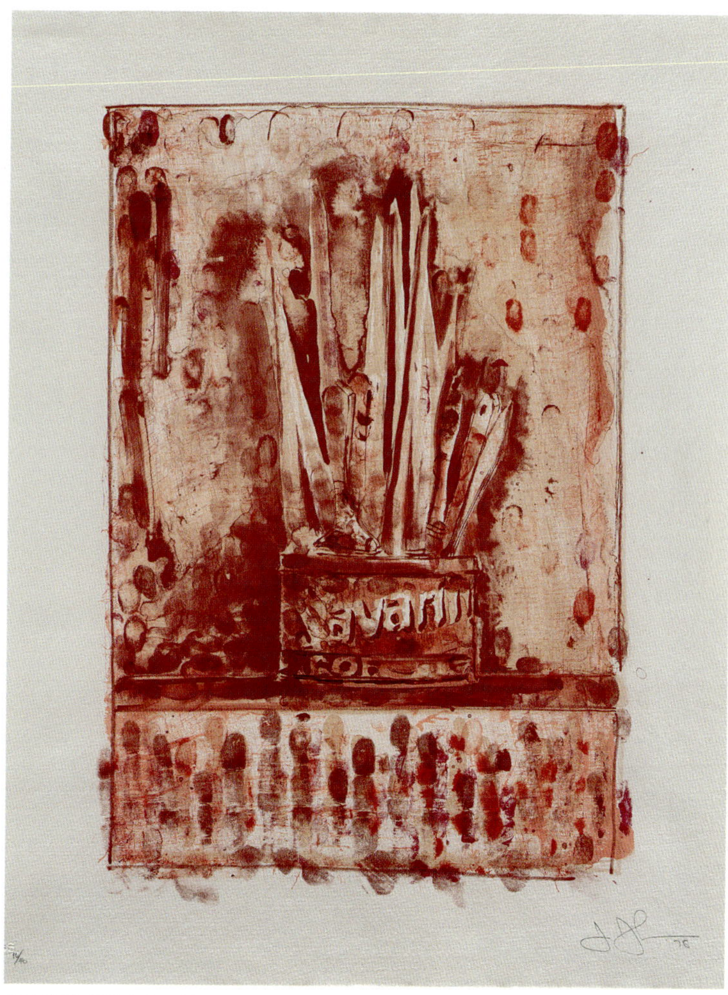

Savarin 3 (Red) 1978

JASPER JOHNS (AMERICAN, B. 1930)

Confounding distinctions between illusion and reality, in 1960 Johns cast in bronze a Savarin coffee can from his studio and the paintbrushes it held and then painted the entire composition, creating a trompe l'oeil sculpture. That Johns used the tools of his trade as a surrogate self-portrait was reinforced by a lithograph of the sculpture he made in 1981 that included an imprint of his arm on the bottom with the initials E.M. This motif referred to an 1895 lithograph by the Norwegian artist Edvard Munch, who placed a skeleton forearm and hand below a haunting depiction of himself.

The Savarin coffee can with brushes, a symbol of the creative act, appears many times in Johns's work in various media, offering a connection to the past and new ways to perceive the image. Large, dominating the space, and viewed straight on, each depiction is really a portrait of the subject. The six lithographs of the 1978 *Savarin Suite* are beautifully printed variations on a theme that explore a range of styles and moods. While *Savarin 4* frames the image in an old-fashioned oval, *Savarin 1,* printed in black, seems brooding, and *Savarin 3,* printed from six plates in shades of red, is ablaze with exuberant and luxuriant color.

LITHOGRAPH, 66 X 52.2 CM (26 X 20-5/8 IN.)

GIFT OF THE PRINT CLUB OF CLEVELAND 1983.219.3

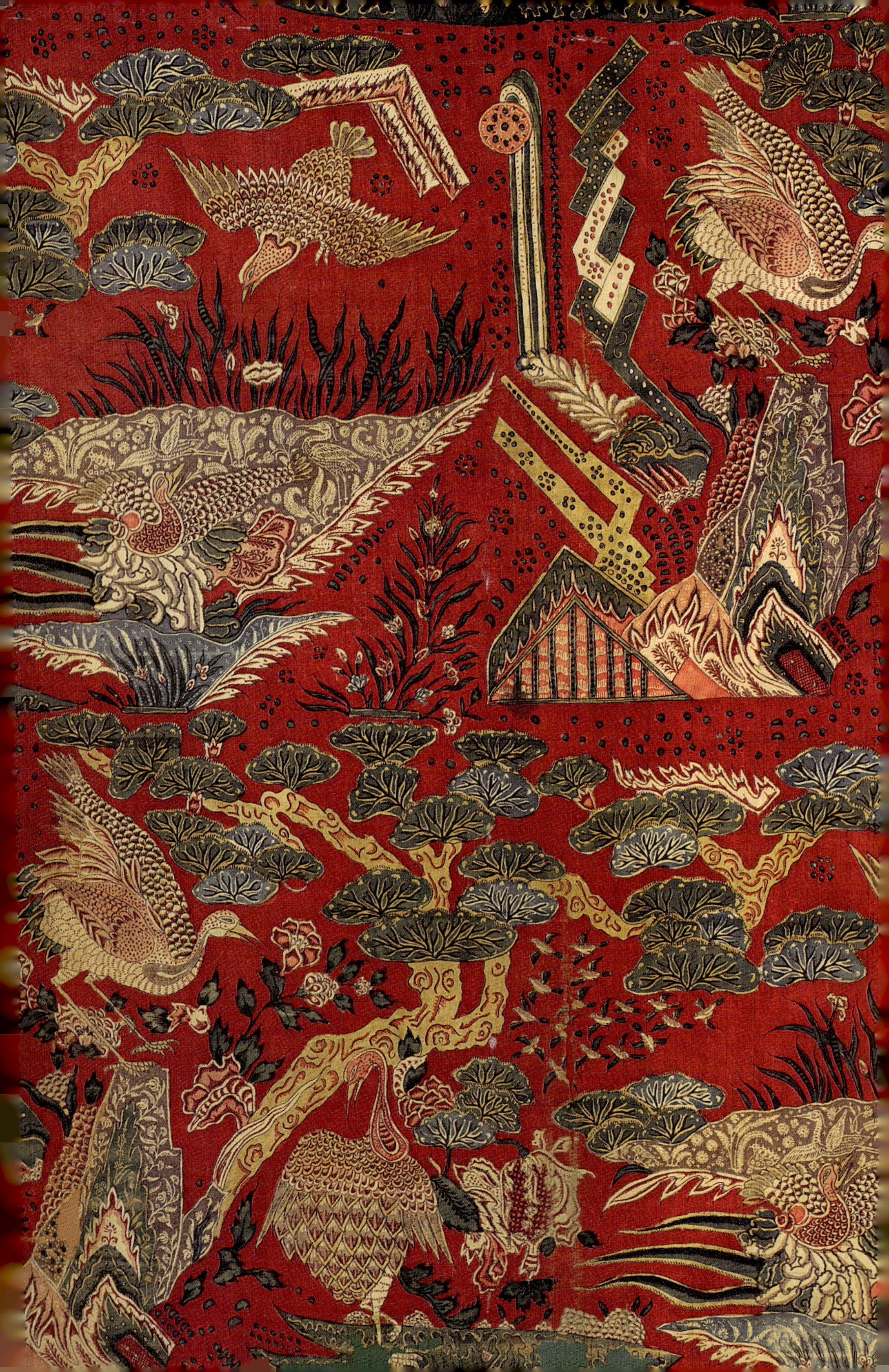

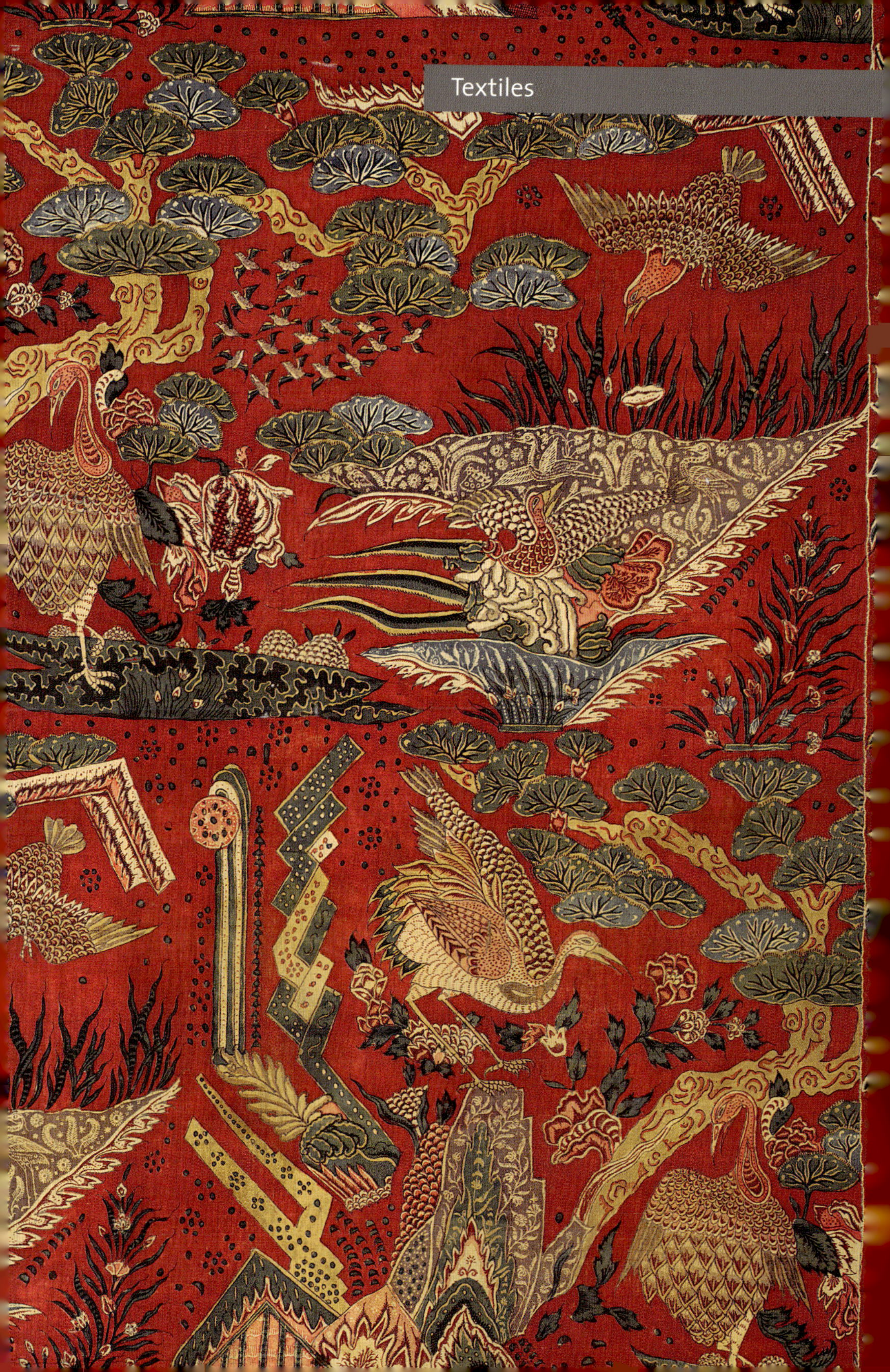

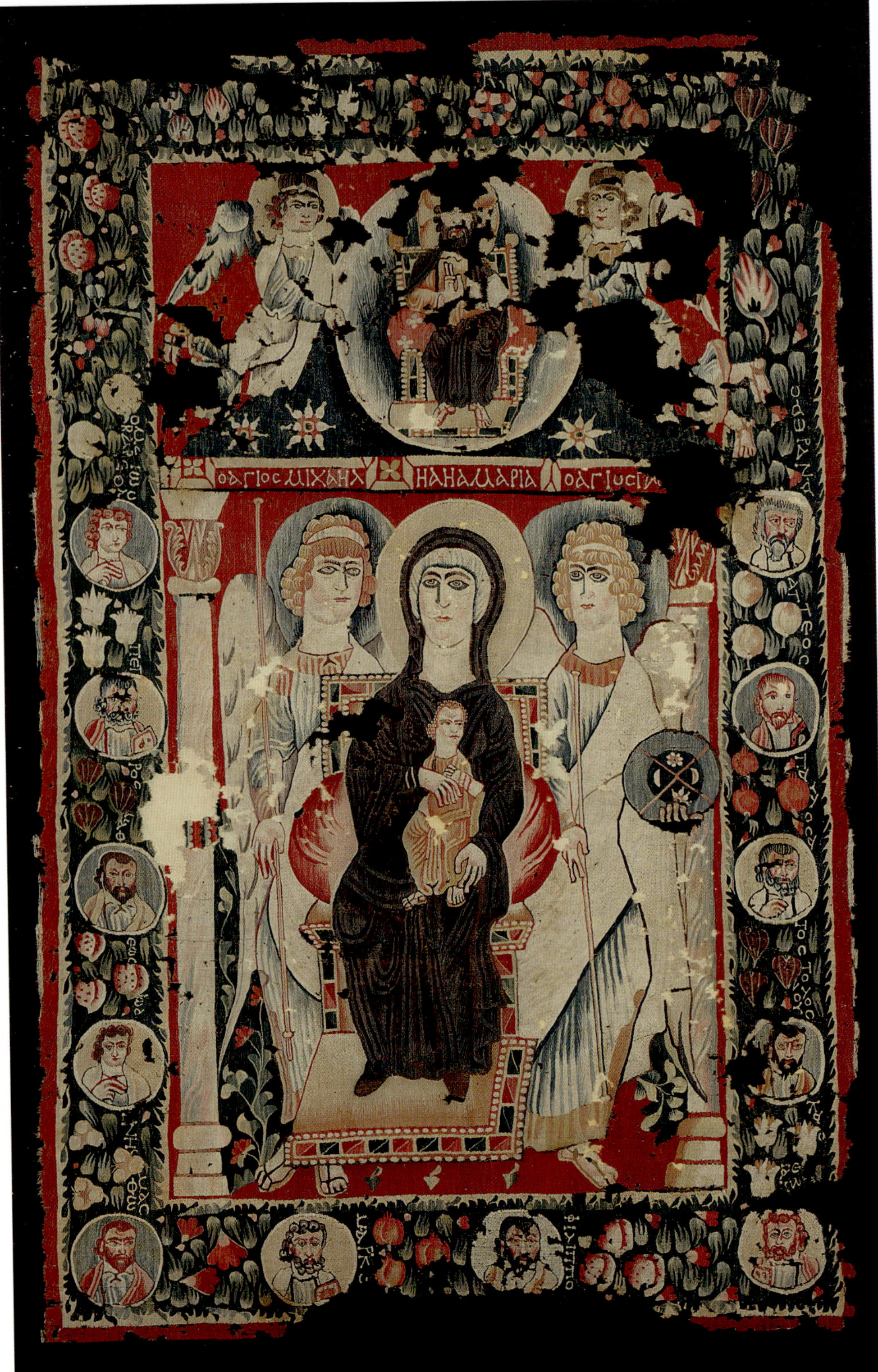
ΟΑΓΙΟΣΜΙΧΑΗΛ
ΗΑΓΙΑΜΑΡΙΑ

Icon of the Virgin and Child
500s
EGYPT, BYZANTINE PERIOD (ABOUT 330–641)

This resplendent woolen tapestry *Icon of the Virgin and Child* is one of the rarest masterpieces of early Christian art in the world. In a composition adopted from imperial Byzantine art, Mary is shown seated with the Christ child on a jeweled throne and flanked by the archangels Michael and Gabriel. Above, the enthroned Christ, supported by two angels, gestures blessings in the starry heavens. A sumptuous frame of fruits and flowers displays busts of the four evangelists and eight of Christ's apostles, each identified by his name in Greek. Christ's humanity and incarnation are emphasized in the lower register while his divine nature is represented in the upper zone.

This portable sacred icon, or holy image of personal devotion, would have been displayed at the front of a public or private place of worship. It is woven with dyed wool in tapestry weave, the equivalent of painting with colored horizontal weft yarns. Delicate effects of shading in the facial features, garments, and vegetation were achieved with at least 20 colors by weaving the panel sideways, as with medieval European tapestries. Since dyes were the costliest expenditure, this monumental tapestry would have been more expensive and luxurious than a painted icon.

SLIT- AND DOVETAILED-TAPESTRY WEAVE; WOOL; 178.7 X 110.5 CM (70-3/8 X 43-1/2 IN.)

LEONARD C. HANNA JR. FUND 1967.144

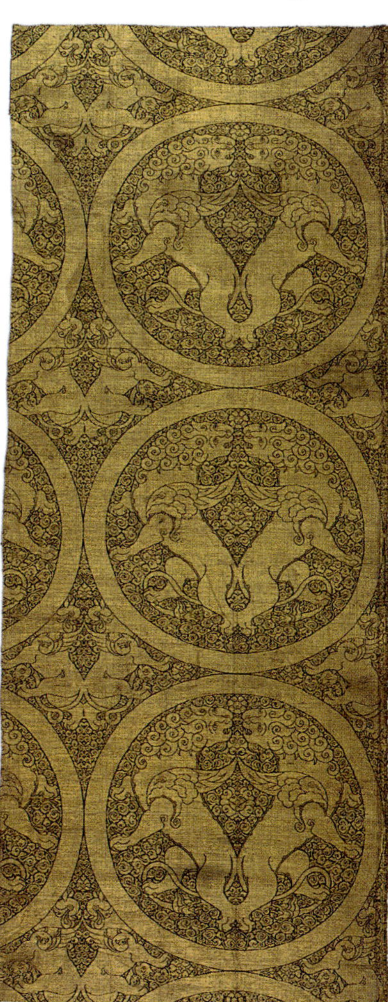

Cloth of Gold: Winged Lions and Griffins about 1240–60
CENTRAL ASIA, ILKHANID PERIOD (1256–1353)

The Mongols created exceptionally sumptuous cloths of gold to symbolize their imperial authority and legitimacy, this being the most resplendent known example. Such splendor was not previously known. Opulent expanses of gold thread enrich the roundels, lions, and griffins in striking contrast with the intricate brown silk foliate ground. The pattern integrates motifs from Iran (paired lions in roundels and paired griffins) and from China (cloud ornaments on the lions' wings). They suggest it was woven in an imperial workshop in Central Asia where Iranian and Chinese craftsmen worked together with local artisans. The gold is on a paper substrate associated with the East whereas animal substrates were used in Islamic lands. It is woven in a new technique, a combination of two weaves known as lampas, developed by Iranian weavers in the 11th century and adopted internationally.

LAMPAS; SILK AND GOLD THREAD; 124 X 48.8 CM (48-7/8 X 19-1/4 IN.)

PURCHASE FROM THE J. H. WADE FUND 1989.50

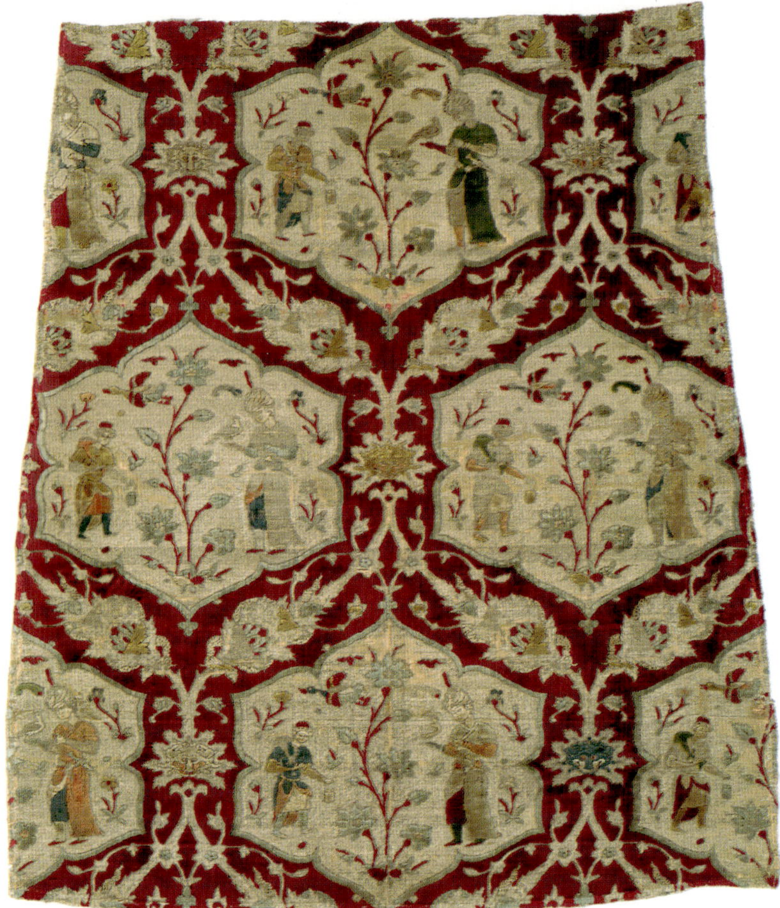

Brocaded Velvet with Falconer and Attendant in Medallions from a kaftan, 1524–76

IRAN, SAFAVID PERIOD (1501–1722)

This signature Safavid velvet displaying a princely falconry scene is celebrated for its refined beauty, meticulous draftsmanship, and exemplary technique with eight colors of velvet pile. A falconer and attendant flank a tall blossoming plant on a golden ground of lobed medallions. The falcon spies a flying duck flushed out by the assistant who carries a bag over his shoulder for the game. Animated foliate vines display leaves bearing lion's masks and black-spotted dragons coiled around larger leaves on the rich crimson velvet ground.

Iranian velvets of the Safavid period are the most colorful velvets ever woven. They have as many as 14 colors of velvet pile instead of only two or three colors. Ingenious Iranian weavers developed the ability to substitute one color of warp pile with another color, called pile-warp substitution. On the back, fringes of cut pile warps occur at the beginning and end of areas of color substitution.

BROCADED VELVET, PILE-WARP SUBSTITUTION; SILK, GILT-METAL THREAD; 79.4 X 66.7 CM (31-1/4 X 26-1/4 IN.) PURCHASE FROM THE J. H. WADE FUND 1944.239

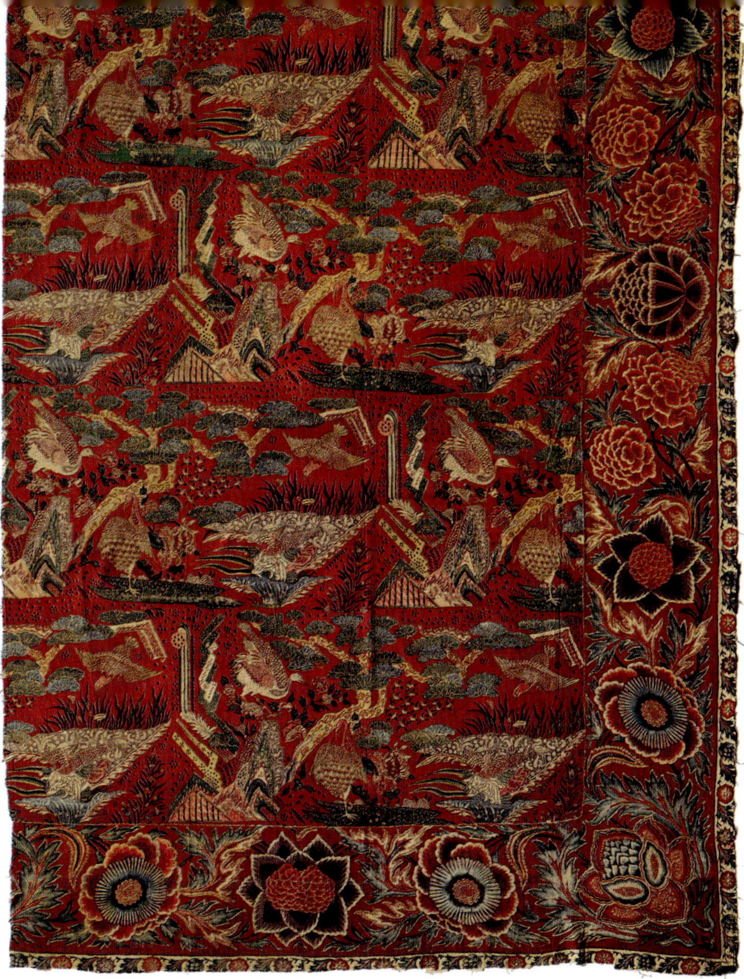

Chintz Bed Cover or Hanging with a Japanese-Inspired Pattern right half, 1700–1750

INDIA, COROMANDEL COAST

Master dyers in India were internationally renowned during the 17th and 18th centuries for rich colorfast cotton cloths known as chintz that were less costly than woven and embroidered textiles but cherished for their vivid decoration. Indian textile manufacturers targeted foreign markets, often copying and adapting samples in specified colors and sizes that were supplied by the dominant Dutch and English trading companies. This superb chintz wall hanging or bed cover features an infrequent Japanese-inspired pattern that the Dutch, who monopolized trade with Japan, would have admired.

The precisely detailed landscape in the field displays Japanese-inspired designs: two birds under a pine tree, a bird flying toward a pool with a nesting bird, and jagged rocks in the center, possibly influenced by Japanese painted and stenciled cottons from Okinawa. The exuberant floral border is sewn to the field, a feature that also occurs on the left half, which is in the Cooper-Hewitt National Design Museum in New York. The border was intended to frame a pattern with comparable blossoms. Seven rich colors—two reds, two blues, purple, brown, green—were created with resists, mordants, and dyes in lengthy labor-intensive processes that represented the finest chintz of the first half of the 18th century.

PLAIN WEAVE: COTTON; DRAWN RESIST, PAINTED MORDANTS, DYED; 284.5 X 136 CM (112 X 53-1/2 IN.)
PURCHASE FROM THE JOHN L. SEVERANCE FUND
2003.43

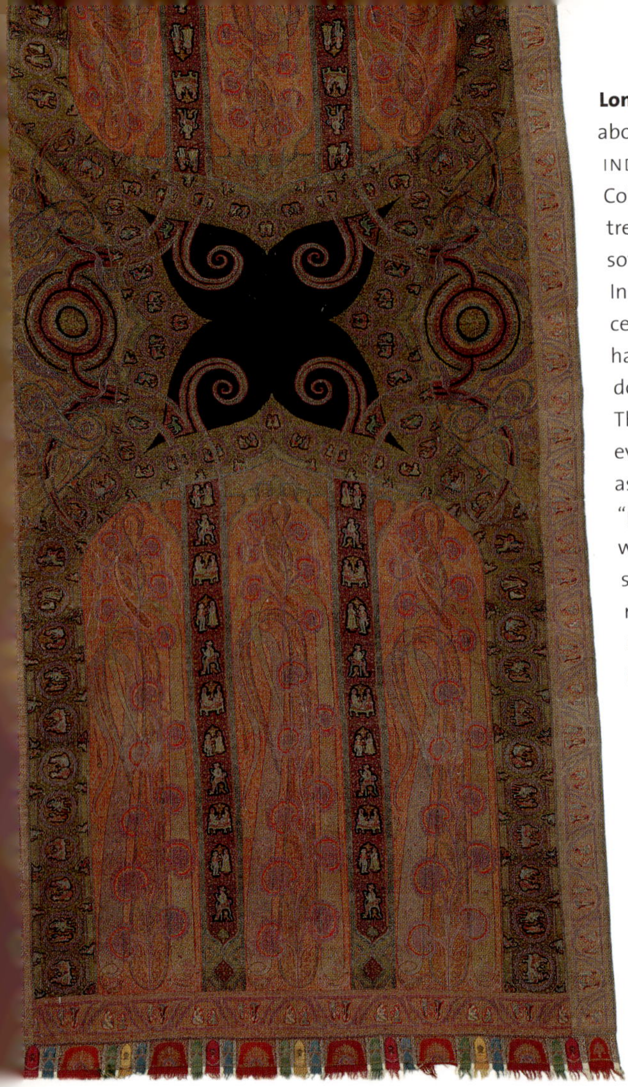

Long Shawl with Woven Figures and Animals

about 1885

INDIA, KASHMIR

Colorful shawls woven in Kashmir were treasured for their lightness, warmth, and softness by Emperor Akbar in 16th-century India and Empress Josephine in early 19th-century France. Their incomparable silky-hair fiber is from the fine undercoat of domesticated Himalayan mountain goats. Their signature decoration, blossoming plants, evolved into composite floral motifs known as *būtā* or *boteh* that are commonly called "paisley" in English after Paisley, Scotland, where they were imitated after their export soared during the 19th century. European manufacturers worked in vain to equal Kashmir originals, woven in the labor-intensive technique of 2/2 twill tapestry weave. In Europe, Kashmir shawls were cherished status symbols of elite ladies and featured in portrait paintings.

More than two hundred finely woven human figures and animals enliven this superlative shawl. Small scenes portray a princely life of drinking, falconry, dancing, and smoking around the center and in the dark stripes alternating with elongated būtās. Nothing comparable is known since figures were invariably embroidered rather than woven. This shawl, which was woven

in many pieces and expertly joined to speed up production in about 1885, was probably made to dazzle the jury at one of the European industrial expositions.

TWILL TAPESTRY WEAVE, DOUBLE INTERLOCKED, PIECED; GOAT HAIR; 354.3 X 141.6 CM (139-1/2 X 55-3/4 IN.)
GIFT OF ARLENE C. COOPER 2006.200

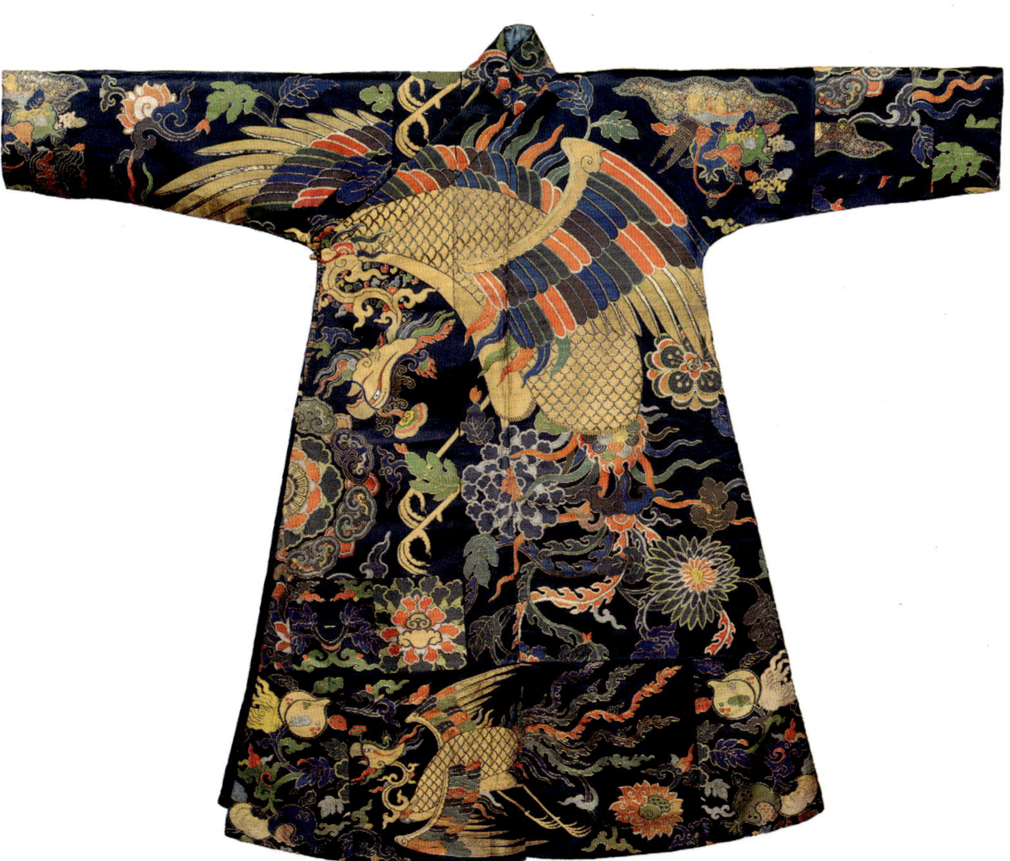

Tibetan Man's Robe (Chuba) late 1600s
CHINA, QING DYNASTY, KANGXI PERIOD (1662–1722)

This sumptuous Tibetan man's robe was a status symbol, political weapon, and hallmark of the finest Tibetan tailoring. It was a symbol of high status for an aristocrat or a high-ranking Buddhist monk, based on its luxurious brocaded silk fabric—a Chinese silk woven for the imperial court in Beijing. Splendid, large gold-thread phoenix have pride of place on the front and back of the robe, complemented by two smaller but equally resplendent phoenix below.

Tibetan robes, called *chubas,* made with cherished Chinese silk were typically pieced together and closed with a belt or sash at the waist. This opulent silk was originally woven for a curtain in the imperial Chinese palace. China used luxury textiles as political weapons in tributary relationships with its frontier areas in order to maintain its position as the center of the civilized universe, a practice continued by the Qing court following those of the Yuan and Ming dynasties. Beijing sent many textiles to Tibet, some as diplomatic gifts and others in trade.

SATIN WEAVE WITH SUPPLEMENTARY WEFT PATTERNING; SILK, GILT-METAL THREAD AND PEACOCK-FEATHERED THREAD; 184 X 129 CM (72-1/2 X 50-3/4 IN.)
NORMAN O. STONE AND ELLA A. STONE MEMORIAL FUND 2007.216

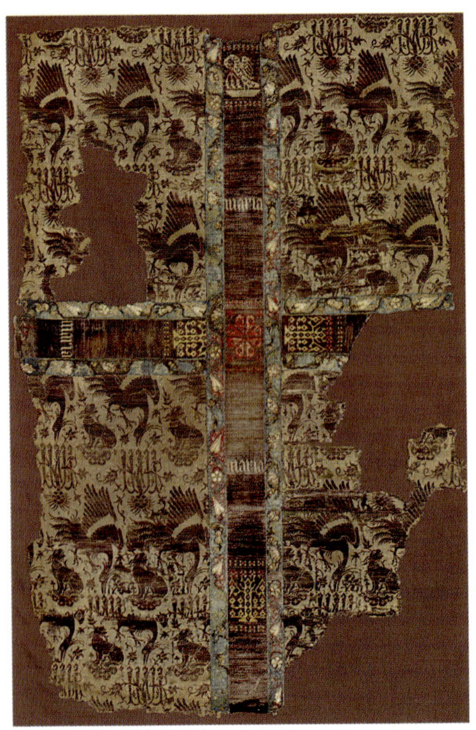

Fragmentary Chasuble with Woven Orphrey Band 1360–1400

ITALY

The second half of the 14th century was one of the great periods of Italian silk design. Drawing on Chinese, Islamic, and European motifs, designers created international designs of beauty and drama. This rare, albeit fragmentary chasuble displays a Chinese phoenix with outstretched wings flying toward a group of pseudo-Arabic letters while a dog snarls at a bird. Although generally decorative rather than legible, Arabic script, which was a symbol of the Holy Land, was incorporated in Italian silk patterns during the 1300s and 1400s and in paintings where it frequently decorated the border of the Virgin's mantle and occasionally her halo.

WOVEN SILK: COMBINATION OF TWO WEAVES (LAMPAS); ORPHREY BAND AND EMBROIDERY BAND: GERMANY, COLOGNE, 1300S; COMPOUND WEAVE (SAMIT); SILK AND GOLD THREAD; 106.7 X 68.6 CM (42 X 27 IN.)

PURCHASE FROM THE J. H. WADE FUND 1928.653

Louis XV Savonnerie Carpet with Royal Arms about 1740–50

SAVONNERIE FACTORY (PARIS), MANUFACTURER; PIERRE-JOSSE PERROT (FRENCH, 1700–1750), DESIGNER

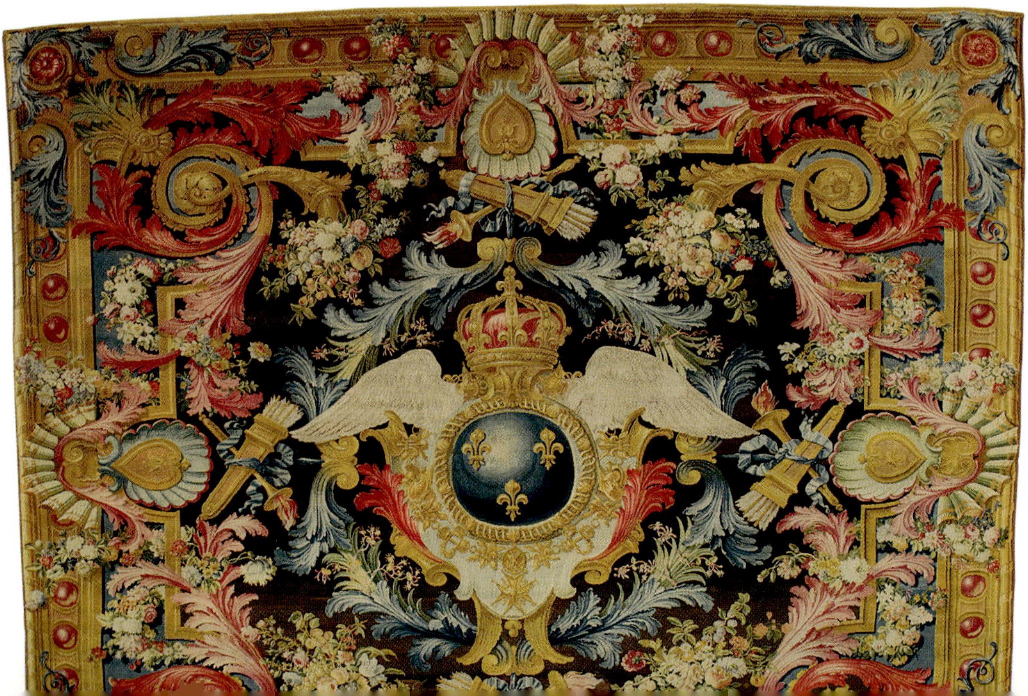

This spectacular carpet, one of three with this royal pattern, was originally designed in 1735 by the prominent Savonnerie artist Pierre-Josse Perrot for Louis XV's dining room at chateau La Muette. The royal arms of France on the orb are

topped by a crown with eagle wings. Cornucopia issue from corner pieces that alternate with military trophies. The lively artistic style was simplified for faster weaving and a brown ground was used to heighten the brilliant colors. The Savonnerie factory was founded in the early 1600s to create French versions of oriental carpets, whose import had created a drain on the economy. The technique, influenced by Turkish carpets, has wool pile formed with symmetrical rug-knots, wool warps, and hemp wefts.

SAVONNERIE KNOTTED PILE (SYMMETRICAL RUG KNOT); WOOL, HEMP; 546 X 615.6 CM (215 X 242-3/8 IN.)

JOHN L. SEVERANCE FUND 1950.8

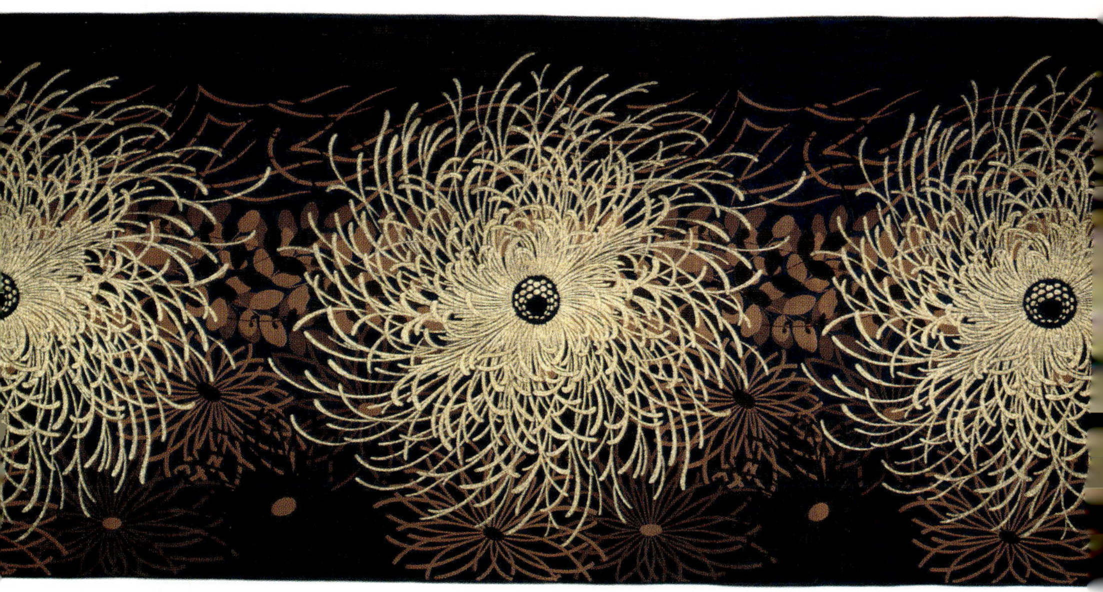

Chrysanthemums 1925

MAISON HENRY BERTRAND (FRANCE), MANUFACTURER

This spectacular design by the French manufacturer Maison Henry Bertrand was shown in Paris in 1925 at the enormously successful Exposition Internationale des Arts Décoratifs et Industriels Modernes, where more than six hundred textile designers exhibited their work in the Grand Palais alone. More than 16 million visitors attended the exhibition, which succeeded in changing the public's taste. Flamboyant golden chrysanthemums of Japanese origin and orange silk lespedeza form this dynamic design on a deep blue silk ground, enlivened by scattered motifs and the texture of the twill-based weave. In Europe, oriental chrysanthemums were recorded in a document in 1689 and cultivated by the 1780s; in 1861 Japanese chrysanthemums imported from Japan were widely admired, especially in France, for their imposing size, varied colors, and variously shaped petals somewhat akin to tousled hair. This lightweight silk with excellent drape may have been designed for evening wear as a flamboyant coat or shawl.

TWILL-BASED JACQUARD WEAVE; SILK AND ARTIFICIAL GOLD THREAD; 325 X 106.7 CM (128 X 42 IN.)

JOHN L. SEVERANCE FUND 2003.42

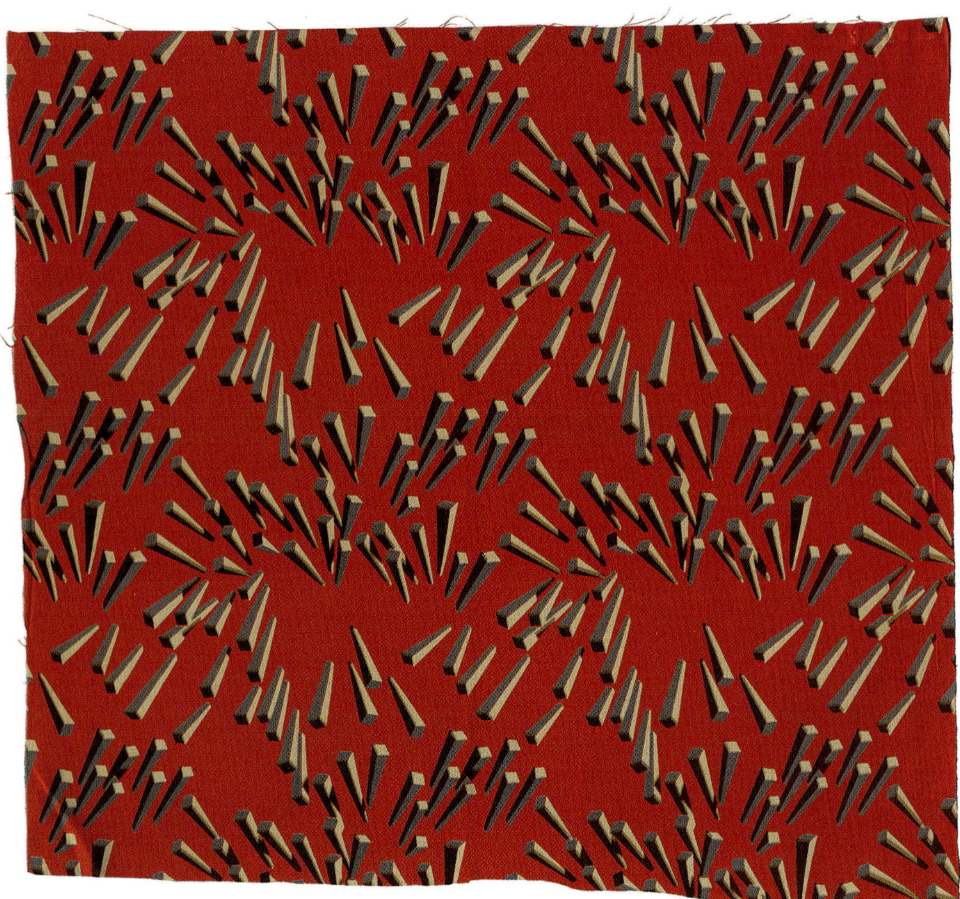

Pegs (Americana Series no. 668) 1927

STEHLI SILKS CORPORATION (AMERICAN), MANUFACTURER; CHARLES BUCKLES FALLS (AMERICAN, 1874–1960), DESIGNER

Although the American government declined to participate in the immensely successful 1925 Exposition Internationale des Arts Décoratifs et Industriels Modernes in Paris because American decorative arts were considered inadequate, the exhibition still had an enormous impact on American design when four hundred objects toured the United States in 1926. It encouraged designers to create interior furnishings in the new modern style of simplicity and directness. *Pegs,* an iconic silk of the early American machine age, features lowly three-dimensional pegs in a dynamic and vibrant pattern. It was designed by Charles Buckles Falls, a poster designer, in 1927 in an Americana series of dress fabrics for Stehli Silks, a progressive manufacturer who gave American artists the freedom to create contemporary American art for American consumers and thereby replace ubiquitous floral patterns. American department stores promoted the new style, following the French example, with huge success. *Pegs* represents the museum's substantial printed collection of American and European modern designs from the late 1920s to the 1950s. That collection was recently enhanced with American printed linens by named designers, two bearing "Good Design" tags indicating that New York's Museum of Modern Art exhibited the pattern at the Merchandise Mart in Chicago between 1950 and 1955 to improve American modern design.

CRÊPE DE CHINE; SILK, PRINTED; 48.9 X 52.1 CM (19-1/4 X 20-1/2 IN.)

GIFT OF THE STEHLI SILKS CORPORATION 1928.587

The Principal Wife Goes On 1984

SHEILA HICKS (AMERICAN, LIVES IN FRANCE, B. 1934)

Few artists created nonutilitarian fabrics until the fiber art movement gained momentum in the 1960s and 1970s, strengthened by exhibitions such as the Cleveland Museum of Art's seminal international *Fiberworks* in 1977. Color, material, line, and form all contribute to the signature sculptural work by the pioneering artist Sheila Hicks, who reinvented the textile tradition while blurring the boundaries among art, design, and architecture. Bundles of natural linen wrapped with intense colors at random intervals were among Hicks's early radical works exhibited in 1969 at the Fourth International Tapestry Biennale in Lausanne. *The Principal Wife Goes On* is one of several dynamic versions made for intimate and public spaces with rich contrasts in texture, color, and movement. Her brilliant, uninhibited explorations in space include worldwide commissions from major corporations and architects created in her atelier in Paris where she has lived since 1964. Her peripatetic creativity was celebrated in the 2011–12 retrospective *Sheila Hicks 50 Years.*

LINEN, RAYON, ACRYLIC YARNS; 254 X 203.2 X 20.4 CM (100 X 80 X 8 IN.)

GIFT OF WATSON K. BLAIR 2011.32

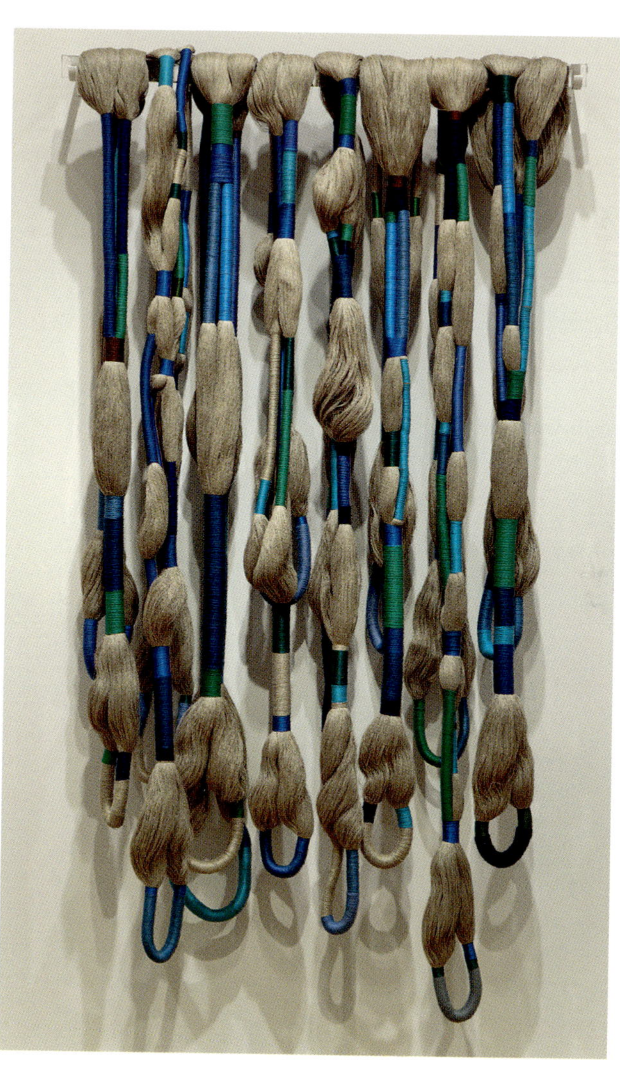

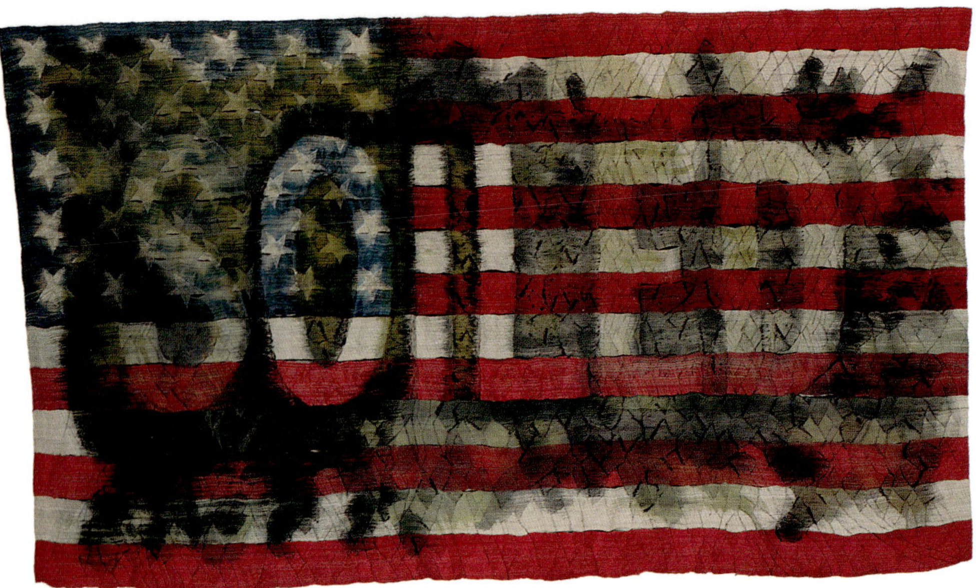

Old Glory 1992

JAMES BASSLER (AMERICAN, B. 1933)

Prompted by the Gulf War in 1990, Los Angeles artist James Bassler spent the year 1992 dyeing linen thread and hand weaving *Old Glory*, a powerful work of art that integrates national identity, politics, and environmental issues in an oil-based economy. Bassler dyed yarns to look soiled from oil, highlighting the letters "oil" in the word "soiled," and wove it in his favorite wedge-weave technique, a type of tapestry weave that can be compared to painting with weft threads. Bassler's distinctive hand-woven style, influenced by his respect for world traditions especially in Navajo and Pre-Columbian textiles, evolved during decades of teaching at UCLA. Artists have used the powerful national symbol of the American flag to convey their sentiments for years, as seen in works by Jasper Johns, Faith Ringgold, Lenore Tawney, and Dread Scott. In 1989, the Supreme Court ruled eloquently on flag desecration: "We are aware that desecration of the flag is deeply offensive to many, but punishing desecration of the flag dilutes the very freedom that makes this emblem so revered and worth revering."

TAPESTRY WEAVE WITH ECCENTRIC WEFTS; LINEN, WAXED; 180.4 X 317.5 CM (71 X 125 IN.)

GIFT OF THE TEXTILE ART ALLIANCE 2005.131

Smoke 2011

PAE WHITE (AMERICAN, B. 1963)

Smoke has been a recurring motif in the work of Pae White, a multimedia artist working in Los Angeles who has explored ways to capture its genuine qualities in various media. This monumental wall hanging, almost 29 feet wide, transforms the elusive motif into a physical image, as if the clouds of smoke have been caught in the computerized-loom woven structure. Magnified plumes of clear smoke curl mysteriously across the wide black expanse while close-up wisps of smoke create an all-over surface of illusory depth. *Smoke* demonstrates White's ability to transform an everyday image into a seductive atmosphere of wonder and spectacle. What White describes as cotton fibers' "dream of becoming something other than itself" is a sensual play of questioning boundaries between different media, between the applied and fine arts, and between different physical conditions.

COMPUTERIZED-LOOM FABRIC, COTTON AND POLYESTER; 438.8 X 874.4 CM (172-3/4 X 344-1/4 IN.)

SEVERANCE AND GRETA MILLIKIN TRUST 2011.203

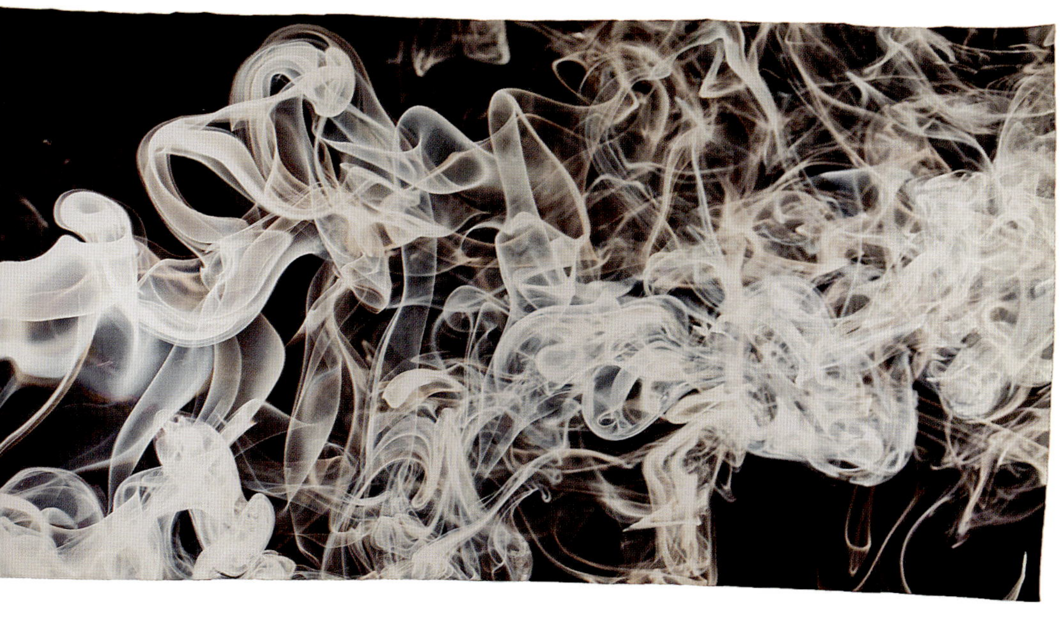

Early Lace

Decorative lace was a status symbol in furnishing fabrics and the dress of European men and women by the 1500s and often more expensive than woven textiles and even jewelry. Its lightness, flexibility, and elaborate decoration with contrasting densities of open and closed areas characterize the two main types, made with a needle and single thread or with multiple threads on bobbins. The widespread popularity of lace drove textile economies in Flanders, Italy, France, and Spain. As a luxury good in Italy during the 1500s, it circumvented laws regulating the use of costly textiles made with silk and gold thread by creating similarly ornate results with inexpensive linen.

The artistic creativity and technical fineness achieved by expert needlewomen is illustrated by several early Italian religious and secular examples from the 1500s and 1600s. A spectacular cover with a bobbin lace border frames the richly varied needle lace and cutwork decoration. A lavishly worked lace flounce with large Renaissance scrolls amid exuberant flora represents superlative Venetian needle lace from 1650 to 1699, called Venetian large point. Religious images depicted the Crucifixion with Mary and St. John beneath the sun and moon in the Venetian flat needlepoint technique. The Old Testament story of Joseph decorates a bobbin lace flounce from a priest's alb worn under a liturgical vestment from Milan. In the initial

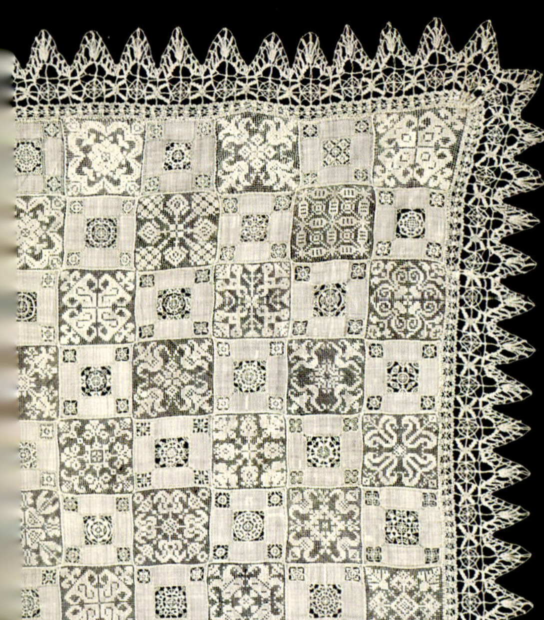

Lace Cover with Embellished Squares, 1500s. Italy. Lace, needle and bobbin: linen; 144.2 x 144.2 cm (56-3/4 x 56-3/4 in.). Gift of Mrs. Edward B. Greene, G. G. Wade, and J. H. Wade Jr. for the Ellen Garretson Wade Memorial Collection 1923.995

Lace Flounce with Renaissance Scrolls, 1650–99. Italy, Venice. Lace, needle: linen; 40.7 x 118.8 cm (16 x 46-3/4 in.). The Frances McIntosh Sherwin Collection 1936.82

scene, the young boy Joseph is presented with his mother Rachel shown reclining on a horse-drawn carriage and his father Jacob while an older brother is seated in the front (on the left).

The Cleveland Museum of Art has one of the world's most significant collections of early lace. J. H. Wade, who donated the land on which to build an art museum, was also a collector. His inaugural gift to the museum, in 1914, was 532 type pieces of lace from the Thomas Wilson collection. Wilson's collection of lace had been assembled for exhibition at the Chicago World's Fair in 1893. In addition to the lace, Wade donated Wilson's collection of books on lace and lace making to the museum's library. Wade also established a trust fund, the income of which was to be used to acquire "European and American paintings, rugs, embroideries, brocades, laces, jewelry, and artistic objects in gold, silver and enamel."

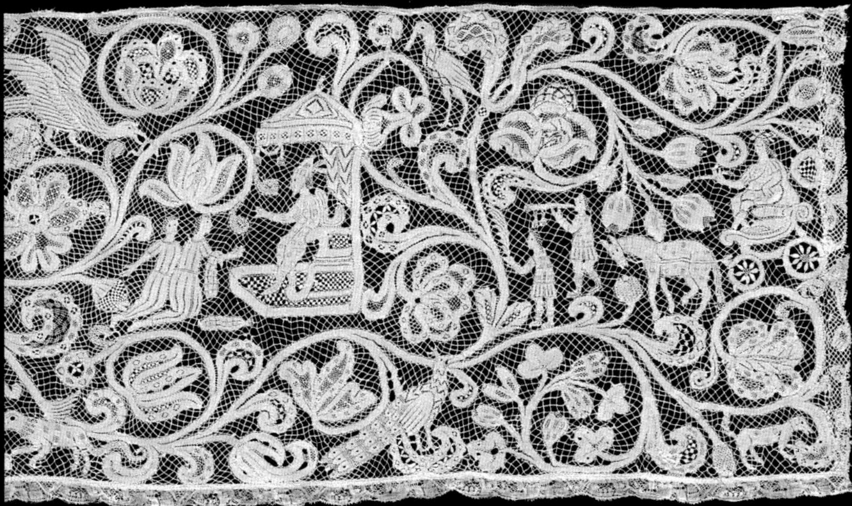

Flounce Depicting the Story of Joseph, 1700s (detail). Italy, Milan. Lace, bobbin: linen; 33.7 x 348 cm (13-1/4 x 137 in.). Gift of Mrs. Edward B. Greene, G. G. Wade, and J. H. Wade Jr. for the Ellen Garretson Wade Memorial Collection 1923.997

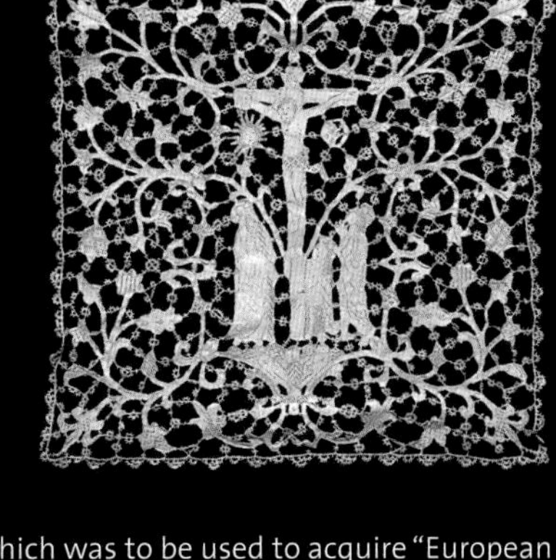

Lace, Crucifixion, 1600s. Italy, Venice. Lace, needle: linen; 15.9 x 15.9 cm (6-1/4 x 6-1/4 in.). Gift of Mrs. Edward B. Greene, G. G. Wade, and J. H. Wade Jr. for the Ellen Garretson Wade Memorial Collection 1923.1026

Level 2

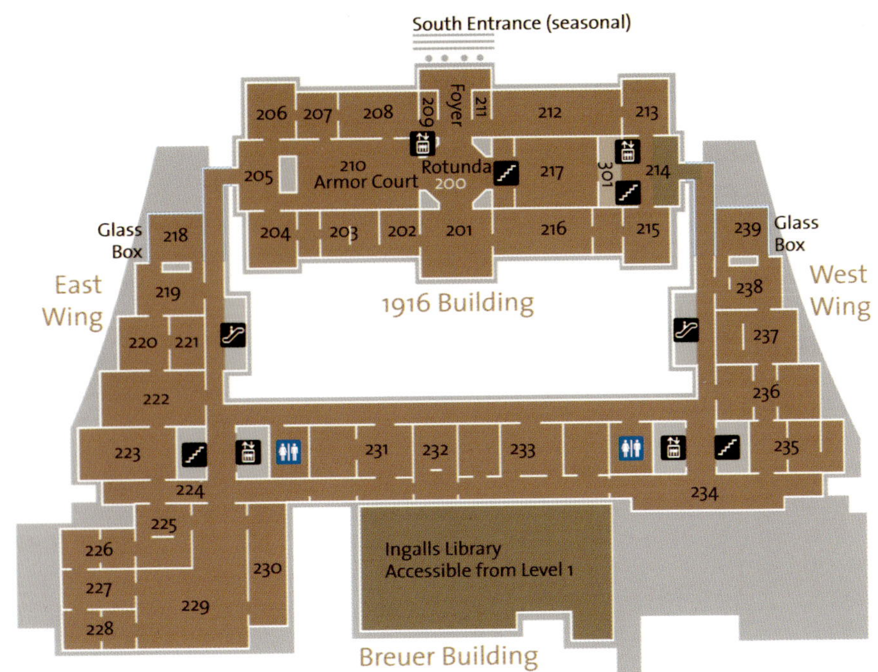

Level 1

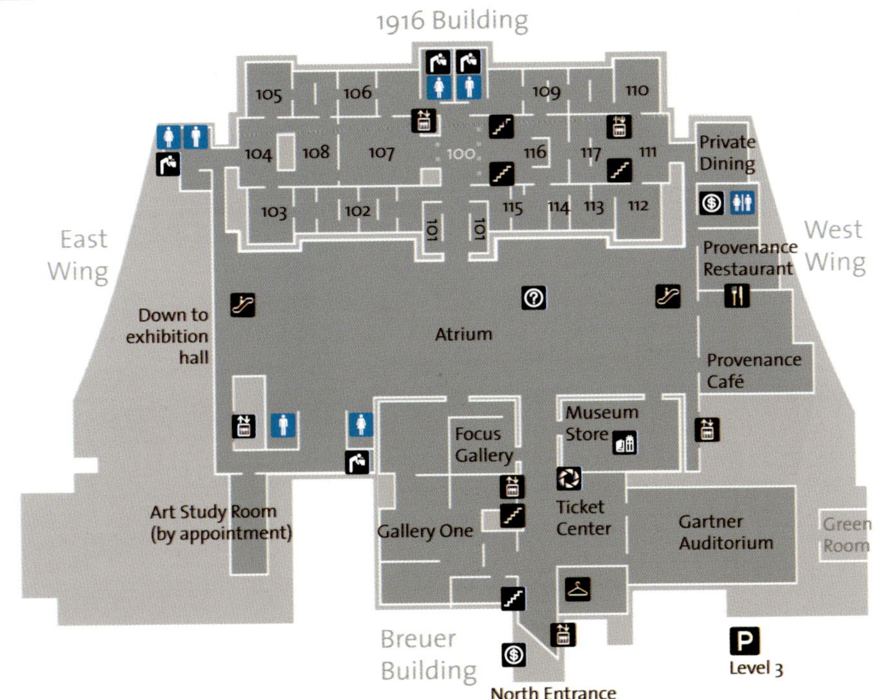

Level One

South Galleries

100 1916 Lobby

101 Prints and Drawings

102–103 Ancient Near Eastern, Greek, and Roman

104–105 Early Christian and Byzantine

106, 109–110 Medieval

107 Ancient Egyptian

108 African

111, 113, 116–117 Renaissance

112 Tapestries

114 Textiles and Manuscripts

115 Islamic

Level Two

South Galleries

200 Rotunda

201–202 Neoclassical

203 British

204–208 American

209 Tiffany

210 Armor Court

211 Fabergé

212, 214–215, 217 Baroque

213 Dutch

216 Rococo

301 Collector's Cabinet

North Galleries

231 Native North American and Pre-Columbian

232 Textiles

233 Japanese and Korean

East Galleries

218 Sculpture

219–220, 223, 225–226 Modern

221 Decorative Art

222 Impressionism

224 Contemporary corridor

227 Abstract Expressionism

228 Cleveland gallery

229 Contemporary

230 Photography

West Galleries

234 Himalayan

235–236 Chinese

237–239 Indian and Southeast Asian

Lower Level

000 Education lobby

001 Exhibition lobby

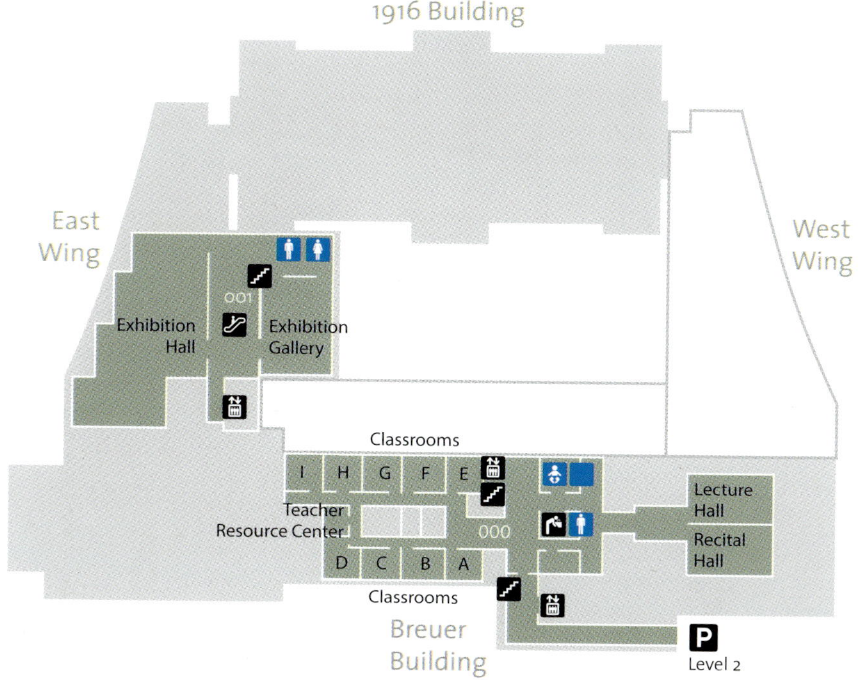

Index

Abbasid period or Aghlabid dynasty, North Africa, Iraq, or Iran, *Two Folios from a Qur'an* 224
Abbasid period or Tulunid period, Egypt, *Pillow Cover* 225
Adnet, Henry 135
Aghlabid dynasty or Abbasid period, North Africa, Iraq, or Iran, *Two Folios from a Qur'an* 224
Akan people, Ghana, *Head* 30
Akotantos, Angelos (attributed to) 262
Angkorean period, Northern Thailand, *Dancing Hevajra* 220
Asuka period or Nara period, Japan, *Buddha of the Future* 235
Ateu Atsa (probably) 33
Audubon, John James 45
Avedon, Richard 315
Aztec style, Mesoamerica, *Seated Male* 329
Baccio dell Porta. *See* Fra Bartolommeo
Bailly, Joseph Alexis (attributed to) 140
Barbari, Jacopo de' 349
Bartlett, Jennifer 120
Bartolommeo, Fra. *See* Fra Bartolommeo
Bassler, James 372
Beaumetz, Jean de 271
Bellows, George 54
Bembe people, Democratic Republic of the Congo, *Plank Mask* 37
Bening, Alexander, and associates 279
Bonnard, Pierre 299
Bonnestrenne, Pierre-François 135
Bonnet, Louis-Marin 353
Bontecou, Lee 114
Boulogne, Valentin de 182
Bourgeois, Louise 120
Bourke-White, Margaret 310
Bouts, Albrecht 277
Brancusi, Constantin 298
Braun, Adolphe 306
Bugatti, Carlo 144
Buonarroti, Michelangelo 155
Burgkmair, Hans 350
Byzantine, Constantinople, *Enthroned Mother of God* 259
Callow, William 163
Campin, Robert 273
Canaletto (Giovanni Antonio Canal) 158
Canova, Antonio 286
Caravaggio 181
Carolingian period, Frankish, *Brooch* 259
Carracci, Annibale 180
Carriera, Rosalba 196
Cesa, Pompeo della 283
Cesati, Alessandro 180
Cézanne, Paul 295
Chardin, Jean-Siméon 193
Chase, William Merritt 50
Chavín style, central Andes, *Head-Shaped Plaque* 331
Chelsea Porcelain Factory, England 136
Chen Hongshou 108
Chimú style, central Andes
Backrest of a Litter 338
Tunic 338
Chokwe people, Angola or Democratic Republic of the Congo, *Comb or Hair Ornament* 40
Chola period, South India
Brahma 206
Nataraja 208
Christus, Petrus (attributed to) 274
Church, Frederic Edwin 48
Classic Veracruz style, Mesoamerica
Ballgame Hip Protector 327
Ballgame Thin Stone Head 328
Claus de Werve 272
Cole, Thomas 46
Colonial Inca style, central Andes, *Half Tunic* 340
Conte style, Panama
Animal-Shaped Ornament 337
Chest Plaque 337
Rod-Shaped Ear Ornament 336
Three Ear Ornaments 336
Two Plaques 336
Cooper, Samuel 196
Coorte, Adriaen 192
Copley, John Singleton 44
Corot, Camille 287
Cosway, Richard 197
Courbet, Gustave 291
Cowan Pottery, United States 148
Cox, John Rogers 59
Cranach, Lucas, the Elder 179
Cromek, Thomas Hartley 162
Dalí, Salvador 300
Daswanth 210
David, Jacques-Louis 287

Death of Adonis 188
Degas, Edgar 166, 293, 354, 356
Dong Qichang 107
Douris (attributed to) 81
Dürer, Albrecht 156, 348
Dumont, François 197
Eakins, Thomas 49
Edo people, Nigeria, *Head* 31
Edo period, Japan, *Standing Figure* 244
Eggleston, William 313
Egypt
Byzantine period, *Icon of the Virgin and Child* 362
dynasty 5, *Head of King Userkaf* 71
dynasty 18: *Head of Amenhotep III* 73; *Nome Gods Bearing Offerings* 74; *Statue of Minemheb* 72
dynasty 21–22, *Coffin of Bakenmut* 25
Ptolemaic dynasty, *Torso of Amenpayom* 76
Ejagham people, Nigeria, *Headdress* 32
Etruscan, Italy, *Cista Handle* 84
Falls, Charles Buckles 370
Farmer, Geoffrey 127
Fast, Omer 125
Flandes, Juan de 280
Flaxman, John 160
Fra Bartolommeo (Baccio dell Porta) 154
Fragmentary Chasuble 368
France
Auvergne, *Virgin and Child* 266
Paris(?), *Table Fountain* 269
Saint-Porchaire, *Ewer* 131
Suite of Furniture and Wall Hangings 132–33
Frankenthaler, Helen 119
Friedlander, Lee 314
Fukae Roshu 245
Gandhara, Pakistan, *Approaching the Bodhi Tree* 201
Gauguin, Paul 293, 355
Gély, Léopold-Jules-Joseph 140
Geometric style, Greece
Bird Pendant 88
Fibula 89
Horse 77
Ornament 89
Zone 88
German, *Pietà* 246
Germany
Augsburg(?), *Field Armor* 282
Hildesheim: *Ceremonial Cross of Count Liudolf* 265; *Ceremonial Cross of Countess Gertrude* 264; *Portable Altar* 265
Swabia, *Christ and Saint John* 267
Gogh, Vincent van 292
Goryeo period, Korea
Arhat 250
Basin 250
Kundika 249
Gossaert, Jan 177
Götz, Joseph Mathias 191
Goya, Francisco de 161
Great Lakes, North America, *Ball-Headed War Club* 342
Greece, Corinth, *Horse* 77
Greek
Crete, *Kriophoros Statuette* 78
Kouros 79
Peloponnese, *Statuette of an Athlete* 80
Statuette of a Nanny Goat 84
Guelph Treasure, Germany 264–65
Gupta period, India, *Head of a Buddha* 202
Gupta period, India or Nepal, *Standing Buddha* 203
Hals, Frans 184
Hardouin, Jules-Michel 134
Hébrard, Adrien-Aurélien 144
Heian period, Japan
Buddhist Tabernacle 236
Mirror 235
Nikko, The Sun Bodhisattva 21
Herter Brothers, United States 142
Hicks, Sheila 371
Hittite, North Syria, *Priest-King or Deity* 68
Hodges, Jim 123
Homer, Winslow 52, 165
Hope, Thomas 139
House of Fabergé, Russia
Kremlin Tower Clock 146
Imperial Red Cross Egg 147
Hoyshala period, southwestern India, *Shiva Bhairava* 209
Hurd, Nathaniel 44
Ilkhanid period, central Asia, *Cloth of Gold* 363
India
central, *Parshva, the 23rd Jina* 206
Coromandel Coast, *Chintz Bed Cover* 365
Kashmir: *Long Shawl* 366; *Standing Shiva Mahadeva* 205
Ingres, Jean-Auguste-Dominique 164

Italy
- *Lace Cover* 374
- Milan, *Flounce* 375
- northern, *Venus with a Burning Urn* 175
- Venice: *Ewer* 130; *Lace Crucifixion* 375; *Lace Flounce* 374

Iztlán del Río style, Mesoamerica, *Seated Couple* 322
Johns, Jasper 169, 359
Jomon period, Japan, *Flame-Style Vessel* 234
Joseon period, Korea
- *Amita (Amitabha)* 252
- *Box* 254
- *Scholar's Accouterments* 255
- *Seven Jeweled Peaks* 254
- *Storage Jar* 253

Joshu 237
Kamakura period, Japan
- *Jar* 240
- *Legends of Yuzu Nembutsu Sect* 239
- *"Secret Five" Bodhisattva* 238

Kano Motonobu (attributed to) 241
Kelly, Ellsworth 116
Kiefer, Anselm 121
Kim Si 253
Kirchner, Ernst Ludwig 296
Koshin 237
Koshun 237
Kosuth, Joseph 117
Krasner, Lee 63
Kusama, Yayoi 114
Kushan period, Afghanistan, *Young Woman* 202
Kushan period, northern India, *Female Devotee* 200
Lalique, René 145
Lange, Michel II (attributed to) 134
Late Roman/Byzantine, Eastern Mediterranean, *Constantinian Pendant and Spacers* 258
Late Roman/Early Christian, Eastern Mediterranean, *Jonah Marbles* 260–61
La Tour, Georges de 186
Lawrence, Jacob 62
Lawrence, Thomas 195
Lewis, Edmonia 48
LeWitt, Sol 122
Li Huayi 111
Liao dynasty, China, *Guanyin* 98
Lipchitz, Jacques 296
Lippi, Filippino 173
Lippi, Filippo 276
Lorrain, Claude (Claude Gellée) 157
Lou, Liza 124
Lucanian, South Italy, *Calyx-Krater* 82
Luntu people, Democratic Republic of the Congo, *Pipe* 41
Maar, Dora 312
Maison Henry Bertrand, France 369
Majiayao culture, Northwest China, *Jar* 92
Malinke people, Mali, *Helmet Mask* 28
Marsh, Reginald 58
Master ES, Germany 346
Master of the Boqueteaux and workshop, France 270
Master of the Royal Plantagenet Workshop, France 263
Matisse, Henri 22, 301
Mauch, Daniel 178
Maya style, Mesoamerica
- *Shell* 324
- *Vessel* 323

Mbuun people, Democratic Republic of the Congo, *Woman's Skirt* 41
Meissonnier, Juste-Aurelle 135
Mena, Pedro de 190
Michelangelo. *See* Buonarroti, Michelangelo
Miller, John Paul 150
Ming dynasty, China
- *Bowl* 103
- *Meiping Vase* 101
- *Stem-Cup* 102
- *Virupa* 221

Mino da Fiesole 172
Minoan, Crete, *Girl* 76
Mir Musavvir (attributed to) 229
Moche style, central Andes
- *Mastiff* 334
- *Nose Ornament* 335

Moholy-Nagy, Lázló 309
Momoyama period, Japan
- *Arrival of "Southern Barbarians"* 243
- *Tea Bowl* 244

Mondrian, Piet 300
Monet, Claude 289, 298
Mount, William Sidney 47
Mughal period, India
- *Alam Shah* 211
- *Angels Bring Food* 212

Nara period or Asuka period, Japan, *Buddha of the Future* 235
Nasca style, central Andes
- *Cloth* 341
- *Shell* 333

Nasca style or Paracas style, central Andes, *Spear Thrower* 341
Neel, Alice 117
Neo-Assyrian, Iraq, *Saluting Protective Spirit* 69
Neo-Sumerian, Iraq, *Statue of Gudea* 67
Nepal, *Bodhisattva Manjushri* 219
Ngbandi people, Democratic Republic of the Congo, *Male and Female Figure Pair* 38
Nok region, Nigeria, *Head* 32
Northern Qi dynasty, China, *Standing Disciple Mahakasyapa* 94
Northern Song dynasty, China
  Brush Washer 99
  Vase 99
O'Keeffe, Georgia 57
Old Shilla period, Korea, *Comma-Shaped Jades* 248
Olmec style, Mesoamerica, *Head Fragment* 323
O'Sullivan, Timothy H. 304
Ottoman period, Turkey, *Large Dish* 231
Pala period, India
  Akshobhya 230
  Vishnu Riding on Garuda 204
Palmer, Samuel 163
Paracas style or Nasca style, central Andes, *Spear Thrower* 341
Paracas style, central Andes, *Tunic* 332
Pataky Polychrome style, Costa Rica or Nicaragua, *Animal Effigy Vessel* 330
Pende people, Democratic Republic of the Congo, *Face Mask* 34
Perrot, Pierre Josse 368
Peyre, Jules-Constant 140
Philippe de Champaigne 189
Picasso, Pablo 167, 294, 297, 358
Pisano, Andrea (attributed to) 268
Policoro Painter (attributed to near) 82
Pollaiuolo, Antionio del 347
Poussin, Nicolas 187
Praxiteles (attributed to) 83
Pre-Angkorean period, Cambodia, *Krishna Govardhana* 214
Pre-Bembe people, Democratic Republic of the Congo, *Male Figure* 36
Prendergast, Maurice 357
Puryear, Martin 122
Qing dynasty, China
  Bowl 103
  Screen with Stand 110
  Tibetan Man's Robe 367
Rauschenberg, Robert 61
Recuay style, central Andes, *Feline Vessel* 335
Reece, Jane 308
Rembrandt van Rijn 351
Renoir, Pierre-Auguste 289
Riemenschneider, Tilman 281
Robbia, Giovanni della 175
Rodin, Auguste 15, 290
Roman
  Italy: *Emperor as Philosopher Probably Marcus Aurelius* 87; *Orestes Sarcophagus* 86
  North Africa, *Portrait Head of Drusus Minor* 85
Roszak, Theodore 60
Ruisdael, Jacob van 187
Ruskin, John 163
Russia, Tula, *Pair of Candelabra* 138
Ryder, Albert Pinkham 53
Safavid period, Iran, *Brocaded Velvet* 364
Şahkulu (attributed to) 230
Sasanian, possibly eastern Iran, *Woman and Water Buffalo Rhyton* 70
Sansovino, Jacopo 177
Sargent, John Singer 51
Sarto, Andrea del 176
Savage, Augusta 58
Savonnerie Factory, France 132, 368
Schreckengost, Viktor 148–49
Seljuk period, Iran
  Inscribed Tombstone 226
  Lion Incense Burner 226
  Luster Dish 227
Senufo people, Ivory Coast
  Helmet 30
  Mother-and-Child Figure 29
Severo da Ravenna 172
Sèvres Imperial Porcelain Manufactory, France 140
Sheeler, Charles 56
Shukei Sesson 242
Siloé, Gil de 278
Sloan, John 55, 357
Smart, John 197
Sommer, William 56
Songye people, Democratic Republic of the Congo, *Male Figure* 35
Sosnowska, Monika 126
Southern Nguni people, South Africa, *Apron* 41
Southern Song dynasty, China, *Basin* 102

Southern Sotho people, Lesotho
Fertility Figure 39
Snuff Container 41
Spero, Nancy 168
Stehli Silks Corp., United States 370
Steichen, Edward 307
Stella, Frank 118
Stieglitz, Alfred 311
Struth, Thomas 317
Sui dynasty, China, *Candlestand* 102
Talbot, William Henry Fox 304
Tang dynasty, China
Bodhisattva 96, 97
Tomb Guardians 95
Teotihuacán style, Mesoamerica, *Mural Fragment* 326
Thailand, probably Shri Thep, *Buddha* 213
Thomas, Hank Willis 319
Tibet
Cosmic Buddha Vairochana 217
Green Tara 218
Vajravarahi 221
Tibet or Central Asia, *Vase, Beaker, and Rhyton* 216
Tiepolo, Giovanni Domenico (Giandomenico) 159
Tiffany, Louis Comfort 143
Tiffany Glass & Decorating Co. 143
Timurid period, Iran
Bookbinding 228
Princely Banquet 229
Tlingit, North America, *Feast Ladle* 339
Toshiko Takaezu 151
Toulouse-Lautrec, Henri de 14
Townsend, Thomas (attributed to) 137
Tulunid period or Abbasid period, Egypt, *Pillow Cover* 225
Turner, Joseph Mallord William 162, 288
Turpin, Pierre 134
Ugolino di Nerio da Siena 268
Ulúa Valley, Mesoamerica, *Vessel* 325
Unified Shilla period, Korea, *Amita (Amitabha)* 248
Vannini, Pietro 275
Velázquez, Diego 183
Vien, Joseph-Marie, the Elder 194
Warhol, Andy 115
Wari style, central Andes, *Sacrificer Container* 333
Watteau, Jean Antoine 352
Weems, Carrie Mae 316
Wen Zhengming 106
West, Benjamin 44
Western Anatolia(?), *Statuette of a Woman* 66
Western Han dynasty, China, *Mat Weight in the Form of a Bear* 94
Western Zhou dynasty, China, *Bell* 93
White, Pae 373
Yan Hui 105
Yayoi period, Japan, *Dotaku* 234
Yi Sumun 251
Yombe people, Democratic Republic of the Congo
Hat 40
Mother-and-Child Figure 34
Yurok style, North America, *Tobacco Basket* 343
Yuan dynasty, China
Bowl 104
Jar 100
Zhang Huan 318
Zhu Bishan (attributed to) 104
Zhu Da 109
Zuni style, North America, *Water Jar* 343
Zurbarán, Francisco de 185

Contributors

Michael Bennett, Curator of Greek and Roman Art

Susan E. Bergh, Curator of Pre-Columbian and Native American Art

Katie Kilroy Blaser, Curatorial Assistant, Asian Art

Anita Chung, Curator of Chinese Art

Mark Cole, Curator of American Painting and Sculpture

Stephen N. Fliegel, Curator of Medieval Art

Jane Glaubinger, Curator of Prints

Stephen Harrison, Curator of Decorative Art and Design

Cory Korkow, Assistant Curator of European Art

Heather Lemonedes, Curator of Drawings

Louise W. Mackie, Curator of Textiles and Islamic Art

Constantine Petridis, Curator of African Art

Sonya Rhie Quintanilla, George P. Bickford Curator of Indian and Southeast Asian Art

William H. Robinson, Curator of Modern European Art

Jon L. Seydl, Paul J. and Edith Ingalls Vignos Jr. Curator of European Painting and Sculpture 1500–1800

Barbara Tannenbaum, Curator of Photography

Reto Thüring, Curator of Contemporary Art

Significant assistance provided by staff members, current and former:

Administration
Jackie Anselmo, Kimberly Grice, Wanda Irwin

Collections Management
Barry Austin, Arthur Beukemann, Joe Blaser, Kurt Hallsmann, Dale Palmer, Andrew Robison, Tracy Sisson

Conservation
Chris Bruns, Stephen Fixx, Robin Hanson, Joan Neubecker, Dave Piurek, Colleen Snyder, Samantha Springer

Curatorial
Joan Brickley, June de Phillips, Bridget Hornberger, Robin Koch, C. Griffith Mann, Amanda Mikolic, Dave Smart, Deirdre Vodanoff, Maggie Wojton

Images and Rights
Rachel Beamer, Elizabeth Saluk

Photography and Imaging
Howard Agriesti, David Brichford, Gary Kirchenbauer, Bruce Shewitz

The Cleveland Museum of Art Board of Trustees